MW01027916

THE EVIDENTIAL ARGUMENT FROM EVIL

The Indiana Series in the Philosophy of Religion
MEROLD WESTPHAL, GENERAL EDITOR

THE

EVIDENTIAL

ARGUMENT

FROM

EVIL

EDITED BY DANIEL HOWARD-SNYDER

Indiana
University
Press

BLOOMINGTON AND INDIANAPOLIS

© 1996 by Indiana University Press

All rights reserved

No part of this book may be reproduced or utilized in any form or by any means, electronic or mechanical, includ-ing photocopying and recording, or by any information storage and retrieval system, without permission in writ-ing from the publisher. The Association of American University Presses' Resolution on Permissions constitutes the only exception to this prohibition.

The paper used in this publication meets the minimum requirements of American National Standard for Information Sciences—Permanence of Paper for Printed Library Materials, ANSI Z39.48-1984.

MANUFACTURED IN THE UNITED STATES OF AMERICA

Library of Congress Cataloging-in-Publication Data

The evidential argument from evil / edited by Daniel Howard-Snyder.
    p.   cm.
   Includes bibliographical references and index.
    ISBN 0-253-32965-5 (alk. paper).   —   ISBN 0-253-21028-3 (pbk. :
alk. paper)
    1. Theodicy. I. Howard-Snyder, Daniel.
BT160.E94   1996
214—dc20
                                            95-11208

1   2   3   4   5   01   00   99   98   97   96

For Frances

CONTENTS

PREFACE

When I was a student at Syracuse University, I once told an acquaintance in the English Department that my dissertation was on the problem of evil. I recall her reply as though I heard it yesterday: "The problem of evil? Isn't that old hat? I mean, what more can be said after Ivan Karamazov?" Apparently, quite a bit. Barry Whitney recently published a bibliography of over 4,200 philosophical and theological writings on the topic, all published from 1960 to 1990. That's nearly one publication every two and a half days. One might rightly wonder how much of this torrent of literature is any good, but one certainly cannot seriously question whether the problem of evil continues to capture the interest of philosophers and theologians alike. It's hardly "old hat."

Philosophical study of the problem of evil has shifted from issues having to do with the compatibility of theism and evil to what is often called "the evidential problem of evil." My aim in collecting the essays of this book has been to bring together recent work on the latter topic. But I didn't want just another collection of previously published pieces. Rather, I wanted a handful of the very best previously published essays to act as a stage upon which dialogue might progress, a place where new work might be done. However, I also wanted a collection that a student or educated layperson could understand, with only minimal assistance from an instructor or a course or two in basic philosophy. Each of the authors has written with these goals in mind. An instructor might easily use many of the essays of this book in an undergraduate course in the philosophy of religion.

A book of this sort requires the cooperation of many individuals. Each new essay was refereed by at least one other contributor, but usually more. Moreover, many other philosophers cajoled, provoked, challenged and otherwise pressed the contributors to do better than they had initially done. It is with heartfelt gratitude that I thank Robert Adams, Mark Brown, David Conway, Mark Cullison, Martin Curd, Evan Fales, Gregory Ganssle, Phillip Goggans, William Gustason, William Hasker, Bruce Hauptli, Frances Howard-Snyder, Hud Hudson, Jeff Jordan, Norman Kretzmann, C. Stephen Layman, Thomas Loughran, Alastair Norcross, David O'Connor, John O'Leary-Hawthorne, John Schellenberg, Stefan Sencerz, James Sennett, Thomas Senor, James Taylor, William Wainwright, Mark Webb, and David Wideker. (If you ought to be on this list, please forgive me my negligence.) For encouragement from the start and for help in other ways, I wish to thank William Alston, Jan Cover, Paul Draper, Janet Rabinowitch, Stewart Thau, Peter van Inwagen, Thomas Trzyna, Merold Westphal, and the departmental staffs of Syracuse University, Wayne State University, and Seattle Pacific University.

Finally, my greatest debt of gratitude is to my best friend and wife, who just reminded me that I have ninety-five midterms to grade by tomorrow. This book is for you, Frances.

DANIEL HOWARD-SNYDER

INTRODUCTION:

The Evidential Argument from Evil

1. The "Problem" of Evil

Evil, it is often said, poses a problem for theism, the view that there is an omnipotent, omniscient, and perfectly good being, "God," for short. This problem is usually called "the problem of evil." But this is a bad name for what philosophers study under that rubric. They study what is better thought of as an argument, or a host of arguments, rather than a problem. Of course, an argument from evil against theism can be both an argument and a problem. Some people realize this for the first time when they assert an argument from evil in print and someone publishes a reply in which numerous defects and oversights are laid bare for the public eye. And if it turns out that there is a God and He doesn't take kindly to such arguments, then an argument from evil might be a big problem, a very big problem, for one who sincerely propounds it. Typically, however, an argument from evil is not thought to be a problem for the atheist. But if not for the atheist, for whom is an argument from evil a "problem"?

Perhaps the theist. The theist, however, may rightly find the premises or inferences of arguments from evil dubious and hence no problem at all. Perhaps, then, an argument from evil is a problem for the theist who finds all its premises and inferences compelling. But even then it might not be a problem, since she might have more compelling grounds to reject the conclusion than to accept all the premises and inferences. Perhaps, then, an argument from evil is a problem for the theist who finds all its premises and inferences compelling and who has lousy grounds for believing theism and she knows it. In that case an argument from evil might be a problem for the theist, at least if she is reasonable. For she might feel strongly inclined to believe there is no God, or at least that, in some sense, she ought to believe that there is no God. No doubt, this could be a troubling state of mind, one that might properly be called a problem. But in that case calling what philosophers study under the name "the problem of evil" a problem is highly misleading. For no philosophers today take the state of mind of the cognitively dissonant theist as their object of study when they study what they refer to as "the problem of evil."

One might think that what philosophers study under the name "the problem of evil" are arguments that should lead the theist to the cognitively dissonant state of mind just sketched, and so, by extension, such an argument is rightly called a problem for the theist. But this rationale for calling what philosophers study under the name "the problem of evil" a problem is highly contentious, to say the least. For an argument from evil *should* lead the theist to cognitive dissonance only if the argument is good, and there is broad disagreement over whether any argument from evil is good. Of course, those convinced that some argument from evil is not defective and that it should lead the theist to cognitive dissonance might properly call it a problem. But why should the rest of us join them? It seems to me, therefore, that we, or at least a great many of us, should stop using "the problem of evil" as a name for what philosophers study under that rubric. If a singular term must be used, "the *argument* from evil" is more apt.

It is customary to distinguish two families of arguments from evil, calling one "logical," "deductive," or "a priori" and calling the other "evidential," "inductive," "empirical," "probabilistic," or "a posteriori." But these too are poor names for that to which they refer. For, if their names are any guide to the contrast (as they are supposed to be), logic is relevant to the members of the first family but not the second, and the members of the second family are meant to be evidence while the first are not. But this is hardly the case. As the chapters in this book indicate, evidential arguments involve quite a bit of logic, both deductive and inductive, and everyone agrees that they must stand up to the canons of logic. And every undeniably logical argument is superlative evidence against theism, if it is a good argument. Moreover, every undeniably logical argument has a premise that can only be known a posteriori, by empirical means, namely, a premise about evil, e.g., that it exists. And every undeniably evidential argument has a premise that can only be known a priori, e.g., a premise about what counts as good evidence or what we rightly expect from God in the way of preventing evil. And many "inductive" arguments from evil are, on the face of it, deductively structured.

So what is this distinction between logical and evidential arguments from evil?

2. Logical Arguments from Evil

Perhaps we can best get at the question by looking at the most famous members of each family. If there is a distinction between logical and evidential arguments from evil, then J. L. Mackie's argument is the paradigm member of the logical family. Mackie asserted that not only can it be shown that

> religious beliefs lack rational support, but that they are positively irrational, that the several parts of the essential theological doctrine are inconsistent with one another, so that the theologian . . . must be prepared to believe, not merely what cannot be proved, but what can be *disproved* from other beliefs that he also holds.[1]

The putative disproof to which Mackie alluded is the problem of evil. As Mackie conceived of it, the problem of evil was "a logical problem, the problem of clarifying and reconciling a number of beliefs" that were "essential parts of most theological positions." The three beliefs he had in mind were these: "God is omnipotent; God is wholly good; and yet evil exists."[2] Mackie was aware that, on the face of it, there was no inconsistency here. Thus, he said, to show it we need some additional premises, or perhaps some quasi-logical rules connecting the terms "good," and "evil," and "omnipotent." These additional principles are that good is opposed to evil, in such a way that a good thing always eliminates evil as far as it can, and that there are no limits to what an omnipotent thing can do. From these it follows that a good omnipotent thing eliminates evil completely, and then the propositions that a good omnipotent thing exists, and that evil exists, are incompatible.

Nearly forty years have passed since Mackie published his famous "logical problem" of evil, as he called it. (So far as I know, this is where we get the name from.) Like logical positivism, Mackie's argument has found its way to the dustbin of philosophical fashions. Why?
Mackie claimed it was *impossible* for

G. God is omnipotent and God is wholly good,

and

E. Evil exists

both to be true. This would be evident, he said, in light of the moral principle

MP1. A good thing always eliminates evil as far as it can,

and the proposition

L. There are no limits to what an omnipotent thing can do.

But G, MP1, and L rule out the possibility of E only if both L and MP1 are necessary truths. If they are not, a wholly good omnipotent thing, say, a person, might permit evil, either because her goodness does not rule out the possibility or because she cannot eliminate evil entirely. Are they both necessary truths? Properly understood, L is.[3] But MP1 is not. If a wholly good person had a morally justifying reason to permit evil she could prevent, she might not eliminate evil as far as she can. A more plausible moral principle for a Mackie-style logical argument from evil is this:

MP2. A wholly good thing eliminates evil as far as it can, unless it has a morally justifying reason not to.

But G, MP2, and L rule out the possibility of E only if it is a necessary truth that there is no morally justifying reason for a wholly good thing to permit preventable evil. However, nothing we know rules out the possibility that there is a morally justifying reason for a wholly good thing to permit evil she could prevent. Indeed, consider the proposition that

J. There is a morally justifying reason for God to permit evil He could prevent, a reason we could not know of, and He permits evil for that reason, and evil results.

Nothing we know rules out J as a possibility; and nothing we know rules out the possibility that G and J are both true. But if both G and J were true, then E would be too. And it would also be true that we could not know the reason God permitted evil. Thus, for all we know, G and E are compatible even if we cannot think of a morally justifying reason for God to permit evil.[4]

Mackie's aim was to "disprove" theism, and thus to show that theistic belief is "positively irrational." Toward that end, his logical argument had a premise that said theism is incompatible with some fact about evil. But note that it was not any old fact about evil that was purportedly incompatible with theism. It was a fact that we know with certainty: that there is evil. Of course, there are other facts that might have served his purposes just as well, e.g., the fact that there is suffering that results from natural disturbances like earthquakes and diseases (so-called "natural evil"), or the fact that a particular infant was intentionally scalded to death with boiling water by its parents on November 24, 1991, in Seattle, or the fact that there is a whole lot of undeserved horrific evil in the world. Each of these facts can be known with certainty. But our present point is this: allowing that Mackie's argument is a guide, we can think of a "logical argument from evil" as one which has a premise that says God and some *known* fact about evil are *incompatible,* and we can think of an "evidential argument from evil" as one that *lacks* such a premise. That is, we should expect that paradigm members of the evidential family will either (i) entirely lack a premise that says that God is incompatible with some fact about evil, or (ii) if they have such a premise, the putative fact about evil cannot be known with certainty, e.g., it might be claimed to be probable to some significant degree, or reasonably believed. As it turns out, this is what we find.

3. Evidential Arguments from Evil

In chapter 1, William Rowe puts the evidential argument from evil roughly like this:

> 1. There exist instances of intense suffering that God could have prevented without thereby losing some greater good.
> 2. God would prevent the occurrence of any intense suffering He could, unless He could not do so without thereby losing some greater good.
> 3. So, God does not exist.

Premise 2 says that the existence of God is incompatible with each instance of preventable intense suffering the permission of which is not required for some greater good. We have here, then, an argument from evil that asserts that the existence of God is *incompatible* with some purported fact about evil. But note that it is *not* a *known* fact. As Rowe points out, "we cannot know with certainty that instances of suffering of the sort described in 1 do occur in the world." Rather, he says, we have "rational grounds" for believing 1, grounds which "render 1 probable to the degree that it is more reasonable to believe 1 than to suspend judgment on 1." So this popular version of the evidential argument conforms to our distinction.

Since 1979, Rowe has articulated two other evidential arguments from evil, both of which he discusses in chapter 14. They rely on the following inference:

P. No good we know of justifies God in permitting E1 and E2
(where E1 and E2 are cases of especially horrific evil); so,
it is quite probable that
Q. No good at all justifies God in permitting E1 and E2.

Both arguments have what amounts to the premise that Q entails there is no God. However, they differ over what bridges the gap between P and Q. One asserts that "we are justified in moving from P to Q in the same way we are justified in making the many inferences we constantly make from the known to the unknown," namely, by way of enumerative generalization. The other employs Bayes's Theorem, and certain argued-for assignments of value to it, to conclude that P makes Q considerably more likely than not. In both cases there is a premise, i.e. Q, that says some purported fact about evil is incompatible with theism. But, again, note that purported fact is *not* known. Rather, Q is argued for in the way suggested. Of course, there are other grounds for believing Q on P. (See, e.g., chapters 10 and 11.) But in each case, Q is based on grounds insufficient for knowing Q with certainty. At best, these arguments make Q likely to a significant degree or reasonable to believe, given P and other information.

Each of the evidential arguments thus far mentioned has a premise that says some fact about evil is incompatible with theism. It is then argued that the fact in question is likely to some degree or another or reasonable to believe, given some other fact which is itself known or argued for. But an evidential argument might not proceed like this. For example, in chapter 14 Rowe defends a Bayesian version of the evidential argument that bypasses Q altogether, one that goes straight from P to the conclusion that theism is probably false. Another example is Paul Draper's argument in chapter 2. Draper asks us to consider a serious alternative hypothesis to theism. He calls it the hypothesis of indifference (HI):

Neither the nature nor the condition of sentient beings on earth is the result of benevolent or malevolent actions performed by non-human persons.

Let O stand for a statement reporting known facts about sentient creatures experiencing pain and pleasure. And let a theistic story be any attempt to explain O in terms of theism. Draper claims that, given what we know apart from O, HI explains O much better than theism. He glosses this as the claim that

C. O is antecedently much more probable on the assumption that HI is true than on the assumption that theism is true.

That is, given what we know apart from O, the probability of O on HI is much greater than the probability of O on theism, or, in short, $\Pr(O/HI) >! \Pr(O/theism)$. Draper's premises are:

1. Given the biological role played by both pain and pleasure in organisms, inde-

pendent of the effect of theistic stories on Pr(O/theism), C is true.
2. Theistic stories do not significantly raise Pr(O/theism).

If C is true, says Draper, we have a prima facie reason to reject theism. For present purposes, note that, even though O is known, Draper's argument does *not* employ a premise that says that theism and O are incompatible. So it too conforms to our distinction between logical and evidential arguments from evil.

While my sampling of arguments is necessarily limited, it seems that we can distinguish arguments from evil along the lines suggested, even though that distinction is badly named. So-called "logical" arguments from evil have a premise that says theism is incompatible with some known fact about evil; so-called "evidential" arguments do not.

While we may easily draw this distinction, we are hard pressed to defend its significance. I'm afraid I don't have much to say about the matter, except for the obvious. I mean, whenever one meets what its author purports to be an *argument* from evil (in contrast with, say, the sort of response to horrendous evil that you might find in Albert Camus's *The Plague* or Elie Wiesel's *Night*), one ought to consider whether the author intends to assert that facts about evil known with certainty are incompatible with theism. If she does, then one should query why the argument is not dubious for the same reason that Mackie's argument from evil is dubious. If she does not—that is, if she intends to say that facts about evil which are known with certainty make theism significantly unlikely, or that theism is incompatible with certain facts about evil that are themselves quite likely—then one needs to think hard about the sorts of issues this book is about.

4. Central Issues in Evidential Arguments from Evil

It would be pointless, and a grave injustice, were I to try here to summarize the work of each contributor. Instead, I shall briefly sketch what I think are some of the main issues at stake in the debate over the evidential argument from evil and where they are discussed in the essays that follow.

4.1 ISSUES COMMON TO EVERY EVIDENTIAL ARGUMENT FROM EVIL

Three fundamental issues arise with respect to every evidential argument from evil.

First, one might argue that even if an evidential argument counts against theism, the *total* evidence makes theism quite likely or sufficiently reasonable to believe. This raises with a vengeance the question of whether, on the whole, the total evidence supports theism. I can't go into that here.[5] Alvin Plantinga, however, gives this question an interesting twist toward the end of chapters 5 and 13. After finding fault with different evidential arguments from evil, he argues that even if they showed what they purported to show *the theist* might well have much better *nonpropositional* grounds for her theistic belief than any argument from evil provides her with *propositional* grounds against it. And whether this is so is largely a matter of whether God has given us certain cognitive powers, as classical theism asserts. Thus, according to Plantinga, whether theistic belief is rendered unreasonable by any evidential argument from evil depends on whether classical theism is true.[6]

A second issue that cuts across versions of the evidential argument from evil is this: suppose we knew of some plausible justifying reason for God to permit the sorts of evil we find in our world, a *theodicy*. In that case, one might think that evil would not count against theism at all. In chapter 3, Richard Swinburne argues that we know of a number of actual greater goods that moral and natural evil serve and that these goods constitute major strands in a viable theodicy. In chapter 4, Eleonore Stump argues that reflection on Aquinas's commentary on Job and his general account of suffering as medicine for a cancer that hinders us from eternal communion with God shows that how we look at suffering is a consequence of much larger issues, specifically, our views about the nature of human happiness and the goal of human life. She urges that to assess the prospects for theodicy we must first resolve these larger issues. I refer the reader to the bibliography for other works of theodicy, e.g., those by Marilyn McCord Adams and John Hick.

Third, evidential arguments from evil purport to show that it is likely to some degree or another that there is no God. But what concept of probability is being used here? I suspect that different concepts are employed in the arguments of, say, Rowe and Draper. Draper explicitly says that he means to be using what is called *epistemic probability*, as opposed to some more objective concept, e.g., statistical probability. Many interesting questions lurk here, some of which are taken up by Draper (chapters 2 and 9), Plantinga (chapters 5 and 13), and Peter van Inwagen (chapters 8 and 12). Be sure to read the notes for these chapters.

4.2 ARGUMENTS FROM INSCRUTABLE EVIL

Let us briefly turn to the most popular version of the evidential argument from evil, the argument that in various ways is defended by Rowe (chapters 1 and 14), Russell (chapter 10) and Gale (chapter 11). They claim that there is no justifying reason for God to permit certain particular horrific evils. At bottom, their basis for saying this is that they cannot see how any reason they know of justifies God in permitting those particular evils, or that no reason they know of does the trick. Call this "the inference from inscrutable to pointless evil." Three main issues lurk here.

First, we need to consider whether there are any plausible reasons that would justify God in permitting the sorts of horrors Rowe et al. point to. Even if we can think of reasons for God to permit moral and natural evil, however, it does not follow that they justify God in permitting any *particular* evil. And it is particular evils that Rowe et al. point to. An interesting question arises: What is it, exactly, that God *must* have a reason to permit? Suppose He has a reason to permit a good deal of undeserved horrific evil. Must He also have a reason to permit each particular horror, or certain narrowly defined kinds of horrific evil, e.g., murder, child abuse, or suffering from disease? Of course, He *might* have such a reason. But Rowe et al. assume that He *must*. This issue is taken up explicitly in note 11 of van Inwagen's chapter 8, note 12 in Russell's chapter 10, van Inwagen's reply to Russell in chapter 12 and in §1 of chapter 15.[7]

The second main issue is raised most explicitly by Rowe (chapters 1 and 14) and William Alston (chapters 6 and 16). While Alston agrees that we cannot see how any reason we know of justifies God in permitting the particular evils Rowe et al. point to, he argues that they wrongly infer that no good we know of justifies God in permitting them, since we are in no position to make that judgment. Our grasp of the nature of some goods we know of may not allow us to assess their value properly. Moreover, our grasp of the conditions of their realization may not allow us to judge that they could have been realized without God permitting the evil in question. Rowe, however, cites several considerations that he believes make it eminently reasonable to affirm that no good we know of justifies God.

The third main issue is whether the inference from inscrutable to pointless evil is any good. One might argue that the best explanation of inscrutable evil is pointless evil (Russell, chapter 10),[8] or that if some good justified God, we would very likely know of it (Gale, chapter 11),[9] or that it is improbable in the extreme that there are goods outside our ken (Gale),[10] or that skepticism follows if we deny that certain horrific evils are not justifiably permitted by God (Russell and Gale), or that we have conducted the relevant search for reasons for God to permit these things (Russell), or that certain assignments to a Bayes theoretic formulation of the argument are justified (Rowe, chapter 14). In different ways, Alston (chapters 6 and 16), Plantinga (chapter 5), Wykstra (chapter 7), and the author of chapter 15 try to contribute to the dual thesis that not only are these bad reasons to draw the inference from inscrutable to pointless evil, but there is good reason to believe that the inference is *positively irrational,* to borrow Mackie's happy phrase.

4.3. EXPLANATORY ARGUMENTS

Contrary to popular opinion, not every evidential argument from evil employs the premise that there is no justifying reason for God to permit certain facts about evil. Recall the argument I attributed to Draper earlier, the conclusion of which is that the Hypothesis of Indifference (HI) explains known facts about sentient creatures experiencing pain and pleasure (O) much better than theism does, which he glosses as the claim that $Pr(O/HI) >! Pr(O/theism)$. A number of interesting issues need further study.

First, one frequently hears that to evaluate the truth of theism we must assess whether it is the best explanation of some relevant range of data. But why suppose that theism is in the business of *explaining* anything, much less various facts about evil? Is theism an explanation? Is theistic belief properly treated as belief that a certain explanation is true, better than its competitors, or some such thing? Draper and others—both theists and nontheists—assume affirmative answers to these questions; but, so far as I know, no one has defended those assumptions in any convincing way. This issue is central to explanatory arguments from evil. For if theism is not properly treated as an explanation (and we need not stoop to neo-

Wittgensteinian perversions to say it is not), then those who cavil at theism for being a bad explanation are caviling up the wrong tree.[11]

Second, in chapter 16, Alston raises a number of considerations that shed doubt on whether Draper's argument really should be thought of as an explanatory argument from evil. At best, Draper focuses on only one factor in determining whether one explanation is better than another. And neither of the explanans he compares—theism and HI—can be properly thought of as explanations, since neither is specific enough to throw any light on why the explanandum, O, occurred. Perhaps there is little point in comparing the explanatory power of theism and HI vis-à-vis O without using theistic or HI-istic stories as bridge principles that shed some light on why O occurred.

Third, is it really true that, given the biological role played by both pain and pleasure in organisms, and that independent of the effect of theistic stories on $Pr(O/theism)$, $Pr(O/HI) >! Pr(O/theism)$? In chapter 2, Draper defends an affirmative answer, while in chapter 13, Plantinga defends a negative one.[12]

Fourth, Draper argued that there were only two viable responses to his argument: (i) refute the argument by telling a theistic story that significantly raised $Pr(O/theism)$, or (ii) make a case for preferring theism to HI that outweighs the prima facie case for preferring HI to theism. According to Peter van Inwagen, this list of responses is incomplete. If we simply could not know whether to expect O on theism, then we would be in no position to judge that $Pr(O/HI) >! Pr(O/theism)$, and this, argues van Inwagen in chapter 8, is indeed the case. In chapters 9, 10, and 11, Draper, Russell, and Gale argue that the epistemic and moral principles van Inwagen uses and assumes lead to objectionable versions of skepticism. Van Inwagen clarifies his view and defends himself in chapter 12.

As a matter of practical necessity I have only gestured at some of the issues that the authors in this book address. Nothing can replace the careful study of their essays, to which I hope my reader now quickly turns.[13]

NOTES

1. J. L. Mackie, "Evil and Omnipotence," *Mind* 64 (1955): 200-212, reprinted in *God and Evil,* ed. Nelson Pike (Englewood Cliffs: Prentice-Hall, 1964), and in *The Problem of Evil,* ed. Marilyn McCord Adams and Robert Adams (Oxford: Oxford University Press, 1991).

2. Of course, anyone modestly acquainted with medieval philosophy will tell you that the proposition that evil exists is not an *essential* part of theism. Perhaps Mackie just meant to voice his conviction that it is exceedingly unreasonable for a theist to deny that evil exists, which seems quite right.

3. See Saint Thomas Aquinas, *Summa Theologica,* I, Q 25, Art. 3, for the sort of understanding that's proper.

4. The point I'm making here was first made, I believe, by Nelson Pike in "Hume on Evil," *Philosophical Review* (1963), reprinted in *God and Evil,* ed. Pike.

5. See Richard Swinburne, *The Existence of God* (Oxford: Clarendon Press, 1979), for a contemporary treatment of the topic.

6. This idea of Plantinga's will be developed more fully in Alvin Plantinga, *Warranted Christian Belief* (Oxford: Oxford University Press, forthcoming). See also William Alston, *Perceiving God* (Ithaca: Cornell University Press, 1992), for what else might be said in defense of nonpropositional grounds for theistic belief.

7. See also Peter van Inwagen, "The Place of Chance in a World Sustained by God," in *Divine and Human Action,* ed. Thomas V. Morris (Ithaca: Cornell University Press, 1988), and "The Magnitude, Duration, and Distribution of Evil: A Theodicy," *Philosophical Topics* 16 (Fall 1988), both in *God, Knowledge, and Mystery* (forthcoming).

8. See also Michael Martin, *Atheism: A Philosophical Justification* (Philadelphia: Temple University Press, 1990), chap. 9.

9. See also William Rowe, "The Empirical Argument from Evil," in *Rationality, Religious Belief, and Moral Commitment,* ed. Robert Audi and William J. Wainwright (Ithaca: Cornell University Press, 1986).

10. See also Michael Tooley, "The Argument from Evil," *Philosophical Perspectives* 5 (1991): 89-134.

11. I do not mean to imply that Draper or anyone else is not aware of the importance of this issue. Indeed, Draper is so fully aware of it that he is the guest editor of a future issue of *Topoi,* the topic of which is "Is Theism a Theory?" See also John O'Leary-Hawthorne and Daniel Howard-Snyder, "Are Beliefs about God Theoretical Beliefs? Reflections on Aquinas and Kant," *Religious Studies* (forthcoming).

12. For another negative answer, see Daniel Howard-Snyder, "Theism, the Hypothesis of Indifference and the Biological Role of Pain and Pleasure," *Faith and Philosophy* (1994).

13. In writing this introduction, I am indebted to Paul Draper, "Probabilistic Arguments from Evil," *Religious Studies* (1993).

THE EVIDENTIAL ARGUMENT FROM EVIL

1.

WILLIAM L. ROWE

The Problem of Evil
and Some Varieties of Atheism

This chapter is concerned with three interrelated questions. The first is: Is there
an argument for atheism based on the existence of evil that may rationally jus- *yes*
tify someone in being an atheist? To this first question I give an affirmative answer
and try to support that answer by setting forth a strong argument for atheism based
on the existence of evil. [2] The second question is: How can the theist best defend
his position against the argument for atheism based on the existence of evil? In
response to this question I try to describe what may be an adequate rational
defense for theism against any argument for atheism based on the existence of evil.
[3] The final question is: What position should the informed atheist take concerning
the rationality of theistic belief? Three different answers an atheist may give to this
question serve to distinguish three varieties of atheism: unfriendly atheism, indifferent atheism, and friendly atheism. In the final part of the paper I discuss and
defend the position of friendly atheism.

Before we consider the argument from evil, we need to distinguish a narrow and a broad sense of the terms "theist," "atheist," and "agnostic." By a "theist"
in the narrow sense I mean someone who believes in the existence of an omnipo-

tent, omniscient, eternal, supremely good being who created the world. By a "theist" in the broad sense I mean someone who believes in the existence of some sort
of divine being or divine reality. To be a theist in the narrow sense is also to be a
theist in the broad sense, but one may be a theist in the broad sense—as was Paul
Tillich—without believing that there is a supremely good, omnipotent, omniscient, eternal being who created the world. Similar distinctions must be made
between a narrow and a broad sense of the terms "atheist" and "agnostic." To be an
atheist in the broad sense is to deny the existence of any sort of divine being or
divine reality. Tillich was not an atheist in the broad sense. But he was an atheist in
the narrow sense, for he denied that there exists a divine being that is all-knowing,
all-powerful, and perfectly good. In this paper I will be using the terms "theism,"
"atheist," "agnosticism," and "agnostic" in the narrow sense, not in the broad sense.

I

In developing the argument for atheism based on the existence of evil, it
will be useful to focus on some particular evil that our world contains in considerable abundance. Intense human and animal suffering, for example, occurs daily
and in great plenitude in our world. Such intense suffering is a clear case of evil.
Of course, if the intense suffering leads to some greater good, a good we could not
have obtained without undergoing the suffering in question, we might conclude
that the suffering is justified, but it remains an evil nevertheless. For we must not
confuse the intense suffering in and of itself with the good things to which it sometimes leads or of which it may be a necessary part. Intense human or animal suffering is in itself bad, an evil, even though it may sometimes be justified by virtue
of being a part of, or leading to, some good which is unobtainable without it. What
is evil in itself may sometimes be good as a means because it leads to something
that is good in itself. In such a case, while remaining an evil in itself, the intense
human or animal suffering is, nevertheless, an evil which someone might be
morally justified in permitting.

Taking human and animal suffering as a clear instance of evil which occurs
with great frequency in our world, the argument for atheism based on evil can be
stated as follows:

> 1. There exist instances of intense suffering which an omnipotent, omni-
> scient being could have prevented without thereby losing some greater
> good or permitting some evil equally bad or worse.[2]
> 2. An omniscient, wholly good being would prevent the occurrence of
> any intense suffering it could, unless it could not do so without thereby
> losing some greater good or permitting some evil equally bad or worse.
> 3. There does not exist an omnipotent, omniscient, wholly good being.

What are we to say about this argument for atheism, an argument based on the
profusion of one sort of evil in our world? The argument is valid; therefore, if we
have rational grounds for accepting its premises, to that extent we have rational

grounds for accepting atheism. Do we, however, have rational grounds for accepting the premises of this argument?

Let's begin with the second premise. Let $s1$ be an instance of intense human or animal suffering which an omniscient, wholly good being could prevent. We will also suppose that things are such that $s1$ will occur unless prevented by the omniscient, wholly good (OG) being. We might be interested in determining what would be a *sufficient* condition of OG failing to prevent $s1$. But, for our purpose here, we need only try to state a *necessary* condition for OG failing to prevent $s1$. That condition, so it seems to me, is this:

> *Either* (i) there is some greater good, G, such that G is obtainable by OG only if OG permits $s1$,[3]
>
> *or* (ii) there is some greater good, G, such that G is obtainable by OG only if OG permits either $s1$ or some evil equally bad or worse,
>
> *or* (iii) $s1$ is such that it is preventable by OG only if OG permits some evil equally bad or worse.

It is important to recognize that (iii) is not included in (i). For losing a good greater than $s1$ is not the same as permitting an evil greater than $s1$. And this is because the *absence* of a good state of affairs need not itself be an evil state of affairs. It is also important to recognize that $s1$ might be such that it is preventable by OG *without* losing G (so condition (i) is not satisfied) but also such that if OG did prevent it, G would be lost unless OG permitted some evil equal to or worse than $s1$. If this were so, it does not seem correct to require that OG prevent $s1$. Thus, condition (ii) takes into account an important possibility not encompassed in condition (i).

Is it true that if an omniscient, wholly good being permits the occurrence of some intense suffering it could have prevented, then either (i) or (ii) or (iii) obtains? It seems to me that it is true. But if it is true, then so is premise (2) of the argument for atheism. For that premise merely states in more compact form what we have suggested must be true if an omniscient, wholly good being fails to prevent some intense suffering it could prevent. Premise (2) says that an omniscient, wholly good being would prevent the occurrence of any intense suffering it could, unless it could not do so without thereby losing some greater good or permitting some evil equally bad or worse. This premise (or something not too distant from it) is, I think, held in common by many atheists and nontheists. Of course, there may be disagreement about whether something is good, and whether, if it is good, one would be morally justified in permitting some intense suffering to occur in order to obtain it. Someone might hold, for example, that no good is great enough to justify permitting an innocent child to suffer terribly.[4] Again, someone might hold that the mere fact that a given good outweighs some suffering and would be lost if the suffering were prevented, is not a morally sufficient reason for permitting the suffering. But to hold either of these views is not to deny (2). For (2) claims only that *if* an omniscient, wholly good being permits intense suffering, *then* either there is some greater good that would have been lost, or some equally bad or worse evil that would have occurred, had the intense suffering been prevented. (2) does not purport to describe what might be a *sufficient* condition for an omniscient, wholly good being to permit intense suffering, only what is a *necessary* condition. So stated, (2) seems to express a belief that accords with our basic moral principles, principles shared by both theists and nontheists. If we are to fault the argument for atheism, therefore, it seems we must find some fault with its first premise.

Suppose in some distant forest lightning strikes a dead tree, resulting in a forest fire. In the fire a fawn is trapped, horribly burned, and lies in terrible agony for several days before death relieves its suffering. So far as we can see, the fawn's intense suffering is pointless. For there does not appear to be any greater good such that the prevention of the fawn's suffering would require either the loss of that good or the occurrence of an evil equally bad or worse. Nor does there seem to be any equally bad or worse evil so connected to the fawn's suffering that it would have had to occur had the fawn's suffering been prevented. Could an omnipotent, omniscient being have prevented the fawn's apparently pointless suffering? The answer is obvious, as even the theist will insist. An omnipotent, omniscient being could have easily prevented the fawn from being horribly burned, or, given the burning, could have spared the fawn the intense suffering by quickly ending its life, rather than allowing the fawn to lie in terrible agony for several days. Since the fawn's intense suffering was preventable and, so far as we can see, pointless, doesn't it appear that premise (1) of the argument is true, that there do exist instances of intense suffering which an omnipotent, omniscient being could have prevented without thereby losing some greater good or permitting some evil equally bad or worse.

It must be acknowledged that the case of the fawn's apparently pointless suffering does not *prove* that (1) is true. For even though we cannot see how the fawn's suffering is required to obtain some greater good (or to prevent some equally bad or worse evil), it hardly follows that it is not so required. After all, we are often surprised by how things we thought to be unconnected turn out to be intimately connected. Perhaps, for all we know, there is some familiar good outweighing the fawn's suffering to which that suffering is connected in a way we do not see. Furthermore, there may be unfamiliar goods, goods we haven't dreamed of, to which the fawn's suffering is inextricably connected. Indeed, it would seem to require something like omniscience on our part before we should lay claim to *knowing* that there is no greater good connected to the fawn's suffering in such a manner than an omnipotent, omniscient being could not have achieved that good without permitting that suffering or some evil equally bad or worse. So the case of the fawn's suffering surely does not enable us to *establish* the truth of (1).

The truth is that we are not in a position to prove that (1) is true. We cannot know with certainty that instances of suffering of the sort described in (1) do occur in our world. But it is one thing to *know* or *prove* that (1) is true and quite another thing to have *rational grounds* for believing (1) to be true. We are often in the position where in the light of our experience and knowledge it is rational to believe that a certain statement is true, even though we are not in a position to prove or to know with certainty that the statement is true. In the light of our past experience and knowledge it is, for example, very reasonable to believe that neither Goldwater nor McGovern will ever be elected President, but we are scarcely in the position of knowing with certainty that neither will ever be elected President. So, too, with (1), although we cannot know with certainty that it is true, it perhaps can be rationally supported, shown to be a rational belief.

Consider again the case of the fawn's suffering. Is it reasonable to believe that there is some greater good so intimately connected to that suffering that even an omnipotent, omniscient being could not have obtained that good without permitting that suffering or some evil at least as bad? It certainly does not appear reasonable to believe this. Nor does it seem reasonable to believe that there is some evil at least as bad as the fawn's suffering such that an omnipotent being simply could not have prevented it without permitting the fawn's suffering. But even if it should somehow be reasonable to believe either of these things of the fawn's suffering, we must then ask whether it is reasonable to believe either of these things of *all* the instances of seemingly pointless human and animal suffering that occur daily in our world. And surely the answer to this more general question must be no. It seems quite unlikely that *all* the instances of intense suffering occurring daily in our world are intimately related to the occurrence of a greater good or the prevention of evils at least as bad; and even more unlikely, should they somehow all be so related, that an omnipotent, omniscient being could not have achieved at least some of those goods (or prevented some of those evils) without permitting the instances of intense suffering that are supposedly related to them. In the light of our experience and knowledge of the variety and scale of human and animal suffering in our world, the idea that none of this suffering could have been prevented by an omnipotent being without thereby losing a greater good or permitting an evil at least as bad seems an extraordinarily absurd idea, quite beyond our belief. It seems then that although we cannot *prove* that (1) is true, it is, nevertheless, altogether *reasonable* to believe that (1) is true, that (1) is a *rational* belief.[5]

Returning now to our argument for atheism, we've seen that the second premise expresses a basic belief common to many theists and nontheists. We've also seen that our experience and knowledge of the variety and profusion of suffering in our world provides *rational support* for the first premise. Seeing that the conclusion, "There does not exist an omnipotent, omniscient, wholly good being," follows from these two premises, it does seem that we have rational support for atheism, that it is reasonable for us to believe that the theistic God does not exist.

II

Can theism be rationally defended against the argument for atheism we have just examined? If it can, how might the theist best respond to that argument? Since the argument from (1) and (2) to (3) is valid, and since the theist, no less than the nontheist, is more than likely committed to (2), it's clear that the theist can reject this atheistic argument only by rejecting its first premise, the premise that there are instances of intense suffering which an omnipotent, omniscient being could have prevented without thereby losing some greater good or permitting some evil equally bad or worse. How, then, can the theist best respond to this premise and the considerations advanced in its support?

There are basically three responses a theist can make. First, he might argue not that (1) is false or probably false, but only that the reasoning given in support of it is in some way *defective.* He may do this either by arguing that the reasons given in support of (1) are *in themselves* insufficient to justify accepting (1), or by arguing that there are other things we know which, when taken in conjunction with these reasons, do not justify us in accepting (1). I suppose some theists would be content with this rather modest response to the basic argument for atheism. But given the validity of the basic argument and the theist's likely acceptance of (2), he is thereby committed to the view that (1) is false, not just that we have no good reasons for accepting (1) as true. The second two responses are aimed at showing that it is reasonable to believe that (1) is false. Since the theist is committed to this view, I shall focus the discussion on these two attempts, attempts which we can distinguish as "the direct attack" and "the indirect attack."

By a direct attack, I mean an attempt to reject (1) by pointing out goods, for example, to which suffering may well be connected, goods which an omnipotent, omniscient being could not achieve without permitting suffering. It is doubtful, however, that the direct attack can succeed. The theist may point out that some suffering leads to moral and spiritual development impossible without suffering. But it's reasonably clear that suffering often occurs in a degree far beyond what is required for character development. The theist may say that some suffering results from free choices of human beings and might be preventable only by preventing some measure of human freedom. But, again, it's clear that much intense suffering occurs not as a result of human free choices. The general difficulty with this direct attack on premise (1) is twofold. First, it cannot succeed, for the theist does not know what greater goods might be served, or evils prevented, by each instance of intense human or animal suffering. Second, the theist's own religious tradition usually maintains that in this life it is not given to us to know God's purpose in allowing particular instances of suffering. Hence, the direct attack against premise (1) cannot succeed and violates basic beliefs associated with theism.

The best procedure for the theist to follow in rejecting premise (1) is the indirect procedure. This procedure I shall call "the G. E. Moore shift," so called in honor of the twentieth-century philosopher, G. E. Moore, who used it to great effect in dealing with the arguments of the skeptics. Skeptical philosophers such as David Hume have advanced ingenious arguments to prove that no one can know of the existence of any material object. The premises of their arguments employ plausible principles, principles which many philosophers have tried to reject directly, but only with questionable success. Moore's procedure was altogether different. Instead of arguing directly against the premises of the skeptic's arguments, he simply noted that the premises implied, for example, that he (Moore) did not know of the existence of a pencil. Moore then proceeded indirectly against the skeptic's premises by arguing:

I do know that this pencil exists.
If the skeptic's principles are correct I cannot know the existence of this pencil.
Therefore,
∴The skeptic's principles (at least one) must be incorrect.

Moore then noted that his argument is just as valid as the skeptic's, that both of their arguments contain the premise "If the skeptic's principles are correct Moore cannot know of the existence of this pencil," and concluded that the only way to choose between the two arguments (Moore's and the skeptic's) is by deciding which of the first premises it is more rational to believe—Moore's premise, "I do know that this pencil exists," or the skeptic's premise asserting that his skeptical principles are correct. Moore concluded that his own first premise was the more rational of the two.[6]

Before we see how the theist may apply the G. E. Moore shift to the basic argument for atheism, we should note the general strategy of the shift. We're given an argument: *p, q,* therefore, *r.* Instead of arguing directly against *p,* another argument is constructed—not-*r, q,* therefore, not-*p*—which begins with the denial of the conclusion of the first argument, keeps its second premise, and ends with the denial of the first premise as its conclusion. Compare, for example, these two:

I.   *p*   II.   not-*r*
         q   *q*
         —   —
         r   not-*p*

$$\text{if } p \text{ then } q \qquad \text{if } p \text{ then } q$$
$$\underline{\quad p \quad} \qquad\qquad \underline{\quad \neg q \quad}$$
$$q \qquad\qquad\qquad \neg p$$

It is a truth of logic that if I is valid, II must be valid as well. Since the arguments are the same so far as the second premise is concerned, any choice between them must concern their respective first premises. To argue against the first premise (*p*) by constructing the counterargument II is to employ the G. E. Moore shift.

Applying the G. E. Moore shift against the first premise of the basic argument for atheism, the theist can argue as follows:

not-3. There exists an omnipotent, omniscient, wholly good being.
2. An omniscient, wholly good being would prevent the occurrence of any intense suffering it could, unless it could not do so without thereby losing some greater good or permitting some evil equally bad or worse.
Therefore,
not-1. It is not the case that there exist instances of intense suffering which an omnipotent, omniscient being could have prevented without thereby losing some greater good or permitting some evil equally bad or worse.

We now have two arguments: the basic argument for atheism from (1) and (2) to (3), and the theist's best response, the argument from (not-3) and (2) to (not-1). What the theist then says about (1) is that he has rational grounds for believing in the existence of the theistic God (not-3), accepts (2) as true, and sees that (not-1) follows from (not-3) and (2). He concludes, therefore, that he has rational grounds for rejecting (1). Having rational grounds for rejecting (1), the theist concludes that the basic argument for atheism is mistaken.

III

We've had a look at a forceful argument for atheism and what seems to be the theist's best response to that argument. If one is persuaded by the argument for atheism, as I find myself to be, how might one best view the position of the theist? Of course, he will view the theist as having a false belief, just as the theist will view the atheist as having a false belief. But what position should the atheist take concerning the rationality of the theist's belief? There are three major positions an atheist might take, positions which we may think of as some varieties of atheism. First, the atheist may believe that no one is rationally justified in believing that the theistic God exists. Let us call this position "unfriendly atheism." Second, the atheist may hold no belief concerning whether any theist is or isn't rationally justified in believing that the theistic God exists. Let us call this view "indifferent atheism." Finally, the atheist may believe that some theists are rationally justified in believing that the theistic God exists. This view we shall call "friendly atheism." In this final part of the paper I propose to discuss and defend the position of friendly atheism.

If no one can be rationally justified in believing a false proposition, then friendly atheism is a paradoxical if not incoherent position. But surely the truth of a belief is not a necessary condition of someone's being rationally justified in having that belief. So in holding that someone is rationally justified in believing that the theistic God exists, the friendly atheist is not committed to thinking that the theist has a true belief. What he is committed to is that the theist has rational grounds for his belief, a belief the atheist rejects and is convinced he is rationally justified in rejecting. But is this possible? Can someone, like our friendly atheist, hold a belief, be convinced that he is rationally justified in holding that belief, and yet believe that someone else is equally justified in believing the opposite? Surely this is possible. Suppose your friends see you off on a flight to Hawaii. Hours after take-off they learn that your plane has gone down at sea. After a twenty-four hour search, no survivors have been found. Under these circumstances they are rationally justified in believing that you have perished. But it is hardly rational for you to believe this, as you bob up and down in your life vest, wondering why the search planes have failed to spot you. Indeed, to amuse yourself while awaiting your fate, you might very well reflect on the fact that your friends are rationally justified in believing that you are now dead, a proposition you disbelieve and are rationally justified in disbelieving. So, too, perhaps an atheist may be rationally justified in his atheistic belief and yet hold that some theists are rationally justified in believing just the opposite of what he believes.

What sort of grounds might a theist have for believing that God exists? Well, he might endeavor to justify his belief by appealing to one or more of the traditional arguments: Ontological, Cosmological, Teleological, Moral, etc. Second, he might appeal to certain aspects of religious experience, perhaps even his own religious experience. Third, he might try to justify theism as a plausible theory in terms of which we can account for a variety of phenomena. Although an atheist must hold that the theistic God does not exist, can he not also believe, and be justified in so believing, that some of these "justifications of theism" do actually rationally justify some theists in their belief that there exists a supremely good, omnipotent, omniscient being? It seems to me that he can.

If we think of the long history of theistic belief and the special situations in which people are sometimes placed, it is perhaps as absurd to think that no one was ever rationally justified in believing that the theistic God exists as it is to think that no one was ever justified in believing that human beings would never walk on the moon. But in suggesting that friendly atheism is preferable to unfriendly atheism, I don't mean to rest the case on what some human beings might reasonably have believed in the eleventh or thirteenth century. The more interesting question is whether some people in modern society, people who are aware of the usual grounds for belief and disbelief and are acquainted to some degree with modern science, are yet rationally justified in accepting theism. Friendly atheism is a significant position only if it answers this question in the affirmative.

It is not difficult for an atheist to be friendly when he has reason to believe that the theist could not reasonably be expected to be acquainted with the grounds for disbelief that he (the atheist) possesses. For then the atheist may take the view that some theists are rationally justified in holding to theism but would not be so were they to be acquainted with the grounds for disbelief—those grounds being sufficient to tip the scale in favor of atheism when balanced against the reasons the theist has in support of his belief.

Friendly atheism becomes paradoxical, however, when the atheist contemplates believing that the theist has all the grounds for atheism that he, the atheist, has, and yet is rationally justified in maintaining his theistic belief. But even so excessively friendly a view as this perhaps can be held by the atheist if he also has some reason to think that the grounds for theism are not as telling as the theist is justified in taking them to be.[7]

In this paper I've presented what I take to be a strong argument for atheism, pointed out what I think is the theist's best response to that argument, distinguished three positions an atheist might take concerning the rationality of theistic belief, and made some remarks in defense of the position called "friendly atheism." I'm aware that the central points of the paper are not likely to be warmly received by many philosophers. Philosophers who are atheists tend to be tough minded, holding that there are no good reasons for supposing that theism is true. And theists tend either to reject the view that the existence of evil provides rational grounds for atheism or to hold that religious belief has nothing to do with reason and evidence at all. But such is the way of philosophy.[8]

NOTES

This essay originally appeared in *American Philosophical Quarterly,* volume 16 (1979). It is reprinted with permission.

1. Some philosophers have contended that the existence of evil is *logically incon-sistent* with the existence of the theistic God. No one, I think, has succeeded in establishing such an extravagant claim. Indeed, granted incompatibilism, there is a fairly compelling argument for the view that the existence of evil is logically consistent with the existence of the theistic God. (For a lucid statement of this argument, see Alvin Plantinga, *God, Freedom, and Evil* (Grand Rapids: Eerdmans, 1977), 29-59). There remains, however, what we may call the *evidential* form—as opposed to the *logical* form—of the problem of evil: the view that the variety and profusion of evil in our world, although perhaps not logically incon-sistent with the existence of the theistic God, provides, nevertheless, *rational support* for atheism. In this paper I shall be concerned solely with the evidential form of the problem, the form of the problem which, I think, presents a rather severe difficulty for theism.

2. If there is some good, *G,* greater than any evil, (1) will be false for the trivial reason that no matter what evil, *E,* we pick, the conjunctive good state of affairs consisting of *G* and *E* will outweigh *E* and be such that an omnipotent being could not obtain it with-out permitting *E.* (See Alvin Plantinga, *God and Other Minds,* Ithaca: Cornell University Press, 1967, 167.) To avoid this objection we may insert "unreplaceable" into our premises (1) and (2) between "some" and "greater." If *E* isn't required for *G,* and *G* is better than *G* plus *E,* then the good conjunctive state of affairs composed of *G* and *E* would be *replaceable* by the greater good of *G* alone. For the sake of simplicity, however, I will ignore this com-plication both in the formulation and discussion of premises (1) and (2).

3. Three clarifying points need to be made in connection with (i). First, by "good" I don't mean to exclude the fulfillment of certain moral principles. Perhaps pre-venting *s1* would preclude certain actions prescribed by the principles of justice. I shall allow that the satisfaction of certain principles of justice may be a good that outweighs the evil of *s1.* Second, even though (i) may suggest it, I don't mean to limit the good in ques-tion to something that would *follow in time* the occurrence of *s1.* And, finally, we should per-haps not fault *OG* if the good *G,* that would be lost were *s1* prevented, is not actually greater than *s1,* but merely such that allowing *s1* and *G,* as opposed to preventing *s1* and thereby losing *G,* would not alter the balance between good and evil. For reasons of simplicity, I have left this point out in stating (i), with the result that (i) is perhaps a bit stronger than it should be.

4. See Ivan's speech in Book V, Chapter IV of *The Brothers Karamazov.*

5. One might object that the conclusion of this paragraph is stronger than the reasons given warrant. For it is one thing to argue that it is unreasonable to think that (1) is false and another thing to conclude that we are therefore justified in accepting (1) as true. There are propositions such that believing them is much more reasonable than dis-believing them, and yet are such that *withholding judgment* about them is more reasonable than believing them. To take an example of Chisholm's: it is more reasonable to suspend judgment on the question of the Pope's whereabouts on that particular date, than to believe that he will be in Rome. Thus it might be objected that while we've shown that believing (1) is more reasonable than disbelieving (1), we haven't shown that believing (1) is more reasonable than withholding belief. My answer to this objection is that there are things we know which render (1) probable to the degree that it is more reasonable to believe (1) than to suspend judgment on (1). What are these things we know? First, I think, is the fact that there is an enormous variety and profusion of intense human and animal suffering in our world. Second is the fact that much of this suffering seems quite unrelated to any greater goods (or the absence of equal or greater evils) that might justify it. And, finally, there is the fact that such suffering as is related to greater goods (or the absence of equal or greater evils) does not, in many cases, seem so intimately related as to require its

permission by an omnipotent being bent on securing those goods (the absence of those evils). These facts, I am claiming, make it more reasonable to accept (1) than to withhold judgment on (1).

6. See, for example, the two chapters on Hume in G. E. Moore, *Some Main Problems of Philosophy* (London: George Allen and Unwin Ltd., 1953).

7. Suppose that I add a long sum of numbers three times and get result *x*. I inform you of this so that you have pretty much the same evidence I have for the claim that the sum of the numbers is *x*. You then use your calculator twice over and arrive at result *y*. You, then, are justified in believing that the sum of the numbers is *not x*. However, knowing that your calculator has been damaged and is therefore unreliable, and that you have no reason to think that it is damaged, *I* may reasonably believe not only that the sum of the numbers is *x*, but also that you are justified in believing that the sum is not *x*. Here is a case, then, where you have all of my evidence for *p*, and yet I can reasonably believe that you are justified in believing not-*p*, for I have reason to believe that your grounds for not-*p* are not as telling as you are justified in taking them to be.

8. I am indebted to my colleagues at Purdue University, particularly to Ted Ulrich and Lilly Russow, and to philosophers at The University of Nebraska, Indiana State University, and The University of Wisconsin at Milwaukee for helpful criticisms of earlier versions of this paper.

PAUL DRAPER

Pain and Pleasure: An Evidential Problem for Theists

I. The Nature of the Problem

I will argue in this paper that our knowledge about pain and pleasure creates an epistemic problem for theists. The problem is not that some proposition about pain and pleasure can be shown to be both true and logically inconsistent with theism. Rather, the problem is evidential. A statement reporting the observations and testimony upon which our knowledge about pain and pleasure is based bears a certain significant negative evidential relation to theism.[1] And because of this, we have a prima facie good epistemic reason to reject theism—that is, a reason that is sufficient for rejecting theism unless overridden by other reasons for not rejecting theism.

By "theism" I mean the following statement:

There exists an omnipotent, omniscient, and morally perfect person who created the Universe.

I will use the word "God" as a title rather than as a proper name, and I will stipulate that necessary and sufficient conditions for bearing this title are that one be an omnipotent, omniscient, and morally perfect person who created the Universe. Given this (probably technical) use of the term "God," theism is the statement that God exists.

Some philosophers believe that the evils we find in the world create an evidential problem for theists because theism fails to explain these evils (or most of what we know about them). (See, for example, Hare 1968.) This position is attractive. It seems to reflect the intuitions of a great many people who have regarded evil as an epistemic problem for theists. After all, the most common way of stating the problem of evil is to ask a why question like "if God exists, then why is there so much evil in the world?" And such questions are either genuine or rhetorical requests for explanation. Moreover, the relevance of theodicies to this alleged problem of evil is quite clear, since a theodicy can very naturally be understood as an attempt to explain certain evils or facts about evil in terms of theism.

But other philosophers who agree that theism fails to explain most of the evils we find in the world deny that this creates an epistemic problem for theists— that is, they deny that this explanatory failure is a prima facie good reason to reject theism. This disagreement has led to a debate over how much evil, if any, theism needs to explain to avoid disconfirmation. (See, for example, Yandell 1969a and 1969b, Kane 1970, Mavrodes 1970, pp. 90-111, Ahern 1971, Hare 1972, and Yandell 1972.)* What the members of both sides of this debate have failed to recognize is that one cannot determine what facts about evil theism needs to explain or how well it needs to explain them without considering alternatives to theism. The important question, a question that David Hume asked (1980, Part XI, pp. 74-75) but that most contemporary philosophers of religion have ignored, is whether or not any serious hypothesis that is logically inconsistent with theism explains some significant set of facts about evil or about good and evil much better than theism does.

I will argue for an affirmative answer to this question. Specifically, I will compare theism to the following alternative, which I will call "the Hypothesis of Indifference" ("HI" for short):

HI: neither the nature nor the condition of sentient beings on earth is the result of benevolent or malevolent actions performed by nonhuman persons.

Unlike theism, HI does not entail that supernatural beings exist and so is consistent with naturalism. But HI is also consistent with the existence of supernatural beings. What makes HI inconsistent with theism is that it entails that, if supernatural beings do exist, then no action performed by them is motivated by a direct concern for our well-being. Now let "O" stand for a statement reporting both the observations one has made of humans and animals experiencing pain or pleasure and the testimony one has encountered concerning the observations others have made of sentient beings experiencing pain or pleasure. By "pain" I mean physical or mental suffering of any sort. I will argue that the pain and pleasure in our world create an epistemic problem for theists by arguing that:

C: HI explains the facts O reports much better than theism does.

One problem with this formulation of C is that the verb "to explain" has a number of distinct but easily confused meanings. For my purposes here, it will suffice to point out that in some instances the claim that one hypothesis explains some observation report much better than another is equivalent in meaning, or at least bears a close conceptual connection, to the claim that the truth of that observation report is much less surprising on the first hypothesis than it is on the second. Since I suspect that it is only in these instances that comparisons of explanatory power support comparisons of probability, I will reformulate C as the claim that the facts O reports are much more surprising on theism than they are on HI, or, more precisely, that the antecedent probability of O is much greater on the assumption that HI is true than on the assumption that theism is true. By the "antecedent" probability of O, I mean O's probability, independent of (rather than temporally prior to) the observations and testimony it reports. So my reformulation of C is best expressed as follows:

C: independent of the observations and testimony O reports, O is much more probable on the assumption that HI is true than on the assumption that theism is true.

For the sake of brevity, I will use P(x/y) to represent the probability of the statement x, *independent of the observations and testimony O reports,* on the assumption that the statement y is true. Using this notation, I can abbreviate C in the following way:

C: P(O/HI) is much greater than P(O/theism).

One last elucidatory remark about C. The probabilities employed in C are epistemic ones rather than, for example, statistical, physical, or logical probabilities.[2] Thus, they can vary from person to person and from time to time, since different persons can be in different epistemic situations at the same time and the same person can be in different epistemic situations at different times. For example, suppose that six hands of poker are dealt. Then the epistemic probability that one hand includes four aces will be different for those players who inspect their hands and find no aces and those players who inspect their hands and discover one or more aces. And the epistemic probability for any of the six players that one hand includes four aces will be different before inspecting his or her hand than after inspecting it.

Now suppose that I succeed in showing that C is true (relative to my own and my readers' epistemic situations). Then the truth of C is (for us) a prima facie good (epistemic) reason to believe that theism is less probable than HI. Thus, since the denial of theism is obviously entailed by HI and so is at least as probable as HI, the truth of C is a prima facie good reason to believe that theism is less probable than not. And since it is epistemically irrational to believe both that theism is true and that it is less probable than not, the truth of C is also a prima facie good reason to reject (i.e., to cease or refrain from believing) theism.

In Section II, I will argue that C is true. However, my argument will depend on the assumption that theodicies do not significantly raise P(O/theism). In Section III, I will defend this assumption. And in Section IV, I will discuss the significance of C's truth.

II. *The Biological Utility of Pain and Pleasure*

The claim that P(O/HI) is much greater than P(O/theism) is by no means obviously true. The fact that O reports observations and testimony about pleasure as well as pain should make this clear. So an argument for this claim is needed. I will argue that it is the biological role played by both pain and pleasure in goal-directed organic systems that renders this claim true. In order to explain precisely why this is so, I will need to introduce a concept of "biological usefulness."

Though no one doubts that organic systems are goal-directed in some objective sense, it is by no means easy to provide a precise analysis of this kind of goal-directedness. As a first approximation, we may say that a system S is "goal-directed" just in case from some property G that S has exhibited or will exhibit, a broad range of potential environmental changes are such that: (i) if they occurred at a time when S is exhibiting G and no compensating changes took place in the parts of S, then S would cease to exhibit G and never exhibit G again, and (ii) if they occurred at a time when S is exhibiting G, then compensating changes would take place in the parts of S, resulting in either S's continuing to exhibit G or in S's exhibiting G once again. (Cf. Boorse 1976 and Ruse 1973.) Notice that to be goal-directed in this sense does not entail direction to the conscious end of some intelligent being. Notice also that the organic world is made up of complex and interdependent goal-directed systems, including ecosystems, populations of organisms, organisms, parts of organisms, parts of parts of organisms, and so on.

I will call the goals to which organic systems are directed in this sense their "biological goals." And I will say that a part of some goal-directed organic system S is "biologically useful" just in case (i) it causally contributes to one of S's biological goals (or to one of the biological goals of some other goal-directed organic system of which it is a part), and (ii) its doing so is not biologically accidental. (It is in virtue of clause ii that, for example, a nonfatal heart attack that prevents a person from committing suicide cannot be called biologically useful.) Notice that much of the pain and pleasure in the world is biologically useful in this sense. Consider, for example, the pain my cat Hector felt when he jumped on top of a hot oven door. Hector's quick response to this pain enabled him to avoid serious injury, and he now flees whenever an oven door is opened. Hector's pain in this case, like much of the pain reported by O, was biologically useful. For it causally contributed to two central biological goals of individual organisms, namely, survival and reproduction, and its doing so was plainly not accidental from a biological point of view. Of course, there is also much pain and pleasure in our world that is not biologically useful: for instance, masochistic pleasure and pain resulting from burns that ultimately prove fatal. (I will sometimes call this kind of pain and pleasure "biologically gratuitous.")

This notion of biological utility enables me to introduce a statement logically equivalent to O that will help me show that C is true. Let "O1," "O2," and "O3" stand for statements respectively reporting the facts O reports about:

> (1) moral agents experiencing pain or pleasure that we know to be biologically useful,
> (2) sentient beings that are not moral agents experiencing pain, or pleasure that we know to be biologically useful, and
> (3) sentient beings experiencing pain or pleasure that we do not know to be biologically useful.

Since O is obviously logically equivalent to the conjunction of O1, O2, and O3, it follows that, for any hypothesis h:

$$P(O/h) = P(O1 \& O2 \& O3/h)$$

But the following theorem of the mathematical calculus of probability holds for epistemic probability:

$$P(O1 \& O2 \& O3/h) = P(O1/h) \times P(O2/h \& O1) \times P(O3/h \& O1 \& O2).[3]$$

Thus, C is true—P(O/HI) is much greater than P(O/theism)—just in case:

> A: $P(O1/HI) \times P(O2/HI \& O1) \times P(O3/HI \& O1 \& O2)$

is much greater than

> B: $P(O1/theism) \times P(O2/theism \& O1) \times P(O3/theism \& O1 \& O2)$.

I will argue that A is much greater than B by arguing that each of the multiplicands of A is either greater or much greater than the corresponding multiplicand of B. As I will explain in Section III, my arguments will assume that theodicies do not significantly raise P(O/theism).

Let us begin with O1, which reports those facts reported by O about humans (who are moral agents) experiencing pain or pleasure that we know to be biologically useful. We know antecedently—that is, we know independent of the observations and testimony O reports—that humans are goal-directed organic systems, composed of parts that systematically contribute to the biological goals of these systems. This seems to give us reason to expect that human pain and pleasure, if they exist, will also systematically contribute to these goals. (And this is, of course, precisely what O1 reports.) But notice that pain and pleasure are in one respect strikingly dissimilar to other parts of organic systems: they have intrinsic moral value. Pain is intrinsically bad, and pleasure is intrinsically good. Does this difference substantially decrease the amount of support that our antecedent knowledge about humans gives to the "prediction" that pain and pleasure, if they exist, will systematically contribute to biological goals? I submit that it does if we assume that theism is true, but does not if we assume that HI is true. It is this difference between HI and theism that makes P(O1/HI) much greater than P(O1/theism).

Allow me to explain. HI entails that, if pain and pleasure exist, then they are not the result of malevolent or benevolent actions performed by nonhuman persons. So on HI, the moral difference between pain and pleasure and other parts of organic systems gives us no antecedent reason to believe that pain and pleasure will not play the same biological role that other parts of organic systems play. Indeed, a biological explanation of pain and pleasure is just the sort of explanation that one would expect on HI. But theism entails that God is responsible for the existence of any pain and pleasure in the world. Since God is morally perfect, He would have good moral reasons for producing pleasure even if it is never biologically useful, and He would not permit pain unless He had, not just a biological reason, but also a morally sufficient reason to do so. And since God is omnipotent and omniscient, He could create goal-directed organic systems (including humans) without biologically useful pain and pleasure. So theism entails both that God does not need biologically useful pain and pleasure to produce human goal-directed organic systems and that, if human pain and pleasure exist, then God had good moral reasons for producing them, reasons that, for all we know antecedently, might very well be inconsistent with pain and pleasure systematically contributing to the biological goals of human organisms. Therefore, we would have much less reason on theism than on HI to be surprised if it turned out that human pain and pleasure differed from other parts of organic systems by not systematically contributing to the biological goals of those systems. Hence, since O1 reports that the pain and pleasure experienced by humans (who are moral agents) do contribute in this way, P(O1/HI) is much greater than P(O1/theism).

One might object that from theism and our antecedent knowledge that goal-directed organic systems exist, we can infer that the biological functions of the parts of those systems are themselves morally worthwhile, which gives us reason on theism that we do not have on HI to expect pain and pleasure to have biological functions. It might be thought that this counterbalances the reasons offered above for concluding that O1 is antecedently much more likely given HI than it is given theism.[4] Now we obviously cannot infer from theism and our antecedent knowledge that the greater the number of functioning parts in an organic system, the more valuable the system. We might be able to infer that organic systems are valuable and that the parts of these systems that have biological functions are valuable because the systems could not exist without functioning parts. But this does not imply that we have as much or even close to as much reason on theism as on HI to expect pain and pleasure to have biological functions. For an omnipotent and omniscient being could produce such systems without biologically useful pain and pleasure. Thus, since a morally perfect being would try to accomplish its goals with as little pain as possible, the value of organic systems gives us no reason on theism to expect pain to have biological functions. And since pleasure has intrinsic value and so is worth producing whether or not it furthers some other goal, the value of organic systems gives us very little reason on theism to expect pleasure to have biological functions.

O2 reports the observations and testimony reported by O about sentient beings that are not moral agents (e.g., young human children and nonhuman animals) experiencing pain or pleasure that we know to be biologically useful. Independent of the observations and testimony O reports, we know that some sentient beings that are not moral agents are biologically very similar to moral agents. Since O1 implies that moral agents experience biologically useful pain and pleasure, this knowledge makes it antecedently likely on HI and O1 that some sentient beings that are not moral agents will also experience biologically useful pain and pleasure. Now at first glance, one might think that this knowledge makes the existence of such pain and pleasure just as likely on theism & O1. After all, from the assumption that theism and O1 are both true, it follows that God has good moral reasons for permitting biologically useful pain. But there is an important difference between the biologically useful pain that O1 reports and the biologically useful pain that O2 reports. Given theism & O1, we have reasons to believe that God permits the pain O1 reports because it plays some sort of (presently indiscernible) moral role in the lives of the humans that experience it. But the pain O2 reports cannot play such a role, since the subjects of it are not moral agents. This difference is plainly not relevant on HI & O1, but it gives us some reason on theism & O1 to expect that the good moral reasons God has for permitting moral agents to experience pain do not apply to animals that are not moral agents, and hence some reason to believe that God will not permit such beings to experience pain. So $P(O2/HI \& O1)$ is somewhat greater than $P(O2/theism \& O1)$.

O3 reports facts about sentient beings experiencing pain or pleasure that we do not know to be biologically useful. This includes much pain and pleasure that we know to be biologically gratuitous, as well as some that is not known to be useful and is also not known to be gratuitous. I will give a two-part argument for the conclusion that $P(O3/HI \& O1 \& O2)$ is much greater than $P(O3/theism \& O1 \& O2)$.

First, we obviously have much more reason on theism & O1 & O2 than we have on HI & O1 & O2 to expect sentient beings (especially nonhuman animals) to be happy—in any case much more happy than they would be if their pleasure were limited to that reported by O1 and O2. Instead, when the facts O3 reports are added to those reported by O1 and O2, we find that many humans and animals experience prolonged and intense suffering and a much greater number are far from happy. In addition, we have more reason on theism & O1 & O2 than on HI & O1 & O2 to expect to discover a close connection between certain moral goods (e.g., justice and virtue) and biologically gratuitous pain and pleasure, but we discover no such connection.

Second, we have, antecedently, much more reason on HI & O1 & O2 than on theism & O1 & O2 to believe that the fundamental role of pain and pleasure in our world is a biological one and that the presence of biologically gratuitous pain and pleasure is epiphenomenal, a biological accident resulting from nature's or an indifferent creator's failure to "fine tune" organic systems. And this is undeniably supported (though not entailed) by what O3 reports. To demonstrate this, a couple definitions are needed. First, by "pathological" pain or pleasure, I mean pain or pleasure that results from the failure of some organic system to function properly. For example, pain caused by terminal cancer and sadistic pleasure are pathological in this sense. And second, by "biologically appropriate" pain or pleasure, I mean pain or pleasure that occurs in a situation which is such that it is biologically useful that pain or pleasure is felt in situations of this sort. For instance, the pain felt by a person killed in a fire is not biologically useful, but it is biologically appropriate because it is biologically useful that humans feel pain when they come in contact with fire. Clearly much of the pain and pleasure reported by O3 is either pathological or biologically appropriate, and very little is known to be both non-pathological and biologically inappropriate.[5] And this is exactly what one would expect if pain and pleasure are fundamentally biological rather than moral phenomena, and so is much more to be expected on HI & O1 & O2 than on theism & O1 & O2.

Therefore, assuming that theodicies do not significantly raise P(O/theism), the first and third multiplicands of A are much greater than the first and third multiplicands of B, and the second multiplicand of A is greater than the second multiplicand of B. And this implies that P(O/HI) is much greater than P(O/theism).

III. *The Moral Value of Pain and Pleasure*

In addition to their biological roles, pain and pleasure also play various moral roles in our world. By appealing to these roles, the theist might hope to explain some of the facts O reports in terms of theism, and thereby render O less surprising on theism than it is initially. This would seem to be the theist's most promising strategy for undermining the argument for C given above. Theodicies can be treated as attempts to carry out such a strategy.[6] While few would deny that most theodicies are rather obvious failures, it is widely thought that plausible theistic explanations of suffering can be constructed by appealing to the intrinsic or instrumental moral value of free will. So it is necessary to determine what effect such theodicies have on P(O/theism). Additionally, it is important to evaluate the increasingly popular position that evidential arguments from evil against theism fail because the disproportion between omniscience and human knowledge makes it quite likely, on the assumption that God exists, that humans would not understand why God permits evil. (For a defense of this position, see Wykstra 1984.)

A. EVALUATING THEODICIES

Explaining some phenomenon in terms of a statement usually involves adding other statements to that statement. This is certainly true in the case of theodicies, which typically add to the claim that God exists the claims that God has a certain goal, that even God must produce or permit certain evils in order to accomplish that goal, and that accomplishing the goal is, from a moral point of view, worth the evils. I will say that a statement h* is an "expansion" of a statement h just in case h* is known to entail h. (Notice that h* can be an expansion of h even if it is logically equivalent to h.) The effect of a theodicy on P(O/theism) can be assessed by identifying an appropriate expansion T_n of theism that the theodicy employs and then using the following principle to evaluate P(O/theism) (cf. Adams 1985, appendix, p. 252): P(O/theism) = (P(T_n/theism) x P(O/T_n)) + (P($\sim T_n$/theism) x P(O/theism & $\sim T_n$)).[7]

I will call this principle the "Weighted Average Principle" ("WAP" for short) because it identifies one probability with a probability weighted average of two others. Roughly, WAP tells us that P(O/theism) is the average of P(O/T_n and P(O/theism & $\sim T_n$). This average, however, is a probability weighted average, the weights of which are P(T_n/theism), and P($\sim T_n$/theism). The higher P(T_n/theism), the closer P(O/theism) will be to P(O/T_n). And the lower P(T_n/theism), the closer P(O/theism) will be to P(O/theism & $\sim T_n$).

WAP clarifies the relationship between theodicies and the argument for C I gave in Section II. For example, suppose that, for some expansion T_n of theism that a certain theodicy employs, P(T_n/theism) is high. My argument for C in Section II ignores this theodicy and so in effect equates P(O/theism) with P(O/theism & $\sim T_n$). Since P(T_n/theism) is high, WAP tells us that P(O/theism) is actually closer to P(O/T_n) than to P(O/theism & $\sim T_n$) (assuming that these are not the same). To successfully defend my assumption in Section II that this theodicy does not significantly raise P(O/theism), I would need to show that P(O/T_n) is not significantly greater than P(O/theism & $\sim T_n$). In other words, I would need to show that, independent of the observations and testimony O reports, we have little or no more reason on T_n than we have on theism & $\sim T_n$ to believe that O is true.

B. FREE WILL AND THE ADVANCEMENT OF MORALITY

Most free will theodicies appeal to a certain sort of moral freedom, which I will call "freedom*." An action is free* only if (i) it is free in an imcompatibilist sense—that is, in a sense incompatible with its being determined by antecedent condition outside the agent's control—and (ii) if it is morally right, then at least an alternative action that is open in an incompatibilist sense to the agent is such that it would be morally wrong for the agent to perform that alternative action. This concept of freedom is used to give the following theistic explanation of immorality. Freedom* has great value (either because morally right actions that are freely* performed are more valuable than right actions that are not freely* performed or because, following Hick 1966, moral virtue that is acquired by freely* performing right actions is more valuable than moral virtue that is not freely* acquired). For this reason, God endows humans with freedom. However, since it is logically impossible to force a person to freely* perform a right action instead of a wrong one, God cannot give humans freedom* and ensure that humans will never perform morally wrong actions.

Unfortunately, humans sometimes abuse their freedom* by performing wrong actions. Nevertheless, God is justified in giving humans freedom* because a world in which humans freely* perform both right and wrong actions is (provided that the balance of right over wrong actions or of morally good humans over morally bad humans is sufficiently favorable) better than a world in which immorality is prevented by withholding freedom* from humans.

Notice that, so far, we have no explanation of the existence of pain. For there are morally right actions and morally wrong actions that do not entail the existence of pain. Wrong actions of this sort include some instances of breaking promises, killing, attempting to cause pain, and depriving someone of pleasure. So God could have given humans freedom* without permitting pain. The first version of the free will theodicy that I will evaluate adds to the above explanation of immorality the proposal that God permits pain in order to advance morality. This proposal can be spelled out in the following way. God wants humans to freely* perform right actions instead of wrong ones. Of course, as mentioned above, He cannot force humans to freely* perform only morally right actions, but He would have some control over the balance of right over wrong actions because even free* choices can be influenced and because God would know what free* choices humans would make (or would be likely to make)[8] in various situations. In particular, God might use pain to influence humans to freely* perform right actions instead of wrong ones. Also, some right actions entail the existence of pain, and God might know prior to creating humans that some or all humans would perform (or would be likely to perform) these right actions if given the chance. Therefore, God might use pain to obtain a more favorable balance of freely* performed right actions over wrong actions.

This version of the free will theodicy employs the following expansion of theism:

T_1: God exists, and one of His final ends is a favorable balance of freely* performed right actions over wrong actions.[9]

I doubt that a consensus could ever be reached about $P(T_1/\text{theism})$. For T_1 presupposes several very controversial metaphysical and ethical positions. For example, it presupposes that the concept of "freedom*" is coherent, that humans have freedom*, and that freedom* is of great value. Since I obviously do not have the space here to discuss how plausible these claims are, I will assume for the sake of argument that $P(T_1/\text{theism})$ is high.

I will argue, however, that $P(O/T_1)$ is not significantly higher than $P(O/\text{theism} \& \sim T_1)$. This implies that, even if $P(T_1/\text{theism})$ is high, our first version of the free will theodicy does not significantly increase $P(O/\text{theism})$. If, as I will assume, it is, morally permissible for God to use pain to advance morality, then we have reason on T_1 that we do not have on theism & $\sim T_1$ to expect that the world will contain both pain that influences humans to perform morally right action and pain that is logically necessary for some of the right actions humans perform. Since O reports the existence of pain of both these sorts, we have a predictive success for the theodicy. But O also reports both that pain often influences humans to perform morally wrong actions and that pain is logically necessary for many of the wrong actions humans perform. And we have reason on T_1 that we do not have on theism & $\sim T_1$ to be surprised by these facts. Furthermore, the observations and testimony O reports provide strong evidence that the world does not presently contain a very impressive balance of right over wrong actions performed by humans and that this is due in part both to a variety of demoralizing conditions like illness, poverty and ignorance, and to the absence of conditions that tend to promote morality. All of this is even more surprising on T_1 than on theism & $\sim T_1$. (Cf. Adams 1985, pp. 250-251.) So T_1's "predictive" advantages are counterbalanced by several serious "predictive" disadvantages, and for this reason $P(O/T_1)$ is not significantly greater than $P(O/\text{theism} \& \sim T_1)$.

C. FREE WILL AND RESPONSIBILITY

Some free will theodicists claim that God gives humans freedom* to bring about suffering (either by producing it or by failing to prevent it) in order to increase the responsibility humans have for their own well-being and the well-being of others and thereby increase the importance of the moral decisions humans make. By an "important" moral decision, these theodicists mean a decision upon which the presence or absence of something of great positive or negative value depends. The key value judgment here is that, all else held equal, the more important the moral decisions we are free* to make, the more valuable our freedom* is. By not preventing us from freely* bringing about evils, including serious ones, God increases our control over how valuable the world is and thereby increases the value of our freedom*. This theodicy employs the following expansion of theism:

> T_2: God exists, and one of His final ends is for humans to have the freedom* to make very important moral decisions.

I will assume, once again, that $P(T_2/\text{theism})$ is high, and I will argue that this second version of the free-will theodicy does not significantly raise $P(O/\text{theism})$ by arguing that $P(O/T_2)$ is not significantly greater than $P(O/\text{theism} \& \sim T_2)$.

I will begin by arguing that Richard Swinburne (1979, Ch. 11) fails in his attempt to extend this theodicy so that it accounts for pain for which humans are not morally responsible. (I will call this sort of pain "amoral pain.") Swinburne believes that free will theodicies that employ T_2 can account for such pain because (i) they explain why God gives humans the freedom* to bring about suffering and (ii) amoral pain is necessary if humans are to have genuine freedom* to bring about suffering. Swinburne defends (ii) in the following way. Freedom* to bring about suffering requires the knowledge of how to bring about suffering. And humans can obtain such knowledge in only one of two ways: either by God telling them how to bring about suffering or by experiencing how this is done. Unfortunately, if God told humans how to bring about suffering, then humans would know that God exists, and hence would have little temptation to do evil and so no genuine freedom* to bring about suffering. So for humans to have such freedom, they must learn by experience how to bring about suffering, and hence must learn this either by observing suffering for which no human is morally responsible or by observing suffering brought about by other humans. But for any particular kind of suffering, there must have been a first time when a human knew how to bring it about despite never having observed suffering of that kind brought about by a human. Hence, if humans are to learn by experience how to bring about suffering, then amoral pain must exist. Therefore, such suffering is necessary for humans to have the freedom* to bring about suffering.

I will make three comments about this argument for (ii). First, even if it is sound, it obviously does not provide an adequate theistic account of amoral pain from which humans gain no new knowledge about how to produce or prevent suffering. Second, even if it is sound, it does not provide an adequate theistic explanation of most of the amoral pain that does give humans new knowledge of this sort. For an omnipotent and omniscient being could have greatly decreased the variety of ways in which humans know how to harm others, and so greatly decreased the amount of amoral pain needed for this knowledge, without decreasing the amount of harm humans can do to others and so without decreasing the amount of control that humans have over the well-being of others. Third, and most importantly, the argument is not sound. As Stump 1983 and Moser 1984 have observed, God could, without permitting amoral pain, give humans the knowledge of how to bring about suffering without revealing His existence and so without undermining human freedom*. For example, as Stump (pp. 52-53) has pointed out, humans might regularly have vivid, message-laden dreams and learn of their reliability, and yet not be compelled to believe in God.

So if this second version of the free will theodicy raises P(O/theism) at all, it is because we have reason on T_2 that we do not have on theism & $\sim T_2$ to expect the existence of pain for which humans are morally responsible. Now, giving humans the freedom* to bring about intense suffering is certainly one way (though not the only way) of giving humans the freedom* to make important moral decisions. So assuming that there is no better way,[10] we have some reason on T_2 to expect humans to have such freedom*, and so reason on T_2 to expect the existence of pain for which humans are morally responsible. But even granting all this, it can be shown that $P(O/T_2)$ is not significantly greater than $P(O/\text{theism} \& \sim T_2)$ by showing that other facts O reports are even more surprising on T_2 than they are on theism & $\sim T_2$.

An analogy between God and a good parent will be useful here. Ironically, such an analogy is often used to defend this sort of theodicy. For example, Swinburne (1979) responds to the objection that God should not give humans the freedom* to seriously harm others by asserting that the objector is asking that God "make a toy-world, a world where [our choices] matter, but not very much" (p. 219). Such a God "would be like the over-protective parent who will not let his child out of sight for a moment" (p. 220). But Swinburne neglects to ask whether or not humans are worthy of the freedom* to seriously harm others. A good parent gradually increases a child's responsibility as the child becomes capable of handling greater responsibility. Children who are unworthy of a certain responsibility are not benefited by parents who give them that responsibility. On the assumption that T_2 is true, one would expect that God would behave like a good parent, giving humans great responsibility only when we are worthy of it. I am not claiming that on T_2 one would expect God to impose a good moral character on humans before He gives them serious responsibilities. Nor am I claiming that creatures who are worthy of great responsibility would never abuse that responsibility. Rather, I am claiming that on T_2 one would expect God to give all or some humans less responsibility—and in particular no ability to do serious evils—until they freely* developed the strength of character that would make them worthy of greater responsibility. And if at some point humans become worthy of and are given great responsibility but nevertheless abuse this responsibility to such an extent that they are no longer worthy of it, then one would on T_2 expect God, like a good parent, to decrease the amount of responsibility humans have until they are worthy of a second chance.

But O conflicts with all of these expectations. Many humans are plainly not worthy of the freedom* to do serious evils. Nor is the human race making any significant amount of moral progress. If God exists, then for centuries He has been allowing his children to torment, torture, and kill each other. Thus, even if they were once worthy of great responsibility, they no longer are, and hence are not benefited by having such responsibility. So like T_1, T_2's predictive advantages are counterbalanced by several serious predictive disadvantages. Therefore, $P(O/T_2)$ is not significantly greater than $P(O/\text{theism} \& \sim T_2)$, and hence this second version of the free will theodicy fails to significantly raise $P(O/\text{theism})$.

D. THE "INFINITE INTELLECT DEFENSE"

Some philosophers think that "evidential arguments from evil" can be refuted by pointing out that since God's knowledge about good and evil is limitless, it is not all that surprising that He produces or permits evils for reasons that are unknown to humans. The expansion of theism suggested here is the following:

> T_3: God exists and has a vast amount of knowledge about good and evil and how they are related that humans do not have.

Since $P(T_3/\text{theism}) = \text{one}$, $P(O/\text{theism}) = P(O/T_3)$. But this does not reveal any defect in my argument for C. For antecedently—that is, independent of the observations and testimony O reports—we have no reason to think that God's additional knowledge concerning good and evil is such that He would permit any of the facts O reports to obtain. Of course, an omnipotent and omniscient being might, for all we know antecedently, have moral reasons unknown to us to permit the evil reported by O. But it is also the case that such a being might, for all we know antecedently, have moral reasons unknown to us to prevent this evil. Indeed, we have no more reason antecedently to believe that such a being would know of some great good unknown to us whose existence entails the existence of the pain O reports than we have reason to believe that such a being would know of some great good unknown to us whose existence entails the nonexistence of the pain or the pleasure O reports. And an omnipotent and omniscient being might very well know of means, far too complicated for humans to understand, by which He could obtain certain goods without the evil O reports. Of course, *given the facts O reports,* we have some reason on T_3 to expect that humans will be unable to produce a plausible theistic explanation of those facts. But HI gives us even more reason to expect this. So human ignorance does not solve the theist's evidential problems.

Hence, none of the theodicies we have considered significantly raises P(O/theism). Therefore, relative to the espistemic situations of those of us who are unable to think of some other much more successful theodicy (i.e., all of us, I suspect), C is true: P(O/HI) is much greater than P(O/theism).

IV. The Significance of the Problem

In *The Origin of Species,* Charles Darwin argued that his theory of the evolution of species by means of natural selection explains numerous facts (e.g., the geographical distribution of species and the existence of atrophied organs in animals) much better than the alternative hypothesis, that each species of plant and animal was independently created by God. (Let us call this latter hypothesis "special creationism.") Darwin's results were significant partly because special creationists at Darwin's time did not have nor were they able to obtain any evidence favoring special creationism over evolutionary theory that outweighed or at least offset Darwin's evidence favoring evolutionary theory over special creationism. For this reason, many theists, while continuing to believe in creationism, which is consistent with Darwin's theory, rejected special creationism. And those theists who were familiar with Darwin's arguments and yet remained special creationists did so at a cost: their belief in special creationism was no longer an epistemically rational one.

Similarly, how significant my results are depends, in part, on how many theists have or could obtain propositional or nonpropositional evidence favoring theism over HI that offsets the propositional evidence, provided by my argument for C, favoring HI over theism.[11] Any theist confronted with my argument for C who lacks such evidence and is unable to obtain it cannot rationally continue to believe that theism is true. It is beyond the scope of this paper to determine how many theists would be in such a position. But I will make four sets of comments that I hope indicate how difficult a theist's search for the needed evidence might be.

First, I do not see how it could be shown that HI is an ad hoc hypothesis or that theism is *intrinsically* more probable than HI. For HI is consistent with a wide variety of both naturalistic and supernaturalistic hypotheses, and it has no positive ontological commitments. Theism, on the other hand, is a very specific supernaturalistic claim with a very strong ontological commitment. Indeed, such differences between theism and HI might very well provide additional evidence favoring HI over theism.

Second, traditional and contemporary arguments for theism are far from compelling—that is, they are far from being so persuasive as to coerce the acceptance of all or even most rational theists. Thus, even if some such arguments were sound, most theists, including many philosophically sophisticated ones, would not recognize this, and hence the argument would not provide them with evidence favoring theism over HI. (The evidence would exist, but they would not *have* it.)

Third, many traditional and contemporary arguments for theism, including many versions of the cosmological argument, the teleological argument, and the argument from consciousness, may not solve the theist's problem even if they are sound and recognized by the theist to be so. For they at most purport to show that an omnipotent and omniscient being exists—not that the being is morally perfect. Suppose then that some such argument is sound. My argument for C would work just as well if HI were replaced with the following hypothesis, which I will call "the Indifferent Deity Hypothesis":

> There exists an omnipotent and omniscient person who created the Universe and who has no intrinsic concern about the pain or pleasure of other beings.

Like theism, this hypothesis entails that an omnipotent and omniscient being exists. So establishing that such a being exists would help the theist only if the theist also has strong evidence favoring theism over the Indifferent Deity Hypothesis.[12]

Finally, religious experiences of the kind appealed to by "Reformed Epistemologists" like Alvin Plantinga (1983) are ambiguous with respect to the moral attributes of the creator. While Plantinga is correct in claiming that theists typically do feel inclined in certain circumstances (e.g., "when life is sweet and satisfying") to think that the creator is morally good, sensitive theists also feel inclined in other circumstances—namely, when they experience poignant evil—to believe that the creator is indifferent to their good or to the good of others. And many atheists have very powerful experiences in which they seem to be aware of the ultimate indifference of nature. These experiences are very common and are very similar phenomenologically to the experiences Plantinga mentions. Moreover, C implies that these "experiences of indifference" are better corroborated than the "theistic experiences" to which Plantinga appeals. Thus, even if Plantinga is correct in thinking that theistic experiences confer prima facie justification on the theist's belief in God, experiences of indifference defeat this justification. Therefore, theistic experiences do not provide nonpropositional evidence that favors theism over HI, or at least none that outweighs the propositional evidence favoring HI over theism provided by my argument for C.[13]

NOTES

This essay originally appeared in *Nous,* volume 23 (1989). Reprinted by permission of Blackwell Publishers.

1. I agree with most philosophers of religion that theists face no serious logical problem of evil. This chapter challenges the increasingly popular view, defended recently by Pargetter (1976), Plantinga (1979), and Reichenbach (1980), that theists face no serious evidential problem of evil.

2. The concept of epistemic probability is an ordinary concept of probability for which no adequate philosophical analysis has, in my opinion, been proposed. As a first approximation, however, perhaps the following analysis will do:

> Relative to K, p is epistemically more probable than q, where K is an epistemic situation and p and q are propositions, just in case any fully rational person in K would have a higher degree of belief in p than in q.

3. One difficulty with the claim that this theorem of the probability calculus is true for epistemic probability is that, since multiplication and addition can only be performed on numbers, it follows that the theorem presupposes that probabilities have numerical values. But most epistemic probabilities have only comparative values. This difficulty can be overcome by interpreting the claim that this theorem is true for epistemic probability as the claim that (i) if each of the probabilities in the theorem have numerical values, then the theorem states the numerical relationships which hold between them, and (ii) if at least one probability in the theorem does not have a numerical value, then all statements of comparative probability entailed by that theorem are true. My reason for believing that this theorem is true for epistemic probability in this sense is that I can find no counterexample to it. I do not place a lot of emphasis on the mere fact that it is a theorem of the probability calculus. For I do not believe that all theorems of the probability calculus are true for epistemic probability.

4. I am grateful to a *Nous* referee for this objection.

5. Even the enjoyment of perceiving beauty may be biologically appropriate. For our enjoyment of clear perception is plausibly thought to be biologically useful, and Guy Sircello (1975, pp. 129-134) gives a very interesting argument for the conclusion that perceiving beauty is a special case of clear perception.

6. The term "theodicy" is often defined as "an attempt to state what God's actual reason for permitting evil is." This definition implies that in order to show that some theodicy is successful, one must show that God exists. I prefer a definition of "theodicy" that avoids this implication. By a "theodicy" I mean an attempt to give a plausible theistic explanation of some fact about evil.

7. More generally, it follows from the probability calculus that $P(O/\text{theism}) = (P(T_n/\text{theism}) \times P(O/\text{theism} \& T_n)) + (P(\sim T_n/\text{theism}) \times P(O/\text{theism} \& \sim T_n))$. WAP replaces $P(O/\text{theism} \& T_n)$ with $P(O/T_n)$ because T_n is an expansion of theism and hence is known to be logically equivalent to theism $\& T_n$.

8. Robert Adams (1977) argues that God, despite being omniscient, would not know what free* choice a particular human would make in a certain situation prior to deciding both to place that human in that situation and to allow him to make that choice. Adams also argues, however, that God would have prior knowledge of what free* choices humans would be likely to make in various situations.

9. A slightly different version of this theodicy employs the following expansion of theism:

> T_1*: God exists, and one of His final ends is a favorable balance of morally good humans whose moral goodness was freely* acquired over morally bad humans.

I suspect that $P(T_1*/\text{theism})$ is greater than $P(T_1/\text{theism})$ because God would be more likely to be concerned about persons than about actions. However, I need not evaluate T_1* separately because I will assume that $P(T_1/\text{theism})$ is high and my arguments concerning $P(O/T_1)$ would work just as well if T_1 were replaced with T_1*.

10. One might challenge this assumption and thereby attack theodicies that employ T_2 in the following way. Choosing whether or not to produce a large amount of pleasure is, all else held equal, a more important moral decision than choosing whether or not to produce a small amount of pain. Hence, it would seem that by increasing our

capacity to produce or prevent pleasure, God could give us the power to make moral decisions about pleasure that are as important as any that we now make concerning pain. It is antecedently likely that such a world would be a better world than one in which humans have the ability to cause others to suffer. Therefore, it is antecedently unlikely that God would use pain to accomplish His goal of giving humans important moral choices.

11. One way of attempting to show that such evidence exists would be to (i) identify an appropriate body of evidence (call it O*) that is broader than O (e.g., a statement reporting the relevant observations and testimony, not just about pain and pleasure but about all intrinsic goods and evils) and then (ii) attempt to show that independent of the observations and testimony O* reports, O* is at least as likely on theism as it is on HI.

12. Swinburne (1979, chap. 5) argues that quasi-theistic hypotheses like the Indifferent Deity Hypothesis are intrinsically much less probable than theism. I do not believe his argument is sound, but if it were, then strong evidence favoring theism over the Indifferent Deity Hypothesis would be available.

13. For criticisms of previous versions of this chapter, I am grateful to Gary Gutting, C. Stephen Layman, Nelson Pike, Alvin Plantinga, Philip L. Quinn, and an anonymous *Nous* referee.

REFERENCES

Adams, Robert M. "Middle Knowledge and the Problem of Evil." *American Philosophical Quarterly* 14 (1977): 109-17.
———. "Plantinga on the Problem of Evil." In *Alvin Plantinga*, ed. James E. Tomberlin and Peter van Inwagen. Dordrecht: Reidel, 1985: 225-55.
Ahern, M. B. *The Problem of Evil.* London: Routledge and Kegan Paul, 1971.
Boorse, Christopher. "Wright on Functions." *Philosophical Review* 85 (1976): 70-86.
Hare, Peter H., and Edward H. Madden. *Evil and the Concept of God.* Springfield: Charles C. Thomas, 1968.
———. "Evil and Inconclusiveness." *Sophia* (Australia) 11 (1972): 8-12.
Hick, John. *Evil and the God of Love.* New York: Harper & Row, 1966.
Hume, David. *Dialogues concerning Natural Religion.* Ed. Richard Popkin. Indianapolis: Hackett, 1980.
Kane, Stanley. "Theism and Evil." *Sophia* (Australia) 9 (1970): 14-21.
Mavrodes, George I. *Belief in God: A Study in the Epistemology of Religion.* New York: Random House, 1970.
Moser, Paul K. "Natural Evil and the Free Will Defense." *International Journal for Philosophy of Religion* 15 (1984): 49-56.
Pargetter, Robert. "Evil as Evidence against the Existence of God." *Mind* 85 (1976): 242-45.
Plantinga, Alvin. "The Probabilistic Argument from Evil." *Philosophical Studies* 35 (1979): 1-53.
———. "Reason and Belief in God." In *Faith and Rationality: Reason and Belief in God*, ed. Alvin Plantinga and Nicholas Wolterstorff. Notre Dame: University of Notre Dame Press, 1983: 16-93.
Reichenbach, Bruce. "The Inductive Argument from Evil." *American Philosophical Quarterly* 17 (1980): 221-27.
Ruse, Michael. *The Philosophy of Biology.* London: Hutchingson, 1973.
Sircello, Guy. *A New Theory of Beauty.* Princeton: Princeton University Press, 1975.

Stump, Eleonore. "Knowledge, Freedom and the Problem of Evil." *International Journal for Philosophy of Religion* 14 (1983): 49-58.

Swinburne, Richard. *The Existence of God.* Oxford: Clarendon Press, 1979.

Wykstra, Stephen J. "The Humean Obstacle to Evidential Arguments from Suffering: On Avoiding the Evils of 'Appearance.'" *International Journal for Philosophy of Religion* 16 (1984): 73-93.

Yandell, Keith E. "Ethics, Evils and Theism." *Sophia* (Australia) 8 (1969a): 18-28.

———. "A Premature Farewell to Theism." *Religious Studies* 5 (1969b): 251-55.

———. "Theism and Evil: A Reply." *Sophia* (Australia) 11 (1972): 1-7.

3.

RICHARD SWINBURNE

Some Major Strands of Theodicy

God is by definition omnipotent and perfectly good. Yet manifestly there is evil of many diverse kinds. It would appear that an omnipotent being can prevent evil if he tries to do so, and that a perfectly good being will try. The existence of such evil appears, therefore, to be inconsistent with the existence of God, or at least to render it improbable.[1] Theodicy is the enterprise of showing that appearances are misleading: that evils of the kind and quantity we find on Earth are neither incompatible with nor render improbable the existence of God.[2] Even if the evils around us do render improbable the existence of God, we may still have stronger evidence to show that there is a God which outweighs the counterevidence, which suffices to make it rational for us to believe that there is a God. My own view, however, is that theodicy is a viable enterprise, that we do not need to rely on stronger evidence for the existence of God to outweigh counterevidence from evil. This paper is a contribution to theodicy. I accept that an omnipotent being can prevent any evil he chooses, but I deny that a perfectly good being will always try to do so. If a perfectly good being is to allow evil to occur, he must have the right to do so, and there must be some good which is brought about by allowing the evil to occur and could not be brought about by him in any better way, and so great that it is worth allowing the evil to occur. If the perfectly good being is also omnipotent (i.e., can do anything logically possible), then it must be logically impossible for him to bring about the greater good in any better way. The condition about the right is important: even if my allowing you to suffer will do you great good, unless I am in some special position in regard to you (e.g., I am your parent), I do not have the right to allow you to suffer. I believe that God does have the right to allow humans (and animals) to suffer for the sake of greater good—to a limited extent and for a limited period (e.g., 100 years per human)—but I shall not argue for that here for reason of space.[3] My concern will be rather with contributing toward showing that evils of the kind and quantity we find on Earth serve greater goods.

I believe that theodicy seems to many people an impossible task because they have a very narrow conception of good and evil—e.g., in extremis, that the only goods are sensory pleasures and the only evils sensory pains. If that conception were correct, then obviously God could create sensory pleasures without creating sensory pains. But that conception is not merely too narrow, it is absurdly too narrow—someone whose conception of the good was thus limited would be a moral pygmy. But when you start having a wider conception of good and evil, theodicy does not seem so impossible a task; it just seems difficult. The difficulty arises because of the variety of the goods and evils and the complexity of the logical relations between them.

My approach in this paper will be to list various good states of affairs (understood in a wide sense, which includes events and actions), which a good God might well seek to bring about and which do in fact occur on Earth, and show how so many of them could not be realized without the occurrence (or possible occurrence) of corresponding evils. (By the "possible occurrence" of some evil I mean some agent, animate or inanimate, having the power to bring about the evil which nothing inside or outside the agent causes the agent either to exercise or not to exercise.) In the course of running through the good states, I shall mention the major evils we find on Earth—both those involving humans and those involving animals—and show that they contribute to goods, in that the goods could not be realized without their actual or possible occurrence or the actual or possible occurrence of evils equally bad. That I hope I shall show fairly conclusively. What I shall also begin to show but could not within the compass of a philosophical paper of normal length possibly show conclusively to those without considerable sympathies toward certain general moral views is that the good states of affairs are so good that it is worth allowing the evils to occur in order to make possible the good states. There are two main reasons why I cannot show the latter conclusively within the stated space. The first of these reasons is that, I believe, there are so many different kinds of good states and so many different ways in which evil is required for their occurrence. For example, I believe that the occurrence of natural evils (i.e., evils such as disease and accidents unpredictable by humans) is required for humans to have the power to choose between doing significant good or evil to their fellows, for the reason that the observation of the processes which produce natural evil is required for humans to have the knowledge of how to do significant evil to their fellows. Without that knowledge the choice between good and evil will not be available. We learn how to poison by observing someone accidentally eating a berry and being poisoned by it; that then puts us in a position deliberately to poison others (by giving them similar berries), or through negligence to allow others to be poisoned, or alternatively to prevent their being poisoned. I believe that what goes for this schematically simple example goes generally, and that evils of the kind and quantity we find around us are required if humans are to have the power to choose between doing good or evil of varied significant kinds to their fellows. It is good that they have this latter choice, as I shall be arguing in due course. But the demonstration that natural evil is required to give us the requisite knowledge is a complicated one which I have expounded elsewhere,[4] and a fuller defense of it would require at least an article of its own. I therefore deprive myself of the strand of theodicy provided by "the argument from the need for knowledge," and rely on other strands.

The second and major reason, however, why I cannot show conclusively within the allotted space that the goods are so great that it is worth allowing the evils which they require to occur is that my assessment of the relative worth of the goods depends on more general moral views which are not fashionable today. Now, people only come to see the strength of a moral position rather different from their initial one as a result of reflection upon their experiences of life or description at some considerable length of real or fictional incidents. The philosopher can assist in the process of reflection or description; but convincing conclusions will not be reached solely by a few pages of rigorous deductive argument, aided by numbered propositions. For those of my readers who have considerable initial sympathy with the general moral views which I shall be expounding, I hope that I shall say enough to clarify and to strengthen those views in such a way as to enable the readers to see that they lead to a viable theodicy. But for the readers without much initial sympathy with the views in question, I hope that I shall say enough to make the readers more sympathetic, and so enable them to see that there are prospects for a theodicy of the kind I shall expound, that theodicy could well be a viable enterprise.[5]

So let's begin to list some goods. I have no general formula for picking out good states of affairs—I believe them to be too diverse to fall under any formula—but I list quite a number of them relevant to theodicy. Perhaps the most basic good of all is the good of the satisfaction of desire, basic in the sense that its goodness makes for the greater goodness of many other states of affairs. A desire, as I understand it, is an involuntary inclination with which an agent finds himself to do some action or to have something happen.[6] Desires may be for almost anything—for mental states, including sensory states, for bodily states, for states of the world far distant from the agent. I may desire to have a certain tingling sensation, or for a piece of poetry to run through my mind, to waggle my ears, to be president of the United States. Or my desires may be focused on others—that my children be happy or successful or inherit my wealth when I am dead.

Enjoyment or pleasure consists in the known satisfaction of present desire. It consists in doing what you are inclined to do, or letting happen what you are inclined to let happen, when you know that you are doing the action or letting the state occur. I enjoy eating cake or playing golf if I'm inclined to do so, do so while inclined, and know that I am doing. I get pleasure out of sitting in the sun if I let myself continue to sit in the sun when inclined so to do (do not struggle against sitting there) and know that is what I am doing. I get pleasure out of being president if I am inclined to be president, and am, and know that I am president. The most primitive kind of pleasure is sensory pleasure, pleasure in the having of certain sensations, the occurrence of which I cannot be mistaken. But the more remote from my immediate environment is the state of affairs on which my inclinations are focused, the more serious is the possibility that I may believe some inclination to be satisfied when it is not. I may believe that I am president when I am not; in that case what I get pleasure from is not being president but believing that I am. I am in one state in which I desire to be—believing that I am. I am in one state in which I desire to be—believing that I am president—but not in another such one—being president. When I am disabused of my false belief, there is nothing left out of which I can get pleasure.

Pleasure is the known satisfaction of present desire. Is there good in the present satisfaction of past desire? I suggest so, if it is uncanceled desire (i.e., the agent hasn't given it up). If, aged five, I long to be an engine driver but I give up this desire when I am aged ten, when I desire to be a naval captain instead; I am then declared medically unfit for the navy when conscription arrives and drafted to become an engine driver instead, there would seem little (if any) good in this. But this is because my earlier desire has been replaced by a different desire. Yet contrast this with the desire of a man for being buried here rather than there when he is dead. Surely it is good that his relatives should bury him here rather than there, even if but for the dead man's known past desire, there would be nothing particularly good about burial here rather than there.

As such, the satisfaction of desire, and above all pleasure, is a good thing. But the satisfaction of certain desires is not a good thing. The satisfaction of desires for things bad in themselves is not good. The satisfaction of a desire that others, or even one's later self, suffer pain, lose their reputation, fortune, or family is a bad thing; and any pleasure derived from these things is not merely not a good, but very much an evil. Only the pervert rejoices at the sufferings of others. Also, I suggest, pleasure is not a good where the belief needed to sustain it is false. The pleasure which a man gets from believing his son to be a successful businessman when in fact he is unemployed is not a good thing. We can see this when we consider that if we had the opportunity to plug into an "experience machine" which would inculcate in us the false beliefs that our desires were currently being satisfied, we would—almost all of us—refrain, under normal circumstances (i.e., unless life without the machine was so intolerable that "plugging in" was the lesser of two evils).

The satisfaction of a strong desire is as such a greater good than the satisfaction of a weak desire. Further, the satisfaction of a desire is the better if it is a desire for a state of affairs good for other reasons. Desires to drink good wine rather than Coca-Cola, to read great novels rather than pornography, to understand quantum physics, or to develop a correct theodicy rather than know Wisden's Almanac by heart are like this, because of the subtlety of the sensitivity we desire to indulge in the former cases, and width and depth of the knowledge we desire to attain in the latter cases. The satisfaction of joint desires—e.g., the desires of two creatures for the common end of their nest being built—is very good because of the goodness of sharing and cooperation. It is better to have a desire for the satisfaction of desire as such—viz., the desire for pleasure in whatever way it can be achieved rather than the desire for a particular sensation—for it shows sensitivity to what is good in the satisfaction of desire. And it is yet better that the desire of one for the satisfaction of the desire of another—e.g., my desire that your desire to eat cream cake be satisfied; or more generally that the desire of a mother for the satisfaction of her offspring's desire be satisfied—than that the desire of each of us to eat cream cake be satisfied. This is because of the goodness of mutual concern and involvement. Much better that my desire that your desire to eat cream cake be satisfied than that the desire of each of us to eat cream cake be satisfied. It follows, because of the goodness of mutual concern, that even better is the satisfaction of joint desires for the satisfaction of the desire of a third creature, e.g., the satisfaction of the desire of both parents for the desired success in examinations of their child. Even better still is the satisfaction of desires to perform actions of certain sorts benefiting oneself and others, to the goodness of which actions (desired or not) I shall come in due course.

In cases such as those just described, where one person, A, desires the satisfaction of the desire of a second person, B, and the desire is satisfied, there is a triple good. There is the primitive good of the satisfaction of B's desire. There is the greater good of the satisfaction of A's desire, greater because A's desire focused on the fulfillment of another's desire (as such, quite apart from what it is) is a desire for a better good than B's desire. And there is the further good for B that A desired his (B's) desire to be satisfied. It is a good for us when other people mind about us. We are fortunate if our happiness gives happiness to others—even if we don't know that it does. We can see this by the fact that we regard ourselves as fortunate when we discover that another was made happy by our being happy; but although the discovery causes us so to regard ourselves, what we regard ourselves as fortunate in respect of is what we discover (not the fact of our discovering it)—and that is something which could occur without our having discovered it.

Just as the satisfaction of desire is good, so is its frustration (i.e., the desire continuing when it is for a present state of affairs but is not known to be satisfied)[7] an evil. Pains are evils because they involve desires for the nonoccurrence of a sensation, which are not satisfied. And an unfulfilled longing to be president is an evil for the same reason.

God has reason to bring about the existence of creatures with desires for good states of affairs which are satisfied. He can do so without any evil occurring so long as the satisfaction is known and immediate. But if the creature continues to exist with his desire unsatisfied or not known to be satisfied, we have immediately the evil of frustrated desire. Yet there is special good in the satisfaction of persisting desire. For a desire which persists through varied experiences and new desires is a thought-through and committed desire. Hence the special good of the satisfaction of an animal's desire for the return of its offspring lost for hours or days, of the satisfaction of the desire for a mate the longing for which has deterred the animal from the search for other goods such as food, and of the satisfaction of the desire for food by those hungry for some hours. The greater good of the satisfaction of persisting desire is greater when what is desired is the success of some action of some kind. It is good that someone persists in attempting to search for food and doesn't just grab it off the table; to stick at trying to learn to type or drive or swim and finally succeed. But the eventual satisfaction of persisting desires involves on the way the evil of temporary frustrations: pangs of hunger on the way to getting food, feelings of exhaustion in the course of the long search for a mate, etc. And note of course that in these as in other cases, the good of the satisfaction of desire does not lie solely in its known satisfaction. It follows that there is significant good in the satisfaction of a persisting desire after the desirer's death. The greater good of the satisfaction of persisting desires is yet greater, the better their object; and so there is special good in the satisfaction of shared persisting desires for the satisfaction of the persisting desire of a third individual, a good which involves more evil on the way. The goodness of the satisfaction of persisting desire is the first aspect of that logical straightjacket which means that good cannot be achieved save through evil and which provides the key to theodicy. God has reason to give to creatures the good of persistent desires, despite the agony of their temporary frustration.

It is not just the satisfaction of desire which is in general a good, and especially when it is of a desire for a state of affairs good for other reasons. The mere having of desire is good, especially when it is desire for a state of affairs good for other reasons. It is good that I want things, long for things, am inclined to try to bring about things. It is better that I be someone to whom things matter rather than a "cold fish" who acts under the guidance of reason alone. Desires in themselves are good, except when they are desires for what is bad; but they are better, the better the states desired. And if my desires are focused on your well-being, that is a good not merely for me but also for you—how lucky we are if people care about us. But there are some desires for what is good which can never be satisfied. The desire to be monogamously married to beautiful Jane for all her adult life is a desire for what is good, and so it is good that both John and George have it. But of course both of their desires cannot be satisfied. Likewise, it is good to desire to be president of the United States for the next four years, to hold a great office of public service; but we can't all occupy the office. A world in which all our desires were satisfied at some time would be a world in which we were deprived of desires for certain great goods, just because we couldn't get them. If God wants to make creatures sensitive to all that is good, He will allow them to have desires which are permanently frustrated. So we are rightly sentenced to ambitions that we cannot achieve, and to the consequent deprivation, and (because of the goodness of true beliefs about these matters) to feelings of failure.

There is also great good in certain emotional states, including desire as well as other elements. It is good that I love all creatures, but especially those with whom I have contact and in particular those greatly dependent on me or on whom I am greatly dependent. It is good that I love these latter more than others—otherwise I do not pay proper tribute to their connection with myself; I trivialize our personal relations. And again, the love that persists despite inadequate response or is evoked by bad states has its own special greatness. It is good that I feel compassion for the sufferer, sadness at failure, and grief at the loss of the departed.[8] Again, these attitudes are good both for him who has these right attitudes and good for him on whom they are focused—very good if the latter knows about them and that gives him some pleasure, but good even if he doesn't—for the reason given earlier. What gives him pleasure is the knowledge of the existence of a good state (e.g., someone else's compassion for him), and that state can exist without his knowing about it. We are fortunate if others mourn for us when we are dead; we can see this by the fact that we regard people as unfortunate if no one is sorry when they die. So too it lessens the evil of the suffering of a fawn caught in a forest fire if others know about this and respond with compassion—both other deer at the time and humans centuries later. Our compassion for sentient creatures is often far too narrow; it needs to extend far over space and time.

A natural reaction to examples such as these is to urge that while compassion may be a good state, which mitigates the evil of suffering, a world would be much better without either of them; and likewise for the other two examples. That reaction seems to me overgeneral—a world without any suffering or in consequence any compassion would not be better than a world with a little suffering and its proper response (other things being equal), and likewise for the other two examples. For compassion is an involvement in the inner life of another in a deep kind of way, which simply cannot be provided by a sharing of their joy. This is because the sufferer is one whose desires are frustrated. He is at his most naked. He has little to cling to by way of a structure of desire being fulfilled or which he may hope can be fulfilled. Our involvement with him is therefore an involvement with him as he is in himself, not as someone who has as it were exteriorized himself in the fulfillment of plans for himself or others, but someone with a unique opportunity to cope with his nakedness. "Sorrow shared is sorrow halved," says the proverb, and it is only doing the sums insofar as they affect the original sufferer who knows of the compassion. If we add the benefit (not altogether an enjoyed benefit) to the sympathizer, the sums may well sometimes come out level. God will not give us endless pain, failure, and felt loss of dear ones in order to allow us to show proper compassion, sadness, and grief; but he may well give us some pain, failure, and felt loss in order to allow us to be involved with each other in ways and at levels we could not otherwise have.

So far I've been concerned largely with the goodness of passive states. But doing is more important than having happen. Causing matters, and above all, intentional actions matter, in particular actions of promoting the goods so far described, and certainly not just because it is good that those goods come about. A good (intentional) action is good to the extent to which it is done intentionally (under the description under which it is good), efficaciously, freely, spontaneously, or contrary to temptation. An action can have all of the first three characteristics, and a free intentional action will be either spontaneous or contrary to temptation, but to the extent to which it has one of the latter characteristics it will lack the other. Performing some intentional action (e.g., I buy your house), I may unintentionally do something else good (e.g., I save you from bankruptcy). Such a good action will derive its goodness not from its intention but from its effect (so long as the effect is closely connected to the intentional action and not a remote effect dependent also on many other and very different causes). What is achieved is a good, and it is also a good for the agent who effected it, even if unintentionally; he is lucky to be a vehicle of benefit. Conversely, an unsuccessful action which aimed at something good is also a good for the agent.[9] It is good that people try to help the starving, even if they don't succeed. We can see the good of unintended success better than in my earlier example by bringing in this latter point, and considering an action which is aimed at a good but fails and is better for having an unintended good result than it would be otherwise. I toil to save a life and fail, but the record of my efforts makes possible the development of a technique for saving other lives in the future. Is that better than if I failed and by chance someone else hit on the new technique? Yes, because my efforts are crowned, and therefore it is a good for me, not merely for those whose lives were ultimately saved. But clearly things are better if the good which I achieve is intended. While it is good that I try to feed the starving, even if I don't succeed, it is better if I do succeed—but not just because it is good that the starving have enough to eat; it is a good for me that I am privileged to help them, that I am of use.

An intended good action is the better if done freely in the sense of not being fully caused.[10] An agent's freely bringing about the good is indeed a good for the agent. It is a good for any agent to have a free choice, for that makes him an ultimate source of the way things happen in the universe. He is no longer totally at the mercy of forces from without, but himself an autonomous minicreator. And if he exercises that choice in forwarding the good, that is a further good for him. But the good of forwarding the good is a lot better if the agent has a free choice between good and evil, not just between alternative goods, for then his choice is deeply significant for the way the world goes. Yet if he is to have a choice between good and evil, he must be subject to temptation, i.e., desires for the evil. An action would not be intentional unless it was done for a reason, i.e., seen as in some way a good thing (either in itself or because of its consequences). And if reasons alone influence actions, that regarded by the subject as most important will determine what is done; an agent under the influence of reason alone will inevitably do the action which he regards as overall the best (or one of the actions, if there are such, which he regards as overall equal best). If an agent is to have a free choice of whether to do an action which he regards as overall, factors other than reason must exert an influence on him. In other words, desires for what he regards as good only in a certain respect, but not overall and so on balance evil, must be influencing him. Then he has a choice of whether to yield to desire or to pursue the best, despite contrary desire, i.e., temptation. Just as if reasons alone influence action, an agent inevitably does what he believes to be the best; so if desires alone influence action, an agent will inevitably follow his strongest desire. Free choice of action only comes in when there is a choice between two actions which the agent regards as equally good, or between two actions which he desires to do equally, or—the serious free choice—between two actions, one of which he desires to do more, and the other of which he believes it is better to do.[11] An agent's free choice of good despite contrary temptation is indeed a good—for the agent. For he has determined the flow of events in favor of the good rather than the bad. And he will have exerted more influence on that flow, the greater the temptation to the bad.

But while the pursuit of the good, despite serious contrary temptation, is a good, so too is the spontaneous pursuit of the good, the pursuit of the good which the agent fully desires to pursue. We value the willingly generous action, the naturally honest, spontaneously loving action. The spontaneous ready pursuit of the good has its own special kind of goodness, which—given the risk that, if he is tempted, the subject will yield to temptation, and a bad act be done and bad consequences follow—I cannot rank as either better or worse than the pursuit of the good, despite contrary temptation. (The spontaneous pursuit of the good may or may not involve a free choice. There may be a free choice between two actions seen as equally good and equally desired; or desire and reason may combine to make one choice inevitable.)

A good action is better, the greater the goals sought and attained. Especially good are supererogatory acts of helping people in great need. And just as it is good that there be a crisscrossing of desires and their satisfaction, so it is good that we seek each other's good and cooperate in seeking the good of others.

Just as having the desire and not merely its fulfillment is a good, so is having the opportunity to pursue the good, even if the opportunity is not taken. As I wrote earlier, having the opportunity to pursue the good intentionally, efficaciously, and freely is indeed a good for the agent; and if he has a free choice between good and evil, that makes him an ultimate source of how things go in the world in a very significant way. That, as we have seen, will involve his being subject to temptation to pursue the evil. The greater the choice of goods and evils we have, and (up to a limit) the greater the genuine freedom provided by serious temptation to pursue the bad instead, the more how the world goes is up to us and so the greater the privilege of our position. It is this which leads to the "free-will" defense of theodicy in respect of moral evil, the evil knowingly caused or constituted by the actions or negligence of human beings. God cannot give us the great good of the possibility of intentional, efficacious, free action, involving a choice between good and evil without at the same time providing the natural possibility (i.e., possibility allowed by natural laws) of evil which he will not prevent (not "cannot prevent" but "will not prevent," in order that the freedom he gives us may be efficacious freedom). The "free-will defense," carefully spelled out, must be a central core of theodicy, as it has been for the last two or three thousand years. But one point of this paper is to stress that the incompatibility of significant efficacious freedom and the absence of a natural possibility of evil is but one aspect of the logical straightjacket of goods which cannot be realized without actual or possible evils.

It is good that the free choices of humans between good and evil should include choices which make a difference to other humans for good or ill. A world where agents can benefit but not harm each other is a world where they have only very limited responsibility for each other. But the good of responsibility for each other is a very great good. We recognize this when we recognize it as a good gift to our own children to give them the responsibility for things, animals, and even other humans, and do not pressure them too much as to how they are to act. But if my responsibility for you is limited to whether or not to give you some quite unexpected new piece of photographic equipment, but I cannot make you unhappy, stunt your growth, or limit your education, then I do not have a great deal of responsibility for you. If God gave agents only such limited responsibility for their fellows, He would not have given much. He would be like a father asking his elder son to look after the younger son, and adding that he would be watching the elder son's every move and would intervene the moment the elder son did a thing wrong. The elder son might justly retort that while he would be happy to share his father's work, he could only really do so if he was left to make his own judgments as to what to do within a significant range of the options available to the father. God, like a good father, has reason to delegate responsibility. In order to allow creatures a share in creation, he has reason to allow them the choice of hurting and maiming, of frustrating the divine plan. Given that human choices are free ones (and I believe that there are reasons for supposing so),[12] then our world is one where humans have deep responsibility for each other.

This responsibility is not limited to the short term. By choices now I can affect the welfare of my own children in years to come; and I and others can make great differences for good or ill to life on this earth in decades to come. And by our choices now—to pursue certain kinds of scientific research and invest our wealth in certain sorts of technology—we may be able in centuries to come to influence for how long the human race lives and on which planet. My claim is that so good a thing is that deep responsibility that there is justification for God's allowing the evils caused by humans to each other (and themselves) to occur.

If an agent is to choose freely between good and evil, he needs, we have seen, to have contrary desires, evil inclinations; and these are themselves evils. I cannot choose freely to give money to the starving rather than hoard it unless I have some inherent miserly inclination, and my having that is itself an evil. For that reason, as well as for the reason of the evil which will be brought about if the agent yields to temptation, there is, as I noted earlier, a special kind of goodness in the good act done naturally and spontaneously without contrary temptation. God has reason to create creatures simpler than ourselves who naturally pursue the good. God has reason to make higher animals who often act spontaneously (without, I assume, free will) to benefit themselves (not just by acquiring food, but by playing and exploring) and others of their kind (mates and offspring whom they feed, clean, protect, etc.) and indeed often other kinds too (e.g., humans). And it is good too that humans often spontaneously pursue the good of their fellows.

What is known as the "higher-order goods defense" draws to our attention the good of performing certain sorts of good action, viz., those done in the face of evils, and of having the opportunity freely to choose to do such actions. There are certain actions which cannot be done unless there is pain and suffering (which I suggest centrally involve frustration of desire) to which they react. Showing sympathy (as opposed to the passive state of feeling compassion), helping the suffering, and showing courage of a certain sort are like this. I cannot show you sympathy unless you are suffering, nor help the suffering unless there is suffering nor bravely bear my pain unless I have pain to bear. The evil of pain is the grit which makes possible the growth of the pearl. Of course, no benevolent creator would multiply pains without limit in order to give creatures the opportunity to show courage, sympathy, and help of this sort. But he might well give us some pain in order to give us the opportunity to perform some actions good in the special way that these actions are good.

In these cases, as with feeling compassion, we are involved with the sufferer (ourself or another) at his lowest. But here we can do something about the situation, not merely have the appropriate feelings. It is good that an agent do good actions, and he expresses his most substantial commitment to the good when he does such actions when it is hardest, when he gets no encouragement from the success of other plans and things are happening to him which he does not desire. He does so when he shows courage of a certain sort. And it is good that others should be involved with people at their most naked making the hard choices, when the sufferer can see the others as concerned for him and not anything slightly exterior to him (aspects of his appearance of success which make him attractive), doing what they can for him and helping him to make the right choices. Help is most significant when it is most needed, and it is most needed when its recipient is suffering and deprived. Whatever it is good that we do, it is good that others help us to do—even if sometimes it is also good that we have available the ever harder choice of showing courage on our own.

Showing sympathy and showing courage are good actions which may be done in the face of the simple natural evil of frustration of desire involved in pain and suffering. But there are good actions of other kinds which can only be done in the face of evil actions of various kinds. I can only make reparation if I have wronged you, or forgive you if you have wronged me. In these cases, while of course it is not overall a good that wrong be done, reparation made and it be forgiven, still these actions do in part compensate for the wrong done. And while the possibility of its misuse provides a reason for God not to create creatures with significant freedom, the possibility of such compensation for misuse reduces the force of that reason. There is some truth, though not as much as the writer of the Exultet supposed, in "O Felix Culpa, quae talem ac tantum meruit habere redemptorem."[13] There are good actions of certain kinds which can only be done in the face of good actions of various kinds—such as showing gratitude, recognition of achievement, and reward; and the possibility of these responses to actions which may themselves be responses to pain and suffering (e.g., showing gratitude to doctors who have worked hard to relieve pain) provides further reason for permitting the pain and suffering.[14]

It is good that some actions, including the actions of animals lacking free will, should be serious actions which involve benefiting despite loss or foreseen risk of loss to themselves and so actions of looking for a mate, despite failure to find; or decoying predators or exploring despite risk of loss of life. But again an action good in this kind of way cannot be done without evil. You cannot intentionally avoid forest fires, or take trouble to rescue your offspring from forest fires, unless there exists a serious danger of getting caught in a forest fire. The action of rescuing despite danger simply cannot be done unless the danger exists—and the danger will not exist unless there is a significant natural probability of being caught in the fire. To the extent that the world is deterministic, that involves creatures actually being caught in the fire;[15] and to the extent that the world is indeterministic, that involves an inclination of nature to produce that effect unprevented by God. Fawns are bound to get caught in forest fires sometimes if other fawns are to have the opportunity of intentionally avoiding fires and if deer are to have the opportunities of rescuing other fawns from fires.[16]

Not all evil actions are actions of agents with free will and so to be justified by the free-will defense. Animals sometimes reject their offspring or hurt other animals.[17] Yet these actions, like physical pain, provide opportunities for good actions to be done in response to them, e.g., make possible adoption of the rejected offspring by other animals, or rescue of the injured by other animals, or the animal courageously coping with his injury or rejection.

I have argued so far for the great good of the having and satisfaction of desire, and shown how the satisfaction of persisting desires and the having of compassionate desires involves the occurrence of various evils. I then went on to show how the great good of having significant free choice involves actual bad desires and the possible occurrence of further significant harm to ourselves and others; and how having the opportunity to show courage or compassion involves the actual occurrence of pain and suffering. I also brought out the lesser value of serious beneficiary action by animals lacking free will.

As with desire, so with action, I have stressed the good for the subject of desire and action of having and satisfying good desires and performing or trying to perform good actions, especially ones whose object is someone else. It is a great good for me to bring the goods of life to others. Helping, contributing, being of use to others, even more than to ourselves, is a great good, a blessing, a privilege—especially if it is by free action, but also if it is by a spontaneous action, a significantly greater good than are the goods (which are indeed goods) of having tingles of sensory pleasure. And, as we have seen, there is special value in helping those who most need help. That helping is an immense good for the helper has always been difficult for humans to see, but it is especially hard for twentieth-century secularized Western people to see. It is however, something quite often near the surface of New Testament writings; and it was aptly summarized by Saint Paul in his farewell sermon to the church at Ephesus when he urged them "to remember the words of the Lord Jesus, how he himself said, It is more blessed to give than to receive" (Acts 20:35).

We don't, most of us, think that most of the time. We think that our well-being consists in the things that we possess or the experiences we enjoy. Sometimes, true, all men find themselves in circumstances in which they ought to give—alas, the starving appear on our doorstep and we ought to give them some of our wealth, perhaps something large which will deprive us of future enjoyments. But that, the common thinking goes, is our misfortune, good for the starving but bad for us. Life would have been better for us if they hadn't turned up on the doorstep. But what the words of Christ say, taken literally, is "not so." We are lucky that they turned up on the doorstep. It would have been our misfortune if there had been no starving to whom to give; life would have been worse for us.

And even twentieth-century people can begin to see that—sometimes—when they seek to help prisoners not by providing more comfortable quarters but by letting prisoners help the handicapped; or when they pity rather than envy the "poor little rich girl" who has everything and does nothing for anyone else. And one phenomenon prevalent in end-of-century Britain draws this especially to our attention—the evil of unemployment. Because of our system of social security the unemployed on the whole have enough money to live without too much discomfort; certainly they are a lot better off than are many employed in Africa or Asia or Victorian Britain. What is evil about unemployment is not so much any resulting poverty but the uselessness of the unemployed. They often report feeling unvalued by society, of no use, "on the scrap heap." They rightly think it would be a good for them to contribute, but they can't.

It is not only intentional actions freely chosen, but also ones performed involuntarily, which have good consequences which constitute a good for the person who does them. If the unemployed were compelled to work for some useful purpose, they would still—most of them—regard that as a good for them in comparison with being useless. Or consider the conscript killed in a just and ultimately successful war in defense of his country against a tyrannous aggressor. Almost all peoples, apart from those of the Western world in our generation, have recognized that dying for one's country is a great good for him who dies, even if he was conscripted.[18] And it is not only intentional actions but experiences undergone involuntarily (or involuntary curtailment of good experiences, as by death) which have good consequences—so long as those experienced are closely connected with their consequences—which constitute a good for him who has them (even if a lesser good than that of a free intentional action causing those consequences, and a good often outweighed by the evil of the experience in question). Consider someone hurt or killed in an accident, where the accident leads to some reform which prevents the occurrence of similar accidents in the future (e.g., someone killed in a rail crash which leads to the installation of a new system of railway signaling which avoids similar accidents in the future). He and his relatives may comment in such a situation that at any rate the victim did not suffer or die in vain. They would have regarded it as a greater misfortune even for the victim if his suffering or death served no useful purpose. It is a good for us if our experiences are not wasted but are used for the good of others, if they are the means of a benefit which would not have come to others without them, which will at least in part compensate for those experiences. It follows from this insight that it is a blessing for a person if the possibility of his suffering makes possible the good for others of having the free choice of hurting or harming him; and if his actual suffering makes possible the good for others of feeling compassion for him, and of choosing to show or not show sympathy or provides knowledge for others. Thus it is a good for the fawn caught in the thicket in the forest fire that its suffering provides knowledge for the deer and other animals who see it to avoid the fire and deter their other offspring from being caught in it. The supreme good of being of use is worth paying a lot to get. It is much better if the being-of-use is chosen voluntarily, but it is good even if it isn't. Blessed is the man or woman whose life is of use.

If A desires the satisfaction of B's desire, the satisfaction of this desire is, I argued, a good for B in having his desire satisfied, a good for A in that his especially good desire is satisfied, and also an additional good for B in that the satisfaction of his desire was something that A cared about. Similarly, and much more so, with intentional actions. If A secures the fulfillment of some desire of B, not merely is it a good for B that his desire is fulfilled, and a good for A that he is the instrument of this, but it is a further good for B that the fulfillment of desire did not come by chance but by A actively seeking his well-being. We are lucky if people mind about us, and the natural expression of minding is seeking well-being. Sometimes those who "don't like to be beholden to others" don't see this. "I wish that I were not so dependent on my parents for money," says the undergraduate. But "so" is the crucial word—dependence can come in irksome forms or be too complete; but how awful it would be if nobody ever cared for us enough to give us anything. Fortunately, if God exists, no human or animal is ever in that position.

In the course of this paper I have run through many good states which we find on Earth and which God might seek to bring about. I have shown how often various evils (or their possibility) are (logically) necessary for their attainment. The evils include moral evils—the harm we humans do to each other or negligently allow to occur—the natural evils of various kinds, both animal and human suffering. The same goods could exist in a world different from ours in which there was less natural evil and more moral evil—e.g., there was so much moral evil in virtue of stronger human desires for evil—that there was no need for so much natural evil if humans were to have the same opportunity for courage in face of pain. But it is far from obvious that such a world would be a better world than ours. In general we need a similar amount of evil if we are to have the similar amount of good by way of the having and satisfaction of desire, and of significant choice and serious beneficiary action. There are also, I believe, other goods and other ways in which evil is necessary for good which I have not described.

None of the goods which I have listed are such that their production would justify God in causing endless suffering, but he does not do that. There is a limit of intensity and above all time (the length of a human life) to the suffering caused to any individual. In the perspective of eternity, the evils of this world are very limited in number and duration; and the issue concerns only whether God would allow such narrowly limited evils to occur for the sake of the great goods they make possible. A central theme of this paper is to draw attention to goods of two kinds which the modern world tends not to notice. It is when you take them into serious account, I suggest, that you begin to realize that not merely are certain evils necessary for certain goods, but they are necessary for goods at least as great as the evils are evil. There is first the good of being of use, or helping, and secondly the good of being helped. God will seek to bestow generously these great blessings.

I have almost always found in discussion of these matters that my opponents are usually happy to grant me, when I bring the suggestion to their attention, that the states which I describe as "goods" cannot be had without the corresponding evils, and quite often happy to grant that the former states are indeed good states and even that a world is not on balance worse for containing a few of these goods in the mildest of forms with the corresponding evils than it would otherwise be. But my opponents usually object to the scale—there are, they claim, too many, too various, and too serious evils to justify bringing about the goods which they make possible. Yet it must be stressed that each evil or possible evil removed takes away one more actual good.

If the fawn does not suffer in the thicket, other deer will not so readily have the opportunity of intentionally avoiding fires; he will not through his suffering be able to show courage or have the privilege of providing knowledge for other deer of how to avoid such tragedies; other deer and humans centuries later will not be able to show compassion for his suffering, etc. The sort of world where so many such evils are removed and which in effect my opponents think that God's goodness requires him to make, turns out—as regards the kinds of good to which I have drawn attention—to be a toy world. Things matter in the kinds of respect which I mention, but they don't matter very much. I cannot see that God would be less than perfectly good if he gave us a world where things matter a lot more than that.

I suggest that the reluctance of my opponents to see that arises primarily from overestimating the goodness of mere pleasure and the evil of mere pain, and grossly underestimating the value of being of use and being helped. Our culture has dulled our moral sensitivities in these respects. Yet even if an opponent allows the formal point that there is great value for the subject in being of use and being helped, he may fail to see that that has the consequence for theodicy which I commend because of two characteristic human vices—short-term and short-distance thinking. He tends to think of the worth of a sentient life as dependent on things that happen during that life and fairly close in space to the life. But once you grant the formal point that things outside a life, e.g., its causes and effects, make a great difference to the value of that life, it seems totally arbitrary to confine those things to ones near to the life in space and time. The sufferings of the Jewish victims of the Nazi concentration camps were the result of a web of choices that stretched back over centuries and continents and caused or made possible a whole web of actions and reactions that will stretch forward over centuries and continents (and the same goes to a lesser extent for the suffering of the fawn). Such sufferings made heroic choices possible for people normally too timid to make them (e.g., to harbor the prospective victims) and for people normally too hardhearted (as a result of previous bad choices) to make them (e.g., for a concentration camp guard not to obey orders). And they make possible reactions of courage (e.g., by the victims), of compassion, sympathy, penitence, forgiveness, reform, avoidance of repetition, etc., stretching down time and space. In saying this, I am not of course saying that those Nazi officials who sent Jews to the concentration camps were justified in doing so. For they had no right whatever to do that to others. But I am saying that God, who has rights over us that we do not have over others, is not less than perfectly good if he allowed the Jews for a short period to be subjected to these terrible evils through the evil free choice of others—in virtue of the hard heroic value of their lives of suffering.

There is no other way to get the evils of this world into the right perspective, except to reflect at length on innumerable very detailed thought experiments (in addition to actual experiences of life) in which we postulate very different sorts of worlds from our own, then ask ourselves whether the perfect goodness of God would require him to create one of these (or no world at all) rather than our own.[19] But I conclude with a very small thought experiment, which may help my opponents to begin this process. Suppose that you exist in another world before your birth in this one and are given a choice as to the sort of life you are to lead. You are told that you are to have only a short life, maybe of only a few minutes, although it will be an adult life in the sense that you will have the richness of sensation and belief characteristic of adults. You have a choice as to the sort of life you will have. You can have either a few minutes of very considerable pleasure of the kind produced by some drug such as heroin, which you will experience by yourself and will have no effects at all in the world (e.g., no one else will know about it); or you can have a few minutes of considerable pain, such as the pain of childbirth, which will have (unknown to you at the time of pain) considerable good effects on others over a few years. You are told that if you do not make the second choice, those others will never exist—and so you are under no moral obligation to make the second choice. But you seek to make the choice which will make your own life the best life for you to have led. How will you choose? The choice is, I hope, obvious. You must choose the second alternative. And it would of course make no difference to your choice if the good effects are to be very distant in time and space from your life.[20]

If we go on to meditate on how we should choose between other alternatives with longer lives or different lives—incarnation as a fawn or a suffering child[21] maybe—against a background of many centuries of effect and cause and place in the web of human and animal society, we may begin to look at things a little more sub specie aeternitatis. If God is generously to give to creatures the privilege of forming other creatures, developing their desires and freedom of choice and informing them about the possible choices open to them, he cannot (for logical reasons) ask the latter before they are born what sort of life they would like to live. He has to make the choice on their behalf, and he will therefore seek to make a choice which, if rational, we might make for ourselves. He sometimes pays us the compliment of supposing that we would choose to be heroes.

For someone who remains unconvinced by my claims about the relative strengths of the goods and evils involved, holding that great though the goods are they do not justify the evils which they involve, there is a fall-back position. My arguments may have convinced the reader of the greatness of the goods involved sufficiently for him to allow that God would be justified in bringing about the evils for the sake of the goods which they make possible, if and only if God also provides compensation in the form of happiness after death to the victims whose sufferings make possible the goods. Someone whose theodicy requires buttressing in this way will need independent reason for believing that God does provide such life after death if he is to be justified in holding his theodicy, and he may well have such reason.[22] While believing that God does provide at any rate for many humans such life after death, I have expounded a theodicy without relying on this assumption. But I can understand someone thinking that the assumption is needed. If, for example, the goods making possible free choice for the Nazi concentration camp guards (in choosing whether to disobey orders), for the Jewish victims (in deciding how to bear their suffering), and for many others involved are not goods great enough to justify God's allowing the Nazis to choose to exterminate Jews, maybe they would be if the evil is compensated by some years of happy afterlife for the Jews involved.

It remains the case, however, that evil is evil, and there is a substantial price to pay for the goods of our world. God would not be less than perfectly good if he created instead a world without pain and suffering, and so without the particular goods which they make possible. Christian tradition claims that God has created worlds of both kinds—our world, and the heaven of the blessed. The latter is a marvelous world with a vast range of possible deep goods, but it lacks a few goods which our world contains, including the good of being able to reject the good. Out of generosity, God might well choose to give some of us the choice of rejecting the good in a world like ours, before giving to those who accept it a wonderful world in which that possibility no longer exists.[23]

NOTES

1. Given that an omnipotent being can prevent and that a perfectly good being will always try to prevent evils of the kind and quantity we find on Earth, the argument from such evils is a conclusive deductive argument against the existence of God. But insofar as it is only probable that an omnipotent being can prevent or that a perfectly good being will try to prevent evils of the kind and quantity we find on Earth, then the conclusion that there is no God will only be probable.

2. Some writers have used "theodicy" as the name of the enterprise of showing God's actual reasons for allowing evil to occur and have contrasted it with a "defense" to the argument from evil to the nonexistence of God which merely shows that the argument doesn't work. See, e.g., Alvin Plantinga, *The Nature of Necessity* (Oxford: Clarendon Press, 1974), 192. Given this contrast, what I am seeking to do is provide a "defense" rather than a "theodicy," but I do so by showing what reasons God could have for allowing evil to occur; I am not, however, claiming that the reasons which I give are God's actual reasons. I believe, however, that my use of "theodicy" is that normal to the tradition of discussion of these issues.

3. For argument on this, see my book *The Existence of God* (Oxford: Clarendon Press, 1979), 216-18.

4. See *The Existence of God*, 202-14. I present the argument at greater length and

defend it against objections in "Knowledge from Experience, and the Problem of Evil" in Wm. Abraham and S. Holtzer, eds., *The Rationality of Religious Belief* (Oxford: Clarendon Press, 1987). While I accept the need for yet further tightening of the argument, to do so would require at least an article devoted entirely to that topic.

5. I plan to write a full-length book on Providence, in which I shall defend the moral views in question at much greater length than I do in this paper.

6. For a fuller account of desire, see my book *The Evolution of the Soul* (Oxford: Clarendon Press, 1986), chap. 6.

7. I stress that the desire is only "frustrated" when it is a (believedly) unfulfilled desire for something to happen now. A desire to go to London tomorrow is today neither satisfied nor frustrated. Of course, some frustrations are so mild that we might hesitate to call them that in ordinary speech—but my unfulfilled mild desire for cream cake is on a continuum with my strong desire that a certain sensation go away, or that peace come to the Middle East; and hence it is appropriate in philosophical discussion to call the former also a case of frustration of desire.

8. The evil is not the death of the loved ones but our being deprived of intercourse with them. Death is simply in itself the point at which the finite good of life comes to an end. Death is only an evil for the dead one if it occurs under certain circumstances (e.g., prematurely, when life's ambitions are suddenly frustrated). That death is not as such an evil (i.e., for the dead one under normal circumstances) but that in many respects it is good that the world contain death, see *The Existence of God*, 193-96.

9. In discussing intentional actions, I am assuming that the agent's moral beliefs are correct. It would complicate the discussion too much to bring in the goodness of actions aimed at some end falsely believed to be good. But I do not believe that this simplification in any way affects the main points of the argument.

10. That is, the agent has libertarian free will—his choices are not fully determined; not just compatibilist free will—no one puts psychological or physical pressure on him to act as he does. Of course, libertarian free will only belongs to an agent choosing intentionally between alternatives; it doesn't belong to any nonmental events, such as the random swervings of atoms, which are not fully caused.

11. There is a further circumstance under which free choice is possible. That is where an agent has a choice between an infinite number of good actions, each of which is, he believes, worse than some other such action; there is, he believes, no best or equal best action. However, since only a being whose power is unlimited in some respect will be in such a situation, humans or animals are never in such a situation; and so for the sake of simplicity of exposition, I ignore this possibility.

12. I have given my reasons for my belief, that they do have such free will elsewhere—see my *Evolution of the Soul*, chap. 13. Insofar as there is reason to suppose that they do not have such free will, the free-will defense will fail.

13. This is the comment of the Exultet, the hymn of the traditional Easter Eve Liturgy, on the sin of Adam: "O happy fault which merited a redeemer so great and of such a kind."

14. For analysis of such notions as reparation, forgiveness, gratitude, and reward, see my *Responsibility and Atonement* (Oxford: Clarendon Press, 1989), chaps. 4 and 5.

15. If the behavior of tossed coins is deterministic, talk about a natural probability of a coin landing heads can only be intelligibly construed as talk about proportions of coins tossed in typical setups which result in heads. ("Natural probability" or "physical probability" is probability in nature in contrast to "epistemic probability," which is probability relative to our knowledge.) See my *Introduction to Confirmation Theory* (Oxford: Methuen, 1973), chaps. 1 and 2.

16. Those familiar with recent philosophical writing on the problem of evil will realize that I choose the example of a fawn caught in a forest fire because of its prevalence in that literature. It was put forward by William Rowe (see chapter 1 in this volume) as an example of apparently pointless evil.

17. It is a mistake, in my view, to regard the killing of one animal by another for food as in itself an evil. To be killed and eaten by another animal is as natural an end to life as would be death by other natural causes at the same age. For, given that animals lack free will and moral concepts, the killing of one by another is as much part of the natural order as is accident or disease not involving its transmission by other animals. And if death by such natural causes is not as such an evil, as I have urged (see note 8), but simply the end of a good, so too with death by predator. Evil comes insofar as there is pain involved in the killing, or offspring are knowingly deprived of a parent. I do not see any very good reason to suppose that invertebrates who do not have a central nervous system similar to that of humans suffer pain, let alone have knowledge. The evil of suffering arises, I suspect, only with the vertebrates and possibly only with mammals. Plausibly, too, since the central nervous systems of other vertebrates and mammals are less developed than ours, their sufferings are less than ours.

18. This good, others have recognized, exists as a this-worldly good, quite apart from any reward for patriotic behavior which might accrue in the afterlife. The hope of such reward was not a major motive among Romans and Greeks who died for their country: "The doctrine of a future life was far too vague among the pagans to exercise any powerful general influence," writes W. E. H. Lecky in his *History of European Morals from Augustus to Charlemagne,* vol. 2 (1899), 3. And he states that "the Spartan and the Roman died for his country because he loved it. The martyr's ecstasy of hope had no place in his dying hour. He gave up all he had, he closed his eyes, as he believed for ever, and he asked for no reward in this world or in the next" (vol. 1, 178). The lines of Horace, "dulce et decorum propatria mori" (it is sweet and proper to die for one's country) in his *Odes* (3.2.13), were written by a man whose belief in personal immortality was negligible—see 3.30, in which Horace sees his "immortality" as consisting in his subsequent reputation and seems to convey the view that dying for one's country was a good for the one who died. It was of course a Socratic view that doing just acts was a good for the one who does them; see Plato, *Gorgias* 479.

19. Note that the issue is not whether this world is the best of all possible worlds. There cannot, I suggest, be a best of all possible worlds, because any world could always be bettered in some respect—see *The Existence of God,* 113-14. The issue is whether there is too much evil in this world, despite the goods it makes possible, for God to create it at all. He may of course create other worlds as well.

20. The thought experiment is only meant to bring out the value of such a life for the sufferer. It is not put forward as a case when God could not produce the good effect in any other way. But it is meant to begin to help us to assess correctly cases of the latter kind.

21. See Ivan's speech in Dostoyevsky's *Brothers Karamazov,* bk. 5, chap. 4.

22. This may, for example, be provided by revelation. On the evidence for revealed truth, see my *Revelation* (Oxford: Clarendon Press, 1992).

23. For comments on earlier drafts of this paper, I thank C. Stephen Layman, Bruce Russell, Eleonore Stump, and Mark O. Webb.

4.

ELEONORE STUMP

Aquinas on the Sufferings of Job

Aquinas wrote commentaries on five books of the Old Testament (Psalms, Job, Isaiah, Jeremiah, Lamentations), two Gospels (Matthew and John), and the Pauline epistles. These biblical commentaries have not received the same sort of attention as some of his other works, such as the *Summa theologiae* or the *Summa contra gentiles,* but they are a treasure trove of philosophy and theology.[1] The commentary on Job in particular is one of Aquinas's more mature and polished commentaries. Unlike many of them, which are preserved in the form of a *reportatio,* a transcription of Aquinas's lecturers by someone who attended them, the commentary on Job is an *expositio,* material reworked and revised by Aquinas himself.[2] The commentary sheds light on Aquinas's understanding of God's providence and especially of the relation between God's providence and human suffering. Aquinas does discuss providence in other works as well, most notably in book 3 of the *Summa contra gentiles,* which is roughly contemporary with the commentary on Job; and he considers problems involving suffering in many of the biblical commentaries, especially those on the Pauline epistles.[3] But the book of Job is the paradigmatic presentation of the problem of evil for anyone trying to reconcile the

existence of God with the presence of evil in the world, and it is therefore particularly interesting to see how Aquinas interprets this book. So, although I turn to
the *Summa contra gentiles* and the commentaries on the Pauline epistles when appropriate, my focus is on Aquinas's commentary on Job.

1. Aquinas's Approach to Job

Contemporary readers tend to think of the subject of the book of Job as
the problem of evil. Since the book itself says that Job was innocent and since the
book is equally clear about the fact that Job's suffering is (indirectly) caused by
God, who grants Satan permission to afflict him, it seems to contemporary readers that the story of Job's suffering is hard to reconcile with the claim that there is
an omnipotent, omniscient, perfectly good God. How could such a being allow an
innocent person to suffer the loss of his property, the death of his children, a
painful and disfiguring disease, and the other sufferings Job endured? And so the
story of innocent Job, horribly afflicted with undeserved suffering, seems to many
people representative of the kind of evil with which any theodicy must come to
grips. But Aquinas sees the problems in the book of Job differently. He seems not
to recognize that suffering in the world, of the quantity and quality of Job's, calls
into question God's goodness, let alone God's existence. Instead Aquinas understands the book as an attempt to come to grips with the nature and operations of
divine providence. How does God direct his creatures? Does the suffering of the
just require us to say that divine providence is not extended to human affairs? Of
course, this question is clearly connected to the one we today generally find in the
book of Job. But the difference between the contemporary approach to Job and the
one Aquinas adopts is instructive for understanding Aquinas's view of the relation
between God and evil.

On Aquinas's account, the problem with Job's friends is that they have a
wrong view of the way providence operates. They suppose that providence assigns
adversities in this life as a punishment for sins and earthly prosperity as a reward
for virtue. Job, however, has a more correct view of providence, according to
Aquinas, because he recognizes that a good and loving God will nonetheless allow
the worst sorts of adversities to befall a virtuous person also. The disputation constituted by the speeches of Job and his friends is a disputation concerning the correct understanding of this aspect of the operations of providence. What is of more
interest to us here than the details of this disputation, as Aquinas understands it, is
his analysis of the reasons the friends take such a wrong view of providence. In connection with one of Eliphaz's speeches, Aquinas says, "If in this life human beings
are rewarded by God for good deeds and punished for bad, as Eliphaz was endeav-
oring to establish, it apparently follows that the ultimate goal for human beings is
in this life. But Job intends to rebut this opinion, and he wants to show that the
present life of human beings doesn't contain [that] ultimate goal, but is related to
it as motion is related to rest and the road to its end."[4]

2. Constraints on Theodicy

Aquinas's idea, then, is that the things that happen to a person in this life can be justified only by reference to her or his state in the afterlife. That a medieval Christian thinker should have an other-worldly view comes as no surprise, but it is at first glance perplexing to see that Aquinas thinks taking the other world into account will settle questions about how providence operates. For we might suppose that even if all that happens in a person's life is simply a prolegomenon to her state in the afterlife, nothing in this claim allays the concerns raised by seeing that in this world bad things happen to good people. Job's comforters take the line they do, that suffering is punishment for sins, just because they see no other way to maintain God's goodness and justice. It's hard to see how indicating the existence of an afterlife would change their minds. Because Aquinas has always in mind the thought that the days of our lives here are short while the afterlife is unending,[5] he naturally supposes that things having to do with the afterlife are more important than the things having to do with this life. But nothing in this attitude of his is incompatible with supposing that if God is good, things in this life ought to go well, at least for the just, if not for everybody.

We might suppose that Aquinas is here presupposing a view familiar to us from contemporary discussions of the problem of evil: God's reasons for allowing suffering are mysterious, and we don't know what sort of justification, if any, there is for God's allowing evil; but the immeasurable good of union with God in heaven recompenses all the finite evils we suffer here.[6] The benefits of the afterlife don't justify God's allowing evil, but they do make up for the suffering of people who experience evil, in the sense that in union with God such people find their sufferings more than compensated. But Aquinas adopts a line different from this. His line makes constructing an adequate theodicy more difficult but also (to my mind) more satisfying if successful. He supposes that *we* can know, at least in general, the good that justifies God's allowing evil. And he accepts basically the same constraints as those some contemporary philosophers insist on: if a good God allows evil, it can only be because the evil in question produces a benefit for the sufferer and one that God could not provide without the suffering.[7]

In his commentary on Romans, Aquinas distinguishes between the way providence works with respect to persons, on the one hand, and the rest of creation, on the other hand. As part of his defense of the line that all things work together for good for those who love God, Aquinas says this:

> Whatever happens on earth, even if it is evil, turns out for the good of the whole world. Because as Augustine says in the *Enchiridion,* God is so good that he would never permit any evil if he were not also so powerful that from any evil he could draw out a good. But the evil does not always turn out for the good of the thing in connection with which the evil occurs, because although the corruption of one animal turns out for the good of the whole world—insofar as one animal is generated from the corruption of another—nonetheless it doesn't turn out for the good of the animal which is corrupted. The reason for this is that the good of the whole world is willed by God for its own sake, and all the parts of the world are

ordered to this [end]. The same reasoning appears to apply with regard to the order of the noblest parts [of the world] with respect to the other parts, because the evil of the other parts is ordered to the good of the noblest parts. But whatever happens with regard to the noblest parts is ordered only to the good of those parts themselves, because care is taken of them for their own sake, and for their sake care is taken of other things. . . . But among the best of all the parts of the world are God's saints. . . . He takes care of them in such a way that he doesn't allow any evil for them which he doesn't turn into their good.[8]

In discussing providence in the *Summa contra gentiles,* he takes the same line. In a chapter headed "Rational creatures are governed for their own sake but others are governed in subordination to them," Aquinas repeatedly argues for the conclusion that "by divine providence, for creatures with intellects provision is made for their own sake, but for other creatures provision is made for the sake of those with intellects."[9]

In fact, Aquinas not only accepts the biblical line that (by divine providence) all things work together for good for those (rational creatures) who love God, but he has a particularly strong interpretation of it. How are we to understand the expression "all things" in this line? he asks in his commentary on Romans. The general claim that for created persons God permits only those evils he can turn into goods for them is, Aquinas says, "plainly true when it comes to the painful evils that [created persons] suffer. That is why it says in the gloss that the humility [of those who love God] is stimulated by their weakness, their patience by affliction, their wisdom by opposition, and their benevolence by animosity."[10] But what about the evils that are sins? Are they also among the things which work together for good for those who love God? "Some people say that sins are not included under 'all things' [in the biblical passage]. . . . But against this is the passage in the gloss: . . . if some among the saints go astray and turn aside, even this God makes efficacious for good for them. . . . [S]uch people rise again [from their fall] with greater charity, since the good of human beings is charity. . . . They return more humble and better instructed."[11]

So Aquinas adopts a line different from the one some contemporary philosophers argue for. He apparently believes that we can and in some cases do know the goods which justify suffering. On the other hand, like some contemporary philosophers, Aquinas feels that (at least for creatures with minds) suffering is justified only in case it is a means to good for the sufferer herself. And Aquinas's examples of such good all have at least a natural, if not a necessary, connection with the evil in question: patience brought about by affliction, humility brought about by the experience of sin and repentance.

What shall we say then about Aquinas's approach to Job? Given his understanding of the constraints governing theodicy, how shall we explain Aquinas's view that the perplexities of the story and the inadequacies of the comforters can all be satisfactorily accounted for by the recognition that there is an afterlife and that rewards and punishments are distributed there rather than in this life? The first part of the explanation comes from Aquinas's attitude toward happiness; the second part stems from his account of suffering.

3. *Aquinas's Attitude toward Human Happiness*

That human beings naturally desire their own happiness is a common-place of Western philosophy. And we also suppose that any good person, but especially a perfectly good divine person, will desire the happiness of other persons. What raises the problem of evil for us is watching cases in which, it seems to us, God isn't doing enough to promote the happiness of his creatures; or is permitting their unhappiness, or even, as in Job's case, is actively conniving at the unhappiness of one of his creatures. But then in order to investigate the problem of evil we need first to be reflective about the nature of human happiness. It is noteworthy that in his long treatment of providence in the *Summa contra gentiles*, Aquinas has virtually no discussion of what we would consider the problem of evil but fifteen chapters on the nature of human happiness.

What exactly happens to Job that makes us wonder about God's good-ness? (We might also ask about what happens to Job's animals, Job's children, or Job's wife, because questions about God's goodness obviously arise in connection with them, too; but I will focus here just on Job.) He loses his animals, the basis of wealth in his society. Afflicted with a miserable skin disease, he loses his health. And he loses his children, all of whom are killed in one day. We might term these losses Job's first-order afflictions. These first-order afflictions are the cause of further, second-order afflictions for him, the most notable of which is his disgrace in his own society. In consequence of the way in which his society interprets his troubles, he becomes a pariah among those who once honored him. And, finally, because Job's friends react very negatively to his insistence that he is innocent, their response to the way in which Job sees his first- and second-order afflictions pro-vides yet more suffering for him, a third-order suffering. Because his reactions to his first- and second-order suffering differ radically from theirs, he finds himself deeply at odds with the very people who might have been a source of comfort to him—first his wife and then the men closest to him. (His conflict with God, to which Aquinas is oblivious, seems to me the most important part of this third-order affliction, but I will leave it to one side here, and not only because Aquinas is insensitive to it. Since this part of Job's misery stems from his inability to under-stand how the God he trusted could let such things happen to him, the enterprise of theodicy is itself an attempt to explain this part of Job's suffering.)

We naturally take Job's losses to constitute the destruction of his happi-ness. But if we look at the chapters on happiness in the *Summa contra gentiles*, we find Aquinas arguing the following claims: happiness does not consist in wealth,[12] happiness does not consist in the goods of the body such as health,[13] and happiness does not consist in honors.[14] Happiness is the greatest of goods, on Aquinas's account, but any good that is not by nature completely shareable, that is, which is such that in giving it to others one has less of it, is only a small good. Most, if not all, the gifts of fortune will therefore count just as small goods, on Aquinas's view. There is enough of medieval Christianity left in twentieth-century Western culture that many of us can read such claims and vaguely affirm them without paying much attention to what they mean. But on this view of Aquinas's, if happiness does not consist in health, honor, or riches, then it doesn't follow that a person who does not have these things is without happiness. It is therefore not immediately clear, contrary to what we unreflectively assume, that Job's happiness is destroyed in consequence of not having these things.

Two things are worth noticing here. First, Aquinas, even with all his otherworldly focus, is not a Stoic. Among the many chapters in *Summa contra gentiles* saying what happiness does not consist in, there is no chapter saying that happiness does not consist in loving relations with other persons. Unlike some ancient philosophers, Aquinas does not understand happiness as a matter of self-sufficiency. So Aquinas's arguments about what happiness does not consist in are apparently not relevant to one of Job's losses, the loss of his children, or to the third-order afflictions of discord with his wife and friends. Second, even if health, honor, riches, and the other things on Aquinas's list don't constitute happiness, it might nonetheless be the case that the loss of them or the presence of their opposites—sickness, disgrace, impoverishment—produces so much pain as to make happiness impossible. On Aquinas's view, human happiness consists in the contemplation of God. Apart from worries over whether human cognitive faculties are capable of contemplating God in this life, one might wonder whether pain and suffering don't interfere with such contemplation. And, in fact, as part of the evidence for the conclusion that true happiness cannot be achieved in this life, Aquinas himself says that weaknesses and misfortunes can impede the functions which must be exercised for happiness.[15] Consequently, even if, as Aquinas thinks, happiness consists in contemplation of God rather than in the gifts of fortune, so that the loss of health or honor or riches doesn't by itself entail the loss of happiness, Aquinas apparently recognizes that it is possible for misfortune in any of its varieties to be an obstacle to happiness. So although it is helpful to understand Aquinas's views of happiness, we also need to consider his account of suffering in order to understand his approach to the book of Job.

4. Aquinas's Attitude toward Pain and Suffering

When from the standpoint of religion we reflect on the many evils of the world—murder, rape, torture, the oppression of apartheid, the evils of nuclear armament, the horrors of Auschwitz and Treblinka—we can hardly avoid wondering how a good God could let such things occur. But another thing to wonder about is the nature of human beings, who in all cultures and all ages can be so vicious to one another. On Aquinas's view, all human beings have a terminal cancer of soul, a proneness to evil which invariably eventuates in sin and which in the right circumstances blows up into monstrosity. On his view, even "our senses and our thoughts are prone to evil."[16] The pure and innocent among human beings are no exception to this claim. When the biblical text says that Job was righteous, Aquinas takes the text to mean that Job was pure by human standards. By the objective, uncurved standards of God, even Job was infected with the radical human tendencies toward evil.[17] No human being who remains uncured of this disease can see God. On Aquinas's view, then, the primary obstacle to contemplation of God, in which human happiness consists, is the sinful character of human beings.

Aquinas thinks that pain and suffering of all sorts are God's medicine for this spiritual cancer; and he emphasizes this view repeatedly. In his commentary on the Apostles' Creed, he says, "If all the pain a human being suffers is from God, then he ought to bear it patiently, both because it is from God and because it is ordered toward good; for pains purge sins, bring evildoers to humility, and stimulate good people to love of God."[18] In his commentary on Thessalonians he says, "As water extinguishes a burning fire, so tribulations extinguish the force of concupiscent desires, so that human beings don't follow them at will. . . . Therefore, [the Church] is not destroyed [by tribulations] but lifted up by them, and in the first place by the lifting up of the mind to God, as Gregory says: the evils which bear us down here drive us to go to God."[19] He comments in great detail on the line in Hebrews: "whom the Lord loves he chastens."[20] "All the saints who have pleased God have gone through many tribulations by which they were made the sons of God."[21] "Since pains are a sort of medicine, we should apparently judge correction and medicine the same way. Now medicine in the taking of it is bitter and loathsome, but its end is desirable and intensely sweet. So discipline is also. It is hard to bear, but it blossoms into the best outcome."[22]

The same general point appears recurrently in the commentary on Job. Arguing that temporal goods such as those Job lost are given and taken away according to God's will, Aquinas says "someone's suffering adversity would not be pleasing to God except for the sake of some good coming from the adversity. And so although adversity is in itself bitter and gives rise to sadness, it should nonetheless be agreeable [to us] when we consider its usefulness, on account of which it is pleasing to God. . . . For in his reason a person rejoices over the taking of bitter medicine because of the hope of health, even though in his senses he is troubled."[23] Even the dreadful suffering Job experiences at the death of his good and virtuous children becomes transformed on this account from the unbearable awfulness of total loss to the bitter but temporary pain of separation. In being united to God in love, a person is also united with others. The ultimate good of union with God, like any great good, is by nature shareable.

In commenting on a line in Job containing the complaint that God sometimes doesn't hear a needy person's prayers, Aquinas says, "Now it sometimes happens that God hearkens not to a person's pleas but rather to his advantage. A doctor does not hearken to the pleas of the sick person who requests that the bitter medicine be taken away (supposing that the doctor doesn't take it away because he knows that it contributes to health); instead he hearkens to [the patient's] advantage, because by doing so he produces health, which the sick person wants most of all. In the same way, God does not remove tribulations from the person stuck in them, even though he prays earnestly for God to do so, because God knows these tribulations help him forward to final salvation. And so although God truly does hearken, the person stuck in afflictions believes that God hasn't hearkened to him."[24]

In fact, on Aquinas's view, the better the person, the more likely it is that he will experience suffering. In explicating two metaphors of Job's,[25] comparing human beings in this life to soldiers on a military campaign and to employees, Aquinas makes the point in this way: "It is plain that the general of an army does not spare [his] more active soldiers dangers or exertions, but as the plan of battle requires, he sometimes lays them open to greater dangers and greater exertions. But after the attainment of victory, he bestows greater honor on the more active soldiers. So also the head of a household assigns greater exertions to his better servants, but when it is time to reward them, he lavishes greater gifts on them. And so neither is it characteristic of divine providence that it should exempt good people more from the adversities and exertions of the present life, but rather that it reward them more at the end."[26]

In his commentary on Thessalonians, Aquinas makes the same sort of point: "Many who are alive [in the eschaton] will be tried in the persecution of Antichrist, and they will surpass in greatness the many who had previously died."[27] And in his commentary on Philippians, he makes the point more generally: "from sufferings borne here a person attains to glory."[28]

With this background, we should not be surprised to find Aquinas affirming Paul's line in Romans that we should be glad of suffering: "It is a sign of the ardent hope which we have on account of Christ that we glory not only because of [our] hope of the glory to come, but we glory even regarding the evils which we suffer for it. And so [Paul] says that we not only glory (that is, in our hope of glory), but we glory even in tribulations, by which we attain to glory."[29]

5. The Oddness of Aquinas's Views

In Plato's *Gorgias* Callicles accuses Socrates of turning the world upside down; if Socrates' views are correct, Callicles says, "Everything we do is the exact opposite of what we ought to do."[30] Aquinas's views here also seem upside down. If he is right, everything we typically think about what counts as evil in the world is the exact opposite of what we ought to think. The topsy-turvy nature of this view of evil in the world is made vivid by a passage in a much earlier commentary on Job by Gregory the Great, whose views on this score are similar to Aquinas's. The ways of Providence are often hard to understand, Gregory says, but they are "still more mysterious when things go well with good people here, and ill with bad people. . . . When things go well with good people here, and ill with bad people, a great uncertainty arises whether good people receive good so that they might be stimulated to grow into something [even] better or whether by a just and secret judgment they see the rewards of their deeds here so that they may be void of the rewards of the life to come. . . . Therefore since the human mind is hemmed in by the thick fog of its uncertainty among the divine judgments, when holy people see the prosperity of this world coming to them, they are troubled with a frightening suspicion. For they are afraid that they might receive the fruits of their labors here; they are afraid that divine justice detects a secret wound in them and, heaping external rewards on them, drives them away from internal ones. . . . Consequently, holy people are more fearful of prosperity in this world than of adversity."[31] In other words, since it is in Gregory's view so difficult to understand how a just and benevolent providence could allow *good* things to happen to good people, when good people see that there is no adversity in their lives, they can't help but wonder whether they aren't after all to be counted among the wicked. For that reason, prosperity is more frightening to them than adversity.

This upside-down view of evil is the foreseeable conclusion of Aquinas's twin accounts of happiness and suffering. True happiness consists in the contemplation of God, shared and enjoyed together by all the redeemed in heaven. But the spiritual cancer which infects all human beings, even those who count as pure and innocent by human standards, makes it impossible for them to be united with God (or with each other) in heaven. Suffering is a kind of medicine for that disease.[32] Furthermore, at least for those who assent to the process and are eventually saved from their sinfulness, there is a direct connection between the amount of suffering in this life and the degree of glory in the life to come. Given such views, the sort of topsy-turvy thought represented by the passage from Gregory the Great is less surprising. If suffering is the chemotherapy for spiritual cancer, the patients whose regimen doesn't include any are the only ones for whom the prognosis is really bad.

This attitude on Aquinas's part also helps to explain his reaction to the book of Job. Like Aquinas, we take the attitude we do toward Job because of the values, the metaphysics, the general worldview we bring to the book. Because *we* assume, unreflectively, that temporal well-being is a necessary constituent of happiness (or even the whole of it), we also suppose that Job's losses undermine or destroy his happiness. Consequently, we wonder how God could count as good if he allowed these things to happen to a good person such as a Job, or we take stories of undeserved suffering to constitute evidence for thinking there is no God. Aquinas, on the other hand, begins with the conviction that neither God's goodness nor his existence are in doubt, either for the characters in the story of Job or for the readers of that story. Therefore, on his view, those who go astray in considering sufferings such as Job's do so because, like Job's comforters, they mistakenly suppose that happiness and unhappiness are functions just of things in this life. And so Aquinas takes the book of Job to be trying to instill in us the conviction that there is another life after this one, that our happiness lies there rather than here, and that we attain to that happiness only through suffering.[33] On Aquinas's view, Job has more suffering than ordinary people not because he is morally worse than ordinary, as the comforters assume, but just because he is better. Because he is a better soldier in the war against his own evil and a better servant of God's, God can give him more to bear here; and when this period of earthly life is over, his glory will also be surpassing.

6.   Concerns about Aquinas's View

For many of us, the reaction to this view of Aquinas's will be indignation. If we take it not as piously platitudinous but as a serious expression of otherworldliness, we are likely to find it so alien to our own sensitivities that we reject it as outrageous. I think that there are two primary forms such a reaction will take.

Our more articulate reaction is likely to center on the thought that this view constitutes a reprehensible callousness toward human affliction and misfortune and a disgusting willingness to accept evil.[34] Concern for others is a good part of what prompts this reaction; the asceticism and otherworldliness of Aquinas's sort of attitude seem to rule out all attempts to alleviate the suffering of other people. And, of course, an emphasis on otherworldliness *has* in the past been used in abominable ways as a basis for exploiting and oppressing the poor and defenseless. When the labor movement in this country was trying to protect workers through unionization, part of its strategy was to cast opprobrium on hope in an afterlife. Instead of offering decent conditions and fair wages, union organizers said, the exploitative bosses held out to their workers the hope of "pie in the sky when we die."

In fact, if what we take away from Aquinas's text is just the general conclusion that on his view pain and adversity are good things, then his view will yield results worthy not only of vituperation but of ridicule as well. We might suppose, for example, that his views entail the claim that anesthetics are to be eschewed[35] or, more generally, that any attempt to palliate or end anyone's pain is a bad thing.

One thing worth noticing at the outset here is that it is perhaps not quite so obvious as we might suppose where callousness lies in this discussion. If, contrary to what Aquinas supposes, human happiness requires the gifts of fortune, then people in contemporary wealthy and developed countries, or just the middle and upper classes in them, will have a vastly greater share of happiness, and the bulk of the world's population will be ruled out of that state. Aquinas's alien otherworldliness at least has the implication that the highest human good of happiness is not another monopoly of the industrialized nations.

But the more detailed and appropriate response to our emotive reaction in both its altruistic and its more general forms consists in seeing that on Aquinas's view suffering is good not *simpliciter* but only *secundum quid*. That is, suffering is not good in itself but only conditionally, insofar as it is a means to an end. "The evils which are in this world," Aquinas says, "aren't to be desired for their own sake but insofar as they are ordered to some good."[36] In itself suffering is a bad thing; it acquires positive value only when it contributes to spiritual well-being. We have no trouble seeing this sort of point when it comes to chemotherapy. In chemotherapy toxic drugs are administered to the patient, and the patient's friends and family are grateful for the treatments; but no one gets confused and supposes that it is then all right to allow the patient to ingest any sort of poisonous substance or that the medical personnel who administer the drugs are as a result in favor of administering poison generally.

It is sometimes easy to confuse conditional goods with nonconditional ones. The development of muscles is a conditional good, to be valued insofar as it contributes to health and strength and their accompanying attractiveness, but steroid users can mistakenly value it as a good in its own right. No doubt, even those steroid users who aren't ignorant of the dangers of steroids would claim that they took the drugs to enhance their bodies. But their behavior belies their explanation and suggests that they have lost sight of the purported purpose; bulking up of muscles appears to have become a good in itself in their eyes, even if it is harmful to health in the long run. Similarly, not eating is good only *secundum quid*, insofar as it leads to a healthier and more attractive body, but anorexics misprogram themselves to value it even when it leads to an ugly destruction of health. An anorexic might believe of herself that she was continuing to diet because dieting is a good means to a more attractive body; but in the face of her distressing skeletal appearance, it would be hard not to suppose that she had lost sight of the goal she professed to want in her obsessed valuing of the means. It is clear from the stories of ascetic excesses in the patristic and medieval periods that it is possible to become confused in the same sort of way about the conditional good of suffering. Simeon Stylites spent thirty-seven years living on top of pillars, the last of which was sixty feet high and only six feet wide. He is reputed to have come close to death on one occasion as a result of wearing next to his skin an abrasive material which grew into the skin and infected it.[37] It seems not unreasonable to take him as a spiritual anorexic, mistaking a conditional good for a nonconditional one. Perhaps he believed of himself that his purpose for self-denial was spiritual progress, but like the anorexic he appears to have become obsessed with the means at the expense of the goal. No doubt, part of what the Renaissance found so repulsive about the Middle Ages was a certain tendency on the part of medievals to engage in prolonged and pointless bouts of self-destructive asceticism.

But how do we know that Simeon Stylites, or one of the other overrigorous ascetics of the patristic period, is the medieval analogue to a neurotic and unstoppable dieter? It is not so hard to know the difference between healthy dieting and anorexia, but how would we know with regard to suffering when it was serving the function of spiritual health and so was good rather than destructive? The answer, I think, is that we can't know. Sometimes in dealing with conditional goods we have to rely on experts. The steroids which some misguided athletes take to their misfortune are also important therapeutic drugs for certain sorts of cancers; but we learn this fact from medical experts, and we have to rely on them to administer the drugs in such a way that they contribute to health rather than destruction. In the case of suffering and its role in redemption, it seems clear that at least in the great majority of cases we don't know enough to turn suffering into a help toward spiritual health. We have to rely, therefore, on God's expertise instead.[38]

How do we avail ourselves of that expertise? How do we know in any given case whether God intends some suffering as a cure for evil or whether a particular degree of suffering won't produce spiritual toxicosis instead? When we see someone suffer as a result of human injustice, then on Aquinas's view (other things being equal) we have a clear obligation to do what is in our power to stop the suffering. Injustice is a mortal sin which separates a person from God; in intervening we help to rescue not only the victim of the injustice but also the perpetrator, whose condition on Aquinas's view is otherwise apparently terminal. Job, in arguing for his innocence, points not just to the fact that he has not exploited any of those dependent on him but that he has even been particularly attentive to the needs of the poor and downtrodden,[39] and Aquinas comments on these passages with evident approval.[40] There is nothing in Aquinas's attitude toward suffering which is incompatible with a robust program of social justice. More generally, one way (though not the only way) to tell if any particular suffering on the part of a given individual is ordained by God to spiritual health is if we try to alleviate that suffering and it turns out not to be possible to do so. Part of what makes Simeon Stylites repulsive to us is that he not only doesn't try to avoid suffering but even deliberately seeks it out for its own sake.[41] Gregory the Great's line, on the other hand, implies that redemptive suffering can't be instigated by us but has to be received from God's hand. Otherwise, the good men who tremble at their prosperity could stop trembling and just flagellate themselves to put a stop to their worrisome lack of adversity.

For these reasons the concern that Aquinas's account prompts indifference to suffering is mistaken; and if our indignation at his views is based on this concern, it is misplaced. But perhaps our negative reaction to Aquinas's account of evil stems from attitudes more complicated and less amenable to crisp articulation. Renaissance attitudes toward the Middle Ages were something like Callicles' reaction to Socrates. The Renaissance thought the Middle Ages had turned human values upside down, and it found medieval worldviews repellent because it saw them as inhuman. As intellectual descendants of the Renaissance (more nearly than of the Middle Ages), we might feel somewhat the same way about Aquinas's view of the world: any life really lived in accordance with this worldview would be wretched, inhumanly repudiating all the loveliness and goodness of this world, unnaturally withdrawing from all that makes life worthwhile.

Aquinas is not oblivious to this problem. For that matter, neither is the apostle Paul. "If in this life only we have hope in Christ," he says, "we are of all people most miserable."[42] In commenting on this passage, Aquinas says, "If there is no resurrection of the dead, it follows that there is no good for human beings other than in this life. And if this is the case, then those people are more miserable who suffer many evils and tribulations in this life. Therefore, since the apostles and Christians [generally] suffer more tribulations, it follows that they, who enjoy less of the goods of this world, would be more miserable than other people." The very fact that Aquinas feels he needs to explicate this point in some detail highlights the difference between our worldview and his; no one has to explain to us that those who suffer more evils in this world are more miserable than others. But what Aquinas goes on to say spells out explicitly the difference between the worldview of his culture and our own. "If there were no resurrection of the dead," he continues, "people wouldn't think it was a power and a glory to abandon all that can give pleasure and to bear the pains of death and dishonor; instead they would think it was stupid." He assumes that Christians are people who do glory in tribulations, and so he ends his commentary on this passage in Corinthians by saying, "And so it is clear that [if there were no resurrection of the dead,] [Christians] would be more miserable than other people."[43]

So Aquinas's account of evil has inherent in it a response to objections of the Renaissance variety. If you suppose that fastfood-munching couch potatoes are just as healthy or healthier than nutrition-conscious physical-fitness advocates, you will of course find all the emphasis of the exercisers on diet and physical training perplexing or neurotic or worse. Denying oneself appealing foods and forcing oneself to sweat and strain in exercise are conditional goods only. Unless you share the view that these things do lead to desirable ends, you won't find them good in any sense. Similarly, if we don't share the worldview that holds that there is an afterlife, that true happiness consists in union with God in the afterlife, and that suffering helps us to attain that happiness, we will naturally find Aquinas's valuing suffering even as a conditional good appalling or crazy.

7. Consolation

Even those who share with Aquinas the conviction that there is an afterlife and that the truest or deepest happiness is to be found in it might nonetheless feel queasy about or alienated from his account of evil. For many people, the supposition that suffering has the therapeutic value Aquinas claims for it will not be enough; they will still feel that there is something frighteningly inhuman in a worldview that tells us not only that the whole of our life on earth will be one prolonged spiritual analogue to chemotherapy but also that we ought to rejoice in that state of affairs. And so they are likely to side with the Renaissance humanist repudiation of such a worldview. I, too, think the Renaissance humanists were right to reject this worldview, but I think it would be a mistake to take it as the correct description of Aquinas's account. There is a more humane side to the medieval view of suffering which the Renaissance humanists missed. As Aquinas explains it, this part of his account applies primarily to the suffering of fully functional adults who are Christians. (I think it is possible to see in Aquinas's thought a way in which to transpose his line so that it applies also to the suffering of children and non-Christian adults.[44] For the sake of brevity, however, I will consider it here only in the form he gives it, in which it applies to Christian adults with normally functioning faculties.)

The missing element has to do with the work of the Holy Spirit. On Aquinas's view, the Holy Spirit works in the hearts of those who believe in God and produces spiritual consolation. The Holy Spirit, Aquinas says, "purges us from sin," "illumines the intellect," "brings us to keep the commandments," "confirms our hope in eternal life," "counsels us in our perplexities about the will of God," and "brings us to love God."[45] The Holy Spirit guides toward truth those whom it fills and helps them to conquer their weaknesses[46] so that they can become the sort of people they are glad to be. Most importantly, the Holy Spirit fills a person with a sense of the love of God and his nearness, so that one of the principal effects of the Holy Spirit is joy.[47]

The Holy Spirit perfects us, both inwardly and outwardly, Aquinas says; and "the ultimate perfection, by which a person is made perfect inwardly, is joy, which stems from the presence of what is loved. Whoever has the love of God, however, already has what he loves, as is said in 1 John 4:16: 'whoever abides in the love of God abides in God, and God abides in him.' And joy wells up from this."[48] "When [Paul] says 'the Lord is near,' he points out the cause of joy, because a person rejoices at the nearness of his friend."[49]

Perhaps there is no greater joy than the presence of the person you love when that person loves you to the fulfillment of your heart's desire.[50] Joy of that sort, Aquinas says, is not destroyed by either pain or tribulation. In order to keep joy whole, even in the adversities of this life, the Holy Spirit protects people against the evils they encounter: "and first against the evil which disturbs peace, since peace is disturbed by adversities. But with regard to adversities the Holy Spirit perfects [us] through patience, which enables [us] to bear adversities patiently. . . . Second, against the evil which arrests joy, namely, the wait for what is loved. To this evil, the Spirit opposes long-suffering, which is not broken by the waiting." In this way and others, Aquinas says, the Holy Spirit makes human joy whole, even in the midst of pain.[51]

But what about Job? we might think at this point. Wasn't he someone who faced his troubles without consolation from God? Aquinas thinks, after all, that God sometimes heeds a suffering person's advantage rather than his prayer, and it is in connection with Job that Aquinas develops that line. If the sufferer can't see that advantage, then, as even Aquinas recognizes, the sufferer may not be consoled but rather be afflicted in spirit also.[52] But I think Aquinas would be inclined to deny our characterization of Job as someone who suffers without divine consolation. One of the longest speeches attributed to God in the Bible is the speech he makes to Job; and when God's speech is finished, what does Job say? "I had heard of you before with the hearing of the ear, but now my eye sees you."[53] Whatever else we need to say about the complicated relations between God and Job, and that is no doubt a great deal, it is clear that with his views of happiness Aquinas would certainly attribute deep, sweet consolation to anyone who could truly claim to be seeing God. Furthermore, part of the point of Christianity, on Aquinas's account, is to make it clear to people that there is a point to suffering, so as to ward off the kind of theological perplexity and anguish many of us think we see in Job. In his passion, Christ not only makes atonement for sinners but also sets them an example, so that they will understand that the path to redemption goes through suffering.[54] The lesson learned for us by Job and the example presented by Christ make it easier for others afterwards, Aquinas thinks, to endure suffering without losing spiritual consolation during the period of pain.[55]

In fact, Aquinas thinks that for Christians the inner sweetness of God's consolation increases directly with the troubles of this life. At the start of his commentary on 1 Thessalonians he quotes with approval the line in 2 Corinthians which says that "as the sufferings of Christ abound in us, so our consolation also abounds by Christ." And in explaining that line, in his commentary on 2 Corinthians, he describes spiritual consolation in this way: "People need to be supported in the evils that happen to them. And this is what consolation is, strictly speaking. Because if a person didn't have something in which his heart could rest when he is overcome with evils, he couldn't bear up under them. And so one person consoles another when he offers him some relief, in which he can rest in the midst of evils. Now there are some evils in which one human being can console us in all [our] evils."[56] Even in our sins, which from Aquinas's point of view are more frightening than adversity, because unlike adversity they separate us from God, even then,

Aquinas holds, we are consoled by God; that is why, Aquinas says, Paul calls him the God of *all* consolation.[57]

The Renaissance saw the Middle Ages as inhuman in part because it no longer shared the medieval worldview and in part because it had missed this side of the medieval story. On Aquinas's account, Christianity does not call people to a life of self-denying wretchedness but to a life of joy, even in the midst of pain and trouble. Without joy, Aquinas says, no progress is possible in the Christian life.[58]

Aquinas's attitude toward evil is clearly as different from our own as Socrates' attitude toward the good life is different from Callicles'. Aquinas's analysis of the reaction of Job's comforters would also, I think, be his analysis of the reaction to evil on the part of those of us concerned with the problem of evil in this culture.

> Human beings are made up of a spiritual nature and of earthly flesh. Consequently, evil for human beings consists in their abandoning spiritual goods, to which they are directed in virtue of [having] rational minds, and their cleaving to earthly goods, which suit them in virtue of [having] earthly flesh.[59]
>
> Job's loquacious friends did not understand the spiritual consolation of Job, and so he adds, "You have put their heart far from learning"—that is, from the spiritual learning [which comes from] you, by which you teach [human beings] to disdain temporal goods and to hope for spiritual ones. And because they put their hope only in things low and temporal, they could not reach a spiritual plane to be placed next to God.[60]

It certainly does seem true, at any rate, that there is a correlation between the degree to which we associate human good with things in this world and the extent to which we see the problem of evil in its contemporary form. The story of the metamorphosis from the medieval worldview to our own is, of course, in large part a matter of a shift from a religious to a secular outlook. But even among Christians we can chart the change from the otherworldly approach of the medievals to the more common contemporary attitudes. We can see this change in its beginnings in, for example, the pious Christian adherents of the *devotio moderna,* a religious movement important in the Netherlands, particularly in the fifteenth century. There was a distinctly nonmedieval attitude in the *devotio moderna* in its tendency to conflate temporal and spiritual goods and in its emphasis on the religious importance of temporal concerns. Commenting on the death of a recently appointed principal of a school for religious instruction, an anonymous adherent of this movement raises the problem of evil in a way which is devout but altogether different from Aquinas's approach. He says,

> Permit me to take a moment here to allude to the wondrous and secret judgments of our Lord God, not as if scrutinizing them in a reproachful way but rather as humbly venerating the inscrutable. It is quite amazing that our fathers and brothers had set out with a single will and labored at their own expense, to the honor of God and for the salvation of souls, to erect a school here in Emmerich to do exercises with boys and clerics. . . . And now after much care

and trouble, everything had been brought to a good state: we had a learned and suitable man for rector, the venerable Master Arnold of Hildesheim. . . . Then, behold, . . . our Lord God, as if totally unconcerned with all that we had in hand, which had just begun to flower, suddenly and unexpectedly threw it all into confusion and decline, nearly reducing it to nothing. For just as the sheep are dispersed when the shepherd is struck down, so when our beloved brother [Master Arnold] died the whole school was thrown into confusion. The youths left in swarms . . . not, it is to be feared, without some danger to their souls. . . . Nonetheless, to [him] be the honor and the glory now and through the ages, to him whose judgments, though hidden, are yet never unjust.[61]

Between the attitude of this author, who finds adversity for God's people fundamentally inexplicable, and the attitude of such medievals as Aquinas or Gregory the Great there is a world of difference.

In this paper I have only expounded Aquinas's views of evil; I have not sought to argue for them, although they seem to me impressive and admirable in many ways. No doubt, a thorough philosophical defense or refutation of his views would require book-length treatment. But what Aquinas's interpretation of Job and his general account of evil show us, whether we are inclined to accept or reject them, is that our approach to the problem of evil is a consequence of our attitude toward much larger issues, such as the nature of human happiness and the goal of human life. To make progress on the problem of evil, in my view, we need to face up to these larger issues in a reflective way. One of the benefits of the history of philosophy, especially the history of philosophy from periods such as the Middle Ages whose cultures are so different from our own, is that it helps us to see the otherwise unnoticed and unexamined assumptions we bring to philosophical issues such as the problem of evil. Aquinas's worldview, characterized by a renunciation of the things of this world and a rush toward heaven, is a particularly good one to juxtapose to the worldview of our culture, steeped in comforts and seeking pleasure. "Theodicies," says Terrence Tilley in his passionate denunciation of them, "construct consoling dreams to distract our gaze from real evils."[62] What reflection on Aquinas's account helps us to see is that in evaluating this claim and others like it, hostile to theodicy, everything depends on what you take to be dream and what you take to be reality.[63]

NOTES

This essay, with minor modifications, originally appeared in *Reasoned Faith*, ed. Eleonore Stump (Ithaca: Cornell University Press, 1993). Reprinted by permission of Cornell University Press.

1. Norman Kretzmann has discussed some of the issues raised in Aquinas's commentary on Romans in a recent paper; see his "Warring against the Law of My Mind:

Aquinas on Romans 7," in *Philosophy and the Christian Faith,* ed. Thomas Morris (Notre Dame: University of Notre Dame Press, 1988), 172-95.

2. This commentary, *Expositio super Job ad litteram,* is available in the Leonine edition of Aquinas's works, vol. 26, and in an English translation: *Thomas Aquinas, the Literal Exposition on Job: A Scriptural Commentary concerning Providence,* trans. Anthony Damico and Martin Yaffe, The American Academy of Religion Classics in Religious Studies (Atlanta: Scholars Press, 1989). The commentary was probably written while Aquinas was at Orvieto, in the period 1261/2-1264. See James Weisheipl, *Friar Thomas D'Aquino: His Life, Thought, andWorks,* 2d ed. (Washington, D.C.: Catholic University of America Press, 1983), 153; see also *Albert and Thomas: SelectedWritings,* ed. Simon Tugwell, Classics of Western Spirituality (Mahwah: Paulist Press, 1988), 223.

3. The commentaries on the Pauline epistles were probably written during Aquinas's second Parisian regency, 1269-1272, and during his subsequent stay in Naples. See Tugwell, *Albert and Thomas,* 248; Weisheipl, *Friar Thomas D'Aquino,* 373.

4. Aquinas, *Expositio super Job,* chap. 7, secs. 1-4, Damico and Yaffe, 145. Although I have preferred to give my own translations, I have found the Damico and Yaffe translation very helpful, and I will give references to this work both to the Latin and to the Damico and Yaffe translation.

5. See, for example, Thomas Aquinas, *Super ad Romanos,* chap. 12, lec. 2.

6. See, for example, Marilyn Adams, "Redemptive Suffering: A Christian Solution to the Problem of Evil," in *Rationality, Religious Belief, and Moral Commitment: New Essays in the Philosophy of Religion,* ed. Robert Audi and William Wainwright (Ithaca: Cornell University Press, 1986), 248-67.

7. See, for example, William Rowe, "The Empirical Argument from Evil," in *Rationality, Religious Belief, and Moral Commitment* (cited in preceding note).

8. Aquinas, *Super ad Romanos,* chap. 8, lec. 6.

9. SCG III, 112. See also *Expositio super Job,* chap. 7, secs. 10-18; Damico and Yaffe, 151, 153.

10. Aquinas, *Super ad Romanos,* chap. 8, lec. 6.

11. Ibid.

12. SCG III, 30.

13. SCG III, 32.

14. SCG III, 28.

15. SCG III, 48.

16. Thomas Aquinas, *Super ad Hebraeos,* chap. 12, lec. 2.

17. Aquinas, *Expositio super Job,* chap. 9, secs. 24-30; Damico and Yaffe, p. 179.

18. For an excellent annotated translation of the text, see Nicholas Ayo, *The Sermon-Conferences of St.Thomas Aquinas on the Apostles' Creed* (Notre Dame: University of Notre Dame Press, 1988). Although I have preferred to use my own translation, I found Ayo's quite helpful, and for this work I give citations both to the Latin and to Ayo's translation. Thomas Aquinas, *Collationes Credo in Deum,* sec. III; Ayo, 40-42. For some reasons for thinking that Aquinas's approach to the problem of evil is right, see my papers "The Problem of Evil," *Faith and Philosophy* 2 (1985): 392-424, and "Providence and the Problem of Evil," in *Christian Philosophy,* ed. Thomas Flint (Notre Dame: University of Notre Dame Press, 1990), 51-91. In those papers I discuss reasons for supposing that a good god would create a world in which human beings have such a cancer of the soul, that suffering is the best available means to cure the cancer in the soul, and that God can justifiably allow suffering even though it sometimes eventuates in the opposite of moral goodness or love of God.

19. There is a translation of this commentary: *Commentary on Saint Paul's First Letter to theThessalonians and the Letter to the Philippians by St.Thomas Aquinas,* trans. F. R. Larcher and Michael Duffy (Albany: Magi Books, 1969). Although I have preferred to use my own translations, I found the Larcher and Duffy translation helpful, and I will give citations for this work and for the commentary on Philippians both to the Latin and to this translation. Thomas Aquinas, *Super adThessalonicenses I,* prologue; Larcher and Duffy, 3.

20. Thomas Aquinas, *Super ad Hebraeos,* chap. 12, lec. 1.

21. Ibid., lec. 2.

22. Ibid.

23. Aquinas, *Expositio super Job,* chap. 1, secs. 20-21; Damico and Yaffe, 89.

24. Aquinas, *Expositio super Job,* chap. 9, secs. 15-21; Damico and Yaffe, 174.

25. Only one of the two metaphors is in the Revised Standard Version, the King James, and the Anchor Bible.

26. Aquinas, *Expositio super Job,* chap. 7 sec. 1; Damico and Yaffe, 146. The idea here seems to be that there are degrees of glory or degrees of reward in heaven, and those persons who are better are given more suffering for the sake of the concomitant greater glory. Presumably, part of what makes such persons better is that they would be willing to accept greater suffering for the sake of greater glory; see the section on martyrs in my paper "Providence and the Problem of Evil" (cited in n. 18). Someone might suppose that Aquinas ought to say not that better people suffer more but rather that worse people, who need more suffering, suffer more. But here I think the analogy with chemotherapy is again helpful. Sometimes the most effective kinds of chemotherapy can't be used on those who need it most because their systems are too weak to bear the treatments, and so the strongest kinds of treatment tend to be reserved for those who aren't too old or too advanced in the disease or too riddled with secondary complications—in other words, for those who are (aside from the particular cancer) strong and robust.

27. Thomas Aquinas, *Super ad Thessalonicenses* I, chap. 4, lec. 2; Larcher and Duffy, p.39.

28. Thomas Aquinas, *Super ad Philippenses,* chap. 3, lec. 2; Larcher and Duffy, p. 102.

29. Thomas Aquinas, *Super ad Romanos,* chap. 5, lec. 1.

30. Plato, *Gorgias* 481C.

31. There is a nineteenth-century translation of this work: *Morals on the Book of Job by Gregory the Great, the First Pope of That Name* (Oxford, 1844). Although I have preferred to use my own translations, I give the reference both to the Latin and to this translation: Gregory the Great, *Moralia in Job,* book 5, introduction; *Morals,* 241-242. The line taken by Gregory has the result that if we come across saintly people who don't suffer much, we should be inclined to wonder whether they really are as saintly as they seem. The implausibility of this line is significantly reduced if we remember that it is possible, Mother Teresa fashion, to be afflicted for the suffering of others as well as for one's own.

32. One shouldn't misunderstand this claim and suppose Aquinas to be claiming that human beings can earn their way to heaven by the merit badges of suffering. Aquinas is quite explicit that salvation is through Christ only. His claim here is not about what causes salvation but only about what is efficacious in the process of salvation. It would take us too far afield here to consider Aquinas's view of the relation between Christ's work of redemption and the role of human suffering in that process. What is important for my purposes is just to see that on Aquinas's account suffering is an indispensable element in the course of human salvation, initiated and merited by Christ.

33. See, for example, *Expositio super Job,* chap. 7, sec. 1, Damico and Yaffe, 145; and chap. 19, 23-29, Damico and Yaffe, 268-71, where Aquinas makes these points clear and maintains that Job was already among the redeemed awaiting the resurrection and union with God. Someone might wonder whether it is possible to maintain this approach to suffering when the suffering consists in madness, mental retardation, or some form of dementia. This doubt is based on the unreflective assumption that those suffering from these afflictions have lost all the mental faculties needed for moral or spiritual development. For some suggestions to the contrary, see the sensitive and insightful discussion of retarded and autistic patients in Oliver Sacks, *The Man Who Mistook His Wife for a Hat* (New York: Summit Books, 1985).

34. For a vigorous response of this sort to all kinds of theodicy, see Terrence W. Tilley, *The Evils of Theodicy* (Washington, D.C.: Georgetown University Press, 1991).

35. As late as the end of the nineteenth century, even *Scientific American* was publishing diatribes against anesthetics (see the quotation in *Scientific American,* August 1991, 14), and the lamentable nineteenth-century animus against anesthetics, particularly in connection with childbirth, often had a religious basis. For a detailed discussion of nineteenth-century attitudes toward anesthetics, see Martin S. Pernick, *A Calculus of Suffering: Pain, Professionalism, and Anesthesia in Nineteenth-Century America* (New York: Columbia University Press, 1985).

36. Thomas Aquinas, *Super I ad Corinthios,* chap. 15, lec. 2.

37. David Hugh Farmer, *The Oxford Dictionary of Saints* (Oxford: Oxford University Press, 1988).

38. Clearly sometimes we do know, or at least have a pretty good idea, as when loving parents deliberately inflict some suffering on their children in response to intolerable behavior on the children's part.

39. Job 31. In supporting Aquinas's line here, I am assuming that sins of thought and deed are worse than the analogous sins of thought alone. That is, I am assuming that someone who is murderous but who is prevented by his friends from acting on his intentions is morally better off than he would be if he had been allowed to go ahead and commit murder. This assumption is widely, though not universally, shared.

40. See also *ST* II-II, 32, 5 and 6, where Aquinas argues that not giving alms, or keeping for oneself more than one needs, can be punished with damnation.

41. Two caveats are perhaps necessary here. (1) Nothing in these remarks should be taken as denigrating asceticism as a whole. Rigorous training, of body or mind, does take self-discipline and, by implication, self-denial. But it is possible to become obsessed with the self-denial itself, so that it effaces the goal for which it was originally intended as a means. There is a difference between anorexia and dieting, and one can see the problems in anorexia without thereby eschewing discipline as regards eating. (2) By saying that Simeon sought suffering for its own sake, I don't mean to deny that he might have believed that the purpose of the ascetic suffering he engaged in was spiritual progress. It seems nonetheless true that many of his actions focus just on inflicting suffering on himself, rather than focusing on the goal to which the suffering was supposed to be a means. It certainly appears as if he lost sight of the professed goal of spiritual well-being in his fixation on mortifying the flesh. I am grateful to Marilyn Adams for comments on this point.

42. 1 Cor. 15:19.

43. Aquinas, *Super I ad Corinthios,* chap. 15, lec. 2.

44. I have discussed ways in which this sort of approach to the problem of evil might be applied to those who aren't adults or to those who aren't Christian in "The Problem of Evil" (see n. 18).

45. Thomas Aquinas, *Collationes Credo in Deum,* sec. 11; Ayo, 116-18.

46. Thomas Aquinas, *Super ad Philippenses,* chap. 1, lec. 2; Larcher and Duffy, 63; also, chap. 1, lec. 3; Larcher and Duffy, 68.

47. See, for example, *Super ad Romanos,* chap. 5, lec. 1.

48. There is an English translation of this work: *Commentary on Saint Paul's Epistle to the Galatians by St. Thomas Aquinas,* trans. F. R. Larcher and Richard Murphy (Albany: Magi Books, 1966). Although I have preferred to use my own translations, I found the Larcher and Murphy translation helpful, and I will give citations for this work both to the Latin and to the Larcher and Murphy translation. *Super ad Galatas,* chap. 5, lec. 6; Larcher and Murphy, 179-80.

49. *Super ad Philippenses,* chap. 4, lec. 1; Larcher and Duffy, 113.

50. Someone might suppose that this statement is false, on the grounds that sometimes pain or sickness makes us just irritable and unable to find any joy or even relief in the presence of a person we love. The mistake in this view can be seen by considering cases of childbirth. In the painful, humiliating, or embarrassing circumstances which sometimes arise in childbirth, a woman may get irritable enough at the father of her child to lash out at him, verbally or even physically. That she wants him there anyway, that his presence

is a great comfort to her underneath and around the irritation, is made manifest by the fact that she still wants him in the delivery room, that she would find his leaving intolerable. Being irritable under pain in the presence of someone you love is compatible with finding great comfort in his presence at another level. It should perhaps also be said, as an additional consideration in this connection, that the degree of joy or comfort one person has at the presence of another will be proportional to the intensity of the love between them.

51. Aquinas, *Super ad Galatas,* chap. 5, lec. 6; Larcher and Murphy, 180. Also, *Super ad Galatas,* chap. 5, lec. 6; Larcher and Murphy, 179; and *Super ad Hebraeos,* chap. 12, lec. 2.

52. Aquinas, *Expositio super Job,* chap. 9, secs. 15-21, Damico and Yaffe, 174.

53. Job 42:5.

54. See, for example, Aquinas, *Collationes Credo in Deum,* sec. 6; Ayo, 69, 73.

55. Aquinas therefore supposes that Job's later return to worldly prosperity is at least in part a divine concession to the fact that Job is part of a pre-Christian culture. "And [Job's return to prosperity] was appropriate to the time, because of the position of the Old Testament in which temporal goods are promised, so that in this way by the prosperity which he recovered an example was given to others, to turn them to God." *Expositio super Job,* chap. 42, secs. 10-16; Damico and Yaffe, 472. It should be said that nothing in Aquinas's position requires him to hold that all Christian adults experience divine consolation in their suffering. For some people, the point of the suffering might be to bring them to the stage where they are able to experience consolation; and even for those people who are well advanced in spiritual or moral progress, consolation can always be warded off by a spirit which refuses it.

56. Aquinas, *Super II ad Corinthios,* chap. 1, lec. 2.

57. Ibid. See also *Super ad Romanos,* chap. 8, lec. 7.

58. *Super ad Philippenses,* chap. 4, lec. 1; Larcher and Duffy, 112.

59. Aquinas, *Expositio super Job,* chap. 1, secs. 6-7; Damico and Yaffe, 79.

60. Aquinas, *Expositio super Job,* chap. 17, secs. 2-9: Damico and Yaffe, 252.

61. *Devotio Moderna: Basic Writings,* trans. John van Engen (New York: Paulist Press, 1988), 151. I am grateful to John van Engen for calling my attention to the intriguing material in this book.

62. Tilley, *The Evils of Theodicy,* 219.

63. I am grateful to Norman Kretzmann for helpful comments on an earlier draft of this paper.

5.

ALVIN PLANTINGA

Epistemic Probability and Evil

The amount and variety of *evil* in our world has often baffled and perplexed believers in God. Evil can occasion deeper problems: faced with the shocking concreteness of a particularly appalling example of evil in his own life or the life of someone close to him, a believer may find himself tempted to take toward God an attitude he himself deplores; such evil can incline him to mistrust God, to be angry with him, to adopt toward him an attitude of suspicion and distrust or bitterness and rebellion. This is a *pastoral,* or *religious,* or *existential* problem of evil.

Many philosophers have argued, however, that evil generates a problem of quite another sort for the theist; indeed, nearly every first course in philosophy includes a session on the so-called "problem of evil." *This* problem is not pastoral or existential but broadly speaking epistemic; it has to do with fulfilling epistemic obligation, or maintaining a rational system of beliefs, or following proper intellectual procedure, or perhaps with practicing proper mental hygiene. The claim is that the evil in our world—including suffering as well as evil properly so-called, that is, wickedness—is both obvious and undeniable; but then belief in God, in the face of such gross and rampant evil, is in some way intellectually dubious, or questionable, or out of order, or worse. I propose to investigate this claim. First, I shall claim that in its most viable form this objection invokes a version of the probabilistic atheological argument from evil. Second, I shall argue that the prospects for this objection are bleak, both from a rough-and-ready intuitive point of view and from the perspectives of the main contemporary accounts of probability. Third, I shall claim that the main contemporary accounts of probability don't provide the resources for a proper discussion of this objection. And fourth, after outlining a more appropriate conception of epistemic probability, I shall try to show that in any event the most important question here does not concern the *propositional* warrant or lack thereof displayed by belief in God; the real question here concerns the *non*propositional warrant, if any, enjoyed by this belief.

I. Evil and Probability

The objector begins with Epicurus's ancient question: If God is omnipotent, omniscient, and wholly good, why is there any evil? "Is he willing to prevent evil, but not able? then he is impotent. Is he able but not willing? then he is malevolent. Is he both able and willing? whence then is evil?"[1] The Christian theist must concede that she doesn't know—that is, she doesn't know in any detail. On a quite general level, she may know or think she knows that God permits evil because he can achieve a world he sees as better by permitting evil than by preventing it; and what God sees as better is, of course, better. But we cannot see why our world, with all its ills, would be better than others we think we can imagine, nor what, in any detail, is God's reason for permitting a given specific evil. Not only can we not see this; we can't, I think, envision any very good possibilities. And here I must remark that many of the attempts to explain why God permits evil—*theodicies,* as we might call them—seem to me shallow, tepid, and ultimately frivolous.

Of course the fact that the theist can't answer Epicurus's question—the fact that for many or most specific evils, she has no real idea what God's reason for permitting that specific evil might be—that fact does not in itself threaten her with irrationality, or cognitive impropriety, or dereliction of epistemic duty, or anything of the sort. Our grasp of the fundamental way of things is at best limited; there is no reason to think that if God *did* have a reason for permitting the evil in question, we would be the first to know. Something further must be added, if an infirmity worth worrying about is to be uncovered. Granted: we don't know why God permits evil; but where, so far, is the problem?

Here the objector is quick to oblige. And (at least until recently) his most popular response has been to offer some version of the *deductive antitheistic argument from evil.* He claims that there are true propositions about the amount and extent of evil—propositions ordinarily conceded to be true by the theist himself—that entail that there is no God, or at any rate no God as conceived by classical theism. If such an argument is correct, then theism is inconsistent in some sense, and hence in some sense not rationally acceptable. Thus, for example, the late J. L. Mackie:

I think, however, that a more telling criticism [of theism] can be made by way of the traditional problem of evil. Here it can be shown, not merely that religious beliefs lack rational support, but that they are positively irrational, that the several parts of the essential theological doctrine are inconsistent with one another.[2]

Mackie goes on to argue that the existence of God is incompatible with the existence of evil; he concludes that since the theist is committed to both, theistic belief is irrational. It ought to be discouraged; and those who accept it, presumably, ought to give it up.

At present, however, I think it is widely conceded that there is nothing like straightforward contradiction or necessary falsehood in the joint affirmation of God and evil;[3] the existence of evil is not incompatible with the existence of an all-powerful, all-knowing and perfectly good God. Accordingly, those who offer an antitheistic argument from evil—call them "atheologians"—have turned from deductive to *probabilistic* arguments from evil. The typical atheological claim at present is not that the existence of God is *incompatible* with that of evil, but rather that the latter offers the resources for a strong probabilistic argument against the former.

There are at least two forms such an argument can take. In the first place, the atheologian can hold that

(1) there is an omnipotent, omniscient, and perfectly good God

is *improbable* or unlikely with respect to

(2) there are 10^{13} turps of evil

(where the *turp* is the basic unit of evil), or perhaps with respect to some other proposition about evil—some proposition specifying some of the varieties of evil to be found (the involuntary suffering of the innocent, for example), or a proposition specifying certain properties of some of the kinds of evils we find. This would be to say that (2) *statically* disconfirms (1); the probability of (2) on (1) is low. On the other hand, the atheologian may want to argue that (2) *dynamically* disconfirms (1); that is, the probability of (1) on (2) together with our background knowledge k is less than that of (2) on k alone, i.e., $P((1)/((2)\&k) < P((1)/k))$.[4] In either case what the atheologian hopes to conclude is that (1) is improbable not just on (2) but on our total evidence.

William Rowe, for example, offers an argument of this type. He claims that it is probable that

(3) there exist instances of intense suffering which an omnipotent, omniscient being could have prevented without thereby losing some greater good or permitting some evil equally bad or worse.[5]

This is probable, he says, because

It seems quite unlikely that *all* the instances of intense suffering occurring daily in our world are intimately related to the occurrence of greater goods or the prevention of evils at least as bad; and even more unlikely, should they somehow all be so related, that an omnipotent, omniscient being could not have achieved at least some of these goods (or prevented some of those evils) without permitting the instances of intense suffering that are supposedly related to them. (Pp. 337-338)

Rowe adds that

(4) an omnipotent, omniscient and wholly good being would prevent the occurrence of any intense suffering it could, unless it could not do so without thereby losing some greater good or permitting some evil equally bad or worse. (P. 336)

And of course if (4) is necessary or obvious and (3) is probable, then it will be improbable that there is such a person as God.[6]

The atheologian, therefore, claims that (1) is improbable with respect to (2) (or some other appropriate proposition about evil). But he doesn't make this point for the sheer academic interest of it; something further is supposed to follow. The fact, if it is a fact, that (1) is thus improbable is supposed to show or help show something normative: that there is something wrong or misguided about belief in God, that it is irrational, or intellectually irresponsible, or noetically second class, or not such as to measure up to the appropriate standards for proper belief. Perhaps the way to put it, borrowing a term from Roderick Chisholm, is to say that this claim—the claim that (1) is improbable with respect to (2)—is invoked to show or help show that belief in God has little by way of *positive epistemic status*[7] for the believer—less than withholding it or accepting its denial would have.

But how shall we evaluate this claim? It isn't just clear or obvious or self-evident, after all, that (1) *is* improbable on (2) (or some other reasonably plausible proposition about evil). Why should we think this true? Suppose we begin by returning to Rowe and his claim that (3) is probable: with respect to *what* is (3) alleged to be probable? Rowe's answer:

First, I think, is the fact that there is an enormous variety and profusion of intense human and animal suffering in our world. Second, is the fact that much of this suffering seems quite unrelated to any greater goods (or the absence of equal or greater evils) that might justify it. And, finally, there is the fact that such suffering as is related to greater good (or the absence of equal or greater evils) does not, in many cases, seem so intimately related as to require its permission by an omnipotent being bent on securing those goods (the absence of those evils). (P. 338)

Speaking of a specific (hypothesized) evil state of affairs involving a fawn burned in a forest fire, Rowe speaks of the fawn's "apparently pointless" (p. 337) suffering; this suffering he says, "was preventable, and so far as we can see, pointless" (p. 337). Rowe's claim is that there is much apparently pointless evil, evil that seems to us to be such that God (if there is such a person) could have had a better world just by deleting or not permitting it. He seems to be arguing that (3) is probable with respect to such propositions as

(5) Many cases of evil are apparently pointless,

i.e., many cases of evil are apparently not such that an omniscient and omnipotent God would be obliged to put up with them in order to achieve a world as good (or nearly as good)[8] as ours.

But how shall we understand Rowe here? Shall we see him as holding that in fact there are many cases of evil such that it is apparent that an omnipotent and omniscient God, if he existed, would not have a reason for permitting them? But this is much too strong; as Stephen Wykstra points out,[9] we could sensibly claim something like this only if we had reason to think that if such a God *did* have a reason for permitting such evils, we would be likely to have some insight into what it is. But if theism is true, then this is false; from the theistic perspective there is little or no reason to think that God would have a reason for a particular evil state of affairs only if we had a pretty good idea of what that reason might be. On the theistic conception, our cognitive powers, as opposed to God's, are a bit slim for that. God might have reasons we cannot so much as understand; he might have reasons involving other free creatures—angels, devils, the principalities and powers of which St. Paul speaks—of which we have no knowledge.

We must stop to look at the matter in a bit more detail. The suggestion is that there are evils such that it is simply apparent that no omnipotent and omniscient being, if there were such a person, would have a good reason for permitting them. Now the claim is not that these evils are such that it is *impossible,* in the broadly logical sense, that there be such a being that had a good reason for them; it *could* be, for example, that there is a being of that sort and some good state of affairs that outweighs the evil in question, which good state of affairs is such that the being in question could not achieve its actuality without permitting the evil in question. The suggestion is not that this is impossible, but that it is apparent to us that it is not in fact so. The idea is that this is in some way obvious to us, or perhaps clear to us upon a modicum of reflection.

But this seems to me clearly false; that is, it seems false that there are evil states of affairs which, while indeed there *could* be an omnipotent, omniscient God who had a good reason for permitting them, are nonetheless such that in fact it is apparent to us that there isn't any such reason—no outweighing good he couldn't achieve without permitting the evil in question, and no evil he couldn't avoid without permitting it. How could such a thing as that be simply *apparent* to us? Consider the case of a child who dies a lingering and painful death from leukemia. True enough: we can't see what reason God, if there is such a person, has for permitting this child to suffer in that way. But (granted that it is indeed possible that he have a reason) can we just *see* that he doesn't have a reason? Perhaps his reason lies in some transaction involving free creatures of sorts we have little conception of. Perhaps God's reason involves a good for other creatures, a good for some other creature such that God can't achieve that good without permitting the evil in question. Or perhaps his reason involves a good for the sufferer, a good that lies in a future life. It is part of Christianity and many theistic religions to suppose that our earthly life is but a small initial segment of our total lives; there is life after death and indeed immortality. And perhaps God's reason for permitting the suffering in question is that there is a good for the child—a good in the afterlife—which involves the uncoerced cooperation of other free creatures, and would not in fact have been forthcoming if the child had not been allowed to suffer in this way. To maintain his position here, the sort of atheologian we are considering would have to hold that it is just *apparent* that there is no such outweighing good. But how could a thing like that just be apparent to us?

I should think

(a) there is no outweighing good for that child

would be apparent only if

(b) there is no outweighing good for the child in an afterlife

were apparent; but clearly it is not. If further argument is required, (b) would be apparent only if either

(c) there is no afterlife

or

(d) even if this child has an afterlife, it will contain no good that outweighs this evil and is such that God could not achieve it without permitting this evil

were apparent; and neither is. So Rowe can't sensibly suppose that it is just apparent that an omnipotent, omniscient person, if there were such a person, would have no reason for permitting this evil.

Shall we take (5) as pointing out, then, just that there are many evils such that we have no idea what God's reason, if any, is for permitting them? That seems right; but (3) is probable with respect to (5) (taken thus) only if we had good reason to think we would be privy to God's reasons for permitting evil, only if there were some reason to think that if we can't see what reason God might have for a given evil, then it is likely that he does not have a good reason. But there is no reason to think such a thing. If indeed there is such a person, a God, an omniscient, omnipotent, eternal person, then in many situations it would probably be difficult for us to see what his reason for what he does would be. Our cognitive powers are at best modest; we do fairly well with respect to medium-size dry goods, as Austin remarks, but of course there may be much God takes into account that is entirely beyond our ken. Perhaps, for example, he is concerned with the welfare of free creatures who are involved in our history but of whom we have at best dim apprehension; perhaps *he* must take into account counterfactuals of freedom involving such creatures, even though *we* have little by way of cognitive access to them.

This is the lesson of the book of Job. Job suffers; his friends Eliphaz the Temonite, Bildad the Shuhite, and Zophar the Naamathite come to comfort and console him. After seven days and nights of silence, what they tell him is that he must be wicked indeed to warrant such great suffering and he should mend his ways. But Job knows he has done nothing particularly heinous or unusually wicked. No doubt "no one does good, no, not one"; but Job is no worse along these lines than others. In particular he isn't a greater sinner than Eliphaz, Bildad, and Zophar. So he thinks God is treating him unjustly in permitting him to suffer in this way. He wants to go to court with God (until he ruefully realizes that God would be prosecuting attorney, judge, jury, and executioner). He can't see any reason why God should allow him to be afflicted as he is; he concludes, unthinkingly, that God doesn't *have* a good reason. As a matter of fact, according to the story, God *does* have a good reason, but the reason involves a transaction among beings some of whom Job has no awareness at all. The point here is that the reason for Job's sufferings is something entirely beyond his ken, so that the fact that he can't see what sort of reason God might have for permitting his suffering doesn't at all tend to show that God has no reason. And when God replies to Job, he doesn't tell him the reason for his suffering (perhaps Job couldn't so much as grasp or comprehend God's reason); instead, God tells him how little he knows (compared to God):

> Then the Lord answered Job out of the tempest: Who is this whose ignorant words darken counsel? Brace yourself and stand up like a man; I will ask questions and you shall answer. Where were you when I laid the earth's foundations? Tell me, if you know and understand! Who settled its dimensions? Surely you should know! Who stretched his measuring line over it? On what do its supporting pillars rest? Who set its cornerstone in place, when the morning stars sang together and all the sons of God shouted for joy? . . . Have you descended to the springs of the sea or walked in the unfathomable deep? Have the gates of death been revealed to you? Have you ever seen the door-keepers of the place of darkness? Have you comprehended the vast expanse of the world? Come, tell me all this, if you know! Which is the way to the home of light and where does darkness dwell? And can you then take each to its appointed bound and escort it on its homeward path? Doubtless you know all this; for you were born already, so long is the span of your life! (Job 38:1-7, 16-31)

Job complains that God has no good reason for permitting the evil that befalls him. He believes that God doesn't have a good reason because he, Job, can't imagine what that reason might be. In reply, God does not tell him what the reason is; instead, he attacks Job's unthinking assumption that if he can't imagine what reason God might have, then probably God doesn't have a reason at all. And God attacks this assumption by pointing out that Job's knowledge is limited along these lines. No doubt he can't think what God's reason might be; but nothing of interest follows from this: in particular it doesn't follow that probably God doesn't *have* a reason. "All right, Job, if you're so smart, if you know so much, tell me about it! Tell me how the universe was created; tell me about the sons of God who shouted with joy upon its creation! No doubt you were there!" And Job sees the point: "I have spoken of great things which I have not understood, things too wonderful for me to know" (42:3).

Say that an evil is *inscrutable* if it is such that we can't think of any reason God (if there is such a person) could have for permitting it. Clearly, the crucial problem for this probabilistic argument from evil is just that nothing much follows from the fact that some evils are inscrutable; if theism is true we would expect that there would be inscrutable evil. Indeed, a little reflection shows there is no reason to think we could so much as grasp God's plans here, even if he proposed to divulge them to us. But then the fact that there is inscrutable evil does not make it improbable that God exists.

If we like, we can put this in terms of the calculus of probability. The conditional probability of inscrutable evil on the existence of God (P(IE/G)) is about the same as the antecedent probability of inscrutable evil (P(IE)); for given our cognitive situation there is good reason to think that if there is such a person as God, there would be evils such that we would be unable to imagine what his reason is for permitting them. Now consider Bayes's Theorem:

$$P(G/IE) = \frac{P(G) \times P(IE/G)}{P(IE)}.$$

Specified to God's existence and the existence of inscrutable evil, what this says is that the conditional probability of the existence of God on the existence of inscrutable evil (P(G/IE)) is equal to the antecedent probability of the existence of God (P(G)) multiplied by the conditional probability of inscrutable evil on the existence of God (P(IE/G)), this product being divided by the antecedent probability of inscrutable evil (P(IE)). What we have seen is that (P(IE/G)) is about the same as P(IE); on the supposition that theism is true, the existence of inscrutable evil is about as likely as it is apart from the consideration of the existence of God. But then

$$\frac{P(IE/G)}{P(IE)}$$

will be nearly equal to 1, in which case P(G/IE) will be nearly equal to (P(G)). That is, the conditional probability of the existence of God on the existence of inscrutable evil is nearly equal to the antecedent probability of the existence of God, so that the existence of inscrutable evil does not significantly disconfirm (i.e., lower the antecedent probability of) the existence of God.

We can see the same point from a slightly different perspective. According to (1), God is omnipotent and omniscient; he is also perfectly good. Now it is initially not implausible to think that a person like that would do away with or prevent the evils that we see. Wouldn't one initially expect that a world created and sustained by an omniscient, omnipotent, and wholly good God would exhibit a lot less evil than our world seems to? At first thought this seems sensible enough.

It is the burden of the free-will defense, however, to show that it is *possible* that God, though omnipotent and omniscient, could not have created a world with as much good as ours displays, but less evil. Let me briefly state a couple of its central ideas.[10] No doubt, for all we know, there are possible worlds in which there exist significantly free creatures—creatures free with respect to morally significant action—all of whom always do only what is right; and no doubt many of those worlds contain as much good as the actual world, but less evil. The question, however, is whether these worlds are such that it was within the power of God to actualize them. According to the free-will defense, it is possible that God could not have brought any of these possible worlds into actuality; it is possible that it was not within the power of God to actualize them. The heart of the free-will defense is the argument that there are possible worlds such that it is not within the power of God to actualize them—and this despite his omnipotence. Say that God *strongly* actualizes a state of affairs *S* if and only if he causes *S* to be actual and causes to be actual every contingent state of affairs that *S* includes. Then God strongly actualizes such states of affairs as *there being a physical universe, there being human beings,* and *Eve's existing.* On the other hand, of course, God does not strongly actualize such states of affairs as *Eve's freely taking the apple,* for if he *causes* her to take the apple, then she does not take it *freely.* Accordingly, there are many possible worlds such that it was not within the power of God to strongly actualize them.

Of course (as the atheologian will be quick to point out), even if God could not have *strongly* actualized such states of affairs, there might still be a way in which he could have brought them into actuality. Thus, for example, perhaps God knew before[11] he created Eve that if he were to create her and place her in a certain situation, a certain set of circumstances *C* (including *there being apples, Eve's being offered an apple, Eve's being free with respect to the action of taking an apple,* and the like) then she would freely take the apple. (Such a proposition is a *counterfactual of freedom:* a proposition that specifies what some creature would freely do or would have freely done under some set of circumstances—typically circumstances that do not or do not yet obtain.)[12] If so, then if he had strongly actualized *C*'s holding, i.e., if he had caused this set of circumstances to obtain, he would have *weakly actualized Eve's freely taking the apple.* God weakly actualizes a state of affairs *S* if and only if he strongly actualizes a state of affairs *S** that counterfactually implies *S;* and it was *within God's power* to weakly actualize a state of affairs *S* only if there is some state of affairs *S** such that (1) it was within God's power to (strongly) actualize *S**, and (2), if he were to have done so, then *S* would have been actual.

Given these ideas, what the free-will defender argues is that there are many possible worlds God could not have weakly actualized. Let T(*W*), for any possible world *W,* be *the largest state of affairs God strongly actualizes in W*—a state of affairs, that is, such that (1) God strongly actualizes it in *W* (that is, it is necessary that if *W* had been actual, then God would have strongly actualized T(*W*)), and (2) it includes every state of affairs God strongly actualizes in *W*. There will in general be a difference between T(*W*) and *W;* if *W* includes some creature's performing a free action of some sort or other, then T(*W*) will be a state of affairs included in but not including *W.* And now let *W* be any such world—i.e., a world that includes some creature's freely performing an action. Then T(*W*) will be included in at least two possible worlds: one in which the creature in question performs the action in question, and one in which she does not. And whether God could have weakly actualized *W* depend upon whether

(6) if God had strongly actualized T(*W*), *W* would have been actual

is true: if it is, then God could have weakly actualized *W;* if not, not.

Now it is possible that (the instantiation of) (6) is not true for any world W in which there are free creatures who always do only what is right, if God had strongly actualized T(W), then W would not have been actual. It could be that no matter what God were to have done, if he had created free creatures and caused them to be free with respect to morally significant actions, they would have done at least some wrong. If so, then it wasn't within the power of God to create a world in which there are significantly free creatures but no moral evil. It is therefore possible that it was not within the power of God to actualize (weakly actualize) a world containing moral good but no moral evil. Furthermore, it is possible that

> (7) For any possible world W which is as good as the actual world but contains less than 10^{13} turps of evil, it is false that if God had strongly actualized T(W), then W would not have been actual.

If (7) is true, then it wasn't within the power of God to create a world as good as the actual world, but less evil. (7) is possible; but if (7) is true, then God could not have created a world as good as ours but with less evil—in which case he might have thought it good to actualize a world containing at least 10^{13} turps of evil.

To return to the probabilistic argument from evil: our question is whether (1) is improbable on (2) (or some other proposition about evil accepted by both theist and atheologian). (7) entails (1), however, so (at any rate according to the probability calculus[13]) (1) is improbable on (2) only if (7) is. But is it? Is (7) improbable with respect to (2), or with respect to (2) conjoined with some other relevant proposition about evil such as Rowe's (5)? I see no reason to think so. It isn't easy to tell; but we could sensibly claim that (7) was improbable with respect to such a proposition only if we had some good ideas as to what God's alternatives and options were. This question, however, is not one on which we have much by way of reliable information. How would we know what would have happened if God had created a world quite different from this one, if he had strongly actualized T(W) for some possible world W in which he strongly actualizes states of affairs quite different from the ones he does in fact strongly actualize? What would lead us to think that there is some world W such that if God had strongly actualized (T(W)), he would have had a world that is better, all things considered, than this one? This is not a question on which it becomes us to have strong opinions. What would be the source of our information? For all we know, there is a great variety of free creatures involved in our history and in the history of our world—creatures of whose nature and activity we are at best but dimly aware. Perhaps there are angels and devils (Satan and his cohorts); perhaps there are the principalities, powers, and dominions of whom St. Paul speaks. We know far too little about the world that is in fact actual, far too little about the sorts of creatures it contains and the counterfactuals of freedom that characterize them, to be justly confident of opinions about God's alternatives. Once we see that (7) is possibly true—once we see that it is possible that it was not within the power of God to create a world as good as ours but with less evil—it no longer seems the least bit obvious that (1) is improbable on (2), or (2) & (5), or (2) and some other relevant proposition about evil; for it isn't the least bit obvious that (7) is improbable on these things.

From a rough-and-ready intuitive point of view, therefore, there is no good reason to hold that (1) is improbable with respect to (2) or some other relevant proposition about evil. So how shall we look further into the matter? What considerations are relevant? How can we penetrate this question? How might the atheologian advance his case? Perhaps the way to make progress is to look more closely at the nature of probability: what is probability, and how does it work? And, from the other side, the theist might wish to know why the atheologian thinks (1)is improbable with respect to (2); this isn't just obvious, after all. Perhaps it will help to look into the nature of probability; perhaps that will help us settle the issue.

Here, however, the atheologian is doomed to disappointment: none of the current conceptions of probability, so far as I can see, gives him a polemical leg to stand on.[14] There are substantially three conceptions of probability lurking in the neighborhood these days, each with its variations. First, there is the personalist conception. Classically, the personalist holds that for each person S there is *credence function*: a function P_s from an appropriate set of propositions—all propositions, or perhaps all the propositions S has heard of, or whatever—into the unit interval. $P_s(A) = n$ expresses something like the degree to which S believes or accepts A; $P_s(A) = 1$ proclaims S's utter and abandoned commitment to A, while $P_s(A) = 0$ does the same for the denial of A;[15] and the conditional probability $P_s(A/B)$ is ordinarily defined as:

$$P_s(A/B) = \frac{P_s(A\&B)}{P_s(B)}$$

(provided $P_s(B)$ does not equal zero).

From the personalist perspective, then, when the atheologian holds that (1) is improbable on (2), he is apparently making a remark about someone's credence function. But *whose* credence function? Given the *theist's* credence function, (1) need not be at all improbable on (2). The theist may very well believe the conjunction of (1) with (2) nearly as firmly as (2) itself; in that case $P_t((1)/(2))$ will be high, so that (1) will not be improbable on (2). Of course (1) will no doubt be improbable on (2) given the *atheologian's* credence function; but if this is what he means when he says that (1) is improbable on (2), then his claim that theism is improbable on evil will be a remark about his own credence function, having all the philosophical interest characteristic of such autobiographical remarks.

On the straightforward personalist account, therefore, the atheologian's claim that (1) is improbable on (2) is of little polemical interest. Of course the personalist typically adds that a *rational* or *reasonable* credence function is *coherent;* it conforms to the probability calculus. (He might also add that a rational person changes belief by way of *conditionalization;* he might add that *diachronic coherence* is another necessary condition of rationality; he might also add that a rational structure of beliefs conforms to van Fraassen's principle *Reflection.*)[16] The atheologian might go on, therefore, to claim that his credence function, on which (1) is improbable on (2), is in fact coherent and hence rational. The suggestion that coherence is *sufficient* for rationality is, of course, at best monumentally dubious; a person's credence function can be coherent even if his beliefs never so much as change in response to changes in his experience. You are climbing Guide's Wall in the Grand Tetons: you have just led the next-to-last pitch and are seated on the belay ledge, enjoying the view and bringing your partner up. At this time *t,* your beliefs are coherent; and you believe (among other things) that the upper snow fields of Mount Owen are in full view to your left, that a couple of hundred feet below there is a hawk floating in lazy circles, that the rock shoes you are wearing are absurdly tight and hurt your left little toe, that it was some three hours ago that you took the boat across Jenny Lake and hiked up Cascade Canyon, and the like. Now suppose (through some cerebral mischance) that your beliefs become fixed at *t,* so that they no longer change in response to changes in your circumstances; they remain exactly as they were at *t.* By way of a desperate attempt at therapy, your relatives take you to a performance of Verdi's *La Traviata* in a nearby town. Their efforts fail; your beliefs remain as before; you continue to believe that you are on Guide's Wall, that Mount Owen is visible just to your left, and the like. Then your beliefs at *t** will still be coherent, and, if coherence is sufficient for rationality, they will be perfectly rational, despite their absurdly bad match with your experience and surroundings. But in fact your beliefs would offer a paradigm case of an irrational system of beliefs; hence coherence doesn't offer even the beginning of a guarantee of rationality. (It is equally clear, I think, that coherence isn't *necessary* for rationality. Coherence requires that one believe the logical consequences of any proposition *p* one believes to at least the degree to which one believes *p;* but surely, for example, a rational human being would not believe recondite theorems of mathematics or even first-order logic to the same degree that he believes such truths as the corresponding conditional of modus ponens or that he has had parents.) But the real problem for the atheological personalist here lies in a different direction: even if there are coherent credence functions according to which $P((1)/(2))$ is low, there are, of course, plenty of other coherent credence functions on which it is high; indeed, there are plenty of perfectly coherent credence functions on which $P((1)/(2))$-1. Here, therefore, we find no apparent way for him to argue that there is something defective or improper or irrational in the theist's accepting both (1) and (2); here there is little hope for the atheologian.

Can he do better by thinking of probabilities as *propensities* or *frequencies?* An initial and formidable problem is that it seems difficult *in excelsis* to see how even to begin to construe the conditional probability of a proposition like (1) on a proposition like (2) in terms of frequencies or propensities. How, from this point of view, are we supposed to attach a probability to such propositions as (1) and (2) and their conjunction? If we could, then clearly enough we could get a probability of (1) on (2); but how are we to do it? Following Wesley Salmon,[17] we might try to see the probability of a proposition like (1) as a matter of the frequency of the attribute *truth* among propositions similar to (1), determining this frequency by determining the proportion of true propositions among those in the class in question whose truth values we know. There are several technical problems here;[18] but the most important problem is as follows. (1), of course, is a member of many impressive classes of propositions: the class of theological propositions, the class of propositions believed by many people, the class of existential propositions, of propositions entailing the existence of a person, and so on. Which of these is the class of propositions relevantly similar to (1)? This is, of course, the dreaded *problem of the single case,* a problem of enormous difficulty for the frequentist bent on assigning a probability to such propositions as (1) or (1)&(2). I see no way of making these assignments in a polemically useful fashion. Salmon, indeed, suggests that the relevant class is the *broadest homogeneous reference class,* i.e., the broadest reference class that is homogeneous (either in fact or as we know) with respect to the relevant attribute, which in this case is truth. But clearly this will be unsatisfactory. The theist thinks that (1) and (2) are both true; he therefore thinks that their conjunction is true; but then the broadest reference class containing (1)&(2) and homogeneous with respect to truth will be the class of true propositions, in which the relative frequency of truth, naturally enough, is 1. But since the same goes for (1), the theist who follows Salmon's directions will hold that $P((1)/(2))=1$, so that the atheological argument can't get off the ground at all.

If anything, it is even harder to see how propensity accounts of probability could be applied to the question whether (1) is improbable on (2); I shall therefore ignore them, turning briefly to the last objectivist theory of probability, the logical theory.[19] On this conception, there is a quasi-logical, wholly objective relation of probability between any two statements, or any two statements of a relevant domain. Probability so thought of may be metaphorically considered as partial entailment, with entailment *simpliciter* the special case in which $P(A/B)=1$. But here the problem is with *absolutely prior* or a priori probabilities: the probability of a proposition on a tautology or other necessary truth. One who embraces the logical theory of probability is committed to the existence of such a priori probabilities; but they raise havoc in the present context. In the first place, the bulk of the theistic tradition has held that God is a necessary being: a being such that there is no possible world in which he does not exist. The proposition that there is such a person, then, is itself either necessarily true or necessarily false. If so, however, then according to the logical theory, the a priori probability of God's existence will be either 1 or 0: 1 if God exists and 0 if he does not. But then it follows by the probability calculus that the same goes for the conditional probability of God's existence on any evidence you care to specify, including (2); this too will be either 1 or 0. How, then, will the atheologian come up with anything like a probabilistic argument from evil?

But suppose we ignore this difficulty; suppose we assume, for the nonce, that God is a contingent being. According to a simple form of Bayes's Theorem,

$$P((1)/(2)) = \frac{P(1) \times P((2)/(1))}{P(2)}$$

where $P(1)$ and $P(2)$ are the intrinsic or a priori probability of these propositions: their probability on tautological evidence such as $P \vee \sim P$. But here we strike a problem of great significance: is there any reason to think that such propositions as (1) and (2) *have* a probability on a tautology or any other necessary truth? Is the idea that there is something like a ratio or proportion m/n such that God exists in m/n possible worlds? I don't see the slightest reason to think there are any such proportions or any such a priori probabilities (unless it is either necessary or impossible that there be such a person as God); in fact there is good reason to think that there aren't any.

A brief argument: if contingent propositions in general have an a priori probability on tautological evidence, then presumably the members of any collection of mutually exclusive and jointly exhaustive propositions of equal content or specificity should have the *same* a priori probability. But then the members of a countably infinite collection of the sort *there are no horses, there is just 1 horse, there are just 2 horses . . .* will all have the same a priori probability, in which case that probability must be zero. (It is for this reason that Carnap and others have held that universal generalizations should be assigned an a priori probability of zero; a universal generalization *All A's are B* is equivalent to the first member [*There are no non-B A's*] of such a set of propositions.) It follows that for any kind of object such that, for any natural number n it is possible that there be just n objects of that kind, the a priori probability, for any number n, that there are just n objects of that kind is zero.[20] Now say that a person S has been *created** by God if and only if S has been created by God, or has been created by some being who has been created* by God. According to traditional theistic ways of thinking of God, it is not possible that God exist and that there also be nondivine persons who have not been created* by God. Still, it is possible (if, as we are assuming, God is not a necessary being) that there be human beings who are not created* by God, because it is possible that God not exist. Indeed, for any number n it is possible that there be n such human beings. The a priori probability that there are no such human beings, then, is zero; hence the a priori probability that there is at least one such person is 1. But then it follows that the a priori probability of the existence of God is zero. On the other hand, it is also possible that there be human beings created by God; for any number n, in fact, it is possible that there be n such human beings. But then the a priori probability that there are no such human beings is zero; hence the a priori probability of the existence of God is 1. So suppose the proposition that there is such a person as God is contingent and has an a priori probability: then it looks as if there is excellent reason to hold that the probability in question is 1, but equally good reason to hold that it is zero.[21] There seems to be no satisfactory way to assign a priori probabilities to this proposition. I am therefore disinclined to think that such propositions have an a priori probability at all.

But let us suppose they do. How would we tell what that probability was? The atheologian will presumably estimate this probability as low; the theist may take it to be high. But how is either to estimate these probabilities? Do we have any way at all of making even a reasonably good guess? Imagine possible worlds as uniformly distributed throughout a sort of bounded logical space (a giant sphere, let's say). What is the proportion of that space occupied by possible worlds in which God exists? The theistic tradition (for the most part) has held that God exists in all possible worlds, but suppose we continue to assume that false: what would a good guess be? 1/4? 1/2? 24/25? It is anyone's guess, and any guess will be about as good as any other. The theist, no doubt, will set this probability fairly high; the atheologian may set it low; and how are we to decide between them?[22] So once again we have the same problem for the atheologian as in the previous case: there is no way here to mount a polemically effective atheological argument. What we take to be the conditional probability of (1) on (2), on the logical conception of probability, will depend in part upon our estimates of the a priori probabilities of (1), (2), and (1)&(2). It is extremely doubtful that there are any such probabilities; but even if there are, there seems no even reasonably uncontroversial way to determine what they are. In particular, the theist and atheological arguer from evil may very well differ radically as to what they are, each being entirely within his rights. So in this case, as in the last, the prospect for a successful probabilistic atheological argument from evil are at best dim.

The problem for the atheologian aiming to offer a cogent probabilistic argument from evil, then, is as follows. From an initial and preanalytic perspective, there seems to be little reason to think (1) is improbable on (2) (or some appropriate substitute), at least once we realize that such propositions as (7) are possibly true and are such that we have no reason to think them improbable on what we know. When we turn to the various extant theories of probability, however, things are even worse for the atheologian. The problem is not that none of these theories seems a successful account of probability; this is indeed true, and is indeed a problem, but of course it is no more a problem for the atheologian than it is for anyone else. We do in fact have some idea of probability and some grasp of probabilities, halting and infirm though it be; and there are many clear cases of improbable propositions, and many clear cases of pairs of propositions one of which is improbable on the other.[23] The problem, rather, is that if any of these theories is true, then there seems to be no way to develop an atheological probabilistic argument from evil.

II. Normative Probability

Personal probability, probability as frequencies, probability as construed on the logical theory—these are all *factual* or *nonnormative* conceptions of probability. There is nothing specifically normative about the fact that my degree of belief for some proposition is r, or that the proportion of A's that are B's (in the actual world, or in physically possible worlds, or in all possible worlds) is r, or that the a priori probability of a proposition A is r. But we may think of probability quite differently. We may think of it as a guide to life, as something like a *degree of rational belief*, as *epistemic probability*. This is a *normative* conception of probability. Probability so thought of is not a merely factual property or relation among propositions; it has to do instead with what is the (or a) right, or correct, or proper, or satisfactory way of holding one's beliefs. Suppose we try to see whether there is hope for progress with our problem by thinking about the matter along these lines.

But first we must try to get a clearer view of epistemic probability. Suppose we begin with a kind of special version of personalism: the probability of A, we might initially say, is something like *the degree to which a rational person would accept A*. Of course this isn't even a decent beginning as it stands; there is no such thing as *the* degree to which a rational person will accept *A;* how firmly she will accept *A* will, of course, depend upon her circumstances. If *S* is examining a large oak from forty yards and knows that her visual faculties are functioning properly, she will no doubt accept the proposition *S is looking at a large tree* more firmly than she would if she were in the basement listening to music with her eyes closed. Hence probability, so taken, will have to be relativized to circumstances. Second, I said we could start with the idea that epistemic probability had to do with *rational* degree of belief; but *rational* isn't quite the right word, if only because of its protean, chameleonic character. Probability has to do, I propose, with the degree of belief that would be accorded a given proposition (relative to circumstances) by someone who was suffering from no cognitive defect of deficiency or dysfunction, *someone whose noetic faculties were functioning properly.* I have tried to develop this notion of proper epistemic function (and its relation to the central concerns of epistemology) elsewhere;[24] here I shall say only the following. *Experience* obviously plays a key role here: the degree to which I accept a proposition, when my faculties are functioning properly, will clearly depend upon the sort of experience I enjoy. First, *sensuous* experience is involved; if my cognitive faculties are functioning as they ought, then the way in which I am appeared to will be crucially relevant to what I believe. But it isn't only sensuous experience that is involved; there is also something like an experienced compulsion or impulsion to believe. Experience is as crucially relevant to the formation of so-called a priori beliefs as to perceptual beliefs and memory beliefs. Thinking of *modus ponens* (or its corresponding conditional) *feels* different from thinking of affirming the consequence; and this difference in phenomenology is intimately connected with our strong tendency to accept the one and reject the other. Here what is involved is not so much sensuous experience as a sort of felt inclination to believe; the proposition in question has a sort of phenomenological attractiveness or compelling character about it.[25]

Epistemic probability thought of in this way is close to a notion of *warrant,* or *positive epistemic status.*[26] The epistemic probability of a proposition for a person at a time is the warrant that proposition has for her then, or the positive epistemic status it has for her then, where positive epistemic status is the property enough of which (together, perhaps, with a fillip to take account of Gettier problems) is sufficient for knowledge. Of course what interests us here is not epistemic probability *tout court,* but epistemic *conditional* probability, the probability of one proposition on another;[27] we are interested in the probability of (1) on (2).

As a first approximation, therefore, we might try thinking of the conditional probability of *A* on *B* as the degree to which a rational person, a person whose faculties were functioning properly, would accept *A* if she accepted *B*. But as before, this will not be satisfactory; the degree to which a rational person will accept a proposition *A,* given that she accepts *B,* will also depend on her circumstances. *A* is, again, the proposition that she perceives an oak tree; *B* is the proposition that nine out of ten trees around here are elms. The degree to which she will accept *A* will depend, not just on her acceptance of *B,* but on, for example, the question whether she can distinguish elms from oaks and what the tree she is examining looks like. She might very well accept A to a high degree, despite her accepting B and despite the apparent improbability of A on B. So initially, and to a first approximation, we must put the matter something like this: the epistemic conditional probability of A on B is the degree to which a rational person, one whose faculties were functioning properly, would accept A given that she accepted B, and given that neither A nor its denial has any other source of positive epistemic status for her. We could also put it like this: the epistemic probability of A on B is the degree of positive epistemic status or warrant A would have for someone whose faculties are functioning properly, who accepts B, considers A in the light of B, believes A on the basis of B, and for whom neither A nor -A has no other source of positive epistemic warrant. A further initial complication: the degree to which she will accept A, under these conditions, also depends upon the degree to which she accepts B; if her confidence in B is limited, so should be her confidence in A. So for present purposes let us say that she is certain of B, accepts it to the maximum degree. The conditional epistemic probability of A on B, then, initially and to a first approximation, is the degree to which a rational person, a person whose faculties are functioning properly, would accept A given that she was certain of B, knew that she accepted B, reflectively considered A in the light of B, and had no other source of warrant or positive epistemic status for A or for its denial.[28]

Now clearly epistemic probability, so conceived, does not conform to the calculus of probabilities. First, there is no reason to think there will be a specific real number registering the probability of A on B for me. It may be that there is no sensible way of assigning real numbers to degrees of belief; my degrees of belief are certainly vague to at least some extent; and perhaps we shall have to remain content with a comparative rather than a quantitative conception of epistemic probability.[29] Second and more important, even if we can quantify degrees of belief, it may be that there is a certain *range* associated with the probability of A on B. Different rational persons might believe A to slightly different degrees, even in relevantly similar epistemic circumstances. Third and much more important: contrary to the probability calculus, it will not be the case that if A entails B (or even if *if A then B* is theorem of first-order logic, or even of propositional logic), then the epistemic probability of B on some proposition C can't be less than that of A on C; even if A entails B, a person whose faculties were functioning perfectly properly could be much more confident of A than of B. B might be extremely complicated, for example, so that he can't easily see that A entails it; or B might not be particularly complicated, but nonetheless such that it isn't just obvious that it is entailed by A. Consider, for example, the proposition that there aren't any nonexistent objects. *Pace* Meinong, the early Russell, Castaneda, and Parsons, this proposition (I believe) is necessarily true and hence entailed by just any proposition. A rational person, however, will probably accept it with somewhat less enthusiasm than, say, the corresponding conditional of *modus ponens,* or the proposition that there is such a country as China. Consider either Goldbach's conjecture or its denial, whichever is true: this proposition will be entailed by just any proposition, but someone whose faculties are functioning properly will probably not accord it much credence. The right sort of experience is not present for it to be self-evident or nearly so; and no one, so far as we know, has been able to produce a proof for it.

Still another example, and one more poignant in the present context: we have been asking whether (1) is improbable on (2). According to the probability calculus, if B is equivalent, in the broadly logical sense, to C, then $P(A/B) = P(A/C)$. But now consider

>(1) there is an omnipotent, omniscient, and perfectly good God,
>(2) there are 10^{13} turps of evil

and

>(8) Possibly, for any possible world W which is as good as the actual world, but contains less than 10^{13} turps of evil, if God had strongly actualized $T(W)$, then W would not have been actual.

According to the probability calculus, the probability of (1) on (2) is equivalent to that of (1) on (2)&(8) (because (8) is necessarily true, so that (2)&(8) is equivalent to (2)); but surely this is at best dubious. Clearly a person whose faculties are functioning properly might never have thought of (8), or might not have realized that it is true, or might not have thought of (8) when estimating the bearing of (2) on (1). Such a person might quite properly be inclined to believe (1), upon thinking about the bearing of (2) on (1), to a certain degree r, but be inclined to believe (1) to quite a different degree upon seeing the truth of (8) and reflecting upon (1) in the light of the conjunction of (8) and (2).

Now suppose we return to the question with which we began: is (1) improbable on (2) (or some other appropriate proposition about evil)? More exactly, given that we agree that it is possible that God, though omnipotent and omniscient, could not have created a world with as much good as the actual world displays but less evil, is (1) improbable on the conjunction of (2) with that proposition? Would a rational person, a person who is in full command of her faculties, one whose faculties are functioning properly, who believed (2) and (8), for whom neither (1) nor its denial had any other source of positive epistemic status, and who had reflected on the question whether (1) was true in the light of (2) and (8)— would such a person be somewhat inclined to accept the denial of (1)? How *do* people think about, react to, (1) in connection with (2)?

Variously. For some, belief in God is if anything strengthened by confrontation with massive evil; there is no record that Mother Teresa's faith in God was weakened by her daily work in the presence of hideous evil, and there are many cases—including some in Auschwitz circumstances—where direct confrontation with appalling evil strengthened rather than weakened belief in God. Someone else may find the evil in question perplexing, but may say to God: "I don't know and can't imagine what reason you have for allowing this particularly heinous evil: but I know that you are perfectly good, just, wise, and loving and so I know that you *have* good reason for it, even if I haven't any idea what it is." Others will initially feel doubts—of God's goodness, or trustworthiness, or existence—but think, e.g., of the marvelous goodness involved and displayed in God's redemptive scheme and then no longer suffer the doubts—or perhaps still suffer them, but still believe. Still another reaction: Job was inclined to mistrust God, to say: "You may be magnificent and wonderful and omniscient and omnipotent and wholly good, and all that, but I don't like what you are doing, and I wish you would let me argue it out with you." And finally, someone without much inclination to believe in God may say: a good, all-powerful, all-knowing God couldn't possibly allow *that;* so there isn't any such person.

Now it is not implausible to see these different reactions and responses as connected with different initial degrees of belief in God; and perhaps someone who wasn't at all strongly inclined to believe would, upon reflecting upon such cases of evil, be inclined to disbelieve—even if she knew about the free-will defense and knew that it is quite *possible* that a perfectly good God allow such evil. But then it follows (by my account above) that (1) is improbable on (2), at least to some degree.

III. *Epistemic Probability and the Probabilistic Argument*

Now suppose we concede (if only for purposes of argument) that (1) is indeed epistemically improbable on (2), or on (2) and (8), or on (2) and (8) and Rowe's (5). I see no reason to think that it is, but let's for the moment nonetheless suppose that it is. What is supposed to follow from that? Why does the atheologian bring this up? How is this to be construed as an objection to theistic belief? How does the atheologian's argument go from there?

Of course he doesn't claim that what follows is that theism is false. What he *is* aiming to argue is that theistic belief, given that we know or believe (2), is somehow out of order or defective; it is not the sort of thing we should be believing. But obviously enough even if (1) is improbable on (2), it doesn't follow that one who accepts both (1) and (2)—and, let's add, sees that (1) is improbable with respect to (2)—has an irrational system of belief or is in any way guilty of noetic impropriety, or that he ought to give up (1). For it could be, of course, that (1) is improbable with respect to (2) but probable with respect to something else we know or believe. I might know, for example, both

(9) Feike is a Frisian and nine out of ten Frisians can't swim

and

(10) Feike is a Frisian lifeguard, and eight out of ten Frisian lifeguards can swim;

it is plausible to hold that

(11) Feike can swim

is probable with respect to (10) but improbable with respect to (9). If, furthermore, (9) and (10) are all we know about Feike's swimming ability, then the view that he can swim is more acceptable for us than the view that he can't, even though we know something with respect to which the former is improbable. Indeed, we might very well *know* both (9) and (11); we might very well know a pair of propositions one of which was improbable with respect to the other.[30] Suppose, therefore, that (1) is improbable with respect to (2) and that I know that it is; it doesn't begin to follow that my noetic structure is in some way flawed by virtue of my continuing to accept (1).

So even if (1) is improbable with respect to (2), it doesn't follow that (1) has little by way of warrant or epistemic probability for me; for it might be warranted by other things I believe. The degree of positive epistemic status it has for me will depend upon its relation to other propositions as well as on its relation to (2). But perhaps here the atheologian will argue that if (1) is indeed improbable on (2), then if the theist cannot produce some evidence *for* the existence of God (some successful version of one of the traditional theistic proofs, for example), then it is reasonable to assume that (1) is improbable, not just on (2) but on the relevant body of *total evidence* for the theist—roughly, the propositions he firmly believes minus (1).[31] And, he adds, if this proposition is improbable on that body of belief, then withholding it has more positive epistemic status for him than accepting it, in which case it would be irrational for him to accept it.

Now as a matter of fact there are very many propositions many or most of us believe with respect to which it is epistemically probable that there is such a person as God. But for now I want to look in a different direction and ask the following question: can we blithely assume that the degree to which I ought to accept (1) (the degree of positive epistemic status it has for me) depends solely upon its relations to other propositions? Can we simply assume that its warrant for me depends solely upon the *propositional* evidence I have for and against it? This assumption is nearly universal in discussions of the problem of evil, but it is surely unwarranted. *Some* beliefs, no doubt, are like that—scientific hypotheses, perhaps—but others are not. The positive epistemic status a proposition has for a person *S* need not depend solely upon the relation of that proposition to the rest of what *S* believes; in addition to the propositional evidence one has, there may also be *non*propositional evidence for or against the belief in question. Consider a person appeared to in that characteristic fashion in which one is appeared to upon seeing a tree. The positive epistemic status the proposition that he sees a tree has, for him, depends upon what his experience is like, how he is being appeared to, as well as upon the relation of the belief in question to his other beliefs. What confers warrant upon the proposition in question, for him, is not simply its relation to other beliefs, but its relation to his experience. Such warrant-conferring experience is nonpropositional evidence; and even if the proposition that he is seeing a tree is improbable on the rest of what he believes, that proposition may nonetheless have a great deal of positive epistemic status for him by virtue of this nonpropositional evidence. Suppose I am applying for an NEH fellowship; I try to bribe you to write me a glowing if inaccurate letter of recommendation. You indignantly refuse, and send a copy of my letter to my chairman. The letter disappears from the chairman's office under mysterious circumstances. I have motive for stealing it, and also opportunity: an extremely reliable and fair-minded member of the department reports having seen me lurking in the neighborhood at about the time the letter must have disappeared. I have been known to commit similar offenses. My colleagues sensibly if sorrowfully conclude that I have stolen the letter and upbraid me for my underhanded ways. I myself, however, clearly remember having spent that entire afternoon on a solitary walk in the woods. I then have a great deal of propositional evidence (all the evidence my colleagues have) for the proposition that I stole the letter; nonetheless on the basis of nonpropositional evidence I know that I did not.

So suppose my belief in God is improbable, not just on (2), but on the relevant total evidence. It doesn't follow that my belief in God is irrational, or evidentially out of order, or of very little positive epistemic status, or that it has no warrant for me, or anything of the sort. Indeed, it doesn't follow that I do not *know* (1). That (1) is improbable on (2) or some other relevant proposition about evil, therefore, is interesting (if true), but in itself shows little or nothing about the positive epistemic status of my belief in God, or about the rationality of accepting such belief. What is at least as important here is the warrant or lack thereof, of belief in God *apart from* any which it or its denial might receive by virtue of (2) and (5) and other propositions I properly or warrantedly believe. Perhaps belief in God resembles certain perceptual beliefs, memory beliefs, certain a priori beliefs and others in being *properly basic* (in the right circumstances);[32] if so, belief in God, like these others, will (under the right conditions) have nonpropositional warrant. When God spoke to Moses from the burning bush, for example, the latter's belief that there is such a person as the former may have had much by way of warrant or positive epistemic status, whether or not Moses had propositional evidence for this belief then.

But what sort of warrant or positive epistemic status might that be? To answer this question, suppose we ask another: how will the atheologian characterize the condition of the person who accepts theistic belief despite its having little or no positive epistemic status or warrant for her? What exactly would be wrong with her? How should we characterize her condition?

One possibility is broadly *internalist*. Perhaps the objector thinks (in Cliffordian fashion) that the theist, under these conditions, is violating some intellectual duty or obligation; perhaps positive epistemic status is to be seen as essentially a matter of fulfilling epistemic obligation; and the claim is that the theist, under the envisaged conditions, is flouting these obligations. Alternatively, perhaps the atheologian means to hold, with Foley,[33] that positive epistemic status is not a matter of fulfilling epistemic duty, but consists instead in following that procedure, with respect to belief formation and maintenance, which according to his own beliefs is best calculated to fulfill his own aims and goals; he adds that the theist's lack of warrant for his beliefs is simply a matter of his failing to follow such a procedure. But are these internalist complaints plausible, at least for most theists? After all, perhaps the believer can't help herself; our beliefs are not for the most part within our direct control, and the amount of indirect control we have over them is at best limited. And what if the theist has carefully and responsibly reflected on the mat-

ter but finds belief in God overwhelmingly plausible? What if she simply finds herself with this strongly held belief and (while, of course, she knows that there are
those who don't concur with her here) sees no more objection to it than to other
beliefs she but not everyone holds—the belief, say, that religious belief ought not
to be inculcated in public schools, or the belief that modern science has on balance
improved the quality of our lives? Then the thing for her to do, presumably, is to
treat it like the rest of her beliefs; it would seem unlikely that she could be properly censured for violating some plausible internalist constraint.

So what criticism might the atheologian sensibly lodge against the theist
who, as he sees it, believes in God in the teeth of the evidence and thus believes
improperly? A more plausible path for him to take, I think, is to claim that the noetic
structure of such a theist displays a certain *defect* or *flaw*. Consider someone who
believes that Paris is less populous than Peoria—not because he has evidence, but
because he has read it in the *National Enquirer* and can't help believing whatever he
reads there. Or consider someone who holds this belief on the basis of a wholly preposterous argument. Perhaps there are no internalist constraints such a person has
failed to meet; nevertheless his intellectual condition is defective in some way. He
displays a sort of deficiency, a flaw, a cognitive dysfunction of some sort. Perhaps he
is like someone who has an astigmatism, or is unduly clumsy, or suffers from arthri-
tis. And perhaps the atheological objector is best construed as holding, not that the
theist in question has violated some epistemic obligation or rule of proper procedure, but that she suffers from a certain sort of cognitive deficiency.

Alternatively but similarly, the idea might be that the theist in question is
laboring under a kind of illusion, a pervasive illusion afflicting the great bulk of
mankind over the great bulk of the time thus far allotted to it. Thus Sigmund Freud
saw religious belief as "illusions, fulfillments of the oldest, strongest, and most
insistent wishes of mankind."[34] He saw theistic belief as a matter of wish fulfillment: paralyzed and appalled by the spectacle of the overwhelming, impersonal
forces that control our destiny mindlessly take no notice, no account, of us and our
needs and desires, the theist invents a heavenly father of cosmic proportions—one
who exceeds our earthly fathers in goodness and love as much as in power and
knowledge. Religion, says Freud, is the "universal obsessional neurosis of humanity," and it is destined to disappear when human beings learn to face reality as it is,
resisting the tendency to edit it to suit their fancies.

Similar views are expressed by Karl Marx:

> Religion . . . is the self-consciousness and the self-feeling of the man who has
> either not yet found himself, or else (having found himself) has lost himself once
> more. But man is not an abstract being. . . . Man is the world of men, the State,
> society. This State, this society, produced religion, produced a perverted world
> conscience, because they are a perverted world. . . . Religion is the sigh of the
> oppressed creature, the feelings of a heartless world, just as it is the spirit of
> unspiritual conditions. It is the opium of the people. The people cannot be really
> happy until it has been deprived of illusory happiness by the abolition of religion.
> The demand that the people should shake itself free of illusion as to its own con-
> dition is the demand that it should abandon a condition which needs illusion.[35]

Note that Marx speaks here of a *perverted* world consciousness produced by a per-verted world. There is a perversion from a correct, or right, or natural condition; this perversion is brought about, somehow, by an unhealthy and perverted social order. From this point of view, the theist is subject to a sort of cognitive dysfunc-tion, a certain lack of cognitive and emotional health; and he believes as he does only because of the power of this illusion, this neurotic condition. He is cognitively unhealthy; in an etymological sense he is insane. His cognitive equipment, we might say, isn't working properly; it isn't functioning as it ought to. If his cognitive equip-ment were working properly—if, for example, it were working more like Marx's—he would not be under the spell of this illusion. He would instead face the world and our place in it with the clear-eyed apprehension that we are alone, and that any comfort and help we get will have to be of our own devising. There is no Father in heaven to turn to, and no prospect of anything, after death, but dissolu-tion. ("When we die," says Michael Scriven in his most memorable lines, "we rot.")

Now of course the theist is likely to be less than enthusiastic about the claim that he suffers from cognitive deficiency just by virtue of being a theist. (It is at most a hyperliberal theologian or two, intent on novelty and eager to concede as much as possible to contemporary secularity, who would embrace such a notion.) As a matter of fact, he may be inclined to see the shoe as on the other foot; he may be inclined to think of the *atheist* as a person who is suffering, in this way, from some illusion, from some noetic defect, from an unhappy, unfortunate, and unnatural condition that has deplorable noetic consequences. He may see the athe-ist as somehow the victim of *sin* in the world—his own sin or the sin of others. According to Saint Paul, unbelief is ultimately a result of sin; it ultimately origi-nates in an effort, as Romans 1 puts it, to "suppress the truth in unrighteousness." And according to John Calvin, God has created us with a nisus or tendency to see his hand in the world around us; a "sense of deity," he says, "is inscribed in the hearts of all." He goes on:

> Indeed, the perversity of the impious, who though they struggle furiously are unable to extricate themselves from the fear of God, is abundant testimony that this conviction, namely, that there is some God, is naturally inborn in all, and is fixed deep within, as it were in the very marrow. . . . From this we conclude that it is not a doctrine that must first be learned in school, but one of which each of us is master from his mother's womb and which nature itself permits no man to forget.[36]

Were it not for the existence of sin in the world, says Calvin, human beings would believe in God to the same degree and with the same natural spontaneity displayed in our belief in the existence of ourselves, other persons, an external world, and the past. This is the natural human condition; it is only because of the unnatural condition—due to sin—in which we find ourselves that many of us find belief in God difficult or offensive or absurd. The fact is, Calvin thinks, one who does not believe in God is in an epistemically defective position—rather like someone who does not believe that his wife exists, or thinks that she is a cleverly constructed robot and has no thoughts, feelings, or consciousness. In this way the believer inverts Freud and Marx, claiming that what they see as sickness is really health and what they see as health is really sickness.

Furthermore, the theist may properly add that belief in God has or may have a great deal of positive epistemic status—at any rate for many believers—apart from whatever propositional warrant it does or does not enjoy. There is a huge variety of perfectly ordinary circumstances and experiences that seem to confer or enhance belief in God: perception of the grandeur and beauties of nature (the mountains; the sea; the delicate, articulate beauty of a tiny flower); guilt, feeling forgiven, danger, gratitude, prayer, listening to Mozart's D minor piano concerto (not to mention *Messiah*), Bible reading, hearing certain kinds of sermons. In these circumstances and many others, belief in God is for many people enhanced. And the main question here: when a person's belief in God begins or is enhanced or supported by any of these, is this a case of cognitive malfunction, or is it a case of cognitive faculties functioning properly? If positive epistemic status consists in a belief's being produced by faculties that are functioning properly,[37] functioning the way they ought to function, then the theist will no doubt hold that belief in God has (or may have) a great deal of warrant or positive epistemic status independent of any it gets by virtue of being believed on the basis of other propositions. So, suppose at any rate for purposes of argument, that (1) is indeed improbable on (2), or on the conjunction of (2) with some other relevant proposition about evil: that fact, if indeed it is a fact, is not taken by itself of much moment. It is only one of several facts that must be taken into account in determining the positive epistemic status enjoyed by belief in God. For all this tells us, it could be that the theist is like someone who has substantial propositional evidence against the claim that pigeons are to be found near Devil's Tower, and no propositional evidence for it; in point of fact, however, he is in full view of the tower and sees several large flocks of pigeons flying around it. He may be like the person who shares with his accusers propositional evidence for the claim that he failed to mail his tax return; he himself, however, clearly remembers that he did. In such a case the belief in question has much by way of warrant or positive epistemic status, despite the propositional evidence against it; no doubt he knows that he mailed it in, despite the propositional evidence against it. And of course the same may be true for belief in God. Our question as to the warrant of theistic belief cannot properly be settled just by examining whether the propositional evidence tells for or against it.[38] We must also look into the question what sort of nonpropositional warrant, if any, such belief enjoys.

But here we see the ontological and ultimately religious roots of the epistemological question as to the warrant or lack thereof for belief in God. What is rational depends upon what sort of beings human beings are; and what you properly take to be rational, at least in the sense in question, depends upon what sort of metaphysical and religious stance you adopt; it depends upon what kind of beings you think human beings are, and what sorts of beliefs their noetic faculties will produce when they are functioning properly. Your view as to what sort of creature a human being is will determine or at any rate heavily influence your views as to what it is rational or irrational for human beings to believe. And so the dispute as to whether theistic belief is rational can't be settled just by attending to epistemological considerations; it is at bottom not merely an epistemological dispute, but an ontological or theological dispute. You may think humankind is created by God in the image of God—and created both with a natural tendency to see God's hand in the world about us and with a natural tendency to recognize that he has indeed been created and is beholden to his creator, owing him worship and allegiance. Then of course you will not think of belief in God as in the typical case a manifestation of wishful thinking or any other kind of intellectual defect. (It is then more like a deliverance of sense perception or memory—or perhaps the faculty responsible for a priori knowledge.) On the other hand, you may think we human beings are the product of blind evolutionary forces; you may think there is no God, and that we are part of a godless universe. Then perhaps you will be inclined to accept the sort of view according to which belief in God is an illusion of some sort, properly traced to a sort of disease or dysfunction on the part of the individual or society.

By way of conclusion then: the atheologian claims that (1) is improbable on (2). This is by no means initially obvious. When we look at the question from the point of view of the main contemporary accounts of probability, furthermore, we find little hope for the atheologian; on each of the current views of probability, the prospects for an atheological argument from evil are at best bleak. We may therefore usefully shift our attention to the broader question of epistemic probability, seeing the warrant conferred upon a proposition by virtue of being believed on the basis of another as a special case of warrant generally. Here we note the following. The centrally important question has to do not with the propositional evidence theistic belief enjoys but with the degree, if any, of warrant or positive epistemic status enjoyed by theistic belief *apart* from any conferred upon it or its denial by other beliefs. Our views as to how much such warrant it has, furthermore, will depend upon what sorts of belief we think are to be found in a healthy or properly functioning human noetic structure; but this, in turn, will depend in part upon whether or not we think theism is true. Hence we see that the question as to the epistemic probability of theistic belief is not metaphysically or religiously neutral; its roots lie deep in metaphysics and theology.[39]

NOTES

This essay originally appeared in *Archivio di filosofia,* volume 56 (1988). It is reprinted with permission.

1. David Hume, *Dialogues concerning Natural Religion,* ed. Richard Popkin (Indianapolis: Hackett, 1985), p. 65.

2. J. L. Mackie, "Evil and Omnipotence," *Mind,* 1955 (widely reprinted). In the posthumous *Miracle of Theism* (Oxford: Clarendon University Press, 1982), Mackie wavers between his earlier claim that the existence of God is straightforwardly inconsistent with that of evil and the claim that the existence of evil is powerful but not conclusive evidence against the existence of God; see pp. 150-75. Also see my "Is Theism Really a Miracle?" *Faith and Philosophy* 3 (1986): 122-23.

3. And (as I see it) rightly so; see my *Nature of Necessity* (Oxford: Clarendon Press, 1974), chap. 9, and *God, Freedom, and Evil* (New York: Harper & Row, 1974, and Grand Rapids: Eerdmans, 1977); also see *Alvin Plantinga,* ed. James Tomberlin and Peter van Inwagen (Dordrecht: Reidel, 1985), 36-55.

4. There are serious problems in saying just what k is in this context: since we know (2), it is part of our background information, in which case (2) cannot dynamically disconfirm (1). The theist, furthermore, may know (1), in which case that is also part of his background information, in which case, again, (2) cannot dynamically disconfirm it. We must think of k as containing neither (1) nor (2), nor, of course, any propositions whose conjunction entails (1) or (2). As a first approximation, perhaps we can think of k as any subset of what we (perhaps the parties to the argument) know that is maximal with respect to entailing neither (1) nor (2).

5. William Rowe, "The Problem of Evil and Some Varieties of Atheism," *American Philosophical Quarterly* 16 (1979): 336; reprinted in this volume as chapter 1. (My (3) is Rowe's (1)).

6. I think there are problems, from Rowe's perspective, with respect to the statement of (3) and (4); see my paper "The Probabilistic Argument from Evil," *Philosophical Studies* 35 (1979), 6-10.

7. For Chisholm's explanation of this term, see Roderick Chisholm, *Theory of Knowledge,* 2d ed. (Englewood Cliffs: Prentice-Hall, 1977), 5ff.

8. See, "The Probabilistic Argument from Evil," 9-10.

9. Stephen Wykstra, "The Humean Obstacle to Evidential Arguments from Suffering: On Avoiding the Evils of 'Appearance,'" *International Journal for Philosophy of Religion* 16 (1984), 85.

10. For a fuller statement, see the items referred to in note 3.

11. Here I assume (what seems to me to be true) that while God is indeed eternal, he is not timeless, "outside of time" in the Boethian sense. (What I say can easily be restated to accommodate the latter view.)

12. Some have objected to the free-will defense on the grounds that it presupposes that there are such things as counterfactuals of freedom, that they have truth values, and that God can know them. It is the atheologian, however, who really needs these suppositions; things are easier, not harder, for the free-will defense if we reject these assumptions.

13. I argue later in this essay that epistemic probability does not in fact conform to the probability calculus; but it is easy to see how to reconstruct the present argument from the perspective of the idea of epistemic probability outlined here.

14. I have argued this point in detail elsewhere ("The Probabilistic Argument from Evil," 10-44); here I briefly recapitulate the main thrust of those arguments and add some new considerations.

15. Following F. P. Ramsey, "Truth and Probability," first published in *The Foundations of Mathematics and Other Logical Essays,* ed. R. B. Braithwaite (New York: Humanities Press, 1950), personalists often suggest that a person S's credence function is determined by the sort of betting behavior in which he would engage in various circumstances. (As a matter of fact, what the personalist must appeal to here is the sort of odds S would post if she were forced to post odds on all the propositions in the domain of P_s.)

16. See B. van Fraassen, "Belief and the Will," *Journal of Philosophy* (1984), 237ff., and David Lewis's diachronic Dutch Book argument in P. Teller, "Conditionalization, Observation, and Change of Preference," in W. L. Harper and C. A. Hooker, *Foundations of Probability Theory, Statistical Inference, and Statistical Theories of Science,* vol. 1 (Boston: Reidel, 1976), 209ff.

17. See Wesley Salmon, *The Foundations of Scientific Inference* (Pittsburgh: University of Pittsburgh Press, 1966), 124ff.

18. See "The Probabilistic Argument from Evil," 44-47.

19. This seems to be the theory of probability embraced by, for example, J. L. Mackie in the probabilistic argument from evil he (apparently) offers in chapter 9 of *The*

Miracle of Theism (Oxford: Clarendon Press, 1982). It is not entirely clear whether what Mackie means to offer is a *probabilistic* atheological argument from evil or a *deductive* argument; see my "Is Theism Really a Miracle?" *Faith and Philosophy* (1986).

20. We could say, if we like, that this probability was *infinitesimal* rather than 0; this wouldn't affect the argument that follows.

21. If we adopt the course suggested in the previous note, then these two probabilities will be infinitesimally close to 0 and 1.

22. Richard Swinburne, in *The Existence of God,* suggests that a priori probability is determined by *simplicity;* for critical comment, see my "Is Theism Really A Miracle?"

23. Of course the pair ((1),(2)) is not one of these; it is by no means obvious that (2) is unlikely or improbable on (1). Here we have a situation in which there is disagreement as to what is probable with respect to what—just the sort of situation that drives us to inquire what probability *is.*

24. There is a brief and savagely truncated account in "Epistemic Justification," *Nous* (1986). A fuller version of the same ideas may be found in "Positive Epistemic Status and Proper Function," *Philosophical Perspectives,* ed. Tomberlin (Northridge: Ridgeview, 1988). [Also: *Warrant and Proper Function* (Oxford: Oxford University Press, 1993). Ed.]

25. See my "Reason and Belief in God" in *Faith and Rationality,* ed. A. Plantinga and N. Wolterstorff (Notre Dame: University of Notre Dame Press, 1983), 57.

26. See the essays referred to in note 24.

27. In what follows I am indebted to Richard Otte; see Otte, "A Theistic Conception of Probability," *Faith and Philosophy* (1987).

28. I must emphasize that this is indeed a first approximation; there remain problems. For example, there is the problem that some propositions such that other propositions may have epistemic probability on them are not such that a human being can rationally believe them: *There are no conscious beings,* for example, or *No one now believes anything.* See my forthcoming book *Warrant,* chapter 9.

29. Following Bas van Fraassen ("Belief and the Will," p. 251) we can then say that a person's beliefs are coherent only if there is at least one probability function P such that $P(A) \geq P(B)$ if it seems more likely to him that A than that B, $P(A/C) > P(B/C)$ if on the supposition that C it seems more likely to him that A than that B, and so forth.

30. Notice that this is impossible on the personalist reading of the matter, since (on this view) all the propositions I know will enjoy the maximum or near-maximum degree of belief and propositions I know will be extremely probable with respect to each other.

31. Strictly speaking, of course, this isn't correct; we must also appropriately delete items of belief that *entail* (1). What is needed (to a first approximation) is a subbody of belief that is relevantly maximal with respect to not entailing (1). This is at best a *first* approximation; other candidates for deletion will be such propositions as *it is more probable that (1) is true than that God has created kangaroos* which we accept only because we believe (1). It is extremely difficult to say precisely what the appropriately reduced body of belief is.

32. See "Reason and Belief in God," esp. pp. 16-38, 47-63, and 73-91.

33. See Richard Foley, *The Theory of Epistemic Rationality* (Cambridge: Harvard University Press, 1987), chap. I.

34. Sigmund Freud, *The Future of an Illusion.*

35. K. Marx, *Introduction to a Critique of the Hegelian Philosophy of Right,* in K. Marx and F. Engels, *Collected Works* (London: Lawrence & Wishart, 1975), vol. 3.

36. John Calvin, Institutes of the Christian Religion, trans. Ford Lewis Battles (Philadelphia: Westminster Press, 1960). Here Calvin speaks of belief in God as "inborn in all, . . . fixed deep within . . ." What he means, I think, is not that belief in God is as such innate or inborn in all; what is thus inborn (in properly functioning human beings) is a tendency to *form* belief in God under appropriate circumstances; see "Reason and Belief in God," pp. 80-82.

37. See note 24.

38. See my "Is Theism a Miracle?"

39. I am indebted for stimulating discussion to Richard Otte, Steven Layman, Paul Draper, and the members of the Calvin College Philosophy Colloquium, especially Del Ratzsch and Stephen Wykstra.

6.

WILLIAM P. ALSTON

The Inductive Argument
from Evil and the Human
Cognitive Condition

I

The recent outpouring of literature on the problem of evil has materially advanced the subject in several ways. In particular, a clear distinction has been made between the "logical" *argument against the existence of God* ("atheological argument") from evil, which attempts to show that evil is logically incompatible with the existence of God, and the "inductive" ("empirical," "probabilistic") argument, which contents itself with the claim that evil constitutes (sufficient) empirical evidence against the existence of God. It is now acknowledged on (almost) all sides that the logical argument is bankrupt, but the inductive argument is still very much alive and kicking.

In this paper I will be concerned with the inductive argument. More specifically, I shall be contributing to a certain criticism of that argument, one based on a low estimate of human cognitive capacities in a certain application. To indicate the point at which this criticism engages the argument, I shall use one of the most careful and perspicuous formulations of the argument in a recent essay by William Rowe (1979).*

> 1. There exist instances of intense suffering which an omnipotent, omniscient being could have prevented without thereby losing some greater good or permitting some evil equally bad or worse.
> 2. An omniscient, wholly good being would prevent the occurrence of any intense suffering it could, unless it could not do so without thereby losing some greater good or permitting some evil equally bad or worse.
> 3. There does not exist an omnipotent, omniscient, wholly good being. (p. 336)

Let's use the term *gratuitous suffering* for any case of intense suffering, E, that satisfies premise 1, that is, which is such that an omnipotent, omniscient being could have prevented it without thereby losing some greater good or permitting some evil equally bad or worse.[1] 2 takes what we might call the "content" of 1 (losing a greater good or permitting some worse or equally bad evil) as a necessary condition for God to have a sufficient reason for permitting E. E's being gratuitous, then, is the contradictory of the possibility of God's having a sufficient reason for permitting it. I will oscillate freely between speaking of a particular case of suffering, E, being gratuitous, and speaking of the impossibility of God's having a sufficient reason for permitting E. I shall call a proponent of an inductive argument from evil the "critic."

The criticism I shall be supporting attacks the claim that we are rationally justified in accepting 1, and it does so on the grounds that our epistemic situation is such that we are unable to make a sufficiently well grounded determination that 1 is the case. I will call this faute de mieux, the *agnostic* thesis, or simply *agnosticism*. The criticism claims that the magnitude or complexity of the question is such that our powers, access to data, and so on are radically insufficient to provide sufficient warrant for accepting 1. And if that is so, the inductive argument collapses.[2]

How might one be justified in accepting 1? The obvious way to support an existential statement is to establish one or more instantiations and then use existential generalization. This is Rowe's tack, and I don't see any real alternative. Thus Rowe considers one or another case of suffering and argues, in the case of each, that it instantiates 1. I will follow him in this approach. Thus to argue that we cannot be justified in asserting 1, I shall argue that we cannot be justified in asserting any of its instantiations, each of which is of the form

> 1A. E is such that an omnipotent, omniscient being could have prevented it without thereby losing some greater good or permitting some evil equally bad or worse.

In the sequel when I speak of being or not being justified in accepting 1, it must be remembered that this is taken to hang on whether one is or can be justified in accepting propositions of the form 1A.

---

*See references at the end of this chapter.

Does the agnostic thesis, in my version, also claim that we are unable to justifiably assert the denial of 1, as we would have to do to develop a successful theodicy? It is no part of my task in this paper to address this question, but I will make a couple of remarks. First, my position is that we could justifiably believe, or even know, the denial of 1, and that in one of two ways. We might have sufficient grounds for believing in the existence of God—whether from arguments of natural theology, religious experience, or whatever—including sufficient grounds for taking God to be omnipotent, omniscient, and perfectly good, and that could put us in a position to warrantedly deny 1. Or God might reveal to us that 1 is false, and we might be justified in accepting the message as coming from God. Indeed, revelation might provide not only justification for denying 1 but also justification for beliefs about what God's reasons are for permitting this or that case of suffering or type of suffering, thereby putting us in a position to construct a theodicy of a rather ambitious sort.[3] If, however, we leave aside the putative sources just mentioned and restrict ourselves to what we can do by way of tracing out the interconnections of goods and evils in the world by the use of our natural powers, what are we to say? Well, the matter is a bit complicated. Note that 1 is an existential statement, which says that there are instances of intense suffering of which a certain negative claim is true. To deny 1 would be to say that this negative claim is false for *every* case of intense suffering. And even if we could establish the nongratuitousness of certain cases by tracing out interconnections—and I don't see that this is necessarily beyond our powers—that would not be sufficient to yield the denial of 1. To sum up: I think that examining the interconnections of good and evil in the world by our natural powers cannot suffice to establish either 1 or its negation.[4] For particular cases of suffering we might conceivably be able to establish nongratuitousness in this way, but what I shall argue in this paper is that no one can justifiably assert gratuitousness for any case.

II

Before setting out the agnostic thesis in more detail and adding my bit to the case for it, let me make some further comments about the argument against which the criticism is directed and variants thereof.

A. The argument is stated in terms of intense suffering, but it could just as well have appealed to anything else that can plausibly be claimed to be undesirable in itself. Rowe focuses on intense suffering because he thinks that it presents the greatest difficulty for anyone who tries to deny a premise like 1. I shall follow him in this, though for concision I shall often simply say "suffering" with the "intense" tacitly understood.

B. Rowe doesn't claim that all suffering is gratuitous, but only that some is. He takes it that even one case of gratuitous suffering is incompatible with theism. I go along with this assumption (though in F, I question whether Rowe has succeeded in specifying necessary and sufficient conditions for gratuitousness, and for God's having a sufficient reason for permitting suffering). As already noted, Rowe does not argue for 1 by staying on its level of unspecificity; rather he takes particular examples of suffering and argues in the case of each that it is gratuitous; from there it is a short step of existential generalization to 1. In Rowe (1979) and subsequent papers, Rowe focuses on the case of a fawn trapped in a forest fire and undergoing several days of terrible agony before dying (hereinafter "Bambi"). In Rowe (1988) he adds to this a (real-life) case introduced by Bruce Russell (1989), a case of the rape, beating, and murder by strangulation of a five-year-old girl ("Sue") by her mother's boyfriend. Since I am specifically interested in criticizing Rowe's argument, I will argue that we are not justified, and cannot be justified, in judging these evils to be gratuitous. It will turn out that some of my discussion pertains not to Rowe's cases but to others. I will signal the reader as to how to understand the dummy designator, "E," in each part of the paper.

C. The argument deals with a classical conception of God as omnipotent, omniscient, and perfectly good; it is designed to yield the conclusion that no being with those characteristics exists. I shall also be thinking of the matter in this way. When I use "God" it will be to refer to a being with these characteristics.

D. There are obvious advantages to thinking of the inductive argument from evil as directed against the belief in the existence of God as God is thought of in some full-blown theistic religion, rather than as directed against what we may call "generic theism." The main advantage is that the total system of beliefs in a religion gives us much more to go on in considering what reasons God might possibly have for permitting E. In other terms, it provides much more of a basis for distinguishing between plausible and implausible theodicies. I shall construe the argument as directed against the traditional Christian belief in God.[5] I choose Christianity for this purpose because (a) I am more familiar with it than other alternatives, as most of my readers will be, and (b) most of the philosophical discussions of the problem of evil, both historically and currently, have grown out of Christian thought.

E. Rowe does not claim to know or to be able to prove that 1 is true. With respect to his fawn example he acknowledges that "perhaps, for all we know, there is some familiar good outweighing the fawn's suffering to which that suffering is connected in a way we do not see" (1979, p. 337). He only claims that we have sufficient rational grounds for believing that the fawn's suffering is gratuitous, and still stronger rational grounds for holding that at least some of the many cases of suffering that, so far as we can see, instantiate 1 actually do so.[6] Not all of Rowe's fellow atheologians are so modest, but I will concentrate my fire on his weaker and less vulnerable version.

F. A final comment will occupy us longer. Rowe obviously supposes, as premise 2 makes explicit, that cases of "gratuitous" evil count decisively against the existence of God. That is, he takes it that an omnipotent, omniscient, and perfectly good God would not permit any gratuitous evil; perhaps he regards this as conceptually or metaphysically necessary. Thus he holds that God could have no other reason for permitting suffering except that preventing it would involve losing some greater good or permitting some equally bad or worse evil.[7] But this is highly controversial. It looks as if there are possible divine reasons for permitting evil that would be ruled out by (2). (i) Suppose that God could bring about a greater good only by permitting any one of several equally bad cases of suffering. Then no one is such that by preventing it He would lose that greater good. And if we stipulate that God has a free choice as to whether to permit any of these disjuncts, it is not the case that to prevent it would be to permit something equally bad or worse; that might or might not ensue, depending on God's choice. But if we are to allow that being necessary for a greater good can justify permission of evil, it looks as if we will have to allow this case as well. (ii) More important, human free will complicates God's strategies for carrying out His purposes. As I will be noting later in the paper, if God has a policy of respecting human free will, He cannot guarantee human responses to His initiatives where those responses would be freely made if at all.[8] Hence if God visits suffering on us in an attempt to turn us from our sinful ways, and a particular recipient doesn't make the desired response, God could have prevented that suffering without losing any greater good (no such good was forthcoming), even though we might reasonably take God to be justified in permitting the suffering, provided that was His best strategy in the situation, the one most likely to get the desired result. (iii) Look at "general policy" theodicies.[9] Consider the idea that God's general policy of, e.g., usually letting nature take its course and not interfering, even when much suffering will ensue, is justified by the overall benefits of the policy. Now consider a particular case of divine nonintervention to prevent intense suffering. Clearly, God could have intervened in this case without subverting the general policy and losing its benefits. To prevent this particular suffering would not be to lose some greater good or permit something worse or equally bad. And yet it seems that general policy considerations of the sort mentioned could justify God in refraining from intervening in this case. For if it couldn't, it could not justify His nonintervention in any case, and so He would be inhibited from carrying out the general policy.[10]

Since my central aim in this paper is not to refine principles like 2 in microscopic detail, I will take a shortcut in dealing with these difficulties. (i) can be handled by complicating the formula to allow the permission of any member of a disjunction, some member of which is necessary for a greater good. Consider it done. (ii) and (iii) can be accommodated by widening the sphere of goods for which the evil is necessary. For cases of the (ii) sort, take the greater good to be having as great a chance as possible to attain salvation, and let's say that this good is attained whatever the response. As for (iii), we can say that E is permitted in order to realize the good of maintaining a beneficial general policy except where there are overriding reasons to make an exception, and the reasons in this case are not overriding. With these modifications we can take Rowe to have provided a plausible formulation of necessary conditions for divine sufficient reasons for permitting E. But if you don't think I have successfully defended my revision of Rowe, then you may think in terms of an unspecific substitute for 1, like "there are instances of suffering such that there is no sufficient reason for God to allow them." That will still enable me to argue that no one is in a position to justifiably assert that God could have no sufficient reason for allowing E.

III

Clearly, the case for 1 depends on an inference from "so far as I can tell, p" to "p" or "probably, p." And, equally clearly, such inferences are sometimes warranted and sometimes not. Having carefully examined my desk, I can infer "Jones's letter is not on my desk." But being ignorant of quantum mechanics, I cannot infer "this treatise on quantum mechanics is well done" from "so far as I can tell, this treatise on quantum mechanics is well done." I shall be contending that our position vis-à-vis 1 is like the latter rather than like the former.

I am by no means the first to suggest that the atheological argument from evil is vitiated by an unwarranted confidence in our ability to determine that God could have no sufficient reason for permitting some of the evils we find in the world. A number of recent writers have developed the theme.[11] I endorse many of the reasons they give for their pessimism. Wykstra points out that our cognitive capacities are much more inferior to God's than is a small child's to his parents; and in the latter case the small child is often unable to understand the parents' reasons for inflicting punishment or for requiring him to perform tasks that are distasteful to him (88). Ahern points out that our knowledge of the goods and evils in the world (54-55) and of the interconnections between things (57, 72-73) are very limited. Fitzpatrick adduces the deficiencies in our grasp of the divine nature (25-28). This is all well taken and, I believe, does provide support for the agnostic thesis. But then why am I taking pen in hand to add to this ever-swelling stream of literature? For several reasons. First, I will not be proceeding on the basis of any general skepticism about our cognitive powers either across the board or generally with respect to God. I will, rather, be focusing on the peculiar difficulties we encounter in attempting to provide adequate support for a certain very ambitious negative existential claim, viz., that there is (can be) no sufficient divine reason for permitting a certain case of suffering, E.[12] I will be appealing to the difficulties of defending a claim of this particular kind, rather than to more generalized human cognitive weaknesses. Second, much of the literature just alluded to has centered around Wykstra's claim that to be justified in asserting 1 it would have to be the case that if 1 were false that would be indicated to one in some way.[13] By contrast I will not be proceeding on the basis of any such unrestrictedly general epistemological principle. Third, I will lay out in much more detail than my predecessors the range of conceivable divine reasons we would need to be able to exclude in order to be justified in asserting 1. Fourth, I can respond to some of the defenses which the likes of Rowe have deployed against the agnostic criticism.

IV

Now, at last, I am ready to turn to my central project of arguing that we cannot be justified in accepting 1A. As already noted, I will be emphasizing the fact that this is a negative existential claim. It will be my contention that to be justified in such a claim one must be justified in excluding all the live possibilities for what the claim denies to exist. What 1A denies is that there is any reason God could have for permitting it. I will argue that we are not and cannot be justified in asserting that none of these possibilities are realized. I will draw on various theodicies to compile a (partial) list of the reasons God might conceivably have for permitting E. That will provide me with a partial list of the suggestions we must have sufficient reason to reject in order to rationally accept 1. Note that it is no part of my purpose here to develop or defend a theodicy. I am using theodicies only as a source of *possibilities* for divine reasons for evil, possibilities the realization of which the atheologian will have to show to be highly implausible if his project is to succeed.

Since I am criticizing Rowe's argument, I am concerned to argue that we are not justified in asserting 1A for the particular kinds of suffering on which Rowe focuses. And we should not suppose that God would have the same reason for permitting every case of suffering.[14] Hence it is to be expected that the reasons suggested by a given theodicy will be live possibilities for some cases of evil and not others. I am, naturally, most interested in suggestions that constitute live possibilities for divine reasons for permitting Bambi's and Sue's suffering. And many familiar theodicies do not pass this test. (This is, no doubt, why these cases were chosen by Rowe and Russell.) Bambi's suffering, and presumably Sue's as well, could hardly be put down to punishment for sin, and neither case could seriously be supposed to be allowed by God for the sake of character building. Nevertheless, I shall not confine the discussion to live possibilities for these two cases. There are two reasons for this. First, a discussion of other theodicies will help to nail down the general point that we are typically unable to exclude live possibilities for divine reasons in a particular case. Second, these discussions will provide ammunition against atheological arguments based on other kinds of suffering.

Thus I shall first consider theodical suggestions that seem clearly not to apply to Bambi or Sue. Here I shall be thinking instead of an adult sufferer from a painful and lengthy disease (fill in the details as you like) whom I shall call "Sam." Having argued that we are not in a position to exclude the possibility that God has reasons of these sorts for permitting Sam's suffering, I shall pass on to other suggestions that do constitute genuine possibilities for Bambi and/or Sue.

V Suffering is God's punishment for Sin

I begin with a traditional theme, that human suffering is God's punishment for sin. Though it hardly applies to Bambi or Sue, it may be a live possibility in other cases, and so I will consider it. The punishment motif has tended to drop out of theodicies in our "soft-on-criminals" and "depravity-is-a-disease" climate, but it has bulked large in the Christian tradition.[15] It often draws the criticism that, so far as we can see, degree or extent of suffering is not nicely proportioned to degree of guilt. Are the people of Vietnam, whose country was ravaged by war in this century, markedly more sinful than the people of Switzerland, whose country was not? But, remembering the warnings of the last section, that does not show that this is never God's reason for permitting suffering, and here we are concerned with a particular case, Sam. Let's say that it seems clear, so far as we can tell, that

Sam's suffering is not in proportion to his sinfulness. Sam doesn't seem to have been a bad sort at all, and he has suffered horribly. Can we go from that to "Sam's suffering was not a punishment for sin," or even to "it is reasonable to suppose that Sam's suffering was not a punishment for sin"? I suggest that we cannot.

First, we are often in a poor position to assess the degree and kind of a certain person's sinfulness, or to compare people in this regard. Since I am thinking of the inductive argument from evil as directed against Christian belief in God, it will be appropriate to understand the punishment-for-sin suggestion in those terms. Two points about sin are particularly relevant here. (1) Inward sins—one's intentions, motives, attitudes—are more serious than failings in outward behavior.[16] (2) The greatest sin is a self-centered refusal or failure to make God the center of one's life. (2) is sharply at variance with standard secular bases for moral judgment and evaluation. Hence the fact that X does not seem, from that standpoint, more wicked than Y, or doesn't seem wicked at all, does nothing to show that God, on a Christian understanding of God, would make the same judgment. Because of (1), overt behavior is not always a good indication of a person's condition, sin-wise. This is not to say that we could not make a sound judgment of a person's inner state if we had a complete record of what is publicly observable concerning the person. Perhaps in some instances we could, and perhaps in others we could not. But in any event, we rarely or never have such a record. Hence, for both these reasons our judgments as to the relation between S's suffering and S's sinfulness are usually of questionable value.

Second, according to Christianity, one's life on earth is only a tiny proportion of one's total life span. This means that, knowing nothing about the immeasurably greater proportion of Sam's life, we are in no position to deny that the suffering qua punishment has not had a reformative effect, even if we can see no such effect in his earthly life.[17]

I might be accused of begging the question by dragging in Christian convictions to support my case. But that would be a misunderstanding. I am not seeking to prove, or give grounds for, theism or Christianity. I am countering a certain argument against Christian theism. I introduce these Christian doctrines only to spell out crucial features of what is being argued against. The Christian understanding of sin, human life, God's purposes, and so on, go into the determination of what the critic must be justified in denying if she is to be justified in the conclusion that Sam's suffering would not have been permitted by God.

VI

I have led off my survey of theodical suggestions with the punishment motif, despite the fact that it is highly controversial and the reverse of popular. Nor would I want to put heavy emphasis on it were I constructing a theodicy. I have put my worst foot forward in order to show that even here the critic is in no position to show that Sam's suffering is not permitted by God for this reason. If the critic can't manage even this, he will presumably be much worse off with more plausible suggestions for divine reasons, to some of which I now turn.

One of the most prominent theodical suggestions is that God allows suffering because He is interested in a "vale of soul making." He takes it that by confronting difficulties, hardships, frustrations, perils, and even suffering and only by doing this, we have a chance to develop such qualities of character as patience, courage, and compassion, qualities we would otherwise have no opportunity to develop. This line has been set forth most forcefully in our time by John Hick in *Evil and the God of Love* (revised edition, 1978), a book that has evoked much discussion. To put the point most generally, God's purpose is to make it possible for us to grow into the kind of person that is capable of an eternal life of loving communion with Himself. To be that kind of person, one will have to possess traits of character like those just mentioned, traits that one cannot develop without meeting and reacting to difficulties and hardships, including suffering. To show that E would not be permitted by God, the critic has to show that it does not serve the "soul-making" function.

To get to the points I am concerned to make, I must first respond to some standard objections to this theodicy.

(1) God could surely just create us with the kind of character needed for fellowship with Himself, thereby rendering the hardships and suffering unnecessary. Hick's answer is that what God aims at is not fellowship with a suitably programmed robot, but fellowship with creatures who freely choose to work for what is needed and to take advantage of the opportunity thus engendered. God sees the realization of this aim for some free creatures,[18] even at the cost of suffering and hardship for all, as being of much greater value than any alternative, including a world with no free creatures and a world in which the likes of human beings come off the assembly line presanctified. As usual, I am not concerned to defend the claim that this is the way things are, but only to claim that we are in no position to deny that God is correct in this judgment. (For a discussion of difficulties in carrying out comparative evaluation of total universes, see the end of section IX.)

(2) "If God is using suffering to achieve this goal, He is not doing very well. In spite of all the suffering we undergo, most of us don't get very far in developing courage, compassion, etc." There are two answers to this. First, we are in no position to make that last judgment. We don't know nearly enough about the inner springs of peoples' motivation, attitudes, and character, even in this life. And we know nothing about any further development in an afterlife. Second, the theism under discussion takes God to respect the free will of human beings. No strategy consistent with that can guarantee that all, or perhaps any, creatures will respond in the way intended. Whether they do is ultimately up to them. Hence we cannot argue from the fact that such tactics often don't succeed to the conclusion that God wouldn't employ them. When dealing with free creatures God must, because of self-imposed limitations, use means that have some considerable likelihood of success, not means that cannot fail. It is amazing that so many critics reject theodicies like Hick's on the grounds of a poor success rate. I don't say that a poor success rate could not, under any circumstances, justify us in denying that God would permit E for the sake of soul making. If we really did know enough to be reasonably sure that the success rate is very poor *and* that other devices open to God would

be seen by omniscience to have a significantly greater chance of success, *then* we could conclude that Hick's line does not get at what God is up to. But we are a very long way indeed from being able to justifiably assert this.

We cannot take the kind of reason stressed by Hick to be a live possibility for the Bambi and Sue cases. The former is much more obvious than the latter, but even in the latter case Sue has no chance to respond to the suffering in the desired way, except in an afterlife, and it strains credulity to suppose that God would subject a five-year old to *that* for the sake of character building in the life to come. Hence once more, and until further notice, we will stick with Sam.

Let's stipulate that Sam's suffering does not appear, on close examination, to be theistically explainable as aimed by God at "soul making." He seems already to have more of the qualities of character in question than most of us, or the amount of suffering seems to be too much for the purpose, or to be so great as to overwhelm him and make character development highly unlikely. And so our best judgment is that God wouldn't be permitting his suffering for that reason. But that judgment is made in ignorance of much relevant information. Perhaps a more penetrating picture of Sam's spiritual condition would reveal that he is much more in need of further development than is apparent to us from our usual superficial perspective on such matters. Since we don't see his career after death, we are in a poor position to determine how, over the long run, he reacts to the suffering; perhaps if we had that information we would see that this suffering is a very important for his development. Moreover, we are in a poor position, or no position, to determine what is the most effective strategy for God to use in His pursuit of Sam. We don't know what alternatives are open to God, while respecting Sam's freedom, or what the chances are, on one or another alternative, of inducing the desired responses. We are in a poor position to say that this was too much suffering for the purpose, or to say how much would be just right. And we will continue to be in that position until our access to relevant information is radically improved.

Thus we cannot be justified in holding that Sam's suffering is not permitted by God in order to further His project of soul making. There is an allied but significantly different theodical suggestion by Eleonore Stump concerning which I would make the same points. Briefly, and oversimply, Stump's central suggestion is that the function of natural evil in God's scheme is to bring us to salvation, or, as she likes to put it, to contribute to the project of "fixing our wills," which have been damaged by original sin. Natural evil tends to prod us to turn to God, thereby giving Him a chance to fix our wills.

> Natural evil—the pain of disease, the intermittent and unpredictable destruction of natural disasters, the decay of old age, the imminence of death—takes away a person's satisfaction with himself. It tends to humble him, show him his frailty, make him reflect on the transience of temporal goods, and turn his affections towards other-worldly things, away from the things of this world. No amount of moral or natural evil, of course, can *guarantee* that a man will seek God's help. If it could, the willing it produced would not be free. But evil of this sort is the best hope, I think, and maybe the only effective means, for bringing men to such a state. (Stump, 1985, p. 409)

Objections will be raised somewhat similar to those that have been made to Hick. A perfectly good God wouldn't have let us get in this situation in the first place. God would employ a more effective technique.[19] There's too much suffering for the purpose. It is not distributed properly. And so on. These will be answered in the same way as the analogous objections to Hick. As for Sam, if we cannot see how his suffering was permitted by God for the reason Stump suggests, I will do a rerun of the parallel points concerning Hick's soul-making suggestion.

Closely related suggestions have been made by Marilyn McCord Adams in her essay "Redemptive Suffering: A Christian Solution to the Problem of Evil" (1986). She takes martyrdom as her model for redemptive suffering, though she by no means wishes to limit her discussion to martyrdom strictly so called: ". . . the redemptive potential of many other cases that, strictly speaking, are not martyrdoms can be seen by extrapolation" (p. 261). In other words, her suggestion is that the benefits for the martyr and others that can flow from martyrdom in the strict sense can also flow from suffering that does not involve undergoing persecution for the faith. Her bold suggestion is that "martyrdom is an expression of God's righteous love toward the onlooker, the persecutor, and even the martyr himself" (257). Here I want to focus on her account of the benefits to the martyr: ". . . the threat of martyrdom is a time of testing and judgment. It makes urgent the previously abstract dilemma of whether he loves God more than the temporal goods that are being extracted as a price . . . the martyr will have had to face a deeper truth about himself and his relations to God and temporal goods than ever he could in fair weather . . . the time of trial is also an opportunity for building a relationship of trust between the martyr and that to which he testifies. Whether because we are fallen or by the nature of the case, trusting relationships have to be built up by a history of interactions. If the martyr's loyalty to God is tested, but after a struggle he holds onto his allegiance to God and God delivers him (in his own time and way), the relationship is strengthened and deepened" (259). Adams is modest in her claims. She does not assert that all cases of suffering are analogous to martyrdom in these respects. "Some are too witless to have relationships that can profit and mature through such tests of loyalty. Some people are killed or severely harmed too quickly for such moral struggles to take place. At other times the victim is an unbeliever who has no explicit relationship with God to wrestle with."[20] However, none of these disqualifications apply to her boldest suggestion, that given the Christian doctrine of the suffering of God incarnate on the cross, "temporal suffering itself is a vision into the inner life of God" (264), a theme that she takes from Christian mysticism. That value of suffering, if such it be, can be enjoyed by any sufferer, whatever the circumstances. To be sure, one might not realize at the time that the suffering has that significance. But if one reaches the final term of Christian development, "he might be led to reason that the good aspect of an experience of deep suffering [the aspect just pointed to] is great enough that, from the standpoint of the beatific vision, the victim would not wish the experience away from his life history, but would, on the contrary, count it as an extremely valuable part of his life" (265). It should also be noted that Adams does not suggest that God's reasons for permitting suffering in any particular case are restricted to one of the considerations she has been presenting, or indeed to all of the points she makes.

If we were to try to decide whether Sam's suffering is permitted by God for any of these reasons, we would be in a poor position to make a negative judgment for reasons parallel to those brought out in the discussion of Hick. Given the limits of our access to the secrets of the human heart and the course of the afterlife, if any, we are, in many instances, in no position to assert with any confidence that this suffering does not have such consequences, and hence that God does not permit it (at least in part) for the sake of just those consequences.

VII

Thus far I have been restricting myself to conceivable divine reasons for suffering that involve the use of that suffering to bring about good for the sufferer. This is obvious except for the punishment reason. As for that one, this claim is equally obvious if we are thinking of punishment in terms of reformation of the punishee,[21] but what about a "retributive" theory, according to which the rationale of punishment is simply that the sinner *deserves* to suffer for his sin, that justice demands this, or that a proportionate suffering for wickedness is intrinsically good? Well, though one might balk at describing this as a *good* for the sufferer, it remains that such good as is aimed at and effected by the punishment, on this conception, terminates with the sufferer and does not extend to the welfare of others.

Where divine reasons are restricted this narrowly, the critic is operating on the most favorable possible terrain. If he has any hope of making his case it will be here, where the field of possibilities that must be excluded is relatively narrow. What we have seen is that wherever the reasons we have canvassed are live possibilities, even this is too much for his (our) powers. Our ignorance of relevant facts is so extensive, and the deficiencies in our powers of discernment are so fundamental, as to leave us without any sufficient basis for saying, with respect to a particular case of suffering, that God does not permit it for reasons such as these.

To be sure, this is cold comfort for the critic of Rowe's argument, since, as noted earlier, the possibilities we have been canvassing do not seem to be live possibilities for Bambi or Sue. The only real chance for an exception is Adams' suggestion that the experience of suffering constitutes a vision of the inner life of God. Since this is not confined to those who identify it as such, it could apply to Sue, and perhaps to Bambi as well, though presumably only Sue would have a chance to recognize and rejoice in it, retrospectively, in the light of the beatific vision. However, I don't want to insist on this exception. Let us say that a consideration of the theodicies thus far canvassed does nothing to show that we can't be justified in affirming an instantiation of 1 for Bambi or Sue.

Nevertheless, that does *not* show that we can be justified in excluding the possibility that God has no patient-centered reason for permitting Bambi's or Sue's suffering. It doesn't show this because we are not warranted in supposing that the possible reasons we have been extracting from theodicies exhaust the possibilities for patient-centered reasons God might have for permitting Bambi's or Sue's suffering. Perhaps, unbeknownst to us, one or the other of these bits of suffering is necessary, in ways we cannot grasp, for some outweighing good of a sort with which we are familiar, e.g., supreme fulfillment of one's deepest nature. Or perhaps it is necessary for the realization of a good of which we as yet have no conception. And these possibilities are by no means remote ones. "There are more things in heaven and earth, Horatio, than are dreamt of in your philosophy." Truer words were never spoken. They point to the fact that our cognitions of the world, obtained by filtering raw data through such conceptual screens as we have available for the nonce, acquaint us with only some indeterminable fraction of what there is to be known. The progress of human knowledge makes this evident. No one explicitly realized the distinction between concrete and abstract entities, the distinction between efficient and final causes, the distinction between knowledge and opinion, until great creative thinkers adumbrated these distinctions and disseminated them to their fellows. The development of physical science has made us aware of a myriad of things hitherto undreamed of, and developed the concepts with which to grasp them—gravitation, electricity, electromagnetic fields, space-time curvature, irrational numbers, and so on. It is an irresistible induction from this that we have not reached the final term of this process, and that more realities, aspects, properties, structures remain to be discerned and conceptualized. And why should values, and the conditions of their realization, be any exception to this generalization? A history of the apprehension of values could undoubtedly be written, parallel to the history just adumbrated, though the archeology would be a more difficult and delicate task.

Moreover, remember that our topic is not the possibilities for future human apprehensions, but rather what an omniscient being can grasp of modes of value and the conditions of their realization. Surely it is eminently possible that there are real possibilities for the latter that exceed anything we can anticipate, or even conceptualize. It would be exceedingly strange if an omniscient being did not immeasurably exceed our grasp of such matters. Thus there is an unquestionably live possibility that God's reasons for allowing human suffering may have to do, in part, with the appropriate connection of those sufferings with goods in ways that have never been dreamed of in our theodicies. Once we bring this into the picture, the critic is seen to be on shaky ground in denying, of Bambi's or Sue's suffering, that God could have any patient-centered reason for permitting it, even if we are unable to suggest what such a reason might be.[22]

This would be an appropriate place to consider Rowe's argument that we can be justified in excluding the possibility that God permits one or another case of suffering in order to obtain goods of which we have no conception. In his 1988 article on the subject, Rowe claims that the variant of 1 there put forward:

Q. No good state of affairs is such that an omnipotent, omniscient being's obtaining it would morally justify that being in permitting E1 or E2 (p. 120)[23]

can be derived probabilistically from:

P. No good state of affairs we know of is such that an omnipotent, omniscient being's obtaining it would morally justify that being's permitting E1 or E2. (p. 121)

I have been arguing, and will continue to argue, that Rowe is not justified in asserting P, since he is not justified in supposing that none of the particular goods we have been discussing provide God with sufficient reason for permitting the suffering of Bambi and Sue. But even if Rowe were justified in asserting P, what I have just been contending is that the argument from P to Q does not go through. In defending the argument Rowe says the following:

> My answer is that we are justified in making this inference in the same way we are justified in making the many inferences we constantly make from the known to the unknown. All of us are constantly inferring from the A's we know of to the A's we don't know of. If we observe many A's and all of them are B's we are justified in believing that the A's we haven't observed are also B's. If I encounter a fair number of pit bulls and all of them are vicious, I have reason to believe that all pit bulls are vicious. (1988, pp. 123-124)

But it is just not true that Rowe's inference from known goods to all goods is parallel to inductive inferences we "constantly make." Typically, when we generalize from observed instances, at least when we are warranted in doing so, we know quite a lot about what makes a sample of things like that a good base for general attributions of the properties in question. We know that temperamental traits like viciousness or affection are often breed-specific in dogs, and so when a number of individuals of a breed are observed to exhibit such a trait it is a good guess that it is characteristic of that breed. If, on the other hand, the characteristic found throughout the sample were a certain precise height or a certain sex, our knowledge indicates that an inference that all members of that breed are of that height or of that sex would be foolhardy indeed. But, as I have been arguing, an inference from known goods lacking J to all goods (including those we have never experienced and even those of which we have no conception) is unlike both the sorts just mentioned in the way they resemble one another, viz., our possession of knowledge indicating which characteristics can be expected to be (fairly) constant in the larger population. We have no background knowledge that tells us the chances of J's being a "goods-specific" characteristic, one that can reasonably be expected to be present in all or most goods if it is found in a considerable sample. Hence we cannot appeal to clearly warranted generalizations in support of this one. Rowe's generalization is more like inferring, from the fact that no one has yet produced a physical theory that will unify relativity and quantum mechanics, the prediction that no one will ever do so, or inferring, in 1850, from the fact no one has yet voyaged to the moon that no one will ever do so. We have no way of drawing boundaries around the total class of goods; we are unable to anticipate what may lie in its so-far-unknown subclass, just as we are unable to anticipate future scientific developments and future artistic innovations. This is not an area in which induction by simple enumeration yields justified belief.[24]

VIII

It is now time to move beyond the restriction on divine reasons to benefits to the sufferer. The theodical suggestions we will be discussing from here on do
not observe this restriction. Since I am moving onto territory less favorable to my
opponent, I must give some indication of what might justify dropping the restriction. For my central purposes in this paper I do not need to show that the restriction is unjustified. I take myself to have already shown that the critic is not entitled
to his "no sufficient divine reasons" thesis, even with the restriction. But I do
believe that the restriction is unwarranted, and I want to consider how the land lies
with respect to conceivable divine reasons of other sorts. As a prelude to that, I
will point out the main reasons for and against the restriction to benefits to the sufferer.

On the pro side, by far the main consideration is one of justice and fairness. Why should suffering be laid on me for the sake of some good in which I will
not participate, or in which my participation is not sufficient to justify my suffering? Wouldn't God be sacrificing me to His own ends and/or to the ends of others
if that were His modus operandi, and in that case how could He be considered perfectly good? As Stump writes,

> Undeserved suffering which is uncompensated seems clearly unjust; but so does
> suffering compensated only by benefits to someone other than the sufferer . . .
> other things being equal, it seems morally permissible to allow someone to suf-
> fer involuntarily only in case doing so is a necessary means or the best possible
> means in the circumstances to keep the sufferer from incurring even greater
> harm.[25]

I agree with this to the extent of conceding that a perfectly good God
would not wholly sacrifice the welfare of one of His intelligent creatures simply in
order to achieve a good for others, or for Himself. This would be incompatible
with His concern for the welfare of each of His creatures. Any plan that God would
implement will include provision for each of us having a life that is, on balance, a
good thing, and one in which the person reaches the point of being able to see that
his life as a whole is a good for him. Or at least, where free creaturely responses
have a significant bearing on the overall quality of the person's life, any possible
divine plan will have to provide for each of us to have the chance (or perhaps many
chances) for such an outcome, if our free responses are of the right sort. Nevertheless, this is compatible with God having as part of His reason for permitting a
given case of suffering that it contributes to results that extend beyond the sufferer.[26] So long as the sufferer is amply taken care of, I can't see that this violates
any demands of divine justice, compassion, or love. After all, parents regularly
impose sacrifices on some of their children for the overall welfare of the family. Of
course, in doing so they are acting out of a scarcity of resources, and God's situation is enormously different in this respect. Nevertheless, assuming that Sue's suffering is necessary even for God to be able to achieve a certain good state of affairs,
then, provided that Sue is taken care of in such a way that she will eventually come

to recognize the value and justifiability of the proceeding and to joyfully endorse it (or at least has ample opportunities to get herself into this position), I cannot see that God could be faulted for setting things up this way.[27]

From now on I will be considering possible divine reasons that extend beyond benefit to the sufferer. Though in line with the previous paragraph I will not suppose that any of these (so far as they exclusively concern persons other than the sufferer) could be God's whole reason for permitting a bit of suffering, I will take it as a live possibility that they could contribute to a sufficient divine reason. The theodicies to be considered now will give us more specific suggestions for Bambi and Sue.

I will begin with the familiar free-will theodicy, according to which God is justified in permitting creaturely wickedness and its consequences because He has to do so if He is to bestow on some of His creatures the incommensurable privilege of being responsible agents who have, in many areas, the capacity to choose between alternatives as they will, without God, or anyone or anything else (other than themselves), determining which alternative they choose. The suggestion of this theodicy is that it is conceptually impossible for God to create free agents and also determine how they are to choose, within those areas in which they are free. If He were so to determine their choices they would, ipso facto, not be free. But this being the case, when God decided to endow some of His creatures, including us, with free choice, He thereby took the chance, ran the risk, of our sometimes or often making the wrong choice, a possibility that has been richly realized. It is conceptually impossible for God to create free agents and not subject Himself to such a risk. Not to do the latter would be not to do the former. But that being the case, He, and we, are stuck with whatever consequences ensue. And this is why God permits such horrors as the rape, beating, and murder of Sue. He does it not because that particular wicked choice is itself necessary for the realization of some great good, but because the permission of such horrors is bound up with the decision to give human beings free choice in many areas, and that (the capacity to freely choose) is a great good, such a great good as to be worth all the suffering and other evils that it makes possible.[28]

This theodicy has been repeatedly subjected to radical criticisms that, if sound, would imply that the value of creaturely free will is not even a possible reason for God's allowing Sue's attacker to do his thing. For one thing, it has been urged that it is within God's power to create free agents so that they always choose what is right. For another, it has been denied or doubted that free will is of such value as to be worth all the sin and suffering it has brought into the world. In accord with my general policy in this paper, I will not attempt to argue that this theodicy does succeed in identifying God's reasons for permitting wrongdoing and its results, but only that the possibility of this cannot be excluded. Hence I can confine myself to arguing that these criticisms do not dispose of that possibility. Though lack of space prevents a proper discussion, I will just indicate what I would say in such a discussion. On the first point, if we set aside middle knowledge as I am doing in this paper, it is logically impossible for God to create beings with genuine freedom of choice and also guarantee that they will always choose the right.

And even granting middle knowledge, Plantinga (1974) has established the *possibility* that God could not actualize a world containing free creatures that always do the right thing. As for the second point, though it may be beyond our powers to show that free will has sufficient value to carry the theodical load, it is surely beyond our powers to show that it does not.[29]

Thus we may take it to be a live possibility that the maintenance of creaturely free will is at least part of God's reason for permitting wrongdoing and its consequences. But then the main reason one could have for denying that this is at least part of why God would allow the attack on Sue is that God could, miraculously or otherwise, prevent any one incipient free human action without losing the value of human free will. Clearly a divine interference in normal human operations in this one instance is not going to prevent even Sue's attacker from being a free moral agent in general, with all that involves. This point is supported by the consideration that, for all we know, God does sometimes intervene to prevent human agents from doing wicked things they would otherwise have done, and, so the free-will theodicist will claim, even if that is the case we do enjoy the incommensurable value of free choice. We can also think of it this way. It is perfectly obvious that the scope of our free choice is not unlimited. We have no effective voluntary control over, e.g., our genetic constitution, our digestive and other biological processes, and much of our cognitive operations. Thus whatever value the human capacity for free choice possesses, that value is compatible with free choice being confined within fairly narrow limits. But then presumably a tiny additional constriction such as would be involved in God's preventing Sue's attacker from committing that atrocity would not render things radically different, free-will-wise, from what they would have been without that. So God could have prevented this without losing the good emphasized by this theodicy. Hence we can be sure that this does not constitute a sufficient reason for His not preventing it.

To be sure, if God were to act on this principle in every case of incipient wrongdoing, the situation would be materially changed. Human agents would no longer have a real choice between good and evil, and the surpassing worth that attaches to having such a choice would be lost. Hence, if God is to promote the values emphasized by the free-will theodicy, He can intervene in this way in only a small proportion of cases. And how are these to be selected? I doubt that we are in a position to give a confident answer to this question, but let's assume that the critic proposes that the exceptions are to be picked in such a way as to maximize welfare, and let's go along with that. Rowe's claim would then have to be that Sue's murder was so horrible that it would qualify for the class of exceptions. But that is precisely where the critic's claims far outrun his justification. How can we tell that Sue falls within the most damaging n percent of what would be cases of human wrongdoing apart from divine intervention? To be in a position to make such a judgment we would have to survey the full range of such cases and make reliable assessments of the deleterious consequences of each. Both tasks are far beyond our powers. We don't even know what free creaturely agents there are beyond human beings, and with respect to humans the range of wickedness, past, present, and future, is largely beyond our ken. And even with respect to the cases of which we are aware, we have only a limited ability to assess the total consequences. Hence, by the nature of the case, we are simply not in a position to make a warranted judgment that Sue's case is among the n percent worst cases of wrongdoing in the history of the universe. No doubt it strikes us as incomparably horrible on hearing about it, but so would innumerable others. Therefore, the critic is not in a position to set aside the value of free will as at least part of God's reason for permitting Sue's murder.

IX

Next I turn to theodicies that stress benefit to human beings other than the sufferer or to humanity generally.[30] And first let's return to Marilyn Adams's discussion of martyrdom (1986). In addition to her account, already noted, of martyrdom as a vehicle of God's goodness to the martyr, she discusses "martyrdom as a vehicle of God's goodness to the onlooker." "For onlookers, the event of martyrdom may function as a prophetic story, the more powerful for being brought to life. The martyr who perseveres to the end presents an inspiring example. . . . Onlookers are invited to see in the martyr the person they ought to be and to be brought to a deeper level of commitment. Alternatively, onlookers may see themselves in the persecutor and be moved to repentance. If the onlooker has ears to hear the martyr's testimony, he may receive God's redemption through it" (p. 257). She also suggests that martyrdom may be redemptive for the persecutor. "First of all, the martyr's sacrifice can be used as an instrument of divine judgment, because it draws the persecutor an external picture of what he is really like—the more innocent the victim, the clearer the focus. . . . In attempting to bring reconciliation out of judgment, God may find no more promising vehicle than martyrdom for dealing with the hard-hearted" (p. 258). (Again, in making these suggestions for a theodicy of suffering, Adams is not restricting their scope to martyrdom strictly so called.) To be sure, sometimes there is no persecutor, but often there is, as in child and wife abuse. And there is always the possibility, and usually the actuality, of onlookers.[31]

Can the critic be justified in holding that Sue's suffering, e.g., would not be permitted by God at least in part for reasons of these sorts? Once more, even if we cannot see that Sue's suffering brings these kinds of benefits to her attacker or to onlookers, our massive ignorance of the recesses of the human heart and of the total outcomes, perhaps through eternity, for all such people, renders us poor judges of whether such benefits are indeed forthcoming. And, finally, even if no goods of these sorts eventuate, there is once more the insoluble problem of whether God could be expected to use a different strategy, given His respect for human free will. Perhaps that was a part of the strategy that held out the best chance of evoking the optimal response from these particularly hard-hearted subjects.

Next I want to consider a quite different theodicy that also sees God's reasons for permitting suffering in terms of benefits that are generally distributed, viz., the appeal to the benefits of a lawlike natural order, and the claim that suffering will be an inevitable byproduct of any such order. I choose the exposition of this theodicy in Bruce Reichenbach's *Evil and a Good God* (1982): "creation, in order to make possible the existence of moral agents . . . had to be ordered according to some set of natural laws" (p. 101). The argument for this is that if things do not happen in a lawlike fashion, at least usually, agents will be unable to anticipate the consequences of their volitions, and hence will not be able to effectively make significant choices between good and evil actions. Reichenbach continues:

> Consequently, the possibility arises that sentient creatures like ourselves can be negatively affected by the outworkings of these laws in nature, such that we experience pain, suffering, disability, disutility, and at times the frustration of our good desires. Since a world with free persons making choices between moral good and evil and choosing a significant amount of moral good is better than a world without free persons and moral good and evil, God in creating had to create a world which operated according to natural laws to achieve this higher good. Thus, his action of creation of a natural world and a natural order, along with the resulting pain and pleasure which we experience, is justified. The natural evils which afflict us—diseases, sickness, disasters, birth defects—are all the outworking of the natural system of which we are a part. They are the byproducts made possible by that which is necessary for the greater good. (100-101)

This is a theodicy for natural evil, not for the suffering that results from human wickedness. Hence it has possible application to Bambi, but not to Sue, and possible application to any other suffering that results from natural processes that are independent of human intentional action.

Let's agree that significant moral agency required a natural lawful order. But that doesn't show that it is even possible that God had a sufficient reason to allow Bambi's suffering. There are two difficulties that must be surmounted to arrive at that point.

First, a natural order can be regular enough to provide the degree of predictability required for morally significant choice even if there are exceptions to the regularities. Therefore, God could set aside the usual consequences of natural forces in this instance, so as to prevent Bambi's suffering, without thereby interfering with human agents' reasonable anticipations of the consequences of their actions. So long as God doesn't do this too often, we will still have ample basis for suppositions as to what we can reasonably expect to follow what. But note that by the same line of reasoning God cannot do this too often, or the desired predictability will not be forthcoming. Hence, though any one naturally caused suffering could have been miraculously prevented, God certainly has a strong prima facie reason in each case to refrain from doing this; for if He didn't He would have no reason for letting nature usually take its course. And so He has a possible reason for allowing nature to take its course in the Bambi case, a reason that would have to be overridden by stronger contrary considerations.

This means that in order to be justified in supposing that God would not have a sufficient reason to refrain from intervening in this case, we would have to be justified in supposing that God would have a sufficient reason to make, in this case, an exception to the general policy. And how could we be justified in supposing that? We would need an adequate grasp of the full range of cases from which God would have to choose whatever exceptions He is going to make, if any, to the general policy of letting nature take its course. Without that we would not be in a position to judge that Bambi is among the n percent of the cases most worthy of being miraculously prevented.[32] And it is abundantly clear that we have and can have no such grasp of this territory as a whole. We are quite unable, by our natural powers, of determining just what cases, or even what kinds of cases, of suffering there would be throughout the history of the universe if nature took its course. We just don't know enough about the constituents of the universe even at present, much less throughout the past and future, to make any such catalogue. And we could not make good that deficiency without an enormous enlargement of our cognitive capacities. Hence we are in no position to judge that God does not have sufficient reason (of the Reichenbach sort) for refraining from interfering in the Bambi case.[33]

But all this has to do with whether God would have interfered with the natural order, as it actually exists, to prevent Bambi's suffering. And it will be suggested, secondly, that God could have instituted a quite different natural order, one that would not involve human and animal suffering, or at least much less of it. Why couldn't there be a natural order in which there are no viruses and bacteria the natural operation of which results in human and animal disease, a natural order in which rainfall is evenly distributed, in which earthquakes do not occur, in which forests are not subject to massive fires? To be sure, even God could not bring into being just the creatures we presently have while subjecting their behavior to different laws. For the fact that a tiger's natural operations and tendencies are what they are is an essential part of what makes it the kind of thing it is.[34] But why couldn't God have created a world with different constituents so as to avoid subjecting any sentient creatures to disease and natural disasters? Let's agree that this is possible for God. But then the critic must also show that at least one of the ways in which God could have done this would have produced a world that is better on the whole than the actual world. For even if God could have instituted a natural order without disease and natural disasters, that by itself doesn't show that He would have done so if He existed. For if that world had other undesirable features and/or lacked desirable features in such a way as to be worse, or at least no better than, the actual world, it still doesn't follow that God would have chosen the former over the latter. It all depends on the overall comparative worth of the two systems. Once again I am not concerned to argue for Reichenbach's theodicy, which would, on the rules by which we are playing, require arguing that no possible natural order is overall better than the one we have. Instead I merely want to show that the critic is not justified in supposing that some alternative natural order open to God that does not involve suffering (to the extent that we have it) is better on the whole.

There are two points I want to make about this, points that have not cropped up earlier in the paper. First, it is by no means clear what possibilities are open to God. Here it is important to remember that we are concerned with metaphysical possibilities (or necessities), not merely with conceptual or logical possibilities in a narrow sense of "logical." The critic typically points out that we can consistently and intelligibly conceive a world in which there are no diseases, no earthquakes, floods, or tornadoes, no predators in the animal kingdom, while all or most of the goods we actually enjoy are still present. He takes this to show that it is possible for God to bring about such a world. But, as many thinkers have recently argued,[35] consistent conceivability (conceptual possibility) is by no means sufficient for metaphysical possibility, for what is possible given the metaphysical structure of reality. To use a well-worn example, it may be metaphysically necessary that the chemical composition of water is H_2O, since that is what water essentially is, even though, given the ordinary concept of water, we can without contradiction or unintelligibility think of water as made up of carbon and chlorine. Roughly speaking, what is conceptually or logically (in a narrow sense of "logical") possible depends on the composition of the concepts, or the meanings of the terms, we use to recognize reality, while metaphysical possibility depends on what things are like in themselves, their essential natures, regardless of how they are represented in our thought and language.

It is much more difficult to determine what is metaphysically possible or necessary than to determine what is conceptually possible or necessary. The latter requires only careful reflection on our concepts. The former requires—well, it's not clear what will do the trick, but it's not something we can bring off just by reflecting on what we mean by what we say, or on what we are committing ourselves to by applying a certain concept. To know what is metaphysically possible in the way of alternative systems of natural order, we would have to have as firm a grasp of this subject matter as we have of the chemical constitution of familiar substances like water and salt. It is clear that we have no such grasp. We don't have a clue as to what essential natures are within God's creative repertoire, and still less do we have a clue as to which combinations of these into total lawful systems are doable. We know that you can't have salt without sodium and chlorine. But can there be life without hydrocarbons? Who knows? Can there be conscious, intelligent organisms with free will that are not susceptible to pain? That is, just what is metaphysically required for a creature to have the essential nature of a conscious, intelligent, free agent? Who can say? Since we don't have even the beginnings of a canvass of the possibilities here, we are in no position to make a sufficiently informed judgment as to what God could or could not create by way of a natural order that contains the goods of this one (or equal goods of other sorts) without its disadvantages.

One particular aspect of this disability is our inability to determine what consequences would ensue, with metaphysical necessity, on a certain alteration in the natural order. Suppose that predators were turned into vegetarians. Or rather, if predatory tendencies are part of the essential natures of lions, tigers, and the like, suppose that they were replaced with vegetarians as much like them as possible. How much like them is that? What other features are linked to predatory tendencies by metaphysical necessity? We may know something of what is linked to predation by natural necessity, e.g., by the structure and dispositional properties of genes. But to what extent does metaphysical possibility go beyond natural possibility here? To what extent could God institute a different system of heredity such that what is inseparable from predation in the actual genetic code is separable from it instead?

Who can say? To take another example, suppose we think of the constitution of the earth altered so that the subterranean tensions and collisions involved in earthquakes are ruled out. What would also have to be ruled out, by metaphysical necessity? (Again, we know something of what goes along with this by natural necessity, but that's not the question.) Could the earth still contain soil suitable for edible crops? Would there still be mountains? A system of flowing streams? We are, if anything, still more at a loss when we think of eradicating all the major sources of suffering from the natural order. What metaphysical possibilities are there for what we could be left with? It boggles the (human) mind to contemplate the question.[36]

The second main point is this. Even if we could, at least in outline, determine what alternative systems of natural order are open to God, we would still be faced with the staggering job of comparative evaluation. How can we hold together in our minds the salient features of two such total systems sufficiently to make a considered judgment of their relative merits? *Perhaps* we are capable of making a considered evaluation of each feature of the systems (or many of them), and even capable of judicious comparisons of features two-by-two. For example, we might be justified in holding that the reduction in the possibilities of disease is worth more than the greater variety of forms of life that goes along with susceptibility to disease. But it is another matter altogether to get the kind of overall grasp of each system to the extent required to provide a comprehensive ranking of those systems. We find it difficult enough, if not impossible, to arrive at a definitive comparative evaluation of cultures, social systems, or educational policies. It is far from clear that even if I devoted my life to the study of two primitive cultures, I would thereby be in a position to make an authoritative pronouncement as to which is better on the whole. How much less are we capable of making a comparative evaluation of two alternative natural orders, with all the indefinitely complex ramification of the differences between the two.[37]

Before leaving this topic I want to emphasize the point that, unlike the theodicies discussed earlier, the natural law theodicy bears on the question of animal as well as human suffering. If the value of a lawful universe justifies the suffering that results from the operation of those laws, that would apply to suffering at all levels of the great chain of being.

X

I have been gleaning suggestions from a variety of theodicies as to what reasons God might have for permitting suffering. I believe that each of these suggestions embodies one or more sorts of reasons that God might conceivably have for some of the suffering in the world. And I believe that I have shown that none of us are in a position to warrantedly assert, with respect to any of those reasons, that God would not permit some cases of suffering for that reason. Even if I am mistaken in supposing that we cannot rule out some particular reason, e.g., that the suffering is a punishment for sin, I make bold to claim that it is extremely unlikely that I am mistaken about all those suggestions. Moreover, I have argued, successfully I believe, that some of these reasons are at least part of possible divine reasons for Rowe's cases, Bambi and Sue, and that hence we are unable to justifiably assert that God does not have reasons of these sorts for permitting Rowelike cases.

However, that does not suffice to dispose of Rowe's specific argument, concerned as it is with the Bambi and Sue cases in particular. For I earlier conceded, for the sake of argument, that (1) none of the sufferer-centered reasons I considered could be any part of God's reasons for permitting the Bambi and Sue cases, and (2) that nonsufferer-centered reasons could not be the whole of God's reasons for allowing any case of suffering. This left me without any specific suggestions as to what might be a fully sufficient reason for God to permit those cases. And hence showing that no one can be justified in supposing that reasons of the sort considered are not at least part of God's reasons for one or another case of suffering does not suffice to show that no one can be justified in supposing that God could have no sufficient reason for permitting the Bambi and Sue cases. And hence it does not suffice to show that Rowe cannot be justified in asserting 1.

This lacuna in the argument is remedied by the point that we cannot be justified in supposing that there are no other reasons, thus far unenvisaged, that would fully justify God in permitting Rowe's cases. That point was made at the end of section VII for sufferer-centered reasons, and it can now be made more generally. Even if we were fully entitled to dismiss all the alleged reasons for permitting suffering that have been suggested, we would still have to consider whether there are further possibilities that are undreamt of in our theodicies. Why should we suppose that the theodicies thus far excogitated, however brilliant and learned their authors, exhaust the field? The points made in the earlier discussion about the impossibility of anticipating future developments in human thought can be applied here. Just as we can never repose confidence in any alleged limits of future human theoretical and conceptual developments in science, so it is here, even more so if possible. It is surely reasonable to suppose that God, if such there be, has more tricks up His sleeve than we can envisage. Since it is in principle impossible for us to be justified in supposing that God does not have sufficient reasons for permitting E that are unknown to us, and perhaps unknowable by us, no one can be justified in holding that God could have no reasons for permitting the Bambi and Sue cases, or any other particular cases of suffering.[38]

This last point, that we are not warranted in supposing that God does not have sufficient reasons unknown to us for permitting E, is not only an essential part of the total argument against the justifiability of 1. It would be sufficient by itself. Even if all my argumentation prior to that point were in vain and my opponent could definitively rule out all the specific suggestions I have put forward, she would still face the insurmountable task of showing herself to be justified in supposing that there are no further possibilities for sufficient divine reasons. That point by itself would be decisive.

XI

In the case of each of the theodical suggestions considered I have drawn on various limits to our cognitive powers, opportunities, and achievements in arguing that we are not in a position to deny that God could have that kind of reason for various cases of suffering. In conclusion it may be useful to list the cognitive limits that have formed the backbone of my argument.

1. *Lack of data.* This includes, inter alia, the secrets of the human heart, the detailed constitution and structure of the universe, and the remote past and future, including the afterlife if any.

2. *Complexity greater than we can handle.* Most notably there is the difficulty of holding enormous complexes of fact—different possible worlds or different systems of natural law—together in the mind sufficiently for comparative evaluation.

3. *Difficulty of determining what is metaphysically possible or necessary.* Once we move beyond conceptual or semantic modalities (and even that is no piece of cake) it is notoriously difficult to find any sufficient basis for claims as to what is metaphysically possible, given the essential natures of things, the exact character of which is often obscure to us and virtually always controversial. This difficulty is many times multiplied when we are dealing with total possible worlds or total systems of natural order.

4. *Ignorance of the full range of possibilities.* This is always crippling when we are trying to establish negative conclusions. If we don't know whether or not there are possibilities beyond the ones we have thought of, we are in a very bad position to show that there can be no divine reasons for permitting evil.

5. *Ignorance of the full range of values.* When it's a question of whether some good is related to E in such a way as to justify God in permitting E, we are, for the reason mentioned in 4, in a very poor position to answer the question if we don't know the extent to which there are modes of value beyond those of which we are aware. For in that case, so far as we can know, E may be justified by virtue of its relation to one of those unknown goods.

6. *Limits to our capacity to make well-considered value judgments.* The chief example of this we have noted is the difficulty in making comparative evaluations of large complex wholes.

It may seem to the reader that I have been making things too difficult for the critic, holding him to unwarrantedly exaggerated standards for epistemic justification. "If we were to apply your standards across the board," he may complain, "it would turn out that we are justified in believing little or nothing. That would land us in a total skepticism. And doesn't that indicate that your standards are absurdly inflated?" I agree that it would indicate that if the application of my standards did have the result, but I don't agree that this is the case. The point is that the critic is engaged in attempting to support a particularly difficult claim, a claim that there isn't something in a certain territory, while having a very sketchy idea of what is in that territory, and having no sufficient basis for an estimate of how much of the territory falls outside his knowledge. This is very different from our more usual situation in which we are forming judgments and drawing conclusions about matters concerning which we antecedently know quite a lot, and the boundaries and parameters of which we have pretty well settled. Thus the attempt to show that God could have no sufficient reason for permitting Bambi's or Sue's suffering is quite atypical of our usual cognitive situation; no conclusion can be drawn from our poor performance in the former to an equally poor performance in the latter.[39]

I want to underline the point that my argument in this paper does not rely on a general skepticism about our cognitive powers, about our capacity to achieve knowledge and justified belief. On the contrary, I have been working with what I take to be our usual nonskeptical standards for these matters, standards that I take to be satisfied by the great mass of our beliefs in many areas. My claim has been that when these standards are applied to the kind of claim exemplified by Rowe's 1, it turns out that this claim is not justified and that the prospects for any of us being justified in making it are poor at best. This is because of the specific character of that claim, its being a negative existential claim concerning a territory about the extent, contents, and parameters of which we know little. My position no more implies, presupposes, or reflects a general skepticism than does the claim that we don't know that there is no life elsewhere in the universe.

This completes my case for the "agnostic thesis," the claim that we are simply not in a position to justifiably assert, with respect to Bambi or Sue or other cases of suffering, that God, if He exists, would have no sufficient reason for permitting it. And if that is right, the inductive argument from evil is in no better shape than its late lamented deductive cousin.

NOTES

"The Inductive Argument from Evil and the Human Cognitive Condition," by William P. Alston, appeared in *Philosophical Perspectives, 5, Philosophy of Religion, 1991* edited by James E. Tomberlin (copyright by Ridgeview Publishing Co., Atascadero, CA). Reprinted by permission of Ridgeview Publishing Company.

1. The term *gratuitous* is used in different ways in the literature. Lately it has sprouted variations (Hasker, 1992). My use of the term is strictly tied to Rowe's 1.

2. Rowe (1979) considers this criticism. Rowe says of it: "I suppose some theists would be content with this rather modest response. . . . But given the validity of the basic argument and the theist's likely acceptance of (2), he is thereby committed to the view that (1) is false, not just that we have no good reasons for accepting (1) as true" (338). No doubt the theist is committed to regarding (1) as false, at least on the assumption that it embodies necessary conditions for God's having sufficient reason for permitting suffering (on which see F in section II of this paper). But Rowe does not explain why he thinks that showing that we are not justified in asserting 1 does not constitute a decisive reason for rejecting his argument.

3. There is considerable confusion in the literature over what it takes to have a theodicy, or, otherwise put, what a reasonable level of aspiration is for theodicy. Even if we were vouchsafed an abundance of divine revelations, I cannot conceive of our being able to specify God's reason for permitting each individual evil. The most that could sensibly be aimed at would be an account of the sorts of reasons God has for various sorts of evil. And a more modest, but still significant, ambition would be to make suggestions as to what God's reasons might be, reasons that are plausible in the light of what we know and believe about God, His nature, purposes, and activities. See Stump, 1990.

4. In arguing for 1, Rowe (1979) proceeds as if he supposed that the only alternatives are (a) its being reasonable to believe 1 and (b) its being reasonable to believe not-1. "Consider again the case of the fawn's suffering. Is it reasonable to believe that there is some greater good so intimately connected to that suffering that even an omnipotent, omniscient being could not have obtained that good without permitting that suffering or some evil at least as bad? It certainly does not appear reasonable to believe this. Nor does it seem reasonable to believe that there is some evil at least as bad as the fawn's suffering such that an omnipotent being simply could not have prevented it without permitting the fawn's suffering. But even if it should somehow be reasonable to believe either of these things of the fawn's suffering, we must then ask whether it is reasonable to believe either of these things of *all* the instances of seemingly pointless human and animal suffering that occur daily in our world. And surely the answer to this more general question must be no. . . . It seems then that although we cannot *prove* that (1) is true, that (1) is a *rational* belief" (337-38). The form of this argument is: "It is not rational to believe that p. Therefore it is rational to believe that not-p." But this is patently lacking in force. There are many issues on which it is rational to believe neither p nor not-p. Take p to be, e.g., the proposition that it was raining on this spot exactly 45,000 years ago.

5. The qualifier *traditional* adheres to the restrictions laid down in D and excludes variants like process theology. Admittedly, the term *traditional Christianity* contains a number of in-house variants, but in this paper I will appeal only to what is common to all forms of what could reasonably be called "traditional Christianity."

6. Rowe does not often use the term *justified belief,* but instead usually speaks of its being "rational" to hold a belief. I shall ignore any minor differences there may be between these epistemic concepts.

7. The point at issue here is whether being nongratuitous in this sense is necessary for divine permission. But there is also a question as to whether it is sufficient. Would any outweighing good for which a particular bit of suffering is necessary, however trivial and insignificant that good, justify that suffering? Suppose that some minor suffering on my part is necessary for my enjoying my dinner to the extent I did, and that the enjoyment outweighs the suffering? Would that give God a reason for permitting the suffering? I doubt it. Again, suppose that E is necessary for some greater good, but that the universe as a whole would be better without E and the greater good than with them? Would God be justified in permitting E? (Note that Rowe's substitute for 1 in Rowe, 1986, is in terms of the world as a whole: "There exist evils that O [God] could have prevented, and had O prevented them the world as a whole would have been better" (228).) However, I am not concerned here with what is sufficient for God to have a reason for permitting evil, only with what is necessary for this.

8. This presupposes that God does not enjoy "middle knowledge." For if He did, He could see to it that suffering would be imposed on people only where they will in fact make the desired response. I owe this point to William Hasker.

9. Such a theodicy will be discussed in section IX.

10. There are also more radical objections to Rowe's 2. I think particularly of those who question or deny the principle that God would, by virtue of His nature, create the best possible universe or, in case there can be no uniquely best possible universe, would create a universe that comes up to some minimal evaluative level. See, e.g., R. Adams (1987). On these views an argument like Rowe's never gets out of the starting gate. Though I have some sympathy with such views, I will not take that line in this paper.

11. See, e.g., Ahern (1971), Fitzpatrick (1981), Reichenbach (1982), Wykstra (1984).

12. To be sure, 1 is in the form of a positive existential statement. However, when we consider an instantiation of it with respect to a particular case of suffering, E, as Rowe does in arguing for it, it turns out to be a negative existential statement about E, that "there is no sufficient divine reason for permitting E." It is statements of this form that, I claim, no one can be justified in making.

13. Wykstra labors under the additional burden of having to defend a thesis as

to the conditions under which one is justified in making an assertion of the form "It appears that p," and much of the considerable literature spawned by his article is taken up with this side issue.

14. Hence the very common procedure, of knocking down theodical suggestions one by one by pointing out in the case of each that there are evils it does not cover, will not suffice to make the critic's case. For it may be that even though no one divine reason covers all cases, each case is covered by some divine reason.

15. It is often dismissed nowadays on the grounds that it presupposes a morally unacceptable theory of punishment, viz., a retributive conception. But it need not make any such presupposition; whatever the rationale of punishment, the suggestion is that (in some cases) God has that rationale for permitting suffering. Though it must be admitted that the "retributive" principle that "it is intrinsically good that persons should suffer for wrongdoing" makes it easier to claim that suffering constitutes justifiable punishment than a reformatory theory does, where a necessary condition for the justification of punishment is the significant chance of an improvement of the punishee. For purposes of this discussion I will not choose between different theories of punishment.

16. I don't mean to suggest that a person's inner sinfulness or saintliness cannot be expected to manifest itself in behavior. Still less do I mean to suggest that one could be fully or ideally living the life of the spirit, whatever her outward behavior.

17. Rowe writes: "Perhaps the good for which *some* intense suffering is permitted cannot be realized until the end of the world but it certainly seems likely that much of this good could be realized in the lifetime of the sufferer. . . . In the absence of any reason to think that O [God] would need to postpone these good experiences, we have reason to expect that many of these goods would occur in the world we know" (1986, 244-45). But why suppose that we are entitled to judge that justifying goods, if any, would be realized during the sufferer's earthly life, unless we have specific reasons to the contrary? Why this initial presumption? Why is the burden of proof on the suggestion of the realization of the goods in an afterlife? Rowe doesn't say, nor do I see what he could say.

18. Actually, Hick is a universalist and believes that all free creatures will attain this consummation; but I do not take this thesis as necessary for the soul-making theodicy.

19. Stump gives her answer to this one in the passage quoted.

20. All these disclaimers may well apply to Sue.

21. Here, of course, as in the other cases in which God's action is designed to evoke a free response from the patient, there is no guarantee that the reformation will be effected. But it still remains true that the good aimed at is a good for the sufferer.

22. There is, to be sure, a question as to why, if things are as I have just suggested they may be, God doesn't fill us in on His reasons for permitting suffering. Wouldn't a perfectly benevolent creator see to it that we realize why we are called upon to suffer? I acknowledge this difficulty; in fact it is just another form taken by the problem of evil. And I will respond to it in the same way. Even if we can't see why God would keep us in the dark on this matter, we cannot be justified in supposing that God does not have sufficient reason for doing so.

23. E1 is Bambi's suffering and E2 is Sue's suffering. There are, of course, various differences between Q and 1. For one thing, Q, unlike 1, makes reference to God's being morally justified. For another, Q has to do with God's *obtaining* particular goods, apparently leaving out of account the cases in which cooperation from human free choice is required. However, these differences are not germane to the present point.

24. Cf. the criticism of Rowe's move from P to Q in Christlieb (forthcoming). Note too that Rowe restricts his consideration of the unknown to "good states of affairs" we do not know of. But, as is recognized in my discussion, it is an equally relevant and equally live possibility that we do not grasp ways in which good states of affairs we know of are connected with cases of suffering so as to provide God with a reason for permitting the latter. Both types of unknown factors, if realized, would yield divine reasons for permitting suffering of which we are not cognizant.

25. Stump (1990), 66. Many other thinkers, both theistic and atheistic, concur in this judgment.

26. Note that I am assuming what seems to be obvious, that God might have a number of reasons for permitting a particular case of suffering, no one of which reasons is sufficient by itself, though the whole complex is. This obvious possibility is often ignored when critics seek to knock down theodical suggestions one by one.

27. In "Victimization and the Problem of Evil" (forthcoming), Thomas F. Tracy persuasively argues that although "God must not actualize a world that contains persons whose lives, through no fault of their own, are on balance an evil (i.e., an intrinsic disvalue) for them rather than a good" (20), nevertheless, we cannot also claim that "God must not actualize a world in which a person suffers some evil E if the elimination of E by God would result in a better balance *for this individual* of the goods God intends for persons and the evils God permits" (23).

28. The reader may well wonder why it is only now that I have introduced the free-will theodicy, since it has such an obvious application to Sue's case. The reason is that I wanted at first to focus on those suggestions that confined the rationale of suffering to benefit to the sufferer.

29. On this point, see the discussion in section IX of our inability to make evaluative comparisons on the scale required here.

30. Or to other creatures. Most discussions of the problem of evil are markedly anthropocentric, in a way that would not survive serious theological scrutiny.

31. These suggestions will draw many of the objections we have already seen to be leveled against Hick's, Stump's, and Adams's sufferer-centered points. See section VI for a discussion of these objections.

32. There are also questions about whether we are capable of making a reasonable judgment as to which cases from a given field have the strongest claim to being prevented. Our capacity to do this is especially questionable where incommensurable factors are involved, e.g., the worth of the subject and the magnitude of the suffering. But let this pass.

33. The reader will, no doubt, be struck by the similarity between this problem and the one that came up with respect to the free-will theodicy. There too it was agreed that God can occasionally, but only occasionally, interfere with human free choice and its implementation without sacrificing the value of human free will. And so there too we were faced with the question of whether we could be assured that a particular case would be a sufficiently strong candidate for such interference that God would have sufficient reason to intervene.

34. Reichenbach, 110-11.

35. See, e.g., Kripke (1972), Plantinga (1974).

36. I hope it is unnecessary to point out that I am not suggesting that we are incapable of making any reasonable judgments of metaphysical modality. Here, as elsewhere, my point is that the judgments required by the inductive argument from evil are of a very special and enormously ambitious type and that our cognitive capacities that serve us well in more limited tasks are not equal to this one. (For more on this general feature of the argument, see the final section.) Indeed, just now I contrasted the problem of determining what total systems of nature are metaphysically possible with the problem of the chemical composition of various substances, where we are in a much better position to make judgments of metaphysical modality.

37. This point cuts more than one way. For example, theodicists often confidently assert, as something obvious on the face of it, that a world with free creatures, even free creatures who often misuse their freedom, is better than a world with no free creatures. But it seems to be that it is fearsomely difficult to make this comparison and that we should not be so airily confident that we can do so. Again, to establish a natural law theodicy along Reichenbach's lines one would have to show that the actual natural order is at least as beneficial as any possible alternative; and the considerations I have been adducing cast doubt

on our inability to do this. Again, please note that in this paper I am not concerned to defend any particular theodicy.

     38. For Rowe's objection to this invocation of the possibility of humanly unenvisaged divine reasons for permitting suffering, and my answer thereto, see the end of section VII.

     39. See the end of section VII for a similar point.

REFERENCES

Adams, Marilyn McCord. "Redemptive Suffering: A Christian Solution to the Problem of Evil." In *Rationality, Religious Belief, and Moral Commitment,* ed. R. Audi and W. J. Wainwright. Ithaca: Cornell University Press, 1986.

Adams, Robert M. "Must God Create the Best?" *The Virtue of Faith and Other Essays in Philosophical Theology.* New York: Oxford University Press, 1987, 51-64.

Ahern, M. B. *The Problem of Evil* (London: Routledge and Kegan Paul, 1971).

Christlieb, Terry. "Which Theisms Face an Evidential Problem of Evil?" *Faith and Philosophy* 9 (1992): 45-64.

Fitzpatrick, F. J. "The Onus of Proof in Arguments about the Problem of Evil." *Religious Studies* 17 (1981): 19-38.

Hasker, William. "The Necessity of Gratuitous Evil." *Faith and Philosophy* 9 (1992): 23-44.

Hick, John. *Evil and the God of Love.* 2d ed. (New York: Harper & Row, 1978).

Keller, James. "The Problem of Evil and the Attributes of God," *International Journal for Philosophy of Religion* 26 (1989): 155-71.

Kripke, Saul A. "Naming and Necessity." In *Semantics of Natural Language,* ed. Donald Davidson and Gilbert Harman (Dordrecht: Reidel, 1972).

Plantinga, Alvin. *The Nature of Necessity.* Oxford: Clarendon Press, 1974.

Reichenbach, Bruce. *Evil and a Good God.* New York: Fordham University Press, 1982.

Rowe, William L. "The Problem of Evil and Some Varieties of Atheism." *American Philosophical Quarterly* 16 (1979): 335-41.

————— "The Empirical Argument from Evil." In *Rationality, Religious Belief, and Moral Commitment,* ed. R. Audi and W. J. Wainwright. Ithaca: Cornell University Press, 1986.

————— "Evil and Theodicy." *Philosophical Topics* 16 (1988): 119-32.

Russell, Bruce. "The Persistent Problem of Evil." *Faith and Philosophy* 6 (1989): 121-39.

Stump, Eleonore. "The Problem of Evil." *Faith and Philosophy* 2 (1985): 392-424.

————— "Providence and the Problem of Evil." In *Christian Philosophy,* ed. Thomas P. Flint (Notre Dame: University of Notre Dame Press, 1990), 51-91.

Tracy, Thomas F. "Victimization and the Problem of Evil." *Faith and Philosophy* 9 (1992): 301-29.

Wykstra, Stephen. "The Humean Obstacle to Evidential Arguments from Suffering: On Avoiding the Evils of 'Appearance.'" *International Journal for Philosophy of Religion* 16 (1984): 73-94.

7.

STEPHEN JOHN WYKSTRA

Rowe's Noseeum Arguments from Evil

In the Midwest we have "noseeums"—tiny flies which, while having a painful bite, are so small you "no see 'um." We also have Rowe's inductive argument for atheism. Rowe holds that the theistic God would allow suffering only if doing so serves some outweighing good. But is there some such good for every instance of suffering? Rowe thinks not. There is much suffering, he says, for which we *see no* such goods; and this, he argues, inductively justifies believing that for some sufferings there *are no* such goods. Since it gives such bite to what we cannot see, I call this a "noseeum argument" from evil.

In 1984, I criticized Rowe's induction using CORNEA, the "Condition of Reasonable Epistemic Access." In brief, CORNEA says that we can argue from "we see no X" to "there is no X" only when X has "reasonable seeability"—that is, is the sort of thing which, if it exists, we *can reasonably expect* to see in the situation. Looking around my garage and seeing no dog entitles me to conclude that none is present, but seeing no flea does not; and this is because fleas, unlike dogs, have low seeability: even if they were present, we cannot reasonably expect to see them in this way. But should we expect God-purposed goods to have the needed seeability? Arguing from the disparity between a creator's vision and ours, I urged not: Rowe's case thus fails CORNEA's seeability requirement.

In reply, Rowe says he accepts CORNEA's seeability test; he argues, however, that his argument passes the test. His central objection is that the disparity between God's vision and ours is "no reason whatever" to think God's purposes would lack the required seeability. But underlying our dispute about this are subtler issues. Rowe correctly sees CORNEA as a strategy for "defeating" inductive justifications. I shall argue, however, that he misportrays CORNEA, and that this is due to an underlying difference in our views of how defeaters work. After clarifying this underlying difference, I shall defend the view of defeaters implicit in CORNEA, and use this to improve the CORNEA critique in view of Rowe's central objection.

1. Rowe's Noseeum Case and the CORNEA Critique

Rowe's noseeum case involves two main claims. The first is that God would allow an instance of intense suffering only if doing so serves some outweighing good obtainable only by God's allowing this (or some comparable) evil.[1] Like many theists, I accept this claim. Rowe's second claim is that some sufferings serve no such God-justifying purpose. The two claims together entail that God does not exist; a theist who accepts the first must thus reject the second. But Rowe supports the second by his noseeum evidence. What is this evidence, then, and how strong is it?

1.1 ROWE'S NOSEEUM ARGUMENT

Rowe gives two formulations of his argument for his second big claim. Both begin with a particular case: a fawn, burned in a distant forest fire, lies in agony for days before dying. We see no good served by God's allowing this suffering. And this, Rowe says, is good reason to conclude that there is no such good. Why is this so?

Rowe's original 1979 article puts the inference in "the Appears Mode." Since we cannot see (or think of) any outweighing good served by the suffering, Rowe says, the suffering surely "does not appear" to serve any such good. But it is a well-known epistemic principle (the "principle of credulity")[2] that if something appears to be a certain way, then, provided there is no counterevidence, it is reasonable for us to believe X is that way. That much suffering does not appear to serve any outweighing good, Rowe claims, gives strong rational support that there is no such good (and so, given his first big claim, no God). Letting e be the fawn's suffering, his key moves are:

(1) We see no good for which God would allow e

to

(1.9) There appears to be no good for which God allows e.

to

(2) There is no good for which God allows e.

Later Rowe formulates this as an induction. A good has J, he stipulates, just in case obtaining it would suffice to justify God in allowing the fawn's suffering. The key inference then is:

(1) All goods we see lack J

to

(2) All goods there are lack J.

(1) and (2) here say the same thing as above. Rowe no longer needs the intermediate (1.9), because this formulation—as he sees it—makes the argument a standard inductive inference of the sort that we rely upon constantly (e.g., in moving from "all copper we have observed is conductive" to "all copper is conductive").[3]

1.2 SUMMARY OF CORNEA

The original CORNEA critique was aimed at the first formulation and sought to block the move from 1 to 1.9. In my view, what made Rowe's initial formulation so seductive was the ambiguous character of the "appears" claim (1.9). On first reading, this claim seems to go little beyond the noseeum facts codified in (1)—we see no point to the suffering, so, "surely," it does not appear that there is any point—the suffering "appears pointless." I argued that the appears-claim goes far beyond the initial facts. For one thing, Rowe (in accord with ordinary English, but not strict philosophical precision) uses "does not appear" to mean "appears not" (just as "Tom does not appear to be sane" ordinarily means "Tom appears not to be sane"). For another, he uses "appears" in its so-called "epistemic" sense rather than its weaker comparative or phenomenological senses; only so can he move (by the Principle of Credulity) from his premise about how things seem (1.9) to his conclusion about how they are (2). These two things mean that his appears claim (1.9) asserts far more than one might first think. Imagine a doctor, squinting at a used hypodermic needle and seeing no germs, inferring first that the needle does not appear to have any germs on it (i.e., that it appears germless), and from this, that it does not have any germs on it (that it is germless). We should, I believe, resist the doctor's inference at the first step: the claim that the needle appears germless is a very big claim quite unwarranted by the doctor's seeing no germs. Similarly, I contended, Rowe's inference must be questioned at its first step. To grant (1.9) lets Rowe not just in the game but ninety-nine yards down the field.

CORNEA, then, is a strategy for evaluating appears claims. Its application to Rowe has three stages.

Stage A propounds CORNEA itself. CORNEA says that a situation of seeing no X justifies one's claiming "it appears there is no X" only if it is reasonable for one to believe that X is something to which we would likely have "epistemic access" in the situation. The official formulation of CORNEA (Wykstra [1984], 85),* applied to Rowe's inference, was:

---

*References not given in the notes will be found in the bibliography at the end of this book.

On the basis of his seeing no God-justifying good served by the fawn's suffering, Rowe is entitled to claim "It appears that there is no such good" only if it is reasonable for Rowe to believe that, given his cognitive faculties and the use he has made of them, if the fawn's suffering served such a good, he would likely see (have epistemic access to) it.

In other words, CORNEA says that Rowe's noseeum situation justifies his appears claim only if *it is reasonable for Rowe to believe that a God-justifying good for the fawn's suffering would likely be "seeable."* Let us call this "the reasonable seeability requirement."[4] My first article (Wykstra [1984], 87) stressed how "reasonable to believe" is to be understood:

> in here requiring that it be "reasonable" for [Rowe] to believe that [a divine purpose would be seeable], I do not mean to require that [Rowe] believe this in any conscious or occurrent way. I mean, roughly, only that should the matter be put to [Rowe], it would be reasonable for him to affirm that the condition is satisfied: that is, no norms of reasonable belief would be violated by his believing this. This need not always involve his having, or being able to produce, an evidential or inferential justification for so believing: in some cases, this might properly be believed in a basic way. But even . . .

Stage B arose from precisely this stipulation. While basic justifiers can make a belief reasonable, they can still be defeated by inference from other beliefs. I thus continued (Wykstra [1984], 87):

> But even in these cases [where reasonableness derives from basic rather than inferential justifiers], if [Rowe] has been made aware of good reasons for thinking a God-justifying good would not likely be seeable, then it will not be reasonable for [Rowe] to believe it likely would be seeable—unless he defeats these reasons with other considerations. And in now applying CORNEA to Rowe's case, I shall provide good reasons for thinking that [a God-justifying good would not likely be seeable].

This passage thus sets forth a principle distinct from CORNEA itself, used to determine whether the reasonable seeability requirement of CORNEA itself is met. Let us call it *"the Adjunct Principle"*:

> If [Rowe] is made aware of good reasons to think[5] that a God-justifying good would not likely be seeable, then conditionally (i.e., "unless [Rowe] defeats these with other considerations"), it is not reasonable for [Rowe] to believe that they likely would be seeable.

Stage C, finally, puts forward a reason to think a God-justifying good for the fawn's suffering would not likely be seeable. The disparity between God's vision and ours, I suggested, is comparable to the gap between the vision of a parent and her one-month-old infant. This gives reason to think that our discerning most of God's purposes are about as likely as the infant's discerning most of the parent's purposes. And this, I claimed by further arguments, gives reason to think that a God-justifying good for the fawn's suffering would not likely be seeable. By the adjunct principle, we can then say that, conditionally, the reasonable seeability condition is not met; by CORNEA itself, Rowe's inference thus fails.

The CORNEA critique can also be applied to the inductive inference version of Rowe's argument.

Stage A becomes: Rowe's premise (1) We see no good with J justifies his conclusion (2) There is no good with J only if it is reasonable for Rowe to believe that if there were a good with J, his noseeum situation would likely be different than (1) asserts.

Stage B, the adjunct principle, becomes:

> If Rowe has reason to think that if there were a good with J, his noseeum situation would likely be the same as 1 asserts, then it is not reasonable for Rowe to believe the above.

Stage C, lastly, would give Rowe "reason to think" that if there were a good with J, his noseeum situation would likely be the same as 1 asserts.

Put more tersely, Stage A says that Rowe's inference from 1 to 2 works only if it is reasonable for Rowe to believe that *if 2 were false, his situation would likely be different than 1 says it is.* Stage B says that it will (conditionally) not be reasonable for Rowe to believe the preceding proposition if Rowe has reason to think that if 2 were false, then 1 would be expectable anyway. And Stage C says that Rowe does have reason to think that if 2 were false, 1 would be expectable anyway. This terse formulation will be most relevant to Rowe's later responses to CORNEA.

1.3 ON "RATIONAL SUPPORT"

Rowe's overall thesis is that our seeing no God-justifying good for much suffering provides "rational support" for the claim that there is no God-justifying good served by such suffering, and hence (given his first big claim) that there is no God. A great deal depends on what we take this to mean. Clearly, Rowe does not mean that noseeum evils raise the probability that there is no such good (and so no God) merely to some small degree. Rather, he is claiming that they are of great evidential weight: they suffice, he says, to make atheism "*altogether* reasonable to believe," and to render theism "an *extraordinary absurd* idea, quite beyond our belief" (Rowe [1979], 337-38). Call this "Rowe's Weightiness Thesis."

Giving a precise construal of Rowe's Weightiness Thesis is not easy. Rowe does not mean that his noseem evidence is so weighty that no possible evidence for God could overcome it. But neither (for reasons too technical to go into here) can he mean only that it is weighty enough to make atheism entirely reasonable and theism beyond belief, if it were the only relevant evidence (so that apart from it, one would be in a total evidential vacuum on the matter).

One plausible construal of Rowe's Weightiness Thesis is that noseeum evidence is weighty enough to "lever" a person from one justified belief-state to a "lower" one. There are three main belief-states to be considered: the state of square belief (that God exists), the state of "nonbelief" (i.e., of being "agnostic" on the matter); and the state of square "disbelief" (i.e., of squarely believing that God does not exist). The Weightiness Thesis is then that noseeum evils are weighty enough to "lever" a reasonable person from one square state to another state.

An analogy may be helpful here. Instead of the proposition that God exists, consider the proposition that some particular husband—Michael Douglas, let us call him—has been faithful. Someone—say, his wife—might squarely believe that Michael is faithful, or she might consider this a fifty-fifty proposition (nonbelief), or she might squarely disbelieve it (i.e, squarely believe that Michael is not faithful). Now let us suppose that his wife, based on her evidence and grounds so far, is properly in one of these states; she then acquires a new piece of evidence. We now have two possibilities. Some evidence—say, finding a long blonde hair on Michael's lapel—might slightly increase the probability that Michael is unfaithful but be nowhere near weighty enough to lever a wife (if she is reasonable) from square belief to square nonbelief or even square disbelief. Other evidence—say, a videotape of Michael hot-tubbing in the altogether with another woman—might be weighty enough to lever a reasonable wife from square belief to square nonbelief, or from square nonbelief to square disbelief, or even all the way from square belief to square disbelief. Rowe's Weightiness Thesis, as I shall construe it, is then that noseeum evils are like the videotape, not like the long hair: they are weighty enough to constitute, as I shall call it, "levering evidence," suffi- cient to move one from one rational square belief-state to another (given ample but not overwhelming warrant for the initial belief-state).[6]

Two further points about levering evidence will aid later discussion. First, given the three main belief-states, we can distinguish several kinds of lever- ing evidence. Levering evidence of the first and second kinds would suffice to lever a reasonable person only "one step"—from proper square nonbelief to proper square disbelief, or from proper square belief to proper square nonbelief, respec- tively. Levering evidence of the third kind would suffice to lever a reasonable per- son "two steps"—from proper square belief to proper square disbelief. Clearly, evidence might be weighty enough to be of the first or second kind, but not the third. It is not clear which kind Rowe means to ascribe to noseeum evidence. If someone adducing evidence regarding Michael were to say (in Rowe's words) that it makes it "altogether reasonable" to believe that Michael is unfaithful, and indeed makes the claim that he is faithful "an extraordinary absurd idea, quite beyond belief," we would certainly construe him as claiming that it is of the first and sec- ond kinds, and perhaps even of the third kind. We shall therefore consider each of these three possibilities in what follows.

A second point concerns how belief-states are to be understood if we suppose that the probability calculus applies to them and to relations of evidential support. Suppose a belief-state of square nonbelief toward some proposition is interpreted as assigning a probability of .5 to that proposition: the proposition is as likely true as not. What probability should then be assigned to represent square belief that the proposition is true, or square belief that it is false? There is, so far as I know, no good answer to this question. My own inclinations are as follows. On one hand, one can believe something—say, that my wife is in Grand Rapids today—while allowing that one might be mistaken; to believe (or disbelieve) thus need not be assigning a probability of 1 (or 0). On the other hand, even a probability well above .5 falls short of amounting to belief. Consider the proposition "This nickel will not come up heads on the next two consecutive throws." There is a probability of .75 that this is true; yet I do not *believe* it is true. If it were to come up heads on both throws, I would not say, "Oh dear, I had a false belief." If we are to assign some probability to *belief* that something is true, it must be a probability not very far from 1—something well above .95, I would think. Disbelief (that is, belief in the denial) of some proposition would be assigned something well under .05.[7] If we are going to try to represent belief probabilistically, we must spread the state of nonbelief, or "agnosticism," over a relatively large part of the interval between 0 and 1 (though the paradigm case would be .5), and confine the states of belief or disbelief near the endpoints of this interval. Levering evidence for atheism of the first, second, and third kinds, then, is evidence sufficient, respectively, to lever an initial belief-state of around .5 to something under .05, or to lever an initial belief-state of over .95 to around .5, or to lever an initial belief-state of around .95 to around .05. In the example above, I think our intuition is that the videotape described would be levering evidence (perhaps even of the third kind); nevertheless, it might still be defeated or outweighed by truly exceptional evidence for her husband's faithfulness.

My primary concern here will be with whether Rowe's noseeum evidence is levering evidence; this, I believe, is the most natural interpretation of his claim that it makes atheism "entirely reasonable to believe," and makes theism "an extraordinary absurd claim, quite beyond belief." We should also ask, however, whether evidence might be less than levering, but still much more than minuscule—say, weighty enough to change the tilt of agnosticism from a completely centered nonbelief (rating theism and atheism each at .5) to agnosticism with a strong tilt toward atheism (say, rating theism at only .25, and atheism at .75). Suppose we call evidence that can do this "tilting evidence." It is tempting to assume that if Rowe's data could be tilting evidence to this degree, it could also be levering evidence of (say) the second kind: both, after all, reduce the probability assigned to theism by about half. I shall, however, question this assumption. A third question will be whether noseeum evidence is relevant evidence at all.

2. Rowe's Rendition and the Great Divide

Before examining Rowe's criticism of the CORNEA critique, it is important to scrutinize his rendition of it. Though Rowe says he accepts CORNEA's basic strategy, we shall see that he omits the "burden of reasonability" that CORNEA places on the proponent. I shall then argue that this reflects a deep difference in our perspectives on defeaters, and that CORNEA has the right perspective.

2.1 ROWE'S RENDITION OF CORNEA

First consider Rowe's rendition of CORNEA as applied to the "appears formulation" of his case. Rowe says the CORNEA critique, when "put in its simplest terms," has two steps (Rowe [1984], 95ff.; Rowe [1986], 237). The first step stipulates that we can go from 1 (we see no good served by the fawn's suffering) to 1.9 (there appears to be no good served by it) only if the requirement is met that:

> (R1) we have no reason to think that *if the fawn's suffering served a God-purposed good, then things would likely strike us in pretty much the* same *(noseeum) way.*

CORNEA's second step, Rowe says, argues that requirement R1 is not met—i.e., that we do *have* reason to think the italicized claim in R1 is true.

Rowe contrasts this two-step strategy with an alternative two-step strategy. The alternative would, as its first step, claim that we can go from (1) to (1.9) only if the requirement is met that:

> (R2) we *have* reason to think that *if the fawn's suffering served some God-purposed good, then it would likely strike us* differently *than it does (i.e., differently from a noseeum way).*

(The alternate strategy would then claim, as the second step, that requirement R2 is not met—i.e., that we do *not* have reason to think the italicized claim in R2 is true.) Rowe asserts that a close reading of the text shows CORNEA's strategy to be of the first sort, basing itself on requirement R1, not R2.

But is Rowe right about this? I do not think so. For CORNEA itself, placing a strong burden of reasonability on Rowe (the proponent), says the noseeum inference works only if it is reasonable for Rowe to believe that if the fawn's suffering serves some God-justifying good, it would likely strike us differently than it does. Of the two strategies Rowe describes, only the second (not the first) comes close to preserving this burden of reasonability that CORNEA itself places on the proponent.[8] And as we shall see, this in turn affects how we interpret the expression "reason to think" in the Adjunct Principle.

Rowe performs the same surgery on CORNEA after shifting to his inductive mode. His noseeum inference is now from (P) "We see no good with J" to (Q) "There is no good with J." He again distinguishes two possible defeater strategies. One holds that the inference works only if the proponent lacks reason to believe that *if Q were not true, P would likely be the* same *as it is.* The second holds that an inference from P to Q works only if the proponent *has* reason to believe that *if Q were not true, P would likely be* different *than it is.* This precisely parallels the two defeater strategies he distinguishes in the appears mode; and here too, Rowe takes seriously only the first,[9] regarding it as the essence of CORNEA. But again this is mistaken: the second strategy is closer to CORNEA, because it comes closest to placing on the proponent the "burden of reasonability" that is central to CORNEA itself.

2.2 ROWE'S UNDERLYING PERSPECTIVE ON DEFEATERS

Rowe sees CORNEA as a strategy for "defeating" his noseeum evidence. He here begins from John Pollock's distinction between "undercutting defeaters" and "rebutting defeaters."[10] Suppose (to steal Pollock's example) you are touring a widget factory, and notice that the widgets on the assembly belt appear red. This prima facie justifies you in believing that the widgets on the belt are red. The justification might, however, be "defeated," and this in two ways. The first is by acquiring further evidence that, contrary to appearances, the widgets are some color other than red. Perhaps a worker assures you that they are really white; perhaps you then notice that they appear white when, at the end of the belt, they drop into the widget box. Such evidence might defeat your initial evidence by outweighing it: it would then be what Pollock calls a "rebutting" defeater. But suppose that, instead of this, you learn only that the belt is illuminated by strong red light (which you know makes nonred objects appear red). This new information is not evidence that the widgets are some color other than red; nevertheless, it renders you no longer justified in believing (from their appearing red) that the widgets are red. It defeats your previously sufficient justification not by outweighing it but by "undercutting" it.

Rowe sees CORNEA as a strategy for defeating noseeum evidence in the sense of providing undercutting defeaters. This seems to me right. But how do undercutting defeaters of inductive evidence work?

To see Rowe's perspective on defeaters, we must begin with his conception of inductive justifiers. In glossing his noseeum inference as inductive, Rowe says ([1988], 123):

> we are justified in making this inference in the same way we are justified in making the many inferences we constantly make from the known to the unknown. All of us are constantly inferring from the A's we know of to the A's we don't know of. If we observe many A's and all of them are B's we are justified in believing that the A's we haven't observed are B's.

I shall refer to a premise of the sort Rowe specifies (a premise characterizing our information about our specific observed sample, e.g., "we have tested many pieces of copper, and all of them were conductive") as the "specific premise" of an inductive argument. Rowe holds, then, that the specific premise of his noseeum argument justifies its general conclusion in the same way that all inductive premises do. But what way is this? Rowe's key claim here is that the specific premise of an induction is "in itself" justifying reason to think the conclusion is true. Consider his reply to Del Lewis, who had objected that Rowe's argument does not work unless a further premise is added (namely, that if there were a point to intense suffering, we likely would know of it). Lewis, Rowe replied ([1988], 132):

> is assuming that if P were *all we knew* relative to the truth or falsity of Q, we would not be rationally justified in believing Q. It is this claim that I am rejecting as false. (My emphasis.)

In rejecting this, Rowe is saying that P by itself—even if it were "*all we know relative to*"Q—would justify our believing that Q. Nothing further is needed.

In the next section I shall criticize this "nothing-further-needed" view of justifiers. Here, note how it leads Rowe to a conception of undercutting defeaters.

Since he takes the specific premise of an adequate induction to be *by itself* reason to believe the conclusion, he holds that one cannot defeat this premise merely by showing that there is some further proposition which we should *refrain* from believing. (The induction, after all, needs nothing further.) Defeating an induction must thus be by addition rather than subtraction—that is, by adding to our belief corpus some further warranted proposition, which has a defeating relation to the induction. Rowe gives no account of this defeating relation, but all his examples are couched to express the idea that it is "by addition." The inference from "all observed pit bulls are vicious" to "all pit bulls are vicious" is, he says, defeated if we acquire the *further* warranted belief that the pit bulls we have observed were all trained for fighting. The inference from "the widgets appear red" to "the widgets are red" is defeated if we acquire a further belief that the widgets are illuminated by red light.

This conception helps us understand Rowe's surgery on CORNEA. The real CORNEA says that for Rowe's inference to work, something further *is* needed: it must be reasonable for Rowe to *believe* the further proposition that if some good did have J, then we likely would see it. Rowe's inference will be defeated if this is subtracted: take it away, CORNEA says, and Rowe's induction collapses of its own weight. This makes no sense, of course, given Rowe's "nothing further needed" conception of induction and induction-defeaters. On his conception, what should really be doing the work is the Adjunct Principle. Why not, then, consider the burden of reasonability that is central to CORNEA as vestigial—just snip it off, and not mention it to the patient? From Rowe's perspective this is an act of charity; the patient may feel differently.

2.3 CORNEA'S PERSPECTIVE ON DEFEATERS

CORNEA embodies a different conception of induction and induction-defeaters. It says that something further is needed for one to move from (P) "We see no good with J" to (Q) "There is no good with J": what is needed is that it be reasonable to believe that if some good did have J, then we likely would see it (instead of having the noseeum data that Rowe adduces). On this conception, we can thus defeat the inference "by subtraction"—that is, by subtracting, from the body of things it is reasonable for us to believe, the proposition that if there were a God-purposed good for the fawn's suffering, it would likely be seeable.

I believe CORNEA's conception is best, even in illuminating the examples of defeaters Rowe provides. CORNEA says an inductive inference from (P) "We see no good with J" to (Q) "There is no good with J" works only if it is reasonable to believe the proposition that *if Q were false, then likely P would be false too.* This proposition is virtually equivalent[11] to the proposition that *if P is true, then Q is likely true.* So all CORNEA really says is that premise P justifies our believing conclusion Q only if it is reasonable for us to believe that if P is true, then Q is likely true. While not earth-shaking, this does illuminate Rowe's examples. The inference from "the widgets appear red" to "the widgets are red" is undercut by learning the "further" defeating proposition about the red light. But why is this a defeater? It is because learning about the red light makes it *no longer* reasonable for us to believe that if these widgets were not red, they likely would appear differently than they do (namely, red). The "further" proposition forces us to subtract, from the corpus of things it is reasonable for us to believe, the proposition identified by CORNEA itself. Similarly, learning that the observed pit bulls were trained for fighting makes it no longer reasonable for us to believe that if some pit bulls were friendly, then likely we'd have something different than the vicious data cited.

So Rowe's examples give no reason to prefer his perspective over CORNEA's. Indeed, do not his examples tell against his own perspective? Can a specific premise P really be levering evidence for Q, if we are avowed agnostics about the conditional that if P is true, then likely Q is true? If we had to suspend judgment about this conditional, would the premise by itself (so that it is, as he says, "all we know relative to the conclusion") do the job? Perhaps it could increase to some degree the probability of the conclusion, but Rowe claims it could justify believing the conclusion. This seems to me mistaken.

3. Enhancing CORNEA: Toward a New Adjunct Principle

Let me summarize. The heart of the real CORNEA was that Rowe's inference works only if it is reasonable (on Rowe's part) to believe that God's purposes for the evils he cites would be seeable. Rowe's inference would be defeated, then, if the critic can give good reason to think God's purposes would be "nonseeable." Hence, the Adjunct Principle:

> If Rowe is made aware of good reasons for thinking that God-justifying goods would lack seeability, then conditionally (i.e., unless Rowe defeats these with other considerations), it is not reasonable for Rowe to believe that these goods would be seeable.

This formulation, however, was seriously ambiguous. To make it more precise we must answer at least three questions. First, what meaning should be assigned to the expression "good reasons for thinking"? Second, exactly what claim must these reasons support? And third, what resources can be used in giving such reasons? My failure to be clear about these matters led to infelicities in my 1984 article, which Rowe's central objection amply exploited. I now want to acknowledge and remove these infelicities, so as to prepare the way for a reply to Rowe's central objection.

3.1 ON "GOOD REASONS FOR THINKING"

My 1984 Adjunct Principle enjoins the critic to give "good reasons for thinking" that God's purposes would lack seeability. But this is open to strong or modest interpretation. It might mean, strongly, giving reasons which justify believing that they would lack seeability. Or, more modestly, it might mean giving reasons which support their lacking seeability, so as to require suspension of belief on this matter.

It is clear, I believe, that CORNEA itself requires only the modest version. For if the critic gives reasons requiring Rowe to suspend belief about whether

God's purposes would be seeable, then the burden of reasonability required by CORNEA will not be satisfied. The stronger version would do more than CORNEA requires; the modest version is entirely sufficient.

In responding to my 1984 critique, however, Rowe interprets "reason to think" in the stronger sense. The reasons I give, he says, are "insufficient to justify the claim" that if O were to exist the sufferings in our world would appear as they do." Did he thereby misinterpret my 1984 Adjunct Principle? Probably not. In my reckless youth, it appears that instead of distinguishing the two versions, I instinctively went for the knock-out punch, trying to justify believing that God's purposes would lack seeability.[12] Rowe's response was tactically correct; but my treatment of the Adjunct Principle was clearly impetuous, going beyond what CORNEA requires.

3.2 WHAT PROPOSITION NEEDS SUPPORT?

The critic, then, can defeat Rowe's inference by giving modest reason to think that God's purposes would lack seeability. But exactly what is the proposition here? There are three confusions we must avoid about this.

We can spot the first by noting that Rowe at one point objects that I give no reason to think that "the goods in virtue of which God permits most suffering" would be in the unseen future (Rowe [1984], 165). But so far as I can find, Rowe argues from the premise that many instances of suffering are noseeums (not that most of them are). By CORNEA, therefore, the critic need only give reason to think that if God exists, God's purposes for allowing many sufferings would be noseeums.

Rowe also argues from a particular evil (the fawn suffering in the distant forest). Must the critic then give modest reason to think that if God exists, it is expectable that this particular case would be a noseeum? I think not. For these particular cases are Rowe-selected incidents; and so far, Rowe has made no pretense of getting them by some method of random sampling. Rather, he picks them because they, of the evils he knows, best support his noseeum argument. If we have reason to think it expectable that God-justifying goods would be beyond our ken for many instances of suffering, then, given plausible assumptions about Rowe's ability to choose telling examples, we have reason to think this expectable for these Rowe-selected cases.

But what does "expectable" mean here? Here again are two options, making ambiguous our earlier discussions.[13] It might mean, strongly, that if God exists, there is a probability of 1 or very nearly 1 that many evils will be noseeums—that (as I shall put it) it is "utterly expectable" that many evils will be noseeums. Or, more modestly, it might mean that if God exists, this is as (or more) likely than not—that is, "entirely unsurprising." Which meaning, we must ask, is required by CORNEA?

I believe only the modest sense is required. For CORNEA says Rowe's induction works only if it is reasonable for Rowe to believe that *if there were God-justifying goods for all sufferings, then, likely, we would not have the noseeum data (many evils being noseeums) we do.* Now if we have modest reason to think that if God exists, it is as likely as not that many evils would be noseeums, then we would have to suspend judgment about this italicized proposition. The burden CORNEA itself places on the proponent thus would not be satisfied. By CORNEA, then, modest reasons would provide an ample defeater to Rowe's inference.

If we suppose the probability calculus applies to relations of evidential support, this conclusion can be reinforced by Bayes's theorem. Bayes's theorem says that the "new probability" of hypothesis H (when evidence e is added to background knowledge k) is equal to the old probability (of H on k alone) times "the relevance quotient." The relevance quotient is the theoretical expectability of e if we assume H is true, divided by its theoretical expectability if we don't assume this. That is:

$$P(H/e\&k) = P(H/k) \times \frac{P(e/H\&k)}{P(e/k)}$$

Now this may seem to imply that modest reasons are really irrelevant. Suppose Rowe faces an urn which he knows contains either 100 black balls, or a mix of 50 black balls and 50 white balls. He randomly draws a ball, and it is black. This datum, he infers, is strong evidence that the urn is the one containing the 100 black balls. We seek to defeat this by pointing out to him that his datum is "entirely unsurprising" on the alternate hypothesis. Rowe might reply by appealing to the relevance quotient. While admitting his datum is entirely unsurprising on the mixed-urn hypothesis, he might note that it is far more expectable—indeed, utterly expectable—on the black-urn hypothesis. Plugging the relevant numbers into the relevance quotient, and making a few calculations, Rowe could then show us that if one initially rated both hypotheses at .5, his datum would alter this to rating the black-urn hypothesis twice as likely to be true as the mixed-urn hypothesis. Bayes's' theorem, he might thus urge, shows that so-called modest defeaters are quite irrelevant.

But this conclusion is askew. For what modest defeaters are relevant *to*, is the claim that Rowe's datum is levering evidence against theism and for atheism.[14] Rowe's datum does indeed (given the initial probabilities) make the black-urn hypothesis "twice as likely" to be true as the mixed-urn hypothesis. But this means only that it raises the black-urn hypothesis from .5 to .66, and lowers the mixed-urn hypothesis from .5 to .33. This is not negligible, but neither does it justify Rowe's *believing* he is facing the black urn, not the mixed urn. His datum justifies not abandoning "agnosticism," but giving a tilt to it.

Is "tilting evidence" enough to sustain Rowe's claim regarding the seriousness of noseeum suffering?[15] Suppose books are being stolen from the library at Mayberry U, and that the thief must be either a student or a faculty member. Andy, the security director, believes that the thief is a student. His assistant Barney, more cynical about professors, rates as roughly equal the "faculty hypothesis" and "student hypothesis." They then find evidence establishing that the culprit is a male. Now Barney (noting that the Mayberry faculty is entirely male), urges that this new datum makes it "entirely reasonable" to believe the faculty hypothesis, and to dismiss the student hypothesis as "an extraordinary absurd idea, quite beyond our belief." Andy rejects this: noting that half the students are also males, he points out that if the thief is a student, it is entirely unsurprising that the thief should be a male. This, he intuitively thinks, shows that the new datum is not nearly so serious as Barney makes it out to be. Bayes's theorem supports Andy's intuition.

4. The Substantive Issue: Answering Rowe's Objection

To show that Rowe's argument fails the reasonable seeability requirement of CORNEA itself, my 1984 article attempted—in accord with the Adjunct Principle—to provide *good reasons to think that if there were God-purposed goods for sufferings, it is expectable that these would often be beyond our ken.* Rowe did not think I succeeded in providing such reasons; but neither of us was entirely clear about what really needs providing. I have thus tried, so far, to answer the preliminary questions concerning, as it were, the ground rules of the inquiry. I now turn to the substantive question: do we have good reasons for thinking that if God-purposed goods exist, it is expectable that they would often be beyond our ken?

4.1 THE PARENT ANALOGY AND ROWE'S OBJECTION

By CORNEA, Rowe's noseeum argument works only if it is reasonable for Rowe to believe that if there were God-purposed goods served by all suffering, it is likely that we would have something different than his noseeum data (many sufferings serving no good we can see). Under the new ground rules, the critic needs to show we have ample reason for thinking that if God-purposed goods exist, it is expectable that they would often be beyond our ken. In 1984 and since then, I relied on the claim that if there is a being who created and sustained this universe around us, the wisdom and vision of this being would be considerably greater than our own. Given what we independently know of our cognitive limits, I suggested that the vision of such a being might well be to ours, as a parent's is to that of a one-month-old human infant. (Readers, I said, "may adjust ages and species" to fit their estimate of how close their knowledge is to omniscience.) I thus argued, by "the Parent Analogy," that if such goods exist:

> it might not be unlikely that we should discern some of them. . . . But that we should discern most of them seems about as likely as that a one-month-old should discern most of his parents' purposes for those pains they allow him to suffer—which is to say, it is not likely at all.

In a subsequent article, I urged that this analogy should be construed as resting not just on God's superior vision, but also on the fact that if theism is true, our universe (and any processes of goods realization in it) is God's creation (Russell and Wykstra [1988], 145-147). The hypothesis of a Laplacean Calculator, having knowledge of the entire future of the universe but no creational role, would not have the same bearing as the theistic hypothesis, positing a creator whose vision laid the axiological foundations of our universe. To explore the import of this for the expectable character of the universe, I distinguished "shallow" from "deep" universes. In the former, observable events are rooted in goods that are "close to the surface," so when we can see an event, we can almost always see any good it serves. In the latter this is not so, because observable events often serve deep goods. The Parent Argument, construed along these lines, holds that the disparity between our cognitive limits and the vision needed to create a universe gives us reason to think that if our universe is created by God it is expectable that it would be deep; this is of course reason to think that if there are God-purposed goods, they would often be beyond our ken.

4.2 ROWE'S DIAGNOSIS: ROWE'S RESTRICTION AND THE FUTURITY OBJECTION

Rowe's criticism of the Parent Argument rested on two key moves. The first was to impose what we might call "Rowe's Restriction." Rowe distinguishes what I shall call "Core Theism"—namely, "the view that O exists, unaccompanied by other, independent religious claims"—from expanded versions of theism, which add to Core Theism further specific claims—about, for example, an afterlife, end times, salvation, and so on. Rowe then claims—invoking in support an earlier article of mine[16]—that to defeat his noseeum evidence, I must give reason to think that his noseeum evidence is expectable relative to the claim of Core Theism alone.

In the paper that Rowe invokes, I did argue that one cannot defeat putative evidence against a hypothesis merely by showing that this evidence is expectable on some arbitrarily expanded version of the hypothesis—that is, the hypothesis conjoined with some entirely ad hoc auxiliary hypotheses. It is not clear, however, that Rowe's restriction follows from this. Here we must distinguish two questions:

(Q1) Is E expectable from the *mere* hypothesis of H? That is, does H tautologously make E expectable?

(Q2) Is E expectable from H *together* with other things which we know independently of commitment to H, and which are not themselves adverse to H in relation to its rivals. That is, does H contingently make E expectable?

Rowe's restriction supposes that a defeating strategy must be based on Q1. It is instructive, however, to compare Core Theism with core claims in science, such as "light is wavelike." Carl Hempel calls these "general theoretical conceptions": while making genuine claims, such claims are, as he puts it, "much too indefinite to yield any specific quantitative consequences."[17] Because of this indefiniteness, the core-wave hypothesis, by itself, does not imply even such rudimentary facts as that light travels in straight lines (casting shadows, etc.), a fact which does, however, follow from standard versions of the rival particle theory. Suppose a particle theorist adduces this fact as levering evidence against the core-wave hypothesis. Given Rowe's Restriction, the only way to defeat the evidence is by showing, in accord with Q1, that, *by itself,* the assumption that light is wavelike gives reason to think light travels in straight lines. In fact, however, wave theorists eventually defeated this evidence using a strategy based on Q2. They argued that given various other things we know (not in themselves adverse to the wave hypothesis), the most plausible specific (or "expanded") versions of the wave hypothesis did make expectable that light should travel in straight lines. A similar strategy is, I believe, appropriate in evaluating Rowe's noseeum evidence.

Rowe's second move is to argue that my Parent Analogy rests on an assumption which, given this restriction, is gratuitous. I begin, he says, from the premise that

(1) O's mind (being omniscient) grasps many goods beyond our ken

and infer that

(2) It is likely that the goods for which O permits many sufferings are beyond our ken.

Now Rowe grants that given Core Theism, 1 is very likely if not certain. But 2, he says, does not follow, for (Rowe [1984], 98):

> the mere assumption that O exists gives us no reason whatever to suppose either that the greater goods in virtue of which he permits most sufferings are goods that come into existence far in the future of the sufferings we are aware of, or that once they do obtain we continue to be ignorant of them and their relation to the sufferings.

The key to Rowe's diagnosis lies in his rationale for accepting (1): he takes (1) as likely or certain (given Core Theism) just because God, if existent, can see the distant future (and goods in it) in a way we cannot. But to get from this to (2) we need a further assumption: that the goods for which God allows many *known* (and hence current or past) sufferings are goods in this unknown (to us) *distant future*. Call this "the Futurity Assumption." Rowe's objection, then, is that Core Theism alone, "the mere assumption of O's existence," gives us no reason to think the Futurity Assumption is true. 1 thus is not reason to think that God-purposed goods for known evils would often be beyond our ken, and the Parent Analogy fails.

Rowe did not think my Deep Universe Enhancement helped here (Rowe [1991], 76-79). The distinction between deep and shallow universes, he says, is purely epistemic—between universes where "it is understandable to us what the goods are that justify God in permitting E1 [the fawn's suffering] and E2 [a case of moral evil], and a world in which we are left without a clue." (He here prefers "morally transparent" and "morally obscure" to my honorific-sounding "shallow" and "deep.") Rowe says:

> Wykstra suggests that God may have had a choice about E1 and E2. On one hand he could have produced a world in which the goods for which he permits these evils are within our ken. . . . On the other, he could have produced a world in which the goods for the sake of which he permits these evils are beyond our ken. Faced with these alternatives, it is highly likely, so Wykstra thinks, that he would choose the latter. Why? (78)

142 / STEPHEN JOHN WYKSTRA

Rowe underscores this question with an argument concerning epistemic suffering. It is clear, he says, that if God allows the fawn's suffering for the sake of deep goods, there will be additional suffering on account of our inability to see God's purpose for it. For this reason, the goods that justify this particular suffering in the deep world would have to be better goods than those which do so in the shallow world. Why then is it so likely that God, faced with the alternative of allowing the particular evil for a good we can see, and allowing it (and the extra second-order suffering) for the sake of a good we cannot see, would choose the latter? Rowe laments: "Unfortunately Wykstra doesn't tell us" (Rowe [1991], 79).

I have two misgivings about this formulation of my argument. It is right, I think, that I did not seek to show that God's choosing the latter is likely; but this is because I left open whether this is a matter of divine choice. We need not here presuppose a voluntarist view of God's creation of a deep rather than shallow universe. One can ask how expectable it is that light should travel in straight lines, if light is made of particles rather than waves, without supposing photons have a choice in this matter. So also we can ask how expectable it is that a universe created by God would be deep, without supposing that this is a matter of divine choice (rather than a result of God's nature). Secondly, even if God does choose in a general way between creating a deep or shallow universe, it does not follow that God has a choice about whether to allow particular Rowean evils for deep or for shallow goods. It may be that certain evils are such that God would allow them only in universes containing goods that are (relative to human cognitive faculties) deep goods; God would then never face the alternatives that Rowe portrays God as choosing between.

I propose, then, to avoid voluntaristic assumptions in formulating the question of what is expectable on theism. This done, is Rowe right in his basic claim that I do not give reasons to think that if God exists, a deep universe is expectable? Well, I do try to give such reasons: that is the point of the Parent Analogy. What Rowe means, no doubt, is that this argument fails. His adamancy about this continues to rest, I believe, on his earlier diagnosis. The Parent Analogy fails, even with the Deep Universe Enhancement, because to get from (1) to (2) one also needs to establish (within the constraints of Rowe's Restriction) the Futurity Assumption. And, says Rowe, "the mere assumption that God exists [Core Theism] gives us no reason whatever to suppose" that the Futurity Assumption is true (Rowe [1986], 238).

4.3 THE FUTURITY ASSUMPTION REEXAMINED

But is this so? Rowe's Restriction, I have already argued, is questionable; a proper inquiry must ask whether, using as resources other things we independently know, we have reason to think that if God exists, it is unsurprising that ours would be a deep universe. Here, as in my 1984 article, I shall draw upon one resource only. In asking whether we should expect a deep or shallow universe relative to Core Theism, we are entitled to appeal to what we independently know of our own cognitive capacities.

Suppose we find, for example, that humans cannot see, by unaided powers, what life will be like N years from now. The question would then be whether we have reason to think that God-purposed goods for sufferings would fall within an N-year horizon. Of course, that this should be the horizon of our cognition does not follow from Core Theism alone (any more than it follows from naturalistic materialism). We might be able to imagine creatures who are like ourselves in other respects, but who have far greater cognitive horizons. But to defeat Rowe's induction, we must ask how expectable it is that God-purposed goods would be within our ken, given what we actually know of our cognitive limits. So if we had reason to think that God-purposed goods would often be beyond an N-year horizon, we have reason to think they would often be beyond our ken.[18]

Given what we actually know of our cognitive limits, then, is it true that Core Theism gives us "no reason whatever" for thinking that God-purposed goods would often lie in the distant future? Suppose one began as an atheist holding some form of naturalism; one then became a theist, embracing Core Theism. If Rowe is correct, one would have no more reason than before to think that if an evil serves some outweighing good, this good would lie in the distant future. But is this so? While there are different versions of naturalism (Sartrean, Russellian, etc.), depending on what other philosophically significant doctrines one adds to it, a central tenet of "Core Naturalism" will surely be Bertrand Russell's claim that the life of humans, fawns, et al.

> is the product of causes which had no pre-vision of the end they were achieving. . . . Man's origin, his hopes and fears, his loves and beliefs, are but the outcome of accidental co-locations of atoms. . . . All the labor of the ages, all the devotion, all the inspirations, all the noonday brightness of human genius, are destined to extinction in the vast death of the solar system. . . . The whole temple of Man's achievement must be buried beneath the debris of a Universe in ruins . . . as omnipotent matter, blind to good and evil, reckless of destruction, rolls on its relentless way.[19]

Would shifting from Core Naturalism to Core Theism, then, increase the probability that if some current suffering serves an outweighing good, it would lie in the distant future?

Here we may recur to the Parent Analogy. If Core Theism is true, the universe itself is the product of God's design, much as the "life situation" of a child is the product of her parent's design. Suppose, then, we are considering an incident of suffering in the life of a child, and the question is raised whether, if there is a good justifying the allowing of this suffering, this good is at all likely to lie in the considerable future. Should our answer to this question be affected by our view as to whether the child's life situation is the result of the planning of parents rather than mere chance? And if so, should it also be affected by our estimate regarding the parents' intelligence, character, and ability? Let us consider these in turn.

As regards intelligence, it is evident that if the child's situation be due to parents of very mean intelligence—or, what is more extreme, the product of no intelligence at all, but instead merely chance—then it becomes correspondingly more unlikely that the rationale for the said event lies in the considerable future.

If the child has parents whom we judge to be half-wits, barely capable of making provision for the day's meals, it will not be thought credible that in some treatment of the child there is served the distant end of the child's university education. (This is more the case if we suppose that the child has no parental superintendence but lives as a young Crusoe, subject only to the elemental forces of nature.) But as we increase the acuteness of the parents' intelligence with regard to their grasp of goods realizable in the considerable future, it becomes correspondingly more likely that in some of their actions toward the child, such goods are served by events in the child's current life situation. So also, insofar as we credit nature with a governor at all, and proportionately as we esteem this governor capable of grasping goods in the considerable future, we *increase* the likelihood that such future goods often have a bearing on current allowings.

But it is not merely intelligence that must affect our judgment here. Parents with the most acute grasp of goods realizable in the child's future might nonetheless show a defect of character, as not to care about these future events in their child's life. Such defect lies not in intelligence but in that common prejudice with respect to the present which treats future events as unreal merely because they are remote. Insofar as we judge the parents so limited, we also decrease our reason to believe that in some present arrangement for their child, their rationale lies in the considerable future. Conversely, insofar as we credit them with unprejudiced and benevolent caring for the future, we increase the likelihood that in many of their present arrangements, contingencies regarding future goods play a significant role.

Thirdly, we might credit the parents with intelligence and with impartial care for the future, and yet deem them to have such limited means at their disposal as to make it unlikely that future goods shape their current dispositions. In some circumstances, parents are barely able to provide for the child's welfare for the coming day; they are wanting in power or ability to act in ways that will intentionally shape events in the considerable future. Insofar as parents are deficient in this regard, we have less reason to think that some current suffering is for the sake of goods in the distant future. Conversely, insofar as we credit them with greater power to act efficaciously with respect to future contingencies, we increase the likelihood that in some of their present arrangements, such future goods play a determinative role.

Thus the likelihood that many treatments of the child are owing to consideration of goods in the considerable future will depend upon three things concerning the parents: their cognitive grasp of future goods, the regard they give to the temporally remote, and their power to shape future events by present actions. Analogously, if our universe is the result of the blind atomic processes, which have no grasp of the future at all, which are entirely indifferent to both remote and immediate goods or evils, suffering or happiness, and which have no power to act intentionally at all, then it is extraordinarily unlikely that many sufferings will serve outweighing goods at all, much less that if they do so, such goods would often be in the distant future. The likelihood of this increases if the world is the result of some being with intelligence and benevolence, and it increases more as we raise our estimate of this being's grasp, caring, and ability with regard to the realization of future goods.

To summarize, then: Rowe's central objection was that Core Theism gives "no reason whatever" to think that the goods served by current evils would often be either in the distant future or for some other reason beyond our grasp. I have argued that this is false. Accepting Core Theism greatly increases our reason to think such goods would often be in the distant future;[20] it thus does give us a great deal more than "no reason whatever" to think these goods would be "deep" goods, often beyond our ken.

Perhaps Rowe meant only to claim that Core Theism provides no reason whatever capable of *justifying* belief that the goods for which God allows current evils would often be deep goods. But this claim, I have shown, is not relevant to defending his noseeum case against a correct deployment of the real CORNEA. CORNEA says that Rowe's noseeum case works only if it is reasonable for Rowe to believe that God-purposed goods would not be deep goods. To defeat Rowe's case, therefore, the critic's reasons need not justify believing these goods would be deep; they need only be enough to require Rowe to suspend belief on whether the goods would be deep.

And do the reasons I have given require Rowe to suspend judgment on this matter? This will depend, of course, on whether Rowe can offer much weightier reasons to place on the other side—whether, that is, he thinks he has much weightier arguments that if Core Theism is true, the goods served by suffering would be not be deep. So far, however, Rowe has not tried to provide such reasons. His surgery on CORNEA and his general conception of defeaters—together with infelicities in my earlier deployment of CORNEA—have led him to try to deflect CORNEA without giving reasons that justify believing such goods would not be deep. I have shown that the real CORNEA, correctly deployed, does not allow him this luxury. He may think the reasons I offer do not come to much. But it doesn't take much to beat nothing.[21]

5. Conclusion

If Rowe's inductive argument from evil is a retreat from the earlier attempted deductive arguments from evil, there are now signs of a further retreat, to "abductive" arguments from evil justifying atheism by way of "inference to the best explanation." On this way of thinking, there are two broad accounts of noseeum evils. One is the naturalist's account: we see no point to such evils because there is no point; they are pointless events in an indifferent universe. The other is the theist's account: behind the universe is God, who cares for us (and sparrows and fawns as well); we cannot, however, see the purposes for which God allows many of the things he does. The Christian specification of theism, in particular, promises no insight into God's purposes, but assurance of his love.

Rowe is right, I think, that in explaining our inability to see a purpose for much suffering, Core Naturalism has an edge over Core Theism. Core Naturalism makes the inscrutability of much evil utterly expectable, while Core Theism makes it, so far as I can now tell, not especially surprising. The question is how much this counts against theism. When some datum is utterly expectable on one hypothesis and not especially surprising on its rival, call it "unbalanced" with respect to the two hypotheses. What evidential force do unbalanced data have? In particular, do unbalanced data have levering power?

I now want to return to my earlier point that there are three questions here, not one. Can an unbalanced datum rightly lever one from square belief to square disbelief? From square belief to square nonbelief? And from square nonbelief to square disbelief? One might think that Bayes's theorem implies that if an unbalanced datum can do the third of these, it can at least do the second. For as we saw, Bayes's theorem says that for any evidential datum e, the new probability of the hypothesis is equal to its initial probability multiplied by a definite fraction, the Keynesian "relevance quotient." Suppose that e can lever one from square agnosticism (rating theism .5) to about half of this (rating theism at, say, about .25). Since rating theism at .25 is nowhere near square atheism, this is actually weaker than levering evidence of the third kind; still, it means e has a relevance quotient of about .5, so must not evidence e also be ample to be levering evidence of the second kind—ample to lever square theism (at, say, .95), to square agnosticism (about .5)?

The answer is no, for the relevance quotient is itself a function of the initial probabilities of the hypothesis. In its properly expanded form, the denominator of the relevance quotient is a weighted summation of the expectabilities of the data on each hypothesis. If there are i possible hypotheses,

$$P(H/e \, \& \, k) = P(H/k) * \left[\frac{P(e/H \, \& \, k)}{\sum_{i=1}^{n} P(e/H_n \, \& \, k) * P(H_n/k)} \right]$$

We can illustrate the result as follows. Suppose Rowe faces an urn, and knows that either (H1) it contains 100 black balls, or (H2) it contains a mix of 20 black balls and 80 white ones. He randomly picks a ball, and it is black. How much does this new datum disconfirm H2? The expanded form of Bayes's theorem yields the following answers. Suppose both hypotheses had initial ratings of .5. The relevance quotient, a little calculation shows,[22] is then .333, so the new datum lowers the probability of H2 from .5 to about .17—producing, as it were, a state of nonbelief with a serious tilt toward atheism. Suppose, however, that one initially had evidence making H2 somewhere nearer a proposition it is reasonable to believe—suppose its initial probability were .99. If the relevance quotient were still 1/3, the datum would now cause our confidence to plummet from .99 to .333. However, Bayes's theorem tells us the relevance quotient is now nowhere near .333. It is, a little calculation will show,[23] instead about .96; the datum thus would only reduce the probability from .99 to about .96.

There are lessons for both believers and nonbelievers here. Believers, if they find that noseeum data give reason to reduce their confidence only a little, might suppose these data should not weigh heavily with nonbelievers either. And nonbelievers, finding that the data make their half-belief plummet nearly to disbelief, might suppose it should take a similar cut from the theist's confidence. If the probability calculus applies to relations of evidential support, then both are mistaken, for as we have seen, unbalanced evidence is like unjust taxes: the less you start with, the bigger a cut it takes.

Failing to see this creates dangers for both sides, but the greater danger is perhaps for nontheists. Seeing how such data cause half-belief to plummet could lead the agnostic to neglect inquiry into the grounds for theism: "Even if I found enough evidence to make theism 99 percent sure, noseeum data would rationally cut this down to 40 percent confidence . . . so what does it matter?" But this, we have seen from Bayes's theorem, is wrong. Unbalanced evidence does not tell against belief nearly as much as it damages half-belief. To overlook anything theism has going for it—by, say, neglecting to make a sincere experiment of faith with theism in its most plausible specifications—is thus dangerous.

Perhaps this lesson of Bayes's theorem calls to mind Jesus's words: "To him who has, more will be given; to him who has not, even what he thinks he has will be taken away." If this seems like unjust taxes, we must also add his other promises: God will not quench a smoldering wick, and "Blessed is the one who hungers and thirsts. . . ." Is it to those who have hunger, then, that more is given? Give us this hunger, Lord, that we may be satisfied.[24]

NOTES

1. To bring out the issues that concern us, I simplify Rowe somewhat, formulating his argument in terms of "God-justifying goods" rather than "God-sufficing goods." The first are goods actually purposed by God, justifying his allowing evil e; the second are goods sufficient to justify God in allowing e, if there is a God, and they were his purpose for allowing e. Confusions about the relations between the two formulations lie behind objections by Richard Swinburne, "Does Theism Need a Theodicy?" *Canadian Journal of Philosophy* (1988); Bruce Russell, "The Persistent Problem of Evil," *Faith and Philosophy* 6 (1989); Daniel Howard-Snyder, "Seeing Through CORNEA," *International Journal for Philosophy of Religion* 32 (1992); and others. I analyze these confusions in "The 'Inductive' Argument from Evil: A Dialogue" (coauthored with Bruce Russell), *Philosophical Topics* 16 (1988): 133-60. Rowe now endorses my analysis, and would not, I think, reject the reformulation of his argument in terms of God-justifying purposes.

2. The principle of credulity is discussed by Richard Swinburne in *The Existence of God* (Oxford: Clarendon Press, 1979), 254-76. I note one defect in Swinburne's formulation in "The Humean Obstacle to Evidential Arguments from Suffering: On Avoiding the Evils of 'Appearance,'" *International Journal for Philosophy of Religion* 16 (1984), section 2.3. Rowe discusses the principle in "Religious Experience and the Principle of Credulity," *International Journal for Philosophy of Religion* 13 (1982), 85-92, and uses it in "Ruminations about Evil," *Philosophical Perspectives* 5 (1991), 71-72.

3. Rowe does not characterize such premises in a terribly exact way, and neither shall I. As Ken Konyndyk pointed out to me, "all observed copper" really should be "all observed copper insofar as we have tested and checked on the matter."

4. I have adjusted these quotations slightly, substituting "Rowe" for "H," "see-ability" for "epistemic access," and "the reasonable seeability condition" for "the epistemic access condition."

5. We shall later see a crucial ambiguity in this formulation of the adjunct principle.

6. This need not mean it could do so for any evidence justifying the initial state, however.

7. In an earlier version of this essay, I at one point indicated that giving theism a likelihood of "say, .17" would qualify as square atheism. Little of substance turned on this, but it now seems to me wildly high. Someone who thought there is a .17 chance that a plane would crash is nowhere near having a square belief that it will not crash. In ordinary contexts, the things we typically squarely believe each day (say, that one is wearing shoes and socks, that it is cloudy outside, etc.) are, in effect, rated so near to 1 as to make no practical difference.

8. To be sure, neither strategy is put in terms of what is "reasonable to believe," referring instead to what one has "reason to think." In conversation, however, Rowe indicated that he had taken these as interchangeable.

9. The manuscript of Rowe's "Evil and Theodicy," *Philosophical Topics* 16 (1988), first enunciating his J mode, was read at Calvin College in 1987. He there stated that he took the first defeater strategy to be a transposition of R1 (his rendition of CORNEA's first step) into the J mode. I suggested the possibility of a more modest defeating strategy, which Rowe acknowledged in note 7 of that paper and note 15 of his "Ruminations about Evil," *Philosophical Perspectives* 5 (1991). Only later did I see the relation of this suggestion to the reasonable seeability requirement of CORNEA itself.

10. See John Pollock, *Knowledge and Justification* (Princeton: Princeton University Press, 1974), 42ff. and *Contemporary Theories of Knowledge* (Totowa: Rowman and Littlefield, 1986), 48ff.

11. As Del Ratzsch pointed out to me, the relation between these is not straightforward in S5. Both the location of the operator "likely" and the import of the subjunctive character would need to be reckoned with in sustaining the claim that these are "equivalent." I believe that this claim, or a close approximation to it, can be sustained; the term "virtually" is meant to cover the finesses this will take.

12. This impetuousness went with another; I urged that the evidence Rowe cites does not even "weakly" disconfirm theism.

13. In introducing CORNEA, for example, I gave three cases where putative data against various hypotheses are undermined by the fact that if H were true, these very data would be expectable. One case involves looking through the door of a cluttered room for a table; not seeing the table does not justify thinking none is there because if one were there, it is still expectable one would not see it. (See "The Humean Obstacle to Evidential Arguments from Suffering," 84.) "Expectable" here would clearly not mean "has a probability of 1 or nearly 1." Similarly, Rowe at one point, in "Evil and the Theistic Hypothesis: A Response to Wykstra," *International Journal for Philosophy of Religion* 16 (1984): 99, says that the fawn's suffering will not disconfirm a hypothesis on which the fawn's suffering "*might well* appear as it does": "might well" seems somewhat weaker than "utterly expectable."

14. But in "The Humean Obstacle to Evidential Arguments from Suffering," I recklessly tried to argue that Rowe's evidence is not even weakly disconfirming evidence against theism. To show this, one would have to show the evidence has a probability of 1 or very close to 1 on theism.

15. A deeper problem is that different types of "improbabilities" are involved in urn cases than in worldview and scientific hypotheses; it is by no means clear that Bayes's theorem applies to both. In urn cases the improbability of drawing a given ball is statistical, based on ratios in population. Consider, in contrast, Newton's 1687 theory of gravitation, which as critics noted could not explain why all the planets orbit the sun in the same

direction and very nearly the same plane. It is not that it predicted some *other* arrangement; rather, it was indifferent to the fact, giving no reason to expect it over thousands of other conceivable arrangements. However, a main rival to Newton's theory, Huygens's vortex-aether hypothesis, did predict common directions of orbits. Since Newton's theory is utterly indifferent to the fact, does it make the fact utterly improbable, just like drawing a white ball out of an urn containing one white ball and a thousand black ones? If so, we should, by Bayes's theorem, treat the fact as massive levering evidence against Newton's theory. Neither Newtonians nor vorticists did treat it this way: that Newton's theory *leaves* the fact improbable (by being indifferent to it) is not the same as its *making* it improbable. Perhaps Bayes's theorem itself casts light on why this is so. Any significant theory, true or false, is indifferent with respect to a great many striking facts, *some* of which its rivals are likely to make expectable. That a theory leaves some facts improbable that a rival predicts is thus what we should expect even if the theory is true: even along Bayesian lines, it is not levering evidence against the theory.

16. "Difficulties in Rowe's Argument for Atheism, and in One of Plantinga's Fustigations against It," read on the *Queen Mary* at the Pacific Division Meeting of the APA, 1983. This paper successfully answered Rowe's first (and never published) objection to CORNEA. Consider, Rowe had objected, any genuine disconfirming evidence E against any hypothesis H. Using CORNEA, the proponent of H can urge that E does not disconfirm hypothesis H', comprising the conjunction of H and E; but since H' entails H, it follows by a well-known theorem of the probability calculus that E cannot then disconfirm H either. I showed that "Rowe's reductio" here rests on an equivocation between two senses of "disconfirm." While E does not dynamically reduce the probability of H' as it does H, H' will nevertheless be (statically) as improbable on E as H, for H' starts off much lower due to its increased content. In his reply to this paper, Rowe cited my analysis as the basis for his claim that the theist cannot just "do a little expanding" to get rid of worrisome evidence.

17. Carl Hempel, *Philosophy of Natural Science* (Englewood Cliffs: Prentice-Hall, 1966), 26.

18. I am here addressing the specific argument that Rowe gives from noseeum evidence, not any argument that might be given from such evidence. This reply would not be apt if someone were to argue that if God exists, he would give us faculties ample to grasp all goods served by current sufferings, out of regard for our potential bewilderment. But Rowe's argument is supposed to be a straightforward induction, like that from "no copper we observe has insulativity" to "no copper has insulativity."

19. Bertrand Russell, "A Free Man's Worship," *Why I Am Not a Christian* (New York: Simon and Schuster, 1957), 107.

20. Of course, it might also be argued that core theism gives us reason to think that such goods would often be beyond our ken for other reasons than their futurity. Moral freedom is a difficult thing to understand; if God has given it to us, it might be hard both to see this and to see what our meaningful exercise requires in the way of God's permitting of moral evils. How much could God prevent us from carrying out evil intentions without jeopardizing freedom? If God exists, it might be hard for us to fathom even those goods which he has woven into the fabric of our current universe.

21. Rowe does claim in "Ruminations about Evil," *Philosophical Perspectives* 5 (1991), 78-79, that a good deal of suffering in this world is occasioned by the fact that we see no good that would justify God in allowing the fawn's suffering. He does not, however, deploy this as justifying reason to think that God would make a deep universe, but only to heighten the need for me to tell why God would choose a world in which the goods that justify E1 or E2 are deep goods, rather than shallow goods. This rests on the misunderstanding of my position already discussed. I do not see how this argument could be redeployed as a good reason for thinking God-purposed goods would usually be within our ken, but I should be happy to see Rowe give it a run.

22. The relevance quotient is then .2 divided by the quantity .5 times 1, plus

.5 times .2.

23. The relevance quotient is now .2, divided by the quantity .01 times 1, plus .99 times .2.

24. For help with this chapter, I wish to thank students Mark Cullison and Ray VanArragon, my colleagues in Calvin's Philosophy Department, Martin Curd, Richard Gale, Daniel Howard-Snyder, and J. L. Schellenberg.

PETER VAN INWAGEN

The Problem of Evil,
the Problem of Air,
and the Problem of Silence

It used to be widely held that evil—which for present purposes we may identify with undeserved pain and suffering—was incompatible with the existence of God: that no possible world contained both God and evil. So far as I am able to tell, this thesis is no longer defended. But arguments for the following weaker thesis continue to be very popular: Evil (or at least evil of the amounts and kinds we actually observe) constitutes evidence against the existence of God, evidence that seems decisively to outweigh the totality of available evidence *for* the existence of God.

In this paper, I wish to discuss what seems to me to be the most powerful version of the "evidential argument from evil." The argument takes the following form. There is a serious hypothesis *h* that is inconsistent with theism and on which the amounts and kinds of suffering that the world contains are far more easily explained than they are on the hypothesis of theism. This fact constitutes a prima facie case for preferring *h* to theism. Examination shows that there is no known way of answering this case, and there is good reason to think that no way of answering it will be forthcoming. Therefore, the hypothesis *h* is (relative to the epistemic situation of someone who has followed the argument this far) preferable to theism. But if *p* and *q* are inconsistent and *p* is (relative to one's epistemic situation) epistemically preferable to *q,* then it is not rational for one to accept *q.* (Of course, it does not follow either that it is rational for one to accept *p* or that it is rational for one to reject *q.*) It is, therefore, not rational for one who has followed the argument up to this point to accept theism.[1]

In Section I, I shall present the version of the evidential argument from evil I wish to discuss. In Section II, I shall explain why I find the argument unconvincing. These two sections could stand on their own, and this paper might have consisted simply of the proposed refutation of the evidential argument from evil that they contain. But many philosophers will find the proposed refutation implausible, owing to the fact that it turns on controversial theses about the epistemology of metaphysical possibility and intrinsic value. And perhaps there will also be philosophers who find my reasoning unconvincing because of a deep conviction that, since evil just *obviously* creates an insoluble evidential problem for the theist, a reply to any version of the evidential argument can be nothing more than a desperate attempt to render the obvious obscure. Now if philosophers are unconvinced by one's diagnosis of the faults of a certain argument, one can attempt to make the diagnosis seem more plausible to them by the following method. One can try to find a "parallel" argument that is obviously faulty and try to show that a parallel diagnosis of the faults of the parallel argument can be given, a diagnosis that seems plausible, and hope that some of the plausibility of the parallel diagnosis will rub off on the original. For example, if philosophers find one's diagnosis of the faults of the ontological argument unconvincing, one can construct an obviously faulty argument that "runs parallel to" the ontological argument—in the classical case, an argument for the existence of a perfect island. And one can then attempt to show that a diagnosis parallel to one's diagnosis of the faults of the ontological argument is a correct diagnosis of the faults (which, one hopes, will be so evident as to be uncontroversial) of the parallel argument. It is worth noting that even if an application of this procedure did not convince one's audience of the correctness of one's diagnosis of the faults of the original argument, the parallel argument might by itself be enough to convince them that there must be *something* wrong with the original argument.

This is the plan I shall follow. In fact, I shall consider *two* arguments that run parallel to the evidential argument from evil. In Section III, I shall present an evidential argument, which I feign is addressed to an ancient Greek atomist by one of his contemporaries, for the conclusion that the observed properties of air render a belief in atoms irrational. In Section IV, I shall present an evidential argument for the conclusion that the observed fact of "cosmic silence" renders a belief in "extraterrestrial intelligence" irrational. Neither of these parallel arguments—at least this seems clear to me—succeeds in establishing its conclusion. In each case, I shall offer a diagnosis of the faults of the parallel argument that parallels my diagnosis of the faults of the evidential argument from evil.

Finally, in Section V, I shall make some remarks in aid of a proposed distinction between facts that raise *difficulties* for a theory and facts that constitute *evidence* against a theory.

I

Let "S" stand for a proposition that describes in some detail the amount, kinds, and distribution of suffering—the suffering not only of human beings, but of all the sentient terrestrial creatures that there are or ever have been.[2] (We assume that the content of S is about what one would expect, given our own experience, the newspapers, history books, textbooks of natural history and paleontology, and so on. For example, we assume that the world was not created five minutes ago—or six thousand years ago—"complete with memories of an unreal past," and we assume that Descartes was wrong and that cats really do feel pain.)

Let "theism" be the proposition that the universe was created by an omniscient, omnipotent, and morally perfect being.[3]

The core of the evidential argument from evil is the contention that there is a serious hypothesis, inconsistent with theism, on which S is more probable than S is on theism. (The probabilities that figure in this discussion are epistemic. Without making a serious attempt to clarify this notion, we may say this much: *p* has a higher epistemic probability on *h* than *q* does, just in the case that, given *h*, *q* is more *surprising* than *p*. And here "surprising" must be understood as having an epistemic, rather than a merely psychological, sense. It is evident that the epistemic probability of *p* on *h* need not be the same for two persons or for the same person at two times.)[4] That hypothesis is "the hypothesis of indifference" (HI):

> Neither the nature nor the condition of sentient beings on earth is the result of benevolent or malevolent actions performed by nonhuman persons.[5]

Here is a brief statement of the argument that is built round the core. We begin with an epistemic challenge to the theist, the presentation of a prima facie case against theism: The truth of S is not at all surprising, given HI, but the truth of S is very surprising, given theism. (For the following propositions, if they are not beyond all dispute, are at least highly plausible. Suffering is an intrinsic evil; a morally perfect being will see to it that, insofar as it is possible, intrinsic evils, if they are allowed to exist at all, are distributed according to desert; an omniscient and omnipotent being will be able so to arrange matters that the world contains sentient beings among whom suffering, if it exists at all, is apportioned according to desert; the pattern of suffering recorded in S is well explained—insofar as it can be explained: many instances of suffering are obviously due to chance—by the biological utility of pain, which is just what one would expect on HI, and has little if anything to do with desert.) We have, therefore, a good prima facie reason to prefer HI to theism.

How shall the theist respond to this challenge? The "evidentialist" (as I shall call the proponent of the evidential argument from evil) maintains that any response must be of one of the following three types:

> —the theist may argue that S is much more surprising, given HI, than one might suppose

—the theist may argue that S is much less surprising, given theism, than one might suppose

—the theist may argue that there are reasons for preferring theism to HI that outweigh the prima facie reason for preferring HI to theism that we have provided.

The first of these options (the evidentialist continues) is unlikely to appeal to anyone. The third is also unappealing, at least if "reasons" is taken to mean "arguments for the existence of God" in the traditional or philosophy-of-religion-text sense. Whatever the individual merits or defects of those arguments, none of them but the "moral argument" (and perhaps the ontological argument) purports to prove the existence of a morally perfect being. And neither the moral argument nor the ontological argument has many defenders these days. None of the "theistic" arguments that are currently regarded as at all promising is, therefore, really an argument for *theism*.[6] And, therefore, none of them can supply a reason for preferring theism to HI.

The second option is that taken by philosophers who construct *theodicies*. A theodicy, let us say, is the conjunction of theism with some "auxiliary hypothesis" h that purports to explain how S could be true, given theism. Let us think for a moment in terms of the probability calculus. It is clear that if a theodicy is to be at all interesting, the probability of S on the conjunction of theism and h (that is, on the theodicy) will have to be high—or at least not too low. But whether a theodicy is interesting depends not only on the probability of S on the conjunction of theism and h, but also on the probability of h on theism. Note that the higher $P(h/theism)$, the more closely $P(S/theism)$ will approximate $P(S/theism \& h)$. On the other hand, if $P(h/theism)$ is low, $P(S/theism)$ could be low even if $P(S/theism \& h)$ were high. (Consider, for example, the case in which h is S itself: even if $P(S/theism)$ is low, $P(S/theism \& S)$ will be 1—as high as a probability gets.) The task of the theodicist, therefore, may be represented as follows: find a hypothesis h such that $P(S/theism \& h)$ is high, or at least not too low, and $P(h/theism)$ is high. In other words, the theodicist is to reason as follows: "Although S might initially seem surprising on the assumption of theism, this initial appearance, like many initial appearances, is misleading. For consider the hypothesis h. The truth of this hypothesis is just what one would expect given theism, and S is just what one would expect [would not at all be that surprising] given both theism and h. Therefore, S is just what one would expect [would not be all that surprising] given theism. And, therefore, we do not have a prima facie reason to prefer HI to theism, and the evidential argument from evil fails."[7]

But (the evidentialist concludes) the prospects of finding a theodicy that satisfies these conditions are not very promising. For any auxiliary hypothesis h that has actually been offered by the defenders of theism, it would seem that either no real case has been made for $P(h/theism)$ being high, or else no real case has been made for $P(S/theism \& h)$ being high—or even too low. Consider, for example, the celebrated free-will defense (FWD). Even if it is granted that $P(FWD/theism)$ is high, there is every reason to think that $P(S/theism \& FWD)$ is low, since of all cases of suffering (a phenomenon that has existed for hundreds of millions of years), only a minuscule proportion involved, even in the most indirect way, beings with free will. And no one has the faintest idea of how to find a proposition that is probable on theism *and,* in conjunction with theism, renders S probable. Therefore, given the present state of the available evidence, our original judgment stands: we have a good prima facie reason to prefer HI to theism. And, as we have seen, we have no reason to prefer theism to HI that outweighs this prima facie reason. It is, therefore, irrational to accept theism in the present state of our knowledge.

II

It will be noted that the evidential argument consists not only of an argument for the conclusion that there is a prima facie case for preferring HI to theism, but also of a list of options open to the theist who wishes to reply to that argument: the defender of theism must either refute the argument or else make a case for preferring theism to HI that outweighs the prima facie case for preferring HI to theism; if the defender chooses to refute the argument, he must do this by producing a theodicy in the sense explained in Section I.

This list of options seems to me to be incomplete. Suppose that one were successfully to argue that S was not surprising on theism—and not because S was "just what one should expect" if theism were true, but because no one is in a position to know whether S is what one should expect if theism were true. (Suppose I have never seen, or heard a description of, Egyptian hieroglyphs, although I am familiar with Chinese characters and Babylonian cuneiform and many other exotic scripts. I am shown a sheet of paper reproducing an ancient Egyptian inscription, having been told that it displays a script used in ancient Egypt. What I see cannot be described as "looking just the way one should expect a script used in ancient Egypt to look," but the fact that the script looks the way it does is not epistemically surprising on the hypothesis that it was a script used in ancient Egypt. I am simply not in a position to know whether *this* is the way one should expect a script that was used in ancient Egypt to look.)[8] If one could successfully argue that one simply could not know whether to expect patterns of suffering like those contained in the actual world in a world created by an omniscient, omnipotent, and morally perfect being, this would refute the evidentialist's case for the thesis that there is a prima facie reason for preferring HI to theism. If one is not in a position to assign any epistemic probability to S on theism—if one is not in a position even to assign a probability range like "high" or "low" or "middling" to S on theism—then, obviously, one is not in a position to say that the epistemic probability of S on HI is higher than the probability of S on theism.[9]

The evidentialist's statement of the way in which the defender of theism must conduct his defense is therefore overly restrictive: it is false that the defender must either make a case for theism or devise a theodicy. At any rate, another option exists as a formal possibility. But how might the defender of theism avail himself of this other option? Are there reasons for thinking that the assumption of theism yields no prima facie grounds for expecting a pattern of suffering different from that recorded by S?

I would suggest that it is a function of what have come to be called "defenses" to provide just such reasons. The word *defense* was first employed as a technical term in discussion of the "logical" version of the argument from evil. In that context, a defense is a story according to which both God and suffering exist, and which is possible "in the broadly logical sense"—or which is such that there is no reason to believe that it is impossible in the broadly logical sense. Let us adapt the notion of a defense to the requirements of a discussion of the evidential argument: a defense is a story according to which God and suffering of the sort contained in the actual world both exist, and which is such that (given the existence of God) there is no reason to think that it is false, a story that is not surprising on the hypothesis that God exists. A defense obviously need not be a theodicy in the evidentialist's sense, for the probability of a defense need not be high on theism.[10] (That is, a defense need not be such that its denial is surprising on theism.) In practice, of course, the probability of a defense will never be high on theism: if the defender of theism knew of a story that accounted for the sufferings of the actual world and which was highly probable on theism, he would employ it as a theodicy. We may therefore say that, in practice, a defense is a story that accounts for the sufferings of the actual world and which (given the existence of God) is true "for all anyone knows."

What does the defender of theism accomplish by constructing a defense? Well, it's like this. Suppose that Jane wishes to defend the character of Richard III and that she must contend with evidence that has convinced many people that Richard murdered the two princes in the Tower. Suppose that she proceeds by telling a story—which she does not claim to be true or even more probable than not—that accounts for the evidence that has come down to us, a story according to which Richard did not murder the princes. If my reaction to her story is "For all I know, that's true. I shouldn't be at all surprised if that's how things happened," I shall be less willing to accept a negative evaluation of Richard's character than I might otherwise have been. (Note that Jane need not try to show that her story is highly probable on the hypothesis that Richard was of good character.) It would, moreover, strengthen Jane's case if she could produce not one story but many stories that "exonerated" Richard—stories that were not trivial variants on one another but which were importantly different.

This analogy suggests that one course that is open to the defender of theism is to construct stories that are true for all anyone knows—given that there is a God—and which entail both S and the existence of God. If the defender can do that, this accomplishment will undermine the evidentialist's case for the proposition that the probability of S is lower on theism than on HI. Of course, these stories will (presumably) be *false* for all anyone knows, so they will not, or should not, create any tendency to believe that the probability of S on theism is *not* lower than it is on HI, that it is about the same or higher. Rather, the stories will, or should, lead a person in our epistemic situation to refuse to make any judgment about the relation between the probabilities of S on theism and on HI.

I shall presently offer such a story. But I propose to simplify my task in a way that I hope is legitimate. It seems to me that the theist should not assume that there is a single reason or a tightly interrelated set of reasons for the sufferings of all sentient creatures. In particular, the theist should not assume that God's reasons for decreeing, or allowing, the sufferings of nonrational creatures have much in common with His reasons for decreeing or allowing the sufferings of human beings. The most satisfactory "defenses" that have so far been offered by theists purport to account only for the sufferings of human beings. In the sequel, I will offer a defense that is directed toward the sufferings of nonrational creatures—"beasts," I shall call them. If this defense were a success, it could be combined with defenses directed toward the sufferings of human beings (like the free-will defense) to produce a "total" defense. This "separation of cases" does not seem to me to be an arbitrary procedure. Human beings are radically different from all other animals, and a "total" defense that explained the sufferings of beasts in one way and the sufferings of human beings in a radically different way would not be implausible on that account. Although it is not strictly to our purpose, I will point out that this is consonant with the most usual Christian view of suffering. Typically, Christians have held that human suffering is not a part of God's plan for the world but exists only because that plan has gone awry. On the other hand:

> Thou makest darkness that it may be night; wherein all the beasts of the forest do move.
> The lions, roaring after their prey, do seek their meat from God.
> The sun ariseth, and they get them away together, and lay them down in their dens. (Ps. 104:20-22)

This and many other Biblical texts seem to imply that the whole subrational natural world proceeds according to God's plan (except insofar as we human beings have corrupted nature). And this, as the Psalmist tells us in his great hymn of praise to the order that God has established in nature, includes the phenomenon of predation.

I will now tell a story, a story that is true for all I know, that accounts for the sufferings of beasts. The story consists of the following three propositions:

(1) Every possible world that contains higher-level sentient creatures either contains patterns of suffering morally equivalent to those recorded by S, or else is massively irregular.

(2) Some important intrinsic or extrinsic good depends on the existence of higher-level sentient creatures; this good is of sufficient magnitude that it outweighs the patterns of suffering recorded by S.

(3) Being massively irregular is a defect in a world, a defect at least as great as the defect of containing patterns of suffering morally equivalent to those recorded by S.

The four key terms contained in this story may be explained as follows.

Higher-level sentient creatures are animals that are *conscious* in the way in which (*pace* Descartes) the higher nonhuman mammals are conscious.

Two patterns of suffering are *morally equivalent* if there are no morally decisive reasons for preferring one to the other, if there are no morally decisive reasons for creating a world that embodies one pattern rather than the other. To say that A and B are in this sense morally equivalent is not to say that they are in any interesting sense comparable. Suppose, for example, that the Benthamite dream of universal hedonic calculus is an illusion and that there is no answer to the question whether the suffering caused by war is less than, the same as, or greater than the suffering caused by cancer. It does not follow that these two patterns of suffering are not morally equivalent. On the contrary: unless there is some "nonhedonic" morally relevant distinction to be made between a world that contains war and no cancer and a world that contains cancer and no war (i.e., a distinction that does not depend on comparing the amounts of suffering caused by war and cancer), it would seem to follow that the suffering caused by war and the suffering caused by cancer *are,* in the present technical sense, morally equivalent.

It is important to note that A and B may be morally equivalent even if they are comparable and one of them involves *less* suffering than the other. By way of analogy, consider the fact that there is no morally decisive reason to prefer a jail term of ten years as a penalty for armed assault to a term of ten years and a day, despite the indubitable facts that these two penalties would have the same deterrent effect and that one is lighter than the other. I have argued elsewhere that, for any amount of suffering that somehow serves God's purposes, it may be that some smaller amount of suffering would have served them as well.[11] It may be, therefore, that God has had to choose *some* amount of suffering as the amount contained in the actual world, and could, consistently with his purposes, have chosen any of a vast array of smaller or greater amounts, and that all of the members of this vast array of alternative amounts of suffering are morally equivalent. (Similarly, a legislature has to choose *some* penalty as the penalty for armed assault, and—think of penalties as jail terms measured in minutes—must choose among the members of a vast array of morally equivalent penalties.) Or it may be that God has decreed, with respect to this vast array of alternative, morally equivalent amounts of suffering, that *some* member of this array shall be the actual amount of suffering, but has left it up to chance which member that is.[12]

A *massively irregular world* is a world in which the laws of nature fail in some massive way. A world containing all of the miracles recorded in the New Testament would not, on that account, be massively irregular, for those miracles were too small (if size is measured in terms of the amounts of matter directly affected) and too few and far between. But a world would be massively irregular if it contained the following state of affairs:

> God, by means of a continuous series of ubiquitous miracles, causes a planet inhabited by the same animal life as the actual earth to be a hedonic utopia. On this planet, fawns are (like Shadrach, Meshach, and Abednego) saved by angels when they are in danger of being burnt alive. Harmful parasites and microorganisms suffer immediate supernatural dissolution if they enter a higher animal's body. Lambs are miraculously hidden from lions, and the lions are compensated for the resulting restriction on their diets by physically impossible falls of high-

protein manna. On this planet, either God created every species by a separate miracle, or else, although all living things evolved from a common ancestor, a hedonic utopia has existed at every stage of the evolutionary process. (The latter alternative implies that God has, by means of a vast and intricately coordinated sequence of supernatural adjustments to the machinery of nature, guided the evolutionary process in such a way as to compensate for the fact that a hedonic utopia exerts no selection pressure.)

It would also be possible for a world to be massively irregular in a more systematic or "wholesale" way. A world that came into existence five minutes ago, complete with memories of an unreal past, would be on that account alone massively irregular—if indeed such a world was metaphysically possible. A world in which beasts (beasts having the physical structure and exhibiting the pain-behavior of actual beasts) felt no pain would be on that account alone massively irregular—if indeed such a world was metaphysically possible.

A *defect in a world* is a feature of a world that (whatever its extrinsic value might be in various worlds) a world is intrinsically better for not having.

Our story comprises propositions (1), (2), and (3). I believe that we have no reason to assign any probability or range of probabilities to this story. (With the following possible exception: if we have a reason to regard the existence of God as improbable, then we shall have a reason to regard the story as improbable.)

We should have reason to reject this story if we had reason to believe that there were possible worlds—worlds that were not massively irregular—in which higher-level sentient creatures inhabited a hedonic utopia. Is there any reason to think that there are such worlds? I suppose that the only kind of reason one could have for believing that there was a possible world having a certain feature would be the reason provided by a plausible attempt to "design" a world having that feature. How does one go about designing a world?

One should start by describing in some detail the laws of nature that govern that world. (Physicists' actual formulations of quantum field theories and the general theory of relativity provide the standard of required "detail.") One should then go on to describe the boundary conditions under which those laws operate: the topology of the world's spacetime, its relativistic mass, the number of particle families, and so on. Then one should tell in convincing detail the story of cosmic evolution in that world: the story of the development of large objects like galaxies and stars and of small objects like carbon atoms. Finally, one should tell the story of the evolution of life. These stories, of course, must be coherent, given one's specification of laws and boundary conditions. Unless one proceeds in this manner, one's statements about what is intrinsically or metaphysically possible—and thus one's statements about an omnipotent being's "options" in creating a world—will be entirely subjective, and therefore without value. But I have argued for this view of the epistemology of modal statements (that is, of modal statements concerning major departures from actuality) elsewhere, and the reader is referred to those arguments. In fact, the argument of those papers should be considered a part of the argument of the present paper.[13]

Our own universe provides the only model we have for the formidable task of designing a world. (For all we know, in every possible world that exhibits any degree of complexity, the laws of nature are the actual laws, or at least have the same structure as the actual laws. There are, in fact, philosophically minded physicists who believe that there is only one possible set of laws of nature, and it is epistemically possible that they are right.) Our universe apparently evolved out of an initial singularity in accordance with certain laws of nature.[14] This evolution is not without its mysteries: the very early stages of the unfolding of the universe (the incredibly brief instant during which the laws of nature operated under conditions of perfect symmetry), the formation of the galaxies, and the origin of life on the earth are, in the present state of natural knowledge, deep mysteries. Nevertheless, it seems reasonable to assume that all of these processes involved only the non-miraculous operation of the laws of nature. One important thing that is known about the evolution of the universe into its present state is that it has been a very tightly structured process. A large number of physical parameters have apparently arbitrary values such that if those values had been only slightly different (very, *very* slightly different) the universe would contain no life, and a fortiori no intelligent life.[15] It may or may not be the "purpose" of the cosmos to constitute an arena in which the evolution of intelligent life takes place but it is certainly true that this evolution did take place and that if the universe had been different by an all but unimaginably minute degree, it wouldn't have. My purpose in citing this fact—it is reasonable to believe that it is a fact—is not to produce an up-to-date version of the Design Argument. It is, rather, to suggest that (at least, for all we know) only in a universe very much like ours could intelligent life, or even sentient life, develop by the nonmiraculous operation of the laws of nature. And the natural evolution of higher sentient life in a universe like ours essentially involves suffering, or there is every reason to believe it does. The mechanisms underlying biological evolution may be just what most biologists seem to suppose—the production of new genes by random mutation and the culling of gene pools by environmental selection pressure—or they may be more subtle. But no one, I believe, would take seriously the idea that conscious animals, animals conscious as a dog is conscious, could evolve naturally without hundreds of millions of years of ancestral suffering. Pain is an indispensable component of the evolutionary process after organisms have reached a certain stage of complexity. And, for all we know, the amount of pain that organisms have experienced in the actual world, or some amount morally equivalent to that amount, is necessary to the natural evolution of conscious animals. I conclude that the first part of our defense is true for all we know: Every possible world that contains higher-level sentient creatures either contains patterns of suffering morally equivalent to those recorded by S, or else is massively irregular.

Let us now consider the second part of our defense: Some important intrinsic or extrinsic good depends on the existence of higher-level sentient creatures; this good is of sufficient magnitude that it outweighs the patterns of suffering recorded by S. It is not very hard to believe (is it?) that a world that was as the earth was just before the appearance of human beings would contain a much larger amount of intrinsic good, and would, in fact, contain a better balance of good over evil, than a world in which there were no organisms higher than worms. (Which is not to say that there could not be worlds lacking intelligent life that contained a still better balance of good over evil—say, worlds containing the same organisms, but significantly less suffering.) And then there is the question of extrinsic value. One consideration immediately suggests itself: intelligent life—creatures made in the image and likeness of God—could not evolve directly from worms or oysters; the immediate evolutionary predecessors of intelligent animals must possess higher-level sentience.

We now turn to the third part of our defense: Being massively irregular is a defect in a world, a defect at least as great as the defect of containing patterns of suffering morally equivalent to those recorded by S. We should recall that a defense is not a theodicy, and that we are not required to argue at this point that it is *plausible to suppose* that massive irregularity is a defect in a world, a defect so grave that creating a world containing animal suffering morally equivalent to the animal suffering of the actual world is a reasonable price to pay to avoid it. We are required to argue only that *for all we know* this judgment is correct.

The third part of our defense is objectionable only if we have some prima facie reason for believing that the actual sufferings of beasts are a graver defect in a world than massive irregularity would be. Have we any such reason? It seems to me that we do not. To begin with, it does seem that massive irregularity is a defect in a world. One minor point in favor of this thesis is the witness of deists and other thinkers who have deprecated the miraculous on the ground that *any* degree of irregularity in a world is a defect, a sort of unlovely jury-rigging of things that is altogether unworthy of the power and wisdom of God. Presumably such thinkers would regard massive irregularity as a very grave defect indeed. And perhaps there is something to this reaction. It does seem that there is something right about the idea that God would include no more irregularity than was necessary in His creation. A second point is that many, if not all, massively irregular worlds are not only massively irregular but massively *deceptive*. This is obviously true of a world that looks like the actual world but which began five minutes ago, or a world that looks like the actual world but in which beasts feel no pain. (And this is not surprising, for our beliefs about the world depend in large measure on our habit of drawing conclusions that are based on the assumption that the world is regular.) But it is plausible to suppose that deception, and a fortiori, massive deception, is inconsistent with the nature of a perfect being. These points, however, are no more than suggestive, and, even if they amounted to proof, they would prove only that massive irregularity was a defect; they would not prove that it was a defect in any way comparable with the actual suffering of beasts. In any case, proof is not the present question: the question is whether there is a prima facie case for the thesis that the actual sufferings of beasts constitute a graver defect in a world than does massive irregularity.

What would such a case be based on? I would suppose that someone who maintained that there was such a case would have to rely on his moral intuitions, or, more generally, on his intuitions of value. He would have to say something like this: "I have held the two states of affairs—the actual sufferings of beasts and massive irregularity—before my mind and carefully compared them. My considered judgment is that the former is worse than the latter." This judgment presupposes that these two states of affairs are, in the sense that was explained above, comparable: one of them is worse than the other, or else they are of the same value (or disvalue). It is not clear to me that there is any reason to suppose that this is so. If it is *not* so, then, as we have seen, it can plausibly be maintained that the two states of affairs are morally equivalent, and a Creator could not be faulted on moral grounds for choosing either over the other. But let us suppose that the two states of affairs are comparable. In that case, if the value judgment we are considering is to be trusted, then human beings possess a faculty that enables them to correctly judge the relative values of states of affairs of literally cosmic magnitude, states of affairs, moreover, that are in no way (as some states of affairs of cosmic magnitude may be) connected with the practical concerns of human beings. Why should one suppose that one's inclinations to make judgments of value are reliable in this area? One's intuitions about value are either a gift from God or a product of evolution or socially inculcated or stem from some combination of these sources. Why should we suppose that any of these sources would provide us with the means to make correct value judgments in matters that have nothing to do with the practical concerns of everyday life? (I do think we must be able to speak of *correct* value judgments if the Problem of Evil is to be of any interest. An eminent philosopher of biology has said in one place that God, if He existed, would be indescribably wicked for having created a world like this one, and, in another place, that morality is an illusion, an illusion that we are subject to because of the evolutionary advantage it confers. These two theses do not seem to me to add up to a coherent position.) Earlier I advocated a form of modal skepticism: our modal intuitions, while they are no doubt to be trusted when they tell us that the table could have been placed on the other side of the room, are not to be trusted on such matters as whether there could be transparent iron or whether there could be a "regular" universe in which there were higher sentient creatures that did not suffer. And if this true, it is not surprising. Assuming that there are "modal facts of the matter," why should we assume that God or evolution or social training has given us access to modal facts knowledge of which is of no interest to anyone but the metaphysician? God or evolution has provided us with a capacity for making judgments about size and distance that is very useful in hunting mammoths and driving cars, but which is of no use at all in astronomy. It seems that an analogous restriction applies to our capacity for making modal judgments. How can we be sure that an analogous restriction does not also apply to our capacity for making *value* judgments? My position is that we cannot be sure, and that for all we know our inclinations to make value judgments are not veridical when they are applied to cosmic matters unrelated to the concerns of everyday life. (Not that our inclinations in this area are at all uniform. I myself experience no inclination to come down on one side or the other of the question whether massive irregularity or vast amounts of animal suffering is the graver defect in a world. I suspect that others do experience such inclinations. If they don't, of course, then I'm preaching to the converted.) But then there is no prima facie case for the thesis that the actual sufferings of beasts constitute a graver defect in a world than does massive irregularity. Or, at least, there is no case that is grounded in our intuitions about value. And in what else could such a case be grounded?

These considerations have to do with intrinsic value, with comparison of the intrinsic disvalue of two states of affairs. There is also the matter of extrinsic value. Who can say what the effects of creating a massively irregular world might be? What things of intrinsic value might be frustrated or rendered impossible in a massively irregular world? We cannot say. Christians have generally held that at a certain point God plans to hand over the government of the world to humanity. Would a massively irregular world be the sort of world that could be "handed over"? Perhaps a massively irregular world would immediately dissolve into chaos if an infinite being were not constantly making adjustments to it. We simply cannot say. If anyone insists that he has good reason to believe that nothing of any great value depends on the world's being regular, we must ask him why he thinks he is in a position to know things of that sort. We might remind him of the counsel of epistemic humility that was spoken to Job out of the whirlwind:

> Gird up now thy loins like a man; for I will demand of thee, and
> answer thou me.
> Where wast thou when I laid the foundations of the earth?
> Declare if thou hast understanding.
> Knowest thou it, because thou wast then born, or because the
> number of thy days is great?
> Canst thou bind the sweet influences of Pleiades, or loose the
> bands of Orion?
> Knowest thou the ordinances of heaven? Canst thou set the
> dominion thereof in the earth?[16]

I have urged extreme modal and moral skepticism (or, one might say, humility) in matters unrelated to the concerns of everyday life. If such skepticism is accepted, then we have no reason to accept the evidentialist's premise that "an omniscient and omnipotent being will be able so to arrange matters that the world contains sentient beings among whom suffering, if it exists at all, is apportioned according to desert." More exactly, we have no reason to suppose that an omniscient and omnipotent being could do this without creating a massively irregular world, and, for all we know, the intrinsic or extrinsic disvalue of a massively irregular world is greater than the intrinsic disvalue of vast amounts of animal suffering (which, presumably, are not apportioned according to desert). If these consequences of modal and moral skepticism are accepted, then there is no reason to believe that the probability of S on HI is higher than the probability of S on theism, and the evidential argument from evil cannot get started. Even if we assume that the probability of S on HI is high (that the denial of S is very surprising on HI), this assumption gives us no reason to prefer HI to theism. If there were such a reason, it could be presented as an argument:

> The probability of S on HI is high.
> We do not know what to say about the probability of S on theism.
> HI and theism are inconsistent.
> Therefore, for anyone in our epistemic situation, the truth of S constitutes a
> prima facie case for preferring HI to theism.

This argument is far from compelling. If there is any doubt about this, it can be dispelled by considering a parallel argument. Let L be the proposition that intelligent life exists, and let G be the proposition that God wants intelligent life to exist. We argue as follows:

> The probability of L on G is high.
> We do not know what to say about the probability of L on atheism.
> G and atheism are inconsistent.
> Therefore, for anyone in our epistemic situation, the truth of L constitutes a prima facie case for preferring G to atheism.

The premises of this argument are true. (As to the second premise, there has been considerable debate in the scientific community as to whether the natural evolution of intelligent life is inevitable or extremely unlikely or something in between; let us suppose that "we" are a group of people who have tried to follow this debate and have been hopelessly confused by it.) But I should be very surprised to learn of someone who believed that the premises of the argument entailed its conclusion.

I will close this section by pointing out something that is not strictly relevant to the argument it contains but is, in my view, of more than merely autobiographical interest. I have not accepted the extreme modal skepticism that figures so prominently in the argument of this section as a result of epistemic pressures exerted by the evidential argument from evil. I was an extreme modal skeptic before I was a theist, and I have, on the basis of this skepticism, argued (and would still argue) against both Swinburne's attempt to show that the concept of God is coherent and Plantinga's attempt to use the modal version of the ontological argument to show that theism is rational.[17]

III

Imagine an ancient Greek, an atomist who believes that the whole world is made of tiny, indestructible, immutable solids. Imagine that an opponent of atomism (call him Aristotle) presents our atomist with the following argument: "If fire were made of tiny solids, the same solids earth is made of, or ones that differ from them only in shape, then fire would not be Absolutely Light—it would not rise toward the heavens of its own nature. But that fire is not Absolutely Light is contrary to observation."[18] From our lofty twentieth-century vantage point, we might be inclined to regard Aristotle's argument as merely quaint. But this impression of quaintness rests on two features of the argument that can be removed without damage to what is, from one point of view anyway, its essential force. The two quaint features of Aristotle's argument, the idea that fire is a stuff and the idea of the Absolutely Light, can be removed from the argument by substituting air for fire and by substituting the behavior we nowadays associate with the gaseous state for the defining behavior of the Absolutely Light (that is, a natural tendency to move upward). The resulting argument would look something like this:

Suppose air were made of tiny solid bodies as you say. Then air would behave like fine dust: it would eventually settle to the ground and become a mere dusty coating on the surface of the earth. But this is contrary to observation.

Well, what is wrong with this argument? Why *don't* the O_2, N_2, CO_2, and other molecules that make up the atmosphere simply settle to the ground like dust particles? The answer is that air molecules, unlike dust particles, push on one another; they are kept at average distances that are large in comparison with their own sizes by repulsive forces (electromagnetic in nature), the strength of these forces in a given region being a function of the local temperature. At the temperatures one finds near the surface of the earth (temperatures maintained by solar radiation and the internal heat of the earth), the aggregate action of these intermolecular forces produces the kind of aggregate molecular behavior that, at the macroscopic level of description, we call the gaseous state.

We can see where the improved version of Aristotle's argument goes wrong. (We can also see that in one minor respect it's better than an ancient Greek could know: if it weren't for intermolecular forces, air molecules would not simply settle slowly to the ground; they would drop like rocks.) But what about our imaginary ancient atomist, who not only doesn't know all these things about intermolecular forces and temperature and so on, but who couldn't even conceive of them as epistemic possibilities? What shall he say in response to the improved version of Aristotle's argument?

In order to sharpen this question, let us imagine that a Greek philosopher called A-prime has actually presented our atomist with the air-and-dust argument, and let us imagine that A-prime has at his disposal the techniques of a late-twentieth-century analytical philosopher. Having presented the atomist with the simple argument that I have given above (the primitive or "whence, then, is air?" version of the Argument from Air), he presses his point by confronting the atomist with a much more sophisticated argument, the *evidential* argument from air. "Let HI, the Hypothesis of Independence, be the thesis that there are four independent and continuous elements, air among them, each of which has *sui generis* properties (you can find a list of them in any reputable physics text) that determine its characteristic behavior. Let S be a proposition that records the properties of air. The simple air-and-dust argument is sufficient to establish that S is not surprising given HI, but is very surprising given atomism. There are only three ways for you to respond to this prima facie case against atomism: you may argue that S is much more surprising, given HI than one might suppose; or that S is much less surprising, given atomism, than one might suppose; or that there are reasons for preferring atomism to HI that outweigh the prima facie reason for preferring HI to atomism that is provided by the air-and-dust argument. The first I shall not discuss. The third is unpromising, unless you can come up with something better than the very abstract metaphysical arguments with which you have attempted to support atomism in the past, for they certainly do not outweigh the clear and concrete air-and-dust argument. The only course open to you is to construct an *atomodicy*. That is, you must find some auxiliary hypothesis *h* that explains how S could be true, given atomism. And you will have to show both that the probability of S is high (or at least not too low) on the conjunction of atomism and h and that the probability of h on atomism is high. While you may be able to find an hypothesis that satisfies the former condition, I think it very unlikely that you will be able to find one that satisfies the latter. In any case, unless you *can* find an hypothesis that satisfies both conditions, you cannot rationally continue to be an atomist."

Whatever else may be said about this argument, A-prime is certainly right about one thing: it is unlikely that the atomist will be able to produce a successful atomodicy. Even if he were told the modern story about air, he could not do it. At least, I don't think he could. What is the epistemic probability on atomism (relative to the epistemic situation of an ancient Greek) of our complicated modern story of intermolecular forces and the gaseous state? What probability should someone who knew nothing about the microstructure of the material world except that it was composed of atoms (it is, of course, our "elementary particles" and not our "atoms" or our "molecules" that correspond to the atoms of the Greeks) assign to the modern story? As far as I am able to judge, the only rational thing such a person could do would be to decline to assign any probability to the modern story on atomism. (The answer of modern science to the air-and-dust argument does not take the form of a story that, relative to the epistemic situation of an ancient Greek, is highly probable on atomism.)

Fortunately for the atomist, A-prime's demand that he produce an atomodicy is unreasonable. The atomist need do nothing more in response to the evidential argument from air than find a defense—or, better, several independent defenses. A defense, of course, is a story that explains how there could be a stuff that has the properties of air (those known to an ancient Greek), given that the material world is made entirely of atoms. A defense need *not* be highly probable on atomism. It is required only that, given atomism, the defense be true for all anyone (*sc.* any ancient Greek) knows.

Here is one example of a defense: air atoms (unlike earth atoms) are spheres covered with a "fur" of long, thin, flexible spikes that are, unless flexed by contact with another atom, perpendicular to the surface of the atom's "nucleus" (i.e., its central sphere); the length of the spikes is large in comparison with the diameters of nuclei, and their presence thus tends to keep nuclei far apart. Since, for all anyone (anyone in the epistemic situation of an ancient Greek) knows, some atoms have such features—if there are atoms at all—the observed properties of air are not surprising on the assumption of atomism. Since there are defenses that are true for all anyone (anyone in the epistemic situation of an ancient Greek) knows, no ancient Greek was in a position to say anything about the probability on atomism of S, the proposition that sums up the properties of air that were known to him. A-prime, therefore, is left with no better argument than the following:

> The probability of S on HI is high.
> We do not know what to say about the probability of S on atomism.
> HI and atomism are inconsistent.
> Therefore, for anyone in our epistemic situation, the truth of S constitutes a prima facie case for preferring HI to atomism.

And this argument is manifestly invalid.

IV

We know how it is that air can be composed of molecules and yet not drift to the ground like dust. This knowledge provides us with a certain rather Olympian perspective from which to view the "Problem of Air." I wish next to examine the epistemic situation of those of our contemporaries who believe that the Milky Way galaxy (ours) contains other intelligent species than humanity. (Since they are our contemporaries, we cannot view their situation from any such Olympian perspective.) Let us confront them with an argument analogous to the argument from evil and the argument from air. The essence of this argument is contained in a question of Enrico Fermi's, a question as pithy as "Whence, then, is evil?": Where are they?

If there are other intelligent species in the galaxy, the overwhelming probability is that at least one intelligent species existed at least a hundred million years ago. There has been life on the earth for at least thirty times that long, and there is nothing magical about the present time. The universe was just as suitable for intelligent life a hundred million years ago, and if the pace of evolution on the earth had been just three or four percent faster, there would have been intelligent life *here* a hundred million years ago. An intelligent and technologically able species will attempt to send messages to other species elsewhere in the galaxy (as we have begun to do). The most efficient way to do this is to send out self-reproaching robotic probes to other stars: when such a probe reaches another star, it makes two or more duplicates of itself out of local materials, and these duplicates proceed to further stars. Then it waits, perhaps for hundreds of millions of years, till it detects locally produced radio signals, at which point it reveals itself and delivers its message. (There are no fundamental technological barriers to this program. At our present rate of scientific progress, we shall be able to set such a process in motion within the next century.) It is not hard to show that the descendants of the original probes will reach every star in the galaxy within fifty million years. (We assume that the probes are capable of reaching one-tenth the speed of light.) But no such probe has revealed itself to us. Therefore, any nonhuman intelligences in the galaxy came into existence less than fifty million years ago. But it is statistically very unlikely that there are nonhuman intelligences *all* of which came into existence within the last fifty million years. (The reasoning is like this: if you know that such people as there are in the Sahara Desert are distributed randomly, and if you know that there are no people in the Sahara except, possibly, within a circular area one hundred miles in diameter that is hidden from you, you can conclude that there are probably no people at all in the Sahara.) Furthermore, it is not merely the absence of robotic probes that should disturb the proponent of "extraterrestrial intelligence." There are also the absence of radio signals from thousands of nearby stars and several of the nearer galaxies[19] and the absence of manifestations of "hyper-technology" like the wide-angle infrared source that would signal the presence of a star that has been surrounded with a "Dyson sphere." We may refer collectively to all of these "absences" as *cosmic silence,* or simply *silence.* (If there are other intelligent species in the galaxy, or even in nearby galaxies, they are *species absconditae.*) The obvious implication of these observations is that we are alone.[20]

Let us call the thesis that there is intelligent life elsewhere in the galaxy "noetism." The above argument, the argument from cosmic silence, provides materials from which the antinoetist may construct an evidential argument against noetism analogous to the evidential argument from evil: "Let the Hypothesis of Isolation (HI) be the hypothesis that humanity is the only intelligent species that exists or has ever existed in the Milky Way galaxy or any of the nearby galaxies. Let S be a proposition that records all of the observations that constitute a failure to discover any manifestation whatever of life, and a fortiori, of intelligent life, elsewhere in the universe. The argument from cosmic silence is sufficient to establish that the truth of S (which, of course, is not at all surprising given HI) is very surprising, given noetism. There are only three ways for you to respond to the argument from cosmic silence: you may argue that S is much more surprising, given HI, than one might suppose; or that S is much less surprising, given noetism, than one might suppose; or that there are reasons for preferring noetism to HI that outweigh the prima facie reason for preferring HI to noetism that is provided by the argument from cosmic silence. The first is no more than a formal possibility. The third is unpromising, unless you can come up with something better than those facile arguments for the prevalence of life in the cosmos that are so popular with astronomers and physicists and so exasperating to evolutionary biologists.[21] The only course open to you is to construct a *noodicy.* That is, you must find some auxiliary hypothesis *h* that explains how S could be true, given noetism. And you will have to show both that the probability of S is high (or at least not too low) on the conjunction of noetism and *h* and that the probability of *h* on noetism is high. While you may be able to find an hypothesis that satisfies the former condition, I think it very unlikely that you will be able to find one that satisfies the latter. In any case, unless you can find an hypothesis that satisfies both conditions, you cannot rationally continue to be a noetist."

The antinoetist is no doubt right in supposing that it is very unlikely that the noetist will be able to construct a successful noodicy. One example should suffice to make the point. Consider the elegantly simple, if rather depressing, Nuclear Destruction Scenario: intelligent species do not last long enough to make much of a mark on the cosmos; within at most a few decades of developing radio transmitters powerful enough to be detected across a distance of light-years (and long before they can make self-reproducing intersidereal robotic probes), they invariably destroy themselves in nuclear wars. It is clear that the Nuclear Destruction Scenario is a failure as a noodicy, for it is not highly probable on noetism (that intelligent species invariably destroy themselves in nuclear wars is not highly probable on the hypothesis that intelligent species exist). The proponents of extraterrestrial intelligence have provided a wide range of possible explanations of "cosmic silence" (intelligence does not necessarily imply technology; the desire to communicate with other intelligent species is a human idiosyncrasy; the most efficient means of intersidereal signaling, the one that all the extraterrestrials actually employ, is one we haven't yet thought of), but it is clear that none of these possible explanations should be regarded as *highly probable* on noetism. We simply do not know enough to make any such probability judgment. Shall the noetist therefore concede that we have shown his position to be irrational? No, for the antinoetist's demand that the noetist produce a noodicy is wholly unreasonable. The noetist need only produce one or more *defenses,* one or more explanations of the phenomenon of cosmic silence that entail noetism and are true for all we know. And this is just what the noetist has done. (I have already mentioned several of them.) Since there are defenses that for all anyone knows are true, no one knows what to say about the probability on noetism of S (the proposition that records all of our failed attempts to discover any manifestation of intelligent life elsewhere in the universe). The antinoetist has therefore failed to show that the truth of S constitutes a prima facie case in favor of preferring HI to noetism.

V

"This is all very well. But evil *is* a difficulty for the theist, and the gaseous state *was* a difficulty for the ancient atomist, and cosmic silence *is* a difficulty for the noetist. You seem to be saying that they can just ignore these difficulties."

Not at all. I have said that these difficulties (I accept the term *difficulty*) do not render their beliefs irrational—not even if they are unable to find arguments that raise the probabilites of their hypotheses relative to the probabilites of competing hypotheses that do not face the same difficulties, and are also unable to devise auxiliary hypotheses that enable them to construct "-dicies." It doesn't follow that they should simply ignore the difficulties. "Well, what *should* they do?"

To begin with, they can acknowledge the difficulties. They can admit that the difficulties exist and that they're not sure what to say about them. They might go on to offer some speculations about the causes of the phenomena that raise the difficulties: mechanisms that would account for the gaseous state, possible conditions that would interfere with communications across light-years, reasons God might have for allowing evil. Such speculations need not be (they almost certainly will not be) highly probable on the "ism" in whose defense they are employed. And they need not be probable on anything that is known to be true, although they should not be improbable on anything that is known to be true. They are to be offered as explanations of the difficult phenomena that are, *for all anyone knows,* the correct ones. In sum, the way to deal with such difficulties is to construct defenses.

"But if a phenomenon is a 'difficulty' for a certain theory, does that not mean that it is evidence against that theory? Or if it is not evidence against that theory, in what sense can it raise a 'difficulty' for the theory? Are you not saying that it can be right to accept a theory to which there is counterevidence when there are competing theories to which there is no counterevidence?"

That sounds good, but it is really a recipe for rejecting just about any interesting theory. Just about any interesting theory is faced with phenomena that make the advocates of the theory a bit uncomfortable, this discomfort being signaled by the tendency to speculate about circumstances consistent with the theory that might produce the phenomena. For any theory that faces such a difficulty, there will always be available another "theory," or at least another hypothesis, that does not face that difficulty: its denial. (The denial of an interesting theory will rarely if ever itself be an interesting theory; it will be too general and nonspecific.) Your suggestion would therefore appear to constrain us never to accept any interesting theory, but always either to accept its denial or else neither the theory nor its denial. The latter will be the more common result, since the denial of a theory can usually be partitioned into interesting theories that face individual difficulties. (For example, the denial of atomism can be partitioned into the following hypotheses: matter is continuous; matter is neither continuous nor atomically structured; matter does not exist. Each of these hypotheses faces difficulties.) This result might be avoided if you placed some sort of restriction on what counted as a "competing theory," but it is not clear what sort of restriction would be required. It will not do simply to rule out the denial of a theory as a competing theory, for contraries of the theory that were very general and nonspecific could produce equally counterintuitive results. If, moreover, you did produce a satisfactory solution to this problem, it is not clear what consequences your solution might have for the evidential argument from evil. Consider, for example, the Hypothesis of Indifference. This is not a very specific thesis: it tells us only that the nature and condition of sentient beings on earth do *not* have a certain (very narrowly delineated) cause. Perhaps it would not count as a proper "competitor" with the quite specific thesis we have called 'theism.' Perhaps it would be a consequence of your solution that only some proposition more specific that HI, some proposition that entailed but was not entailed by HI, could properly be in competition with theism. And this proposition might face difficulties of its own, difficulties not faced by HI.

But we may answer your question more directly and simply. A difficulty with a theory does not necessarily constitute evidence against it. To show that an acknowledged difficulty with a theory is not evidence against it, it suffices to construct a defense that accounts for the facts that raise the difficulty. (This thesis by no means provides an automatic "out" for a theory that is confronted with some recalcitrant observation, for a defense is not automatically available to the proponents of every theory that is confronted with a recalcitrant observation. A defense may not be improbable, either on the theory in whose cause it is employed or on anything we know to be true. In a particular case, it may be that no one can think of any hypothesis that satisfies these two conditions, and what was a mere difficulty of a theory will thereby attain to the status of evidence against the theory. It is perhaps worth pointing out that two or more difficulties may jointly constitute evidence against a theory, even if none of them taken individually counts as evidence against it. This could be the case if the defenses that individually "handle" the difficulties are inconsistent, or if—despite the fact that none of the defenses taken individually is improbable—their conjunction is improbable.)

The central thesis of this paper may be usefully summarized in the terminology that has been introduced in the present section: While the patterns of suffering we find in the actual world constitute a *difficulty* for theism and do not constitute a difficulty for the competing hypothesis HI, they do not—owing to the availability of the defense[22] I have outlined—attain to the status of *evidence* that favors HI over theism. It follows that the evidential argument from evil fails, for it is essential to the evidential argument that those patterns of suffering be evidence that favors HI over theism.[23]

NOTES

"The Problem of Evil, the Problem of Air, and the Problem of Silence," by Peter van Inwagen, appeared in *Philosophical Perspectives, 5, Philosophy of Religion, 1991,* edited by James E. Tomberlin (copyright by Ridgeview Publishing Co., Atascadero, CA). Reprinted by permission of Ridgeview Publishing Company.

1. My formulation of this argument owes a great deal to a recent article by Paul Draper, "Pain and Pleasure: An Evidential Problem for Theists," *Nous* 23 (1989): 331-50. I do not, however, claim that the argument I shall present is Draper's intricate and subtle argument, or even a simplified version of it. (One important difference between the argument discussed in the present paper and Draper's argument is that the latter makes reference to the distribution of both pain and pleasure, while the former makes reference only to the distribution of pain.) Nevertheless, I hope that the version of the evidential argument from evil that I shall discuss is similar enough to Draper's that what I say about my version will at least suggest strategies that the theist can employ in dealing with Draper's argument. Draper (p. 332) credits Hume with being the first to ask the question whether there is "any serious hypothesis that is logically inconsistent with theism [and] explains some significant set of facts about evil . . . much better than theism does." (See *Dialogues concerning Natural Religion,* Part XI.)

2. In Draper's argument, the role that corresponds to the role played by S in our argument is played by a proposition O that reports "both the observations one has made of humans and animals experiencing pain or pleasure and the testimony one has encountered concerning the observations others have made of sentient beings experiencing pain or pleasure" (p. 332). I find that the argument goes more easily if it is stated in terms of the probability (on various hypotheses) of the pattern of suffering that it is reasonable to believe that actual world exhibits, rather than in terms of the probability (on those hypotheses) of the observations and testimony on which our reasonable belief in that pattern rests. I do not think that this modification of Draper's strategy leaves me with an argument that is easier to refute than the argument that would have resulted if I had retained this feature of his strategy.

3. Cf. Draper, p. 331. Perhaps we should add that this being has not ceased to exist, and has never ceased to be omniscient, omnipotent, or morally perfect.

4. Cf. Draper, pp. 333 and 349 (note 2). Some difficulties with the notion of epistemic probability are discussed in note 7 below.

5. Cf. Draper, p. 332.

6. It is a currently popular view that one can have reasons for believing in God that are of a quite different kind from "arguments for the existence of God." For a sampling of versions of this view, see the essays by the editors and the essay by William P. Alston in Alvin Plantinga and Nicholas Wolterstorff, eds., *Faith and Rationality: Reason and Belief in God* (Notre Dame: University of Notre Dame Press, 1983). My own position on this matter is that some version of this view is right, and that there are reasons for believing in God that are of the general kind described by Plantinga, Wolterstorff, and Alston. I believe, moreover, that these reasons not only can provide one with adequate justification for being a the-

ist in the absence of a prima facie case against theism, but are strong enough to override any conceivable prima facie case against theism. (For a contrary view—which I believe rests on a misunderstanding—see Draper, pp. 347-48.) But I shall not defend this thesis here, since the point of the present paper is that the patterns of suffering that exist in the actual world do not constitute even a prima facie case against theism.

7. I prefer to formulate the evidential argument from evil in terms of epistemic surprise rather than in terms of high and low epistemic probability. (Draper's essay suggested this use of the concept of "surprise" to me. Although his "official" formulation of his argument is in terms of epistemic probability, he frequently employs the notion of "surprise" in his informal commentary on the argument. Indeed, at one place—see p. 333— he comes very close to explaining epistemic probability as I did in the text: by equating "has a lower epistemic probability" with "is more surprising.") Let me attempt to explain why I am uneasy about formulating the argument in terms of probabilities. If the argument is so formulated, it would appear to depend on the validity of the following inference-form: p; the probability of p on q is much higher than the probability of p on r; q and r are inconsistent; therefore, there exists a prima facie reason (viz., that p) for preferring q to r. The trouble with this inference-form is that the probability of p may be very low on q despite the fact that p is not at all *surprising* on q. For example, the probability of the hypothesis that the unobservable card that Alice is holding is the four of clubs is quite low on the hypothesis that she drew the card at random from a standard deck, but the former hypothesis is not at all surprising on the latter. Now let S be some true proposition that has a low probability on theism, but is not at all surprising on theism. I should think that the proposition that states the exact number of dogs would do: in "most" possible worlds in which God exists, the number of dogs is not the actual number. It is clear that the following facts do not comprise a prima facie case for preferring "S and God does not exist" to "God exists": S; the probability of S on "S and God does not exist" is much higher than the probability of S on "God exists." "S and God does not exist" and "God exists" are inconsistent.

These considerations show that the use of the language of high and low probabilities in formulating the evidential argument from evil is a source of possible confusion. Since, however, my criticisms of the argument have nothing to do with this point, I shall continue to employ this language. But I shall employ it only as a stylistic device: anything I say in this language could easily be restated in terms of epistemic surprise.

8. I can have *some* epistemically warranted expectations about how what I see displayed on the sheet of paper will look: it must in some sense "look like writing"—it can't be a detailed drawing of a cat or a series of a thousand identical marks. Similarly, I can have *some* epistemically warranted expectations about how suffering will be distributed if there is a God. I would suppose, for example, that it is highly improbable on theism that there be sentient creatures and that all of them be in excruciating pain at every moment of their existence.

9. Well, one might somehow know the probability of S on theism as a function of the probability of S on HI; one might know that the former probability was one-tenth the latter, and yet have no idea what either probability was. But that is not the present case. The evidentialist's argument essentially involves two independent probability judgments: that the probability of S on HI is at least not too low, and that the probability of S on theism is very low.

10. Indeed, in *one* sense of probability, the probability of a defense may be very low on theism. We have said that a defense may not be *surprising* on theism, but, as we saw in note 7, there is a perfectly good sense of probability in which a proposition that is not at all surprising on theism may nevertheless be very improbable on theism. If the defender of theism had at his disposal a very large number of defenses, all of them inconsistent with the others and none of them epistemically preferable to any of the others, it is hard to see why he should not conclude that (relative to his epistemic situation) the probability of any given one of them was very low on theism.

11. Peter van Inwagen, "The Magnitude, Duration, and Distribution of Evil: A

Theodicy," *Philosophical Topics* 16 (1988), pp. 161-87. See especially pp. 167-68. Failure to appreciate this consideration is a weak point in many versions of the evidential argument from evil. Consider, for example, William L. Rowe's much-discussed article "The Problem of Evil and Some Varieties of Atheism," *American Philosophical Quarterly* 16 (1979): 335-41. In this article, Rowe employs the following premise:

> An omniscient, wholly good being would prevent the occurrence of any intense suffering it could, unless it could not do so without losing some greater good or permitting some evil equally bad or worse.

If there are alternative, morally equivalent amounts of (intense) suffering, then this premise is false. To make this point more concrete, let us consider Rowe's famous case of a fawn that dies in prolonged agony of burns that it suffers in a forest fire caused by lightning. God, I concede, could have miraculously prevented the fire, or miraculously saved the fawn, or miraculously caused its agony to be cut short by death. And, I will concede for the sake of argument, if He had done so, this would have thwarted no significant good and permitted no significant evil. But what of the hundreds of millions (at least) of similar incidents that have, no doubt, occurred during the long history of life? Well, I concede, He could have prevented any one of them, or any two of them, or any three of them . . . without thwarting any significant good or permitting any significant evil. But could he have prevented all of them? No—not without causing the world to be massively irregular. And, of course, there is no sharp cut-off point between a world that is massively irregular and a world that is not—just as there is no sharp cut-off point between a penalty that is an effective deterrent for armed assault and a penalty that is not. There is, therefore, no *minimum* number of cases of intense suffering that God could allow without forfeiting the good of a world that is not massively irregular—just as there is no shortest sentence that a legislature can establish as the penalty for armed assault without forfeiting the good of effective deterrence.

     12. See my essay "The Place of Chance in a World Sustained by God" in Thomas V. Morris, ed., *Divine and Human Action: Essays in the Metaphysics of Theism* (Ithaca: Cornell University Press, 1988), 211-35.

     13. Peter van Inwagen, "Ontological Arguments," *Nous* 11 (1977): 375-95; review of *The Coherence of Theism* by Richard Swinburne, *Philosophical Review* 87 (1979): 668-72. See also George Seddon, "Logical Possibility," *Mind* 81 (1972): 481-94.

     14. These laws, being quantum mechanical, are indeterministic. God could not, therefore, have "fine-tuned" the initial state of a universe like ours so as to render an eventual universal hedonic utopia causally inevitable. It would seem to be almost certain that owing to quantum-mechanical indeterminacy, a universe that was a duplicate of ours when ours was, say, 10^{-45} seconds old could have evolved into a very different universe from our present universe. (There is also the point to be considered that there probably *was* no initial state of the universe.) Would it be possible for an omniscient and omnipotent being to create a universe that evolved deterministically out of a carefully selected initial state into an hedonic utopia? This question raises many further questions, most of which cannot be answered. Nevertheless, the following facts would seem to be relevant to an attempt to answer it: life depends on chemistry, and chemistry depends on atoms, and atoms depend on quantum mechanics (classically speaking, an atom cannot exist: the electrons of a "classical" atom would spiral inward, shedding their potential energy in the form of electromagnetic radiation, till they collided with the nucleus), and quantum mechanics is essentially indeterministic.

     15. This fact has been widely remarked on. See, e.g., John Leslie, "Modern Cosmology and the Creation of Life," in Ernan McMullin, ed., *Evolution and Creation* (Notre Dame: University of Notre Dame Press, 1985), 91-120.

     16. This is not properly speaking a quotation; it is, rather, a selection of verses from Chapter 38 of the Book of Job. It comprises verses 3, 4, 21, 31, and 33.

     17. See the article and review cited in note 13.

174 / PETER VAN INWAGEN

18. Cf. *De Caelo* IV, especially 309ª18-310ª13.

19. This latter fact is very important in the debate about extraterrestrial intelligence. If someone in our galaxy aimed a powerful signal at, say, the Andromeda galaxy, then, two million years later, anyone in the Andromeda galaxy who aimed a sensitive receiver precisely at our galaxy would detect that signal. When we aim a sensitive receiver precisely at the Andromeda galaxy, however, we detect no signal. Therefore no one on any planet circling any of the hundred billion or more stars in the Andromeda galaxy was aiming a signal at the Milky Way galaxy two million years ago. (This argument actually depends on the false assumption that all of the stars in the Andromeda galaxy are equally distant from us, but the essential point of the argument is sound.)

20. For an excellent popular article on the search for extraterrestrial intelligence, see Gregg Easterbrook, "Are We Alone?" *Atlantic,* August 1988, 25-38.

21. See, for example, Ernst Mayr, "The Probability of Extraterrestrial Intelligent Life," in Michael Ruse, ed., *Philosophy of Biology* (New York: Macmillan, 1989), 279-85.

22. Are there other defenses—other defenses that cover the same ground as the defense I have presented in Section ll? I should like to think so, although I have not had any very interesting ideas about how additional defenses might be constructed. I should welcome suggestions.

23. This paper was read at Brandeis University. The author wishes to thank the members of the Brandeis Philosophy Department, and especially Eli Hirsch, for their helpful comments and criticisms.

9.

PAUL DRAPER

The Skeptical Theist

The term *skeptical theist* is apt to be misleading. If one can resist the temptation to dismiss it as oxymoronic, then one is likely to associate it with fideism. But the theists whose views I intend to discuss are not fideists and accordingly do not defend theism by defending a general skepticism about human cognitive powers. Rather, their skepticism is supposed to extend only so far as nonskeptical standards of rationality demand. This is far enough, they believe, to undermine probabilistic arguments from evil against theism, but not far enough to undermine all rational grounds for theistic belief. By distinguishing different types of probabilistic arguments from evil, I will show that these skeptical theists have not yet solved the evidential problem of evil and that certain forbidding obstacles stand between them and future success.

I

Most skeptical theists attack probabilistic arguments from evil by arguing for something like the following skeptical thesis, which I will call "skeptical thesis #1" or "ST1" for short:

ST1: Humans are in no position to judge directly that an omnipotent and omniscient being would be unlikely to have a morally sufficient reason to permit the evils we find in the world.[1]

For example, William Alston defends this thesis by claiming both that various theodical suggestions cannot be rejected as improbable and (more plausibly I think) that we are in no position to judge as improbable the statement that there are unknown morally sufficient reasons for an omnipotent and omniscient being to allow the evils we find in the world.[2]

What troubles me most about the position of skeptical theists like Alston is not ST1, but rather the inference from ST1 to the conclusion that all probabilistic arguments from evil fail. One is reminded of those philosophers who attack one teleological or cosmological or ontological argument for theism and then conclude that *the* teleological or *the* cosmological or *the* ontological argument fails. Alston, for example, says that "if [ST1] is right, the inductive argument from evil is in no better shape than its late lamented deductive cousin."[3] There is very good reason to believe that Alston takes the consequent of this conditional to be as general as it appears. For although his article focuses on William Rowe's argument from evil, he makes it clear at the outset that he is using Rowe's specific formulation of the argument to defend a general criticism of *the* argument—i.e., of all formulations of the argument. But then accepting his inference requires a considerable leap of faith. For it requires one simply to assume that all probabilistic arguments from evil must reject ST1—that they all must show that it is unlikely that an omnipotent and omniscient being would have a morally sufficient reason to permit certain evils. And Alston offers no reason for thinking that this assumption is true.

Although, as I will show later, this assumption is false, it is not an unnatural assumption for contemporary philosophers of religion to make. Consider the context in which the debate about probabilistic arguments from evil arose. Probabilistic arguments have replaced what are sometimes called "logical" arguments from evil—arguments that attempt to demonstrate the falsity of theism by proving that it is logically incompatible with some known fact about evil. Logical arguments from evil are thought to have the following structure. Let "E" stand for one's favorite fact about evil. Let "G" stand for (traditional) theism, which is the view that there exists an omnipotent, omniscient and morally perfect being who created the universe. One could demonstrate that G is false if one could demonstrate that the following statement is necessarily false or at least that it is false:

M: An omnipotent and omniscient being would have a morally sufficient reason for allowing E.

If one could prove that M is necessarily false, then (since it is a necessary truth that a morally perfect being would not permit E unless it had a morally sufficient reason to do so) G would be disproved by virtue of its inconsistency with E. If one could prove that M is false, then G would be disproved by virtue of its inconsistency with the conjunction of E and the denial of M.

Logical arguments from evil are a dying (dead?) breed. One reason for this is the following. Since even an omnipotent being's power would have logical limitations, such a being could produce goods that logically entail the existence (or possibility) of E only by allowing E (or its possibility). So, for all we know, even an omnipotent and omniscient being might be forced to allow E for the sake of obtaining some important good. Our knowledge of goods and evils and the logical relations they bear to each other is much too limited to prove that this could not be the case. In short, logical arguments from evil are thought to fail because of a nonprobabilistic skeptical thesis: given our cognitive limitations, we are in no position to prove that M is false.

ST1 is more ambitious: given our cognitive limitations, we can't even show that M is improbable. The reason it is tempting to treat ST1 as a reply to all probabilistic arguments from evil is that it is natural to assume that probabilistic arguments from evil have the same basic structure as logical arguments from evil are thought to have, the only difference being that whereas the latter sort of argument aspires to certainty—M is certainly false—the former aspires only to probability—M is probably false. To put the point another way, a familiarity with the literature on logical arguments from evil may seduce one into thinking that there is only one available strategy for constructing probabilistic arguments from evil: show that G is improbable by showing that M or some statement that M entails is improbable. ST1, if true, can be used to refute all probabilistic arguments from evil employing this particular strategy.

Another reason it is easy to overestimate the apologetic power of ST1 is that almost all contemporary proponents of arguments from evil employ this strategy. Indeed, in a recent article, Michael Tooley claims that "there is general agreement concerning the basic structure of the argument from evil"[4] and that "one guiding idea is that the core argument should turn upon the existence of what might be called *unjustified* evils, where an evil counts as unjustified, in the present context, if an omnipotent and omniscient being could have prevented it, and would not have been justified in not doing so."[5] The best known defender of such a strategy is William Rowe. He chooses a particularly inscrutable evil as his replacement for E, and then argues for the conclusion that the following statement is prima facie probable:

> Q: No good state of affairs is such that an omnipotent, omniscient being's obtaining it would morally justify that being's permitting E.[6]

He must believe that M entails ~Q (otherwise he couldn't conclude that G is prima facie improbable); so his argument for the prima facie probability of Q is in effect an argument for the prima facie improbability of M.[7] If ST1 could be shown to be true, then Rowe's argument would fail.

Although it is, for the reasons just given, tempting to think that all probabilistic arguments from evil must reject ST1, this is actually not the case. Not all such arguments attempt to show that G is prima facie improbable by attempting to show that M is prima facie improbable. For example, my own probabilistic argument from evil employs a quite different strategy.[8] This strategy was, so far as I know, first used by David Hume. In Part XI of *Dialogues Concerning Natural Religion,* Hume argues that theism is prima facie improbable because the hypothesis that the first causes of the universe are neither benevolent nor malevolent explains the pattern of pain and pleasure in the world much better than theism does. I don't think his argument succeeds, but not because anything is wrong with his strategy. His strategy is to show that a serious hypothesis that is logically inconsistent with theism explains some significant set of facts about evil and good much better than theism does. The idea is that if one could do this, then one would have a prima facie good reason to believe that this alternative hypothesis is more probable than theism and hence that theism is probably false. Arguments like this, which I call "Humean" probabilistic arguments from evil, do not rely, either explicitly or implicitly, on a premise asserting that an omnipotent and omniscient being would probably not have a morally sufficient reason to permit certain facts about good and evil. Of course, if the theist could construct a very successful theodicy and thereby prove that an omnipotent and omniscient being probably would have such a reason, then Humean arguments from evil would be in trouble. But Humean arguments do not depend on showing that there probably is no such reason. Indeed, the skeptical claim that we can't directly assess the probability of there being such a reason sounds more like an admission that theism is doomed to explanatory inferiority than like a powerful retort.[9] After all, we also can't assess how likely it is that God would have a good reason to create a world in which there exists a high degree of similarity in the biochemistry of life. But that does nothing to undermine the argument that since evolution theory explains this high degree of similarity much better than the theory that each species was independently created by God, the former theory is, other evidence being equal, more probable than the latter.

II

Of course, the skeptical theist might admit that ST1 can't be used against Humean arguments but maintain that a new skeptical thesis can be designed especially for them. Thus, Humean arguments could be refuted if the following skeptical thesis could be defended successfully:

> ST2: Humans are in no position to compare theism's ability to explain certain facts about good or evil to some other hypothesis's ability to explain those facts.

In the remainder of this essay, I will investigate whether or not ST2 or some similar skeptical thesis could be used effectively against my own Humean argument from evil. I am indebted to Peter van Inwagen for making me realize that such an investigation is needed. In a richly suggestive recent article, he attacks a Humean argument from evil by defending a skeptical thesis similar to ST2.[10] It is important to recognize, as van Inwagen does, that the particular argument he discusses differs in several important ways from my own argument. For example, I cash out explanatory superiority in terms of antecedent conditional epistemic probabilities while van Inwagen appeals to a notion of epistemic surprise.[11] (A third type of Humean argument would refuse to replace "explains.") Despite these differences, van Inwagen hopes that what he says about the particular argument from evil he discusses "will at least suggest strategies that the theist can employ in dealing with Draper's argument."[12] I believe that van Inwagen's discussion does suggest a strategy for attacking my argument. I will begin my investigation by describing that strategy.

The central claim of my argument is the following:

C: O is antecedently much more likely on HI than on G.

"O" stands for a statement reporting the observations and testimony upon which one's knowledge about the pattern of pain and pleasure in the world is based. By "antecedently" I mean "independent of the observations and testimony O reports." HI is the hypothesis of indifference, the statement that neither the nature nor the condition of sentient beings on earth results from actions performed by benevolent or malevolent nonhuman persons. For the sake of convenience, I will abbreviate C as follows:

C: $P(O/HI) >! P(O/G)$.

">!" means "is much greater than," and "$P(x/y)$" stands for the antecedent probability of x given y.

If we revise ST2 so that it applies specifically to my argument, we obtain the following:

> ST3: Humans are not in a position to compare the antecedent probability of O on G to the antecedent probability of O on HI.[13]

To show that ST3 is true, one would have to show, at least implicitly, that something is wrong with my argument for C. This argument has two parts. The first part (see section II of "Pain and Pleasure") consists of an argument based on the biological utility of pain and pleasure for the conclusion that, prior to considering (or independent of) the effect of theodicies on $P(O/G)$, C is true. So one possible way of defending ST3 would be to try to show that this argument is flawed, that one should be skeptical about the relevance of the biological utility of pain and pleasure to C. The second part of my argument for C (see section III of "Pain and Pleasure") consists in an argument for the conclusion that theodicies do not significantly raise $P(O/G)$. Thus, another possible way of defending ST3 would be to attack this argument by trying to show that one should be skeptical about how much theodicies raise $P(O/G)$.

But neither of these strategies is suggested by van Inwagen's article. He maintains that *defenses* provide reasons for believing that his skeptical thesis is true, where "a defense is a story that accounts [in terms of theism] for the sufferings of the actual world" and which (given the existence of God) is true "for all anyone knows."[14] In "Pain and Pleasure," I defined a theodicy as an attempt to explain certain facts about evil (I should have added "or good" here) in terms of theism. On this definition, defenses are a proper subclass of theodicies. They are theodicies that are true for all anyone knows. To permit a distinction between theodicies and defenses, I will now call attempts to explain certain facts about evil or good in terms of theism "theistic stories" instead of "theodicies." Using this terminology, my argument for C is based on the following two premises:

C1: Independent of the effect of theistic stories on P(O/G),
P(O/HI) >! P(O/G).
C2: Theistic stories do not significantly raise P(O/G).

The strategy suggested by van Inwagen's paper is to point out that C doesn't follow from C1 and C2 and then show that the additional premise needed is false. This additional premise is:

C3: Theistic stories do not render ST3 true.

C3 is needed because theistic stories that do not raise P(O/G) might still undermine my argument from evil by making skepticism about the truth of C reasonable.

Let's say that a theistic story is a "successful theodicy" if it renders C false by significantly raising P(O/theism). If, on the other hand, a theistic story justifies skepticism about C by rendering ST3 true, then I will call that story a "successful defense." My task, then, is to investigate whether or not any theistic story is a successful defense. I will divide this investigation into two parts. In section III, I will try to determine what conditions a theistic story must satisfy in order to be a successful defense. And in section IV, I will address the question of whether any theistic stories satisfy those conditions.

III

I will begin by stating two necessary conditions for a theistic story (D) to be a defensive success. One is that we be unable to assign any specific range of values (like "low" or "high") to P(D/G)—to the antecedent probability of the story conditional on theism.[15] The meaning of *antecedent* here is the same as before: "independent of the observations and testimony O reports." I will call a theistic story that satisfies this condition an "aprobable" story. A second condition is that P(O/HI) must not be much greater than P(O/D&G): O must not be antecedently much more probable on HI than on D conjoined with theism. I will call a theistic story that satisfies this condition a "good" story.

One part of the requirement that a theistic story be aprobable is that we not be able to assign it a low antecedent probability on theism.[16] But this requirement also implies that we not be able to judge this probability to be high or middling. Any such judgment would be incompatible with the story's supporting ST3. For example, if we can judge that the antecedent probability of some story given theism is very high and it is also a good story, then, although this would be a good reason for rejecting my claim that P(O/HI) is much greater than P(O/G), it would not be any reason at all for believing that ST3 is true—that we are not in a position to compare P(O/G) and P(O/HI). Such a story would be a successful theodicy rather than a successful defense.[17]

The second condition is that a story be good—the antecedent probability of O given the conjunction of theism and the story must be as great as or at least not much less than the antecedent probability of O given HI. Intuitively, the idea of this second condition is that it is not enough to respond to a theistic story by saying "for all I know that story is true." One must be able to add, "and if it is true then theism accounts for O just as well as (or at least not significantly worse than) HI does." Consider, for example, the following story: There are nonhuman persons who, because of their wickedness, want pain and pleasure to be distributed in something like the way O reports. I can certainly imagine someone arguing for the conclusion that this story (call it D*) is aprobable: one might plausibly claim that, given theism, we have no reason to believe that such mean-spirited spirits exist and no reason to believe they don't. Suppose, for the sake of argument, that D* is aprobable. Can we conclude that P(O/G) and P(O/HI) cannot be compared? Of course not. One needs a better story than this. There is very good reason to think that God would not permit some of his creatures to suffer or feel less pleasure than they otherwise would solely for the purpose of satisfying the wicked desires of other creatures. Thus, P(O/D*&G) is no higher than P(O/G) was before considering D*, and hence the (alleged) fact that we cannot assess P(D*/G) is irrelevant—it does nothing to justify skepticism about C.

Some light can be shed on the conditions of aprobability and goodness by what I called in "Pain and Pleasure" "the weighted average principle" or "WAP":

$$P(O/G) = (P(S/G) \times P(O/S\&G)) + (P(\sim S/G) \times P(O/\sim S\&G)).$$

WAP is formulated a bit differently here—the second term in the righthand side of the equation is P(O/S&G) instead of P(O/S)—because I am not assuming in this paper that a theistic story entails theism. In "Pain and Pleasure" I used WAP to assess the effect of a theistic story on the antecedent probability of O given theism.[18] WAP explains quite nicely why the conditions of aprobability and goodness are each necessary for a theistic story to be a successful defense. If a good story were not aprobable, then WAP could be used to assess its effect on P(O/G) and hence it would not support ST3. If, on the other hand, an aprobable story were not good, then our inability to assess P(D/G) wouldn't be an obstacle to comparing P(O/G) to P(O/HI): WAP implies that such a story wouldn't significantly raise P(O/G) no matter what value we assigned to P(D/G).

WAP does not, however, tell us whether the conditions of aprobability and goodness are jointly sufficient for establishing ST3. This is because we are not in this context using WAP and D to make an initial assessment of P(O/G). Rather, we are using WAP to see if D changes P(O/G). If D is a good aprobable theistic story, then WAP does not tell us whether the correct conclusion to draw is that it does not change P(O/G) and hence that C remains true or that we should now refuse to compare P(O/G) with P(O/HI).[19] Fortunately, we do not need WAP to determine whether or not the conditions of aprobability and goodness are jointly sufficient for establishing ST3. A few simple analogies will suffice to show that they are not—that additional conditions are necessary.

My first analogy involves the following two hypotheses:

> Brownism (B): Other things being equal, John would much rather live in a brown house than in a yellow one.
> Yellowism (Y): Other things being equal, John would much rather live in a yellow house than in a brown one.

Suppose John builds himself a house and paints it yellow. Let "E" stand for a statement reporting his choice of color. Now consider the claim that independent of the observations and testimony upon which one's knowledge of E is based, E is much more likely given yellowism than given brownism. (I will abbreviate this claim as follows: P(E/Y) >! P(E/B).) Prior to considering any "brownistic stories," this claim is clearly true. Now suppose a brownist offers the following brownistic story:

> D: The yellow paint John bought was on sale; no other color was on sale; and John would rather live in a yellow house than miss a chance to save money on his paint purchase.

This is a good brownistic story: P(E/Y) is not much greater than P(E/B&D). Suppose further that this story is aprobable. (This requires a little effort, but perhaps it's not impossible.) Should we conclude that we just don't know whether or not P(E/Y) >! P(E/B)? I think a negative answer is clearly correct so long as we have, antecedently, no more reason given B to believe that D is true than to believe that the following parallel story is true:

> A: The yellow paint John bought was not on sale; there was, however, a sale on brown paint; and John had a very strong desire to save money on his paint purchase.

We might call such a story a "counterdefense." Notice that, while P(E/D&B) is much greater than P(E/B) was prior to considering D and A, P(E/A&B) is much less than P(E/B) was prior to considering D and A.

Consider another example. The following two hypotheses have both had their advocates:

> Smokism (S): Smoking is no threat to one's health.
> Realism (R): Smoking is hazardous to one's health.

The following discovery seemed to support R over S:

> E: A much higher percentage of smokers get lung cancer than nonsmokers.

At least prior to considering any smokistic stories, P(E/R) >! P(E/S). Suppose, however, that the tobacco industry had defended their product by offering the following smokistic story:

> D: People who are genetically predisposed to getting lung cancer are much more likely to become smokers (e.g., because this predisposition is genetically linked to an ability to enjoy the smell and taste of tobacco).

This is a good smokistic story, and it is easy to imagine a person's being unable to assess its antecedent probability given S—that is to say, it isn't that difficult to imagine D's being aprobable for someone. Does this mean that person should light up? No, because the following counterdefense is available:

> A: People who are genetically predisposed to getting lung cancer are much less likely to become smokers (e.g., because this predisposition is genetically linked to an inability to enjoy the smell and taste of tobacco).

We have, antecedently, no more reason given S to think that D is true than to think that A is true. And while P(E/D&S) is much greater than P(E/S) was prior to considering D and A, P(E/A&S) is much lower than P(E/S) was prior to considering D and A. So D's aprobability and goodness does not justify skepticism about the claim that P(E/R) >! P(E/S).[20]

One last example. Let "K" stand for the now discredited view that the entire physical universe, including the earth, was created by God less than 10,000 years ago. Let "M" stand for the view that the universe is more than a million years old. Finally, let "E" stand for a statement reporting the observations and testimony upon which our knowledge of fossils, very deep river canyons (which would take more than a million years to form if they were formed by erosion), and distant stars (some of which are more than one million light-years from earth) is based. An argument could be constructed to show that prior to considering K-istic stories, P(E/M) >! P(E/K).

Now suppose a K-ist proposes the following K-istic story:

> D: Some great unknown good depends both upon God's creating fossils and very deep river canyons when he created the earth, and his temporarily increasing the speed at which light travels from distant stars so that it reaches the earth in a few thousand years.

Upon considering this story, which is a good K-istic story and is also aprobable if any theistic story is, should we now be skeptical about the claim that P(E/M) >! P(E/K)? Hardly, for we have, antecedently, no more reason given K to believe that D is true than to believe that the following story is true:

> A: Some great unknown good depends upon God's not creating fossils and very deep river canyons when he created the earth, and his not temporarily increasing the speed at which light travels from distant stars so that it reaches the earth in a few thousand years.

184 / PAUL DRAPER

What these examples show is that finding a good aprobable theistic story D does not suffice to establish ST3, unless that story is not undermined by a counterdefense, where a counterdefense is a parallel story A about which the following two things can be said. First, one has, antecedently, no more reason given theism to believe that D is true than to believe that A is true. (This condition should be interpreted in such a way that A would fail to satisfy it if one had no reason to believe that D or A is true, no reason to believe that D is false, and some reason to believe that A is false.) Second, while $P(O/D\&G)$ is much greater than $P(O/G)$ was prior to considering theistic stories and counterdefenses, $P(O/A\&G)$ is much less than $P(O/G)$ was prior to considering theistic stories and counterdefenses. Let's call a theistic story that is not undermined by a counterdefense an "undefeated" theistic story.

Are the three necessary conditions considered thus far sufficient for defensive success? I don't believe so, because the position that they are sufficient has the absurd implication that finding evidence for a theistic story could put theists in a worse position than they were in prior to finding that evidence. For suppose that some aprobable undefeated theistic story D just barely satisfies the condition of goodness—$P(O/G\&D)$ is less than $P(O/HI)$, but (just barely) not significantly less. If these three conditions were sufficient, then theists armed with D could relax—$P(O/G)$ and $P(O/HI)$ would now be incommensurable. But suppose that these theists later find evidence for D, evidence that renders $P(D/G)$ just slightly greater than $1/2$. Applying WAP, it would follow that $P(O/G)$ is close to a straight average of $P(O/D\&G)$ and $P(O/\sim D\&G)$, which, since D just barely satisfies the condition of goodness, would be significantly less than $P(O/HI)$.

If the three conditions discussed so far are not jointly sufficient, then what else is needed? Van Inwagen suggests (unintentionally) one possible answer to this question. He says or implies more than once that when it comes to defenses, the more the better: the theist's case would be strengthened if she could produce not one story but many *independent* stories, stories that are not trivial variants of one another but rather are importantly different. At first glance, this seems to be an odd position to take. It is clear how having more than one good theistic story whose antecedent probability given theism can be assessed might help: the disjunction of several such stories might be antecedently probable given theism even though no single story is antecedently probable given theism. But when the stories are aprobable, it's not so clear why there is strength in numbers. Van Inwagen himself offers only one (two-part) theistic story, so I find it puzzling that he thinks additional stories would be helpful. After all, if a single theistic story can render $P(O/G)$ and $P(O/HI)$ incommensurable, then additional stories can't make them *more* incommensurable. Perhaps, however, there is something to van Inwagen's intuition. If my initial reasons for claiming that $P(O/HI) >! P(O/G)$—the ones based on the biological utility of pain and pleasure—are strong ones, then a single good aprobable undefeated theistic story won't by itself justify skepticism about that claim. But perhaps many such stories would.[21]

IV

Let's assume for the sake of argument that numerous good aprobable undefeated theistic stories would suffice to justify ST3. Has even a single such story been told? Instead of trying to prove of every theistic story ever told that it fails to satisfy at least one of the three conditions in question, I will discuss only a few theistic stories and use them to illustrate just how difficult it is to satisfy all three of these conditions.

The basic problem confronting the skeptical theist is that good stories tend not to be both aprobable and undefeated. Consider, for example, the following two theistic stories:

> D1: An omnipotent and omniscient being would have a morally sufficient reason to permit O to be true.
>
> D2: An omnipotent being would have the power to produce a good beyond our ken that logically requires O's truth and that is vastly greater in value than any good with which we are familiar.

Although neither D1 nor D2 entails O when conjoined with G, each is, I believe, a good theistic story. Each may also be aprobable. (Notice that the claim that D1 is aprobable is closely related to ST1.) But clearly neither is undefeated. The problem with D1 and D2 is that one has, antecedently, no more reason given theism to believe that they are true than to believe that the following three stories are true:

> A1: An omnipotent and omniscient being would have no morally sufficient reason to permit O.
>
> A2a: There is some unknown good that logically entails ~O and is vastly more valuable than any good with which we are familiar.
>
> A2b: There is some unknown evil that O logically entails and that is vastly worse than any evil with which we are familiar.

A1 clearly undermines D1, and D2 is undermined both by A2a and by A2b. The lesson of D1 and D2 is that while it is very easy to construct good theistic stories by appealing to unspecified great goods or by mentioning O in an entirely ad hoc fashion, it is also very easy to construct successful counterdefenses for such stories.

Now let's examine some theistic stories that appeal to free will. I discussed the following story in "Pain and Pleasure," where I stipulated that an action is free* if it is free in the incompatibilist sense and either it or some alternative action open to the agent would have been morally wrong to perform:

> D3: God exists, and one of his final ends is a favorable balance of freely* performed right actions over wrong actions.

Notice that while it is at least arguable that this story is aprobable and undefeated, this story is clearly not a good one. We have, antecedently, no reason to think that the distribution of pain and pleasure reported by O is well-suited for advancing morality. Some of the pain and pleasure reported by O has a positive influence on people's moral decisions, but much of it is demoralizing. Of course, we could make this theistic story good by building more into it:

> D4: God exists; one of his final ends is a favorable balance of freely* performed right actions over wrong actions; and the best way for God to achieve this end is to permit pain and pleasure to be distributed more or less in the way O reports.

But D4 is neither aprobable nor undefeated. It is improbable for the same reasons that D3 is not good. And it is undermined by the following counterdefense:

> A4: God exists; one of his final ends is a favorable balance of freely* performed right actions over wrong actions; and the best way for God to achieve this end is to permit pain and pleasure to be distributed in some other way than O reports.

Would it help to add a chapter on nonhuman free creatures to the story? Try the following:

> D5: God exists; one of his final ends is a favorable balance of freely* performed right actions over wrong actions; the moral agents performing free* actions in the general vicinity of earth include nonhuman persons—demons and angels, principalities and powers, spirits and spooks, and the like; and the best way for God to achieve this end is to permit pain and pleasure to be distributed more or less in the way O reports.

A better case for the aprobability of D5 can be made than can be made for the aprobability of D4. One might argue that since we have no idea what nonhuman moral agents are like or what might influence them to be virtuous, we are not in a position to judge that the antecedent probability of D5 given theism is low or middling or high. But even if this argument is convincing, nothing is gained, since we have (antecedently) no more reason to believe that D5 is true than to believe that the following story is true:

> A5: God exists; one of his final ends is a favorable balance of freely* performed right actions over wrong actions; the moral agents performing free* actions in the general vicinity of earth include nonhuman persons—demons and angels, principalities and powers, spirits and spooks, and the like; and the best way for God to achieve this end is to permit pain and pleasure to be distributed in some other way than O reports.

Van Inwagen's theistic story combines the free-will defense to account for human suffering with an appeal to natural law to account for the suffering of other animals. He never states his version of the free-will defense. The versions stated above fare no better as accounts of the human suffering reported by O than as accounts of all of the suffering reported by O. I don't see any reason, however, why the second part of his theistic story can't stand on its own, since it focuses on higher-level sentient creatures and that includes humans. This part of his story consists of the following three propositions:

(1) Every possible world that contains higher-level sentient creatures either contains patterns of suffering morally equivalent to those recorded by [O], or else is massively irregular.

(2) Some important intrinsic or extrinsic good depends on the existence of higher-level sentient creatures; this good is of sufficient magnitude that it out-weighs the patterns of suffering recorded by [O].

(3) Being massively irregular is a defect in a world, a defect at least as great as the defect of containing patterns of suffering morally equivalent to those recorded by [O].[22]

Let's call the conjunction of these three propositions "D6." D6 is rather easily undermined by the following counterdefense:

A6: Many possible worlds containing higher-level sentient creatures are not massively irregular and are such that there are morally decisive reasons for pre-ferring the patterns of suffering in them to those reported by O.

We have, antecedently, no more reason to accept D6 than to accept A6. Indeed, the opposite may be true, since A6 is so much less specific than D6—it is consis-tent with both the truth and the falsity of the second and third propositions com-prising D6. (Additional successful counterdefenses could be constructed using stories parallel to the second and third parts of D6.)[23]

Of course, many other theistic stories have been told, and the fact that none of the six stories I have discussed here are aprobable, good, and undefeated does not show that these other stories do not fare better. So I conclude here with a challenge to the skeptical theist to produce some good, aprobable, and undefeated theistic stories. In the absence of such stories, skepticism about my claim that P(O/HI) >! P(O/G) is not warranted. Nor can skepticism about the significance of this claim be defended by complaining that real theists are not generic theists—that Christian theists, for example, should be able to employ Christian doctrines in their explanatory hypothesis (including doctrines about human suffering and plea-sure and about the relative unimportance of those animals not made in God's image). This complaint overlooks the fact that Christian theism and other specific theisms obviously entail theism and hence can't be more probable than theism. Thus, any good reason to think that (generic) theism is improbable is an equally good reason to think that Jewish or Christian or Muslim theism is improbable. Of course, brand-name theists are welcome to avail themselves of various doctrines in replying to my argument. They may use any or all of their religious beliefs to try to explain the pattern of pain and pleasure we observe in the world in terms of the-ism. But then these beliefs must be treated like any other theistic story. Either they are successful theodicies or successful defenses or they are no help at all.

V

I have shown that the sort of skeptical thesis defended by Alston is useless against Humean evidential arguments from evil. I have also shown that theists must overcome some forbidding obstacles if they want to refute my particular Humean argument by constructing defenses. For it is by no means an easy task to devise a theistic story that is aprobable, good, and undefeated. And a single story of this sort would not be enough.

But matters may be even worse for the theist. The skeptical theist is trying to walk a tightrope—to use skepticism to defend a position that seems to many to be a paradigm case of something one should be skeptical about. There is some risk that this strategy may backfire. For example, it is consistent with my response to skeptical theism in this paper to grant that the skeptical theist is not mistaken in thinking that we should be skeptical about claims that if God exists, then he would be likely to have certain goals and to perform certain actions to accomplish those goals. But many arguments for theism rely on such claims. For example, many rely on claims that God would be likely to create a world which contains order or beauty or conscious beings. Others rely on claims that God would be likely to want to reveal himself to us by speaking through prophets or performing miracles. Skeptical theists, if they are to be consistent, must treat such claims with skepticism. And such skepticism may very well be justified. After all, how can we make such claims when we have no idea what an omnipotent and omniscient being's options would be? Furthermore, successful theodicies would seem to be out of the question if we are in no position to judge that a God would be likely to use evil to pursue such and such a goal.

These last remarks are, of course, too sketchy to be anything more than suggestive. But surely there's something to this line of thought. For example, it is hardly surprising that Richard Swinburne is not a skeptical theist, that he tries to solve the problem of evil the old-fashioned way—with a theodicy (see chapter 3 in this book). Skeptical theism is, I believe, incompatible with his brand of natural theology. So skeptical theism is a double-edged sword. And the sharper edge may be the one threatening the theist.[24]

NOTES

1. I say "directly" here because defenders of this thesis should not and often do not deny that this judgment could (in principle) be inferred from a separate determination of the likelihood of theism. If, for example, one could show on other grounds that theism is very improbable and naturalism very probable, then one could infer that it is unlikely that there is a sufficient divine reason for the evils we observe. Of course, making an inference like this is consistent with the evils providing no evidence at all against theism.

2. See William P. Alston, "The Inductive Argument from Evil and the Human Cognitive Condition," chapter 6 in this book.

3. Ibid.

4. Michael Tooley, "The Argument from Evil," *Philosophical Perspectives* 5 (1991): 94.

5. Ibid., 95.

6. William L. Rowe, "Evil and Theodicy," *Philosophical Topics* 16 (1988): 119-32.

7. Rowe's argument, like most other probabilistic arguments from evil, purports to show only that M or theism is prima facie improbable. To show that M or theism is improbable all things considered would require assessing all of the available evidence for theism.

8. Paul Draper, "Pain and Pleasure: An Evidential Problem for Theists," chapter 2 in this book. I will henceforth abbreviate this title as "Pain and Pleasure."

9. For a more detailed discussion and analysis both of the two different general strategies discussed in this section and of Rowe's and Hume's arguments in particular, see my "Probabilistic Arguments from Evil," *Religious Studies* (1993).

10. Peter van Inwagen, "The Problem of Evil, the Problem of Air, and the Problem of Silence," chapter 8 in this book.

11. Van Inwagen believes that Humean arguments formulated in terms of epistemic surprise are superior to ones formulated in terms of antecedent conditional probabilities. He argues for this as follows:

> Now let S be some true proposition that has a low probability on theism, but is not at all surprising on theism. I should think that the proposition that states the exact number of dogs would do. . . . It is clear that the following facts do not comprise a prima facie case for preferring "S and God does not exist" to "God exists": S; the probability of S on "S and God does not exist" is much higher than the probability of S on "God exists;" "S and God does not exist" and "God exists" are inconsistent. (p. 172, n. 7)

I believe that van Inwagen is correct that these three facts do not constitute a *prima facie* case against theism. But that's because "S and God does not exist," unlike HI, is (relative to S) an ad hoc rather than a serious alternative to theism. Indeed, it wouldn't matter if we said these facts do constitute a prima facie case against theism. After all, such a case could easily be defeated by ingeniously conjoining theism with S! This powerful new theory would stack up pretty well against "S and God does not exist" when it comes to predicting S. What's more, it would win hands down against atheism—hence we would have a prima facie case against atheism and hence for theism that is just as strong as the argument from dogs against theism! Van Inwagen says that the trouble with formulating the argument in terms of antecedent conditional probabilities is that something can be antecedently improbable on q and not be at all surprising on q. In fact, that's exactly the trouble with formulating the argument in terms of epistemic surprise. Consider, for example, the special creationist who claims that a high degree of similarity in the biochemistry of all known life forms is not surprising on special creationism and hence provides no evidence favoring evolution theory over special creationism. His premise is correct, but his inference is faulty. The antecedent probability of such a high degree of similarity is very high given evolution theory. And while a high degree of similarity is not at all surprising on special creationism, it is antecedently improbable on special creationism because it is no more likely on special creationism than a high or middling or low or very low degree of similarity. So this evidence against special creationism would likely not be appreciated unless one is careful to evaluate the evidence using antecedent conditional probabilities rather than a notion of epistemic surprise.

12. Van Inwagen, n. 1.

13. Van Inwagen would have us infer ST3 from another skeptical thesis:

> ST4: We are not in a position to assign any (antecedent) epistemic probability at all to O on G.

I choose not to do this because it would weaken the theist's case. The reason for this is that there is no natural interpretation of ST4 that renders it both plausible and such that ST3 follows from it. According to one interpretation (which van Inwagen clearly does not intend), it states that we are not in a position to assign a numerical value to the antecedent probability of O on G. This is obviously true, but it is equally obvious that ST3 does not follow from it. We can make comparative judgments of epistemic probability even if we cannot assign numerical values to the probabilities being compared—indeed, even if these probabilities have no numerical values. A second interpretation of ST4 (which seems to be how van Inwagen understands it) is that we cannot assign a numerical probability or even a probability range (like "low" or "high" or "middling") to O on G. But surely this is mistaken. Given how specific O is, it is rather obvious that $P(O/G)$ and $P(O/HI)$ are both very low (which is, of course, consistent with $P(O/HI)$ being proportionately much greater than $P(O/G)$). But more importantly, even if ST4 were true on this second interpretation, ST3 would not follow from it. For one can make a comparative judgment like "O is antecedently much more probable on HI than on G" without assigning any such probability range to the statements being compared. Indeed, my argument for C is essentially comparative in nature. I argue directly for the conclusion that the ratio of $P(O/HI)$ to $P(O/G)$ is high rather than drawing any inference from two separate conclusions about $P(O/HI)$ and $P(O/G)$. (Cf. van Inwagen, n. 9.) A third interpretation of ST4 is that we can't make any judgment at all, including any comparative judgment, about $P(O/G)$. Obviously ST3 follows from ST4 on this interpretation. But on this interpretation, ST4 is clearly false. Surely we can judge that the epistemic probability of O on G is less than 1 or greater than the epistemic probability of O on ~O. In any case, it would be needlessly ambitious to argue for ST4 interpreted in this way, since what needs to be shown to undermine my argument from evil is that one specific comparative judgment cannot be made, namely, the judgment that O is antecedently much more probable on HI than on G.

14. Van Inwagen, chapter 8.

15. If we have a number of theistic stories, $D_1 \ldots D_n$, that are pairwise mutually exclusive and antecedently equally probable given theism, then $P(D_i/G)$ will be low for each D_i, but the disjunction $D_1 \vee \ldots \vee D_n$ may itself be aprobable and hence may itself function as a potentially successful defense. (Cf. van Inwagen, n. 10.)

16. Van Inwagen states this first part in the following way: "A defense may not be improbable, either on the theory in whose cause it is employed, or on anything we know to be true." Putting aside the shift from "we must not be able to judge that it is improbable" to "it must not be improbable," what he should have said is that a defense may not be (antecedently) improbable on the theory *conjoined* with our background knowledge. I omit "conjoined with our background knowledge" when I state this condition because, given how I use probability talk, it would be redundant. When I use terms like *probable,* no implicit abstraction from one's background knowledge or any other aspects of one's epistemic situation is intended. This is true whether I am speaking of conditional or unconditional probabilities. That's why, when I want to consider probabilities that do involve a *partial* abstraction of some sort—e.g., probabilities independent of the observations and testimony O reports—I refer to them as "antecedent probabilities" so it is clear that such an abstraction is being made.

17. Van Inwagen is a bit unclear about all this. While he says that a defense *must* not be improbable, he says that a defense *need* not be probable. He also says that defenses will not *in practice* be probable because, if they were, the theist would employ them as theodicies. I don't know what to make of this. Surely van Inwagen doesn't believe that it is up to the theist whether to employ a probable theistic story as a successful theodicy or as support for ST3!

18. When I say "effect" here, I mean to imply that such theistic stories can in principle change $P(O/G)$. If tomorrow I were to confront for the first time a successful theodicy—a theistic story T that is antecedently very probable on theism and which is such that $P(O/T\&G)$ is as great as or at least not much smaller than $P(O/HI)$, then I would conclude on the basis of WAP, not that I had previously misjudged $P(O/G)$, but rather that $P(O/G)$ is no longer much less than $P(O/HI)$. This is not to deny that WAP is true for epistemic probability. It does, however, restrict the field of propositions over which WAP is defined to ones that have actually been considered. But this is only sensible. If God exists,

then I suppose he has a great theistic story to tell, but his existence doesn't guarantee that, relative to our epistemic situations, P(O/G) is high.

19. It would be unwise for theists to challenge this point. For just as WAP relates P(O/G) to P(D/G), Bayes's theorem relates P(G/O) to P(O/G):

$$P(G/O) = \frac{P(G) \times P(O/G)}{P(O)}.$$

Thus, suppose that skepticism about P(D/G) commits us to skepticism about P(O/G) by virtue of WAP. Then (since P(G) < 1 and P(O/~G) > O) skepticism about P(O/G) commits us to skepticism about P(G/O) and hence to skepticism about the probability of theism by virtue of Bayes's theorem. And skepticism about the probability of theism commits us to skepticism about theism. For if one is in a position to judge that theism is true, then one must also be in a position to judge that theism is more probably true than false.

20. Cf. George Schlesinger, *The Sweep of Probability* (Notre Dame: University of Notre Dame Press, 1991), 196-97.

21. It is worth noting that van Inwagen's two analogies don't undermine my analysis in this section. The argument from air is a weak argument, but not because of van Inwagen's defense. (Indeed, far from being aprobable, the atomistic story van Inwagen tells has an antecedent probability of 0 on ancient atomism, since atoms are "voidless" and hence can't be flexible.) There are many things I find puzzling about this argument. For example, why should an ancient atomist deny that air atoms are all settled to the ground? Couldn't he say that, like water, we move through air by displacing these atoms? But waiving questions like these, the main problem with the argument is that the "Hypothesis of Independence" simply says that there are four independent and continuous elements, air among them, each of which has *sui generis* properties. But this hypothesis doesn't explain the properties of air better than (or if we look at all the properties of air, even as well as) atomism. Of course, we could build those properties into the hypothesis, but then it would be hopelessly ad hoc. One might object that my Hypothesis of Indifference is also not very specific. But the Hypothesis of Indifference does not explain any facts reported by O by itself. Rather, it is our background knowledge about the goal-directedness of organic systems that allows for an explanation of the observed pattern of pain and pleasure in terms of the Hypothesis of Indifference but not in terms of theism. (See "Pain and Pleasure," Section II.) The fact that the Hypothesis of Indifference is not very specific (it is consistent with naturalism and a variety of supernaturalist hypotheses) and has no ontological commitments makes it initially much more probable than a very specific, ontologically committed, supernaturalist hypothesis like theism. This shows how serious an evidential problem the theist faces. It is a rare advantage to find a very general hypothesis that can explain a significant body of facts much better than a very specific one! The argument from silence against noetism is relatively weak because of a fairly successful "noodicy": it is antecedently very likely that intelligence need not lead to both technology of the right sort and a desire to communicate with life on other planets. If it weren't for several accidents of history, culture, and environment, it wouldn't have led to these things on earth! Of course, cosmic silence is some evidence favoring the Hypothesis of Isolation over noetism. But it's not very strong evidence. The ratio of the antecedent probability of cosmic silence on the Hypothesis of Isolation to the antecedent probability of cosmic silence on noetism is greater than one, but it is not very high. (Bayes's theorem implies that ratios—not differences—are what is important for assessing the strength of the evidence here.)

22. Van Inwagen, chapter 8.

23. Notice that the first conjunct of D6 makes a modal claim that we have, antecedently, absolutely no reason to accept. The second proposition appeals to an unknown good that for some unknown reason depends on the existence of higher-level sentient animals. And the third proposition makes a value judgment—the judgment that

being massively irregular is at least as great a defect in a world as the defect of containing patterns of suffering morally equivalent to those recorded by O—that we have no good reason for believing to be true. (I assume here that neither the fact that *some* massively irregular worlds are massively deceptive nor the *aesthetic* intuitions of certain anal-retentive deists who cringe at the unloveliness of irregularity provides us with a good reason for believing that this judgment is true.) Given all this, and given that each of the conjuncts mentions O in an ad hoc way anyway, it's hard to see what advantage D6 has over D1 and D2. If anything, its appeal to various controversial metaphysical and moral theses makes its aprobability more open to challenge than the aprobability of D1 and D2.

24. I am grateful to Bruce Hauptli for helpful comments on an earlier version of this paper.

10. BRUCE RUSSELL

Defenseless

I

Evidential arguments from evil against the existence of God often take the following form:

1. If God exists, there is no gratuitous evil, that is, evil which God would have no morally sufficient reason to allow.
2. But there is gratuitous evil.
3. So God does not exist.

They are evidential because of the nature of the arguments given for the second premise. Those arguments are probabilistic or epistemic in nature, starting from the fact that even after careful reflection we see no morally sufficient reason for God to allow certain kinds, instances, amounts, or patterns of suffering or from that suffering itself. And they move from those starting points to the conclusion that there is gratuitous evil either by induction or by abduction, that is, by an inference to the best explanation. We can capture these four kinds of evidential arguments from evil by means of the following matrix:

	Inductive	Abductive
Start from the fact that we see no point to allowing certain instances, amounts, types, or patterns of suffering	(1)	(2)
Start from the fact that there are certain instances, amounts, types or patterns of suffering.[1]	(3)	(4)

William Rowe has given a version of the evidential argument from evil that is in category (1). He argues that because the goods we know of provide no morally sufficient reason for allowing certain instances of suffering, we have good reason to believe that no goods provide such reason and hence good reason to believe that allowing the suffering is not morally justified. Critics have responded that our knowledge that the goods we know of do not justify allowing the suffering gives us reason to believe that no goods do only if we have good reason to believe that the sample of goods we know of is a representative sample, and we have no good reason to believe it is.[2] An argument that has been given to show we have no reason to believe the sample is representative is that "goods beyond our ken have no chance of belonging to Rowe's sample [of goods which could justify allowing the suffering]; so the sample is not random."[3]

But when considering whether the sample is representative we need to take account of goods beyond our ken only if there is reason to believe there are any. Consider a parallel case. Suppose we look all around the world and find no blue crows. Suppose someone argues that the sample is not representative because there are no crows in our sample that hide whenever anyone is looking for them. We could rightly object that we have every reason to believe our sample is representative unless there is reason to believe there are such elusive crows "beyond our powers to observe them." Similarly, the defender of the evidential argument from evil can object that we have every reason to believe the sample is representative unless there is reason to believe that there are goods beyond our ken.

Still, there seems something right about this general line of criticism. If we encounter aliens whom we find to be trustworthy and they show us a type of animal we have never seen before (call them zagaloops), we are not justified in believing that none are red on the grounds that none of the many we saw were red. If we have no idea whether the sample is representative or not, then we should suspend judgment on whether none are red. Similarly, *if* we have no idea whether the reasons we have considered for allowing suffering are representative or not, we should suspend judgment on whether none are morally sufficient to justify allowing the relevant suffering. For now I will leave it an open question whether we do have good reason to believe that the sample is representative. After discussing type-2 arguments I will argue that we do.

II

What about type-2 and type-4 arguments? How do they fare? They both rest on something like the following principle:

P1: S is justified in believing p if and only if p is part of the best explanation of what S has observed.

("Observed" should be construed broadly to include, e.g., testimony or accounts a person has heard or read.) Now S might be justified in believing p relative to S's observations and S* justified in believing not-p even though their immediate observations are alike. For instance, S and S* might look through a telescope at the same spot in the night sky and both see nothing. Suppose on the basis of other considerations S* is justified in believing that the telescope they are looking through is so weak that they could not see a planet even if one were where they are looking but, on different grounds, S is justified in believing that the telescope is powerful enough to spot a planet. Then, though S and S* have the same type of perceptions on looking through the telescope, S is justified in believing that there is no planet in the area but S* is not.

So P1 makes justification relative to the total evidence the subject has. But it does not make it subjective. I am assuming that whether some hypothesis best explains what someone observes does not depend on whether that person *thinks* it best explains it. Rather, whether it does is an objective matter, though it is very difficult to specify in any detail what makes one explanation better than another.

Type-2 and type-4 arguments differ only in what they take the explanandum to be, that is, in what they set out to explain. In type-2 arguments the starting point is our failing to see the point of certain instances, amounts, types, or patterns of suffering. In type-4 arguments, it is that suffering itself or, if everything must ultimately be grounded in observations, our observations of that suffering. Our observations of suffering are one thing, our failure to see a reason for it another, just as our observations of a killing are one thing and our failure to see a reason for it another.

In type-2 arguments it is claimed that the best explanation of our failure to see a point to the relevant suffering is that there is none. The theist's competing explanation is that there is a morally sufficient reason but it is beyond our ken.[4] Which is the best explanation of our failing to see a point to certain kinds or instances of suffering, the explanation that there is no point or the explanation that there is but it is beyond our ken?

To answer this question it might help to introduce Bayes's Theorem:

$$P(H/e\&k) = \frac{P(H/k) \times P(e/H\&k)}{P(e/k)}.$$

This theorem says that the probability of some hypothesis, H, on certain evidence, e, and background knowledge (or justified beliefs), k, is a function of how likely that hypothesis is on background knowledge alone [P(H/k)], of how likely that evidence is given that hypothesis and the background knowledge [P(e/H&k)], and of how likely the evidence is on the background knowledge alone [P(e/k)]. Suppose we let e = the statement that even after much careful reflection we see no point to certain instances, amounts, types or patterns of suffering, H = there is no point to that suffering, k = whatever justified background beliefs we have, and T = there is a reason for that suffering that is beyond our ken. Then whether it is more reasonable to accept H or T on e&k will be a question of whether P(H/e&k) > P(T/e&k). And given Bayes's Theorem, that question amounts to the question, "Which of the right sides of the following two equations is greater?"

$$(1)\ P(H/e\&k) = \frac{P(H/k) \times P(e/H\&k)}{P(e/k)}$$

$$(2)\ P(T/e\&k) = \frac{P(T/k) \times P(e/T\&k)}{P(e/k)}.$$

Now surely P(e/T&k) > P(e/H&k). If there is a reason but it is beyond our ken, then it is very likely, even certain, that we won't see one even after careful reflection. It is also very likely that we won't see one if there is none, but one cannot rule out the possibility of illusion: we might think we see a reason when really there is none. So P(e/H&k) < P(e/T&k) and if that is true H is a better explanation on e&k only if P(H/k) > P(T/k).

There is a point worth noting here: the role of apparently pointless evil has lost its importance in the argument from evil.[5] It is admitted that our failure to see the point of certain evils is at least as likely on the theist's hypothesis that there is a reason for it which is beyond our ken as it is on the hypothesis that there is no reason for it. The issue now turns on the question of which of those two competing hypotheses is more likely to be true *on background evidence*.

While this point is worth noting, it is not surprising. Suppose someone holds that God created the universe 100 years ago. The following facts count strongly against the view that God created the universe 100 years ago: the fact that there seem to be books and newspapers over 100 years old, that they recount incidents that occurred even before that, that there are deep river valleys and that mountains seem to have suffered the effects of erosion. However, suppose a person who holds the view that God created the universe 100 years ago also holds that he created it with all its seeming signs of age. Assume that if we object that God would not deceive us that way, the person responds that although deception is *prima facie* wrong, there can be moral reasons which favor deception so that, all things considered, it is not wrong. And suppose that person adds that, for all we know, there are such reasons beyond our ken which would justify God in deceiving us about creating the universe 100 years ago. Since it is just as likely that we would observe what we do on the 100-year theory as on our ordinary view about the age of the universe, if it is more reasonable to accept the ordinary view, it must be because the view that the universe was created 100 years ago by a God who has reasons beyond our ken for deceiving us is less likely on background evidence or knowledge than the ordinary view. And surely it is less likely whatever it is that makes it so.

Is the view that there is a God who, for reasons beyond our ken, allows the suffering which appears pointless to us any different epistemically from the view that there is a God who created the universe 100 years ago and, for reasons beyond our ken, has deceived us into thinking it is older? It does not seem to be. We reject the 100-year theory partly because it must hold that in the last 100 years the signs of erosion have been caused by natural events but before that they were caused by God's creative act. The naturalistic theory which says that the causes have always been of the same sort seems simpler and so more reasonable to accept.

But this difference between the standard view of the age of the universe and the 100-year theory can't amount to much for theists who hold that a creation took place at some (remote) time in the past. For those theists will also hold that from some point onwards, leaving aside miraculous interventions and the actions of free agents, events have natural causes but before that time they do not. So for theists who hold that God created the universe, they will have to reject the 100-year theory on the grounds that it is not reasonable to believe that God deceived us in creating the universe 100 years ago for some reason beyond our ken. But if it is not reasonable to believe that God deceived us, for some reason beyond our ken, when he created the universe, it is not reasonable to believe that there is some reason beyond our ken which, if God exists, would justify him in allowing all the suffering we see.

Both the view that God created the universe 100 years ago and, for reasons beyond our ken, deceived us in doing that and the view that there are reasons beyond our ken that would justify God, if he exists, in allowing all the suffering we see are like the view that there are blue crows beyond our powers of observation. Once we have conducted the relevant search for crows (looking all over the world in different seasons and at crows at different stages of maturity), we are justified in virtue of that search in believing there are no crows beyond our powers of observation which are relevantly different from the crows we've seen. If after the relevant search we weren't justified in believing that, then we would have to remain skeptical about all generalizations about crows. What else could we do that would justify us in believing there are no crows beyond our powers of observation that are relevantly different from the crows we've seen? How else could we be justified in believing that there are no very shy, very cunning, very able crows that are blue but hide whenever we try to look for them? Similarly, once we've conducted the relevant search for moral reasons to justify allowing the relevant suffering (thinking hard about how allowing the suffering would be needed to realize sufficiently weighty goods, reading and talking to others who have thought about the same problem), we are justified in believing that there are no morally sufficient reasons for allowing that suffering.

To see this, let us suppose the opposite, that is, that even after failing to find sufficiently weighty moral reasons to justify God's allowing, say, the brutal rape, beating, and murder of a little girl we are *not* justified in believing there are none. It will follow that we are also not justified in believing that some human being who could easily have stopped the heinous crime did something wrong in failing to intervene. After all, the same reason that justifies God in not intervening,

if God exists, may be the reason why the human onlooker should not have intervened. Of course, since the human onlooker will not be able to give that reason in
defense of his inaction, it will not be *his* reason for doing nothing; it will not be
what motivated him to refrain from intervening. But we can distinguish between
the evaluation of the person and his motives and the evaluation of his act. For
instance, we think that it is morally permissible for a person to give to charity even
if his reason for doing that is to get a break on his taxes. I am arguing that if we are
not justified in believing that no reason would justify God in allowing the brutal
rape and murder, then we are not justified in believing that no reason would justify the onlooker in allowing that same act. The reason beyond our ken that would
justify God in allowing it could be the same reason which would justify the
onlooker. For all we know, both the onlooker and God had to refrain from intervening for the little girl to have union with God or for her killer to develop spiritually. How can we be justified in rejecting these possibilities as reasons for the
onlooker not to intervene if we cannot be justified in rejecting them as sufficient
reasons for God not to intervene?[6]

The fact that we cannot expect to discern *God's* reasons (his motives)
for allowing the murder, but can expect to discern *the onlooker's* has no bearing on
the question at issue. The question at issue is whether we must be unable to judge
that there are no *justifying* reasons for human nonintervention if we are unable to
judge that there are none for Divine nonintervention. I have argued that we must.
Moral skepticism about God's omissions entails moral skepticism about our own
omissions.

We are now in a position to see how closely type-1 and type-2 arguments
are connected. Failure to find any blue crows after the relevant search gives us reason to believe that there are no blue crows that we have failed to observe. Barring
other reasons for thinking there are, we should believe our sample is representative and that the best explanation of our failure to see any blue crows is that there
are none. Similarly, failure to find any morally sufficient reasons for allowing certain instances, amounts, or types of suffering, after trying hard to come up with
them, gives us reason to believe there are none. Barring other reasons for thinking
there are, we should believe our sample of reasons is representative and that the
best explanation of our failure to find a justifying reason is that there are none.

After the relevant search has taken place, the burden of proof is on the
opponents to show that our sample is not representative. But before such a search
has taken place, the burden of proof is on those who offer an evidential argument—
as the example involving the little animals in the extraterrestrial land shows. Because
we have not looked all over the extraterrestrials' planet at Zagaloops, we have no
idea whether the bunch we have been shown is a representative sample. Hence, our
conclusion that none are red, since none we've seen are red, is not justified even if
there is no reason to think that the bunch we've seen is *not* representative.

There is no general truth about whether inductions and abductions are
innocent until proven guilty or guilty until proven innocent. Rather, they are innocent until proven guilty *if they are based on a relevant search* and guilty until proven
innocent *if they are not based on such a search.* Surely the appropriate search regard-

ing moral reasons is an intellectual one, one that in this context involves trying to think of reasons which would justify allowing a certain course of action. That is why the burden of proof is on the theists to show that there is reason to think that there are moral reasons beyond our ken relevantly unlike the ones we have already considered if they hope to undercut the evidential argument. Paradoxically, the best explanation for apparently pointless suffering is that it has no point even though it is at least as likely that it would appear that way given that there is a point beyond our ken as given that there is no point whatsoever.

Having defended both type-1 and type-2 arguments from evil, I now want to turn to a type-4 argument and defend it.

III

Suppose this time we let e = a proposition that describes in some detail the amount, kinds, and distribution of suffering—the suffering not only of human beings but of all the sentient terrestrial creatures that there are or ever have been. e is not now a proposition about our failure to see a point to that suffering. Let T = theism, the hypothesis that there exists an omnipotent, omniscient, and morally perfect person who created the universe and HI = the hypothesis of indifference, that is, the hypothesis that neither the nature nor the condition of sentient beings on earth is the result of benevolent or malevolent actions performed by nonhuman persons. In this discussion I will ignore our background knowledge, k, and assume that T is just as likely as HI on k, that is, that $P(T/k) = P(HI/k)$. Then the question is whether $P(HI/e)$ is greater than $P(T/e)$, and, as we have seen, those two probabilities are a function of other probabilities as the following two formulas indicate.

$$(1)\ P(HI/e) = \frac{P(HI) \times P(e/HI)}{P(e)}$$

$$(2)\ P(T/e) = \frac{P(T) \times P(e/T)}{P(e)}.$$

Peter van Inwagen says that theists can try to show $P(e/HI)$ is lower, or that $P(e/T)$ is higher, than one might suppose.[7] According to him, showing that $P(e/T)$ is higher than one might suppose amounts to giving a theodicy, to giving reasons why God would allow all the suffering we see, where those reasons are likely on theism. In other words, a theodicy requires offering some auxiliary hypothesis, h, such that $P(e/T\&h)$ and $P(h/T)$ are both high. Van Inwagen is not optimistic about the prospects of giving a successful theodicy, since there is no reason to think $P(h/T)$ is high when $P(e/T\&h)$ is, and so proposes to give only a defense, that is, he only tries to show that we are in no position to judge $P(h/T)$ and so in no position to judge $P(T/e)$.[8]

In light of these failures, van Inwagen pursues a more modest strategy, a defense rather than a theodicy. He thinks we will be in no position to judge that e is more likely on HI than on T if we can find an h such that h is not unlikely on anything we know, e is very likely on T&h, and h is true, for all anyone knows, given T. In other words, he thinks we will be in no position to judge $P(e/T)$, and so in no position to judge that $P(HI/e) > P(T/e)$, if we can find an h such that h is not unlikely on anything we know, $P(e/T\&h)$ is high, and, *for all anyone knows*, $P(h/T)$ is high.[9]

The story he tells, and claims is true for all anyone knows, to defend against the atheist's arguments involving the suffering of animals is that there are certain higher-order goods that could only exist if higher-level sentient creatures do and

> (1) Every possible world that contains higher-level sentient creatures either contains patterns of suffering morally equivalent to those recorded by S [our e], or else is massively irregular.
> (2) Some important intrinsic or extrinsic good depends on the existence of higher-level sentient creatures; this good is of sufficient magnitude that it outweighs the patterns of suffering recorded by S.
> (3) Being massively irregular is a defect in a world, a defect at least as great as the defect of containing patterns of suffering morally equivalent to those recorded by S.[10]

It is impossible to argue against van Inwagen's (1) by claiming there are possible regular worlds with different laws of nature, and without earthquakes, tornadoes, and the like, without taking on his modal skepticism, that is, his view that we can't be justified in believing that a world is possible without being able to offer a plausible "design" of that world, and I am not prepared to take that on. But (1) is open to criticism even granting his modal skepticism. There seem to be more alternatives for God than the ones van Inwagen imagines. Perhaps God can only choose *to create* either a world with regularities or one with massive irregularities but another possible world is one where God creates a world with regularities and intervenes more than he now does, if he exists, but not so much as to produce *massive* irregularities. Perhaps no one can complain if God creates a world in which everyone's life is good on balance for him, anymore than a child can complain that he should not have been born if his life is on balance good for him. But a child can complain that his parents should have intervened more than they did to prevent awful things from happening to him even if their failure to intervene did not make his life on balance not worth living. Likewise, we can complain that God has not intervened more than he has, if he has intervened at all, even if (contrary to all evidence) everyone's life is on balance good for him.

So the complaint is that there is a possible world that contains at least one less case of terrible suffering and that God, if he exists, would be morally required to bring about that world. This world would not contain *massive* irregularities so it is irrelevant whether massive irregularity in a world is a defect and a graver defect than massive suffering. Furthermore, van Inwagen's modal skepticism does not prevent us from being justified in believing there is such a possible world because we can "design" such a world: it is just like the actual world except that there is one more case of awful suffering that is miraculously prevented in that world. And because it differs so little from the actual world our moral intuitions should be reliable: a world with one less instance of a brutal beating, rape and murder of a little girl is morally better than one with such an instance, whether that suffering is prevented by God or some human being. And if God exists he would be obligated to prevent it, not because a person is *always* obligated to prevent more rather than less suffering in realizing some good end,[11] but because a person is always obligated to prevent more rather than less terrible suffering in realizing such an end, provided that preventing that suffering does not appear to approach some threshold beyond which terrible consequences will ensue.

Van Inwagen has no adequate response to someone who says that, if God exists, he would be obligated to reduce *to some extent* the level of terrible suffering that exists in the actual world.[12] Neither the violation of the laws of nature nor the interference with people's freedom that would be required would be so great as to justify God's failing to intervene.

While van Inwagen does not directly respond to this objection, his colleague, William Alston, does. Alston thinks we are in no position to judge that God would be obligated to reduce the level of terrible suffering. He argues that, for all we know, it was necessary to allow a child or a fawn to suffer to realize some outweighing good. So atheists are not justified in claiming it was not necessary.

The goods Alston considers fall into four categories which are captured by the following matrix:

	Goods we know of	Goods we don't know of (those beyond our ken)
The good is primarily of benefit to the sufferer	(a)	(b)
The good is *not* primarily of benefit to the sufferer	(c)	(d)

Goods which fall into category (a) include fulfilling one's own deepest nature and having a vision of the inner life of God; those that fall into category (c) include the free will, or freedom of action, of people other than the sufferer. I won't consider all of Alston's arguments, particularly those that appeal to goods in category (a), because I believe that William Rowe has convincingly argued that at most Alston has shown that it is logically possible, or has not been proven false, that God must allow all the suffering there is in order to benefit the sufferer.[13] But to undercut the atheist's claim that we are justified in believing that some of that suffering is not needed to benefit the sufferers, Alston must show more, namely, that it is a *live* possibility that God's allowing that suffering is needed to benefit the sufferers, that is, that we have no good reason to believe it is not so needed.

The more interesting cases fall in class (c). Alston says atheists are not justified in believing that preventing one more instance of a brutal rape and murder, or of a fawn's suffering, is not needed to realize some outweighing good for others because in order to be so justified they would have to know that those cases were "among the n percent of the cases most worthy of being miraculously prevented."[14] And in order to know that Alston says we would have to be able to survey all the cases, past, present, and future, to see if the particular one fell into the relevant n percent.

But it is ludicrous to think we would have to do that survey to be justified in believing God should have intervened. There are cases involving human intervention where if the number of interventions surpassed a certain level such bad consequences would ensue that no further interventions should take place. An example Steve Wykstra and I have used involves the police setting up checkpoints to find drunken motorists.[15] Suppose we know that if more than some indeterminate number of people are stopped they will become so hostile, because of delays, that more people will be killed by those drivers than would be killed by drunken drivers if fewer were stopped. In other words, suppose we know that if more than m percent of drivers are stopped, for some indeterminate m, more harm on balance will be produced. Still, we can be justified in believing that we are beneath the relevant threshold, where the bad effects start to outweigh the good, even if we don't know exactly where that threshold is. Provided we have some reason to think that stopping people at some low level, L, has a deterrent effect on drunken driving—is doing some good—and there is no evidence that bad effects are occurring at level L, we are justified in believing that the police should be stopping people at least at level L. Similarly, we can be justified in believing that if God exists, he would reduce by at least one instance the terrible suffering there is, since there is no reason to think that doing that would have awful results and good reason to think it would have a very good effect.

It might be objected that if one less evil were prevented by God we would still think that one less than that should be prevented and on and on.[16] My reply is that we would think that until we came to a point where it was doubtful whether important goods would be lost, or significant evils produced, if more evils were prevented, that is, until it seemed a relevant threshold were being approached. But that just means that the argument that says that if God exists he should have prevented at least one more instance of terrible suffering would be sound when applied in other possible worlds that are quite similar to our world. That is no objection to its soundness when applied to this world. Suppose a farmer strikes his mule 100 times. It can be reasonable of me to believe that the farmer should have struck his mule at least one less time even if it would also have been reasonable for me to believe he should have struck it one less time had he struck it only 99 times. And that will be true even if I do not know exactly how many fewer times the farmer should have struck his mule.

IV

Van Inwagen thought that there was some auxiliary hypothesis, h, which we are in no position to judge improbable on theism or anything else we know and is such that the pattern of suffering there is in the world is not improbable on theism and that hypothesis. For him h amounted to the following: it is better to have a world with sentient creatures and a certain amount of suffering than one without either (because of the intrinsic goods that can only exist if sentient creatures exist) and, as far as we know, there are no other morally mandatory possible worlds that contain sentient creatures and a different pattern of suffering (as far as we know, other such worlds contain either massive irregularity or at least as bad a pattern of suffering). I have argued that h is improbable on what we know, since we know there is a possible world that contains just one less instance of terrible suffering, that that world is not massively irregular, and that a wholly good being would be morally required to bring it about if he knew about it and could. Hence, T&h is improbable on what we know. According to Bayes's Theorem

$$(1)\ P(HI/e\&k) = \frac{P(III/k) \times P(e/HI\&k)}{P(e/k)}$$

$$(2)\ P(T\&h/e\&k) = \frac{P(T\&h/k) \times P(e/T\&h\&k)}{P(e/k)}.$$

Since HI, the hypothesis that the lives of sentient beings are not the result of actions by benevolent or malevolent nonhuman persons, is not improbable on what we know while T&h is, and P(e/HI&k) is about equal to P(e/T&h&k), Bayes's Theorem can be used to show that P(HI/e&k) > P(T&h/e&k), and that it is more reasonable to accept HI than T&h on evil and our background knowledge.

I have only considered a particular h. Might not a different hypothesis do the job van Inwagen hoped that his h would do? I do not see how it could, since it seems nearly certain on what we know that a world just like this one but with one less instance of terrible suffering would be so much better morally than this world that a wholly good being would be morally required to bring it about if he knew about it and was able to. Hence, any hypothesis that implied that this was not nearly certain would be improbable on what we know. And if an hypothesis is improbable on what we know, it cannot serve as an adequate defense of theism. That is because a defense requires that theism be conjoined with an hypothesis to explain the pattern of suffering there is and if that hypothesis is improbable on what we know, then the conjunction of theism and that hypothesis will also be improbable on that background knowledge.

Theists might respond that it is *not* nearly certain on what *they* know that if God exists there would be at least one less instance of terrible suffering—or at least not on what they are justified in believing. It is true that if there are reasons for the existence of God that are weightier than the reasons in favor of the view that, if God exists, there would be at least one less case of awful suffering, then that view will not be probable on the *total* evidence. I doubt that any reasons for God's existence are weightier, and that the total evidence for sophisticated theists and atheists is different, but that is beside the point in this discussion. All I have been arguing is that *if* there are *no* weightier grounds for belief in the existence of God, then the three types of evidential arguments against the existence of God I have considered will give theists and atheists alike sufficient reason to believe that God does not exist. In other words, recent attempts at *undercutting* these arguments will fail, though attempts at *overriding* them may succeed. Because the hypotheses which are offered to save theism are unlikely on what we know, theism is defenseless against the evidential arguments from evil.[17]

NOTES

1. Paul Draper, in "Pain and Pleasure: An Evidential Problem for Theists," chapter 2 in this book, and in "Probabilistic Arguments from Evil," *Religious Studies* (1993), gives versions of the evidential argument that fall in category (4). I consider the arguments I have given in Bruce Russell, "The Persistent Problem of Evil," *Faith and Philosophy* 6 (1989) and Bruce Russell and Stephen Wykstra, "The 'Inductive' Argument from Evil: A Dialogue," *Philosophical Topics* 16 (1988), to fall in category (2). I believe William Rowe's version of the argument from evil falls in category (1). See Rowe, "The Problem of Evil and Some Varieties of Atheism," chapter 1 in this book; "Evil and Theodicy," *Philosophical Topics* 16 (1988); and "William Alston on the Problem of Evil," in *The Rationality of Belief and the Plurality of Faiths*, ed. Thomas D. Senor (Ithaca: Cornell University Press, 1995). I do not know of anyone who has presented an argument in category (3).

2. William P. Alston, "The Inductive Argument from Evil and the Human Cognitive Condition," chapter 6 in this book, and Draper, "Probabilistic Arguments from Evil," sec. III, B, make the same point.

3. Draper, "Probabilistic Arguments from Evil," 19.

4. See ibid., 14-15, for a discussion of this competing explanation.

5. It would be a mistake to think that the argument does not depend at all on the existence of apparently pointless suffering. The argument that the universe is over 100 years old depends on our observations of apparent signs of age since without those observations there would be nothing for the competing hypotheses about the age and origin of the universe to explain. Similarly, if there was no apparently pointless evil, there would be nothing for the competing hypotheses about the existence or nonexistence of justifying reasons to explain.

6. It should be apparent that I am not arguing that it would be wrong of God to allow the suffering of the little girl since it would be wrong of us. Rather, I am arguing that the method for determining the moral status of that omission is the same in either case. See Russell and Wykstra, "The 'Inductive' Argument from Evil: A Dialogue," 141-42, for a similar point.

7. In Peter van Inwagen, "The Problem of Evil, the Problem of Air, and the Problem of Silence," chapter 8 in this book. I take the statements of HI and e from that chapter. Van Inwagen does not refer to Bayes's Theorem as I have, but the use of Bayes's Theorem allows one to see clearly all the relevant factors that go into judging whether theism or atheism best explains the evil we see. It helps prevent concentration on just one of the factors, in particular, on $P(e/T)$.

8. Traditionally in a defense one tries to show that the existence of God is *not incompatible* with the existence of all the evil we see. To do that one needs to find a proposition that is itself logically possible, is compatible with the existence of God, and is such that evil is *not impossible* on that proposition and theism. Van Inwagen extends the notion of a defense to include attempts to show that the existence of God is *not improbable* on all the evil we see. He tries to find a proposition whose probability on theism we are in no posi-

tion to judge (and so is, in that sense, not improbable on theism), which is not improbable on anything else we know to be true (ibid.), and is such that evil is *not unlikely,* and in fact is likely, on that proposition and theism. In this paper I am using "defense" in van Inwagen's extended sense.

9. Van Inwagen's locution "for all anyone knows" is ambiguous. Understood one way, we might think that *for all anyone knows,* P(h/T) is high if h is as likely as not given theism, that is, if P(h/T) = 0.5. But then we would be in a position to judge h on theism, which van Inwagen wants to exclude in a defense. I will understand "for all we know" to mean "we don't know." Hence, to say that *"for all anyone knows,* P(h/T) is high" will mean "we don't know how likely h is on theism." No doubt van Inwagen will object to versions of the argument from evil that assume some definite number for P(h/T) on the grounds that we are in no position to judge what that number is and so it is inappropriate to assign 0.5 to P(h/T).

10. Ibid.

11. Van Inwagen himself criticizes these grounds in arguing that a judge does nothing wrong in imposing, say, a \$25 parking fine when he could have done as much good on balance by imposing a fine of \$24.99. Still, as van Inwagen also notes, a judge does wrong if he imposes a grossly excessive fine, one that is much too great given the end to be served and the offense committed. See van Inwagen, "The Magnitude, Duration, and Distribution of Evil: A Theodicy," *Philosophical Topics* 16 (1988): 167-68.

12. In note 11 of "The Problem of Air," van Inwagen argues that "There is, therefore, no *minimum* number of cases of intense suffering that God could allow without forfeiting the good of a world that is not massively irregular—just as there is no sharp cut-off point between a penalty that is an effective deterrent for armed assault and a penalty that is not." I take this to imply that there is no *maximum* number of cases of God's intervening to prevent intense suffering that at the same time avoids introducing massive irregularity. That may be true but even if it is, it is irrelevant. We can know that some penalty (say, a fine of \$1) is not an effective deterrent to armed robbery even if there is no sharp cut-off point between penalties that are effective deterrents and those that are not. (A large grey area between known effective deterrents and known ineffective deterrents does not imply that we cannot know that some deterrents are effective and some are not.) Similarly, we can know that God could have intervened "one more time" to prevent intense suffering without introducing massive irregularity even if we do not know exactly, or even roughly, how many times he could intervene without introducing massive irregularity. And we can also know that since he could have intervened more without producing massive irregularity, he should have.

13. See Rowe, "William Alston on the Problem of Evil."

14. Alston, "The Inductive Argument from Evil." He only says this of the case involving the fawn but he says something similar about the case involving the little girl in Flint. There he says that we would have to show that that case "is among the n percent worst cases of wrongdoing in the history of the universe."

15. Russell and Wykstra, "The 'Inductive' Argument from Evil: A Dialogue," 140-41.

16. This objection was offered by an anonymous reviewer and by James Paternoster, a student in my seminar on the problem of evil in winter term, 1993.

17. I am indebted to David Conway, William Hasker, Daniel Howard-Snyder, David O'Connor, John O'Leary-Hawthorne, William Rowe, and the students in my seminar on the problem of evil, winter, 1993, for helpful comments on and criticisms of earlier drafts of this paper. I am grateful to my colleague Stefan Sencerz for discussing with me the connection between moral skepticism about reasons which would justify divine nonintervention and a similar skepticism about human nonintervention.

11.

RICHARD M. GALE

Some Difficulties in
Theistic Treatments of Evil

That the world contains the evils it does obviously poses a challenge to traditional theism. For some it is *logical* in that a contradiction is supposed to be deducible from the coexistence of God and evil. Almost everyone now believes that adequate defenses have been devised to neutralize this challenge, a defense being a description of a possible world containing both God and the evils in question. In such a world God has a morally exonerating excuse for permitting these evils. In particular, it is claimed that the free-will defense, in at least one of its many versions, succeeds in reconciling God's existence with moral evil—evil that is attributable to creaturely misuse of free will. In my book, *On the Nature and Existence of God,* I argued that no version of this defense works, and thereby the logical problem posed by moral evil is still with us. This, however, will not be my concern in this paper.

Evil also can be seen as posing an *evidential* challenge because the evils found in the world are supposed to lower the probability that God exists, and, for some atheologians, so much so that it is less than one-half. There are two different theistic responses to this challenge. The strongest response takes the form of a theodicy, which is a defense plus some argument for thinking that the possible world in which God and evil coexist is the actual world. The weaker response, which I will call "defensive skepticism," is either (i) a defense coupled with an argument for our not being cognitively capable of finding out whether or not the possible world described in this defense is the actual world or (ii) just an argument for our not being cognitively capable of determining whether or not any evil is "gratuitous" in the sense that there is not in fact, though there could be, a circumstance that would constitute a morally exonerating excuse for God's permitting it.

The purpose of this paper is to explore some outstanding difficulties with the theodicies and defensive skepticisms developed in the preceding essays, as well as elsewhere in the extant literature. It is no part of its purpose to settle anything. My aim is just to keep the fire of controversy burning brightly, hopefully as an aid to some student who is faced with the challenge of having to write a paper based on the views expressed in some of the chapters in this volume.

1. The Defensive Skepticism Response

There is a strong and weak version of the evidential argument from evil. Both begin with a proposition, E, which reports all of the apparently gratuitous evils of which we humans know, a gratuitous evil being one that logically excludes God's existence because it has no justification, not being necessary for the realization of an outweighing good or the prevention of a greater evil.[1] E also reports everything that we humans know about their causes and consequences, among which there is nothing that would render these evils nongratuitous. It is claimed that it can be inferred from E, by the ordinary rules of inductive reasoning, that it is probable or highly likely that these evils are gratuitous. From this the weak version infers that relative to our total background knowledge, K,[2] the prior probability that God exists, G, is lowered by E—if $P(G/K)=n$, then $P(G/K$ and $E)<$ n—the strong version that it is lowered to less than $1/2$—$P(G/K$ and $E)<1/2)$.[3]

The response of defensive skepticism to both versions is that our cognitive abilities preclude our ever being justified in making any claims, probabilistic or otherwise, about whether an evil is gratuitous. The more convincing version of defensive skepticism lists all of the defenses, $D_1, \ldots . D_n$, which we can imagine, among which is the catch-all compensation-in-an-afterlife one, which works even for the Bambi and Sue type cases.[4] It then goes on to argue that for each evil described by E there is some defense in this set that does not entail G, has a reasonably high degree of probability relative to G, and whose actuality we human beings are not cognitively capable of determining, from which it is concluded that we are not epistemically justified in claiming that any of the evils reported by E is gratuitous. As a result, we cannot be justified in claiming that any evil, however extensive and seemingly gratuitous, lowers the probability that God exists relative to K.[5] Letting D' stand for all the defenses invoked to deal with the various evils reported by E, $P(G/K)=P(G/K$ and E and $D')=n$. For every member of D' Alston, in chapter 6, claims to "have drawn on various limits to our cognitive powers, opportunities, and achievements in arguing that we are not in a position to deny that God could have that kind of reason for various cases of suffering."

Without the argument for our inability to determine whether or not D' is true, the floodgates are open to a complete skepticism, at least in regard to any contingent proposition, since for any such proposition, p, no matter how high its probability (or improbability) relative to our background knowledge K and certain empirical evidence r that confirms (or disconfirms) p, there is some possibly true proposition q, such that $P(p/K$ and r and $q)=P(p/K)$. What the skeptical response requires is that it is not epistemically possible for us humans to be justified or warranted in asserting q, and this supposedly is not the case for every contingent proposition. As Alston puts it, the difference between the negative existential proposition based on E—that God has no justification for allowing the evils reported by E—and ordinary empirically based negative existentials is that for the former, unlike the latter, we have "a very sketchy idea of what is in that territory" and "no sufficient basis for an estimate of how much of the territory falls outside" our knowledge.

The less convincing response makes no effort to present a defense and instead argues only that our cognitive limitations make it impossible for us to be justified in asserting that every possible defense is a member of $D_1, \ldots, D_n$, thereby leaving open the possibility of there being an adequate defense which we are not up to imagining, no less determining to be actually true. The heart of this response is that God is morally inscrutable to us because our cognitive limitations make it unlikely that we would be able to fathom God's reason for permitting some apparently gratuitous evil. Some of the skeptical defenders in this volume give both types of response.

It now will be shown that: (i) the defensive skeptic's argument for our not being cognitively capable of determining whether a given defense is actual not only precludes the sort of natural theology endorsed by many defensive skeptics but, more seriously, admits of generalization into an argument for a complete, across-the-board skepticism; (ii) the claim that God's morally exonerating reasons for permitting seemingly gratuitous evils are inscrutable to us renders communion with God impossible, in opposition to the very purpose for which the theist claims that God created us humans; (iii) there are grounds for doubting the modal sanity of some skeptical defenders in this volume; and (iv) defensive skepticism cheapens the religious life by making it too easy.

(i) The defensive skeptic, such as van Inwagen, prevented E from lowering the probability of G relative to K by finding some cognitively inscrutable proposition D that has a reasonably high degree of probability relative to G such that $P(G/K)=P(G/K$ and E and D). A parallel argument can be constructed to show that every proposition is such that we humans could not be epistemically justified in making any claim, probabilistic or otherwise, about its truth value. And this is complete skepticism of the most radical sort.

Take any ordinary negative existential proposition, p, for example, that there is no lion in this room. Let r be a report of the failure of numerous normal observers in seemingly standard conditions to detect any lion in the room. The reasonable thing to say is that r lowers the probability of p relative to our background knowledge K—if $P(p/K)=n$, then $P(p/K$ and $r)<n$. But wait a minute. There is

some proposition, q, that there exists a maximally great evil demon (one who has all of the divine perfections save for being all-bad rather than all-good), which does not entail p, has a reasonably high degree of probability relative to p, and whose truth we humans are not cognitively capable of determining, since, like God, the demon is an omniscient supernatural entity.[6] Since it is fairly likely that the evil demon would fool us about the truth of p by bringing it about that r (that's how he gets his kicks), we are not justified in taking r to lower the probability of p relative to K—$P(p/K)=P(p/K$ and r and q). Obviously, this parallel argument can be generalized so as to apply to every proposition, even necessary ones that have apparent cartesian certainty.

To illustrate just how real the latter danger is and give some evidence for the existence of this evil demon, I relate a real-life conversation that my neighbor, Norb Weikers, overheard when he visited his father in a home for the aged. A visitor went up to two elderly lady residents and asked where the dining room was. The first lady responded, "How would I know. I'm only here for the first time," and then her friend chimed in, "And I wouldn't know. I'm not even here for the first time." If there had been a third lady in the group, she no doubt would have topped them all by declaring, "And how would I know. I don't even exist now." (The problem with Descartes's philosophy is that he never hung out at this home for the aged.)

(ii) It is claimed by several authors in this volume that we are not capable of fathoming God's morally exonerating reason(s) for permitting the evils reported by E and thereby are unfit to determine that D' is exhaustive of all possible defenses. As Stephen Wykstra puts it, because God's wisdom is to ours "as an adult human being's is to a one-month-old infant's . . . for any instance of intense suffering, there is good reason to think that if there is an outweighing good of the sort at issue, we would not have epistemic access to this. . . ."[7] Plantinga's rhetorical understatement that "there is no reason to think that if God *did* have a reason for permitting the evil in question, we would be the first to know" endorses this.[8] Sometimes an analogy is drawn between morality and material objects in regard to their having a hidden depth beneath their surface appearances which can be unearthed only through extensive inquiry. Wykstra and Bruce Russell, in spite of their sharp differences, agree that "if our universe is the creation of God, it would likely have great 'moral depth'" in that "many of the goods below its puzzling observable surface, many of the moral causes of God's current allowings and intervenings, would be 'deep' moral goods."[9] Alston further develops this analogy between the physical world and morality in respect to their having a hidden nature that is gradually brought to light by painstaking investigation.

> The development of physical science has made us aware of a myriad of things hitherto undreamed of, and developed the concepts with which to grasp them— gravitation, electricity, electro-magnetic fields, space-time curvature, irrational numbers, and so on. It is an irresistible induction from this that we have not reached the final term of this process, and that more realities, aspects, properties, structures remain to be discerned and conceptualized. And why should values, and the conditions of their realization, be any exception to this

generalization? A history of the apprehension of values could undoubtedly be written, parallel to the history just adumbrated, though the archeology would be a more difficult and delicate task.[10]

What Alston and Wykstra and Russell really are doing is likening morality to a "natural kind"—a kind of entity possessed of an essential nature that is to be unearthed by scientific inquiry, there being some analogous method of inquiry into the inner, hidden nature of morality to that employed in science. But morality is a paradigm of a nonnatural kind, one whose "nature," that is, basic principles and rules, is completely on the surface, patently obvious to the gaze of all participants in the moral language game. A hidden morality is no morality. *Pace* Alston, there is no "history of the apprehension of values . . . parallel to the history" of scientific discovery. The "discovery" that love is better than hate because it is more affectionate is quite different from the discovery of the molecular structure of matter. There is a history of philosophizing about the nature of morality, but this second-order investigation is not remotely analogous to that of science and has made not one whit of difference in the manner in which we, on the ground level, wield moral concepts in our social interactions. To be sure, some of our primitive progenitors in the evolutionary process did not recognize any moral rules and principles, but that no more shows that we had to perform inquiries over a long period of time analogous to those employed by scientists to discover the inner nature of morality than does the fact that they blew their nose on the ground while we use Kleenex show that we had to inquire deeply into the nature of nose blowing. No doubt we have a heightened moral sensitivity relative to them, but that is not due to our having unearthed the deep, hidden nature of morality.

That morality be on the surface, common knowledge of all, is an empirical presupposition for our playing of the morality language game, the purpose of which is to enable us to modify and control each other's conduct by the use of generally accepted rules and principles of moral evaluation, thereby effecting more satisfactory social interactions. It also is required for our entering into relationships of love and friendship with each other. Such relationships require significant commonality of purposes, values, sympathies, ways of thinking and acting, and the like. The major problem faced by the moral-inscrutability-of-God version of defensive skepticism is that it seems to preclude our being able to enter into such relationships with God, thereby undercutting the very purpose for which God created us according to theism, namely to enter into a communal relation of love with God. Some amount of inscrutability is not only allowable but even desirable in love and friendship relationships. What would love be if there weren't a core of mystery to the beloved? But how mysterious, how totally other, can the beloved be?

Not all kinds of moral inscrutability preclude a love relationship. It is important to distinguish between the moral rules and principles employed by a person and the manner in which she applies them to specific cases based on her knowledge of the relevant circumstances, this being a casuistic issue. A distinction can be made between moral principle inscrutability and casuistic inscrutability. That another person is casuistically inscrutable to us need not prevent our entering into a communal love relationship with it, provided it is far more knowledge-able than we are about relevant worldly conditions, such as God, an omniscient being, is supposed to be. But moral principle inscrutability of a certain sort does rule out such a relationship. While we need not understand all of the beloved's moral reasons for her behavior, it must be the case that, *for the most part,* we do in respect to behavior which vitally affects ourselves. One thing, and maybe the only thing, that can be said in favor of the theodicy favored by fundamentalists accord-ing to which all the evils reported by E result from the Fall and are messages from God to show us how lost we are without him, is that it does not run afoul of this requirement. We can hardly love someone who intentionally hurts us and keeps his reasons a secret unless for the most part we know his reasons for affecting us as he does and moreover know that they are benevolent. *Pace* Plantinga, there is good reason to think that if God *did* have a reason for permitting evil, at least those that vitally concern us, "we would be the first to know," at least for the most part.

(iii) Another tactic employed by defensive skeptics is to call into question the modal intuitions that underlie the atheologian's claim that the evils reported by E are gratuitous because God *could have* prevented them by creating human beings who would not be subject to disease, animals that would not prey on each other, sentient beings who would not evolve, if they evolve at all, by a painful evolution-ary process, and selectively intervening to protect innocent persons from the harmful effects of tornadoes and earthquakes, or, better yet, not including these natural disasters in his plan of creation, and so on.

Peter van Inwagen employs several strategies to counter these atheologi-cal modal intuitions. First, he demands that the atheologian give us a reason for thinking that there are worlds of the sort just described, and then claims that "the only kind of reason one could have for believing that there was a possible world having a certain feature would be the reason provided by a plausible attempt to 'design' a world having that feature," this requiring that a detailed description be given of the causal structure and boundary conditions of that world.[11]

It should be noted, first, that van Inwagen operates with a double stan-dard, for he does not require that the theist who says that it is possible for God to create a universe *ex nihilo* by his will alone give a reason for this based on a "design" of how his creative will brings about worldly effects. Furthermore, this demand seems to be an affront to God's omnipotence. Consider the sad case of the man who is hired by the R&D department of GE to come up with ideas for new prod-ucts. His first day on the job he calls in his subordinates and tells them to design and build a machine that will wash, dry, and iron clothes without the need for either water or any power source. When asked how this is to be done, he replies, "Look, I'm just an idea man. The details are your problem." Not surprisingly, he did not last long at GE. His only problem is that he is not omnipotent. For being omnipotent means not only "never having to say you're sorry" but also never hav-ing to say how, that is, being able to get away with being just an idea man. Why can't God create a bunch of hot shot engineers, omniscient ones, and then say, "Let there be a machine that washes, dries, and irons clothes without the need for water or any power source," leaving it up to these omniscient engineers to work out the details, or simply say, without the need for any middlemen, "Let there exist tigers and lions that are not carnivorous."

Underlying van Inwagen's demand that the atheologian spell out all the messy causal and boundary conditions of these better alternatives to the actual world are the modal intuitions of the scientific essentialist. Just as it might be metaphysically necessary that gold has the atomic structure that it does and thereby the causal capacities it has, it could be metaphysically necessary that tigers possess a certain biological makeup that causally requires them to be carnivorous.[12] If so, not even God in his omnipotence is able to create noncarnivorous tigers, any more than he can create gold that has a different atomic weight and number than it actually has. It is not necessary for van Inwagen to argue for this version of scientific essentialism but only to make the more modest claim, as he does, that it is true for all we can know. Some might view this subjugating of God's omnipotence to what is metaphysically possible as an unacceptable departure from the orthodox view of his omnipotence, but the more powerful objection is that the introduction of the issue of metaphysical necessity based on essentialism is a red herring. The atheologian who faults God for not creating the world with the harmless "tigers" in it or the "water" that does not drown us though it quenches our thirst could care less whether the "tigers" and "water" that populate this world really are tigers and water, rather than some exotic species of Putnam's twin-earth-type tigers and water. What is wanted is a world with things that behave very much like ordinary tigers and water do but with some important differences. That these differences, as van Inwagen correctly points out, require a world with a radically different causal structure, which might rule out their being tigers or water, is irrelevant to the atheologian's normative rank ordering of the worlds in question.

Van Inwagen is not without a comeback to this. He challenges the atheologian's modal intuition that God could have created a complex world with a different causal structure than that of the actual one: "For all we know, in every possible world that exhibits any degree of complexity, the laws of nature are the actual laws. There are, in fact, philosophically minded physicists who believe that there is only one possible set of laws of nature, and it is epistemically possible that they are right." He also calls into question "the evidentialist's premise that 'an omniscient and omnipotent being will be able so to arrange matters that the world contains sentient beings among whom suffering, if it exists at all, is apportioned according to desert.'" He urges that we adopt the standpoint of "extreme modal . . . skepticism (or, one might say, humility) in matters unrelated to the concerns of everyday life," such as those about which the atheologian speculates. In the spirit of defensive skepticism he asks rhetorically, "Assuming that there are 'modal facts of the matter,' why should we assume that God or evolution or social training has given us access to modal facts knowledge of which is of no interest to anyone but the metaphysician."[13]

Van Inwagen's modal "modesty" about matters that don't practically concern us threatens to put us philosophers out of work, though that is not in itself an argument against what he says.[14] Not surprisingly, he does not adhere to his own skeptical strictures. He is a self-servingly selective modal skeptic who makes demands of the atheologian that he does not of the theist. Theism makes many modal claims, for example that it is possible for an immaterial being to create worldly things *ex nihilo by* the mere act of willing them, that it is possible that certain purported defenses are true, but one does not find van Inwagen extending his modal "modesty" to them. But the really serious problem with his defensive modal skepticism concerns the modal intuitions that underlie it—that it is possible, for all we can know, that there could not exist a complex world in which different causal laws held than those that hold in the actual world (or that there could not exist sentient beings whose suffering is apportioned according to desert).

I not only disagree with van Inwagen's modal intuitions but fear that he suffers from a serious modal affliction, in spite of his being an excellent philosopher from whom I have learned much. In *On the Nature and Existence of God,* I tried to resolve my modal disagreements with the likes of van Inwagen and Phil Quinn through my modal intuition bowl, but it proved a bust. The networks dropped us because there wasn't enough violence, just a bunch of out-of-shape guys, with the exception of Al Plantinga, who looks like he can jump tall mountains in a single bound, staring at each other and emphatically asserting back and forth, "It *is* possible that p," "No it isn't!"

I have decided to take a more radical, therapeutic approach and have founded the EMDS (Extreme Modal Deficiency Syndrome) Foundation. EMDS is no respecter of rank or philosophical orientation—even tenured analytic philosophers have come down with it. It is tragic to realize that there are people like Peter (my poster person) who cannot modalize as normal people do, or, as we at the Foundation prefer to say, are modally other-abled. I plead with you to fight EMDS with a checkup and a check. First, be on the lookout for the seven warning signals of EMDS; for example, if you answer "Yes" to the question "Is it possible that God couldn't create a world with a different causal structure than that of the actual world?" or if you aren't puzzled by the name of the TV show "Mission Impossible," you've got it bad. Second, mail your check to me at the University of Pittsburgh, Pittsburgh, PA 15260, payable to me, but be sure to write on your check that it is for deposit only in the EMDS Foundation account, since I might get confused after waiting on a long bank line and mistakenly deposit it in my own account. (Beware of fraudulent EMDS Foundations, many of which have 13244 and 46556 zip codes.) Your generosity will make it possible not only for research to continue on the cause and hopefully the prevention or cure of EMDS but also for us, in the meantime, to keep Peter comfortable in our EMDS Foundation Hospital by piping soothing Mantovani music into his room, putting him in the sun for an hour each day, and, most important, carefully screening his reading material so that he won't come upon a sentence such as "It is possible that all human beings always freely do what is morally wrong," which might cause a relapse of such severity that shock therapy will be required—he'll have to be put in the same room as the two elderly ladies in the home for the aged. (Peter, no doubt, has a special room reserved for me in his EMDS Foundation hospital, replete with piped-in music of some of my favorites—"Liberace plays the Classics" and "Lawrence Welk: Down and Dirty with the Lennon Sisters"—as well as other amenities.)

(iv) The upshot of defensive skepticism is that the probability of G relative to K is not lowered one iota by E. This will come as news to the working theist who sees the evils reported by E as counterevidence to G that tries her faith. The response of defensive skeptics, such as Plantinga (chapter 5), is to make a distinction between the pastoral and epistemic problem of evil. What this amounts to, though they wouldn't want to put it this bluntly, is that the working theist whose faith is strained or endangered by the evils which directly confront her is emotionally overwrought and not able to take the cool stance of the epistemologist of religion and thereby see that these evils, however extensive and seemingly gratuitous, are really no challenge to her theistic beliefs. Since she is unable to philosophize clearly at her time of emotional upset, she needs the pastor to hold her hand and say whatever might help her to make it through the night and retain her faith in God.

There is a problem here; however, it is not a pastoral problem but a problem with the pastor and defensive skeptic who runs such a line. Her crisis of faith, although rationally explainable in terms of psychological causes, is not rationally justified because it rests upon the epistemically unwarranted belief that the evils confronting her probably are gratuitous or, at least, counterevidence to G. It also follows that her emotion of horror at the evil of the holocaust, for example, is equally irrational because based on the epistemically unwarranted belief that the apparent gratuitousness of this evil lessens the likelihood that G is true. Rationally speaking, she ought not to feel horror at the holocaust! Let us hope that she gives her pastor, or any defensive skeptic she can lay her hands on, a good punch in the nose.

Defensive skepticism is an ivory tower invention of the detached epistemologist of religion that is completely out of touch with the grimy realities of everyday religious faith and experience. By neutralizing the dramatic bite of evil, it makes it too easy to have religious faith, as Kierkegaard might say. The same holds, only more so, for theodicists. O Lord, save us from theodicists and defensive skeptics.

2. Theodicies

I will conclude by taking a few potshots at the unconscionably lax requirements or standards, both epistemic and axiological, for a theodicy which are upheld by different authors in this volume. Epistemic laxness has to do with insufficiently high standards of proof or confirmation for a theodicy, axiological laxness with insufficiently strong demands being placed upon God's benevolence.

2.1 EPISTEMIC LAXNESS

This problem is acute in van Inwagen's 1988 article "The Magnitude, Duration, and Distribution of Evil: A Theodicy."[15] He begins with the reasonable claim that a theodicy, although it must go beyond being a mere claim of logical possibility, which is what a defense is, need not be based upon a knock-down argument or proof that the described state of affairs is actual. Unfortunately, when he gets down to spelling out the epistemic standards for a theodicy, it is not clear how they differ from those for a defense.

He claims that his theodicy is "a story about God and evil" that gives a "plausible account of God's reasons for allowing the existence of evil."[16] Now there are stories and there are stories. For Parmenides and Plato, a cosmological "story" is an empirically vouchsafed one which fails to measure up to the standard of apodictic certainty required for true knowledge. There are, on the other hand, purely fictional stories. Van Inwagen's story is an embellishment upon the data of Christian revelation, and he tells those "who do not share my allegiance to these data . . . to regard this paper as providing one more defense. . . ."[17] This makes it appear as if what counts as a theodicy is relative to one's subjective beliefs. The fear that his criterion for a theodicy is purely subjective is reinforced by his later claim to have produced a theodicy that "provides plausible—at any rate, I find them plausible—answers to four pointed questions about the magnitude, duration, and distribution of evil."[18] There are further indications that van Inwagen's requirements for a theodicy are about as lax as those for a defense. He calls a theodicy a "just-so story" (after Dennett), in which "just-so stories are tales told to illustrate possibility" against some background beliefs.[19] The background beliefs for his theodicy are based on Christian revelation, but he says nothing in support of them.

2.2 AXIOLOGICAL LAXNESS

It is easy to construct a theodicy, as well as a defense, if you demand little of an omnibenevolent being, thus the point of the bumper sticker "God exists. He just doesn't want to get involved." Richard Swinburne, in *The Existence of God,* understands by "God's being perfectly good . . . that he does no morally bad action" (p. 8), to which he later adds "and does any morally obligatory action" (p. 92). This requires of an omnibenevolent being only that it keep its nose clean, not that it perform acts of supererogation, which plainly is too undemanding a standard for being omnibenevolent. Many an S.O.B. satisfies this duty-based requirement.

The most egregious abuse of God's omnibenevolence occurs in van Inwagen's fundamentalist type of theodicy. So twisted do I find the moral intuitions that underlie it that I have decided to start an EMIDS (Extreme Moral Intuition Deficiency Syndrome) Foundation. Jerry Lewis wasn't available. All of the evils reported by E are a result of the first generation of humans freely rebelling against God: "Their ruin was in some way inherited by all of their descendants."[20] There is no attempt to show that the descendants are in any way blameworthy or morally responsible for these sins, and yet they are the victims of this "hereditary ruin." But this seems unfair in just the same way as it is to keep in the whole class for the misdeeds of a single person. The whole idea of a deity who is so vain that if his children do not choose to love and obey him he will bring down all sorts of horrible evils on them and their innocent descendants is horrendous. Think of what we would say about a human father who treated his children in this way.

Van Inwagen adds an original moral horror of his own creation to this orthodox theodicy. One of the ways in which God makes it clear that man cannot live apart from him is to create a system of chance evils, the victims of which can be and often are innocent persons.

> Among the natural consequences of the Fall is the following evil state of affairs: Horrors happen to people without any relation to desert. They happen simply as a matter of chance. It is a part of God's plan of Atonement that we realize that a natural consequence of our living to ourselves is our living in a world that has that feature.[21]

Van Inwagen papers over the problem of fairness by the following referential equivocation:

> *we* complain that some of us—quite often the good and wise and innocent—fall into the pits. God's response to this complaint, according to the theodicy I propose, is this: "*You* are the ones who made yourselves blind"[22]

(in which the pits represent chance evils and our being blind represents our being defenseless before these evils as a result of hereditary ruin). The use of "we" refers to the innocent descendants of the original culprits who are doing the complaining, but the use of "You" by God refers to the original perpetrators. Herein God is depicted as confounding the perpetrators with their innocent descendants, which is surprising given his omniscience. (I suspect that the equivocation is the fault of van Inwagen rather than God.)

Let us have faith that van Inwagen's god does not exist, and, if it does, our duty is to resist it with all of the energy and courage we can muster.

NOTES

1. In opposition to this, an anonymous reader of my essay gave the following argument for there being gratuitous evil if God exists. If it were obvious that all cases of natural evil were necessary, then humans would have no reason to try to diminish evil or to develop traits such as charity, fortitude, and sympathy, which are necessary for soul-making. This response confounds the human with the divine perspective and the commitments and duties that they involve. While God is permitted to allow evils that are necessary for human soul-building, it does not follow that we ought not try to eliminate and prevent such evils.

2. E must not be in K, although propositions that are possibly supportive of theism, such as descriptions of natural order, purpose and beauty, can be included.

3. William Alston, throughout "The Inductive Argument from Evil and the Human Cognitive Condition," chapter 6 in this book, is guilty of attacking a straw-man evidential argument, one that is required to establish "that no one is in a position to justifiably assert that God *could have* no sufficient reason for allowing E" (my italics). But all the evidential argument tries to do is to show that it is improbable that there is *in fact* such a reason, not that there could not be.

4. Another catch-all defense, which has been overlooked, is that all sentient

creatures undergo reincarnation and that the suffering of seemingly innocent sentient beings, such as Bambi and Sue, as reported in chapter 6, is justified because of transgressions committed in previous incarnations.

5. This is the strategy employed by Peter van Inwagen in "The Problem of Evil," chapter 8 in this book.

6. This demon faces a problem of gratuitous good (a good that is not necessary for the realization of an outweighing evil or the prevention of a greater good), analogous in all respects to that of gratuitous evil for God and permits exactly parallel defensive skepticism response—how can we be justified in saying that we humans have exhausted all the possible demonodicies, and, even if we could, we would not be cognitively up to determining whether these demonodicies hold in the actual world. There is the catch-all demonodicy for every apparently gratuitous good—it is necessary for the realization of an outweighing evil in an afterlife. Furthermore, we never could be justified in asserting G, thereby denying the existence of the demon, on the basis of worldly goods, such as natural beauty, purpose, order, etc., thereby destroying natural theology.

7. Stephen Wykstra, "The Humean Obstacle to Evidential Arguments from Suffering: On Avoiding the Evils of 'Appearance,'" *International Journal for Philosophy of Religion* 16 (1984): 88.

8. Alvin Plantinga, "Epistemic Probability and Evil," chapter 5. See also van Inwagen, chapter 8.

9. Bruce Russell and Stephen Wykstra, "The 'Inductive' Argument from Evil: A Dialogue," *Philosophical Topics* (1988): 146-47.

10. Alston, chapter 6.

11. Van Inwagen, chapter 8. In "The Magnitude, Duration, and Distribution of Evil: A Theodicy," *Philosophical Topics* 16 (1988): 170, van Inwagen writes: "if you think that it would be possible to design a planet, and a universe to contain it, that was both capable of supporting human life and contained no earthquakes or tornadoes, I can only point out that you have never tried."

12. Van Inwagen, in his review of Richard Swinburne's *Coherence of Theism, Philosophical Review* 88 (1979): 671, claims to be unable to imagine that the moon is made of cheese because to do so would require imagining all sorts of countercausal things about cheese, for example, that there is "a way to preserve a piece of cheese in broiling heat, freezing cold. . . ."

13. Van Inwagen, chapter 8.

14. One wonders just how van Inwagen will be able to draw a line between issues that practically concern us and those that interest only the "metaphysician." Certainly, modal issues pertaining to what God can do are of practical concern, but they are about as eruditely metaphysical as anything could be. On the other hand, material objects are part of our familiar, everyday world, and yet there are seemingly unanswerable modal questions about their conditions of identity and individuation.

15. It should come as a shock that van Inwagen should argue three years later in chapter 8 for defensive skepticism, since the latter's claim of our cognitive inability to find out anything about supernatural things seems to preclude construction of a theodicy—yet another instance of the use of double standards in theistic responses to evil. His undue laxness in epistemic standards for a theodicy might be due to a recognition of this apparent inconsistency.

16. Van Inwagen, "The Magnitude, Duration, and Distribution of Evil," 162.

17. Ibid.

18. Ibid., 183.

19. Ibid., 186. A further indication of laxness is given by his use in chapter 8 of parallel arguments against the evidential argument from evil. In one he attempts to show that the evidential argument from evil is just as bad as the argument against Greek atomism based on its inability to explain the behavior of air. (Actually, it was the inability of Greek atomism to explain living things and especially liquids that was the major reason for

its rightful rejection.) The inability of Greek atomism to explain these facts constitutes a "difficulty" for but does not count as "evidence against" Greek atomism. Herein van Inwagen is playing humpty-dumpty with language. Responsible historians of science, such as Stephen Toulmin and June Goodfield in *The Architecture of Matter* (Chicago, 1962), 56-72, make it clear that these recalcitrant facts counted as decisive evidence against *Greek* atomism. It is completely gratuitous for van Inwagen to say that it is "our 'elementary particles' and not our 'atoms' or our 'molecules' that correspond to the atoms of the Greeks." For their atoms correspond to or are identical with entities postulated by modern atomic theory only in the eliminative sense in which Zeus's thunderbolts are nothing but the flow of ionized particles. There just aren't any elementary particles in the world of the sort described by Greek atomism—things with hooks on them, etc.

20. Van Inwagen, "The Magnitude, Duration, and Distribution of Evil," 165.
21. Ibid., 183.
22. Ibid., 182. My italics.

12

PETER VAN INWAGEN

Reflections on the Chapters by Draper, Russell, and Gale

In "The Problem of Evil, the Problem of Air, and the Problem of Silence" (chapter 8 [EAS]), I left the notion of epistemic probability at a more or less intuitive level. Reflection on Professor Draper's essay "The Skeptical Theist" in the present volume (chapter 9) and a letter from Alvin Plantinga have convinced me that the main point I was trying to make was obscured by my failure to discuss this notion systematically—and by my shifting back and forth between the notions of epistemic surprise and epistemic probability. In this paper I shall discuss epistemic probability at some length, and I shall not mention "surprise" at all.

In the first section, I argue that judgments of epistemic probability can best be understood as epistemic judgments about nonepistemic (or "real, objective") probabilities. I go on to show how to reconstruct Draper's "evidential challenge" in such a way that it refers not to epistemic probabilities but to epistemic judgments about nonepistemic probabilities. I then present a restatement of the central argument of my chapter 8 specifically tailored to the reconstructed version of Draper's challenge. In Section II, I shall explain why I do not find any materials in "The Skeptical Theist" from which an effective answer to the restated version of my argument could be constructed. In Section III, I shall explain why—despite what is said in "The Skeptical Theist"—I continue to regard Draper's theses on how epistemic challenges must be met as intolerably restrictive.

I

How shall we understand the notion of the epistemic probability of a proposition? Draper proposes that we understand this notion in terms of the "degree of belief" that a fully rational person would have in the proposition in a given "epistemic situation."[1] Draper's account applies only to the relative magnitudes of the epistemic probabilities of pairs of propositions. But a generalization of his idea is possible if we remember that philosophers of probability have sometimes attempted to spell out degrees of belief behaviorally, in terms of the odds that the believer would be willing to give on a bet. The generalization may be formulated by reference to the bets of an "ideal bookmaker." If I am an ideal bookmaker, then I accept bets at my discretion; I'm interested only in maximizing my winnings (I have no other interest in money); I need fear no losing streak, however long, for I can borrow any amount at no interest for any period; I am in a situation in which it is possible to settle any bet objectively; my "clients" always pay when they lose, and they never have "inside information"—that is, information not available to *me*—about the matter being betted on . . . and so on (add such further clauses as you deem necessary). Suppose also that there is only one way for an "ideal bookmaker" to accept a bet: people come to him and say things of the form, "I'll bet you *k* dollars that *p*. Will you give me odds of *m* to *n*?" "I'll bet you ten dollars that the sun will not rise tomorrow. Will you give me odds of 10 to 1?" This is equivalent to: Will you agree to pay me one hundred dollars if the sun does not rise tomorrow, provided that I agree to pay you ten dollars if it does?) When a bet is offered in this form, an "ideal bookmaker" must either take it or leave it; no negotiation about the odds or anything else is allowed. (An ideal bookmaker never declines a bet because of the amount the bettor puts on the table; no bet is too small, and—because of his enviable credit situation—no bet is too large.)

Now that we have the concept of an ideal bookmaker, we may define epistemic probability. Before stating the definition, I will give an example that illustrates the intuitions that underlie the definition. Suppose a fair die is to be thrown. What is the "epistemic probability" (relative to my present epistemic situation) of its falling 2, 3, 5, or 6? The following thought experiment suggests a way to approach this question. I imagine that I am an ideal bookie, and I say to myself, "Suppose someone said to me, 'I'll bet you ten dollars [or whatever; the amount is irrelevant] that the die will fall 2, 3, 5, or 6.' What odds should I be willing to give him (assuming that I am fully rational)?" If there is nothing very unusual about my present epistemic situation, the answer is obvious: I should be willing to give him any odds lower than 1 to 2. (I should, for example, accept the bet if he proposed odds of 9 to 20; I should be willing to pay him $4.50 if the die fell 2, 3, 5, or 6, provided that he agreed to pay me ten dollars—the amount of his bet—if it fell 1 or 4.) I therefore—it seems evident—manifest in my behavior a belief that "it's 2 to 1 that" the die will fall the way he has bet; that is, I must regard the probability of the die's falling 2, 3, 5, or 6 as equal to 2/3. And this value—it seems evident—should be the "epistemic probability" of the die's so falling for someone in my epistemic situation. The intuitions behind these judgments may be generalized and the generalization treated as a definition:

> The epistemic probability of p relative to (the epistemic situation) K $=_{df}$ (1) 0 if a fully rational ideal bookmaker in K would be willing to give any odds to a client who bet that p; (2) 1 if there are no odds that a fully rational ideal bookmaker in K would be willing to give to a client who bet that p; (3) $n/(m+n)$ otherwise, where m and n are determined as follows: m to n are the highest odds that have the following property: a fully rational ideal bookmaker in K would be willing to give a client who bet that p any odds lower than those odds.

What shall we say about *conditional* epistemic probabilities? I propose the following. If K is the epistemic situation of some person at the world w, let K&p be what is common to that person's epistemic situations in all the worlds closest to w in which he rationally believes that p. (Roughly, K&p is the epistemic situation that someone whose actual epistemic situation is K would be in if he rationally believed that p.) Let us then say that the conditional epistemic probability of p on q relative to K is equal to the epistemic probability of p relative to K&q. Consider, for example, the epistemic probability (relative to my actual epistemic situation) of the proposition that my wife has quit her job, on the (false) hypothesis that she has just told me that she has quit her job. I would go about estimating this probability as follows: I would first try to determine what I could about the nature of the closest worlds in which I rationally believe that my wife has just told me that she has quit her job (I suppose these would be the closest worlds in which she just *has* told me that); I would then imagine myself conducting in one of these worlds an "ideal bookie" thought experiment like the one imagined above (I should have to assume that the differences among my epistemic situations in the *closest* worlds are irrelevant to the assignments of odds: that the thought experiments would yield the same odds in all those worlds); I would go on to calculate the epistemic probability for me in those worlds of the proposition that my wife had just quit her job. When I try all this, I do not feel lost; I am fairly confident in my judgment that the conditional probability I am calculating has a value of unity or so near unity that I may as well treat it as unity for any practical purpose.

Does this account of epistemic probability at least approximate to what Draper means by epistemic probability? I think so, but there is an annoying technical adjustment that must be made before this statement has any chance of being correct. Draper's presentation of his "evidential challenge" requires that the probability of O on theism be (prima facie) pretty low. But I try a thought experiment. I ask myself, suppose that I rationally believed that theism was true; what odds would I give someone who bet that O was true? Well, I *do* rationally believe that theism is true, so what odds would I in fact give? The answer is: either no odds at all—because I am *certain* that O is true—or at any rate very long odds indeed. Or so I judge. It may be that I am wrong in thinking that I rationally accept theism. It may be that in all of the closest worlds in which I rationally accept theism, I observe a hedonic utopia, and would give any odds to someone who proposed a bet that O was true. But I do in fact believe that I rationally accept theism, and I shall hardly be impressed by an argument for the irrationality of my accepting theism that proceeds from a premise that is inconsistent with this belief. But Draper (fortunately) does not really ask me *actually* to accept the thesis that P(O/ theism) is low. Rather, he asks me (in effect) to imagine that I am in a different epistemic situation, and argues that if I were in that situation, I should accept this thesis. He asks me (in effect) to "subtract" O from my present epistemic situation, and to understand his judgments of epistemic probability as relative to the resulting epistemic situation—my "corrected epistemic situation," so to call it.[2] (Someone who was in my corrected epistemic situation in the actual world would have led a sheltered life indeed!) Now I am not sure that everything Draper says or implies about my corrected epistemic situation is coherent. One's being in this situation by definition implies that one has almost no knowledge of the actual distribution of pain and pleasure in the natural world, and yet Draper's arguments for the correctness of the judgments of epistemic probability he endorses imply that someone in my corrected epistemic situation would possess knowledge of the biological utility of pain and pleasure that (so far as I can see) would be impossible without extensive knowledge of the distribution of pain and pleasure in the natural world. I will not make anything of this, however, for, even if these observations are correct, Draper's argument can be stated in a way that does not involve the difficulty I think I see.

In my view, Draper makes his argument needlessly complicated by framing it in terms of the concept of epistemic probability. I will, as I promised, reconstruct his argument in terms of epistemic judgments about nonepistemic probabilities. The reconstructed argument is a more straightforward argument, and it does not require the evaluation of probabilities relative to an epistemic situation that no one is in fact in.

Let us return to the case in which I have judged that, in a bet on a die's falling a certain way, it would be rational for me to take the bet at any odds less than 1 to 2 (and at no higher odds). Let us ask a simple, obvious question: *Why,* exactly, would that be the rational determination of the odds I should accept? Only one answer seems plausible: Because I judge that it is rational for me to accept the thesis that the *real, objective* probability of the die's falling 2, 3, 5, or 6 is 2/3. If I did not make that judgment (perhaps because I had reason to believe that the die was biased) I should not take the bet at all, or I should figure the odds differently. In my view, this answer may be generalized: epistemic probabilities exist only in cases in which it is possible to make reasonable judgments about certain real, objective probabilities. (I accept this rather vague principle despite the fact that there are tricky problems about how to apply it in certain cases. A rational ideal bookie would be willing to give you any odds lower than 9 to 1 on a bet that the billionth digit in the decimal part of π—as yet not calculated—would turn out to be '6.' But the real, objective probability of its being '6' is either 0 or 1; whichever it is, it is certainly not 0.1, which is, by our definition, the epistemic probability relative to our present epistemic situation that the billionth digit in the decimal part of π is '6.' I believe, however, that the rationality of those odds does depend on the fact that a certain judgment of real, objective probability is rational. Something like this one: in general, the real, objective probability of someone's winning a bet about the value of some as yet uncalculated digit in the decimal part of π is 0.1.)

Epistemic probability, then, is not a "ground floor" concept—either in epistemology or in the philosophy of probability. Epistemic probability is to be explained in terms of the concept of real, objective probability and some epistemic concept or concepts, such as the concept of rational belief. Consequently, anyone who refuses to believe in real, objective probability should refuse to believe in epistemic probability as well. In typical cases, the only possible way to arrive at the conclusion that m to n are the highest odds such that a rational ideal bookie would accept a bet that p at any odds lower than m to n is first to determine what it is rational to believe that the real, objective probability of p is. (Then one calculates as follows: If this probability is i/j, set $m=j-i$ and $n=i$.) In *all* cases, a rational judgment about the real, objective probability of *some* proposition is required.

In my reconstruction of Draper's argument, I shall not speak of epistemic probabilities but rather of epistemic judgments about real, objective probabilities. (And these epistemic judgments will be made from the point of view of our actual epistemic situation, and not the epistemic situation of someone who is ignorant of the actual patterns of suffering in the natural world.) In other words, in the reconstructed argument, reference to epistemic probabilities will be eliminated in favor of reference to the concepts I have defined epistemic probabilities in terms of.

Before presenting the reconstructed argument, however, I must say something about "real, objective probability"—or, as I shall say, "alethic probability" (on the model of "alethic modality"). What I shall say represents my own understanding of this thorny concept. (Those who prefer some other account may be able to adapt what I say about Draper's arguments and the arguments of EAS with no important modification.) The account I shall give presupposes some sort of modal realism, and it presupposes that real, objective probabilities attach not only to propositions about cards and dice and balls in urns and nuns over fifty who die in motorcycle accidents (that is, not only to propositions concerning the probability of choosing an object having a certain property when one chooses at random a member of a large set of actual objects), but to a much wider class of propositions. Examples of propositions in this wider class are the proposition that my wife will quit her job within six months (the probability of this proposition is not to be identified with the probability of, for example, a forty-nine-year-old psychiatric nurse's quitting his or her job within six months, despite the fact that my wife is a forty-nine-year-old psychiatric nurse, and the same point applies to any large, well-defined set of objects to which she belongs); the proposition that God exists; the proposition that there are vast amounts of animal suffering in nature.

Let us suppose that some sets of possible worlds have unique *measures;* these measure the proportion of logical space (of the whole set of worlds) occupied by these sets.[3] And let us further suppose that all of the sets of worlds in which we shall be interested in this paper are among those that have such measures. The alethic probability of a proposition is the measure of the set of worlds in which it is true. The conditional alethic probability of the proposition p on the proposition q (where the set of worlds in which q is true is not of measure 0) is the proportion of the region of logical space occupied by worlds in which q is true that is occupied by worlds in which p is true.[4] For example, if 13 percent of the region occupied by worlds in which A is true is occupied by worlds in which B is true, then the conditional alethic probability of B on A is 0.13. In the sequel, I shall frequently use phrases of the form, 'the proportion of the p-worlds that are q-worlds.' Such phrases are to be understood as abbreviations of the corresponding phrases of the form 'the proportion of the region of logical space occupied by worlds in which p is true that is occupied by worlds in which q is true.'

An example may help to tie this together. The conditional alethic probability of the proposition that there is intelligent life on other planets in the galaxy on the proposition that Project Ozma has negative results before the turn of the century is the proportion of the (Project Ozma has negative results before the turn of the century)-worlds in which there is intelligent life on other planets in the galaxy.

We make judgments of alethic probability, both in everyday life and in the sciences. (Or we do in effect. The concepts I have introduced may not be part of the cognitive repertory of most people, but most people make judgments that entail and judgments that are entailed by propositions that are alethic probability judgments in the present sense.)[5] And it would seem that very often such judgments are justified. For example, I judge that the conditional alethic probability of the sun's rising tomorrow on the present state of things is nearly unity, that the conditional alethic probability that the number of Douglas firs in Canada is odd is 0.5 on the proposition that I am in my present epistemic situation, that the unconditional alethic probability of a's being actual (where 'a' is a proper name of the actual world) is 0, and that the conditional alethic probability of there being intelligent bacteria on the proposition that there exists a physical universe is 0. Of course I could be wrong about these things; I *could* be wrong about almost anything. Nevertheless, I could give cogent arguments (or so they seem to me) in support of these probability judgments, and I *believe* that they are fully justified. But there also seem to be cases in which one is simply not in a position to make any judgment about the probabilities of certain propositions. This is hardly surprising. One reason it should not be regarded as surprising can be easily grasped by reflection on the fact that probability judgments are judgments of proportion, judgments about the proportion of a region of logical space that is occupied by some subregion of that region. And—leaving aside for the moment the particular case of judgments about proportions of logical space, and considering judgments of proportion in the abstract—it is evident that there are cases in which we are not in a position to make certain judgments of proportion.

I have drawn one of the numbers from 0 to 100 in a fair drawing from a hat, but I am not going to tell you what it is. I have put that many black balls into an empty urn and have then added 100-minus-that-many white balls. Now: What proportion of the balls in the urn are black? You have no way of answering this question: no answer you could give is epistemically defensible: "35 percent" is no better than "6 percent"; "about half" is no better than "about a quarter"; "a large proportion" is no better than "a small proportion," and so on.[6]

Ask me what proportion of the galaxies other than our own contain intelligent life, and I'll have to say that I don't know; no answer I could give is epistemically defensible for me. The answer could be "all" or "none" or "all but a few" or "about half." I see no reason to prefer any possible answer to this question to any of its equally specific competitors. Or such is my judgment. I could be wrong about the implications of what I think I know, but, then, as I say, I could be wrong about almost anything.

I conclude, therefore, that there are cases in which one is not in an epistemic position to give any answer to a question of the form "What proportion of the F's are G's?" There would seem to be no reason to suppose that this general principle about judgments of proportionality is inapplicable in the case of regions of logical space. And it seems evident that it does apply in that case.

What proportion of the possible worlds in which things happen exactly as they have happened in the actual world before 1993 are worlds in which there is a devastating thermonuclear war between 1993 and 2093? In what proportion of them is there discovered a surveyable proof of the Four-Color Theorem during that period? I, at least, do not profess to have any idea about what the right answers to these questions are. That is, I do not profess to have any idea of the probability (conditional on things being as they now are) of the occurrence of a thermonuclear war or the discovery of a surveyable proof of the Four-Color Theorem during the next hundred years. In what proportion of the worlds in which I am now in my present actual epistemic situation does either of these things happen in the next hundred years? Again, I have no idea.

There are, therefore, cases in which someone is not in a position to make any judgment about the proportion of the worlds having the feature F that also have the feature G—just as there are cases in which someone is not in a position to make any judgment about the proportion of the galaxies that have a certain feature. And just as one may offer cogent arguments for the conclusion that no one is in an epistemic position to make any judgment about what proportion of the galaxies have a certain feature, there are cases in which one may offer cogent arguments for the conclusion that no one is in an epistemic position to make any judgment about what proportion of the worlds that have F also have G. In general, such arguments will not be proofs. They will have to be judged by the same standards that we employ in evaluating philosophical or political or historiographical arguments. The standards that are appropriately applied to such arguments are like the standards that are appropriately applied in the cases of arguments for nominalism or the military value of the Stealth bomber or the importance of the exhaustion of the Spanish silver mines for an understanding of late Roman politics.

I will present my reconstructed version of Draper's argument "directly" in terms of the idea that I have used to explain alethic probability: that regions of logical space have measures having the features I have specified. It will be seen that this allows us to bring to bear on the evidential problem of evil our intuitive capac-

226 / PETER VAN INWAGEN

ities for making judgments of relative size and proportion. This will be useful, because we have employed these intuitive capacities all our lives in our reasoning about regions of ordinary, physical space and about sets of discrete items.

Here is the argument. Consider three regions of logical space, those in which, respectively, O, theism, and HI are true. (I will identify a proposition with the region of logical space in which it is true. This identification is an aid to concision and is not essential to the argument. Given this identification, p & q is simply the region of logical space common to p and q.) And let us assume that HI and theism are of the same size, or at least that neither is significantly larger than the other. Given what it seems reasonable to expect if theism is true and what it seems reasonable to expect if the Hypothesis of Indifference is true, there is a good prima facie case for saying that the proportion of HI that overlaps O is much larger than the proportion of theism that overlaps O. Given that HI and theism are of the same size, it follows that the part of O that overlaps HI is much larger than the part of O that overlaps theism. We may represent this diagrammatically (two features of the diagram are without significance: the way the diagram represents the size of O relative to the sizes of HI and theism, and the way it represents the proportion of O that overlaps neither HI nor theism):

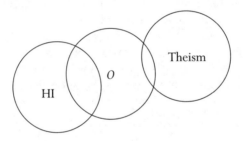

The actual world, a, must fall within O. Hence, in the absence of further relevant considerations, the thesis that a falls within HI is epistemically preferable to the thesis that a falls within theism. (Compare the following judgment about physical space: if a meteor has fallen somewhere within the United States, then, in the absence of further relevant considerations, the thesis that it has fallen in Texas is epistemically preferable to the thesis that it has fallen in Rhode Island.) But if p and q are inconsistent, and p is epistemically preferable to q, then it is not reasonable to accept q. Hence, the theist who wishes to be reasonable must find "further relevant considerations." The theist must either refute the strong prima facie case for the thesis that the above diagram correctly represents the relative sizes of the region HI & O and the region theism & O, or the theist must accept the diagram and present an argument for theism, an argument for the conclusion that a falls within theism[7] (and hence within theism & O, a very small region of logical space). If the diagram is correct, therefore, an argument for theism would be in effect an argument for the conclusion that a falls within a very small region of logical space (relative to the "competing" regions that surround it). It would, in consequence, have to be a very strong argument to carry much conviction, and even weak arguments for theism (as opposed to arguments for the existence of a designer of the world or a first cause or a necessary being) are in short supply.

The theist, therefore, has only one option: to refute the prima facie case for the correctness of the probability judgments displayed in the diagram. There is, in practice, only one way to do this.[8] The theist must find a region of logical space *h* that has the following two features:

> —*h* overlaps a large proportion of theism;
> —*O* overlaps a large proportion of theism & *h*.[9]

This will force us to redraw the diagram (the reader is invited to try it), since it will have the consequence that theism must overlap a significantly larger part of *O*. We should then have to admit that (given that HI and theism are of equal size) the prima facie case for the conclusion that the proportion of HI that overlaps *O* is much larger than the proportion of theism that overlaps *O* has been overcome.

Here is a spatial analogy. Two nonoverlapping storm systems of equal size, East and West, overlap the United States. There is a prima facie case for the thesis that the proportion of West that overlaps the U.S. is much larger than the proportion of East that overlaps the U.S. Therefore, the part of the U.S. that overlaps West ("U.S./West") is, prima facie, much larger than the part of the U.S. that overlaps East ("U.S./East"). Therefore, in the absence of further relevant considerations, the thesis that a particular person, Alice (whom we know to be somewhere in the U.S.), is in U.S./West is epistemically preferable to the thesis that Alice is in U.S./East. Therefore, anyone who believes that Alice is in U.S./East is unreasonable, unless he can do one of two things: give an argument for the conclusion that Alice is in U.S./East (and it will have to be a fairly strong argument, owing to the fact that U.S./East is known to be considerably less than half the U.S.), *or* find a geographical region *r* that has the following two features:

> —*r* overlaps a large proportion of the total region occupied by East;
> —the U.S. overlaps a large proportion of the region common to *r* and the total region occupied by East.

If we could find such a region, then, because East and West are of equal size, we should have refuted the prima facie case for the thesis that the proportion of West that overlapped the U.S. was much larger than the proportion of East that overlapped the U.S.

This is how I would represent, in terms of (our epistemic judgments about) alethic probabilities, Draper's version of the evidential argument from evil. Or, rather, this is how I would represent its overall structure. There is a lot that could be said to put flesh on these bones, and much of it could be read off Draper's original paper, simply by making some fairly mechanical adjustments in terminology. I have been interested here in finding a reconstruction of the argument that I am confident I have a fairly clear understanding of, rather than in presenting a really finished argument.

Now let us see how the reasoning set out in my chapter 8 looks when it is applied to the reconstructed argument.

II

The most important thing I tried to do in chapter 8 may be described in our present terminology as follows: to argue for the proposition

> We are not in an epistemic position to judge that only a small proportion of theism overlaps S.[10]

I proposed (in effect) the following principle:

> We are not in a position to judge that only a small proportion of the p-worlds are q-worlds if there is a proposition h that has the following two features:
> —a large proportion of the p & h-worlds are q-worlds;
> —we are not in a position to make a judgment about the proportion of the p-worlds that are h-worlds.[11]

This principle is simply an application to the special case of judgments concerning proportions of regions of logical space of a general form of reasoning that we should find it very hard to reject in the case of other sorts of judgment of proportion. Let us consider two examples, one involving proportions of geographical regions, and the other involving proportions of finite sets of discrete items.

> We are not in a position to judge that only a small proportion of Spain is arable if, for a certain geographical region R, Spain and R overlap and most of the Spain-R overlap is arable and we are not in a position to make any judgment about the proportion of Spain that overlaps R.

> We are not in a position to judge that only a small proportion of the balls now in the urn are black if some balls have just been added and if most of the balls that were just added are black and we are not in a position to make any judgment about the proportion of the balls now in the urn that were just added.

Both of these judgments seem undeniably correct. (They would be correct even if we knew that no part of Spain outside R was arable, and that none of the original balls in the urn was black.)

In chapter 8, I posed a certain hypothesis I shall call D (for 'defense').[12] I argued that a very high proportion of the theism & D-worlds are S-worlds (all of them, as far as I can judge) and that no one is in an epistemic position to offer any answer to the question, What proportion of the theism-worlds are D-worlds?[13]

If I am right about D, it follows (by the above epistemic principle) that no one is in a position to judge that only a small proportion of the theism-worlds are S-worlds.[14] And, therefore, no one is in a position to judge that the proportion of the HI-worlds that are S-worlds is "much greater" than the proportion of the theism-worlds that are S-worlds.[15]

I see nothing in "The Skeptical Theist" to undermine either the general epistemic principle I have appealed to or my application of it. Draper offers three counterexamples to what he supposes to be the general epistemic strategy of "The Problem of Evil, the Problem of Air, and the Problem of Silence."[16] I have the space to examine only one of them. I choose the "smoking" example. (I record my conviction, without supporting argument, that an examination of the other two would yield similar results.) Consider the following propositions:

> SS   Smoking is safe (i.e., does not *cause* serious diseases)
> SH   Smoking is hazardous
> MLC   Smokers get lung cancer much more frequently than nonsmokers

Draper begins by pointing out that the following probability judgment is prima facie correct:

P(MLC/SH) >! P(MLC/SS).

I agree. When I think about it, it seems to me that the proportion of the smoking-is-hazardous-worlds in which smokers get lung cancer much more frequently than nonsmokers is—unless there is some relevant factor that I have not thought of—far greater than the proportion of the smoking-is-safe-worlds in which smokers get lung cancer much more frequently than nonsmokers. (If I were asked to defend this judgment, I would list possible kinds of explanation of smokers' getting more lung cancer than nonsmokers that did not depend on the causal agency of the habit itself, and argue that, because these explanations postulated very special sets of circumstances, they were intrinsically improbable. But my argument would, in the last analysis, have to be based on intuitive judgments of probability.)[17] Having called attention to the prima facie correctness of this judgment, Draper argues that (if the epistemic strategy of chapter 8 could be applied in the case of any evidential challenge) someone who believed that smoking was safe could defend his belief against an evidential argument based on this judgment simply by contriving the following "defense":

> GENET: Lung cancer is due to genetic causes, and people who are genetically predisposed to lung cancer are genetically predisposed to smoke.

If this were so, it would certainly be a grave blow to, if not a refutation of, my argument. For I not only accept his contention that the above probability judgment is prima facie correct, but I would agree that if this judgment is prima facie correct, then, unless one can discover either a pretty strong argument for the conclusion that smoking is safe or some way to overcome the prima facie correctness of the probability judgment, then it is not reasonable for one to believe that smoking is safe. (It does not follow that it would be reasonable for someone who had no relevant evidence but MLC to believe that smoking was dangerous. Our real-world knowledge that smoking is dangerous is based on the work of epidemiologists who have done far more than establish a positive correlation between smoking and cancer. They, have, for example, discovered evidence that conclusively rules out GENET.) And Draper is certainly right to contend that merely calling attention to the hypothesis I have labeled GENET does nothing to undermine the prima facie correctness of the probability judgment.

But *am* I committed to the thesis that GENET can be used as a "defense" to block a Draper-style evidential argument for the thesis that it is not reasonable to believe that smoking is safe? An argument parallel to my counterargument to the evidentialist argument from evil (one that employed GENET in the role I gave to D) would go like this:

> We are not in an epistemic position to judge that only a small proportion of the SS-worlds are MLC-worlds, owing to the fact that most SS & GENET-worlds are MLC-worlds, and we are not in an epistemic position to make any judgment about the proportion of the SS-worlds that are GENET-worlds.

But we *are* in an epistemic position to make a judgment about the proportion of the SS-worlds that are GENET-worlds. We are in epistemic position to make the judgment that this proportion is very low. Surely only a very small proportion of the worlds in which smoking is safe are worlds in which there is such a thing as lung cancer and it has a genetic cause and the very same factors that genetically predispose people to get lung cancer also genetically predispose people to smoke? (What proportion of the worlds in which it's safe to wear gold jewelry are worlds in which skin cancer has a genetic cause and the very same genetic factors that predispose people to skin cancer also predispose them to enjoy wearing gold jewelry?) Suppose that you know that you are somehow to be "placed" in a world in which smoking is safe, a world that has been chosen at random from among all the worlds in which smoking is safe. How likely do you think it is that you will find that in this world lung cancer exists, has a genetic cause, and, moreover, a genetic cause that predisposes people to smoke? *I* wouldn't bet on this complex of factors turning up. I suppose my reasoning is that in general, in the absence of further considerations, worlds in which two things that are logically and causally unrelated (save, possibly, by a common cause) have a common cause must be "rare"; worlds in which a taste for avocadoes and the enjoyment of medieval Latin lyrics have a common cause (genetic or social or whatever) do not, I would judge, collectively take up much logical space. In any case, if I were not in a position to judge that only a small proportion of SS-worlds were GENET-worlds, I should not have been able to give the argument that convinced me that Draper's initial probability judgment was prima facie correct: I should not have been able to say, "the proportion of the smoking-is-hazardous-worlds in which smokers get lung cancer much more frequently than nonsmokers is—unless there is some relevant factor that I have not thought of—far greater than the proportion of the smoking-is-safe-worlds in which smokers get lung cancer much more frequently than nonsmokers." I was able to make this judgment only because I was able to judge that the proportion of smoking-is-safe-worlds in which smokers get lung cancer much more frequently than nonsmokers is low. And I should not have been able to make this judgment if I were not in a position to judge that only a small proportion of SS-worlds are GENET-worlds.[18] Indeed, much of the argument of the present paragraph is no more than a spelling out of the reasons I had initially for accepting the prima facie credibility of the judgment 'P(MLC/SH) >! P(MLC/SS).'[19]

III

With some risk of oversimplification, we may call the following statement Draper's Thesis:

> If the probability judgment 'P(p/q) >! P(p/r)' (where p is known to be true and q and r are incompatible and there is no reason to suppose that the unconditional alethic probability of r is significantly greater than that of q) is prima facie correct, this fact confronts the r-ist with an evidential challenge that can be met in only two ways: The r-ist must either present a fairly strong argument for r or else must discover an r-dicy (this last term being a generalization of 'theodicy' in Draper's technical sense).

I continue to insist that Draper's Thesis is overly restrictive. My discussions of "the Problem of Air" and "the Problem of Silence" in chapter 8 were intended to make this conclusion plausible.

I can discuss what Draper says in "The Skeptical Theist" concerning the Problem of Air or I can discuss what he says concerning the Problem of Silence. I do not have sufficient space for an adequate discussion of both. I choose to discuss the latter. (Not that I don't have plenty to say about the former.)

Carl Sagan, let us suppose, assents to the thesis that there is intelligent life elsewhere in the galaxy ("noetism"). But there is the fact of cosmic silence; and there is the fact that cosmic silence seems prima facie to be much more probable on the Hypothesis of Isolation (that we are "alone") than it is on noetism; and there is the fact that there seems to be no reason to think that the unconditional alethic probability of noetism is significantly greater than that of HI; and there is the fact, or let us suppose there is, that Sagan has no very strong argument for noetism; and there is the fact that he can devise no "noödicy," no hypothesis h such that h is highly probable on noetism and such that "cosmic silence" is highly probable on the conjunction of noetism and h. Do these facts together entail that his assent to noetism faces an epistemic challenge that cannot be met, and that he should therefore withdraw this assent? No, say I, for there is an hypothesis h (there are in fact several) such that "cosmic silence" is highly probable on the conjunction of noetism and h and also such that no one is in a position to say what the probability of h on noetism is. Therefore, I reason, no one is in a position to say that the probability of cosmic silence on noetism is small. It should be stressed that the conclusion of this piece of reasoning is not that Sagan's belief *is* reasonable. (There are presumably those who would say that the fact that he has not got a strong argument for noetism is by itself enough to render his belief in noetism unreasonable.) It is not even that the fact of cosmic silence does not entail that his belief is unreasonable. It is rather that a certain argument does not show that his belief is unreasonable.[20]

Draper does not believe, or so I would interpret what he says, that Sagan's belief is unreasonable. But he sees Sagan's epistemic options differently from the way I do. He argues that there is an hypothesis that Sagan can appeal to that satisfies the conditions for being a (fairly) successful noödicy:

> The argument from silence against noetism is relatively weak because of a fairly successful "noödicy": it is antecedently very likely that intelligence need not lead to both technology of the right sort and a desire to communicate with life on other planets. If it weren't for several accidents of history, culture, and environment, it wouldn't have led to these things on earth! Of course, cosmic silence is some evidence favoring the Hypothesis of Isolation over noetism. But it's not very strong evidence. The ratio of the antecedent probability of cosmic silence on the Hypothesis of Isolation to the antecedent probability of cosmic silence on noetism is greater than one, but it is not very high.[21]

What exactly is the argument here? Let us remember that for h to be a noödicy it must have this feature: the probability of the proposition that our civilization, a civilization that . . . (insert here a description of our level of technological development and the history to the present date of Project Ozma and all other relevant facts) will have observed, as of this date, no signs of extraterrestrial intelligence is high on the conjunction of noetism and h. What noödicy does Draper propose? To take him at his word, it is this:

> Intelligence need not lead to both technology of the right sort and a desire to communicate with life on other planets.

But I see no reason to think that cosmic silence is highly probable on the conjunction of this proposition and noetism. If, out of thousands of intelligent species, *one* never developed the relevant technology and desires, it would be true that intelligence *need not* lead to these things. Even if we knew that this proposition was true, therefore, this knowledge would not put us in a position to assign a high probability to cosmic silence. It would, therefore, seem reasonable to suppose that a successful noödicy must be a stronger proposition, something like this:

> In the case of only a very small proportion of intelligent species does intelligence lead to both technology of the right sort and a desire to communicate with life on other planets.[22]

But let us not forget the second requirement on a successful noödicy: it must be highly probable on noetism. Draper says of his proposed noödicy that it is antecedently very likely that it is true. I would translate this thesis into my terminology as follows: its probability, conditional on our present relevant knowledge (minus our knowledge of the fact of cosmic silence), is high. I am willing to grant that if it is reasonable for us to make this probability judgment, then it is reasonable for us, now, to judge that the conditional alethic probability of the proposed noödicy on noetism is high. But why are we supposed to think that it is reasonable for us to make this probability judgment? *Is* it "antecedently very likely" that the proposed noödicy is true? I can't see why anyone would think so. Suppose me to be ignorant of the fact of cosmic silence. If God told me, when I was in that epistemic situation, that there were millions of intelligent species in the universe and asked me what proportion of them I thought would at some point in their "careers" develop high technology and a desire to communicate with other intelligent species, what could I say but "*Thou* knowest, Lord"? I suppose that if I had to guess, I wouldn't make the guess "Very low," since the only intelligent species whose course of development I am familiar with *has* developed these features. (But that is a pretty feeble consideration.) And I doubt whether any human being is in a better position to answer this question than I am.

Draper, it will be remembered, makes the following remark: "If it weren't for several accidents of history, culture, and environment, it [intelligence] wouldn't have led to these things on earth!" If this is taken as an argument for the thesis that in only a very small proportion of intelligent species does intelligence lead to both technology of the right sort and a desire to communicate with life on other planets (I expect Draper intended it only as an argument for the "need not" proposition), it is not cogent. Species typically last more or less unchanged for many millions of years—particularly if they do not develop industrial pollution and thermonuclear weapons. Suppose that the "accidents of history, culture, and environment" to which Draper alludes had not happened and that we had, as of this date, not advanced beyond the technological level of the ancient Mediterranean civilizations. What is the probability on this supposition that we should *never* develop an advanced technology—not, literally, in a million years? If this probability is high, think how fantastically low the probability of what actually happened is: the development by *Homo sapiens* of an advanced technology within a few thousand years of the invention of agriculture and the wheel and writing! (If there are evidential difficulties with any thesis discussed in this paper, the thesis that there was only a low probability—on, say, the way things were in 1000 B.C.—of humanity's ever, in the course of its entire span of existence, achieving a high technology must face some of the gravest ones!) We must remember that such evidential difficulties as noetism may face are almost totally insensitive to the outcome of disputes about how long, on the average, it takes a species that does develop a high technology to do so. Suppose we somehow knew that the pace of our technological development has been of extraordinarily improbable rapidity, and that, if there are any other intelligent species, those that develop a high technology will, on average, take about a million years (from the time, say, of their invention of writing) to do so. Anyone who, in this imaginary epistemic circumstance, accepts noetism, faces an evidential challenge from the fact of cosmic silence that is essentially the same as the one that any actual believer in noetism faces.

Draper has failed to discover a noödicy, but he has no reason to be embarrassed by this failure for, or so it seems to me, it is quite evident that no human being is in an epistemic position to discover a noödicy. We simply do not *know* enough to discover one. But then, if Draper's Thesis is correct, it follows that "Sagan's" belief is unreasonable. Although I do not share this belief, it does not seem to me to be unreasonable. At any rate, it is not shown to be unreasonable by the mere fact of his being unable to perform the quite impossible task of discovering a noödicy. (It would interest me to learn whether Draper thinks that anyone *has* ever met any evidential challenge to some belief by discovering a "-dicy.") I conclude that Draper's Thesis is false.

IV

My comments on Professor Russell's chapter 10 will be entirely concerned with one of his notes (number 12).[23] In that note, Russell seems simply to deny the conclusion of my argument without any discussion of the argument. (I mean my argument in note 11 of chapter 8 and the similar argument in the paper cited in that note.) Let me present an imaginary situation and ask Russell what he would do if he were in that situation.

Atlantis is sinking. Russell is in command of the last refugee ship. There are one thousand people left in Atlantis (all men, let us say). They are standing in a queue—position in the queue was determined by a fair lottery and is now unalterable—on the dock, clamoring for admission to his ship. Russell must admit the first n men in the queue ($0 \leq n \leq 1000$); the value of n has been left entirely to his discretion. If he takes no refugees on board, he and his (crewless, fully automated) ship will *certainly* reach the mainland safely. Each refugee he admits will reduce the chances of a safe arrival of the ship at the mainland by 0.1 percent. (Thus, if he takes only the first man in the queue, the two of them will have a 99.9 percent chance of a safe arrival; if he takes everyone, the ship will *certainly* sink; if he leaves behind only the last man in the queue, there is a 99.9 percent chance the ship will sink.) A very distressing moral problem faces Russell, and I do not know what I should do if I were in his place. But the following statement seems to be reasonable:

> Whatever the morally acceptable course(s) of action for someone in Russell's situation may be, none of the following is morally acceptable: to take none of the refugees; to take only a handful of them; to leave none of them behind; to leave only a handful of them behind.

It follows from this statement that whatever it is that Russell should do, it will have this consequence: He will have to close the hatch in the face of someone whose admission would not significantly decrease the ship's chances of reaching the mainland safely.[24] (If you think that 0.1 percent would be a significant decrease in the ship's chances, increase the number of refugees till each man admitted causes only what you would regard as an insignificant decrease in the ship's chances.) This example is artificial only in its simplicity. There are certainly real moral problems that are similar in structure, although an adequate statement of any of them would require a lot of qualification and detail.

If the defense I proposed in chapter 8 is true (that is, if the three statements it comprises are true), then God is in a precisely analogous moral situation. Although He may have miraculously saved all manner of fawns from forest fires, if

He is to preserve the lawlike regularity of the world there must come a point at which He will refrain from saving a fawn (or whatever) even though performing this act of mercy would not significantly decrease the lawlike regularity of the world. This "must" is the must of logical necessity, which constrains even an omnipotent being.

V

I once heard Keith Lehrer say, speaking of the late and much lamented James Cornman, "You either love him or you hate him. I *love* Jim Cornman."

I *love* Richard Gale.

No, honestly, Richard, I really mean it. You're a great guy and a good philosopher, no matter what everyone says.

But seriously, folks . . .

Richard (chapter 11) has learned from Stephen Potter, or has perhaps discovered independently, the following trick of disputation: "to say something so absolutely inappropriate on about five levels simultaneously that it seems hopeless even to try to answer back." (The respected music critic, in cocktail party conversation, admits that he isn't really too keen on Wagner; Potter's colleague induces "conversational paralysis" by replying, "But Wagner's worth five hundred of your modern jazz saxophonists.") This technique is displayed with particular brilliance in Richard's final section on theodicy, but good use of it is made throughout his chapter. I have, however, been able to escape conversational paralysis on a few points, and I will attempt to stammer out some replies.

(1) Would my general strategy for dealing with Draper's "evidential challenge" lead to radical skepticism if consistently applied? No. As I said, a "defense" may not be improbable on anything we think we know. (The point is made in various ways in many places.) And all "Cartesian" hypotheses (hypotheses about evil geniuses, brains in vats, and so on) are highly improbable on what we think we know, for we think we know that the vast majority of our perceptual beliefs about our immediate surroundings are true. (I do not say that this statement constitutes a cogent reply to the standard arguments for "Cartesian" skepticism. I do say that it's true.) And the defense presented in my chapter 8 is not improbable on anything we think we know. Or, if Richard thinks it is, he should have argued for that conclusion. I *did* argue, and at great length, that my defense is not improbable on anything we think we know, and my argument did not (as Richard suggests) depend on the defense's incorporating any sort of reference to in-principle-unobservable supernatural entities. My defense, in fact, refers only to the physical world and the character of physical law and to values. (And it does not presuppose any particular theory about values. It does not, for example, presuppose a "nonnaturalistic" theory of the nature of value.)

(2) Richard, twice at least, accuses me of a double standard, of requiring atheists to prove things when I don't require theists to prove the theses that occupy the corresponding or analogous places in their worldview. This is a misunderstanding. I do not require atheists, qua atheists, to prove *anything*. I have been

addressing a certain argument against theism, and I have contended (whether rightly or wrongly) that there is a hole in the argument if certain things are not proved, or at least cogently argued for. If a theist were to offer an argument against atheism, I would hold that argument to the same standard. I have in fact done something very much like that: I have deployed "modal skepticism" against an argument of Plantinga's for the conclusion that belief in God is rational, and against an argument of Swinburne's for the conclusion that the concept of God is coherent.[25] I was an agnostic when I presented these arguments, but I accept them still. I accept (the propositions that are, *per accidens*) the *conclusions* of Plantinga's and Swinburne's arguments, but I think that each of the arguments has a hole in it, a hole that could be filled only by arguing for a certain modal proposition (and which has not been filled and in my opinion can't be).

Here is an analogy. You say to St. Thomas, "There's a hole in your argument because you haven't shown that an infinite regress of causes is impossible." Thomas replies, "You're holding me to a different epistemic standard from the one you hold the atheist to: You don't demand that the atheist show that an infinite regress is possible." This would be a relevant reply if the atheist had published an argument for atheism that depended on the possibility of an infinite regress of causes, and if you had been maintaining that the atheist's argument was better than Thomas's, and if you had indeed demanded that Thomas show that an infinite regress was impossible and had not demanded that the atheist show that an infinite regress was possible. But if the only topic under discussion is whether Thomas's argument establishes its conclusion, then the protest that I have put into Thomas's mouth makes no sense at all.

Let us remember that the only conclusion of chapter 8 was that a certain evidential argument from evil does not succeed—that it doesn't even come close to succeeding. But it is perfectly consistent with this conclusion to suppose that God does not exist, or that the concept of God is incoherent, or that, whether or not God exists, belief in God is not reasonable, or even that *some* evidential argument from evil shows that belief in God is not reasonable. (Similarly, someone who maintained that Thomas's argument failed because it did not provide any good reason to think that an infinite regress of causes was impossible could consistently maintain that a First Cause existed—or even that a First Cause could be shown to exist by *some* causal argument.)

(3) I think that it will be evident to the unbiased reader of this book— indeed to a goodly portion of its biased readers—that although I have presented arguments for modal skepticism, Richard neither says what those arguments are[26] nor presents any reason to suppose that we have the capacity to make judgments about modal matters that are remote from the concerns of everyday life. He does, however, suggest that I am selectively skeptical about modality, and to this charge I will respond.

I will begin by making it clear that by "modal skepticism" I do not mean the thesis that none of the modal judgments we make is justified. I make all sorts of modal judgments and (or so I believe) they are mostly true, and (or so I believe) I am fully justified in thinking that they are mostly true. (That I might not have been a philosopher, for example, or that there might have been more dogs in Paris in 1933 than there in fact were or that there cannot be liquid wine bottles.) In addition, there are many modal propositions that I am pretty sure are true, although I am not as sure about them as I am about the propositions I have just listed: that I could not have been a woman, for example, or that the earth could not have had a satellite the size of the actual moon that was made of green cheese. These last two judgments are not "remote from ordinary life" in at least one good sense: very straightforward scientific considerations, things you can learn from actual textbooks, underlie my belief that these things are probably absolutely impossible.[27] I therefore do not regard myself as someone who, in Richard's words, "cannot modalize like normal people do." I can, and so can Richard. What he *can't* do, apparently, is to discriminate those cases in which his modal judgments are products of his ordinary human powers of "modalization" from those that are based on his immersion in a certain philosophical environment—an environment composed of philosophers who unthinkingly make all sorts of fanciful modal judgments because *they've* always been surrounded by philosophers who unthinkingly make the same sorts of fanciful modal judgments. He is as unaware of his immersion in this environment as a fish is of its immersion in water. He is unaware that the modal beliefs he expresses or presupposes when he says, "We'd have had more room if we'd moved the table up against the wall" (e.g., that it was possible for the table to be up against the wall), and the modal beliefs he gives such confident expression to in his writings on philosophical theology have quite different sources. The former have their source in our ordinary human powers of "modalization" (for all that, they are not philosophically uncontroversial: they would be disputed by Spinoza); the latter have their source in his professional socialization, in (to borrow an expression of Rorty's) what his peers will let him get away with saying. He could be compared with a Greek mariner of Homeric times who thinks that his (well-grounded) belief that the mountain that has just appeared on the horizon is about thirty miles away and his belief that the sun is about thirty miles away stem from the same source, to wit, his ability to judge distance by eye.

That, at any rate, is my considered and sincerely held opinion. Perhaps it's not very nice of me actually to express it, but there doesn't seem to be any rule in force in this discussion that forbids saying things that it isn't very nice to say.

"Modal skepticism," as I use the term, is a thesis about the scope and limits of our ordinary human powers of "modalization." It is roughly this: If the subject matter of *p* is remote from the concerns of everyday life, then our ordinary human powers of "modalization" are not reliable guides to the modal status of *p*. (But this statement of the thesis is not quite right. We certainly know the modal status of 'If God exists, then there is an immaterial being' and the "subject matter" of this proposition is, no doubt, remote from the concerns of everyday life.)

Now what of Richard's charge that I am selectively skeptical about modality? Don't I (as a theist) hold all sorts of opinions about the modal status of various propositions that could not—if the modal skepticism I endorsed when I was criticizing the evidential argument from evil is correct—have their source in our ordinary human powers of "modalization"? I do indeed. Richard cites the possibility of creation ex nihilo, an excellent example. Another good example, which I mention because I have written on it extensively, is this: it is possible that there exists a necessary concrete being. In my work on the ontological argument,[28] I have argued at length that our ordinary human intellectual powers are inadequate to the task of discovering whether it is possible for there to be a necessary concrete being. And yet I believe that there *is* a necessary concrete being and a fortiori believe that it is possible for there to be one. But I do not stand convicted of inconsistency, for I do not claim to have discovered that it was possible for there to be a necessary concrete being by holding the concept of a necessary concrete being before my mind and applying to it my ordinary human powers of "modalization." I believe it to be possible that there is a necessary concrete being because I believe it to be true that there is one. And I believe it to be true that there is one on the basis of a divine self-revelation (or at least I *believe* that that is why I believe this).[29] There is nothing at all puzzling about the idea of knowing the modal status of a proposition without having applied one's powers of "modalization" to it. It is really a very common occurrence. I believe that it is possible for human beings to know what the stars are made of because I know that they do know this, and not because I have held the concept of a human being who knows what the stars are made of before my mind and applied to it my powers of "modalization." I could list several important mathematical theorems to each of which I stand in the following epistemic relation: I know that it is true (and therefore possibly true) because it has been endorsed by people my epistemic community recognizes as competent mathematicians, and they (so I believe) know it to be true on the basis of mathematical reasoning that I am incapable of following. In general, for almost every theological proposition that I claim to know is possibly true and which I could not know was possibly true by means of my ordinary human powers of "modalization," I would claim the following: this statement is *in fact* true and I know it to be true and this knowledge essentially involves testimony, testimony that derives ultimately from divine revelation. (But there is at least one important *false* theological proposition that I believe I know to be possibly true and which I could not have known was possibly true without some help from divine revelation: that God did not create anything.) If Jane is a proponent of the evidential argument from evil and if she claims to know that—for example—a hedonic-utopia-without-massive-irregularity is possible because one actually exists somewhere, and claims to know this on the basis of some sort of testimony (perhaps June told her and Feigl told June and Maxwell told Feigl and Maxwell was told by creatures from Arcturus), then my argument from modal skepticism would be simply irrelevant to her claim. There might, of course, be other grounds on which it should be judged doubtful.

Richard, no doubt, regards my claim to be the recipient of a divine revelation as not only doubtful but ludicrous, just as I should regard as ludicrous someone's claim to have been told by the Arcturans that there was a hedonic utopia somewhere out beyond Sagittarius. But the question whether my claim is defensible is not to the present point, for the truth of that claim is not among the premises of this paper or of chapter 8. Here I am defending myself against a charge of selective skepticism about the scope and limits of our powers of "modalization," and I am simply pointing out that I do not claim that, e.g., my belief that *creatio ex nihilo* is possible is based upon an exercise of those powers. Even if I am deceived and the revelation that I hold to be the ground of that belief is a fable, my scepticism about our powers of "modalization" is not selective. I was a modal skeptic before I was a theist, and I have always applied this skepticism uniformly and consistently to the claims of theists (Plantinga and Swinburne) and atheists.[30]

NOTES

1. Paul Draper, "Pain and Pleasure," chapter 2, note 2, in this book.

2. Cf. Draper, "Pain and Pleasure": "I will use $P(x/y)$ to represent the probability of the statement *x, independent of the observations and testimony O reports*, on the assumption that the statement *y* is true." (Italics in original.)

3. We adopt the following conventions concerning constraints on the notion of the measure of a set of worlds. All measures are real numbers between (and including) 0 and 1 (there are, therefore, no infinitesimal measures); the measure of the whole of logical space is 1 and the measure of the empty set is 0; if a set (*sc.* of worlds) has a measure, then its union with a set *x* has a measure iff *x* has a measure; if a set is exhaustively decomposed into a finite number of non-overlapping subsets each of which has a measure, the measure of this set (by the previous statement it has a measure) is the sum of the measures of those subsets; if a set of measure *P* has *n* members, where *n* is finite (and not 0), an *m*-membered subset of that set has the measure $m\,P/n$; if there are infinitely many possible worlds, any set of lower cardinality than the whole set has measure 0. It should be noted that these statements *define* "measure" only if the number of possible worlds is finite. If there are infinitely many worlds—and surely there are?—the notion of the measure of a set of worlds gets most of such content as it has from the intuitive notion of the proportion of logical space that a set of worlds occupies. I shall sometimes speak of the proportion of logical space that a set of worlds occupies as its *size*. "Size" in this sense must be carefully distinguished from cardinality. The cardinality of a set may indeed be said to measure its "size" in one perfectly good sense of the word, but there are other measures of the "sizes" of certain sets, measures that are in general independent of cardinality. In point-set topology, for example, regions of space are identified with sets of points, and some regions are assigned such cardinality-independent measures of size as length, area, and volume. There is obviously a close conceptual connection between such measures and the concept of probability. Suppose, for example, that darts are thrown at a wall "at random" or "without bias" (i.e., by a method that favors no point on or region of the wall). The probability that a given dart that strikes the wall will strike a given region of the wall is the proportion of the whole wall that is occupied by that region: the ratio of the area of that region to the area of the whole wall. It is this conceptual connection between probability and area (and length and volume) that is the reason for the heuristic utility of thinking of the set of all worlds as forming a space such that many of its subsets may be assigned measures of size that (like length, area, and volume in respect of sets of points in space) are not in general functions of their cardinality. Just as two sets of points of the same cardinality may be "spread out" in such a way as to occupy different proportions of some region of the plane, so two sets of worlds of the same cardinality may be "spread out" in such a way as to occupy different proportions of logical space. Do we understand these ideas, the idea of sets of worlds being "spread out in logical space" and the idea of their having measures that depend not only on their cardinalities but also on the way they are spread out? In my view, we understand them as well or as badly as we understand the assign-

ment of (real, objective) numerical probabilities to propositions like "My wife will quit her job within six months" or "God exists" or "There exist vast amounts of animal suffering in the natural world." This, at any rate, is true in my case.

4. Or, equivalently, the ratio of the measure of the set of worlds in which both p and q are true to the measure of the set of worlds in which q is true. This definition (in either form) can have counterintuitive consequences if the number of worlds is infinite and q is true in only a finite number of worlds. Consequently, one might want to define conditional probability "separately" for this case. I shall not bother about this very special case.

5. I concede that "pure" judgments of unconditional alethic probability are pretty rare, since the unconditional alethic probability of most propositions that interest us is either very, very large or very, very small. The true unconditional alethic probability of the proposition that the sun will rise tomorrow is (I should imagine) very, very small, since the portion of logical space in which the sun so much as exists is (I should imagine) very, very small—perhaps of 0 measure. (Stephen Hawking has said that it is quite plausible to suppose that the set of worlds in which there is organic life is of 0 measure.) And, if this is so, then the unconditional alethic probability of the *denial* of this proposition is very, very large; perhaps 1. I take it that when we apparently say that certain propositions have real, objective probabilities like 2/3 or 0.7116, we are actually making this statement about their conditional probability on some "understood" proposition—perhaps in many cases the proposition that records the state of things in the actual world at the time of utterance. And this would also seem to be the case even with many judgments that apparently assign propositions unconditional probabilities close to 0 or 1. For example, the judgment that the (real, objective) probability that the sun will rise tomorrow is very near to unity is best understood as the judgment that in almost the entirety of that region of logical space in which things are as they are at present in the actual world, the sun rises tomorrow.

The judgments of real, objective probability that a rational bookmaker uses to calculate odds are usually judgments conditional on an hypothesis involving his epistemic situation at the time of the calculation. When, for example, he judges that the real, objective probability of *this* die's falling 2, 3, 5, or 6 a moment from *now* is 2/3, he is not judging that this or any die that way a moment from now in two-thirds of the whole of logical space (or even in two-thirds of the region of logical space in which things are exactly as they are at present in the actual world, for that might be false given strict, causal determinism—which he may not be in a position to rule out); rather he is judging that in two-thirds of the region of logical space in which he is in *this* epistemic situation and *this* die (or perhaps the die that plays *this* role in relation to someone in this epistemic situation?) is thrown in a moment, it falls 2, 3, 5, or 6.

6. More exactly, no answer is better than any *equally specific* competing answer. Of course there are answers like "between 1 percent and 90 percent" that have a pretty good crack at being right. But this answer is no better than "between 7 percent and 96 percent" or "either between 4 percent and 6 percent, or else between 10 percent and 97 percent."

7. Or, more generally, an argument for some thesis that would undermine the prima facie credibility of the proposition that HI is epistemically preferable to theism. Arguments for the conclusion that a does not fall within HI or for the conclusion that it is more plausible to suppose that a falls within theism than within HI are other possibilities. For the sake of simplicity, I will not discuss other possibilities.

8. Of course there is the formal possibility that one might find some reason to reject the assumption that HI and theism are of about equal unconditional alethic probability, that they are regions of logical space of about the same size. The ontological argument is, in effect, an argument for the conclusion that theism (minus the creation clause) spans the whole of logical space, and thus is much larger than HI (which would presumably be the empty set of worlds if the ontological argument is sound). But every version of the ontological argument is either invalid or depends on a premise that enjoys an epistemic position no better than that of theism, whatever that position may be. No other known argument or consideration seems even relevant to the task of showing that the unconditi-

tional alethic probability of theism is significantly greater than the unconditional alethic probability of HI.

9. Or a proportion that is not too small. I will ignore this refinement.

10. At this point, I abandon Draper's '*O*' for my '*S*,' simply because I am more comfortable thinking in terms of the distribution in logical space of certain patterns of suffering than in terms of the distribution of the sort of evidence on which we base our judgments about the actual pattern of suffering. But I don't think that this makes much difference, really, for I assume that—here I neglect the fact that *O* is defined in relation to both pleasure and suffering, and not to suffering alone—the measure of the set of worlds in which *O* is true and *S* is not 0 or very, very close to 0.

11. Suppose that someone were to argue that this principle, even if it were correct, could not be used to block an evidential challenge to theism, owing to the fact that P(*S*/HI) could be "much larger than" P(*S*/theism) even if P(*S*/theism) were fairly high. (The former might be, say, 0.9 and the latter 0.6.) I do not think that *Draper* would argue this way. If I understand him, he argues that P(*O*/HI) is, prima facie, much greater than P(*O*/theism) because, prima facie, the former is at least not too small, and the latter is very small indeed. However this may be, I should not regard a Draper-style "epistemic challenge" as very impressive unless "much larger than" implied (at least) "several times larger than." If it could be somehow demonstrated to me that P(*S*/HI) = 0.9 and P(*S*/theism) = 0.6, I should not regard this as a demonstration that it was unreasonable to accept theism in the absence of a strong argument for theism. I shall assume that if P(*p*) is "much larger than" P(*q*), this implies that P(*q*) is "small"—even if P(*q*) = 1.

12. In chapter 8, I was not perfectly consistent in the matter of whether the term 'defense' applied to the conjunction of theism and the "auxiliary hypothesis" or to the auxiliary hypothesis alone. It does not make much difference which way the term is used, but I ought to have been consistent. The "defense" I actually proposed—the conjunction of propositions (1), (2), and (3)—is a defense in the latter sense.

13. At any rate, my arguments, if they are correct, show that no one is in a position to rule out the answer "all of them." It may be that one could give a plausible a priori argument for the conclusion that various modal considerations entail that the answer must be "all of them" or "none of them." But a dispute about this point would be of no consequence. If the answer to the question, What proportion of the balls now in the urn were just added? were known to be either "all of them" or "none of them," that would not affect the validity of the conclusion that we are not in a position to judge that only a small proportion of the balls now in the urn are black.

14. It also follows that D has no epistemic probability on theism (relative to our epistemic situation)—nor does D have an epistemic probability on, say, the totality of what science makes it reasonable for us to believe at the present time. It is easy to see that there are propositions that have no epistemic probability. Remember the case in which I chose a number *n* (0 ≤ *n* ≤ 100) at random, and placed *n* black balls and 100-*n* white balls in an empty urn. What is the epistemic probability (relative to a situation in which one knows just this much) of the proposition that the first ball drawn from the urn will be black? A rational ideal bookie, contemplating this situation, will see that because he has no way to determine what the real, objective probability of the first ball's being black is, he has no way to set odds. (Do not confuse this case with the following case: the number *n has not yet been drawn* and the bookie is told that it will be and then the urn prepared and then a ball drawn. In *this* case, the real, objective probability that the ball will be black is 0.5, and the bookie would take the bet at any odds less than even odds.) Although one way of setting the odds is *objectively* better than any of the others (if, for example, the number of black balls in the urn is in fact 36, the best course is to accept a bet that the first ball will be black at any odds lower than (100-36)/36 or 16/9 and at no higher odds), the bookie has no way of *knowing* which way of setting the odds is objectively the best. An ideal bookie who was forced, in this epistemic situation, to post odds for a bet that the first ball would be black could only *choose at random* the odds at which he would accept the bet. No odds, therefore,

are *the* odds that a rational ideal bookie in this situation *would* set, and, as a consequence, the proposition that the first ball drawn will be black has no epistemic probability relative to this epistemic situation. A more interesting, if more problematic example: In my view, the proposition that a surveyable proof of the four-color theorem will be discovered in the next century has no epistemic probability (relative to my present epistemic situation) on any proposition I know or believe to be true.

15. In note 9 to chapter 8 I wrote:

> Well, one might somehow know the probability of S on theism as a function of the probability of HI on theism; one might know that the former probability was one-tenth the latter, and yet have no idea what either probability was. But that is not the present case. The evidentialist's argument essentially involves two independent probability judgments: that the probability of S on HI is at least not too low, and that the probability of S on theism is very low.

This concession now seems to me to have been needless (although the point about the independence of the two probability judgments is certainly correct). If I know that probability A is ten times probability B, then I know that B is less than or equal to 0.1, and I *am,* therefore, in a position to make a judgment about the magnitude of B. If one is not in a position to judge that the probability of B is low, then it cannot be true that one knows that some other probability is ten times greater than B. If one is not in a position to judge that the proportion of Spain that is arable is low, then it cannot be that one knows that the proportion of France that is arable is ten times the proportion of Spain that is arable. (See note 11.)

16. Or to an improved version of it. I ignore the improvements, which I believe to be unnecessary, and, in fact, to involve a condition that could not possibly be fulfilled.

17. I have been asked how a modal skeptic like myself can consistently regard such reasoning as justified. The answer is simple. I am a modal skeptic only about matters remote from everyday life, and that is not the case in the present example. What *justifies* my intuitive judgments of probability in the present case, I do not know. In other words, I do not know how to refute the thesis that the modal (and probabilistic) intuitions we employ in everyday life are unjustified. I would point out, however, that there is an impressive convergence of judgment about modal and probabilistic theses of the sort that we make in everyday life, and that there is no such convergence in the case of modal and probabilistic judgments about matters remote from everyday life.

18. In my view, this judgment does not depend upon my knowledge of the relation between smoking and cancer. It is simply an application of very general and abstract principles about causal relations (primarily the "low probability of common cause" principle that I appealed to earlier in the paragraph to which this note is appended), principles that I may very well know a priori. Whether or not my knowledge of them is a priori, it is certainly knowledge that I possessed before I first learned of the correlation between smoking and cancer.

19. I ought to say something about Draper's argument for the conclusion that my way of dealing with the evidential argument from evil has the "absurd implication" that the acquisition of evidence for D could leave the theist in a worse epistemic position than he was in when he had no evidence for D. But I have failed to follow the crucial last step of the argument, the step contained in the words "which, since D just barely satisfies the condition of goodness, would be significantly less than P(O/HI)." (In this note, I will use Draper's symbols.) I'll try to explain my difficulty. Let us introduce a few numbers to focus our thoughts. Suppose that P(O/HI) is 0.8 and P(O/ G&D) is 0.79. Suppose that we have discovered a body of evidence that has led us to peg P(D/G) at 0.51. (Such a body of evidence, by the way, contrary to what Draper seems to imply, could not consist entirely of evidence that favored D. If *p* is, to use Draper's term, "aprobable" for one, and if one then turns up a body of evidence consisting entirely of observations that favor *p,* this could only lead one to con-

clude that, for some n between 0 and 1, P(p) lies between n and 1. A body of evidence that led one to peg P(p) at 0.51 would have to include observations that led one to conclude that the probability of p was no higher than 0.51, and observations that *favored p* could not do that.) Since P(D/G) is close to ½, so is P(ÿD/G). It follows by the Weighted Averages Principle that P(O/G) is close to ½P(O/D & G) ÷ ½P(O/ÿD & G). But why should it follow from this—here's where I fail to follow Draper's reasoning—that P(O/G) is significantly less than 0.8 (= P(O/HI))? This would follow only if P(O/ÿD & G) were significantly less than 0.81. And why should we suppose *that?* There is certainly no mathematical reason to do so: it is easy to construct a model on which P(D/G) = 0.51, P(O/D & G) = 0.79, and P(O/ÿD & G) = 1. Then P(O/G) = (0.51 ¥ 0.79) + (0.49 ¥ 1)—close to ½ (0.79) + ½ (1)—or about 0.89, a figure that is significantly *greater* than 0.8.

20. The corresponding points apply to chapter 8. The conclusion of that chapter is not that assent to theism *is* reasonable. (There are those who say that the fact that the theist has no strong argument for theism is by itself enough to render the theist's belief unreasonable.) It is not even that S does not entail that the theism is unreasonable. It is rather that a certain argument—Draper's argument, or at least my version of it—does not show that theism is unreasonable.

21. "The Skeptical Theist" (chapter 9 in this book), note 21.

22. It is not at all clear that cosmic silence really is highly probable on the conjunction of this stronger hypothesis and noetism. Recall the "self-reproducing robotic probe" scenario. If even *one* intelligent species had initiated the program imagined in this scenario (and had done so more than fifty million years ago), we'd know about them. And many experts judge that (1) any species with a high technology and a desire to make contact with other intelligent species would eventually initiate such a program, and (2) it is highly likely that if there are *any* intelligent species other than humanity, there were some of them more than fifty million years ago.

23. Editor's note: In an earlier draft of this essay, van Inwagen had more to say about Russell's essay. Due to constraints on space, it was cut, along with over 30,000 words from other new essays in the book.

24. It seems evident to me that whatever it is that Russell should do, the actual concrete action he performs will have to be to some degree "arbitrary," for it seems evident to me that the correct principles of morality, together with all of the facts, are not going to endorse one and only one imperative of the form 'Admit the first n men in the queue.' And yet, in the end, he will have to admit the first n men in the queue, for some n. But whether what Russell should do would have to be to some degree arbitrary does not affect the point of the example: even if the correct moral principles and the facts tell him to admit (say) exactly 217 refugees, he will still have to close the hatch in the face of someone whose admission would not significantly decrease the ship's chances of reaching the mainland safely.

25. See "Ontological Arguments," *Nous* 11 (1977): 375-95, and my review of Swinburne's *Coherence of Theism, Philosophical Review* 88 (1979): 668-72.

26. Gale's discussion of "scientific essentialism" is of no relevance whatever to those arguments.

27. For a discussion of the "green cheese" example, see the review of Swinburne's *Coherence of Theism* cited in note 25.

28. See "Ontological Arguments," cited in note 25, and *Metaphysics* (Boulder: Westview Press, 1993), chap. 5.

29. Not that I think that God has explicitly endorsed the proposition that He is a necessary being somewhere in scripture or in the proceedings of some ecumenical council (I do not claim to be a direct or proximate recipient of divine revelation on these matters). I believe that God is a necessary being on the basis of philosophical reflection on what (I believe) God has explicitly revealed about Himself in scripture and tradition.

30. I wish to thank Evan Fales, James Sennett, James Taylor, and, especially, Alvin Plantinga for comments which have, I believe, greatly improved this paper; at any rate, they have led to extensive revisions.

13.

ALVIN PLANTINGA

On Being Evidentially Challenged

1. The Argument Initially Stated

Pain and pleasure, says Paul Draper, constitute an evidential problem for theists.[1] What precisely is the problem?

> The problem is not that some proposition about pain and pleasure can be shown to be both true and logically inconsistent with theism. Rather, the problem is evidential. A statement reporting the observations and testimony upon which our knowledge about pain and pleasure is based bears a certain significant negative evidential relation to theism.

What is that statement, and what is the significant negative evidential relation it bears to theism? As for the former,

> Now let "O" stand for a statement reporting both the observations one has made of humans and animals experiencing pain or pleasure and the testimony one has encountered concerning the observations others have made of sentient beings

experiencing pain or pleasure. By "pain" I mean physical or mental suffering of any sort.

So O is the statement that bears a significant negative evidential relation to theism. Note that O is person relative: each of us will have her own O, and my O may differ from yours. My O, we might say, sets out the facts about the magnitude, variety, distribution, duration, and the like (for short, the "disposition") of pleasure and pain as I know them.

Now what is the significant negative evidential relation to theism in which O stands? Here Draper bows in the direction of David Hume: most contemporary philosophers of religion (unlike Hume) "have failed to recognize that one cannot determine what facts about evil theism needs to explain or how well it needs to explain them without considering alternatives to theism." The important question is "whether or not any serious hypothesis that is logically inconsistent with theism explains some significant set of facts about evil or about good and evil much better than theism does."

The answer to this important question, says Draper, is that indeed there is such a hypothesis, one that is both inconsistent with theism and explains some significant facts about good and evil much better than theism does. This is the "Hypothesis of Indifference" (HI for short):

> HI: neither the nature nor the condition of sentient beings on earth is the result of benevolent or malevolent actions performed by nonhuman persons.

HI, of course, is inconsistent with theism (taking the latter to entail that the world has been created by a person who is wholly good as well as omnipotent and omniscient). And now Draper's claim:

> C: HI explains the facts O reports much better than theism does.

What is it for a proposition to "explain" something like the facts that O reports?

> I will reformulate C as the claim that the facts O reports are much more surprising on theism than they are on HI, or, more precisely, that the antecedent probability of O is much greater on the assumption that HI is true than on the assumption that theism is true.

I take it the more precise formulation is the operative one here; we must therefore ask what this "antecedent probability" is. "By the 'antecedent' probability of O," says Draper, "I mean O's probability, independent of (rather than temporally prior to) the observations and testimony it reports."

Finally, the probability in question is *epistemic* probability, not (for example) logical, statistical, or physical probability. And what is epistemic probability?

> The concept of epistemic probability is an ordinary concept of probability for which no adequate philosophical analysis has, in my opinion, been proposed. As a first approximation, however, perhaps the following analysis will do:

> Relative to K, p is epistemically more probable than q, where K is an epi-
> stemic situation and p and q are propositions, just in case any fully rational
> person in K would have a higher degree of belief in p than in q.

As Draper says, epistemic probability is an ordinary concept that is difficult to
analyze or explain; suppose we provisionally accept Draper's proposed first
approximation.[2] I take it there is an implicit restriction to *human* persons; how
things might go with other rational creatures is not our present concern. What
does K include; what goes into an epistemic situation? We shall have to return to
this question later; for now let's say initially that K, for a given person S, would
include at least some of the other propositions S believes, as well as the experiences S is undergoing and perhaps has undergone; it would also include what S
remembers, possibly a specification of S's epistemic environment, and no doubt
more besides.

   Now we see the general shape of the argument: the first premise is C, the
claim that HI explains O much better than theism does—that is, the antecedent
epistemic probability of O given HI is much greater than the antecedent probability of O given theism. And second, if C is true, says Draper, then "we have a prima
facie good epistemic reason to reject theism—that is, a reason that is sufficient for
rejecting theism unless overridden by other reasons for not rejecting theism." Here
he is apparently relying on a general principle; perhaps something like

> (1) For any propositions P and Q and person S, if S believes P and Q and there is
> a serious hypothesis R that is incompatible with P and such that the epistemic
> probability of Q with respect to R for S is much greater than the epistemic prob-
> ability of Q with respect to P for S, then S has a prima facie good epistemic rea-
> son to reject P.

So Draper's claim is that HI explains O much better than theism does; since HI is
a serious hypothesis and is inconsistent with theism, we have a prima facie good
reason for rejecting theism:

> Suppose that I succeed in showing that C is true (relative to my own and my
> reader's epistemic situations). Then the truth of C is (for us) a prima facie good
> (epistemic) reason to believe that theism is less probable than HI. Thus, since the
> denial of theism is obviously entailed by HI and so is at least as probable as HI,
> the truth of C is a prima facie good reason to believe that theism is less probable
> than not. And since it is epistemically irrational to believe both that theism is true
> and that it is less probable than not, the truth of C is also a prima facie good rea-
> son to reject (i.e., to cease or refrain from believing) theism.

2. The Argument Examined

   This is a subtle and powerful challenge; it deserves a closer look. The
argument has two premises, C and (1). Suppose we begin with (1).

2.1 ON BEING EVIDENTIALLY CHALLENGED

Draper argues that P(O/HI) is much larger (with respect to the theist's epistemic situation) than P(O/theism); I shall give some reasons later for thinking that false. But suppose it were true: what kind and how much of a challenge to theistic belief would this be? How widespread is this evidential disability? Before we can answer this question, we must ask another: what is a *serious* alternative hypothesis? Draper answers this question elsewhere: "Specifically, one hypothesis is a 'serious' alternative to another only if (i) it is not ad hoc—the facts to be explained are not arbitrarily built into it—and (ii) it is at least as plausible initially as the other hypothesis."[3] Condition (i) requires no present comment, but what about condition (ii)? How are we to understand "plausibility" here? I think Draper means to abstract from specific epistemic situations: the plausibility of a hypothesis depends not on considerations such as the specific evidence (propositional and nonpropositional) I may have for or against it (else HI might not be nearly as plausible, for me, as theism), but on more general considerations such as its scope, how it fits in with what is generally known (a hypothesis entailing that the world is flat wouldn't be plausible), and the like. We don't have an account of plausibility that is at all precise or specific, but perhaps we don't need one for present purposes.

So suppose we say that a proposition *P* is *evidentially challenged* for *S* if it satisfies the antecedent of (1): *P* is evidentially challenged for a person *S* if and only if *S* believes *P* and there are propositions *Q* and *R* such that *S* believes *Q*, *R* is incompatible with *P*, and *Q* is much more probable with respect to *R* than with respect to *P*. What (1) claims is that if a proposition *P* is evidentially challenged for *S*, then *S* has a prima facie good epistemic reason for rejecting *P*—for being agnostic with respect to it or believing its denial. Is this really true? Is being evidentially challenged a serious handicap?

Well, how widespread is it? How many of my beliefs *are* evidentially challenged, for me? More, perhaps, than we might initially think. For example, here are three more propositions related, for me, as are theism, O and HI: (1) George is a non-Catholic, (2) George is a professor at Notre Dame, and (3) George is a Catholic academic. I believe both (1) and (2); but (2) is much more likely (perhaps a million times more likely) on (3), a proposition incompatible with (1), than it is on (1). Does this fact give me a good reason to reject (1)? (Should I reconsider: George is a professor at Notre Dame, after all, and that is enormously more likely on (3) than on (1). So maybe he's really a Catholic?). Not clearly.

Indeed, I think it likely that everything I believe—in any event every belief of mine that is possible in the broadly logical sense—is also evidentially challenged. I don't know how to give a *proof* of this claim (it probably isn't worth spending a whole lot of time trying to find a general proof); but it certainly seems likely to be the case. So, for example, let *P* be the proposition that I am now typing at my computer and let *Q* be the proposition that the lilacs are blooming in my backyard. *Q* is improbable on *P* (sadly enough, most of the time when I am typing on my computer, the lilacs aren't blooming): as *R*, choose the proposition I and some dinner guests are in the backyard (out of reach of my computer) admiring the lilacs. Clearly Q is much more likely with respect to R than with respect to P (I hardly ever admire the lilacs with dinner guests while typing at my computer). The proposition that I am now typing on my computer is therefore evidentially challenged; does this give me much of a prima facie reason to reject it?

Alternatively, let P be the proposition that London, England, is larger than London, Ontario, and let Q be the proposition that yesterday afternoon I was in the north half of the woods behind my house. I believe both of these propositions. Q is unlikely on P; I am seldom in those woods (though if I am I am likely to be in the north half). And let R be the proposition that yesterday afternoon I went for a walk in the woods behind my house in order to try to recover from the shock of learning that as a matter of fact London, England, is *smaller* than London, Ontario. P is evidentially challenged, but the challenge doesn't give me much of a reason to doubt it.

I think you get the picture. For any proposition I believe (so long as it is not logically impossible) I can find an evidential challenge. And this leads me to think that a challenge of this sort is not very significant *by itself or in the general case.* If every or nearly every proposition I believe faces an evidential challenge, then I don't learn much of interest about theism in learning that it too faces such a challenge. Indeed, O itself, the proposition recording what I've learned by observation and testimony of the pattern of pain and pleasure, faces an evidential challenge. Let Q be as above, the proposition that yesterday afternoon I was in the north half of the woods behind my house; this is improbable with respect to O, but probable with respect to *yesterday afternoon, while walking in the woods behind my house, I suddenly realized that O is false,* which is of course incompatible with O.

Under what conditions (if any) would a challenge of this sort be significant? What sorts of beliefs are such that their being subject to an evidential challenge gives us serious reason to doubt them? Here we think first of scientific hypotheses. I propose a hypothesis to explain the behavior of gases: you point out that certain data are more probable with respect to another hypothesis incompatible with mine; that certainly seems to be a strong prima facie reason to doubt my hypothesis.

But here we must be careful. *Every* scientific hypothesis I believe (like the rest of what I believe) faces an evidential challenge, and in most cases those evidential challenges cast almost no doubt on the hypothesis. For example, I believe that Newtonian mechanics is pretty nearly correct for everyday objects and velocities. Returning to the previous example, however, it is unlikely, with respect to Newtonian mechanics, that yesterday I should have been in the north half of the woods behind my house, but likely that I should have been there with respect to the proposition that yesterday afternoon I took a walk in the woods in order to recover from the shock of learning that Newtonian mechanics isn't anywhere nearly correct for everyday objects and velocities. Does that give me a reason to doubt Newtonian mechanics? Probably not.

Why not? There are at least two reasons. To facilitate discussion, suppose we say that when a hypothesis P is evidentially challenged for S, the other proposition Q that S believes is the *datum* and the proposition R incompatible with P with respect to which Q is much more likely than it is with respect to P is the *alternative hypothesis*. Now obviously enough a hypothesis like Newtonian mechanics is not obliged to account for or predict something like the fact that I was in the north half of the woods yesterday; that is not the business it is in. It doesn't matter that this datum is improbable on Newtonian mechanics, and the fact that it is casts no doubt on it. For each scientific hypothesis, there will be a body of data (past and future) such that the success of the hypothesis depends upon how well it explains that data (the data *relevant* to the theory); and the datum in question is not relevant to Newtonian mechanics. Similarly, for an evidential challenge to have any force, the alternative hypothesis must also be relevant. (The denial of Newtonian mechanics isn't, presumably, a relevant alternative, and, as Draper in effect points out, we don't get a relevant alternative hypothesis by conjoining the denial of Newtonian mechanics with the proposition that I was in the woods yesterday.) Of course we don't so far know what *relevance* is (we have only given it a name); and it is a monumentally nontrivial matter to say what it consists in.

But perhaps we need not carry this discussion further for present purposes. Let's pretend that we know (at least roughly and to a zeroeth approximation) what relevance is. And say that a proposition P is *relevantly challenged* when it faces an epistemic challenge in which Q is a *relevant* datum and R a *relevant* alternative hypothesis. Now many scientific hypotheses (at least on the most usual stories) get all or nearly all of their epistemic probability from the fact that they account for the relevant data;[4] and a proposition of that sort is heavily challenged indeed by a relevant evidential challenge. If I discover that a belief of *this* sort is subject to an evidential challenge, then I do indeed have substantial evidence against it and a good prima facie reason to give it up.

So what we have so far is that a proposition's being subject to a relevant evidential challenge is serious evidence against it if it is a scientific hypothesis and is such that the evidence for it is just the fact that it properly explains the data in question and perhaps does so better than any relevant alternative hypothesis. But (to return to Draper's evidential challenge) it is an enormous and in my opinion wholly false assumption to think that belief in God, or more broadly, the larger set of Christian (or Jewish or Muslim) beliefs of which belief in God is a part, is, at any rate for most believers, relevantly like a scientific hypothesis. The evidence for these beliefs is not the fact (if it is a fact) that they properly explain some body of data. For most believers, theistic belief is part of a larger whole, a Christian or Muslim or Jewish whole, and is not accepted as anything like a scientific hypothesis. That is, it is not accepted as an *explanation* of anything;[5] and its evidence does not consist in the fact that it nicely explains some body of data.

But does this fact, crucially important as it is, deliver theism from Draper's evidential challenge? Is it *only* scientific hypotheses for which (relevant) evidential challenges are serious? No. Suppose you are under the impression that your friend Paul has been vacationing on Cape Cod for the last couple of weeks, but you get postcards from him, all of which were mailed from Grand Teton National Park; he doesn't say in the postcards where he is, but he does note the remarkably dry air, as well as the great differences between day and nighttime temperatures. Then I think your belief that he is vacationing at Cape Cod is seriously challenged (a relevant alternative hypothesis being that he is vacationing in the Tetons). This is true even though the warrant for your belief that he was vacationing on the Cape didn't arise as a result of its properly explaining data of one kind or another. (You have a rather indistinct memory of his telling you so.) So it isn't just scientific hypotheses that can be called into question by virtue of facing a relevant evidential challenge. (What does seem more likely is that a relevant evidential challenge is serious only if the challenged belief doesn't have much warrant that comes from sources other than its explaining some body of data.)

Well, then, what about theism? Suppose Draper is right: suppose the probability of O on theism is much less than that of O on HI; would that constitute a relevant evidential challenge? That depends on whether O is a relevant datum and HI a relevant alternative hypothesis for theism.[6] Since we don't have much of an idea of what relevance is, that question may be a little difficult. But let's agree that O is indeed relevant. What about HI? Here I have my doubts. HI is equivalent to the denial of theism conjoined with the proposition that the nature and condition of sentient beings isn't due to the benevolent or malevolent action of any other nonhuman persons either. One doesn't ordinarily think of the denial of a hypothesis as a relevant alternative hypothesis; what about the denial of the hypothesis conjoined with something else? But rather than pursue that question, suppose we concede for purposes of argument that HI, like O, is relevant to theism. If so, then HI and O meet the initial conditions for presenting theism with a relevant evidential challenge; what remains to be seen is (1) whether in fact O *is* much more probable with respect to HI than with respect to theism, (2) whether, if it is, there are other data much more probable with respect to theism than with respect to HI, and (3) whether theism has much by way of warrant that doesn't arise from its nicely explaining a body of data. Let's begin with the first of these questions.

2.2 IS C TRUE?

Draper restates C as C*: "the antecedent probability of O is much greater on the assumption that HI is true than on the assumption that theism is true" and argues for it as follows. First, he introduces the notion of *biological usefulness:* "a part of some goal-directed organic system S is 'biologically useful' just in case (i) it causally contributes to one of S's biological goals (or to one of the biological goals of some other goal-directed organic system of which it is a part), and (ii) its doing so is not biologically accidental."[7] Second, O (which, you recall, reports roughly what you know about the pattern of pain and pleasure among sentient creatures on earth) can be partitioned into three propositions, O1, O2, and O3: O1 states what O says about the pattern, with respect to *moral agents,* of pain and pleasure that we know to be biologically useful; O2 states what O says about the distribution, with respect to sentient beings that are *not* moral agents, of pain and pleasure we know to be biologically useful; and O3 states what O says about the pattern with respect to sentient beings generally (moral agents or not) of pain and pleasure we *don't* know to be biologically useful. O is logically equivalent to the conjunction of O1 with O2 and O3; but then (where *h* is any proposition) by the probability calculus,[8]

P(O1 & O2 & O3/h) = P(O1/h) × P(O2/h & O1) × P(O3/h & O1 & O2).

Hence C* is true if and only if

(2) P(O1/HI) × P(O2/HI & O1) × P(O3/HI & O1 & O2)

is much greater than

(3) P(O1/theism) × P(O2/theism & O1) × P(O3/theism & O1 & O2).

And Draper argues that (2) *is* much greater than (3); he argues that the first and third multiplicands of (2) are much greater than the corresponding multiplicands of (3), and that the second multiplicand of (3) is greater (although not necessarily much greater) than the second multiplicand of (3).

Before examining his argument, we must first briefly note a couple of preliminaries. First, remember that a proposition has epistemic probability *for a person S;* we aren't asking whether, say, P(O1/HI) is much greater than P(O1/theism) *simpliciter,* but whether it is much greater *with respect to a given epistemic situation.* (Since Draper claims that his argument presents an evidential problem for *theists,* this would presumably be the epistemic situation of a typical theist, or of most or many theists, or something of the sort.) Different people have different epistemic situations; P(O1/HI) is different with respect to different situations; hence P(O1/HI) may be quite different for you than for me. In order to simplify matters, I shall conduct the discussion relative to my own epistemic situation, although of course I am hoping it will be easy enough to apply the results to *your* epistemic situation.

Second, when I ask what P(O1/theism) is, I am not, of course, to say that it is unity, on the grounds that I *know* O1 to be true.[9] No doubt I *do* know O1 to be true, but I am to estimate this probability, as Draper says, "independent of the observations and testimony O reports," and hence with respect to an epistemic situation different from my own. *Which* epistemic situation? Perhaps we can make an initial stab as follows: suppose we assume, for purposes of carrying on the argument, that we can speak of one epistemic situation's being similar to another, and indeed can compare degrees of likeness here, so that we can say of three epistemic situations *A, B,* and *C* that *A* is more similar to *B* than *C* is. Then perhaps we could add that the sort of epistemic situation with respect to which I am to evaluate the epistemic probability of O is one that is, among epistemic situations that do not include the belief that O1, maximally similar to mine. This raises further problems: *are* there epistemic situations distinct from but maximally similar to mine? And which respects of similarity are to be weighted most heavily? Different weightings will result in very different values for (O1/HI). But these are problems with the whole notion of epistemic probability; we don't have to solve all the problems connected with that vexed notion before considering Draper's argument.

Third, how shall I estimate P(O1/HI), relative to my epistemic situation? I am a theist; therefore I don't believe HI, and in fact believe that it is false. So of course I can't just add it to my epistemic situation and try to estimate P(O1/HI) with respect to the result: that result would be a disgusting hodgepodge. Follow-

252 / ALVIN PLANTINGA

ing the previous suggestion, perhaps we must ask what P(O1/HI) would be relative to an epistemic situation that was maximally similar to mine among epistemic situations including HI.

Returning to Draper's argument: as we saw, he proposes to argue that (2) is much more probable than (3) by arguing that the first and third multiplicands of (2) are much greater than their counterparts in (3) and that the second multiplicand of (2) is greater than that of (3). I shall consider only what he has to say about the first and third multiplicands.

2.3 IS P(O1/HI) >! P(O1/THEISM)?

O1, you recall, is a proposition reporting what you (or I) know by way of observation and testimony about the pattern, with respect to moral agents, of pain and pleasure that we know to be biologically useful. So the question is whether this pattern is very much more probable, for me, on HI than on theism. Draper thinks it *is* much more probable. Why so? Because (a) we know that human beings are goal-directed organic systems; (b) this leads us to expect that the distribution of pain and pleasure among human beings would systematically contribute to the achievement of the organic goals of human beings; and (c) that is just what O1 shows. So the probability of O1 on HI is relatively high. But on theism things are quite different. That is because pain and pleasure have an *evaluative* or axiological dimension: pain is bad and pleasure is good. Consequently, "we would have much less reason on theism than on HI to be surprised if it turned out that human pain and pleasure differed from other parts of organic systems by not systematically contributing to the biological goals of those systems. Hence, since O1 reports that the pain and pleasure experienced by humans (who are moral agents) do contribute in this way, P(O1/HI) is much greater than P(O1/theism)."

But is this really so? Suppose we look a bit further. I agree that we shouldn't be particularly surprised, given theism, if pain and pleasure did not systematically contribute to those biological goals (and let's suppose that the main relevant biological goals, as Draper seems to think, are survival and reproduction). But this is in large part because one doesn't really know what to expect God to do. We would of course expect that he would choose the best alternative, if indeed there is a best, but we don't know nearly enough to know what that best alternative might be. So we wouldn't be particularly surprised if it turned out that pain and pleasure did not systematically contribute to the goals of survival and reproduction.

But something similar seems to me to be true on HI. Consider an epistemic situation that contains the belief that HI and is otherwise as much like mine as possible: with respect to such an epistemic situation it would not, I think, be at all overwhelmingly probable that pleasure and pain contribute systematically to the organic goals of survival and reproduction on the parts of moral agents.

There are several reasons. For one thing, I am strongly inclined to believe that there are moral agents—angels and devils—who are sentient beings but for whom pleasure and pain don't play much of a biological role at all. But of course the moral agents we know best are human beings, so suppose we stick to them. As

Draper says, we do indeed know of many human phenomena that contribute to the organic goals of survival and reproduction; but we also know of much that does not so contribute, or prima facie does not so contribute, or at any rate is such that we do not know that it *does* so contribute. Thus, for example, *morality* plays an enormously important role in human life; much of what it enjoins and much of our response to what it enjoins doesn't at all obviously contribute to the biological goals of survival and reproduction. Many human beings display a powerful sense of justice and fierce determination to follow it where it leads; they are willing to devote enormous time and energy and sometimes their very lives to trying to right wrongs, defend the weak, uproot a wicked and unjust social system. On the face of it, most of this seems to have very little to do with contributing to such biological goals as survival and reproduction.

Many human beings are also deeply altruistic: there are Mother Teresa and the little sisters of the poor; there are the Jesuit missionaries of the sixteenth century and the Methodist missionaries of the nineteenth; there are enormous numbers of people who have risked or given their lives to save others from accident, disease, and attack. Most of us, in fact, display altruistic impulses; most of us at one time or another are prepared to help others who need help, even at considerable cost to ourselves. These are things people do; but they too seem to have little connection with survival and reproduction.

There is also religion. Being religious is a nearly universal human characteristic; it commands great loyalty and devotion; over the world and at all times past and present most people have been prepared to devote time, energy, and material resources to the service of religious goals. Many have chosen lives of celibacy in the service of what they take to be true religion; and some have been prepared to sacrifice their very lives to what they see as its proper practice. Once more, these religious activities don't seem to contribute to such biological goals as reproduction and survival.

There are many other characteristically human activities and phenomena that apparently do not (or do not apparently) contribute to those biological goals. Literature, poetry, music, art, mathematics, logic, philosophy, nuclear physics, evolutionary biology, play, humor, exploration, and adventure—these are phenomena of enormous significance in human life. Indeed they are among the most important and significant of all the things we human beings do. But again, they don't seem in any direct way to contribute to survival and reproduction.

So many of the most important human phenomena do not appear to contribute, in any systematic way, to these biological goals. Of course some urge a biological explanation of these phenomena: contrary to initial appearances, they say, they really *do* contribute to survival and reproduction; and therein lies their real significance. But most of these "explanations" range from the dubious to the preposterous.[10] In any event, that is how they seem to *me,* and it is my epistemic situation that is at issue here.

There are, then, many human phenomena, and indeed phenomena widely thought to be of the greatest significance, that do not, or prima facie do not, or at any rate are not known to contribute systematically to those biological goals.

Therefore, with respect to my epistemic situation and HI, it would not be particularly surprising, so it seems to me, if the distribution of human pleasure and pain did not contribute in this way to the biological goals of survival and reproduction.[11] Relative to my epistemic situation, P(O1/HI) does not seem much greater, if greater at all, than P(O1/theism).

2.4 IS P(O3/HI & O1 & O2) >! P(O3/THEISM & O1 & O2)?

Well, why should we think so? Draper's argument is twofold. In the first place, on theism and O1 and O2, he says, it is probable that sentient creatures in general would be happy;[12] on HI & O1 & O2 this is not so; and in fact they are not in general happy. Secondly,

> we have, antecedently, much more reason on HI & O1 & O2 than on theism to believe that the fundamental role of pain and pleasure in our world is a biological one and that the presence of biologically gratuitous pain and pleasure is epiphenomenal, a biological accident resulting from nature's or an indifferent creator's failure to "fine tune" organic systems;

and, he adds, "this is undeniably supported (though not entailed) by what O3 reports."

Turn to the second reason first. The claim is that with respect to the theist's epistemic situation, it is very likely on HI & O1 & O2 that the fundamental role of pleasure and pain in our world is a biological one; on theism & O1 & O2 this is not particularly likely. Now it isn't entirely easy to evaluate this suggestion. HI is in the neighborhood of a disjunction of naturalism with indifferent creationism, the proposition that we have been created by one or more morally indifferent beings. I believe that on *naturalism* & O1 & O2 it is likely that the fundamental role of pain and pleasure in our world is biological, but I can't see that the same goes for *indifferent creationism*. And how are these—naturalism and indifferent creationism—to be weighted? How would they be weighted in an epistemic situation that contained the belief that HI but was otherwise as much as possible like mine? Which would be more probable, and how much more probable? I really haven't the faintest idea how to answer those questions.

But let's suppose for purposes of argument that Draper is right: on HI and O1 and O2 but not on theism & O1 & O2 there is excellent reason to believe that the fundamental role of pleasure and pain, in our world, is biological. Now Draper thinks "this is undeniably supported (though not entailed) by what O3 reports." But *is* it really supported? We must note the enormous diversity and variety of human pleasure and pain; much of it doesn't seem to have any direct connection at all with such biological goals as survival and reproduction. Think again of the pleasure and pain, the suffering and joy that go with morality and religion, not to mention friendship, art, science, music, literature, play, humor, and the like. How much of the pleasure and pain that I experience in a day is biologically useful or significant? Maybe I dribble hot water on my hand while trying to make tea: that pain is biologically useful, as is the pleasure of a good meal, sexual pleasure, the satisfied glow following vigorous exercise, and perhaps (but also perhaps not) the pain and sadness upon hearing of a friend's serious and possibly fatal disease. But most of the pleasure and pain of my day isn't like that.

Take the pleasure first: there is enjoying the company of family and friends, amiable banter with genial colleagues, a good laugh with a friend, satisfaction in finishing a paper, delight in getting the first copies of a pair of books I've been working on for years, delight in some new accomplishment on the part of one of my children (or students or friends), delight in a glorious spring day, satisfaction in noting that (after about eight years) the lilacs have finally decided to bloom, a gleam of malicious pleasure in seeing just how bad some of the arguments against mind-body dualism really are, pleasure in hearing from someone on e-mail, in anticipating an upcoming rock-climbing trip (or remembering one of twenty years ago), exalting in a bit of Mozart, satisfaction at working out a philosophical problem, or in coming to new (for me, anyway) insight, or in learning something interesting and important, delight in the sight of someone or something beautiful, feeling, during morning devotions, just a glimmer (seldom more) of the Psalmist's joy and delight in the Lord, feeling a wholly inadequate bit of gratitude for God's presence in my life and for the splendid offer of grace to me and those I love and others, sometimes feeling just a bit of that ultimate safety, that knowledge that nothing can go really wrong, finally and irretrievably wrong, for God's children in God's world.

On the other side, there is fear that I'll once more make an ass of myself in an upcoming sticky situation, embarrassment at some foolish or ill-conceived thing I've said, pique or disappointment or sorrow over something I've done wrong, something I've failed at, something where I should have known better (or worse (contrary to Socrates), where I knew better but did it anyway), a bit of sorrow for sins that seem to stick to me like glue decade after decade, sardonic disappointment when I come to see the devious and subtle way in which I have once more deceived myself (and others) trying to make myself look good, sorrow and disappointment that I don't make more progress on the tough road of sanctification, worry that I'll never get to finish the books and projects I have in mind, a pang of real fear when I think of old age and what it brings, anger and sorrow over my father's more than half a century of suffering from manic depressive psychosis (why the hell should he have to suffer like that for so long? what can that possibly be good for?), pain when I think of my children's sorrow and sadness because of the handicaps of *their* children, anger upon hearing of a fresh atrocity in former Yugoslavia, or Los Angeles, disgust that I can't seem to control my appetite, incipient fury upon reading of yet another case of horrifying child abuse (I'd like to get a baseball bat and show that bastard what it feels like to be abused!), mixed sorrow and anger when I hear of another person whose important work in God's kingdom has been destroyed or compromised by some sexual or other wrongdoing, a pang of envy when one of my friends does something terrific, something I wish I'd done, followed by a prick of conscience and a pang of guilt for being envious instead of delighted, frustration that I can't get something properly figured out, distress at feeling stupid when I can't understand something that I'm pretty sure makes good sense, and so on.

None of this seems at all directly connected with the satisfaction of those biological goals. In fact the vast bulk of pleasure and pain in my life seems to have little connection with those goals; and I suspect the same goes for others. Again, some people will argue that in fact the pleasure and pain that go with these things *is* biologically useful; but again, most of these arguments seem at best doubtful and at worst plainly foolish. Perhaps we can say, with Draper, that it isn't known that these *don't* have a biological explanation; but of course it is also not known that they *do*. Furthermore, it is my epistemic situation that is at issue; I don't in fact believe that these pleasures and pains do have a biological explanation, and think it rather unlikely that they do. So (contrary to Draper) I do not think that what O3 reports at all strongly supports (with respect to my epistemic situation) the claim that the fundamental role of pleasure and pain (at least in the lives of human beings) is biological. *This* reason for thinking P(O3/(HI & O1 & O2)) much greater than P(O3/(theism & O1 & O2)), therefore, seems to me mistaken.

Suppose we turn now to Draper's *other* reason for thinking P(O3/(HI & O1 & O2)) much greater than P(O3/(theism & O1 & O2)): this is the claim that sentient creatures are not in general happy, while on theism & O1 & O2, but not on HI & O1 & O2, we would expect them to be so. Now first, it isn't easy to be at all sure whether or not sentient creatures are in general happy: how would we know a thing like that? We don't know nearly enough about the inner lives of non-human creatures. (We do have such expressions as "Happy as a clam," and "Snug as a bug in a rug," but what do we really know here? How happy is your average housefly?) We do better with other human beings; but even here our knowledge of the interior lives of others is at best fragmentary and crude. What seems fairly clear is that most of us display a complex mixture of joy and sorrow; we are happy part of the time and unhappy part of the time; for many of us, sorrow predominates, but for others joy or contentment is uppermost; and most of us, I suppose, think our lives on balance happy enough so that we have little interest in terminating them. So I can't rely at all heavily on the suggestion that sentient beings are mostly unhappy.

But what is really interesting here is the claim that on theism & O1 & O2 (with respect to the theist's epistemic situation) it is probable that most sentient creatures would be happy. Is this really true? Perhaps this is so with respect to the epistemic situation of someone who is an *austere* theist: someone who is a theist, that is, but does not accept any of the additional beliefs that characterize Christians, Jews, Muslims, and most other theists. But of course the vast majority of theists are not austere theists. And many, perhaps most, theists take it as part of their background information that our world is a *fallen* world. Human beings, and perhaps others among God's rational and moral creatures, have *sinned;* as a result our world is fallen, broken, in need of restoration; and human beings and perhaps other sentient creatures are in need of repentance, reconciliation, salvation. Given this, however, we shouldn't really expect that human beings and other sentient creatures would be happy in their earthly lives. Part of my epistemic situation is the belief that the world is indeed fallen. Hence it isn't true, so far as I can see, that relative to my epistemic situation, the probability of most sentient creatures' being happy is high with respect to theism & O1 & O2; furthermore it is doubtful that it is higher on theism & O1 & O2 than on HI & O1 & O2.

But am I not somehow begging the question by bringing in these other religious beliefs, such as that God's creatures have fallen into sin? Well, why so? Can't I use all that I believe in this context? The question is how these probabilities stand with respect to my epistemic situation; the belief that the world is fallen is certainly part of that epistemic situation. But aren't these beliefs connected with theism in such a way that I wouldn't hold them if I were not a theist? Perhaps; but exactly how is that relevant? Before turning to this very important congeries of questions, however, I want to consider a defeater for the prima facie reason Draper thinks he's offered for rejecting theistic belief.

3. Other Evidence

It is far from obvious, so I've argued, that P(O/theism) is much higher, with respect to the theist's epistemic situation, than P(O/HI). As a matter of fact, there is little difference, particularly in view of the rest of what most theists believe. (I realize there is a promissory note to discharge here.) But I believe there is also other evidence here, other evidence of the very sort Draper calls attention to. This evidence supports theism as opposed to HI (and indeed outweighs the evidence, if any, provided by Draper's evidential challenge). The evidence in question consists of propositions I believe that are far more probable on theism than on HI (if we like, we could think of them as evidential challenges to HI). I mention just a couple of these, because I am out of space; there is of course vastly more to be said.

First, what precisely is it that O reports? Well, it reports the distribution of pain and pleasure (with respect to all sentient beings) that I have myself observed, together with what I know or believe by testimony—what other people tell me, what I read in the newspapers or in textbooks in various areas of biology, etc. But of course what I learn in this way isn't nearly all that I believe about the pattern of pain and pleasure. For I also believe in eternal life. The precise contours of this are certainly obscure, but it includes an eternity of bliss for enormous numbers of God's creatures. If it also includes separation from God and accompanying sorrow and emptiness for others, that will be so only if it is in accord both with divine justice and with divine love. Call the whole pain-and-pleasure pattern I accept "O+": O+ includes or entails O and a great deal more.[13] Still further, O+ is vastly more probable, epistemically speaking, on theism than on HI. That is, the whole pattern of pleasure and pain that I think the world displays is much more probable on theism than on HI. Furthermore, O+ isn't just any old proposition; it is one that *entails* (and is not entailed by) O. This is important; what it means is that any evidence offered against theism by the fact (as for purposes of argument we are temporarily conceding) that O is more probable on HI than on theism is outweighed by the fact that O+ is more probable on theism than on HI.

There is much else I believe that is vastly more probable on theism than on HI. I believe that human beings have fallen into sin but can achieve salvation and eternal life through Jesus Christ, who suffered and died as a propitiation for our sins. These things are not logically incompatible with HI, but they certainly seem vastly less probable with respect to it than with respect to theism.[14]

"But," comes the rejoinder, "isn't there something question-begging or dialectically deficient in appealing in this context to such beliefs as that ours is a fallen world, or O+, or to such specifically Christian beliefs as those of Incarnation and Atonement? This is circular; or if it isn't circular, then at least it has the form of a closed curve in space (as Quine says in another connection). For surely you wouldn't believe these things if you didn't believe theism." Perhaps that is so; but how is it relevant? Well, perhaps as follows. The whole point of Draper's argument is to try to show that the theist who doesn't have other evidence—evidence that counterbalances or outweighs the evidence against theism provided by the fact (as we are assuming) that O is more likely on HI than on theism—holds irrational views or in some related way suffers from some epistemic deficiency. He therefore offers what he takes to be some evidence against theism. Now suppose I replied by deducing something from theism—something such that my only evidence for it is theism or my evidence for theism—and then proposed *that* as counterevidence. That would be dialectically reprehensible, because this "evidence" would be relevant and usable only if it did not suffer from the same deficiency that Draper proposes to pin on my theistic belief. But if its only warrant just *is* my theism, or my warrant for my theism, then if my theism suffers from that deficiency, so does this "evidence." To proceed in this way would be to ignore Draper's claim, or assume that it is false.

Of course I *didn't* deduce these things from theism; the latter doesn't entail these more specifically Christian beliefs. Still, let's concede, for the moment, that the Christian beliefs are rational, for me, only if theism is.

4. Nonpropositional Evidence

What we have been thinking about so far, of course, is *propositional* evidence for and against theism, evidence from other things the theist believes. And so far as propositional evidence goes, it seems to me that theism, with respect to my epistemic situation, does at least as well as HI—at any rate if the theist can properly appeal to such other things he believes as O+, the fall into sin of some of God's rational creatures, the Atonement, and the like. Some of these things entail theism; others don't, but are such that they would be epistemically probable for a person only if theism were probable for that person. But can the theist properly appeal to these beliefs in responding to Draper's challenge? Well, why not? Take the ones that entail theism: Draper points out that they won't be any more epistemically probable, for a theist, than theism itself; so a challenge to theism is also a challenge to them. This is correct; but of course it is also true that theism won't be any *less* epistemically probable, for the theist, than they are; so any epistemic probability *they* have will be transferred to theism itself. The same is true for those Christian doctrines I've cited that do not entail theism: they can contribute to the epistemic probability of theism, as we have seen, by way of being such that they are much more probable, on theism, than on HI or other propositions incompatible with theism. Now all of this pertains to *propositional* evidence for and against theism; but the most important question here, I think, concerns the *nonpropositional* evidence, if any, for and against both theism and those other Christian beliefs. Is there nonpropositional evidence for or against theism? And consider those other Christian beliefs: is there nonpropositional evidence for and against them? To translate this question into Draper's framework: are there nonpropositional features of my epistemic situation that confer epistemic probability, for me, on theism and other Christian beliefs, or on their denials?

I have run out of space and shall have to be ridiculously brief and dogmatic.[15] I find myself with belief in God; I also hold such beliefs as that human beings have fallen into sin, that God was in Christ, reconciling the world to himself, and that we can receive the benefit of that reconciliation by faith. So far as I can see, I don't believe these propositions on the evidential basis of other propositions I believe, although, of course, they form part of a connected and coherent network of beliefs. Now, are these beliefs epistemically rational relative to my epistemic situation? According to Draper's conception of epistemic probability, that depends on whether a fully rational person in my epistemic situation would accept them. Well, would she?

Here I think there are at least two questions, an internal question and an external question. The first question is whether I am rational in holding my beliefs in the sense in which whether for all I can tell from the inside, so to speak, my beliefs meet the appropriate internal standards—whether I am within my intellectual rights in believing as I do, whether I have properly taken account of other things I know, whether I have paid proper attention to objections and to what others say—whether, in a word (or two), I have done my epistemic best, or at least as well as I can be expected to do. I read the Bible; I find myself enthusiastically assenting to the good news of the Gospel; am I doing my epistemic best? This is a complicated question; my "epistemic best" depends among other things on the rest of what I believe. But, if I have carefully considered the objections to what I believe, and (finding them wanting) am still convinced, what more can I do? (I believe that I am a substance that endures, lasts through time; if I carefully consider Parfittian objections but am still convinced, what more can I do?) I think about some of the great evils the world regularly displays: famine, flood, pestilence, starvation, warfare, the horrifying ways in which human beings sometimes treat each other; I may be moved to ask myself whether God really does love us. But then I think of the Incarnation and Atonement (I don't know *why* God permits all this evil, but He is himself willing to suffer unthinkable agony to give us a way out); and the doubts may disappear. Am I not doing my epistemic best here? What more am I supposed to do?

The other question is external. It is really the question of warrant: the question whether my beliefs have that quality or quantity enough of which is sufficient, along with truth, to guarantee knowledge. What is that quality? As I see the matter, one of my beliefs has warrant just if it is produced by cognitive faculties functioning properly in an appropriate cognitive environment according to a design plan successfully aimed at truth.[16] (There are of course other views as to what warrant is, but what follows will hold for most of them.) Now, does my belief, e.g., that Jesus Christ is the divine son of God who became incarnate, suffered and died, and rose again to enable us to have life—does this belief have warrant? Well, it does, if there is such a thing as the internal testimony of the Holy Spirit, which enables Christians to grasp, understand, and believe what the Lord proposes to teach us in the Scriptures—and if the proposition in question is one of the ones the Holy Spirit thus enables us to know.[17] And what about my belief that there is such a person as God? Does this have warrant, i.e., warrant it gets independently of being accepted on the evidential basis of other propositions I believe? Again, it does, if there is such a thing as the *Sensus Divinitatis* of which Calvin speaks, and if this belief of mine is a result of the working of that faculty (and not, as Freud suggests, a result of wishful thinking or some other source of neurotic belief).

But *is* there such a thing as the Internal Testimony of the Holy Spirit, and *is* there such a thing as the *Sensus Divinitatis*? And do they teach us what Christians take them to teach? These are the important questions; but they take us well beyond epistemology into metaphysics, or religion, or theology, or all three. To determine whether there is nonpropositional warrant for Christian and theistic belief, we have to determine whether Christian and theistic beliefs are true; the question whether there is nonpropositional evidence for these propositions is not theologically or religiously neutral.

By way of conclusion: I think we can see that the issues to which Draper directs our attention are fundamentally issues of coherence; they have to do with relationships among the propositions theists typically believe. Draper's claim, from this perspective, is that the typical theist's set of beliefs is in a certain way incoherent: there are probabilistic relations among them of such a sort as to make her beliefs unstable. Draper claims this gives her a reason for rejecting her belief in God. I've argued that Draper's claims here are probably mistaken: if we take into account all that a typical theist believes, including (in the case of Christian theists) beliefs about sin, Incarnation, Atonement, eternal life, and the like, the alleged incoherence seems to disappear.

Of course a theist who concurred with Draper, agreeing that the alleged incoherence is real, has options. Draper says she has a reason to reject belief in God; but she could also extirpate the incoherence not by rejecting theism but by rejecting some of the other beliefs involved—O itself, for example. Here it may be protested that we *know* O, so that it is not a good candidate for rejection. This brings us to a wholly different set of topics and questions, questions and topics that take us beyond coherence into the neighborhood of warrant. I believe these are the more important questions here. The more important questions have to do not with whether my belief in God is coherent with my other beliefs but with whether my belief in God has warrant, warrant of its own, so to speak, warrant that it doesn't get by being appropriately related to the other propositions I believe. This question, however, takes us well beyond our present set of questions; it takes us from epistemology into metaphysics.

NOTES

1. Paul Draper, "Pain and Pleasure: An Evidential Problem for Theists," chapter 2 in this volume.

2. For a fuller account of a closely related notion, that of epistemic conditional probability, see chaps. 8 and 9 of my *Warrant and Proper Function* (New York: Oxford University Press, 1993).

3. Paul Draper, "Probabilistic Arguments From Evil," *Religious Studies* (1993).

4. This really isn't exactly right. Special Relativity, for example, gets its warrant for me not from the fact that it properly accounts for those data but from the fact that I have been told and believe that it does; but trying to put the matter more accurately would take us too far afield. See my *Warrant and Proper Function,* chap. 4.

5. See my "Is Theism Really a Miracle?" *Faith and Philosophy* 3 (1986).

6. In stating the matter this way I am not, of course, suggesting that theism is a hypothesis for most theists; as I said, it certainly isn't.

7. The interconnected notions of goal-directness, function, proper function, dysfunction, and the like are extremely hard to explain in naturalistic terms (see my *Warrant and Proper Function,* chap. 11). I believe Draper's account of biological usefulness is inadequate (because his account of goal direction is); this inadequacy, however, does not affect his argument.

8. For the moment let's go along with the dubious assumption that epistemic probability conforms to the probability calculus.

9. Here we encounter the so-called "problem of old evidence"; see, for example, Daniel Garber, "Old Evidence and Logical Omniscience in Bayesian Confirmation Theory," in *Testing Scientific Theories,* ed. John Earman (Minneapolis: University of Minnesota Press, 1983).

10. For a good example of something falling into the latter category, see Herbert Simon, "A Mechanism for Social Selection and Successful Altruism," *Science* 250 (1990): 1665ff. Simon argues that the explanation of the behavior of those who, like Mother Teresa, devote their lives to helping others, is "docility" and "limited rationality." See my "Evolution, Neutrality, and Antecedent Probability: A Reply to Van Till and McMullin," *Christian Scholar's Review* 21 (1991): 83.

11. And of course as a matter of fact only some pain and pleasure thus contributes (or is thus known to contribute); there is an enormous amount of pain and pleasure that is intimately connected with morality, art, literature, religion, and the like and doesn't seem to be connected in any direct way with survival and reproduction.

12. Note that Draper isn't speaking just of pain and pleasure narrowly conceived; he speaks also and more broadly of happiness and sorrow.

13. And of course we can state O+ in such a way that it doesn't entail theism.

14. There are many other things I believe that (as it seems to me) are much more likely on theism than on HI. For example, I am inclined to think that there would be no such things as right and wrong, moral obligation, or permission if HI were true. (I've heard the arguments against this thesis, but am wholly unconvinced.) But of course I also believe that there is such a thing as right and wrong and moral obligation and permission. So this too is something I believe that (as I think) is much more probable with respect to theism than with respect to HI.

15. My hope is to look into these matters at more satisfying length in *Warranted Christian Belief,* the third volume of my Gifford Lectures.

16. For a development and explanation of this enigmatic pronouncement, see my *Warrant and Proper Function,* chaps. 1 and 2.

17. This is a broadly Protestant way of thinking of the matter; of course Roman Catholics, Orthodox, and other Christian groups have slightly different accounts of the warrant enjoyed by Christian belief.

14.

WILLIAM L. ROWE

The Evidential Argument from
Evil: A Second Look

I

It is as misleading to speak of *the* evidential argument from evil as it is to speak of *the* cosmological argument. Just as there are distinct arguments that qualify as cosmological arguments, there are distinct arguments that qualify as evidential arguments from evil.[1] My purpose here is to look again at an evidential argument from evil that I first presented in 1979.[2] Since that time I have made several changes in that argument in an effort to make it clearer and to patch up weaknesses in earlier statements of it. Starting with the latest published account of the argument, I will discuss some important criticisms of it and will continue my efforts to clarify, simplify, and strengthen the argument.

The latest formulation I have given of the evidential problem of evil goes something like this.[3] (E1 is the case of a fawn trapped in a forest fire and undergoing several days of terrible agony before dying. E2 is the case of the rape, beating, and murder by strangulation of a five-year-old girl.)[4]

P: No good we know of justifies an omnipotent, omniscient, perfectly good being in permitting E1 and E2;
  therefore,
Q: no good at all justifies an omnipotent, omniscient, perfectly good being in permitting E1 and E2;
  therefore,
not-G: there is no omnipotent, omniscient, perfectly good being.

The first inference, from P to Q, is, of course, an inductive inference. My claim was that P makes Q probable. The second inference, from Q to not-G, is deductive.

Against this argument from evil a variety of criticisms are possible. One might claim (1) that none of us is in a position to be justified in believing P. One might claim (2) that the inference from P to Q is not a good inductive inference, that P does not make Q more probable than not. So, one cannot be justified in believing Q on the basis of P. One might claim (3) that even though the inference from P to Q is a good inductive inference, we have reasons (defeaters) on the basis of which it is rational to refrain from accepting Q on the basis of P. Finally, one might claim (4) that not-G does not deductively follow from Q because two possibilities are not excluded. First, (4a) it could be that the prevention of some worse evils is what justifies God in permitting E1 and E2.[5] Second, (4b) it could be that in a world with free, morally responsible creatures God needs to permit the occurrence of unjustified evil (gratuitous evil).[6]

Criticisms that have been advanced against this version of the evidential argument from evil have focused mainly on (1) and (2). Although several important papers have developed such criticisms, special mention should be made of William Alston's essay "The Inductive Problem of Evil and the Human Cognitive Condition" (chapter 6 in this volume) and several papers by Stephen Wykstra.[7] Obviously, the whole issue of whether what we know about evil in our world makes it likely that the theistic God does not exist is quite complex and cannot be satisfactorily addressed in any single essay. But I will undertake here to answer some serious objections concerning the inference from P to Q (raised by Alston, Wykstra, and others) and some serious objections concerning P itself (mostly raised by Alston). After discussing two preliminary matters, I will take up the objections to the inference from P to Q, later turning to some issues concerning P itself.

II

Initially, we need to do two things. First, we need to specify just what P and Q assert. Although I have endeavored to do this in earlier writings on this topic, I don't think I have been as clear as is necessary. So I want to begin with this task, departing somewhat from earlier formulations. Second, we need to settle on our background information, connecting it to the question of God's existence in a way that will make our discussion relevant to the dispute between theists and nontheists over the problem of evil.

As we've already noted, at least initially our discussion revolves around two particular evils, E1 (Bambi) and E2 (Sue). What is it that P affirms about E1 and E2? P says *no good we know of* justifies an omnipotent, omniscient, perfectly good being in permitting E1 and E2. What then does P entail? P entails that among the good states of affairs that we know of (however dimly or through a glass darkly) none is such that it justifies an omnipotent, omniscient, perfectly good being in permitting E1 and E2. So long as we keep in mind the features of the being in question, we can abbreviate our formulation of P as follows:

P: No good we know of justifies God in permitting E1 and E2.

Since we are talking about a good that justifies God in permitting E1 *and* E2, we should allow, if not expect, that the good in question would be a *conjunctive* good. Perhaps there is a good we know of that justifies God in permitting E1. Perhaps there is some other good we know of that justifies God in permitting E2. If so, then we will allow that it is true that some good we know of (a conjunction of the goods in question) justifies God in permitting E1 and E2. It should be obvious that I am trying to pose a serious difficulty for the theist by picking a difficult case of natural evil, E1 (Bambi), and a difficult case of moral evil, E2 (Sue). Should no good we know of justify God in permitting either of these two evils, P is true.

What counts as a "good we know of"? I do not mean to limit us to goods that we know to have occurred. Nor do I mean to limit us to those goods and goods that we know will occur in the future. I mean to include goods that we have some grasp of, even though we have no knowledge at all that they have occurred or ever will occur. For example, consider the good of Sue's experiencing complete felicity in the everlasting presence of God. Theists consider this an enormous personal good. I have no doubt that it is. So, even though we don't have a very clear grasp of what this great good involves, and even though we don't know that such a good state of affairs will ever obtain, we do mean to include the good of Sue's experiencing complete felicity in the everlasting presence of God as among *the goods we know of.* Of course, if the good in question never does occur, then it is not a good that justifies God in permitting E1 or E2. So if some good state of affairs we know of does justify God in permitting E1 or E2, that good state of affairs must become actual at some point in the future, if it is not already actual.

Under what conditions would P be true? P says that there is no good we know of that justifies God in permitting E1 and E2. One condition that would render P true is the nonoccurrence of the known good (supposing there is just one) whose occurrence would justify God in permitting E1 or E2. Suppose that among all known goods only Sue's experiencing eternal felicity in the presence of God is such that its occurrence would justify God in permitting E2 (Sue's suffering on being brutally beaten, raped, and strangled). If this good never occurs, P is true. As I indicated earlier, a good state of affairs justifies God in permitting some actual evil only if that good state of affairs occurs. Second, we should note that the nonexistence of God is also a sufficient condition of the truth of P. For the realization of a known good justifies God in permitting E1 or E2 only if God exists. To see this, consider the *negation* of P. The negation of P asserts that God exists and that some good known to us justifies him in permitting E1 and E2. Since the negation of P is false if God does not exist, P will be true if God does not exist.[8]

Having spent some time clarifying P, we can be brief with Q.

Q: No good at all justifies an omnipotent, omniscient, perfectly good being in permitting E1 and E2.

So long as we keep in mind the features of the being in question, we can abbreviate our formulation as follows:

Q: No good justifies God in permitting E1 and E2.

As with P, we should note that if God does not exist, Q is true. For given that E1 and E2 exist, if God does not exist then it is not the case that there is an omnipotent, omniscient, perfectly good being who is justified in permitting E1 and E2 by virtue of realizing some good. Another way of seeing this point is to note that the *negation* of Q asserts that God exists and that there is a good that justifies God in permitting E1 and E2. Since the negation of Q is false if God does not exist, Q is true if God does not exist.

I turn now to the background information k on which we will rely in forming judgments about how likely P, Q, and G (God exists) are. What will k include? I take it as important here that k be restricted almost entirely to information that is shared by most theists and nontheists who have given some thought to the issues raised by the problem of evil.[9] To this end, we will want to include in k our common knowledge of the occurrence of various evils in our world, including E1 and E2, as well as our knowledge that the world contains a good deal of evil. k will also include our common understanding of the way the world works, the sorts of things we know to exist in the world, along with our knowledge of many of the goods that occur and many of the goods that do not occur. Of course, k will not include the information that God exists or the information that God does not exist.

If we conceive of k in the way just suggested, what assignment should be given to the probability that God exists, given k, Pr(G/k)? Many nontheists hold that the enormous amount of evil in our world, particularly instances of horrendous human or animal suffering such as E1 and E2, make the existence of the theistic God unlikely. Many theists and some nontheists, however, will disagree with this assessment. On the other hand, many theists will argue that the mere existence of a world (or the order in the world) makes the existence of God likely. But some theists and many nontheists will disagree with this assessment. In order not to beg any of these questions, I will assign a probability of 0.5 to Pr(G/k), and, of course, 0.5 to Pr(~G/k). We will say that k by itself makes neither God's existence nor his nonexistence more likely than not. This need not be understood as denying what some nontheists hold concerning the possible negative evidential impact of the existence and multitude of horrendous evils in the world. Nor need it be understood as denying what some theists hold about the possible positive evidential impact of the existence of a world exhibiting order, etc. What it does indicate is that these different aspects of k—if they do impact positively or negatively on the likelihood of God's existence—in some way balance out so that the totality of k leaves the probability of the existence of God at 0.5.[10]

Will k include the information that ordinary religious experiences and mystical religious experiences occur? Insofar as the inclusion of such information raises the probability of G on k above 0.5 we will have to exclude it. This may seem arbitrary and harmful to the theist's position. But it need not be construed in that way. If it should turn out that we have reason to believe that P is true and that P lowers the probability of God's existence, it is open to the theist to reply that the addition to k of our information concerning the occurrence of ordinary and mystical religious experiences restores the balance or even tips the scales in favor of theism. As I endeavored to make clear in "The Problem of Evil and Some Varieties of Atheism," I have *not* argued that no matter what other evidence a person has, the argument from evil will still make it unreasonable for that person (who understands the argument from evil and accepts the grounds for its premises) to believe in God. For one might have stronger evidence for the existence of God than is provided by the problem of evil for the nonexistence of God.[11]

k will not, of course, include either P or Q. Moreover, so that we do not beg an important question central to the criticism that P is not a good reason for Q, k will not include any explicit claim as to whether the goods we know are representative of all the goods there are.

III

We want to discover the answer to four questions:

1. Does P make Q more likely than it would otherwise be? That is, is $Pr(Q/P\&k) > Pr(Q/k)$?
2. Does P make Q more likely than not? That is, is $Pr(Q/P\&k) > 0.5$?[12]
3. Does P make G less likely than it would otherwise be? That is, is $Pr(G/P\&k) > Pr(G/k)$?
4. Does P make G less likely than not? That is, is $Pr(G/P\&k) > 0.5$?[13]

In this section we will give reasons for an affirmative answer to the first question and note a difficulty in one attempt to provide an affirmative answer to the second question.

To begin our investigation, let's consider what Bayes's Theorem tells us about $Pr(Q/P\&k)$, the probability of Q given P and k. According to Bayes's Theorem,

$$Pr(Q/P\&k) = Pr(Q/k) \times \frac{Pr(P/Q\&k)}{Pr(P/k)}.$$

By reflecting on this equation, can we make any progress toward answering either of our first two questions? I believe we can. First, all of us will certainly agree that $Pr(Q/P\&k) < 1$. Indeed, according to Alston and others, we have no reason at all to think that $Pr(Q/P\&k)$ isn't less than 0.5. Moreover, since Q entails P, $Pr(P/Q\&k) = 1$. Now, since $Pr(Q/P\&k) < 1$ and $Pr(P/Q\&k) = 1$, it follows that

$$Pr(Q/k) < Pr(P/k).^{14}$$

It is also clear that our background information k does not entail P, so $Pr(P/k)$ does not equal 1. And from the conjunction of $Pr(P/Q\&k) = 1$, $Pr(Q/k) < Pr(P/k)$, and $Pr(P/k) < 1$, it follows that

$$Pr(Q/P\&k) > Pr(Q/k).$$

So, we have reached a definitive answer to our first question. P does make Q more likely than it would otherwise be.

But what of our second question? Does P make Q more likely than not? In an earlier paper[15] I gave an affirmative answer to this question and endeavored to support that answer with an argument I've since come to believe is inadequate. I noted first that the inference from P to Q is like an inference from "All the A's we've observed are B's" to "All A's are B's." I then argued that if we have observed many A's and found all of them to be B's, we have a prima facie good reason to believe that the A's we haven't observed will likely be B's as well. Thus we have a prima facie good reason to believe that all A's are B's.

I now think this argument is, at best, a weak argument.[16] To shore it up we would need some reason to think it likely that the goods we know of (the A's we've observed) are representative of the goods there are (the A's there are). Noting the variety of goods we know of would be relevant to this task. Having a good argument to think that most goods are known to us would also be relevant.[17] But I now propose to abandon this argument altogether and give what I believe is a better argument for thinking that P makes Q more likely than not. Consideration of this new argument, however, must be postponed until we have discovered the answers to questions 3 and 4, the questions that are of ultimate interest to us.

IV

If we substitute G (God exists) for Q (No good justifies God in permitting E1 and E2) in our earlier representation of $Pr(Q/P\&k)$ according to Bayes's Theorem, we get the following:

$$Pr(G/P\&k) = Pr(G/k) \times \frac{Pr(P/G\&k)}{Pr(P/k)}.$$

Recall that from our earlier discussion of k, $Pr(G/k) = 0.5$. Also note that *if* $Pr(P/k) > Pr(P/G\&k)$ *then* $Pr(G/P\&k) < Pr(G/k)$. (The general point here is that G makes P less likely than it would otherwise be if and only if P makes G less likely than it would otherwise be.) So, *if* we can succeed in showing $Pr(P/k) > Pr(P/G\&k)$ *then* we will have established an important point about what can be inferred from P. For we will have shown, first, that given k, P makes G less likely than it would otherwise be, $Pr(G/P\&k) < Pr(G/k)$, and, second, that given k, P makes G less likely than not, $Pr(G/P\&k) < 0.5$. (This part follows from the first part and the fact that $Pr(G/k) = 0.5$.)[18] But can we establish that $Pr(P/k) > Pr(P/G\&k)$? I believe we can.

Let's begin by considering $Pr(P/G\&k)$. In the end we shall discover that it will not matter much what value is assigned to $Pr(P/G\&k)$, so long as it is less than 1.[19] But for the moment it will be instructive to assign it a value of 0.5. Theodicists who believe that there are goods that we know of that could justify God in permitting E1 and E2 may think that $Pr(P/G\&k) < 0.5$. Other theists who find themselves quite incapable of thinking of any good whose realization might be God's reason for permitting E1 and E2 would undoubtedly be sympathetic to the assignment of 0.5, and may even think that it should be somewhat higher than that.[20] But for instructive purposes, let's assume that $Pr(P/G\&k) = 0.5$. If so, can we determine $Pr(P/k)$? Or, if we cannot determine $Pr(P/k)$, can we at least determine that it is > 0.5? The truth is that given that $Pr(G/k) = 0.5$ and given that $Pr(P/G\&k)$ is 0.5, we can determine exactly what $Pr(P/k)$ is. To see this, let's first establish that $Pr(P/k)$ must lie somewhere between a low of 0.25 and a high of 0.75. We establish this by using the rule of elimination to determine the value of $Pr(P/k)$:

$$Pr(P/k) = [Pr(G/k) \times Pr(P/G\&k)] + [Pr(\sim G/k) \times Pr(P/\sim G\&k)].$$

Since $Pr(G/k)$ and $Pr(P/G\&k)$ are both 0.5, we have 0.25 on the left side of the plus sign. And since $Pr(\sim G/k) = 0.5$ and $Pr(P/\sim G\&k)$ must lie somewhere between zero and 1, it follows that on the right side of the plus sign the number must be somewhere between zero and 0.5. Therefore, $Pr(P/k)$ is somewhere between 0.25 and 0.75.

Now if we could go no further toward establishing $Pr(P/k)$, very little of interest could be established concerning $Pr(G/P\&k)$. But we can go further. In fact, we can establish that if both $Pr(G/k)$ and $Pr(P/G\&k) = 0.5$, then $Pr(G/P\&k) = 0.333$.[21] This can be shown once we note that $Pr(P/\sim G\&k) = 1$. For, as we earlier noted, P is entailed by $\sim G$. So, since P is entailed by $\sim G$, $Pr(P/\sim G\&k) = 1$.

If both $Pr(G/k)$ and $Pr(P/G\&k) = 0.5$, $Pr(P/k) = 0.75$, with the result that $Pr(G/P\&k) = 0.333$. And this shows us a general truth: given that $Pr(G/k) = 0.5$ and $Pr(P/G\&k) < 1$, P not only lowers the probability of G, it also makes G lower than 0.5. But we need to distinguish these two results. The first, that P lowers the probability of G, makes G less likely than it would otherwise be, is bound to be true provided that $Pr(P/G\&k) < 1$. For given that $Pr(P/G\&k) < 1$ (as almost all would agree), it must be that $Pr(P/k) > Pr(P/G\&k)$. And, if $Pr(P/k) > Pr(P/G\&k)$ then $Pr(G/P\&k) < Pr(G/k)$—no matter what $Pr(G/k)$ happens to be. The second, that P makes G lower than 0.5, does depend to some degree on our original assignment of 0.5 to $Pr(G/k)$. If we sufficiently increase $Pr(G/k)$, then although $Pr(G/P\&k)$ will always be lower than $Pr(G/k)$, it will rise above 0.5. And this is what we should expect. For if the existence of God is sufficiently probable apart from the negative impact of P, then the existence of God may still be more probable than not even when the negative impact of P is taken into account. No one should disagree with this result.

To sum up then: Since $Pr(Q/P\&k) < 1$ and $Pr(P/k) < 1$, it follows that

1. $Pr(Q/P\&k) > Pr(Q/k)$.

And given that $Pr(G/k) = 0.5$ and that $Pr(P/G\&k) < 1$, we have established two other important points.

2. $Pr(G/P\&k) < Pr(G/k)$.
3. $Pr(G/P\&k) < 0.5$.

What we have yet to establish is

4. $Pr(Q/P\&k) > 0.5$.

Let's return to our first formula concerning $Pr(Q/P\&k)$:

$$Pr(Q/P\&k) = Pr(Q/k) \times \frac{Pr(P/Q\&k)}{Pr(P/k)}.$$

Since $Pr(P/Q\&k) = 1$, we can eliminate it from the formula with the following result:

$$Pr(Q/P\&k) = \frac{Pr(Q/k)}{Pr(P/k)}.$$

Relying on our earlier stipulation that $Pr(G/k) = 0.5$ and $Pr(\sim G/k) = 0.5$, we can use the rule of elimination to determine the value of $Pr(Q/k)$. We have the following:

$$Pr(Q/k) = [Pr(G/k) \times Pr(Q/G\&k)] + [Pr(\sim G/k) \times Pr(Q/\sim G\&k)].$$

On the left side of the plus sign, we have 0.5×0, for the conjunction (G&k) entails that Q is false.[22] On the right side of the plus sign we have 0.5×1, for Q is entailed by $\sim G$. So $Pr(Q/k) = 0.5$. If we accept the earlier assignment of 0.5 to $Pr(P/G\&k)$, then $Pr(P/k) = 0.75$, with the result that $Pr(Q/P\&k) = 0.666$. But aside from this argument, it is evident that $Pr(P/k) > Pr(Q/k)$.[23] So, given that $Pr(P/k) < 1$, if $Pr(Q/k) = 0.5$, it follows that $Pr(Q/P\&k) > 0.5$. In fact, if our argument is correct, $Pr(Q/P\&k) = 1 - Pr(G/P\&k)$, and this will be true no matter what non-zero assignments less than 1 are made to $Pr(P/k)$, $Pr(G/k)$, and $Pr(Q/k)$.

Returning to our summing up, we can now add

4. $Pr(Q/P\&k) > 0.5$

to our list of propositions we have established given that $Pr(G/k) = 0.5$ and that $Pr(P/G\&k) < 1$. This is the better argument I mentioned earlier for the view that

P not only makes Q more likely than it otherwise would be but also makes it more likely than not.[24]

Return now to the formulation of the argument at the beginning of this chapter. The argument proceeds inductively from P to Q and deductively from Q to ~G. Given the discussion in sections II and III, it is clear that we can simplify the argument considerably by bypassing Q altogether and proceeding directly from P to ~G. And that is what I now propose to do. Our evidential argument from evil, therefore, can now be stated more succinctly as

> P: No good we know of justifies God in permitting E1 and E2.
>   therefore, it is probable that
> ~G: There is no omnipotent, omniscient, perfectly good being.

So far, we have not considered what justification we might have for the initial premise P. As I noted earlier, we need to consider this issue in the light of objections raised by Alston in "The Inductive Problem of Evil and the Human Cognitive Condition." What we have been considering is the justification we have for the claim that P makes ~G probable. And what we have seen is that given that the probability of G on our background information k is 0.5, there is a compelling argument that P makes ~G more probable than G. So it does seem that we are justified in holding not only that P makes G less likely than it would otherwise be, but also justified in holding that P makes G less likely than ~G. But we need to look more deeply into the degree of support P provides for ~G, particularly in light of Wykstra's penetrating discussions of this point.

V

I refer the reader to Wykstra's new essay (chapter 7 in this volume), "Rowe's Noseeum Arguments from Evil," for a full explication of CORNEA (Condition of Reasonable Epistemic Access) and his current understanding of its application to my inference from P to ~G.[25] But in brief it comes to this: Wykstra's CORNEA, as he now explains it, tells us that we are entitled to believe Q (or ~G) on the basis of P only if it is reasonable for us to believe that

> If P is true, it is likely that Q (~G) is true.

As he puts it: "So all CORNEA really says is that premise P justifies our believing conclusion Q only if it is reasonable for us to believe that if P is true, then Q is likely true." Since we have deleted Q from our statement of the evidential argument, we can take the proposition in question to be:

> If P [No good we know of justifies God in permitting E1 and E2], it is likely that ~G [There is no omnipotent, omniscient, perfectly good being].

In his 1984 paper, to which I responded, Wykstra argued that given God's omniscience and that he is the creator of all that is, it is *quite likely* that the goods for the sake of which he permits many sufferings would be altogether *beyond our ken*. Noting my claim that in a great many cases of evil the justifying goods are nowhere within our ken, he remarked:

> The linchpin of my critique has been that if theism is true, this is *just what one would expect;* for if we think carefully about the sort of being theism proposes for our belief, it is *entirely expectable*—given what we know of our cognitive limits—that the goods by virtue of which this Being allows known suffering should very often be beyond our ken. [26]

In his new essay for this volume he argues that it is not necessary for him to take such a strong position. He now holds that it would be sufficient to take a more "modest" approach, arguing that *it is just as likely as not* that these goods should be beyond our ken. So, instead of arguing that it is *quite likely* that the goods for the sake of which God permits many sufferings would be *beyond our ken,* Wykstra now opts for the more modest claim that it is *as likely as not* that these goods would be *beyond our ken.* He also argues that I cannot simply take the inference from P to ~G as a good inference, one we are entitled to make unless someone shows that we are not. Finally, he finishes his new essay by reworking and defending his analogy between God and the good parent who often acts in ways the child cannot understand.

Let's first consider his point that for my argument to work *it must be reasonable to believe* that if P is true then it is likely that ~G, that it is not sufficient just to claim that we are entitled to believe it unless we have a good reason not to believe it, thus throwing all the burden on the theist to argue that P's being true does not make it likely that God does not exist. I agree with Wykstra that it must be reasonable to believe that if P is true then it is likely that ~G. And I hope that the first several sections of this chapter show that relative to background information k, on which G is as likely as not, P does make it likely that ~G. But this is a somewhat complicated matter and we need to look at it a bit more fully.

Given the level playing field assumption that the probability of God's existence is 0.5 relative to the theist's and nontheist's shared background information k, we raised the question of whether P makes ~G unlikely. We saw that *whatever probability (less than 1) we assign to G on k,* it will be the case that $Pr(G/P\&k)$ is lower than $Pr(G/k)$.[27] We then saw, of course, that $Pr(G/P\&k) < 0.5$. Have we then satisfied Wykstra's requirement that it be reasonable to believe that if P is true then it is likely that ~G? This depends on how we understand Wykstra's requirement. We've shown that it is reasonable to believe that P lowers the probability of G. We've shown that on our background information k, it is reasonable to believe that if P is true ~G is more likely than not. But have we shown that relative to background information k it is reasonable to *believe* that if P is true G is unlikely? Well, it might seem that we have. But suppose we put Wykstra's requirement like this. It must be reasonable to believe that *P is a good reason to believe that G is false.* Have we shown that the conjunction P&k is a good reason to believe ~G? If we have, then we may conclude that it is reasonable to believe that P is a good *prima facie* reason to believe that G is false. But what we have shown is that the conjunction P&k is a

272 / WILLIAM L. ROWE

good reason to believe that G is *less likely than not*. And to have a good reason to believe that G is less likely than not is not the same as having a good reason to believe that G is false. For suppose we establish that $Pr(G/P\&k) = 0.45$. If we do *establish* this, then we may agree that P is a good reason to believe that G is less likely than not. But we would require something more than this for P to be a good reason to believe that G is false. 0.45 is so close to 0.5 that the rational thing to do would be to suspend judgment about the truth or falsity of G. And I think what Wykstra requires of me is some reason to think that the probability of G on P&k is low enough for P to be a good reason to believe that G is false. Have I provided any such reason?

We've taken note of two major points in Wykstra's essay. First, we've seen that he holds that my evidential argument succeeds only if it is reasonable for me to believe that if P is true it is likely that ~G. Second, we've seen that he thinks that if the considerations he brings forth (the parent-child analogy, the moral depth line, etc.) suffice to show that if G is true P is *just as likely as not* (the "modest" attack), this will render it *unreasonable* for me to believe that if P is true it is likely that ~G. Concerning the first point, I've responded by noting (a) that P lowers the probability of G, and (b) that given k, P makes G less probable than not. The remaining issue is *how low* G must be on P&k for P&k to be a good reason to believe ~G. On this last point, we might settle on something like ~G being twice as likely as G. If so, then given our level playing field assumption, $Pr(G/k) = 0.5$, I believe I can satisfy Wykstra's requirement. For I think we have reason to believe that $Pr(P/G\&k)$ is no greater than 0.5. And given that $Pr(G/k) = 0.5$ and that $Pr(P/G\&k)$ is no greater than 0.5, it follows that $Pr(G/P\&k)$ is no greater than 0.333.

It is clear, however, that Wykstra thinks that a probability of 1/3 is not low enough to justify disbelief. He holds, I believe, that if the initial probability of G on k is 0.5 and the probability of P on G & k is 0.5, then, although P lowers G's likelihood to 1/3 and increases ~G's likelihood to 2/3, thus making ~G twice as likely as G, P does not sufficiently lower G's probability to justify abandoning agnosticism and taking up atheism. I have some sympathy for this view. Using some concepts employed by Chisholm, so long as we had only k to go on we might say that believing theism was not more reasonable than believing atheism, and believing atheism was not more reasonable than believing theism. Adding P to k, however, shifts things in favor of atheism. It is now more reasonable to believe atheism than it is to believe theism. But this may be true without it being true that it is now more reasonable to believe atheism than it is to withhold judgment on the matter of God's existence (agnosticism). How much must P lower G's probability in order for Wykstra to think that we are justified in moving from agnosticism to atheism, assuming that our initial position was one of agnosticism? It may well be that there is no sharp cut-off point here. But even if there is, Wykstra's view is that the cut-off point is less than 1/3. In the penultimate version of his paper he suggested that if the initial probability of a hypothesis is 0.5 and some evidence lowers its probability to 0.2, this entitles a shift from "square agnosticism" to "semi-square atheism"; whereas if the evidence lowers its probability to 0.17, this entitles a shift from "square agnosticism" to "square atheism."[28] But in the final version he suggests that "levering evidence," evidence sufficient to lever a belief-state from square agnosticism to square atheism, must lower the probability of theism virtually to 0, "to something under .05." In support of this rather strict view of what constitutes "levering evidence," Wykstra remarks: "In ordinary contexts, the things we typically squarely believe each day (say, that one is wearing shoes and socks, that it is cloudy outside, etc.) are, in effect, rated so near to 1 as to make no practical difference."[29] I think Wykstra's examples here are typically cases of knowledge, rather than belief in the absence of knowledge. Typically, I know that I'm wearing socks and shoes. Typically, when outdoors I'm in the position to know that it is cloudy (when it is). But when clouds are dark and I hear what sounds like thunder, I may form the belief that it will rain soon. Is my belief that it will rain soon rated something well above .95? I don't think so. But this is a minor point. The important point here is Wykstra's observation that evidence that lowers an initial probability from 0.5 to 1/3 falls somewhat short of "levering evidence." I believe Wykstra is right about this point. Given our judgments about the probability of G on k and the probability of P on G & k, P is evidence for atheism. But it is not "levering evidence"; it does not justify a shift from square agnosticism to square atheism.

   In reply to this interesting criticism, I have two points to make. First, it must be acknowledged that P does lower the probability of G. (Theists have been rather reluctant to acknowledge that the evils in our world, or what we have reason to believe about some of them, render God's existence less likely than it would otherwise be.) And if we start with our judgments about the probability of G on k and the probability of P on G & k, P lowers G's probability *significantly,* making ~G twice as likely as G. Although it does not lower G's probability sufficiently to move one from square agnosticism to square atheism, it does make it more rational to believe atheism than to believe theism. Second, we should remember that we are here considering one *particular argument* from evil, an argument based on the claim that no good we know of provides sufficient justification for God to permit two instances of evil, E1 and E2. As I suggested in an earlier essay,[30] there are two basic types of arguments from evil, one beginning from the fact that there exist evils "that seem to us to serve no good whatever, let alone one that is otherwise unobtainable by omnipotence," and the other that starts "from the somewhat less complex fact that the world contains vast amounts of intense human and animal suffering." In reaching any *overall conclusion* as to the force of the evidential argument from evil on the rationality of belief in God, we need to consider arguments of the second type as well. And the important point for our purposes here is that unlike the argument I've presented—resting as it does on a statement, P, that is not a part of k—arguments based simply on the existence of evils we know to occur are based on statements already contained in k. For k includes information about the kinds, amounts, and distribution of evils and goods in the world. Since I do think arguments based on our shared information about the kinds, amounts, and distribution of evils and goods in the world do have merit, I earlier noted in an endnote that my own view is that $Pr(G/k) < 0.5$. Suppose that after a thorough investigation of arguments of this sort we were to come to the conclusion that

Pr(G/k) < 0.5. What bearing would this have on the argument that I have given in this chapter? It would mean that Pr(G/P&k) < 0.333. How much less would depend on how low the probability of G on k is and how low the probability of P given G and k is. If Pr(G/k) = 0.2 and Pr(P/G&k) = 0.25, Pr(G/P&k) would be < .06. Of course, even if we were to agree to all this, we would not have answered Wykstra's point that my argument from P to ~G does not suffice to *leverage* us from square agnosticism to square atheism. For, since we are no longer taking Pr(G/k) to be 0.5, we are not beginning with square agnosticism. But if we were then to introduce k' as k *minus* the information about the kinds, amounts, and distribution of evils and goods in the world, we could then say that given Pr(G/k') as 0.5, the *combination* of the two sorts of arguments from evil may suffice to move us from square agnosticism to square atheism.

Wykstra's second point, his "modest" attack, turns out to be too modest to do much good. If all Wykstra does is establish that if God exists it is just as likely as not that P, we will be left with the result that Pr(G/P&k) = 0.333. Of course, since we've agreed that a probability of 0.333 is not sufficiently low to warrant belief in atheism, as opposed to belief that atheism is epistemically preferable to theism, Wykstra can rest content that my argument is insufficient to justify a move from square agnosticism to square atheism. But, as I've pointed out, the argument would still show that P *significantly lowers* the probability of G and makes belief in atheism more reasonable than belief in theism. To do anything more, Wykstra needs to revert to his *strong* attack and argue that Pr(P/G&k) is very high. Even if he is entirely successful in doing so, however, so long as Pr(P/G&k) < 1, it will still be true that Pr(G/P&k) < 0.5, that atheism is more probable than not. But if Wykstra succeeds in showing that Pr(P/G&k) is *very high,* Pr(G/P&k) will be quite close to 0.5. And this, of course, is not unimportant. For it would show that P does not *significantly lower* the probability of G.

Two questions remain:

Are there good reasons for believing that Pr(P/G&k) is very high?
Are there good reasons for believing that P is true?

In the next two sections I will take up these questions.

VI

Wykstra believes that if God exists it is quite likely that the goods for the sake of which he permits many instances of suffering (including Bambi's and Sue's) are beyond our ken. He argues from what he calls "the parent analogy." In his 1984 essay he claimed that our discerning most of these goods is "about as likely as that a one-month-old should discern most of his parents' purposes for those pains they allow him to suffer—which is to say, it is not likely at all."[31] In his new essay, he further develops and defends this argument from analogy.[32]

Before examining Wykstra's analogical argument for the view that Pr(P/G&k) is quite high, it will be helpful to see the bearing of this point on our evidential argument from evil. If God exists then some good justifies him in permitting Sue's horrendous suffering on being beaten, raped, and strangled. Either that good is a good we know of or it is not. Suppose that P is true, that *no good we know of* justifies God in permitting the sufferings of Bambi and Sue. Would this fact be a good reason for thinking it likely that God does not exist? As we've seen, this depends to a considerable extent on the degree to which P lowers the probability of G. Of course, P *does* lower the probability of G. But our question is whether it *significantly lowers* the probability of G. And the importance of Wykstra's parent analogy argument is that if it is correct we have a reason to think that P does not significantly lower the probability of G. So, much hangs on whether it can be successfully shown that if G is true, P is just what one would expect, that G makes P quite likely. We must now explore Wykstra's argument to this effect.

Is our intellectual grasp of goods for the sake of which God (if he exists) permits horrendous human and animal suffering *analogous* to a one-month-old infant's intellectual grasp of his parents' purposes for those pains they allow him to suffer? It hardly seems so. For a one-month-old infant hasn't developed the *concepts* necessary for even contemplating the proposition that good purposes may justify parents in permitting pains.[33] Adult human beings, on the other hand, have the intellectual equipment to distinguish intrinsic goods from extrinsic goods, to distinguish different kinds of intrinsic goods, to recognize certain intrinsic goods as superior to others, to form an idea of goods that have never been experienced by living human beings on earth (e.g., total felicity in the eternal presence of God), and to make some reasonable judgments about what goods an omnipotent being would (or would not) be able to bring about without permitting various instances of horrendous suffering. Of course, we have to allow that there may be kinds of intrinsic goods we have not thought of. But we do have reason to believe both that every intrinsic good necessarily involves conscious experience and that the highest intrinsic good human beings are capable of involves conscious experience of God. So, we know of many goods and we know of some of the very highest goods that human beings can experience. Why then does Wykstra believe that the parent analogy provides a strong argument for the view that the goods that justify God in permitting much horrendous suffering will be goods of which we have no knowledge?

Wykstra argues that the greater the degree of the parents' intelligence, care for the future life of the child, and ability, the more likely it is that their permitting present sufferings of the child serves goods in the *distant future*. Since God has unlimited intelligence, cares infinitely about the totality of each creature's life, and is unlimited in power, the argument from analogy implies that the goods justifying God in permitting horrendous human and animal suffering are often likely to be realized in the distant future.

What are we to make of this argument? Well, I don't think we should dismiss it out of hand simply because a parent's intelligence, loving concern for her children, and ability to provide are finite, whereas these features in God are infinite. But we should note that these differences make for significant disanalogies between the loving parent and God. The following are *often true* of the loving parent but are very likely *never true* of God:

A. The parent does not prevent the child's suffering (due to disease, etc.,) simply because the parent is *unaware* of the cause of the suffering or *unable* to prevent the suffering.

B. The parent does not prevent the child's suffering because the parent has other duties to fulfill that preclude her from being in a position to prevent the suffering. Unlike God, parents cannot be everywhere at once.

C. The parent permits present sufferings for distant goods not because these goods are incapable of existing sooner, or better for being distant, but because of insufficient intelligence and ability to realize the goods in the present or near future.

But let's put aside these disanalogies and focus on what is, I believe, the major weakness of the argument based on the analogy between God and the loving parent. What happens when a loving parent intentionally permits her child to suffer intensely for the sake of a distant good that cannot otherwise be realized? In such instances the parent attends directly to the child throughout its period of suffering, comforts the child to the best of her ability, expresses her concern and love for the child in ways that are unmistakably clear to the child, assures the child that the suffering will end, and tries to explain, as best she can, why it is necessary for her to permit the suffering even though it is in her power to prevent it. In short, during these periods of intentionally permitted intense suffering, the child is *consciously aware* of the direct presence, love, and concern of the parent, and receives *special assurances* from the parent that, if not why, the suffering (or the parent's permission of it) is necessary for some distant good.

If we do apply the parent analogy, the conclusion about God that we should draw is something like the following: When God permits horrendous suffering for the sake of some good, if that good is *beyond our ken,* God will make every effort to be consciously present to us during our period of suffering, will do his best to explain to us why he is permitting us to suffer, and will give us special assurances of his love and concern during the period of the suffering.[34] Since enormous numbers of human beings undergo prolonged, horrendous suffering without being consciously aware of any such divine presence, concern, and explanations, we may conclude that if there is a God, the goods for the sake of which he permits horrendous human suffering are more often than not goods we know of. In any case, I think we are justified in concluding that we've been given no good reason to think that if God exists the goods that justify him in permitting much human and animal suffering are quite likely to be beyond our ken.[35]

VII

At long last we come to the question of P itself. What reason do we have to believe that *no good we know of justifies God in permitting E1 and E2?* The main reason to believe P is this: When we reflect on some good we know of we can see that it is very likely, if not certain, that the good in question *either* is not good enough to justify God in permitting E1 or E2 *or* is such that an omnipotent, omniscient being could realize it (or some greater good) without having to permit E1 or E2. Consider, for example, Sue's pleasure upon receiving some toys on her fourth birthday. Clearly that pleasure is not good enough to justify the permission by God of what we can only suppose to be her terror and pain on being brutally beaten, raped, and strangled when she was five years old. And if we begin to reflect on the various kinds of goods we know of, we will come to the sound judgment that many of them are not good enough to justify anyone in permitting E1. Similar remarks can be made concerning various kinds and degrees of goods relative to the terrible pain Bambi endures for several days upon being badly burned in the forest fire. In short, we can see that various kinds of goods we know of simply aren't good enough to justify permitting horrendous evils such as E1 and E2. On the other hand, for those goods we know of that do seem to *outweigh* either E1 or E2, reflection on them leads us to the judgment that it is very likely, if not certain, that an omnipotent being could have realized the goods in question (or some better goods) without having to permit E1 or E2. Consider, for example, Sue's experiencing complete felicity in the eternal presence of God. While this good may justly be held to outweigh almost any horrendous evil that may befall Sue in her earthly life, it strains credulity to think that it is beyond the power of God to realize this good without having to permit Sue's being brutally beaten, raped, and strangled at the age of five years. It might be suggested that had Sue continued to live out her life she would have freely chosen to harden her heart against God with the result that she would have precluded herself from experiencing complete felicity in the eternal presence of God. Let this be so. If God knows this, he might then have some reason to permit her death at the age of five. On the other hand, it hardly makes sense for God to give us the freedom to develop into beings who have hardened our hearts against him and his eternal kingdom and then act to prevent us from having the chance to exercise that freedom. Moreover, we might expect that God could have brought about circumstances in which Sue would have freely refrained from hardening her heart against God. But suppose that God does have reason to permit Sue's death at an early age. Does God then have a sufficient reason to permit her to die by being brutally beaten, raped, and strangled? Clearly, given his omnipotence he could have realized her early death by more humane means. So, even when we consider some good we know of that does seem to outweigh E2, we have good reason to believe that if God could realize that good, he could realize it without permitting E2. And what of Bambi's terrible suffering? What good do we know of that outweighs it and is such that God could not have realized it without permitting E1? When we reflect on any good we know of and consider Bambi's excruciating suffering, reason cries out that it is very likely, if not certain, that either the good is not good enough or God could have realized it without having to permit E1 (or something else as bad or worse).

In "The Inductive Argument from Evil and the Human Cognitive Condition" (chapter 6 in this volume), William Alston does a masterful job of surveying the terrain of goods we know of in search of some good whose realization might justify God in permitting E1 or E2. Although the overall purpose of his essay is to *establish* that none of us is or can be justified in believing that no good justifies God in permitting E1 or E2, my interest here concerns only that part of his essay that focuses on P (No good we *know of* justifies God in permitting E1 and E2).[36] In pursuing our question of whether we are justified in believing that P is true, we can do no better than to critically examine Alston's discussion of this issue.

A major part of Alston's project is to consider familiar Christian theodicies and to explore their possible application to Bambi and Sue. These theodicies divide into those proposing divine reasons for suffering that are concerned with possible goods to those who endure the suffering and those proposing divine reasons for suffering concerned with possible goods not restricted to the sufferers. Examples he gives of the first sort are punishment for sin, soul-making, and having a vision of the inner life of God. Examples he gives of the second sort are the value of free will, benefits to those who cause or witness the suffering, and the value generated by a lawlike, natural order.

Alston emphasizes that he is considering Christian theodicies only as *live possibilities* for divine reasons for permitting evil. He is not undertaking to show that any of these theodicies is correct. Since he does not spell out what he means by a live possibility in this context, I shall take a live possibility here to be something that we have no good reason to believe would not wholly or partially justify an omniscient, omnipotent, wholly good being in permitting some evil. The question then becomes whether any or all of the theodicies are live possibilities *for Bambi and Sue*. If they are not live possibilities, if they are implausible suggestions as to what might justify an omnipotent, omniscient being in permitting Bambi and Sue, then, insofar as his use of Christian theodicies is concerned, Alston will not have shown that no one is justified in believing P to be true.

So far as goods for the sufferer are concerned, Alston believes that the prominent Christian theodicies *fail* to provide live possibilities for the cases of Bambi and Sue. But he thinks that he can establish that some goods we are familiar with (for example, the supreme fulfillment of one's nature) are such that we've no good reason to think that an omnipotent, omniscient being can obtain them without having to permit Bambi's and Sue's sufferings. But apart from noting that it is logically possible that Bambi's and Sue's sufferings are required for the fulfillment of their natures, Alston does little or nothing by way of "establishing" that we are not justified in precluding familiar goods like the supreme fulfillment of Bambi's nature or Bambi's having a vision of God from providing an omnipotent, omniscient being with a morally sufficient reason to permit Bambi's excruciating torment and death.

The major theodicy concerned with a good that extends beyond the sufferer is the free-will theodicy. I will here consider Alston's efforts to use this theodicy to establish that we cannot be justified in believing P.[37] According to this theodicy, God is justified in permitting evil actions and their consequences because he has bestowed on some of his creatures genuine freedom in a range of actions, and it is a conceptual impossibility for God to create a free agent with respect to some action and also determine the agent to choose (not choose) to perform the action. So, according to this theodicy, God permits certain horrors to occur because to prevent them would be to prevent a certain degree of freedom in his creatures. Against this theodicy, Alston notes that it has been argued (1) that God could have created free creatures who always choose to do what is right, and (2) that permitting free will with respect to certain actions at certain times isn't worth the horrendous evils (for example, Sue's suffering) that result from the use of that freedom. Concerning the first objection, Alston points out that if we set aside middle knowledge, as he does in the chapter, God would not be able to create beings with genuine freedom and "guarantee" that they will always choose to do what is right. And he further notes that even if we grant middle knowledge, Plantinga "has established the *possibility* that God could not actualize a world containing free creatures that always do the right thing."

Before considering his response to the second objection, we should note two points here. First, to conduct his case on the *assumption* that there is no middle knowledge considerably weakens Alston's argument. For there is no consensus on whether middle knowledge is possible. And if middle knowledge is possible, then we have reason to think that an omnipotent, omniscient being could have created a world with less evil, but as much good, as our world contains.[38] Nor will it do to emphasize that Plantinga has established the *possibility* that even with middle knowledge God could not have created a world with free creatures that always do the right thing. For Alston needs to show that even with middle knowledge it remains a *live possibility* that God could not have created a world with free creatures who always do what is right. But all that Plantinga has shown is that it is a *logical possibility* that such would be the case. And here again, I'm afraid, we have a slide on Alston's part from what is a logical possibility to what is a live possibility, from what is broadly logically possible to what we have no good reason for thinking isn't so. Indeed, that such a slide has occurred is indicated by the sentence with which Alston begins his very next paragraph. "Thus we may take it to be a *live possibility* that the maintenance of creaturely free will is at least part of God's reason for permitting wrongdoing and its consequences" (emphasis mine).

Suppose we endeavor to apply the free-will theodicy to the case of Sue's suffering on being beaten, raped, and strangled. The first question we need to ask is whether the possession of free will is something that is *in itself* of such great value as to merit God's permission of the horrendous moral evils in the world. I think the answer must be no. We should distinguish the intrinsic value of possessing free will from its extrinsic value. The mere possession of free will does not strike me as itself having much in the way of intrinsic value.[39] But the possession of free will does seem necessary to attaining states that are of great intrinsic value. Thus, if we can agree that free will is necessary for the existence of things of great intrinsic value, we can agree that an omnipotent, omniscient, perfectly good being would likely endow his creatures (or some of them) with free will, provided that it does result to a sufficient degree in the things of great intrinsic value for which its possession was intended. But, of course, it is sometimes right to curtail a particular exercise of free will when one foresees or predicts that its exercise is evil and/or will result in considerable suffering. Since curtailing a particular exercise of free will does not significantly diminish a person's overall degree of freedom, the question at hand is whether it is rational to believe that an omnipotent, omniscient, perfectly good being would have prevented the particular exercise of free will (if that is what it was) Sue's attacker engaged in when he brutally beat, raped, and strangled the five-year-old child. As Alston puts the issue:

> presumably a tiny additional constriction such as would be involved in God's preventing Sue's attacker from committing that atrocity would not render things radically different, free-will-wise, from what they would have been without that. So God could have prevented this without losing the good emphasized by this theodicy. Hence we can be sure that this does not constitute a sufficient reason for His not preventing it. (113, above)

Alston, however, thinks that the preservation of Sue's attacker's free will is a *live possibility* for at least part of God's reason for permitting the suffering Sue undergoes at the hands of her attacker. For he reasons that the value of free will is such that God can intervene in only a small proportion of cases.

> Rowe's claim would then have to be that Sue's murder was so horrible that it would qualify for the class of exceptions. But that is precisely where the critic's claims far outrun his justification. How can we tell that Sue falls within the most damaging n percent of what would be cases of human wrongdoing apart from divine intervention? To be in a position to make such a judgment we would have to survey the full range of such cases and make reliable assessments of the deleterious consequences of each. Both tasks are far beyond our powers. (ibid.)

Alston's point seems to be this: God cannot intervene in all cases of the use of free will in doing evil that results in suffering, for this would severely limit human capacity to choose between good and evil. God, then, would intervene only in a certain percentage (n) of such cases. The cases in which God intervenes would be selected so as to minimize human suffering overall or to maximize human welfare. And we simply don't know enough about what would be cases of human wickedness (past, present, and future) apart from divine intervention to determine whether or not Sue's case would be included among the percentage of cases God would select to eliminate. Alston states:

> Hence, by the nature of the case, we are simply not in a position to make a warranted judgment that Sue's case is among the n percent worst cases of wrongdoing in the history of the universe. No doubt it strikes us as incomparably horrible on hearing about it, but so would innumerable others. Therefore, the critic is not in a position to set aside the value of free will as at least part of God's reason for permitting Sue's murder. (114)

Does this argument *establish* that we aren't justified in excluding the value of human free will as part of God's reason for permitting Sue's suffering? Well, if the basic premise of Alston's argument is correct, the argument does establish just that. For to be so justified, Alston requires that we compare the episode involving Sue with the whole range of cases of human wrongdoing in the universe (past, present, and future) that would occur apart from divine intervention in order to determine whether Sue's case is sufficiently bad to warrant God in setting aside the value of free will in that case. And, of course, no human being knows enough to engage in such a comparison. But I do not think this knowledge is required. The free-will theodicy is built around the idea that the possession of freedom to do good and evil is a good *in each person* that God creates. What is important, there-fore, is that each person have some measure of freedom to do good and evil. Now, as Alston will readily admit, (1) we don't possess unlimited freedom, and (2) it is sometimes right to curtail someone's freedom in order to prevent some horren-dous evil act that results in considerable suffering to an innocent person. But if God were to select some person and effectively prevent that person from ever choosing to do an evil deed that results in suffering to an innocent person, we can agree that this might severely diminish the value of that person's freedom to do good and evil. So God has a reason to permit each person to effectively engage in doing good and evil acts. Of course, God would be able to intervene in some of those acts without significantly diminishing the person's general freedom to do good and evil. What, then, do we have to make a judgment about in order to deter-mine whether the prevention of Sue's attacker's freedom to brutally beat, rape, and strangle Sue would have severely diminished the value of that person's free-dom to do good and evil? Do we have to compare it with all the cases of human wrongdoing, past, present, and future, as Alston claims? Clearly not. What is at issue here is not some sort of amount of freedom to do good and evil in the entire universe, past, present, and future. What is at issue here is the degree and value of Sue's attacker's freedom to do good and evil. Would this particular intervention severely diminish the value of that individual's overall degree of freedom to do good and evil? And if it would, is the value of that individual's overall degree of freedom to do good and evil worth the price of permitting the act in question? Per-haps some rational judgments are required about these questions in order for us to be justified in taking Sue's suffering as an instance of gratuitous suffering. But this is a far cry from having to do a survey of all human acts of wickedness in the uni-verse, past, present, and future.[40]

We've had a look at Alston's efforts to single out *among goods we know of* some live possibilities for a sufficient reason for God to permit Bambi's or Sue's suffering. Concerning goods we know of that are restricted to the sufferer, Alston concedes that "none of the sufferer-centered reasons I considered could be any part of God's reasons for permitting the Bambi and Sue cases." And because it would be wrong for God to permit horrendous suffering *solely* for the benefit of others, Alston concludes "that nonsufferer-centered reasons could not be the whole of God's reasons for allowing any case of suffering." So, Alston's final con-clusion is that he must appeal to goods *beyond our ken* in order to argue that we can-not be justified in believing that God has no sufficient reason to permit E1 or E2. Thus, quite apart from the specific criticisms I have presented against his attempts to provide live possibilities for God's reasons to permit E1 and E2, Alston concedes that he hasn't shown that we cannot be justified in believing that no good we *know of* justifies God in permitting E1 and E2.

Of course, it's one thing for the most talented philosophers and theologians to fail to show that we aren't justified in believing P, and another thing for us to be justified in believing P, and still another thing for us to *show* that we are justified in believing P. And I must confess that I know of no way to *prove* that P is true. What we do have is genuine knowledge that many goods we know of are insufficient to justify God in permitting E1 or E2. In addition we have very good reason to believe that many other goods we know of could be realized by an omnipotent, omniscient being without his having to permit E1 and E2 (or something just as bad). And, finally, we have the failure of theodicists to show how any of the goods we know of can plausibly be held, separately or collectively, to constitute a sufficient reason for God to permit E1 or E2. All this, I believe, gives us good reason to believe that P is true.

VII

The evidential problem of evil derives its strength from our almost inescapable conviction that among the goods that fall within our intellectual grasp none can reasonably be thought to constitute God's justifying reason for permitting such horrendous evils as E1 and E2. For if we divide the possible justifying goods into those that fall within our intellectual grasp and those utterly beyond our ken, and then discover that none of the goods in the first category are justifying for God with respect to such horrendous evils, we significantly lower the likelihood of God's existence. This is particularly so if our antecedent expectations are that the justifying goods are as likely to fall in the first category as in the second.

Tough-minded theists have held that the facts about evil in our world do not render God's existence less likely than not. Indeed, some have held that the facts about evil do not even make God's existence less likely than it would otherwise be. In this chapter I have argued that these views are seriously mistaken. Given our common knowledge of the evils and goods in our world and our reasons for believing that P is true, it is *irrational* to believe in theism unless we possess or discover strong evidence in its behalf. I conclude, therefore, that the evidential argument from evil is alive and well.[41]

NOTES

1. See Bruce Russell's chapter 10 in this volume for a classification of several kinds of evidential arguments from evil.

2. William L. Rowe, "The Problem of Evil and Some Varieities of Atheism," *American Philosophical Quarterly* 16 (1979): 335-41; chapter 1 in this volume.

3. See William L. Rowe, "Evil and Theodicy," *Philosophical Topics* 16 (1988): 119-32, and "Ruminations about Evil," *Philosophical Perspectives* 5 (1991): 69-88.

4. William Alston uses "Bambi" to refer to E1 and "Sue" to refer to E2. See

Alston, "The Inductive Argument from Evil and the Human Cognitive Condition," chapter 6 in this volume.

5. This objection can be remedied by complicating P and Q so that they include some clause concerning the prevention of some equal or worse evils. For sake of simplicity, I ignore this complication. See note 2 of "Evil and Theodicy," 131-32.

6. For an interesting development of this objection, see William Hasker, "The Necessity of Gratuitous Evil," *Faith and Philosophy* 9 (1992): 23-44. I discuss Hasker's view in "Ruminations About Evil."

7. See Stephen Wykstra, "The Humean Obstacle to Evidential Arguments from Suffering: On Avoiding the Evils of 'Appearance,'" *International Journal for Philosophy of Religion* 16 (1984): 73-93. This essay, along with my reply, is reprinted in *The Problem of Evil*, ed. M. M. Adams and R. M. Adams (Oxford University Press, 1990). Also see Wykstra's co-authored piece (with Bruce Russell), "The 'Inductive' Argument from Evil: A Dialogue," *Philosophical Topics* 16 (1988): 133-60, as well as his chapter 7 in this volume. Also see Terry Christlieb, "Which Theisms Face an Evidential Problem of Evil?" *Faith and Philosophy* 9 (1992): 45-64, Paul Draper, "Probabilistic Arguments from Evil," *Religious Studies* 28 (1992): 303-17, and James Sennett, "The Inscrutable Evil Defense," *Faith and Philosophy* 10 (1993): 220-29.

8. It is important not to confuse P with

P*: No good we know of *would* justify God *(if he exists)* in permitting E1 and E2.

While P must be true if God does not exist, P* may be false if God does not exist. For even though God does not exist, it could still be true that if he did exist some good we know of would justify him in permitting E1 and E2. To avoid any confusion of P with P*, it will be helpful to keep in mind that the sentence "No good we know of justifies God in permitting E1 and E2" is here being used to express the negation of the following proposition:

God exists & there exists a good we know of & that good justifies him in permitting E1 and E2.

9. The information that *I exist near the earth's surface* is not shared by most theists and nontheists. But we may well include such information in k, since most of us (at some time) know a proposition that corresponds to the one I know. It is also understood here that k includes certain stipulated information. In particular, k includes our information concerning E1 (the case of Bambi) and E2 (the case of Sue).

10. My own view is that $\Pr(G/k) < 0.5$. For I think the information we possess concerning the abundance of various evils in the world renders G unlikely. And I do not think the other information in k manages to counterbalance the weight of our information about the abundance of evils in the world. But for purposes of finding a starting point for the "theist-nontheist dialogue" I am here putting this view aside, although I will return to it later.

11. In "The Problem of Evil and Some Varieties of Atheism," I made use of what I called "the G. E. Moore shift" to show how belief in God can be sustained as rational by having stronger evidence for God's existence than the evidence from evil constitutes for God's nonexistence.

12. Alternatively, is $\Pr(Q/P\&k) < \Pr(\text{not-}Q/P\&k)$?

13. Alternatively, is $\Pr(G/P\&k) < \Pr(\text{not-}G/P\&k)$?

14. If $\Pr(Q/k) = \Pr(P/k)$ then $\Pr(Q/P\&k)$ would be 1, which we know it not to be. If $\Pr(Q/k) > \Pr(P/k)$ then $\Pr(Q/P\&k)$ would be > 1, which is impossible.

15. "Evil and Theodicy," 123-24.

16. If we have observed many A's and all of them are B's, this fact will make the proposition "All A's are B's" more likely than it would otherwise be. But one proposition

may make another more likely than it would otherwise be without making it more likely than not.

17. Michael Tooley advances such an argument in "The Argument from Evil," *Philosophical Perspectives* 5 (1991): 114-15.

18. This point is important, in part, because its first part has been denied by some in writing on the problem of evil. For example, Wykstra, in his 1984 essay, "The Humean Obstacle to Evidential Arguments from Suffering: On Avoiding the Evils of 'Appearance,'" argued that propositions like P do not even "weakly disconfirm" G. A proposition weakly disconfirms a second proposition if, given the first, the second proposition is less likely than it otherwise would be.

19. That is, it won't matter if all we are trying to show is that $\Pr(G/P\&k) < 0.5$. As we shall see later, for the resolution of other important issues it matters a great deal what value is assigned to $\Pr(P/G\&k)$.

20. Some theists hold that although $\Pr(P/G\&k)$ is at least 0.5, for all we know $\Pr(P/G\&k) = 1$. See, for example, Daniel Howard-Snyder, "Inscrutable Evil and the Silence of God," doctoral dissertation, Syracuse University, 1992. Assuming these theists will agree to an assignment of 0.5 to $\Pr(G/k)$, we can characterize this view as holding the following propositions: (1) unless the conjunction of G and k *entails* P, P lowers the probability of G, (2) if $\Pr(P/G\&k) < 0.5$ then P lowers the probability of G anywhere from 0.333 to 0, (3) we have a sufficient reason to believe that $\Pr(P/G\&k)$ is not less than 0.5, (4) we are completely in the dark as to what assignment between 0.5 and 1 belongs to $\Pr(P/G\&k)$, and therefore, (5) we can be *confident* that if P lowers the probability of G, it does not lower it beyond 0.333. This view clearly merits consideration. Here I will only note that it is somewhat odd to suggest that human reason is *fully adequate* to determine that $\Pr(P/G\&k)$ cannot be a decimal point below 0.5, but *utterly inadequate* to judge whether it is closer to 0.5 than it is to 1.

21. Strictly speaking, this isn't exactly right. $\Pr(G/P\&k) = 1/3$. But for reasons of uniformity I will continue to use the approximate decimal equivalent.

22. Common to most theists and nontheists is a principle (a necessary truth) to the effect that if God exists and some horrendous evil exists then there is some good whose realization justifies God in permitting that evil. Given G&k, it follows that God exists and that E1 and E2 exist. And given the principle just noted, it will follow that there is some good that justifies God in permitting E1 and E2. But if this is so, Q is false. For Q says that no good justifies God in permitting E1 and E2.

23. "Evil and Theodicy," 123-24.

24. As with our conclusion that $\Pr(G/P\&k) < 0.5$, our conclusion that $\Pr(Q/P\&k) > 0.5$ depends to some degree on our original assignment of 0.5 to $\Pr(G/k)$.

25. Actually, Wykstra applies CORNEA to my inference from P to Q. But his point remains the same when extended to my more succinct statement of the argument which bypasses Q with a direct inference from P to ~G. For some important criticisms of Wykstra's CORNEA, see Daniel Howard-Snyder, "Seeing through CORNEA," *International Journal for Philosophy of Religion* 32 (1992): 25-49.

26. Italics mine. I have taken this remark from the reprint of Wykstra's 1984 essay in *The Problem of Evil,* ed. M. M. Adams and R. M. Adams, 159.

27. It is taken for granted here that $\Pr(P/G\&k) < 1$.

28. See note 7 of "Rowe's Noseeum Arguments from Evil," chapter 7 in this book.

29. Ibid.

30. William L. Rowe, "The Empirical Argument from Evil," in *Rationality, Religious Belief, and Moral Commitment,* ed. Robert Audi and William J. Wainwright (Ithaca: Cornell University Press, 1986), 245-47.

31. Quoted in his new essay written for this volume (chapter 7).

32. See chapter 7.

33. We should note that Wykstra invites us to adjust the infant's age beyond his

one-month suggestion. But it is striking, nevertheless, that he thinks the one-month age is appropriate for his analogy.

34. If the good is one we know of, then we have some chance of recognizing that good as one that may well be God's reason for permitting the suffering in question, thus reducing the need for God to attend to us directly, providing us with special assurances and explanations of why the suffering (or his permission of it) is necessary for some good.

35. Theists may say that there are special reasons applying to God, but not to loving parents, that prevent him from making his loving concern for our sufferings apparent to us, thus adding a further epicycle to the theistic response to evil. Tough-minded theists may insist that it is human perversity itself that prevents God from responding to human suffering in the way the loving parent responds to her child's suffering. Tender-minded theists may say that our freedom in relation to God would be destroyed if he were not to remain hidden during our times of apparently pointless travail and suffering. For helpful discussions of questions concerning the hiddenness of God, see Daniel Howard-Snyder, "The Argument from Divine Hiddenness" and John Schellenberg, *Divine Hiddenness and Human Reason* (Ithaca: Cornell University Press, 1993).

36. I have critically discussed Alston's essay in Rowe, "William Alston on the Problem of Evil," in *The Rationality of Belief and the Plurality of Faiths,* ed. Thomas D. Senor (Ithaca: Cornell University Press, 1994). A good bit of my discussion here is taken from that paper.

37. For an examination of his discussion of other theodicies that emphasize a good not restricted to the sufferer, see my essay "William Alston on the Problem of Evil."

38. For a brief discussion of this point, see my essay "Ruminations about Evil," 74-76.

39. Thus, it seems to me that the free-will theodicy needs to be included within something like Hick's soul-making theodicy, a theodicy that stresses some intrinsic goods for which free will is a necessary condition.

40. One might argue that were God to intervene in Sue's case He would have to intervene in every similar case, with the result that no human being would be free to do evil acts of the kind represented by Sue. I respond to an argument of this sort in connection with Alston's discussion of the theodicy that rests on the need for the world to operate in accordance with relatively stable laws of nature. See "William Alston on the Problem of Evil."

41. For comments on earlier drafts of this chapter, I am grateful to Martin Curd, Paul Draper, William Gustason, Bruce Russell, Dan Howard-Snyder, Eleonore Stump, William Wainwright, and David Widerker.

15.

DANIEL HOWARD-SNYDER

The Argument from Inscrutable Evil

But there are the children, and what am I to do about them? That's a question I can't answer. For the hundredth time I repeat, there are numbers of questions, but I've only taken the children, because in their case what I mean is so unanswerably clear. Listen! . . . what have the children to do with it, tell me, please?[1]

§1 Inscrutable Evil

1. Only those lacking moral sensibilities, or those with twisted views of providence, could fail to feel the anguish apparent in Ivan Karamazov's question. At least when most of us reflect on each of the particular horrors he describes— e.g., the boy eaten alive by the general's hunting hounds or the girl habitually beaten, thrashed, and kicked by her parents "until her body was one bruise," or some other brutal, debilitating, and undeserved evil—we find ourselves frustrated, unable to grasp what reasons God would have for permitting innocent children to suffer. As Ivan puts it, "it is beyond all comprehension that they should suffer." Their suffering is, in a word, *inscrutable*.

An argument frequently found on the lips of atheists lurks nearby. We might put it like this: "If God exists, He *must* have some reason for permitting, e.g., the boy to be eaten alive by the general's hounds. But no reason we know of justifies his permitting that evil. So it is very likely that there is no God." But *must* God have a reason to permit *that* evil, if He exists?

Suppose God has a reason to permit that particular boy to be eaten alive at some time and place or other. Must He also have a reason to permit him to be eaten alive, *then and there,* at that particular time and place, rather than some other time and place? Of course, He might have such a reason. Perhaps God's purposes call for the boy to suffer right then and there. But *must* He have such a reason? I can't see why. Indeed, to suppose He must is like supposing that in addition to having a reason to allow her team to play, a scrupulous basketball coach must also have a reason to allow her team to play *now* on *that* court, which is plainly false.

Now let's suppose God has a reason to permit some people or other to be eaten alive, undeservedly. Must He also have a reason to permit *that boy* to be eaten alive? Again, He might have such a reason. Perhaps there is no better way for His purposes to be fulfilled. But *must* He have a reason to permit *him* rather than, say, his sister, who is equally undeserving? Surely not. To suppose He must is like supposing that in addition to having a reason to permit her players to sprain their ankles, our scrupulous coach must also have a reason to permit *Joshua* to sprain his ankle, which is not true.

Now let's suppose that God has a reason to permit people to undergo intense, debilitating and undeserved suffering. Must He also have a reason to permit them to be *eaten alive* when they have done nothing to deserve it? Again, He might have such a reason in a particular case. But *must* He? Think of it this way. Suppose there are discrete, narrowly circumscribed, comparable sorts of undeserved horrific evil, natural kinds, if you will: being eaten alive, being burned to death, suffering from fatal leukemia, and so on. For each kind, must God have a reason to permit an instance of *that kind* rather than some other kind? I can't see why. To suppose He must is like supposing that in addition to having a reason to permit her players to injure themselves, our scrupulous coach must also have a reason to permit them to sprain their ankles, another to twist their knees, another to break their fingers, and so on, which is clearly false.

It seems, therefore, that God need not have a reason to permit the boy to be eaten alive *then and there;* nor must He have reason to permit *the boy* to be eaten alive; nor must He have a reason to permit anyone to be *eaten alive.* As astonishing as it initially sounds, God need not have a reason to permit *that* evil, in any natural sense in which the demonstrative "*that* evil" might be used.

2. Perhaps the reader will think that I have attacked a straw man. No philosophically sophisticated atheist asserts of any particular evil that God must have a reason to permit *it,* rather than some other particular evil. Rather, she will say that if God exists, then some good justifies Him in permitting *that evil or some equally bad or worse evil.*[2]

But even this sophisticated appeal to particular horrors far exceeds its warrant. That's because it presupposes a highly questionable thesis, namely, that there is an amount of horrific evil whose permission is sufficient for the realization of God's purposes in permitting such evil and such that slightly less would not do. To see that this appeal to particular horrors depends on this presupposition, suppose it is false. That is, suppose that there is *no* amount of horrific evil whose permission is sufficient for the realization of God's purposes and such that slightly less would not do. Now, surely God justifiably permits some, perhaps even a good deal of, horrific evil.[3] It follows that each particular horror has this feature, call it *R*: God could have prevented it without forfeiting any good, and if He has prevented it, He need not have permitted some other comparably bad evil in order that His purposes might have been achieved. Then the fact that the boy's being eaten alive has R would not entail that God does not justifiably permit it. That is, *if* there is *no* amount of horrific evil God would have to permit in order for His purposes to be realized and such that slightly less would not do, then it is *false* that, for any particular horror, if God exists, some good justifies Him in permitting it or some equally bad or worse evil. So the sophisticated appeal to particular horrors depends on the presupposition in question.

What should we make of this presupposition? In an attempt to answer the question, consider how it might be used in other contexts. For example, imagine someone arguing like this: "We can't see how any good we know of justifies the state in imposing *that* minute of Jim Bakker's jail sentence, *or some minute of equally bad or worse punishment*. After all, the state could have prevented that minute without forfeiting any good for which it imposes jail sentences for fraud, and it need not have permitted any other minute or comparably bad punishment in order that its purposes in imposing jail sentences for fraud to succeed. So, very likely, no good justifies the state in keeping Bakker in jail for that minute, or some comparably bad minute." How should one sympathetic with the state respond to this argument? Surely like this. You presuppose that there is an amount of jail time sufficient for the state's purpose in imposing penalties on fraud and such that slightly less would not do. But doubtless, some goods (e.g., deterrence) justify the state in imposing some time in jail for fraud, perhaps even a good deal of time. Thus, each minute of any particular jail sentence has this feature, call it R': the state could have prevented it without forfeiting any good, and if the state had prevented it, it (the state) need not have permitted some other minute of comparably bad punishment in order that its purposes might have been achieved. Hence, the face that *that* minute of Jim Bakker's jail sentence has R' does not entail that the state does not justifiably permit it. That is, it is *false* that if the state is a perfect administrator of justice informed by mercy, then some good justifies it in permitting that minute, or some minute of comparably bad punishment.[4]

We must be careful not to generalize hastily here. Just because it seems obvious that, in some cases, there is no amount of suffering sufficient for someone's purposes in permitting it and such that slightly less would not do does not mean that every case is like that. We need not, however, draw such a conclusion to feel troubled about the sophisticated appeal to particular horrors. For if we are to endorse that strategy reasonably, we will need some good reason to presuppose that God's purposes in permitting horrific evil *must* be such that there *is* an amount of horrific evil God would have to permit in order for His purposes in permitting such evil to be realized and slightly less would not do. I, for one, am less than sanguine about the prospects for articulating such a reason.

Lest I be misunderstood, let me underscore that I have *not* claimed that there is no amount of horrific evil God would have to permit in order for His purposes to be realized such that slightly less would not do; nor have I claimed that it is false that, for each particular horror, if God exists, then some good justifies Him in permitting it or some equally bad or worse evil. Rather, I think that if one says that, for each particular horror, God exists only if some good justifies Him in permitting it or some equally bad or worse evil, then, on pain of inconsistency, one must also say that there is an amount of horrific evil God would have to permit in order for His purposes to be realized such that slightly less would not do. But, since we have no idea whether the latter is true, we have no idea whether the former is true. Thus, we should not use the former as a premise in an argument from evil, as do Rowe, Russell, and others who appeal to particular horrors.

3. I can imagine the following response to this line of thought: "The atheist need not appeal to particular horrors. They are not essential to her argument. They merely serve to illustrate the kind of evil *the amount of which* is not justifiably permitted by God: the sort of especially destructive and debilitating undeserved suffering that makes us cringe when we see the starving on television, visit a children's hospital, or dwell on what it was like in the Nazi camps and adjacent medical wards. While the appeal to particular horrors is a red herring, the appeal to the amount of horrific evil most certainly is not. For even if there is no smallest amount of horrific evil God had to permit in order to achieve His purposes, if He could have achieved those purposes with *a lot* less than there is, then surely He would have. To suppose otherwise is like supposing that if there is no smallest number of minutes that sufficed for the state's purposes in imposing jail sentences for fraud, then it would justifiably lock up Bakker for twelve consecutive life sentences." I concur wholeheartedly.

Call the argument latent in this response the *Argument from Inscrutable Evil:*

I. We cannot see how any good we know of justifies God in permitting so much horrific evil rather than a lot less.
So, it is quite likely that
Q. No good justifies God in permitting so much horrific evil rather than a lot less.
M. If God exists, then some good justifies Him in permitting so much horrific evil rather than a lot less.
So, it is quite likely that there is no God.[5]

What should we make of this argument? M is necessarily true. But why believe I? And why think that the inference from I to Q is reasonable?

4. The best reason to believe I is this. God has a reason to permit so much horrific evil rather than a lot less only if there is some sufficiently weighty good that could not be realized if He permitted a lot less. But each sufficiently good state of affairs we can think of—call them *theodical goods*—is such that we cannot see how

it would fail to be realized if God permitted a lot less horrific evil. To see this, consider some significant amount of horrific evil. Perhaps this will do. Read Martin Gilbert's *The Holocaust,* Raul Hilberg's *The Destruction of the European Jews,* and Robert Jay Lifton's *The Nazi Doctors* to get a sense of the repugnance and the enormity of the suffering and evil involved in the Nazis' attempt to purge Eastern Europe of "non-Aryans." Read Elie Wiesel's *Night* for a firsthand account of what it was like for one of the "lucky ones," a survivor of Auschwitz and Buchenwald. Much of the suffering of the victims of the Holocaust was undeserved and so horrifyingly evil that it defies adequate description.

One might agree with this last judgment yet object that, compared to the suffering of all creatures throughout time, the amount the Holocaust victims suffered is very little, a mere drop in a vast ocean of evil. Hence, in permitting *that much* more suffering, God is not permitting *a lot* more. But here we must remember that whether an amount of suffering is "a lot" depends not only on how much suffering there is all told but also on the kind of thing it is. Mindful of this second measure, we cannot doubt that the amount of suffering experienced by the Holocaust victims, the amount of sheer evil perpetrated at that place and time, was a lot.

Now, God could have prevented a lot of horrific evil by preventing the Holocaust. (But He need not have. He could have exercised His providence here and there over the course of a few millennia to prevent roughly the same amount.) Had He done so, would some sufficiently great good have been prevented or objectionably reduced? For example, would our having a significant say about the sorts of people we become have been prevented, or would the degree to which we have such power been objectionably reduced? I cannot see how. The perpetrators still would have had it in their power to abuse, maim, hate, and kill in a variety of other more mundane circumstances. And similarly for the victims and observers: they too would have had plenty of opportunity to respond virtuously to the vicissitudes and hardships of a mundane life even if God had prevented the Holocaust. (I suspect that any temptation to think otherwise betrays the false belief that having a significant say about the sorts of persons we become is an all-or-nothing affair: either we have complete control over the matter or we have none. This is not only false—having a significant say about the sorts of persons we become is a matter of degree—it also contradicts Christian doctrine. The Church teaches that the Holy Spirit restrains evildoers and assists those who wish to receive God's grace, even though each of us who has a say about it is responsible for the sort of person they become.) So how would our having a significant say about the sorts of persons we become have been prevented or objectionably reduced if God had prevented the Holocaust? I cannot see how. I just don't see it. And the same goes for other theodical goods, including their conjunction. The atheist, I think, is right: every theodical good we know of is such that we cannot see how it would fail to be realized if God permitted a lot less horrific evil. That is, I is true. There is inscrutable evil.

4. I frequently hear four objections to the Argument from Inscrutable Evil. (i) "The phrase 'so much horrific evil rather than a lot less' is too vague to be of any use." Vague it is, but its use is no more objectionable in I than the analogous phrase is in the claim that we can't see how a father's purposes in grounding his

daughter for coming in late require that he ground her for four hundred consecutive days rather than a lot less. (ii) "If we cannot see how any reason we know of
justifies God in permitting a lot less horrific evil, then we cannot see how any reason we know of justifies God in permitting any horrific evil *at all,* which, as you've
said, is false." But that's like supposing that if we cannot see how any reason justifies a father in giving his three-year-old daughter forty lashes for running across a
busy street, then we cannot see how any reason justifies disciplining her at all. (iii)
"We cannot, upon any amount of reflection, *just see* how all those goods we know
of could be realized even if God permitted a lot less horrific evil. For all we know,
that suffering is necessary, in ways we don't know of, for the realization of some
familiar goods." Although some atheists sometimes assume that they can just see
such things, the atheist need not say that we can "just see" how all those goods we
know of could be realized even if God permitted a lot less horrific evil. She need
only claim that *we are unable to see* how permitting a lot less would *not* be enough
in order for those goods we know of to be realized. (iv) "If God had prevented the
Holocaust, He would have deceived us. He would have made it appear that sin did
not lead to destruction and suffering." But our sinful condition would have been
apparent even if God had prevented the Holocaust. To suppose otherwise is like
supposing that our condition is not now apparent if, unbeknownst to us, God in
His gracious providence won't allow an all-out global nuclear war.

M and I are the only premises. They are both true. That leaves the infer-
ence from I to Q, or as I shall call it, *the inference from inscrutable to pointless evil.* The
Argument from Inscrutable Evil hangs on whether this inference is reasonable. Is
it? I shall examine six reasons for thinking it is.

§2 Reasons Why Inscrutable Evil Justifies Belief in Pointless Evil

1. "Suppose we look all around Washington State and find no blue crows.
If we have good reason to believe that the crows we have seen constitute a representative sample of the state's population of crows, then we rightly infer that it is
very likely that there are no blue crows, unless we have comparable reason to
believe that some blue crows cannot be detected by us. Do we have good reason
to believe that the crows we have seen constitute a representative sample? Of
course. For in looking all around the state, we have conducted a search that is relevant to finding blue crows. Thus, since we have no good reason to believe there
are undetectable blue crows, we should infer that, very likely, there are no blue
crows in Washington. Similarly, we have conducted an appropriate search for goods
that would justify God in permitting so much horrific evil rather than a lot less but
we have found none. The appropriate search in this case is an intellectual one: trying to think of goods that would justify allowing a certain course of action, talking
to others and reading what has been said about the matter. That search has left us
empty-handed. And we have no reason to think that there are goods outside our
ken that would justify God in permitting so much horrific evil rather than a lot
less. Thus, we have good reason to believe that those goods we know of constitute

a representative sample of all the goods there are. Hence the inference from inscrutable evil to pointless evil is justified."[6]

Reply. Why suppose that looking around Washington is the appropriate search for blue crows? Because that way we will very likely see them if there are any. And why suppose that an intellectual search is the "appropriate" search for goods that would justify God in permitting so much horrific evil rather than a lot less? Surely because by thinking, talking, and reading we will very likely comprehend such God-justifying reasons if there are any. Now, while we have good reason to believe that blue crows are the sorts of things we will see by looking around (without this assumption the analogy is a nonstarter), what reason is given to think that by thinking, talking, and reading about the matter, we will very likely comprehend God-justifying goods, if there were any? None. The fact of the matter is that we have good reason to believe that an intellectual search is the appropriate search for God-justifying goods only if we have good reason to believe that we would very likely comprehend those goods by thinking, talking, and reading about the matter—but the analogy fails at this crucial point. At best, it only highlights what it would take to be justified in believing that the inference from inscrutable to pointless evil is reasonable.

2. "Suppose that even after failing to find a justifying good for God to permit, say, the Holocaust, it is *not* reasonable to infer that there is no such good. What follows? It follows that it is *not* reasonable for us to believe that some human onlooker who could have but did not intervene did something wrong in failing to intervene, even if we can't think of any good that would justify the onlooker in failing to intervene. For, after all, the same good that would justify God in not intervening, were He to exist, *may* be the good for the sake of which the human onlooker should not have intervened. The good beyond our ken that would justify God in allowing the Holocaust *could* be the same good that would justify the onlooker. For all we know, both the onlooker and God had to refrain from intervening for the victims to have union with God or for the perpetrators to develop spiritually. We cannot be justified in rejecting these possibilities for the onlooker not to intervene if we cannot be justified in rejecting them as possibilities for God not to intervene. Moral skepticism about God's omissions entails moral skepticism about our own omissions."[7]

Reply. Note, firstly, that it is false that if some good justifies God's failure to intervene, then it can justify the onlooker's failure to intervene. As Steve Layman pointed out in conversation, whether that's the case depends on what the good is. Some goods—e.g., permitting the wages of human sinfulness to be manifest—are such that they justify God in permitting considerable cruelty even though it is our job to interfere with that cruelty whenever we can. However, the chief trouble is that the argument assumes that we are justified in believing the onlooker behaved wrongly only if we are justified in believing that there is no good beyond our ken that *could* justify her not intervening. But that's surely false. Since the onlooker is one of us, we are familiar with the goods for the sake of which *she* would permit the Holocaust. They are goods we know of. If none of them did the trick, we would rightly infer that she behaved wrongly; she has no moral justification for her failure to intervene. Indeed, even if we were *certain* that there was some good beyond our ken that *could* justify her failure to intervene, we would rightly infer that she behaved wrongly since it would not be for the sake of any good outside our ken that she permitted it. But we wrongly draw the analogous inference about God. We jest if we say that if He existed, since He would be one of us, it is not for the sake of some good outside our ken that He would permit the Holocaust.

3. Suppose that the hypothesis that there is no point better explains inscrutable evil than the theist's hypothesis, the hypothesis that there is a God who, for the sake of some good beyond our ken, permits so much horrific evil rather than a lot less. In that case it is reasonable to think that the inference from inscrutable to pointless evil is justified. But, is this the case?

One might argue for an affirmative answer like this: "It is very likely, even certain, that there would be inscrutable evil given the theist's hypothesis. Thus, inscrutable evil is at least as likely on the theist's hypothesis as it is on the hypothesis that there is no point. Hence, given Bayes's Theorem, we should infer that which of these two competing hypotheses is more likely given inscrutable evil—and hence which is a better explanation of inscrutable evil—hangs entirely on which is more likely *on background evidence*. Since the hypothesis that there is no point seems simpler and so more reasonable to accept than the theist's hypothesis, the hypothesis of pointless evil better explains inscrutable evil than the theist's hypothesis."[8]

Reply. At least three difficulties beset this argument, even if we put aside our worries about the enormously problematic thesis that theism is a theory.

First, the argument is a non sequitur. Since the theist's hypothesis entails the existence of God, it has much more explanatory power than the mere hypothesis that there is no point to inscrutable evil. But let's suppose, for the sake of argument, that the hypothesis of pointless evil is embedded in some competing worldview which is at least as explanatorily powerful as the theist's hypothesis.

The second trouble is that the argument assumes that, all else being equal, of two competing hypotheses the simpler is preferable. What does this mean? In what does the simplicity of a hypothesis consist? And supposing we can settle that question, why think that simplicity is to be preferred? Those who endorse this argument don't even bother to gesture toward answers to these questions; indeed, they don't even raise the questions. This is unconscionable, given the attention that simplicity as a criterion of theory choice has received in the latter half of this century.[9] Let's look into the matter for a moment. Let's say that hypothesis h1 is simpler than hypothesis h2 if and only if were h1 true, then there would be fewer entities per se, fewer kinds of entities, and mathematically simpler modes of behavior between them, than if h2 were true. And let's leave aside worries about what mathematical simplicity is, and whether and how these criteria ought to be weighted.[10] Views of the value or preferability of simplicity divide over whether simplicity is truth-conducive. The tradition has it that the simple is the sign of the true. Hence, of two hypotheses, all else being equal, the simpler is more likely to be true. But why believe this? The best argument I've seen is that the simpler hypothesis will, so to speak, assert that there are fewer things, and the more things that you quantify over the more likely you are to make a mistake. This is a bad argument. For if it is the case that the more things you quantify over the more likely it is that you are mistaken, then the proposition that there is nothing is, a priori, more likely to be true than the proposition that there is something. But that is false. Only one possible world has nothing and infinitely many have something—the sheer statistical unlikelihood that there be nothing renders it much less likely that there be nothing than that there be something. Indeed, we have here not only the refutation of an argument for the claim that the simple is the sign of the true; we have a positive argument against it![11] Perhaps whether the simple is the sign of the true is not to be decided a priori. But in that case, it seems that whether, all else being equal, the simpler hypothesis is more likely to be true depends on the way the world is. If there are many things, you would be ill-advised to choose a theory that says there are few things over a theory that says there are many, at least if you wish to choose a true theory.

But perhaps we're thinking of simplicity incorrectly. Most philosophers of science these days regard simplicity as an intrinsic value that, in part, defines the goals of science. It is not valuable because it is truth-conducive but because the simpler hypothesis is more "pleasing to the mind" than its competitors, as Copernicus is reported to have said, or because it is more intelligible to us. But if we understand the value of simplicity in these ways, then even if the hypothesis of pointless evil is simpler than the theist's hypothesis, that fact is irrelevant to our concerns. We want to be justified in *believing* that the hypothesis of pointless evil is more likely than the theist's hypothesis given inscrutable evil. That a proposition is more pleasing or intelligible to us only justifies our preferring it to be true. To think otherwise is to imply that, all else being equal, a religion is less likely to be true than its denial if it postulates that we are ruined creatures unable to fix ourselves on our own, or if it postulates that some of the Deity's nature and some of his ways are beyond our capacity to fathom. This is manifestly absurd. At any rate, even if these nonalethic conceptions of the value of simplicity do not render the comparative simplicity of the theist's hypothesis and the hypothesis of pointlessness irrelevant to our concerns, it isn't clear that the latter is more simple *in these senses* than the former. The theist's hypothesis and its implications provide me and many others with a source of great comfort and aesthetic delight, whereas the hypothesis of pointless evil and its implications are deeply disturbing and ugly. Moreover we have no difficulty understanding why it is that smart humans know more than their cognitively deficient friends; hence, the idea that an omniscient being has purposes outside our ken is just as intelligible an explanation for inscrutable evil as that there are no such purposes.

In short, I doubt that the simple is the sign of the true. And, if it is not, then either the simplicity of a hypothesis is irrelevant to assessing whether the hypothesis of pointless evil better explains inscrutable evil than the theist's hypothesis or the former is no more simple than the latter.

The third, and most important, problem is that the argument under discussion gives inscrutable evil a very minor role to play. Indeed, it relegates it to the mere status of an occasion to consider whether theism better explains its domain than its competitors. Of course, we didn't need inscrutable evil to consider that question! Moreover, proponents of arguments from evil typically think that certain facts about evil suffice for a high degree of justified atheistic belief. The explanatory argument given on behalf of the inference from inscrutable to pointless evil makes the argument hang on a slew of other considerations that have nothing to do with evil. Inscrutable evil becomes, at best, only a small part, a very small part, in the overall case for atheism, certainly insufficient for justified atheistic belief.[12]

Let's look at some more promising strategies. Some people suggest that our belief that Q is justified *not* on the basis of I but on the basis of

> P. No reason we know of justifies God in permitting so much horrific evil rather than a lot less.

I and P are not the same claim. I says that *we cannot see how* any reason we know of justifies God; P says that *in fact* no reason we know of does the trick. Whether I is a good reason to believe P or whether belief in P is otherwise justified I shall set aside.[13] Suppose P is true. Does P justify our believing Q?

4. "The inference from P to Q is justified, since it is like the many justified inferences we constantly make from the known to the unknown. If we observe many A's and they are all B's, then, lacking reason in any particular case to doubt the inference, we justifiedly infer that all A's are B's."[14]

Reply. Suppose we have no special reason to doubt the inference from P to Q. Does it follow that we justifiedly believe Q on the basis of P? Arguably not. Universal generalizations are risky business. It takes very little to err. That's why we teach our introductory students that universal generalizations are justified only if we have good reason to believe that the observed A's are strongly representative of all A's. Without good reason to believe that the sample is representative of the entire population or that we very likely know all of the A's, we rightly resist the temptation to generalize. At best, this argument shows the sort of think that is needed in order to be justified in believing Q on the basis of P. The next two arguments attempt to fill that gap.

5. "(1) The goods for the sake of which God permits human suffering involve the conscious experiences of the sufferers. (2) We know the conscious experiences of the sufferers. (3) So, if such goods occur, we would quite likely know them now. (4) So, P makes Q quite likely."[15]

Reply. Two worries arise. First, premise (1) is suspect. God might well permit human suffering for the sake of goods that have nothing to do with the sufferer's conscious experience, or for the sake of goods whose goodness consists in the conscious experience of all humans, indiscriminately, not just the sufferers. Second, waiving that worry, to assess this argument properly, we must distinguish *good-tokens,* instances or occurrences, from *good-types,* kinds of goods, and conscious experience *tokens* from conscious experience *types.* Clearly, the argument is about good-types and types of conscious experience; otherwise, premise (2) would be false: there are too many tokenings of conscious experience for any of us to know even a fraction of them. So we must read (2) as "We know the types of conscious experience of the sufferers." But in that case, the lack of explicit quantifiers in (2) raises some nontrivial questions: How many of the types of conscious experience that humans *can* enjoy do we know of? A few? Half? The vast majority? All? Are the ones we *do* know of representative of the whole lot? Are there goods outside our ken that would be or could just as well be realized in an afterlife? These are not triflied worries. Without answers, we unjustifiedly affirm (2).

6. "We would rightly infer that P makes Q quite likely if we had good reason to think that, all things considered, it is very unlikely that there are goods other than the ones, we know of. Here's such a reason: (1) Only a minuscule number of states of affairs that human beings have discovered over the course of their history are good in themselves, and (2) in the past 3,000 years no intrinsic goods have been discovered. So, (3) it is improbable in the extreme that there are intrinsic goods other than those we know of."[16]

Reply. This argument assumes that intrinsic goods come in rather "thick" conceptual slices, so that they are countable and very few have been discovered in a very long time. However, if intrinsic goods are better conceived as very "thinly" sliced, then (1) and (2) are dubious. But set aside this trifle.[17] Suppose (1) and (2) are both true. Do they warrant an inference to (3)? That all depends.

Consider the following speculative sketch of the development of our species' ability to conceive of good states of affairs: "After the Mesozoic and Caenozoic eras, *Homo erectus* followed Australopithecus to be succeeded by Pre-Mousterian man between 100,000–200,000 B.C. The remarkable thing about the brain in *Homo sapiens* was that with its development came a capacity hitherto unpossessed by any terrestrial creature: a capacity to conceive of some states of affairs as good and others as bad. The development of this capacity was slow and halting. Late in his career, Neanderthal man developed a tendency to have pleasant feelings and proto-proattitudes when he thought of things he was attracted to, and their opposite when he thought of things he was averse to. And here our development remained for many millennia. Not until around 50,000–70,000 B.C. did a terrestrial creature consciously move from the thought 'I don't like it' to the thought 'That sort of thing is bad,' hence that if an action led to pain, that was a reason not to do it. (Given the appropriate changes, similarly for pleasure.) Here again, though, another gap in our moral development occurred. It wasn't until about 35,000–40,000 B.C. that *Homo sapiens* was able to divorce the concept of the good from pleasure and the concept of the bad from pain, but, with this break the possibility of generalizing the concepts of good and bad was realized. It wasn't long before it was recognized that the natural necessity to band in groups was not only conducive to survival, but offered something that often involved pleasure, but was more than or beside that. Somewhere near 28,000 B.C. friendship was conceived and recognized as good, and loneliness bad. Then, near 22,000 B.C. an alarming incidence of intergroup conflict and subsequent slavery of war prisoners brought *Homo sapiens* to form the concept of freedom and soon after to recognize its value and the disvalue of unwanted force and coercion. Near this time, the concepts of truth and falsity were also honed, and something quite like that contrast was dimly recognized. By about 17,000 B.C. the distinction between what is reasonable and what is not was fully conceived, the former recognized at its best in knowledge. During this period, *Homo sapiens* also began to recognize various attitudes and dispositions as conducive to strong familial and communal bonds—courage, honesty, and kindness, for example. Only later, though, about 13,000 B.C., did some members of the species recognize fidelity and respect for proper authority as good things, and trained their young to recognize them too. A great stagnancy in the discovery of goods followed this period. It took the innovative minds of early Greek, Indian, and broadly Asian civilizations—circa 8,000 B.C.—to conceive of and articulate the goodness of temperance, proper pride, shame, justice, and piety, and the badness of incontinence, self-abasement, shamelessness, injustice, and impiety. And it wasn't until some 2,000–3,000 years ago that the goodness of selfless charity and humility were clearly discerned, as well as the badness of lust and avarice. Most members of the species have yet to catch on to these latest developments."

Call this speculative archaeology of value "the Story." I have no idea whether the Story is true. But one notable feature it has is that, if it is true, the discovery of what is good by our ancestors spanned tens of thousands of years dotted with millennia-long gaps when nothing new was learned. (Substitute your own story, provided it has this feature.) Do we have any reason to doubt the Story? Certainly not a priori. There is no reason to suppose that our concepts of good states of affairs come in a tightly bound package so that we can't have one without having them all. (In this connection we might also reflect on the development in a child's awareness of goods). Do we have some reason a posteriori to doubt the Story? Not that I know of. What skeletal remains, relics, cave drawings and manuscripts we have provide no reason at all to believe that the ability of *Homo sapiens* to conceive of what is good did not involve sporadic, lengthy progress, although certainly *some* development took place. Indeed, given that the human brain evolved over tens of thousands of years, and given that with that development arose the capacity to conceive of various goods, we should only expect something like the Story to be true. At least, given what we have to go on in the way of archaeological and paleontological data, it would not be surprising if a progression of the sort indicated by the Story occurred.

This modest observation is relevant to the argument under discussion. Not only do we have no reason to doubt the Story; it is neither laughable nor ad hoc nor incompatible with or unlikely given premises (1) and (2). But most importantly, the conjunction of (1), (2), and the Story entails the *denial* of the conclusion of the argument. (Moreover, as Frances Howard-Snyder mentioned to me, at best, the argument under consideration only shows that we have already discovered all the intrinsic goods we are *presently capable* of discovering, just as, say, cats have already discovered all the intrinsic goods that they are presently capable of discovering.) In that case, we should not infer that it is "improbable in the extreme" that there are goods other than the ones we know of. The better part of wisdom seems to be that we should withhold judgment on the matter.

§3 A Warning against Level Confusions

1. Suppose there is no reason to think the inference from I or P to Q is justified. We might infer that we cannot justifiedly believe in pointless evil on the

basis of (I) or (P). For, after all, we justifiedly believe *p* only if we justifiedly believe that *our belief that p is justified on g* (our grounds for believing p), and this we do not justifiedly believe in this case.

We must be cautious here. We must not confuse the conditions for justifiedly believing a lower-level proposition *p* with the conditions for justifiedly believing its higher-level sibling, *our belief that p is justified*. Arguably, we cannot justifiedly believe *our belief that p is justified* unless we have good reason to believe *our belief that p is justified on g*. But if we cannot justifiedly believe the lower-level *p* unless we have good reason to believe *our belief that p is justified on g*, wholesale skepticism looms large.[18]

For, firstly, we justifiedly believe *our belief that p is justified on g* only if we justifiedly believe that some justification relation, R, holds between g and p. Epistemologists disagree about what R is, but everyone agrees that the expression of it involves some considerably sophisticated concepts and some, namely, process reliabilists, say that it involves an extremely complicated (and as yet unknown) story about how we acquire information about the world. But if we must have a grip on some pretty sophisticated concepts or if we must understand the information-processing capacities of the human brain in order to believe justifiedly that *our belief that p is justified on g,* then only the conceptually sophisticated elite or (future) neuroscientists and empirical psychologists would justifiedly believe the most mundane lower level propositions. Secondly, we justifiedly believe *our belief that p is justified on g* only if we justifiedly believe *g bears R to p*. Since we don't justifiedly believe propositions of the form *g bears R to p* without grounds, the condition in question applies to our grounds for believing it, call it *g1*. Thus, we must justifiedly believe that *g1 bears R to "g bears R to p."* It is evident that the reiterative nature of the principle in question entails that we must have infinitely many beliefs right now to believe justifiedly the most mundane matters. It also entails that we must believe indefinitely many propositions the entertaining of each of which would require more time than there is between now and when the physical universe will collapse in on itself again. And herein lies the worry: we are finite creatures. We are unable to grasp infinitely many propositions in a moment since we cannot take them all in at once; and no one has enough time to take them in one at a time, so to speak. Moreover, none of us has the time to grasp a proposition the entertaining of which would require a lifespan much longer than the age of the universe. But, of course, we cannot believe what we cannot grasp. Thus, possessing infinite many beliefs and believing very "long" propositions are beyond our powers. If such powers are required to justifiedly believe something, then none of us is ever justified in believing anything.[19]

Perhaps we can make sense of our having infinitely many beliefs if we distinguish occurrent from nonoccurrent beliefs. One has the nonoccurrent belief that *p* if one is disposed to affirm *p* upon entertaining it. Thus, even if we have only a finite mental capacity, we can have infinitely many nonoccurrent beliefs because we are disposed to affirm infinitely many propositions.

Two problems arise for this argument. First, we must distinguish dispositionally believing something from possessing a disposition to affirm something. I might well fail to believe something even though I am disposed to affirm it. When

I was six, I would have affirmed that you have a nose on your face, had I been asked, but I may not have believed it (e.g., I may not have known of you). Second, even if nonoccurrent beliefs are dispositions to affirm propositions, it does not follow that we can have infinitely many beliefs *of the sort in question:* indefinitely many of them will be so "long" that we simply could not be disposed to affirm them—we would die before we finished trying to entertain them![20]

To avoid the skeptical consequences of the epistemic requirement in question, we must *not* say that we justifiedly believe Q on the basis of I or P only if we justifiedly believe that *our belief that Q is justified on I or P;* at least we must not say this on the basis of a *general* requirement of the sort I have been criticizing.

2. My hedging here raises an important question: is it arguable that the move from I or P to Q is an instance of a special sort of inference, one that *does* require that one justifiedly believe that *one's belief that Q is justified on I or P?* Perhaps. We know that universal generalizations are quite risky. It takes just one unknown x or one unknown A that is B to err. Without anything else to go on— e.g., that the goods we know of are representative—this fact arguably undermines whatever justification the inference from I or P to Q might otherwise have. Thus, to defeat this underminer one might urge that we must justifiedly believe that *our belief that Q is justified on I or P.* If that is right, epistemic standards ordinarily applicable only to higher level propositions arguably apply to the lower level Q.

If we accept the argument of the preceding paragraph, then, given the paucity of reason to think belief in Q is justified on the basis of I or P, we might stop right here. But that would be to quit prematurely. Perhaps one day someone will construct a reason to believe that the inference from I or P to Q is justified. Then, barring defeaters, the inference will be fully justified. It behooves those who care to prepare for the day! More importantly, perhaps, it is of interest not only to consider what can be said for the inference but also what can be said against it.

I now return to my focus on the inference from I to Q. What follows applies, mutatis mutandis, to the inference from P to Q.

§4 *Inscrutable Evil Does Not Justify Belief in Pointless Evil*

1. If we can show that some necessary condition on justifiedly inferring pointless evil from inscrutable evil is not met, we will have reason to reject the inference. Consider this candidate: I justifies believing Q only if we have no good reason to be in doubt about whether I would very likely be false, if Q were false. That is, the inference from inscrutable to pointless evil is justified only if we have no good reason to be in doubt about whether, if some reason justified God in permitting so much horrific evil rather than a lot less, we would quite likely see how it justified Him. This condition on justifiedly believing Q on I is an instance of the epistemic principle that

> EP. *We cannot see an x* justifies believing *there is no x* only if we have no good reason to be in doubt about whether we would very likely see x, if there were one.

(Don't confuse "to be *in* doubt about" with "to doubt that.") What should we make of EP?

Its initial plausibility can be illustrated by its ability to explain our commonsense judgments about many cases. Looking out your study window in broad daylight, you cannot see any rabbits in the freshly mown field across the street. Are you justified in believing there are none there? No. The field is large and rabbits are small and their coloring blends with the color of hay. You have good reason to be in doubt about whether you would see a rabbit in the field even if one were there. Or, imagine a student who, inspired by your first-day lecture, actually does the next day's reading. He comes across that dense passage in the *Euthyphro* that begins: "But if the god-beloved and the pious were the same, and the pious were loved because it was pious, then. . ." He hasn't the foggiest idea what Socrates is getting at. Even so, he should not infer that these sentences have no sense. For he knows that he is new to philosophy and unfamiliar with the context in which Socrates speaks. This constitutes good reason to be in doubt about whether he would discern the meaning of the text even if it did make sense. EP nicely explains our intuitions about such cases.

While this is some endorsement of EP, such data underdetermine theory; it would be nice if EP were supported by some more basic principles to which we are wed. Happily, it is. We all agree that if we have good reason to be in doubt about whether the basis of our belief makes what we believe very likely, then given that the reason is weighty enough, any justification our belief might have otherwise had on that basis is undermined. Thus, if we have good reason to be in doubt about whether *we cannot see an x* makes *there is no x* quite likely, our belief that *there is no x* will not be justified on that basis. Of course, *we cannot see an x* makes *there is no x* quite likely only if we would quite likely see an x if there were one. It follows that we have good reason to be in doubt about whether *we cannot see an x* makes *there is no x* quite likely if we have good reason to be in doubt about whether we would quite likely see an x if there were one.

2. Thus, a question confronts us: do we have sufficient reason to be in doubt about whether I would very likely be false if Q were false?

Keep in mind here that we have no reason at all to think that we would very likely be able to grasp the good for the sake of which God permitted so much horrific evil rather than a lot less. Thus, it will take relatively little to be rightly in doubt about the matter. Moreover, we need to remember the oft-mentioned point that compared to God's, our cognitive powers are quite limited. If there were goods outside our ken, He would have access to them. And if they were great enough to justify the permission of so much horrific evil rather than a lot less, it would hardly be surprising if His purposes involved them. Our question, then, is this: have we reason to suppose that there are goods of which we are ignorant and, if so, have we reason to suppose that they would be good enough to figure in God's purposes in permitting horrific evil? Aside from good reason to think God exists, we do not have sufficient reason to suppose that *there are* goods outside our ken; nor do we have sufficient reason to think that if there were goods of which we are ignorant, they *would be* good enough to figure in God's purposes. What we do have, though, is sufficient reason to think that it would not be surprising if there were goods outside our ken and that if there were such, it would not be surprising if they were good enough to figure in God's purposes. At least two arguments are relevant here.

The Progress Argument. Knowledge has progressed in a variety of fields of inquiry, especially the physical sciences. The periodic discovery of previously unknown aspects of reality strongly suggests that there will be further progress of a similar sort. Since future progress implies present ignorance, it is very likely that there is a good deal of which we are now ignorant. Now, what we have to go on in charting the progress of axiological discovery by our ancestors is meager, to say the least. Indeed, given the scant archaeological evidence we have, and given paleontological evidence regarding the evolutionary development of the brain in *Homo sapiens,* it would not be surprising at all that humans discovered various intrinsic goods over tens of thousands of years dotted by millennia-long gaps in which nothing was discovered. (Recall the point of "the Story" in §2.6.) Hence, given what we have to go on, it would not be surprising if there has been the sort of periodic progress that strongly suggests that there remain goods to be discovered. Thus it would not be surprising if there are goods of which we are ignorant, goods of which God (if such there be) would not be ignorant. Moreover, nothing we reasonably believe rules out the possibility that there are goods outside our ken; and nothing we reasonably believe rules out the possibility that some of them actually obtain, or will obtain, and that if we fully grasped them, we would clearly see that they justify God's permission of so much horrific evil rather than a lot less.

The Argument from Complexity. One thing that Mozart's Violin Concerto No. 4, Ste. Michele's Cabernet Sauvignon (Reserve), and the best sort of love have in common when compared to "Chopsticks," Boone's Hill wine, and puppy love is that each illustrates the fact that the goodness of a state of affairs is *sometimes* greater, in part, because it is more complex. Now, since horrific evil is so bad, it would take correspondingly greater goods to justify God's permitting so much of it rather than a lot less. Hence, it would not be surprising if God's reasons for permitting so much horrific evil rather than a lot less have to do with goods whose complexity is beyond our grasp.

These arguments *jointly* constitute a good reason to be in doubt about whether it is quite likely that we would discern those goods for the sake of which God permits so much horrific evil rather than a lot less. Thus, in conjunction with EP, we rightly conclude that the inference from inscrutable to pointless evil is not justified.

§5 *Two Objections and a Clarification*

1. "In the Progress Argument, the sort of progress that motivates the inference to the likelihood that there are aspects of reality of which we are ignorant is best seen in the physical sciences. Our knowledge of the physical world has exploded in leaps and bounds over the past four centuries in large part because of technological advances. We have developed telescopes to see into the vast reaches of the cosmos, microscopes to delve into the recesses of the microcosm, particle

accelerators to smash the atom, and so on. Indeed, without these instruments, there would have been little progress in our discovery of black holes, the molecule, the color spectrum, bosons, etc. By refining this technology, progress in the physical sciences was made possible. But there is no analogue to the technology of science in the area of values. And this isn't surprising. Whether something is intrinsically good is a matter of necessity to be discerned by the comprehending intellect, a tool of axiological discovery that was available to the ancients as well as us. That's why intrinsic goods we know were known by ancient Greeks, Chinese, etc. So, there are two crucial disanalogies between the physical sciences, where the sort of inference to ignorance you draw is at its strongest, and the discovery of value."[21]

Reply. This objection fastens on irrelevant features of the analogy between progress in the physical sciences and progress in the discovery of values. The fact that technology is unlike the intellect or that "the ancients" discerned goods we do is beside the point. It is the fact that there has been *periodic* progress that makes it very likely that aspects of physical reality remain to be discovered. Similarly, the fact that it is not surprising if there has been periodic progress in the history of our discovery of value makes it remarkably unsurprising if there is more of value than meets the mind's eye.

2. "The crucial premise in the Argument from Complexity is that value is sometimes a function of complexity. That's surely right, as reflection on the comparative value of a slug and one of us suggests. But why suppose that complexity would hinder us from discerning value? Consider, for example, the value of friendship and love. While we might be able to say a few trite things about our social and emotional needs and our capacities for meeting them, most of us could not begin to articulate what it is about us that makes them possible. But we can still recognize the goodness of friendship and love. So even if we are ill-equipped to grasp very complex states of affairs, that does not render us incapable of grasping their goodness. You are wrong, therefore, to assume that we would be unable to recognize the value of a state of affairs if its complexity exceeded our grasp. Without that assumption, the Argument from Complexity doesn't even get off the ground."

Reply. To begin with, note that while the complexity of a state of affairs *need not* adversely affect our ability to recognize its value, it *can* and *sometimes does*. Of course, I cannot convince you that there are complex states of affairs whose value we fully recognize but whose complexity hinders such recognition by showing you one. Instead I will show that complexity can, and sometimes does, hinder the discernment of value.

First, there is the general phenomenon of the complexity of something hindering our view of some important feature it has, e.g., the complexity of an argument hindering our ability to discern its validity, or the complexity of your opponent's strategy hindering your ability to discern that unless you move your knight to queen's side bishop 5, her next move is checkmate. But, more to the point, why can a child discern the literary merits of a comic book but not *Henry V*? Why can a child clearly discern the aesthetic value of a toffee but not coho salmon served with a lemon-dill sauce, lightly buttered asparagus al dente and a dry riesling? Why can a child recognize the value of his friendship with his buddy next door but not the full value of his parents' love for each other? Surely because *Henry V,* fine cuisine, and adult love involve much more than he is able to comprehend. And this is true of adults as well, as reflection on our progress in understanding the complexity of various things of value reveals. For example, periodically reflecting on the fabric of our relationships with those whom we most love, we might well find strands and shades that when brought to full light permit us to see love as more valuable then we had once thought. If the failure to grasp the more complicated aspects of our relationships can prevent a proper appreciation of love's value, surely the failure to grasp the complexity of a state of affairs might well hinder us from discerning its goodness. For similar reasons an astronomer may appreciate more fully than we the wonders of the night sky, and a chess master the beauty of chess. Value is often veiled in complexity.

   3. The question to which the Progress Argument and the Argument from Complexity are addressed is this: *do we have* good enough reason to be in doubt about whether I would very likely be false if Q were false? Do we have good enough reason to be in doubt about whether it is highly likely that we would grasp the goods for the sake of which God permitted so much horrific evil if indeed there were such goods? A more fundamental question, however, is this: what would *be* good enough reason to be properly in doubt about whether I would very likely be false if Q were false? Certainly this would do: good reason to think that *it is not very likely that I would be false were Q false.* At least three options appear here: reason to believe that, if Q were false, nevertheless, I would very likely be *true,* or reason to believe that if Q were false, I would be *just* as likely to be true as to be false, or reason to believe that I would be *at least* as likely to be true as to be false.[22] We do not, however, need good reason to think that it is not highly likely that I would be false were Q false in order to be properly in doubt about whether I would very likely be false if Q were false. We can rightly be in doubt about the matter even if we have no good reason at all to think that it is *not* highly likely that I would be false were Q false.

   Here's what I have in mind. Imagine that we thoroughly investigate the likelihood of inscrutable evil on the assumption that there is a God-justifying good and we discover that for any argument we consider, countervailing considerations rightly compel us to question the import of that argument. Suppose each of the arguments for concluding that the likelihood of inscrutable evil on not-Q is low are questionable. And suppose that each of the arguments for concluding that the likelihood of inscrutable evil on not-Q is high are questionable. And suppose that each of the arguments for concluding that it is false that the likelihood of inscrutable evil on not-Q is low are questionable. In this last connection, let's suppose that if the Progress Argument works, then we can use an analogue to argue that it would not be surprising if there were undiscovered kinds of evils which, if we knew of them, we would clearly see that they are not justifiably permitted by God. And let us acknowledge that we have no reason to think that there is a lawlike connection between the greatness of a good and the greatness of its complexity. Hence, even if it would not be surprising that a considerable degree of complexity were to attend those goods great enough to justify God, we have no idea how much complexity that might be, whether it would be more or less than the complexity of goods that are within our ken whose complexity does not hinder our discernment of their value. We might think that considerations such as these neutralize the force of the Progress Argument and the Argument from Complexity.[23] Given these suppositions, should we infer that we have no good reason to be in doubt about whether it is highly likely that we would grasp those goods for the sake of which God would permit so much horrific evil rather than a lot less? Should we say that despite our inability to see our way clearly here, we have no good reason to be in doubt about whether I is highly likely to be false if Q is false? Of course not. We should say that we have good reason to be in doubt about whether I would very likely be false if Q were false. I do not mean that we thereby have good reason *to doubt* that I would very likely be false if Q were false, i.e., to think that proposition false. Rather, I mean that if what we have to go on in assessing the likelihood of I on not-Q is so muddy that we don't know what to say about it, then we should be *in doubt* about the matter, and in particular, in doubt about whether I would very likely be false if Q were false. We should confess that given our best efforts, we cannot at this time, with the information we have, judge that the probability of I on not-Q is "high" or "low" or "middling." We should simply admit that we are nonplussed.

§6 A Row-style Bayesian Argument

In "The Evidential Argument from Evil: A Second Look," Rowe uses Bayes's Theorem to argue that "the evidential argument from evil is alive and well."[24] It will be useful to see how my case bears on that version of the evidential argument. Applied to our concerns, Bayes's Theorem says

$$\Pr(Q/I\&k) = \frac{\Pr(Q/k) \times \Pr(I/Q\&k)}{[\Pr(Q/k) \times \Pr(I/Q\&k)] + [\Pr(\text{not-}Q/k) \times \Pr(I/\text{not-}Q\&k)]}$$

We need to assign three values: $\Pr(I/Q\&k)$, $\Pr(Q/k)$, and $\Pr(I/\text{not-}Q\&k)$.

Pr(I/Q&k). If no good justifies God in permitting so much horrific evil rather than a lot less, then no good we know of does the trick. That is, Q entails I. So, $\Pr(I/Q\&k) = 1$.

Pr(Q/k). What value we assign all depends on what is in our background knowledge, k. Alvin Plantinga insists that the theist properly brings to the matter the proposition that God exists. Of course, theism entails not-Q. Thus, if Plantinga is right, the theist properly says that $\Pr(Q/k) = 0$. But let us follow Rowe instead and consider the question in light of the epistemic situation of one who judges that theism and its denial are equiprobable after weighing all the other considerations she has for and against the existence of God. That is, allowing G to stand for "God exists," let us consider the question in light of this assignment of values: $\Pr(G/k) = .5$ and $\Pr(\text{not-}G/k) = .5$. Call this *the agnostic stance.* (This is not the only stance an agnostic can take. He might have no idea what probabilities to assign the different considerations for and against theism, and hence acknowledge that he is in no position to affirm that theism and its denial are equiprobable). Now, suppose we agree with Rowe that G is true if and only if Q is false, and that

$$Pr(Q/k) = [Pr(G/k) \times Pr(Q/G\&k)] + [Pr(not\text{-}G/k) \times Pr(Q/not\text{-}G\&k)].$$

$Pr(G/k) \times Pr(Q/G\&k) = 0$ since G entails not-Q, and thus $Pr(Q/G\&k) = 0$. And, $Pr(not\text{-}G/k) \times Pr(Q/not\text{-}G\&k) = .5$ since not-G&k entails Q, and, from the agnostic stance, $Pr(not\text{-}G/k) = .5$. Thus, $Pr(Q/k) = .5$, and hence $Pr(not\text{-}Q/k) = .5$.

 Pr(I/not-Q&k). The argument of sections 4 and 5 shows that we should be in doubt about whether $Pr(I/not\text{-}Q\&k)$ is low. We just do not have enough to go on to assign a probability. An important question arises: if the agnostic is really in the dark about what value to assign $Pr(I/not\text{-}Q\&k)$, does she reasonably believe Q on the basis of I anyway? The answer is unequivocally negative.[25] From the agnostic stance, the inference from inscrutable to pointless evil is not justified.[26]

7. Inscrutable Evil and the Silence of God

 1. I imagine that something like the following objection will have occurred to the reader: "Suppose we have good reason to be in doubt about whether we would be able to grasp God's purposes in permitting so much horrific evil, if indeed He were justified in doing so. And suppose that if we had nothing else to go on, this fact would undermine whatever justification the inference from inscrutable to pointless evil might have otherwise had. But we do have something else to go on here, namely this. If there were a God, He would make His love, and hence Himself, sufficiently evident so that no reasonable person doubted His existence (especially given the horrific evil in the world). But this He has not done. However, if He did make His love so manifest, no reasonable person would infer Q, even if I were true. Thus, even if I would *certainly* be true were Q false, that is no reason to be in doubt about whether I made Q quite likely. The point here might be put like this: Even if we cannot grasp the goods that justify God in allowing so much horrific evil rather than a lot less, we might still know *of* them. God could ensure we know *that* such goods exist, *that* the innocent will, in the long run, be compensated for their suffering. It would be enormously comforting to a lot of people if He did this, and it would prevent many people from losing their faith. Given our present cognitive capacities, the most obvious way for Him to ensure that we know these things is for Him to make His love, and hence Himself, sufficiently well known to us. Indeed, we rightly expect this of Him in light of the horrific suffering and subsequent doubt we experience.

 Consider an analogy. Suppose some parents remove a huge infected boil from the tiny arm of their boy without any anesthetic. He can't see how their cutting away at his bicep, digging out the roots and violently squeezing the gaping hole in his arm will help matters. By his lights, aspirin and Band-Aids, although inconvenient, did just fine. Now, suppose that instead of warmly wrapping him in their arms and reassuringly stroking his hair as he cried so there could be no doubt of their love and good intentions, his parents held him down, lanced the boil, dressed his arm, and walked away. And suppose this appearance of a lack of concern for his interest in being assured of their love for him is a common feature of his relationship with them, and their relationship with his siblings. What would we make of his reasoning as follows: "I know I'm too young to be able to understand my parents' reason for cutting off my boil, if indeed they have one. But they know I don't understand how it serves any good purpose. And they are able to overcome my inclination to doubt their goodness by clearly assuring me of their love, even if I cannot grasp their purposes. But they do nothing. If only they would wrap me in their arms, that would be enough. But I haven't even this to go on." I should think that the boy might well justifiedly infer that his parents had no reason to lance his boil, even though he has good reason to suspect his ability to discern his parents' good purposes, if such they had. For they fail to assure him of their love, and if they did love him, they would be much more forthcoming about it, especially in light of his inability to understand the suffering they have caused him. Of course, if they did make their love manifest in an understandable way to him, then, since he is a reasonable lad, he would not infer that the operation was pointless even if he could not see the point of it. In that case, the inscrutability of his parents' purposes would not lead him to believe the operation was pointless (if indeed it had a point). Thus, his inability to discern their purposes would be no reason for him to be in doubt about whether the inscrutability of their purposes made it quite likely that the operation was pointless.

So it is with the inference from I to Q. Horrific evil abounds. We do not see how God is justified in permitting so much of it rather than a lot less. Although we are rightly in doubt about our ability to discern such things, we wrongly infer that I does not justify belief in Q. For that inference may be drawn in light of the fact that unlike the boy's parents, God *would* assure us of His love, and hence His existence, especially in the midst of our suffering and ignorance. But He is silent.

2. Central to *The Objection,* as I shall call it, is what many regard as an independent argument for atheistic belief. One way to put it is this: If God exists, then He is perfect in love. Thus, He would want to relate personally to those capable of such a relationship, especially given the horrific suffering in the world. Such a relationship requires belief that God exists. But, it is very likely that some capable people inculpably lack theistic belief. Therefore, it is very likely that there is no God. Call this the *Argument from Divine Silence.* (Elsewhere I call it the Argument from Divine Hiddenness.)

I want to stress three features of its relation to the Argument from Inscrutable Evil. A proper appreciation of these features will, I hope, forestall the worry that, at best, The Objection is an instance of a well-known sophistical strategy: if you don't know what to say to an objection to what you've said, change the topic.

i. The Objection works only if the Argument from Divine Silence works. If the Argument from Divine Silence works, one might worry that inscrutable evil is a useless cog in the Argument from Inscrutable Evil, quite a paradoxical result! After all, one might think, the Argument from Divine Silence saves the inference from inscrutable to pointless evil. But this worry is unfounded. God's failure to make Himself more evident than He should cannot plausibly be construed *by itself* as a basis to infer pointless evil. It's not the right sort of fact. Inscrutable evil, on the other hand, is.

ii. Even if the Argument from Divine Silence is sufficient reason to believe atheism, it is not used in The Objection in that way. The Objection is not "Well, OK. The Argument from Inscrutable Evil doesn't justify atheistic belief. But look here, the Argument from Divine Silence does." Rather, the Argument from Divine Silence is used to *defeat* what would otherwise undermine our justifiedly inferring pointless evil on the basis of inscrutability. You might say that it preserves the justifying power of inscrutable evil vis-à-vis pointless evil, that it permits inscrutable evil to contribute to justifying atheistic belief in spite of my case against it. So the Argument from Divine Silence has two jobs in the cumulative case for atheism. During the day, it is a reason in its own right for atheistic belief, but it moonlights as a defeater of a defeater.

iii. The Argument from Divine Silence, however, does not moonlight for free. It gets something out of its relationship to inscrutable evil. If it lowers the probability of theism at all, the Argument from Divine Silence lowers the probability of theism much more than it otherwise would given that there is inscrutable evil. To see why, imagine that some people capable of a relationship with God inculpably lack theistic belief, but there is no inscrutable evil either because there is no horrific evil at all, or because, although there is as much horrific evil as there actually is, everyone understands how God would be justified in permitting so much rather than a lot less. If in our hypothesized situation there were as much horrific evil as there actually is and we all understood God's purposes, we would all see how some very weighty reasons justified God in permitting so much horrific evil rather than a lot less. In that case, surely, our cognitive powers would be dramatically improved, so much so, I conjecture, that we would be much more likely to grasp how God would be justified in permitting inculpable nonbelief. Indeed, perhaps the same reasons would apply in both cases. On the other hand, if our hypothesized situation were free of horrific evil, then the silence of God would not be nearly as potent as it otherwise would be. To see this point, note that even when those who love us are not causally relevant to our suffering, we rightly expect their comfort and care. For on such occasions we need both to be looked after and assured of their concern for our well-being. This need is magnified when they are the ones who permit or cause our suffering and magnified again when we don't understand why they are allowing or doing it. So there is a special urgency for God to be forthcoming about His love, if He exists. Given inscrutable evil, His failure to manifest Himself and His love is all the more striking.

So we cannot simply dismiss The Objection as a rhetorical sleight-of-hand. If we reject the Argument from Inscrutable Evil along the line I have suggested, we must show not only that the reasons offered on behalf of the inference from inscrutable to pointless evil are defective but also that we have reason to be in doubt about whether we would be able to discern God's purposes—we must also meet the challenge of the Argument from Divine Silence.[27,28]

NOTES

1. Fyodor Dostoyevsky, "Rebellion," *The Brothers Karamazov,* trans. C. Garnett (New York: Random House, Modern Library, 1950).
2. See William Rowe, "The Problem of Evil and Some Varieties of Atheism," chapter 1 in this book, 3.
3. Why is God justified in permitting *any* undeserved horrific evil? Well-known theodicies suffice.
4. The thrust of § 1.1 and § 1.2 is due to Peter van Inwagen. See van Inwagen, "The Magnitude, Duration, and Distribution of Evil: A Theodicy," *Philosophical Topics* 16 (1988): 167-68; "The Place of Chance in a World Sustained by God," in *Divine and Human Action,* ed. Thomas V. Morris (Ithaca: Cornell University Press, 1988), esp. 230ff.; and "The Problem of Evil, the Problem of Air, and the Problem of Silence" (chapter 8 in this book), note 11.
5. A charitable eye will see that, for the most part, what I say about this argument applies, with obvious changes, to a formally analogous argument that appeals to particular horrors.
6. This is how Bruce Russell argues in "Defenseless," chapter 10, 197.
7. Ibid., 197–98.
8. Ibid., 196–97.
9. Mary Hesse's article, "Simplicity," in *The Encyclopedia of Philosophy,* is a nice place from which to start thinking about the matter.
10. This is, roughly, Richard Swinburne's view of the matter. See Swinburne, "Does Theism Need a Theodicy?" *Canadian Journal of Philosophy* 18 (1988): 305, and *The Existence of God* (Oxford: Clarendon Press, 1979), 52.
11. Talking with Frances Howard-Snyder helped me see this point.
12. For more on this point, see the articles referred to in note 26.
13. But I must say this. In "The Evidential Argument from Evil: A Second Look" (chapter 14, 277), Rowe countenances the suffering of a five-year-old Flint girl, whom he names Sue, who was viciously beaten, raped, then strangled by her mother's boyfriend. He says that "the main reason" to believe that no good we know of justifies God in permitting Sue's suffering is this: every outweighing good that we know of, e.g., Sue's experiencing complete felicity in the eternal presence of God, is such that God could realize it without having to permit her to suffer so horribly. Why is that? Rowe says it is because God is omnipotent. But this is like arguing that God could create *ex nihilo* a genuine U.S. dime, for, after all, He is omnipotent. Both appeals to omnipotence are fallacious: it must first be argued that the states of affairs envisaged are real possibilities. For, in Aquinas's words, "power is said in reference to possible things" (*Summa Theologica,* I, Q 25, Art. 3). Thus, in His omnipotence, God has the *power* to realize Sue's complete felicity in His eternal presence without permitting her to suffer as she did only if it is *possible* for Sue to be in that state without God's permitting her to suffer like that. Rowe needs to argue that it is possible for Sue to be in a state of complete felicity in God's eternal presence without Him permitting her to suffer like that. Now perhaps Rowe failed to argue for this possibility because he thinks it is so blindingly obvious that only one caught in a perverse sort of modal skepticism could fail to believe it. But I beg to differ. To be sure, nothing we know about God's nature entails that He must permit Sue to suffer like that in order for her (or for any of us) to experience complete felicity with Him forever. But who could seriously claim that they understand God's nature sufficiently well to grasp what union with Him involves? It wouldn't be surprising at all if there were aspects of His being that we cannot fathom and in virtue of which union with Him required that He permit each of those whom He loved to suffer greatly. This is not modal skepticism. This is a right recognition of our ignorance of the divine nature. We should be reticent, therefore, to claim that it is possible for Sue to experience eternal felicity in the presence of God forever without being permitted to suffer very horribly. We should likewise be reticent to affirm (P).

14. See Rowe, "Evil and Theodicy," *Philosophical Topics* 16 (1988): 123-24, and "Ruminations About Evil," *Philosophical Perspectives* 5 (1991): 73.

15. See Rowe, "The Empirical Argument from Evil," in *Rationality, Religious Belief, and Moral Commitment,* ed. Robert Audi and William J. Wainwright (Ithaca: Cornell University Press, 1986), 124.

16. See Michael Tooley, "The Argument from Evil," *Philosophical Perspectives* 5 (1991): 111-16.

17. For more on this matter, see Michael Stocker, *Plural and Conflicting Values* (New York: Oxford University Press, 1990), especially "Plurality and Choice," and Alasdair MacIntyre, *After Virtue* (Notre Dame: University of Notre Dame Press, 1981), 63-64.

18. Level confusions are not uncommon in criticism of the evidential argument from evil. The most explicit one is in Delmas Lewis, "The Problem with the Problem of Evil," *Sophia* (Australia) 22 (1983): 30. See also Keith Yandell, "Gratuitous Evil and Divine Existence," *Religious Studies* 25 (1988): 18-20. But most frequently, level confusions lurk behind stated conditions for justifiedly believing the lower-level proposition that *there is pointless evil,* conditions that, without special reason, ought only to be applied to justifiedly believing the higher-level proposition that *the belief that there is pointless evil is justified.* While I cannot be sure of their intentions, the following authors lay down conditions which seem to be motivated by level confusions (at least, they do not evince an awareness of the need to argue that conditions appropriate for justifiedly believing higher-level propositions apply to the lower-level proposition that *there is pointless evil*): F. J. Fitzpatrick, "The Onus of Proof in Arguments about the Problem of Evil," *Religious Studies* 17 (1981): 29; Alvin Plantinga, "Epistemic Probability and Evil," chapter 5 in this book; James Sennett, "The Inscrutable Evil Defense," *Faith and Philosophy* 10 (1933): 223. Level confusions even seem to find their way into the most unlikely of places, Alston's "The Inductive Argument from Evil and the Human Cognitive Condition," chapter 6 in this book. Note the general condition Alston lays down for justified enumerative induction. But see his response to this charge, "Some (Temporarily) Final Thoughts on Evidential Arguments from Evil," chapter 16 in this book.

19. For more on level confusions, see William Alston, "Level Confusions in Epistemology," *Epistemic Justification* (Ithaca: Cornell University Press, 1989), and "Higher Level Requirements for Epistemic Justification," in *The Opened Curtain,* ed. K. Lehrer and E. Sosa (Boulder: Westview Press, 1991).

20. For more on the infinite belief thesis, see Robert Audi's very fine "Believing and Affirming," *Mind* (1983).

21. See Rowe, "William Alston on the Problem of Evil," in *The Rationality of Belief and the Plurality of Faiths,* ed. Thomas D. Senor (Ithaca: Cornell University Press, 1995).

22. To say that p is *at least* as likely as not is not to say that p is *just* as likely as not. To say that p is just as likely as not is to say that the probability of p is .5. To say that p is at least as likely as not is to say that the probability of p is somewhere in the vicinity of .5 to 1.

23. Wes Morriston suggested these considerations to me.

24. See chapter 14 in this book.

25. I haven't the space to address all of Rowe's specific arguments.

26. But what about *the atheistic stance?* It is an interesting question whether and how the atheist can be justified in believing that there is pointless evil on the basis of inscrutable evil. If she makes the initial probability assignments Rowe does, then inscrutable evil contributes little, if any, justification to her belief in pointless evil. It seems there are just two alternatives, then. Either she should not take seriously theistic stories in which God is justified, and thus assign a low probability to Pr(I/not-Q&k), or else she should assign theism a low antecedent probability, i.e., a high probability to Pr(Q/k). Either way, the argument from evil does not provide atheists with as much epistemic punch as they have tended to think. For more on this matter, see my "God, Schmod and Gratu-

itous Evil," *Philosophy and Phenomenological Research* (1993), and "On the A Priori Rejection of Evidential Arguments from Evil," *Sophia* (1993), both co-authored with John O'Leary-Hawthorne.

27. The best book on the Argument from Divine Silence is J. L. Schellenberg, *Divine Hiddenness and Human Reason* (Ithaca: Cornell University Press, 1993). See also my review of his book in *Mind* (1995), and "The Argument from Divine Hiddenness."

28. For comments on previous drafts of this chapter, I am grateful to William Alston, Martin Curd, Phillip Goggans, Frances Howard-Snyder, Hud Hudson, Steve Layman, Wes Morriston, and William Rowe. I am also grateful to audiences at the Northwest Conference on Philosophy, the Philosophy Department at Purdue University, and the Pacific Division Meetings of the American Philosophical Association.

16.

WILLIAM P. ALSTON

Some (Temporarily) Final Thoughts on Evidential Arguments from Evil

I

I have been assigned the unenviable job of "clean-up hitter." The baseball metaphor, though of obvious application, can be misleading in more than one way. So far from aiming to bring the previous batters home (to their intended destination,) my efforts will be much more often directed to stranding them on the base paths. Moreover, the targets of my discussion are largely drawn from the opposing team, the members of which are bending their efforts to keeping me from making solid contact with the ball. Perhaps a more felicitous term for the assignment would be "groundskeeper." My assignment is to restore the playing field to its pristine state after the depredations wrought by my predecessors.

Extricating myself from these athletic metaphors, it goes without saying that any "final word" on this topic is final only until the next round of comment and countercomment. My aim in this terminal chapter is to draw some of the threads of the previous chapters into the fabric I am inclined to weave. No doubt, many of my colleagues would discern a different pattern. More specifically, I will offer some second thoughts on my essay reprinted in this volume, then seek to do a better job of bringing out what I take to be the fatal weakness in evidential atheological arguments from evil, commenting, along the way, on various points in the foregoing chapters.

II

The main reason why my 1991 essay (reprinted here as chapter 6) is not more successful is that I was trying to do two quite different things that did not smoothly blend into a unified presentation. First, I wanted to neutralize the arguments of Rowe and Russell, arguments based on particularly refractory cases of evil. Second, I wanted to use various theodicies for a purpose for which they were not intended, viz., as a source of *possibilities* for God's purpose in permitting various evils, possibilities that, so I claimed, we cannot be in an epistemic position to dismiss. I endeavored to use the second project as a way of carrying out the first. But this turned out not to be a very effective way of dismantling their arguments. Indeed, I candidly acknowledge in the essay that from the theodicies I consider we can glean at most some unexcludable possibilities for part of God's reasons for allowing the particular cases of evil they focus on. I appeal to the live possibility of divine reasons unenvisaged by us to take up the slack, and I still think it is sufficient to take up whatever slack there is, including 100 percent if needed. But I now prefer to drop the rehearsal of theodicies and criticize the Rowe-Russell arguments in a somewhat different way.

III

As already indicated, I want to do a better job of bringing out the ineffectiveness of arguments that start from our inability to discern a sufficient reason God might have for permitting certain evils. But since I will be concentrating on versions of the argument Rowe has already published, I should first explain why I do not abandon that project and concentrate instead on the somewhat different Bayesian argument he presents in this volume in "The Evidential Argument from Evil: A Second Look" (chapter 14). Rowe's stated motivation for this replacement concerns his disenchantment with the enumerative induction from (P) "No good we know of justifies an omnipotent, omniscient, perfectly good being in permitting E1 and E2 (the sufferings of Bambi and Sue)" to (Q) "No good at all justifies an omnipotent, omniscient, perfectly good being in permitting E1 and E2." He now holds that though this induction increases the antecedent probability of Q, it does not, as it stands, make Q more likely than not.[1] The new argument aims to show both that P, together with background evidence, renders Q more likely than not, and that P, with background evidence, renders theism less likely than not. If the latter succeeds, we can bypass Q altogether in the argument against theism from P. Before turning to the issues I will discuss in detail I will briefly indicate why I do not find this new argument convincing.

Like most Bayesian arguments directed to controversial philosophical positions, Rowe's relies on questionable probability assignments. The assignments I am inclined to question are the following:

1. Pr (G(theism)/k(background evidence)) = .5.
2. Pr (P/not-G&k) = 1.
3. Pr (P/G&k) = .5.

Though 1 is controversial, I don't choose to rest my case, even in part, on contesting it. I will focus on 2 and 3.

My point about 2 is not that the assignment is unjustified, *as Rowe construes the propositions involved.* My objection is to one of the construals. Rowe's basis for 2 is that P is entailed by not-G. Consider how P must be understood if this entailment is to hold. P is the denial of some proposition, and if it is to be entailed by not-G, that proposition has to be committed to G. Rowe spells out not-P as a conjunction.

I. God exists, and some good known to us justifies him in permitting E1 and E2.

The denial of this conjunction, P, is a disjunction of the negations of the conjuncts.

II. Either God does not exist, or no good known to us justifies God in permitting E1 and E2.

So construed, Rowe is clearly right in judging that not-G entails P.

But although II allows Rowe to make probability assignment 2, which is crucial for his argument, it is untenable on other grounds. The first thing to note is that II is compatible with:

III. There are known goods that *would* be sufficient to justify God in permitting E1 and E2 if God should exist.

II is compatible with III since the truth of the first disjunct would be sufficient for II's truth.[2] If God does not exist, II is thereby true, and would still be true even if there are known goods that *would* justify God in permitting E1 and E2. But then an argument for not-G from P, on this reading of P, i.e., on II, is *not* an argument from evil, at least not an argument from evil of the sort Rowe presumably means to be giving, at least not an argument of the sort he has given in the past. For the basis of *that* sort of argument is the contention that no known goods would justify God in permitting E1 and E2. Thus when P is construed such that it is compatible with the denial of that basis, something has gone seriously amiss with the enterprise.

But what if Rowe denies that the sort of argument he intends to be giving now is one that essentially depends on the denial of III? The trouble with that is that the support he actually gives for P runs as follows:

The main reason to believe P is this. When we reflect on some good we know of we can see that it is very likely, if not certain, that the good in question *either* is not good enough to justify God in permitting E1 or E2 *or* is such that an omnipotent, omniscient being could realize it (or some greater good) without having to permit E1 or E2.

What these considerations directly support is not-III, and hence Rowe can hardly claim that his argument does not depend on not-III. Moreover, if he is to claim that these considerations establish P, as presently construed, i.e., as II, he owes us an argument that P follows from, or at least is strongly supported by, not-III.

Mark Brown pointed out to me that Rowe might attempt to justify the derivation as follows. A denial of III as just formulated would read:

> IV. There are no known goods that *would* be sufficient to justify God in permitting E1 and E2 if God should exist.

Let's say that this is equivalent to the following subjunctive conditional:

> V. If God should exist, there are no known goods that would be sufficient to justify Him in permitting E1 and E2.

Let's further take V to entail the material conditional:

> VI. If God exists, there are no known goods that would be sufficient to justify Him in permitting E1 and E2.

And this is equivalent to the disjunction:

> VII. Either God does not exist, or there are no known goods that would be sufficient to justify Him in permitting E1 and E2.

And if we make the existential commitment of the second disjunct explicit, this is Rowe's P on the present interpretation, i.e., II.

The weak point in this argument is the claim that IV is equivalent to V or to any other subjunctive conditional. IV makes a categorical statement as to the nonexistence of anything of a certain sort in the actual world. It does not make this nonexistence contingent on the holding of some condition (God's existence) that, so far as it says, may or may not hold. Thus the derivation of P (on the present interpretation) from not-III never really gets started.[3]

The third assignment—Pr (P/G & k) = .5—damages the argument for another reason: it is question begging. Some, like Wykstra, will object that .5 is much too low a value, since they hold that theism leads us to expect that many of God's reasons for permitting evil will not be apparent to us.[4] But I think we are in no position to make any such probability assignment, even a rough, approximate one. As I argued in "The Inductive Argument from Evil and the Human Cognitive Condition,"[5] and as I hope to clarify below, we are in no position to judge whether among the goods known to us there are any that figure in a justifying reason God has (would have) for permitting one or another evil. Since this is at least one of the positions that Rowe must discredit if his argument is to be cogent, I regard any assignment of a probability to (P/G & k) to beg the question against one of the major opposing positions. Since I can't go along with two of the three antecedent conditional probability assignments that are crucial to Rowe's Bayesian argument, I find it unsuccessful. That throws me back to a consideration of the simpler argument that, to put it roughly, moves from what we can discern of possible sufficient divine reasons for permitting certain evils to a conclusion as to whether there are such reasons.[6]

IV

In Rowe's essay "The Problem of Evil and Some Varieties of Atheism,"[7] the first premise of the argument is:

> 1. There exist instances of intense suffering which an omnipotent, omniscient being could have prevented without thereby losing some greater good or permitting some evil equally bad or worse.

Rowe then argues for 1 by maintaining that there are instances of suffering that, so far as we can see, satisfy 1, e.g., the fawn (which I call "Bambi") trapped in a forest fire. From "Evil and Theodicy"[8] on, he uses what he considers a more discriminating formulation, distinguishing goods known to us from all others. Simplifying by taking the avoidance of a greater evil as special case of realizing a greater good, he argues for the functional equivalent of premise 1 in the previous argument as follows:

> P. No good state of affairs we know of is such that an omnipotent, omniscient being's obtaining it would morally justify that being's permitting E1 or E2.

Therefore:

> Q. No good state of affairs is such that an omnipotent, omniscient being's obtaining it would morally justify that being in permitting E1 or E2.

Rowe's argument for P is pretty much the same as before. The inference of Q from P is presented as a run-of-the-mill enumerative induction.

Although Rowe 1988 looks superior since it more finely discriminates aspects of the problem, it has led him to slight crucial problems. Moreover, Rowe 1979 provides a better starting point for the argument. Let me explain why.

The main trouble with Rowe 1988 is that it encourages the false belief that the only movement from the known to the unknown required by the argument is that involved in taking goods we know about as a representative sample of all goods (representative at least for their capacity to provide justifying reasons for permitting the evils on which Rowe concentrates). It encourages the supposition that we can tell whether *known goods* could provide God with a justifying reason for permitting certain evils. It is goods that fall beyond our ken that are a problem. But in fact there are two areas in which it is important to distinguish between what we know and what we do not know. By Rowe's lights, for God to be justified in permitting an evil there must be a sufficiently great good for the sake of which God permits it, *and it must be the case that that good could not have been realized without permitting that evil.* In looking for possible divine reasons for permitting evil, we must not only consider what candidate goods are out there, but also *what the conditions of realization of those goods are,* conditions that even Omnipotence would have to respect. And since there are both these aspects to the problem, we have to consider what we do and do not know about the conditions of realization of goods as well as about what goods there are. If we can't see any justifying reasons for God to permit Bambi's suffering, we have to consider not only whether there are goods we are not aware of that might figure in such reasons, but also whether there are conditions of realization of goods of which we are ignorant, conditions of realization *both of goods we are not cognizant of and of goods we are cognizant of.* Under the second heading, we have to consider whether some good we do have some conception of—eternal blessedness in heaven, for example—has, unbeknownst to us, some kind of suffering or God's permission thereof as a necessary precondition. This consideration is as crucial to the problem as considering whether there may be goods, undreamed of by us, that play a justifying role.[9]

Because there is just as big a problem in moving from known interconnections to all interconnections as there is in moving from known goods to all goods, the argument can be more fruitfully addressed in something more like its 1979 form. Rowe's empirical base can be put as follows: As far as he can see, on careful reflection, there is no known good, i.e., anything we can envisage that we can see to be good, such that it is true both that (a) God could not realize it without permitting Bambi's or Sue's suffering, and (b) it is of such magnitude that God could reasonably take its realization to outweigh (or neutralize) the disvalue of Bambi's or Sue's suffering.[10] The crucial problem is that of moving from "so far as one can see no good satisfies both (a) and (b)" to the conclusion that "no good satisfies both (a) and (b)." This requires us not only to consider the possibility that some good that is totally outside our ken satisfies both (a) and (b), but also the possibility that some good we can envisage satisfies both conditions, even though we cannot see that it does.

I concede that Rowe is not idiosyncratic in failing to "see," with respect to any envisaged good, that it satisfies both (a) and (b). If I thought that this failure was due to a lack on his part, and that others can see what he cannot, I would not view the problem as basically a matter of whether we can infer "It isn't there" from "We can't see it." I agree that we cannot discern any sufficient divine reason for permitting Bambi's and Sue's suffering.

V

Now I come to the basic claim of this chapter. Given that we cannot see, of any divine reason we can envisage, that this reason would justify God in permitting Bambi's or Sue's suffering, does this justify us in supposing that there is no divine reason that would justify such a permission? Are we warranted in making this step from "I can't see any" to "There isn't any"? My contention is that we are not.

My reasons for believing this are not original. They have to do with our cognitive powers, vis-à-vis the reasons an omnipotent, omniscient, perfectly good being might have for His decisions and actions. I simply hope to bring out more clearly and in more detail than heretofore the basic lines of this insight, while avoiding distracting side issues.

Think of the matter in this way. We are considering whether the fact that we cannot see what sufficient justifying reason an omniscient, omnipotent being might have for doing something provides strong support for the supposition that no such reason is available for that being. I think the absurdity of the claim that it does provide strong support is evident on the face of it. But perhaps a series of analogues will make the matter clearer for those who disagree. There are various distinguishable aspects of the situation with which we are concerned here. We can find analogues for each of these aspects, analogues in which it is, I hope, obvious that we are not justified in the inference in question.

A. The most salient feature of the inference from "I can't see any sufficient reason for God to permit this evil" to "There is no sufficient reason for God to permit this evil" is that we are taking the insights attainable by finite, fallible human beings as an adequate indication of what is available in the way of reasons to an omniscient, omnipotent being. This aspect of the matter has not escaped the attention of critics of the argument. Ahern points out that our knowledge of the good and evils in the world and of the interconnections between things is very limited. Fitzpatrick adduces the deficiencies in our grasp of the divine nature. Wykstra and Plantinga point out that our cognitive capacities are much more inferior to God's than is a small child's to his parents.[11] I find these remarks to be generally well taken, though I am not sure that the limitations of our grasp of the divine nature is directly relevant to the issue. My version will be most similar to Wykstra's approach, but I will steer clear of his small child analogy, because, though I find it apt, it is also disanalogous in ways that leave loopholes for the opponent, as Rowe points out in his chapter 14 in this volume (274–76).

Suppose I am confronted with the activity or the productions of a master in a field in which I have no expertise. This may involve a scientific theory or experiment, a painting, a musical composition, an architectural design, or a chess move. I look at a theory of quantum phenomena and fail to see any reason for the author to draw the conclusions he draws. Does that entitle me to suppose that he has no sufficient reason for his conclusions? It certainly doesn't if I lack the requisite expertise. How could I expect to discern his reasons if I am too ignorant of the subject to follow what is going on? The same point is to be made of the following situations: (1) Lacking any training in or appreciation of painting, I fail to see why Veronese organized the figures in a certain painting as he did. Does that give me the right to conclude that he had no sufficient reason for doing so? (2) Being in the same position with respect to music, I fail to see any reason for Mozart to develop a theme as he did. Ditto. (3) Having only the sketchiest grasp of chess, I fail to see any reason for Karpov to have made the move he did at a certain point in a game. Does that entitle me to conclude that he had no good reason for making that move?

I take it that it will be beyond controversy that the answer to each of these questions is a resounding no. And why shouldn't the same response be made to the inference from "I can't see any sufficient reason for God to permit the sufferings of Bambi and Sue" to "God has no sufficient reason to do so"? Here too a judgment is made in the absence of any reason to suppose one has a sufficient grasp of the range of possible reasons open to the other party. Surely our purchase on what reasons God might have for His actions is as inadequate as the grasp of the judger in the other cases. Surely an omniscient, omnipotent being is further removed from any of us in this respect than a brilliant physicist is from one innocent of physics, or a Mozart is from one innocent of music, or Karpov is from a neophyte. Surely the extent to which God can envisage reasons for permitting a given state of affairs exceeds our ability to do so by *at least as much* as Einstein's ability to discern the reason for a physical theory exceeds the ability of one ignorant of physics.

B. The above analogies were maximally similar to the target situation. They, like the latter, involved judgments concerning the reasons someone else might have for a line of action. As such they are well suited for bringing out a crucial feature of our target case—the incapacity of the judge to make a sound judgment. But less close analogies can bring out other aspects of the situation. Another prominent feature of our central case is that it involves trying to determine whether there is a so-and-so in a territory the extent and composition of which is largely unknown to us. Or at least it is a territory such that we have no way of knowing the extent to which its constituents are unknown to us. How can we possibly think that we have a reliable internal map of the diversity of considerations (even limiting this to values and the conditions of their realization) that are available to an omniscient being? Given what we know of our limitations—the variety of questions we don't know how to answer, the possibilities we can't exclude of realms of being to which we have no access, our ignorance even of many of the details of human history, and so on—how can we suppose that we are in a position to estimate the extent to which the possibilities we can envisage for divine reasons for permitting evils even come close to exhausting the possibilities open to an omniscient being? It is surely the better part of wisdom to acknowledge that we are groping in the dark in assessing the extent to which we can survey the whole field.

And now for the analogies. This is like going from "We haven't found any signs of life elsewhere in the universe" to "There isn't life elsewhere in the universe." It is like someone who is culturally and geographically isolated going from "As far as I have been able to tell, there is nothing on earth beyond this forest" to "There is nothing on earth beyond this forest." Or, to get a bit more sophisticated, it is like someone who reasons "We are unable to discern anything beyond the temporal bounds of our universe," where those bounds are the big bang and the final collapse, to "There is nothing beyond the temporal bounds of our universe."

These examples involve a "territory" in the literal sense of a spatial or a temporal "region." But there are analogous cases in which the "territory" is of a more conceptual sort. Can we anticipate future intellectual or artistic developments? No, at least not in any detail; for if they were predicted in detail, they would already have occurred and would not be future. Even very unspecific predictions are risky at best and often turn out to be incorrect. Consider the eighteenth-century confidence that all that remained for physics to do was to tidy up and extend Newtonian mechanics and Comte's example of a useless metaphysical speculation in science—the chemical composition of the stars! Who in the late nineteenth century could have foreseen the development of atonal music, not to mention the still weirder developments that have been assaulting our ears in this century. Our inability to survey the "space" of possible future developments and segregate them into the more or less likely subverts any attempt to argue from "So far as I can see there will not be such-a-such a type of development" to "There will not be any such development." Again, can there be intelligent beings with some non-hydrocarbon-based chemistry? We don't have a clue as to how to assess the possibilities and probabilities here. The fact that we don't see how non-hydrocarbon-based animal life is possible is little ground to suppose that it is not possible. These cases are closely analogous to our situation with respect to determining whether God has a justifying reason for permitting Bambi's or Sue's suffering, on the basis of our inability to ascertain such a reason. Here too we are in no position to map the "territory" of possible reasons. We lack the resources to determine the extent to which the possibilities we can envisage and understand exhaust the field, and to determine the extent, variety, and detailed constitution of the terra incognita.

These analogies warn us not to make our cognitive limitations a recipe for what there is. If we are unable to map the territory within which to look for something, we are correspondingly unable to infer from our inability to find something that there isn't one there. It will be instructive to look at Bruce Russell's objection to this position, expressed in chapter 10 of this volume:

> the view that there are reasons beyond our ken that would justify God, if he exists, in allowing all the suffering we see [is] like the view that there are blue crows beyond our powers of observation. Once we have conducted the relevant search for crows (looking all over the world in different seasons and at crows at different stages of maturity), we are justified in virtue of that search in believing there are no crows beyond our powers of observation which are relatively different from the crows we've seen. . . . Similarly, once we've conducted the relevant search for moral reasons to justify allowing the relevant suffering (thinking hard about how allowing the suffering would be needed to realize sufficiently weighty goods, reading and talking to others who have thought about the same problem), we are justified in believing that there are no morally sufficient reasons for allowing that suffering. (197)

The crow search is crucially different from the divine reasons search in just the respect brought out by this second set of analogies. The territory of the search is well mapped. Furthermore, we know that, by the nature of the beast, a crow is open to sensory observation, given suitable conditions. Hence, given a careful enough search, we can be amply justified in supposing that there are no blue crows. But the search for divine reasons differs in just these respects. We have no idea how to map the relevant territory—what its boundaries are and what variety it contains. Nor can we be assured that the cognitive powers we possess are sufficient for detecting the quarry if it exists. Hence, contrary to what Russell intended, the crow case nicely displays the defect of the inference in question.

In Alston 1991, I presented some considerations that were designed to indicate the rationality of supposing that there is an indefinitely large realm of facts, evaluative and otherwise, that lie beyond our ken. The pervasive phenomenon of human intellectual progress shows that at any given time in the past there were many things not known or even conceived that came to be conceived and known at a later stage. The induction is obvious. It would be highly irrational to suppose that we have reached the limit of this process and have ascertained everything there is to be learned. This creates a presumption that with respect to values, as well as their conditions of realization, there is much that lies beyond our present grasp.

Several critics have found fault with this line of reasoning, but they have generally misread the argument. Here is an example from Richard Gale's essay in this volume (chapter 11):

> What Alston [is] doing is likening morality to a "natural kind"—a kind of entity possessed of an essential nature that is to be unearthed by scientific inquiry, there being some analogous method of inquiry into the inner, hidden nature of morality to that employed in science. But morality is a paradigm of a nonnatural kind, one whose "nature," that is, basic principles and rules, is completely on the surface, patently obvious to the gaze of all participants in the moral language game. A hidden morality is no morality.[12] *Pace* Alston, there is no "history of the apprehension of values . . . parallel to the history" of scientific discovery. (210)

The misreading here comes from supposing that the intellectual progress to which I appeal is entirely or mostly a matter of discovering the essential nature of some natural kind. But if one will go back to the relevant passage of Alston 1991, one will see that my main emphasis was on advances—getting into a position to conceptualize aspects of the world that were previously hidden from us, rather than discovering the inner nature of a kind of thing with which we were already familiar. Indeed, my initial examples, omitted from Gale's quotation, were of conceptual developments in philosophy. My argument was not specially concerned with scientific advances.

But leaving aside issues of Alstonian exegesis, I cannot agree that this appeal to "moral language games" scotches the idea of moral progress, much less progress in the apprehension of values generally. Let's agree that membership in a moral community requires the internalization of certain basic moral rules, principles, and concepts. But that does not preclude the realization of new principles and values, any more than the fact that membership in a scientific community requires the internalization of certain concepts, "paradigms," methods, etc. precludes new scientific discoveries. A language game approach fails to support Gale's ironclad moral conservatism.

I have been arguing that we are not in a position to assert that there are no sufficient justifying reasons for God to permit Bambi's and Sue's suffering. I have not argued that we cannot discern such reasons, but rather that we should not expect to be able to discern such reasons if they exist. (I have not argued that it is *impossible* for us to discern God's reasons, only that our failure to do so is no indication of their nonexistence). I take seriously the possibility that God would not make us privy to His reasons for permitting a particular case of suffering, would not even communicate those reasons to the sufferer herself.[13] And theism has been attacked on just this point. Some argue that it is incompatible with the goodness of God to leave us in ignorance as to why He permits us to suffer.[14] Surely, these people say, a loving Father would explain to His children why He is allowing them to undergo their suffering if He could. And since God is omnipotent and omniscient, He could certainly do so. My response to this is that our ignorance of God's reasons for permitting our sufferings is just one more instance of evil the reason for permitting which we cannot see. Hence the present objection simply amounts to saying that my position implies that there is a certain kind of evil God's reason for permitting which we cannot discern. But of course! That's not an objection; it's a restatement of the common starting point from which my opponents and I go in opposite directions.

Russell maintains that if "after failing to find sufficiently weighty moral reasons to justify God's allowing [Sue's suffering] we are *not* justified in believing there are none" "it will follow that we are also not justified in believing that some human being who could easily have stopped the heinous crime did something wrong in failing to intervene." An obvious retort, as Russell notes, is that "we cannot expect to discern *God's* reasons (his motives) for allowing the murder, but can expect to discern *the onlooker's*." But he holds that this "has no bearing on the question at issue. The question at issue is whether we must be unable to judge that there are no *justifying* reasons for human nonintervention if we are unable to judge that there are none for divine nonintervention. I have argued that we must" (chapter 10). The argument is that if God could have justifying reason for allowing the brutality, so could the human onlooker, for that same reason could justify both noninterventions. But this badly misconstrues moral justification. Whether I am morally justified in doing something is not a function of whether there are objective facts that could be used by *someone* as a morally good reason for doing it. It is rather a function of whether *I* have such a morally good reason for doing it. And it is quite possible (highly likely, I would say) that God should have such a reason that no human being could have—either because we are incapable of grasping the reason or because the reason concerns features of God's relation to the situation that we cannot share.

This completes my case for the thesis that the fact that we are unable to see any justifying reason for God to permit Bambi's or Sue's suffering gives us no reason of any weight to suppose that God has, or would have if He existed, no justifying reason for these permissions. Being unable to estimate the extent to which what we can discern exhausts the possibilities, we are in no position to suppose that our inability to find a justifying divine reason is a sufficient ground for supposing there is none. We are in the kind of situation illustrated by the analogues I have set out.[15]

I would like to stress that my argument is neither based on, nor does it issue in, a generalized skepticism. For that matter, it is not based on, nor does it support, a general theological skepticism. It is compatible with our knowing quite a bit about the divine nature, activities, purposes, and relations with humanity. The conclusion of the argument is only that we are unable to form sound judgments on whether there are justifying reasons for God's permitting certain evils. Indeed, it is crucial to my argument to contrast our cognitive situation vis-à-vis divine reasons for evil with our cognitive situation vis-à-vis many other things, highlighting the unfavorable state of the former by contrast with our epistemically favorable condition in the latter. I make this point because more than one critic of Alston 1991 has made it a reproach to my position that it leads to general skepticism. (See, for an example, Gale, chapter 11.)

VI

I will now apply the contentions of section V to Rowe's arguments for atheism. In Rowe 1979 the "evidential" premise was:

> 1. There exist instances of intense suffering which an omnipotent, omniscient being could have prevented without thereby losing some greater good or permitting some evil equally bad or worse.

The above considerations subvert Rowe's argument for 1: "Since the fawn's intense suffering was preventable [by God] and, so far as we can see, pointless, doesn't it appear that premise (1) of the argument is true. . . ?" They are designed to show that the fact that we are unable, even on the most careful reflection, to discern any point to the fawn's suffering (i.e., any good reason God would have for allowing it) does not justify the claim that it has no point.

The application to the 1988 argument is more complicated. In Rowe 1988 the argument is set up as follows.

> P. No good state of affairs we know of is such that an omnipotent, omniscient being's obtaining it would morally justify that being's permitting E1 or E2.
> Therefore:
> Q. No good state of affairs is such that an omnipotent, omniscient being's obtaining it would morally justify that being in permitting E1 or E2.

From Q we infer that no such being exists, since there would be no suffering that this being is not morally justified in permitting.

This structuring of the argument, I have argued, gives the false impression that the main problem is one of generalizing to all goods from known goods, whereas the main problem is not that but rather the inference from "We cannot discern any way in which God would be morally justified in permitting E1 or E2" to "There is no such way." When we apply my objections to this latter inference to the 1988 version of Rowe's argument, we get the following:

First, my objection hits at Rowe's case for P itself. That case is substantially equivalent to his case for 1 in Rowe 1979. To repeat once more his new summary statement in his chapter 14 in this volume:

> When we reflect on some good we know of we can see that it is very likely, if not certain, that the good in question *either* is not good enough to justify God in per-

mitting E1 or E2 *or* is such that an omnipotent, omniscient being could realize it (or some greater good) without having to permit E1 or E2.

This support for P does not explicitly involve an inference from "I can't see any way in which this good would justify God in permitting E1 or E2" to "This good does not justify God in permitting E1 or E2." Indeed, Rowe 1988 explicitly disavows any reliance on such an inference:

> I don't mean simply that we can see how some good we know about (say, my enjoyment on smelling a good cigar) would justify an omnipotent being's permitting E1 or E2. I mean that we can see how such a good would not justify an omnipotent being's permitting E1 or E2.

Here Rowe denies that he is moving from "Can't see" to "Isn't." Still, that inference is implicit. In claiming that for any good we can envisage he can see that realizing that good would not morally justify God in permitting E1 or E2, he is relying on what he can "see," on careful reflection, to be all the relevant considerations. Hence, if he is unwarranted in moving from that to "The obtaining of no such good would justify God in permitting E1 or E2," his case for P is without force. So if I have subverted that move, I have subverted Rowe's case for P.

One might think that my objections to this last inference do not have the force I was claiming for them in section V, when, as here, the discussion is restricted to goods we can envisage. For in those cases are we not in a position to judge whether the realization of any such good would justify God in permitting certain cases of evil, even if we are not in such a position vis-à-vis goods generally?

In a word, "no," for two reasons. The first reason has to do with our "knowledge" of the goods. Rowe rightly says that he does "not mean to limit us to goods that we know to have occurred" or "to those goods and goods that we know will occur in the future. I mean to include goods that we have some grasp of, even though we have no knowledge at all that they have occurred or ever will occur." Moreover, Rowe is thinking of good-types rather than good-tokens. For when he considers a good that, so far as he knows, never has occurred and never will occur, he cannot be directing his thought to some particular token. Finally, he does not require any particular degree of adequacy of grasp of the good in question. He says that he will include "experiencing complete felicity in the everlasting presence of God" as a known good, "even though we don't have a very clear grasp of what this great good involves."

These clarifications imply that a good's being "known" does not necessarily put us in a favorable position to assess its magnitude and hence does not necessarily put us in a favorable position to say whether its obtaining would justify God's permitting a certain evil (assuming it could not be realized by God without His permitting that evil). Note that when Rowe contends, with respect to specific goods, that they are not of sufficient worth for their realization to justify permitting Bambi's or Sue's suffering, he always picks good-types with many tokens of which he is familiar, e.g., his enjoyment of smelling a good cigar or Sue's pleasure upon receiving some toys. Surely we are not in nearly as good a position to assess the degree of value of goods we have never experienced as we are with those we have experienced. This point clearly applies to "experiencing complete felicity in the everlasting presence of God," where "we don't have a clear grasp of what this great good involves." Although, as this example suggests, deficiencies in our grasp of the details of a good tend to go along with lack of experience of tokens, we have more of a grasp of some unexperienced goods than of others, just because some unexperienced goods have a stronger analogy with experienced ones. I have a much better grasp of the good of writing great poetry than I do of complete fulfillment of my nature, even though I have experienced neither. To sum up, when we consider unexperienced goods of which we have only a minimal grasp—and it may be that the livest candidates for goods the realization of which would justify God in permitting suffering all fall within this class—we are in a bad position to determine whether the magnitude of the good is such as to make it worthwhile for God to permit a certain evil in order to make its realization possible.[16]

However, the main bar to our being justified in accepting P (and this is the second reason) has to do with the state of our knowledge of the conditions of realization for various goods. Here the extent of our grasp of one or another good is very important. We have a pretty good handle on the conditions under which Rowe's favorite—the enjoyment of smelling a good cigar—would be realized. But when it comes to *experiencing complete felicity in the eternal presence of God,* we have clearly gotten out of our depth. Perhaps we can make a stab at enumerating states of character that would fit someone for this and those that would interfere with it, but for all we know there are other conditions for this supreme fulfillment of which we have little or no idea. And what about the states of character just alluded to, e.g., pride and humility? We undoubtedly have some idea as to social influences, interpersonal interactions, lines of conduct, regimens, etc., that are conducive to one or the other. But our understanding of all this is fragmentary, being largely limited to natural, this-worldly factors, in contrast to supernatural influences that might be involved in God's plans, such as the sanctifying activity of the Holy Spirit. I am not trying to show that there *are* conditions of realization that are unknown to us. On the contrary. By mentioning such putative possibilities, I mean to indicate that we are not in a position to determine the extent to which there are such additional conditions and what they are. Hence we are in no position to assert, with respect to a given good that is not disqualified by a low degree of value, that a certain kind of suffering is not required for the realization of that good.

We are frequently reminded that the attainment of a particular good justifies God's permission of a certain evil only if an omnipotent being could not realize that state of affairs without permitting that evil or some evil just as bad or worse. And that is a stringent requirement indeed. But this is to take too piecemeal an approach. Suppose God permits certain evils to befall Sam because He sees those evils are needed to turn Sam in the direction of spiritual development, which in turn is required for the supreme consummation of eternal loving communion with Himself. Presumably God could realize this last end without these prerequisites. He could bring it about by fiat that Sam is in that condition. Does that show that the reason for permitting those evils is not justifying? No. For it may be that if God were to confer the beatific vision by arbitrary fiat, rather than as the outcome of a "natural"[17] course of development, that would militate against other features of the divine master plan. For example, it might violate regularities that are needed for some other purpose.[18] Hence, even if God could achieve the particular good without permitting this evil, or some evil equally bad or worse, doing so might involve too much a sacrifice elsewhere in the scheme. It may be that if we specify the justifying good in global enough terms, it would include everything that is relevant to the case. Thus, with respect to this case we could specify the good in question not just as Sam's enjoying eternal loving communion with God but as Sam's attaining this *in a certain way*. But if we were to beef up the specification so that it includes everything relevant, it might be too comprehensive for us to comprehend. When we are at the level of the specific, limited sorts of good Rowe and others mention, the point made in this paragraph holds.

Thus, when we consider what we justifiably believe about "known" goods, there are two factors that can prevent us from justifiably accepting P. First, our grasp of the nature of the good may not be sufficient for us to assess it properly for degree and kind of value. Second, our grasp of the conditions of its realization may not be sufficient for us to say with justified confidence that God could have realized that good without permitting the evil in question and without making too much of a sacrifice of good (or prevention of evil) elsewhere in the scheme.

So much for P. Now since, on my view, the crucial inference is from "We can't find a reason" to "There isn't one," rather than from "No known goods constitute a reason" to "No goods constitute a reason," the burden no longer rests on an enumerative induction from known goods to all goods; hence questions of representativeness of samples and the like no longer bulk large. Indeed, as I construe the argument there is no way of structuring it so that the distinction between known and unknown goods plays an important part. The most we can do with that distinction is the following: The consideration of known goods, I have urged, leaves us with uneliminated possibilities for a sufficient justifying reason for God's permitting some evil. When we then consider the idea that there may be values that are currently not even conceived or envisaged by us, that simply widens the gap between "We can't discern a sufficient divine justifying reason for permitting the evil" and "There is no such reason." For since we cannot be justified in denying that there are values we have not discerned, and since if any of those values should provide God with a justifying reason for permitting a certain evil we would not be able to discern it, that gives us an additional reason for supposing that "We can't discern a reason" does not provide strong support for "There is no such reason."

But even though the known-unknown good distinction can play no major role in the discussion, I still want to maintain, as I did rather briefly in Alston 1991, that as the argument is set up in Rowe 1988, the enumerative induction from P to Q is weak. Rowe claimed that "we are justified in making this inference in the same way we are justified in making the many inferences we constantly make from the known to the unknown. . . . If I encounter a fair number of pit bulls and all of them are vicious, I have reason to believe that all pit bulls are vicious."

In Alston 1991 I take up this example to make the point that we have general reasons for thinking that marked temperamental features are breed specific in dogs. Hence if all or most of the members of a given breed we have observed display a certain temperament, we are on solid ground in taking our sample to be representative of the breed in this regard. I contrasted this with Rowe's generalization from known goods to all goods by making the same kind of point I have been making in this chapter concerning our inability to "map" the relevant "territory": "We have no way of drawing boundaries around the total class of goods; we are unable to anticipate what may lie in its so-far-unknown sub-class." Thus we are not in the kind of position for generalizing from a sample that we are in when making an inductive generalization about temperamental features of a breed of dogs from a proper sample of that breed.

Unfortunately, my formulation there, though ambiguous on this point, could well be interpreted as claiming that anyone making an inductive generalization has to *justifiably believe* that his sample is representative in the relevant respect in order to be justified in making the inductive generalization and hence in believing the conclusion on the basis of that induction.[19] Such a strong higher-level requirement would not be satisfied by most inductive conclusions we ordinarily judge to be sound. For most (relatively naive) inducers are innocent of any justified beliefs about representativeness of samples, innocent, in fact, of any such beliefs at all. Hence I am anxious to avoid holding individual inducers responsible for having sufficient justification for a higher-level belief about the representativeness of their samples.

Well, then, exactly what am I requiring for a sound inductive inference? I can take the consideration of this question as an opportunity to be more explicit as to what I claim Rowe, or anyone else, lacks in inferring "God would have no sufficient reason for permitting E1 and E2" from "I can see no sufficient reason for permitting E1 and E2." I have spoken in terms of our (anyone's) not being in a "position" to take our inability to see any such reason as a sufficient basis for supposing there is no such reason. But what is it to be in a "position" to do this? Just what is it, in my view, that we lack and that we must have in order to be justified in affirming "There is no such reason"?

Going back to my "territory" metaphor, we can distinguish a more subjective and a more objective sense in which there might be an adequate "mapping" of the territory, one that must "be there" if we can warrantedly take our inability to find something as a good reason for supposing it isn't there. The more subjective sense is the one I have just rejected—the subject's being justified in beliefs about the territory that imply that one's inference basis is sufficiently representative of that territory. The most objective sense is this: one's sample being in fact representative of the territory, whether one knows this, justifiably believes it, or believes it at all. That isn't the sense I want either. To condemn my opponent on those grounds would be to claim that in fact what we can discern about these matters is not a fair representation of what is there. And, of course, I don't want to claim that, for I have argued that we are in no position to determine whether or not that is the case.

So how is my position to be understood? The preceding paragraph naturally suggests that what I need is something between the subjective and objective extremes; and that is where I shall look. The clue to the via media lies in the social dimension of knowledge. When I say that *we* are in no position to suppose that what we can discern is an adequate guide to what God can discern, the plural form of the first-person pronoun is no mere *façon de parler*. What it takes for *me* to be in a position to make that inference is that there are, in the larger community with which I am at least potentially in effective contact, persons who have sufficient reason to think that what we can discern of justifying reasons is an adequate guide to what justifying reasons God has available to Him. In another version of this general idea, *this is known* (within my community), even if I personally do not have that knowledge. The social availability of a justification for supposing my sample to be representative is something that is objective vis-à-vis me and any other individual cognitive subject, though, since it is a fact about human knowledge of (justified belief about) the world, rather than a fact about that world itself, it is not as severely objective as the second alternative I rejected earlier. By this device I am enabled to steer between the Scylla of requiring higher level knowledge of each believer and the Charybdis of making assumptions about the real state of affairs with respect to the human and divine situation vis-à-vis justifying reasons. Each of us is in no position to infer "God has no reason" from "We can't see any reason that He has," just because none of us is justified in supposing that our insights into these matters are a sufficient guide to the way it is with God.[20]

This completes my current criticism of the view that from the fact that, so far as we can see, there are no justifying reasons for God to permit Bambi's or Sue's suffering, we may reasonably conclude that there are no such reasons.

VII

Finally, I want to say something about the explanatory argument developed by Paul Draper.[21] Draper considers an hypothesis that is an alternative to theism, viz., the "Hypothesis of Indifference" (HI):

> HI: Neither the nature nor the condition of sentient beings on earth is the result of benevolent or malevolent actions performed by nonhuman persons.

He then argues that HI explains O (the facts about the distribution of pain and pleasure in the world)[22] much better than theism. And from this he infers that we have a prima facie good reason to believe that theism is less probable than HI. As Russell notes in chapter 10, we could also mount an argument of this general sort in which the explanandum is the fact that we can't discern any sufficient justifying reason for God's permitting certain cases of suffering, rather than O.

In his new contribution to this volume (chapter 9), Draper takes me to task for supposing that my claim that we are unable to determine whether God would have a justifying reason to permit certain evils implies that "all probabilistic arguments from evil fail." He points out correctly that this thesis does not tell at all against explanatory arguments like his, for such arguments do not depend on supposing that "it is unlikely that an omnipotent and omniscient being would have a morally sufficient reason to permit certain evils." It is true that in Alston 1991 I use the terms *inductive, empirical,* and *probabilistic* indifferently to characterize the kind of argument I am criticizing, and then at the end of the essay talk as if the considerations adduced there dispose of all such arguments. This was sloppy of me. I never meant to be discussing explanatory arguments, even by implication, though I can see how my words might lead someone to think so.

But what about explanatory arguments like Draper's? Draper takes it that the fact that HI explains O much better than theism tells significantly against theism. But, as Plantinga points out in "On Being Evidentially Challenged" (chapter 13), this depends on the relevance of this explanatory task to the evaluation of theism, and that is a complicated matter. Here I shall pursue some other issues.

First, does Draper really succeed in comparing two *explanations* of O? Just what are these alleged explanations? The only thing he does to identify them is to say that they are provided by theism and HI respectively. But that does not suffice to specify any particular explanations. This can be seen by noting that the following are two different explanations of O:

1. God permits O to be the case so that human beings will have a chance to develop good moral characters.
2. God permits O to be the case so that the creation may exhibit as much variety as possible.

These are both theistic explanations of O, but they are by no means the same explanation. Thus merely citing theism, i.e., stating that O is due to God, does not suffice to *explain* O. At most, it indicates where we are to look for an explanation but without actually providing an explanation of that sort. It only says that the explanation is of some theistic sort.

The same point is to be made vis-à-vis the alleged explanation by HI. HI merely stipulates that O is not due to the actions of nonhuman persons. That obviously leaves a tremendous field of possibilities open. Until the field is considerably narrowed down, we don't have any particular explanation of O. Is O due to blind chance, to the inevitable workings of mechanical forces, to some Bergsonian élan vital, or what? Simply to invoke HI is to tell us one kind of thing that is not involved. It is to rule out one large class of explanations, including those that count as theistic. But an innumerable throng is left.

Draper may insist that he has indeed specified two explanations. It is just that he has not spelled them out completely. Many things we count as explanations leave loose ends dangling. We explain an instance of corrosion by citing the presence of an acid, without spelling out the chemical laws involved. We explain the bridge's collapse by citing an abnormal load without specifying the magnitude of the load or saying how much the bridge is capable of supporting. Why don't Draper's explanations exemplify the same kind of incompleteness?

The answer is that there is a difference between an incomplete explanation and no explanation at all. A genuine explanation throws light on the explanandum; it enables us to see why it happened or was brought into being. The incomplete explanations just cited do that. They genuinely throw light on why the thing in question happened. But neither theism nor HI throws light in the same way on the fact that O obtains. They merely tell us, in the case of theism, the kind of being that is ultimately responsible and, in the case of HI, the kind of being that is not ultimately responsible. This would be like saying of the growth of plants that it is due to the sun, without saying what it is about the sun and its activity that brings this about. It would be like saying of certain administrative arrangements that they were instituted by Mr. Carter without saying anything about why he did so or for what purpose. And as for HI, we don't get even that much. The "HI explanation" is like saying of those administrative arrangements that they were not instituted by Mr. Carter, and letting it go at that.

So if Draper wants to maintain that theism suffers epistemically because some other explanation of O is markedly superior to a theistic explanation, he will have to give us a theistic and a nontheistic explanation to work with. Otherwise, he is just beating the air to no purpose.

But perhaps it is a mistake to think that Draper seriously means to be talking about explanation. In Draper 1989, after formulating "C: HI explains the facts O reports much better than theism does," Draper goes on to explain his use of "explain" as follows:

> I will reformulate C as the claim that the facts O reports are much more surprising on theism than they are on HI, or, more precisely, that the antecedent probability of O is much greater on the assumption that HI is true than on the assumption that theism is true. By the "antecedent" probability of O, I mean O's probability independent of (rather than temporally prior to) the observations and testimony it reports.

He further lays it down that "The probabilities employed in C are epistemic ones rather than, for example, statistical, physical, or logical probabilities." And in a note to this statement he writes:

> The concept of epistemic probability is an ordinary concept of probability for which no adequate philosophical analysis has, in my opinion, been proposed. As a first approximation, however, perhaps the following analysis will do:
>> Relative to K, p is epistemically more probable than q, where K is an epistemic situation and p and q are propositions, just in case any fully rational person in K would have a higher degree of belief in p than in q.

The reason this indicates that Draper is not seriously concerned with explanation is that there is no sense of *explain* in which "P explains x better than Q" *means* "The antecedent probability of x is greater on P than on Q." First of all, there are many cases of epistemic probability in which there is no explanatory relation at all. Consider inductive generalization. The antecedent probability of "This specimen of copper melted at 327 degrees C" is greater on "Copper always melts at 327 degrees C" than on "Copper sometimes melts at 327 degrees C." But neither of the latter goes any way at all toward explaining the fact that this specimen of copper melted at 327 degrees C. And going the other way, "Copper always melts at 327 degrees C" has a higher probability on "All observed samples of copper melted at 327 degrees C" than on "Half of the observed samples of copper melted at 327 degrees C." And even more obviously the behavior of the observed samples contributes nothing to the explanation of the general fact. To take another kind of example, the probability of "Robinson shot the victim" is greater on "Potter (an eminently respectable citizen with no self-interest in the matter) testified that he saw Robinson shoot the victim" than on "Wheelwright (a convicted criminal who is trying to get the best plea bargain) testified that he saw Robinson shoot the victim." But in neither case does the testimony do anything to explain the fact that Robinson shot the victim. This point could be illustrated by many other sorts of cases.

Secondly, comparative goodness of explanations doesn't always hang on the comparison of antecedent probability of the explanandum on the explanans. Sometimes it hangs on how well the explanans fits in with the rest of our knowledge, whether the fact cited by the explanans actually obtains, comparative simplicity of the rivals, and many other things. Thus the failure of my amplifier has at least as great a probability on the hypothesis of gremlins as on the hypothesis of a defective transistor. But we would prefer the latter explanation for the first two reasons just mentioned.

The moral of this is that one can't define *explain* in any way that strikes one's fancy. The term *explain* is certainly not perfectly precise; nor does it have only one meaning. But there are limits to its correct use. And Draper, I fear, has not identified even one meaning of "P explains x better than Q." At most, he has identified one factor that contributes to explanatory superiority.

This suggests that we should forget about explanation and take Draper to be concerned only with epistemic probability. How does the argument stack up in that case? Not very well. Draper supposes that whenever a set of facts, F, has a higher "antecedent probability" on q than on p, where q is inconsistent with p and is a "serious" hypothesis, then we have a prima facie good (epistemic) reason to reject q.[23] For counterexamples to this claim, see Plantinga's "On Being Evidentially Challenged" (chapter 13).[24]

NOTES

1. William L. Rowe, "William Alston on the Problem of Evil," in *The Rationality of Belief and the Plurality of Faiths*, ed. Thomas D. Senor (Ithaca: Cornell University Press, 1994).

2. In note 8, ibid., Rowe contrasts his construal of P with not-III (in a slightly different wording) and explicitly disavows the latter as his understanding of P.

3. I am indebted to Rowe for pointing out some mistakes in two earlier attempts to say what is wrong with his present reading of P.

4. This is not quite accurate. As I will stress later, the category of justifying goods known to us is by no means identical to the category of justifying *reasons* known by us.

5. *Philosophical Perspectives* 5 (1991); chapter 6 in this volume. Hereafter I will refer to this article as "Alston 1991."

6. One would like to determine just how this new argument of Rowe's is related to his earlier inductive argument from P to Q. For example, one would like to know whether the soundness of that induction is somehow presupposed in this Bayesian argument. To go into the matter thoroughly would be a major undertaking for which there is no room in this chapter. I will just point out that my objection to a probability assignment for P/G&k is closely related to my objections to supposing that our inability to see a sufficient reason for God's permitting E1 and E2 provides no substantial basis for supposing that there is no such reason.

7. *American Philosophical Quarterly* 16 (1979); chapter 1 in this volume. Hereafter I refer to this article as "Rowe 1979."

8. *Philosophical Topics* 16 (1988). Hereafter I refer to this article as "Rowe 1988."

9. I am far from suggesting that Rowe is unaware of this. On the contrary, in presenting his case for P (for 1 in Rowe 1979), he often proceeds by attending to both facets of the question as to whether any known goods would provide God with a sufficient justifying reason for permitting, e.g., Bambi's suffering. In the passage I have quoted in which Rowe presents his case for P, he addresses himself to both facets of the problem. Nor is this a recent reform on his part. See Rowe 1988, 120-21, and Rowe 1979. Indeed, in the latter passage Rowe focuses exclusively on the conditions of realization rather than on the nature of the good. So if Rowe consistently exhibits awareness of both aspects of the problem, why am I making such a big deal out of this? Because the way his argument is structured from 1988 on inevitably focuses on the inference from known goods to all goods, and tends to divert us from the need to consider what we know about the conditions of realization. For example, in his new contribution to this volume (chapter 14) he asks, "Under what conditions would P be true?" He mentions two conditions: (1) "the nonoccurrence of the known good (supposing there is just one) whose occurrence would justify God in permitting E1 or E2"; (2) "the nonexistence of God." Nothing is said about the conditions of realization of the good. True, Rowe does not claim that this list is exhaustive, but it is significant that he omits the crucial condition that his structuring of the argument tends to deemphasize. Again, while Rowe has been quite concerned to defend his inference from "no known goods justify the permission" to "no goods justify the permission," he exhibits no such concern for the equally problematic inference from "our knowledge of interconnections does not indicate that the permission of E1 or E2 would be necessary for God to realize some sufficiently great good" to "there are no such interconnections."

10. I have represented Rowe's empirical base more modestly than he does. I have presented that base as "No good satisfies (a) and (b), so far as he can tell on careful reflection." But what he maintains is that on reflection "we can see [of any good we can envisage] that it is very likely, if not certain, that the good in question either is not good enough to justify God in permitting E1 or E2 or is such that an omnipotent, omniscient being could realize it (or some greater good) without having to permit E1 or E2" (chapter 14; see also Rowe 1988, 120). Where I specify Rowe's starting point as a statement about what is the case *so far as he can see,* he claims that it is reasonable to believe that this is the case, that on reflection he can see it as "very likely, if not certain." I do not accept these more ambitious claims. In contesting them, I shall push the discussion back to what I take to lie behind them, viz., that no known goods satisfy both (a) and (b), so far as he can see on careful reflection. Rowe, I am supposing, takes this to adequately support the claim that no known good satisfies both (a) and (b). It is this inference that I will assess.

11. M. B. Ahern, *The Problem of Evil* (London: Routledge and Kegan Paul, 1971), 54-55, 57, 72-73; F. J. Fitzpatrick, "The Onus of Proof in Arguments about the Problem of Evil," *Religious Studies* 17 (1981): 25-28; Stephen J. Wykstra, "The Humean Obstacle to Evidential Arguments from Suffering: On Avoiding the Evils of 'Appearance,'" *International Journal for Philosophy of Religion* 16 (1984): 88, and Wykstra's chapter 7 in this volume; Alvin Plantinga, "Epistemic Probability and Evil," chapter 5 in this volume.

12. Gale, as well as the others I am about to discuss on this topic, lump all consideration of values under the rubrics of "morality," "moral philosophy," "moral values," "morally significant values," and the like. They all seem to suppose that any value (or disvalue) that can have a bearing on moral decisions, i.e., any value, is properly termed "moral." That seems to me, at best, infelicitous. I prefer to use *moral* in a more discriminating fashion. But to avoid confusion I will go along with my opponents on this point and pretend that the topic of values generally can be treated as part of morality.

13. Note that, unlike Wykstra, I do not argue that there is an antecedent probability that many of God's reasons for permitting evil would be hidden from us. I see no general theological or other reasons for expecting this. It is just that, along with Rowe, I hold that in many cases of evil we do not, in fact, see what reasons would justify God in permitting them. Hence, if God exists, His reasons for these permissions are in fact hidden from us.

14. Rowe, chapter 14, and Gale, chapter 11.

15. Let me emphasize that the analogues are not presented as an argument for my thesis. They do not *show* that the discernment-of-divine-reasons case is analogous to them in the relevant respects. I did not present them to do that job. Rather, they are designed to help us see the features of the divine reasons case to which they are analogous.

16. Another complexity here is that whether it is worth enduring the suffering to achieve the good depends not just on the general type to which the good belongs but also on the degree of it, where it is something that admits of degrees, as "felicity" does. To give Rowe the benefit of the doubt, let's assume that he is playing fair with the theist by considering in each case the maximum degree of the good.

17. I.e., in accord with the natural potentialities and capacities of the subject, without violating the subject's nature.

18. If I were attempting to lay out a plausible scenario for the divine master plan, this last suggestion would be woefully deficient. But I am only concerned here to indicate abstract possibilities in order to suggest that we are not in a position to tell whether they are realized in some form or other; I am not concerned to spell out the details of a particular possible realization.

19. See, e.g., Daniel Howard-Snyder, "Inscrutable Evil and the Silence of God," doctoral dissertation, Syracuse University, 1992, §20. To make this supposition would be tantamount to requiring S's being justified in believing that *S is justified in believing that p* for it to be the case that S is justified in believing that p, and thus to fall into the sort of "level confusion" against which I have repeatedly warmed by confreres. See Alston, "Level Confusions in Epistemology," *Epistemic Justification* (Ithaca: Cornell University Press, 1989).

20. The immediate inspiration for this move is the notion of a belief's being "objectively evidence essential" in Stephen Wykstra, "Toward a Sensible Evidentialism: On the Notion of 'Needing Evidence,'" in *Philosophy of Religion,* ed. William Rowe and William Wainwright (New York: Harcourt Brace Jovanovich, 1989). A more remote inspiration is the emphasis on a social "division of labor" in Hilary Putnam, "The Meaning of 'Meaning,'" in *Language, Mind, and Knowledge,* ed. K. Gunderson (Minneapolis: University of Minnesota Press, 1975).

21. Paul Draper, "Pain and Pleasure: An Evidential Problem for Theists," *Nous* 23 (1989); chapter 2 in this volume. Hereafter I shall refer to this article as "Draper 1989."

22. O is "a statement reporting both the observations one has made of humans and animals experiencing pain or pleasure and the testimony one has encountered concerning the observations others have made of sentient beings experiencing pain or pleasure."

23. I'm not sure just what it takes for an hypothesis to be "serious," but let's say that it requires at least that the hypothesis not be known to be false and that in the epistemic situation in question it seems to be a live possibility.

24. For comments on and discussion of various parts of this chapter, I thank Mark Brown, Paul Draper, Daniel Howard-Snyder, and William Rowe.

BIBLIOGRAPHY

ALICIA McKISSEN, KELLIE HOLZER, AND DANIEL HOWARD-SNYDER
Essays reprinted in this volume are marked by an asterisk.

Ackerman, Robert. "An Alternative Free Will Defense." *Religious Studies* 18 (1982): 365-72.

Adams, Marilyn McCord. "Hell and the Justice of God." *Religious Studies* 11 (1975): 433-47.

—————— "Redemptive Suffering: A Christian Solution to the Problem of Evil." In *Rationality, Religious Belief, and Moral Commitment,* ed. Robert Audi and William J. Wainwright. Ithaca: Cornell University Press, 1986.

—————— "Duns Scotus on the Goodness of God." *Faith and Philosophy* 4 (1987): 486-505.

—————— "Problems of Evil: More Advice to Christian Philosophers." *Faith and Philosophy* 5 (1988): 121-43.

—————— "Theodicy without Blame." *Philosophical Topics* 16 (1988): 215-45.

—————— "Horrendous Evils and the Goodness of God." *The Aristotelian Society Supplementary Volume* 63 (1989): 297-310.

—————— "Sin as Uncleanness." *Philosophical Perspectives* 5 (1991): 1-27.

—————— "God and Evil: Polarities of a Problem." *Philosophical Studies* 69 (1993): 167-86.

—————— "The Problem of Hell: A Problem of Evil for Christians." In *Reasoned Faith,* ed. Eleonore Stump. Ithaca: Cornell University Press, 1994.

—————— and Robert Adams, eds. *The Problem of Evil.* New York: Oxford University Press, 1990.

Adams, Robert M. "Must God Create the Best?" *Philosophical Review* 81 (1972). Also in Robert M. Adams, *The Virtue of Faith.* New York: Oxford University Press, 1987, 51-64.

—————— "Middle Knowledge and the Problem of Evil." *American Philosophical Quarterly* 14 (1977): 109-17. Also in *The Virtue of Faith,* 77-93.

—————— "Existence, Self-Interest, and the Problem of Evil." *Nous* 13 (1979). Also in *The Virtue of Faith,* 65-76.

—————— "Plantinga on the Problem of Evil." In *Alvin Plantinga,* ed. James E. Tomberlin and Peter van Inwagen. Dordrecht: Reidel, 1985, 225-55.

Ahern, M. B. *The Problem of Evil.* London and New York: Routledge and Kegan Paul and Schocken Books, 1971.

Aiken, Henry David. "God and Evil: A Study of Some Relations between Faith and Morals." *Ethics* 68 (1958): 77-97.

Allen, Diogenes. "Theodicies: Rebuttals to a Challenge." In *The Reasonableness of Faith: A Philosophical Essay on the Grounds for Religious Beliefs.* Washington, D.C.: Corpus Books, 1968.

———— "Natural Evil and the Love of God." *Religious Studies* 16 (1980): 439-56.

*Alston, William. "The Inductive Argument from Evil and the Human Cognitive Condition." *Philosophical Perspectives* 5 (1991): 29-67.

Andre, Shane. "The Problem of Evil and the Paradox of Friendly Atheism." *International Journal for Philosophy of Religion* 17 (1985): 209-16.

Anglin, William. "Evil Is Privation." *International Journal for Philosophy of Religion* 13 (1982): 3-12.

Appleby, Peter C. "Reformed Epistemology, Rationality and Belief in God." *International Journal for Philosophy of Religion* 24 (1988): 129-41.

Aspenson, Steven S. "Reply to O'Connor's 'A Variation on the Free Will Defense.'" *Faith and Philosophy* 6 (1989): 95-98.

Ayers, Robert H. "A Viable Theodicy for Christian Apologetics." *Modern Schoolman* 52 (1975): 391-403.

Baldwin, Dalton D. "Evil and Persuasive Power: A Response to Hare and Madden." *Process Studies* 3 (1973): 259-72.

Banning, Andrew, "Professor Brightman's Theory of a Limited God: A Criticism." *Harvard Theological Review* 27 (1934): 145-68.

Barnhart, J. E. "An Ontology of Inevitable Moral Evil." *Personalist* 47 (1966): 102-11.

———— "Persuasive and Coercive Power in Process Metaphysics." *Process Studies* 13 (1973): 153-57.

———— "Theodicy and the Free Will Defense: Response to Plantinga and Flew." *Religious Studies* 13 (1977): 439-53.

Basinger, David. "Evil as Evidence against the Existence of God: A Response." *Philosophy Research Archives* 4 (1978), no. 1275.

———— "Human Freedom and Divine Omnipotence: Some New Thoughts on an Old Problem." *Religious Studies* 15 (1979): 491-510.

———— "Christian Theism and the Free Will Defense." *Sophia* (Australia) 19 (1980): 20-33.

———— "Must God Create the Best Possible World? A Response." *International Philosophical Quarterly* 20 (1980): 339-42.

———— "Evil as Evidence against God's Existence." *Modern Schoolman* 58 (1981): 175-84.

———— "Determinism and Evil: Some Clarifications." *Australasian Journal of Philosophy* 60 (1982): 163-64.

———— "Plantinga's 'Free-Will Defense' as a Challenge to Orthodox Theism." *American Journal of Theology and Philosophy* 3 (1982): 35-41.

———— "Divine Omniscience and the Best of All Possible Worlds." *Journal of Value Inquiry* 16 (1982): 143-48.

———— "In What Sense Must God Do His Best? A Response to Hasker." *International Journal of Philosophy of Religion* 18 (1985): 161-64.

———— "Divine Power: Do Process Theists Have a Better Idea?" In *Process Theology,* ed. Ronald Nash. Grand Rapids: Baker, 1987, 197-213.

———— "Evil and a Finite God: A Response to McGrath's 'Evil and the Existence of a Finite God.'" *Philosophy Research Archives* 13 (1987-88): 285-87.

———— Review of David Ray Griffin's *Evil Revisited: Responses and Reconsiderations. Faith and Philosophy* (1993): 275-79.

———— "Divine Omniscience and the Soteriological Problem of Evil: Is the Type of Knowledge God Possesses Relevant?" *Religious Studies* 28 (1992): 1-18.

Basinger, Randall, and David Basinger. "Divine Omnipotence: Plantinga vs. Griffin." *Process Studies* 11 (1981): 11-24.

———— "Divine Determinateness and the Free Will Defense." *Philosophy Research Archives* 8 (1982), no. 1517.

Bauckham, Richard. "'Only the Suffering God Can Help': Divine Impassibility in Modern Theology." *Themelios* 9 (1984): 6-12.

———— "Theodicy from Ivan Karamazov to Moltmann." *Modern Theology* 4 (1987): 83-97.

Beaty, Michael D. "The Problem of Evil: The Unanswered Questions Argument." *Southwest Philosophy Review* 4 (1988): 57-64.

Benditt, Theodore. "A Problem for Theodicists." *Philosophy* 50 (1975): 470-74.

Bennett, Philip W. "Evil, God and the Free Will Defense." *Australasian Journal of Philosophy* 51 (1973): 39-50.

Bertocci, Peter A. "Idealistic Temporalistic Personalism and Good-and-Evil." *Proceedings of the American Catholic Philosophical Association* 51 (1977): 56-65.

Betty, L. Stafford. "Making Sense of Animal Pain: An Environmental Theodicy." *Faith and Philosophy* 9 (1992): 65-82.

Beversluis, John. "Grief." *C. S. Lewis and the Search for Rational Religion.* Grand Rapids: Eerdmans, 1985.

Bishop, John. "Compatibilism and the Free Will Defence." *Australian Journal of Philosophy* 71 (1993): 104-20.

———— "Evil and the Concept of God." *Philosophical Papers* 22 (1993): 1-15.

Boer, Steven. "The Irrelevance of the Free Will Defense." *Analysis* 38 (1978): 110-12.

Brecher, Robert. "Knowledge, Belief, and the Sophisticated Theodicist." *Heythrop Journal* 17 (1976): 178-83.

Brightman, Edgar Sheffield. *The Problem of God.* New York: Abingdon, 1930.

Brown, Patterson. "Religious Morality." *Mind* 72 (1963): 235-44.

Brummer, Vincent. *Speaking of a Personal God: An Essay in Philosophical Theology.* New York: Cambridge University Press, 1993.

Buber, Martin. *Good and Evil.* New York: Charles Scribner's Sons, 1952.

Burch, Robert. "Plantinga and Leibniz's Lapse." *Analysis* 39 (1979): 24-29.

Burgess-Jackson, Keith. "Free Will, Omnipotence, and the Problem of Evil." *American Journal of Theology and Philosophy* 9 (1988): 175-85.

Burke, Michael B. "Theodicy with a God of Limited Power: A Reply to McGrath's 'Atheism or Agnosticism.'" *Analysis* 47 (1987): 57-58.

Burkle, Howard. *God, Suffering, and Belief.* Nashville: Abingdon, 1977.

Burns, J. Patout. "Augustine on the Origin and Progress of Evil." *Journal of Religious Ethics* 16 (1988): 9-27.

Burrell, David. "Maimonides, Aquinas and Gersonides on Providence and Evil." *Religious Studies* 20 (1984): 335-52.

Burt, Donald X. "The Powerlessness of God or of Man." *Proceedings of the American Catholic Philosophical Association* 46 (1972): 142-48.

Buttrick, George A. *God, Pain and Evil.* Nashville: Abingdon, 1966.

Cahill, Lisa Sowie. "Consent in Time of Affliction: The Ethics of a Circumspect Theist." *Journal of Religious Ethics* 13 (1985): 22-36.

Cahn, Steven M. "Cacodaemony." *Analysis* 37 (1977): 69-73.

Calvert, Brian. "Descartes and the Problem of Evil." *Canadian Journal of Philosophy* (1972): 117-26.

———— "Dualism and the Problem of Evil." *Sophia* (Australia) 22 (1983): 15-28.

Campbell, Keith. "Patterson Brown on God and Evil." *Mind* 74 (1965): 582-84.

Campbell, Richmond. "God, Evil and Humanity." *Sophia* (Australia) 23 (1984): 21-35.

Capitan, William H. "Part X of Hume's Dialogues." *American Philosophical Quarterly* 3 (1966): 82-86.

Carson, D. A. *How Long, O Lord?* Grand Rapids: Baker, 1991.

Cartwright, Nancy. "Comments on Wesley Salmon's 'Science and Religion.'" *Philosophical Studies* 33 (1978): 177-83.

Chakraborty, Nirmalya. "If There Be a God, from Whence Proceed So Many Evils?" *Indian Philosophical Quarterly* 20 (1993): 125-43.

Chaves, Eduardo O. C. "Logical and Semantical Aspects of the Problem of Evil." *Critica* 10 (1978): 3-42.

Chernoff, Fred. "The Obstinance of Evil." *Mind* 89 (1980): 269-73.

Chisholm, Roderick M. "The Defeat of Good and Evil." *Proceedings and Addresses of the American Philosophical Association* 42 (1968-69): 21-38.

Christlieb, Terry. "Which Theisms Face an Evidential Problem of Evil?" *Faith and Philosophy* 9 (1992): 45-64.

Chryssides, George D. "Evil and the Problem of God." *Religious Studies* 23 (1987): 467-75.

Chrzan, Keith. "Linear Programming and Utilitarian Theodicy." *International Journal of Philosophy of Religion* 20 (1986): 147-57.

———— "The Irrelevance of the No Best Possible World Defense." *Philosophia* (Israel) 17 (1987): 161-67.

———— "Hudson on 'Too Much' Evil: Response to Hudson's 'Is There Too Much Evil in the World.'" *International Philosophical Quarterly* 27 (1987): 203-6.

———— "Plantinga on Atheistic Induction." *Sophia* (Australia) 27 (1988): 10-14.

———— "When Is a Gratuitous Evil Really Gratuitous?" *International Journal for Philosophy of Religion* 24 (1988): 87-91.

———— "God and Gratuitous Evil: A Reply to Yandell." *Religious Studies* (1991): 99-103.

———— "Comment on Langtry's 'God, Evil and Probability.'" *Sophia* (Australia) 32 (1993): 54-58.

———— "Necessary Gratuitous Evil." *Faith and Philosophy* (1994): 134-37.

Clark, Kelly James. "Evil and Christian Belief." *International Philosophical Quarterly* 29 (1989): 175-89.

Clark, Stephen R. L. "God, Good and Evil." *Proceedings of the Aristotelian Society* 77 (1976-77): 247-64.

Cobb, John G. *God and the World.* Philadelphia: Westminster Press, 1969.

———— "The Problem of Evil and the Task of Ministry." In *Encountering Evil,* ed. Stephen T. Davis. Atlanta: Knox Press, 1981: 167-80.

Conway, David A. "The Philosophical Problem of Evil." *International Journal for Philosophy of Religion* 24 (1988): 35-66.

Cooper, K. J. "Here We Go Again: Pike vs. Plantinga on the Problem of Evil." *International Journal for Philosophy of Religion* 14 (1983): 107-16.

Copp, David. "Leibniz's Theory That Not All Possible Worlds Are Compossible." *Studia Leibnitiana* 5 (1973): 26-42.

Coughlan, Michael J. "Moral Evil without Consequences?" *Analysis* 39 (1979): 58-60.

———— "The Free Will Defense and Natural Evil." *International Journal for Philosophy of Religion* 20 (1986): 93-108.

———— "In Defense of Free Will Theodicy." *Religious Studies* 23 (1987): 543-54.

Crenshaw, James. *Theodicy in the Old Testament.* Philadelphia: Fortress Press, 1983.

Crisp, Roger. "The Avoidance of the Problem of Evil: A Reply to McGrath." *Analysis* 46 (1986): 160.

Davies, Martin. "Determinism and Evil: Some Clarifications." *Australasian Journal of Philosophy* 58 (1980): 116-27.

Davis, Douglas P. "The Privation Account of Evil: H. J. McCloskey and Francisco Suarez." *Proceedings of the American Catholic Philosophical Association* 61 (1987): 199-208.

Davis, John W. "Going out the Window: A Comment on Tweyman's 'Humes's Dialogues on Evil.'" *Hume Studies* 13 (1987): 86-97.

Davis, Stephen T. "A Defense of the Free Will Defense." *Religious Studies* 8 (1972): 335-43.

———— "Why Did This Happen to Me?—the Patient as a Philosopher." *Princeton Seminary Bulletin* 65 (1972): 61-67.

———— "God the Mad Scientist: Process Theology on God and Evil." *Themelios* 5 (1979): 18-23.

————, ed. *Encountering Evil: Live Options in Theodicy.* Atlanta: Knox Press, 1981.

———— "The Problem of Evil in Recent Philosophy." *Review and Expositor* 82 (1985): 535-48.

De Beausobre, Julia. "Creative Suffering." *Theoria to Theory* 12 (1978): 111-21.

Dedek, John F. "Intrinsically Evil Acts: An Historical Study of the Mind of St. Thomas." *Thomist* 43 (1979): 385-413.

DeRose, Keith. "Plantinga, Presumption, Possibility, and the Problem of Evil." *Canadian Journal of Philosophy* 21 (1991): 497-512.

Dilley, Frank B. "Fool-Proof Proofs of God?" *International Journal for Philosophy of Religion* 8 (1977).

———— "A Modified Flew Attack on the Free Will Defense." *Southern Journal of Philosophy* 20 (1982): 25-34.

———— "Is the Free Will Defense Irrelevant?" *Religious Studies* 18 (1982): 355-64.

———— "The Free-Will Defence and Worlds without Moral Evil." *International Journal for Philosophy of Religion* 27 (1990): 1-15.

Dore, Clement. "Plantinga on the Free Will Defense." *Review of Metaphysics* 24 (1971): 690-706.

———— "Ethical Supernaturalism and the Problem of Evil." *Religious Studies* 8 (1972): 97-113.

———— "Do Theodicists Mean What They Say?" *Philosophy* 48 (1974): 357-74.

———— "Do Theists Need to Solve the Problem of Evil?" *Religious Studies* 12 (1976): 383-90.

———— "Does Suffering Serve Valuable Ends?" *Theism.* Dordrecht: D. Reidel, 1984.

*Draper, Paul. "Pain and Pleasure: An Evidential Problem for Theists." *Nous* 23 (1989): 331-50.

———— "Evil and the Proper Basicality of Belief in God." *Faith and Philosophy* 8 (1991): 135-47.

———— "Probabilistic Arguments from Evil." *Religious Studies* 28 (1993): 303-17.

Drum, Peter. "The Intrinsic Value of Pain." *Sophia* (Australia) 31 (1992): 97-99.

Dupre, Louis. "Evil—a Religious Mystery." *Faith and Philosophy* 7 (1990): 261-80.

Ehman, Robert R. "On Evil and God." *Monist* 47 (1963): 478-87.

Evans, G. R. *Augustine on Evil.* Cambridge: Cambridge University Press, 1982.

Evans, J. N. "LaFollette on Plantinga's Free Will Defense." *International Journal for Philosophy of Religion* 14 (1983): 117-22.

Fackenheim, Emil L. "The Holocaust and Philosophy." *Journal of Philosophy* 82 (1985): 505-14.

Fales, Evan. "Antediluvian Theodicy: Stump on the Fall." *Faith and Philosophy* 6 (1989): 320-29.

———— "Should God Not Have Created Adam?" *Faith and Philosophy* 9 (1992): 192-208.

Farmer, H. H. *The World and God.* New York: Harper, 1935.

Farrell, P. M. "Evil and Omnipotence." *Mind* 67 (1958): 399-403.

———— "Freedom and Evil." *Australasian Journal of Philosophy* 36 (1958): 216-21.

Farrer, Austin. *Love Almighty and Ills Unlimited.* London: Collins, 1962.

Feinberg, John S. *The Many Faces of Evil: Theological Systems and the Problem of Evil,* 2nd ed. Grand Rapids: Zondervan, 1994.

Felt, James W. "God's Choice: Reflections on Evil in a Created World." *Faith and Philosophy* 1 (1984): 370-77.

Ferre, Frederick. "Theodicy and the Status of Animals." *American Philosophical Quarterly* 23 (1986): 23-34.

Ferre, Nels. *Evil and the Christian Faith.* New York: Harper, 1947; Books for Libraries Press, 1971.

Fisher, Peter F. "Milton's Theodicy." *Journal of the History of Ideas* 17 (1956): 28-53.

Fitzpatrick, F. J. "The Onus of Proof in Arguments about the Problem of Evil." *Religious Studies* 17 (1981): 19-38.

Flemming, Arthur. "Omnibenevolence and Evil." *Ethics* 9 (1986): 261-81.

Flew, Antony. "The 'Religious Morality' of Mr. Patterson Brown." *Mind* 74 (1965): 578-81.

———— "Compatibilism, Free Will, and God." *Philosophy* 48 (1973): 231-44.

———— "The Free Will Defence." *God, Freedom and Immortality: A Critical Analysis.* Buffalo:

Prometheus, 1984. (Originally published as *The Presumption of Atheism,* Elek Books, 1976, 81-99.)

Flint, Thomas P. "Divine Sovereignty and the Free Will Defense." *Sophia* (Australia) 23 (1984): 41-52.

Ford, Lewis. "Divine Persuasion and the Triumph of Good." *The Christian Scholar* 50 (1967): 235-50.

Forrest, Peter. "The Problem of Evil: Two Neglected Defenses." *Sophia* (Australia) 20 (1981): 49-54.

Forsyth, P. T. *The Justification of God: Lectures for War-Time in a Christian Theodicy.* London: Duckworth, 1916.

Frankenberry, Nancy. "Some Problems in Process Theodicy." *Religious Studies* 17 (1981): 179-97.

Friedman, R. Z. "Evil and Moral Agency." *International Journal for Philosophy of Religion* 24 (1988): 3-20.

Fulmer, Gilbert. "Evil and Analogy." *Personalist* 58 (1977): 333-43.

——— "John Hick's Soul-Making Theodicy." *Southwest Philosophical Studies* 7 (1982): 170-79.

Gale, Richard M. "Freedom and the Free Will Defense." *Social Theory and Practice* (Fall 1990): 397-423.

——— *On the Nature and Existence of God.* New York: Cambridge University Press, 1991.

Galligan, Michael. *God and Evil.* New York: Paulist Press, 1976.

Gan, Barry L. "Plantinga's Transworld Depravity: It's Got Possibilities." *International Journal for Philosophy of Religion* 13 (1982): 169-77.

Garcia, J. L. A. "Goods and Evils." *Philosophy and Phenomenological Research* 47 (1987): 385-412.

Garcia, Laura L. "A Response to the Modal Problem of Evil." *Faith and Philosophy* 1 (1984): 378-88.

Geach, Peter. *Providence and Evil.* Cambridge: Cambridge University Press, 1977.

Geach, Peter, and Gilbert Fulmer. "An Exchange between Peter Geach and Gilbert Fulmer." *Southwestern Journal of Philosophy* 11 (1980): 165-70.

Geisler, Norman L. *The Roots of Evil.* Probe Ministries International, 1978.

Gellman, Jerome I. "A New Look at the Problem of Evil." *Faith and Philosophy* 9 (1992): 209-15.

Gelven, Michael. "The Meanings of Evil." *Philosophy Today* 27 (1983): 200-221.

Glatzer, Nahum, ed. *Dimensions of Job: A Study and Selected Readings.* New York: Schocken Books, 1969.

Gordis, Robert. *The Book of God and Man: A Study of Job.* Chicago and London: University of Chicago Press, 1978.

Gordon, David. "Is the Argument from Evil Decisive?" *Religious Studies* 19 (1983): 407-10.

Gordon, Jeffrey, "The Dilemma of Theodicy." *Sophia* (Australia) 23 (1984): 22-34.

Grave, S. A. "On Evil and Omnipotence." *Mind* 65 (1956): 259-62.

Gregory, Peter N. "The Problem of Theodicy in the *Awakening of Faith.*" *Religious Studies* 22 (1986): 63-78.

Griffin, David R. "Divine Causality, Evil, and Philosophical Theology: A Critique of James Ross." *International Journal for Philosophy of Religion* 4 (1973): 168-86.

——— *God, Power, and Evil: A Process Theodicy.* Philadelphia: Westminster Press, 1976.

——— "Creation out of Chaos and the Problem of Evil." In *Encountering Evil,* ed. Stephen T. Davis. Atlanta: Knox Press, 1981, 101-36.

——— "Actuality, Possibility, and Theodicy: A Response to Nelson Pike's 'Process Theodicy and the Concept of Power.'" *Process Studies* 12 (1982): 168-79.

——— *Evil Revisited: Responses and Reconsiderations.* Albany: SUNY Press, 1991.

Grigg, Richard. "Theism and Proper Basicality: A Response to Plantinga." *International Journal for Philosophy of Religion* 14 (1983): 123-27.

Grover, Stephen. "Satisfied Pigs and Dissatisfied Philosophers: Schlesinger on the Problem of Evil." *Philosophical Investigations* 16 (1993): 212-30.

Grunbaum, Adolf. "God and the Holocaust." *Free Inquiry* 8 (1987-88): 23.

Guirdham, Arthur. "Evil and Disease." *Systematics* 11 (1974): 267-76.

Guleserian, Theodore. "God and Possible Worlds: The Modal Problem of Evil." *Nous* 17 (1983): 221-38.

Halberstam, Joshua. "Philosophy and the Holocaust." *Metaphilosophy* 12 (1981): 277-83.

Hall, Thor. "Theodicy as a Test of the Reasonableness of Theology." *Religion in Life* 43 (1974): 204-17.

Hallett, Garth L. "Evil and Human Understanding." *Heythrop Journal* (1991): 467-76.

Hare, Peter. Review of David Ray Griffin, *God, Power, and Evil. Process Studies* 7 (1977): 44-51.

———— Review of George Schlesinger, *Religion and Scientific Method. Metaphilosophy* 11 (1980): 292-95.

Hare, Peter H., and Edward H. Madden. "Why Hare Must Hound the Gods." *Philosophy and Phenomenological Research* 29 (1969): 456-59.

———— "Evil and Inconclusiveness." *Sophia* (Australia) 11 (1972): 8-12.

———— "Evil and Persuasive Power." *Process Studies* 2 (1972): 44-48.

Harrison, Peter. "Theodicy and Animal Pain." *Philosophy* 64 (1989): 79-92.

Hartshorne, Charles. "A New Look at the Problem of Evil." In *Current Philosophical Issues: Essays in Honor of Curt John Ducasse,* ed. F. C. Dommeyer. Springfield: Charles C. Thomas, 1966, 201-12.

———— "The Dipolar Conception of Deity." *Review of Metaphysics* 21 (1967): 273-89.

Hasker, William. "On Regretting the Evils of This World." *Southern Journal of Philosophy* 19 (1981): 425-37.

———— "Must God Do His Best?" *International Journal for Philosophy of Religion* 16 (1984): 213-24.

———— "Suffering, Soul-Making, and Salvation." *International Philosophical Quarterly* 28 (1988): 3-19.

———— "The Necessity of Gratuitous Evil." *Faith and Philosophy* 9 (1992): 23-44.

———— "Providence and Evil: Three Theories." *Religious Studies* 28 (1992): 91-105.

Hatcher, William S. "A Logical Solution to the Problem of Evil." *Zygon* 9 (1974): 245-55.

———— "The Relative Conception of Good and Evil." *Zygon* 10 (1975): 446-48.

Hauerwas, Stanley. *Suffering Presence: Theological Reflections on Medicine, the Mentally Handicapped, and the Church.* Notre Dame: University of Notre Dame Press, 1985.

———— "God, Medicine, and the Problem of Evil." *Reformed Journal* 38 (1988): 16-22.

———— *Naming the Silences: God, Medicine, and the Problem of Suffering.* Grand Rapids: Eerdmans (1990).

Hebblethwaite, Brian. *Evil, Suffering, and Religion.* New York: Hawthorne Books, 1976.

Hedentius, Ingemar. "Disproofs of God's Existence?" *Personalist* 52 (1971): 23-43.

Hershbell, Jackson P. "Berkeley and the Problem of Evil." *Journal of the History of Ideas* 31 (1970): 543-54.

Hick, John. "The Problem of Evil." In *The Encyclopedia of Philosophy,* ed. Paul Edwards. New York: Macmillan and Free Press, 1967, 136-41.

———— "The Problem of Evil in the First and Last Things." *Journal of Theological Studies* 19, part 2 (1968): 591-602.

———— "God, Evil and Mystery." *Religious Studies* 3 (1968): 539-46.

———— Review of E. H. Madden and P. H. Hare, *Evil and the Concept of God. Philosophy* 44 (1969): 160-61.

———— "Freedom and the Irenaean Theodicy Again." *Journal of Theological Studies* 21, part 2 (1970): 419-22.

———— "God, Evil and Mystery." In *God and the Universe of Faiths,* ed. John Hick. London and New York: Macmillan and St. Martin's Press, 1973.

———— "Coherence and the God of Love Again." *Journal of Theological Studies* 24, part 2 (1973): 522-28.

———— "The Problem of Evil." *Philosophy of Religion,* 2nd ed. Englewood Cliffs: Prentice-Hall, 1973, 36-43.

———— "Evil and Incarnation." In *Incarnation and Myth: The Debate Continued,* ed. Michael Gouldner. London: SCM, 1979.

———— *Evil and the God of Love.* 2d. ed. New York: Harper & Row, 1978.

———— "Remarks." In *Reason and Religion,* ed. Stuart Brown. Ithaca: Cornell University Press, 1977.

———— *Faith and Knowledge.* 2d ed. London: Macmillan, 1988.

Hicks, David C. "Moral Evil as Apparent Disvalue." *Religious Studies* 13 (1977): 1-16.

Higgins, David. "Evil in Maritain and Lonergan." In *Jacques Maritain,* ed. J. Knasas. Notre Dame: University of Notre Dame Press, 1988, 235-42.

Hitterdale, Larry. "The Problem of Evil and the Subjectivity of Values Are Incompatible." *International Philosophical Quarterly* 18 (1978): 467-69.

Hoitenga, Dewey. "Logic and the Problem of Evil." *American Philosophical Quarterly* 4 (1967): 114-26.

Howard-Snyder, Daniel. "Seeing through CORNEA." *International Journal for Philosophy of Religion* 32 (1992): 25-49.

———— "Theism, the Hypothesis of Indifference and the Biological Role of Pain and Pleasure." *Faith and Philosophy* (forthcoming).

———— Review of J. L. Schellenberg, *Divine Hiddenness and Human Reason, Mind* (forthcoming).

Howard-Snyder, Frances and Daniel. "The Christian Theodicist's Appeal to Love." *Religious Studies* 29 (1993): 185-92.

———— "How an Unsurpassable Being Can Create a Surpassable World." *Faith and Philosophy* (1994).

Hudson, Yeager. "Is There Too Much Evil in the World?" *International Philosophical Quarterly* 25 (1985): 343-48.

———— "Response to Chrzan's 'Hudson on "Too Much" Evil.'" *International Philosophical Quarterly* 27 (1987): 207-10.

———— "The Problem of Evil." *The Philosophy of Religion.* Mountain View: Mayfield, 1991, 117-33.

Hughes, Charles T. "Theism, Natural Evil, and Superior Possible Worlds." *International Journal for Philosophy of Religion* 31 (1992): 45-51.

Humber, James M. "Response to Gale's 'Freedom and the Free Will Defense.'" *Social Theory and Practice* (Fall 1990): 425-33.

Hutcheson, Peter. "Omniscience and the Problem of Evil." *Sophia* (Australia) 31 (1992): 53-58.

Jooharigian, Robert Badrik. *God and Natural Evil.* Bristol: Wyndham Hall Press, 1985.

Kane, G. Stanley. "Theism and Evil." *Sophia* (Australia) 9 (1970): 14-21.

———— "Soul-Making Theodicy and Eschatology." *Sophia* (Australia) 9 (1970): 24-31.

———— "The Concept of Divine Goodness and the Problem of Evil." *Religious Studies* 11 (1975): 49-71.

———— "The Failure of Soul-Making Theodicy." *International Journal for Philosophy of Religion* 6 (1975): 1-22.

———— "The Free-Will Defense Defended." *New Scholasticism* 50 (1976): 435-46.

———— "Evil and Privation." *International Journal for Philosophy of Religion* 11 (1980): 43-58.

Kaufman, Gordon D. "God and Evil." In *God the Problem.* Cambridge: Harvard University Press, 1972.

Kekes, John. "The Problem of Good." *Journal of Value Inquiry* 18 (1984): 99-112.

———— "Understanding Evil." *American Philosophical Quarterly* 25 (1988): 13-24.

———— *Facing Evil.* Princeton: Princeton University Press, 1990.

Keller, James A. "The Problem of Evil and the Attributes of God." *International Journal for Philosophy of Religion* 26 (1989): 155-71.

Khatchadourian, Haig. "God, Happiness and Evil." *Religious Studies* 2 (1966): 109-20.

Kielkopf, Charles F. "Emotivism as the Solution to the Problem of Evil." *Sophia* (Australia) 9 (1970): 34-38.

King, James T. "The Problem of Evil and the Meaning of Good." *Proceedings of the American Catholic Philosophical Association* 44 (1970): 185-94.

———— "The Meta-Ethical Dimension of the Problem of Evil." *Journal of Value Inquiry* 5 (1971): 174-84.

King-Farlow, John. "Must Gods Madden Madden?" *Philosophy and Phenomenological Research* 29 (1969): 451-55.

———— "Through a Glass Darkly: God and Evil." *Reason and Religion.* London: Darton, Longman, and Todd, 1969.

———— "Cacodaemony and Devilish Isomorphism." *Analysis* 38 (1978): 59-61.

———— "Evil: On Multiple Placings in Time and Space." *Sophia* (Australia) 25 (1986): 44-46.

Kivy, Peter. "Voltaire, Hume, and the Problem of Evil." *Philosophy and Literature* 1 (1977): 211-24.

Kondoleon, Theodore J. "Moral Evil and the Existence of God: A Reply." *New Scholasticism* 47 (1973): 366-74.

———— "More on the Free Will Defense." *Thomist* 47 (1983): 1-42.

Kraemer, Eric, and Hardy Jones. "Freedom and the Problems of Evil." *Philosophical Topics* 13 (1985): 33-49.

Kretzmann, Norman. "God among the Causes of Moral Evil: The Hardening of Hearts and Spiritual Blinding." *Philosophical Topics* 16 (1988): 189-214.

———— "A General Problem of Creation." In *Being and Goodness,* ed. Scott MacDonald. Ithaca: Cornell University Press, 1990.

———— "A Particular Problem of Creation." In *Being and Goodness.*

Kroon, Frederick W. "Plantinga on God, Freedom, and Evil." *International Journal for Philosophy of Religion* 12 (1981): 75-96.

Kropf, Richard W. *Evil and Evolution: A Theodicy.* Cranbury: Associated University Press, 1984.

Kvanvig, Jonathan. *The Problem of Hell.* New York: Oxford University Press, 1993.

LaCroix, Richard R. "Unjustified Evil and God's Choice." *Sophia* (Australia) 13 (1974): 20-28.

LaFollette, Hugh. "Plantinga on the Free Will Defense." *International Journal for Philosophy of Religion* 11 (1980): 123-32.

Langton, Douglas. "The Argument from Evil: Reply to Professor Richman." *Religious Studies* 16 (1980): 103-13.

Langtry, Bruce. "God, Evil and Probability." *Sophia* (Australia) 28 (1989): 32-40.

———— "Some Internal Theodicies and the Objection from Alternative Goods." *International Journal for Philosophy of Religion* 34 (1993): 29-39.

LaPara, Nicholas. "Suffering, Happiness and Evil," *Sophia* (Australia) 4 (1965).

Larue, Gerald A. "The Book of Job on the Futility of Theological Discussion." *Personalist* 45 (1964): 72-79.

Lewis, C. S. *A Grief Observed.* New York: Bantam Books, 1961.

———— *The Problem of Pain.* New York: Macmillan, 1962.

Lewis, Delmas. "The Problem with the Problem of Evil." *Sophia* (Australia) 22 (1983): 26-36.

Lomasky, Loren E. "Are Compatibilism and the Free Will Defense Compatible?" *Personalist* 56 (1975): 385-88.

Londis, James J. "God, Probability and John Hick." *Religious Studies* 16 (1980): 457-63.

Lovin, Keith. "Plantinga's Puddle." *Southwestern Philosophical Studies* 4 (1979): 103-8.

Lugenbehl, Dale. "Can the Argument from Evil Be Decisive after All?" *Religious Studies* 18 (1982): 29-35.

Mackie, J. L. "Evil and Omnipotence." *Mind* 64 (1955): 200-212. Also in *The Problem of Evil,* ed. Michael Peterson, and *The Problem of Evil,* ed. Marilyn McCord Adams and Robert Adams.

————— "Theism and Utopia." *Philosophy* 37 (1962): 153-58.

————— Review of Hick's *Evil and the God of Love. Philosophical Books* 3 (1966): 17.

————— "The Problem of Evil." *The Miracle of Theism.* Oxford: Clarendon Press, 1982.

McCabe, Herbert. "God: Evil." *New Blackfriars* 62 (1981): 4-17.

McCloskey, H. J. "God and Evil." *Philosophical Quarterly* 10 (1960): 97-114.

————— "The Problem of Evil." *Journal of Bible and Religion* 30 (1962): 187-97.

————— "Evil and the Problem of Evil." *Sophia* (Australia) 5 (1966): 14-19.

————— *God and Evil.* The Hague: Martinus Nijhoff, 1974.

McCullagh, C. Behan. "Evil and the Love of God." *Sophia* (Australia) 31 (1992): 48-50.

McGrath, P. J. "Evil and the Existence of a Finite God." *Analysis* 46 (1986): 63-64.

————— "Is There a Problem of Evil?" *Philosophical Quarterly* 39 (1989): 91-94.

McHarry, John D. "A Theodicy." *Analysis* 38 (1978): 132-34.

McKenzie, David. "A Kantian Theodicy." *Faith and Philosophy* 1 (1984): 236-48.

McKim, Robert. "Worlds without Evil." *International Journal for Philosophy of Religion* 15 (1984): 161-70.

————— "The Hiddenness of God." *Religious Studies* 26 (1990): 141-43.

————— Review of J. L. Schellenberg, *Divine Hiddenness and Human Reason. Faith and Philosophy* (forthcoming).

MacKinnon, Donald. "Evil and the Vulnerability of God." *Philosophy* 62 (1987): 102.

McMahon, William E. "The Problem of Evil and the Possibility of a Better World." *Journal of Value Inquiry* 3 (1969): 81-90.

McNaughton, David. "The Problem of Evil: A Deontological Perspective." In *Reason and the Christian Religion,* ed. Alan Padgett. Oxford: Clarendon Press, 1994, 329-51.

McWilliams, Warren. "Divine Suffering in Contemporary Theology." *Scottish Journal of Theology* 33 (1980): 35-53.

Madden, Edward, and Peter Hare. *Evil and the Concept of God.* Springfield: Charles C. Thomas, 1968.

————— "Evil and Inconclusiveness." *Sophia* (Australia) 11 (1972): 8-12.

Maker, William A. "Augustine on Evil: The Dilemma of the Philosophers." *International Journal for Philosophy of Religion* 15 (1984): 149-60.

Maritain, Jacques. *St. Thomas and the Problem of Evil.* Milwaukee: Marquette University Press, 1942.

————— *God and the Permission of Evil.* Milwaukee: Bruce, 1966.

Markham, Ian. "Hume Revisited: A Problem with the Free Will Defense." *Modern Theology* (1991): 281-90.

Martin, Michael. "Is Evil Evidence against the Existence of God?" *Mind* 87 (1978): 429-32.

————— "God, Satan and Natural Evil." *Sophia* (Australia) 22 (1983): 43-45.

————— "The Coherence of the Hypothesis of an Omnipotent, Omniscient, Free and Perfectly Evil Being." *International Journal for Philosophy of Religion* 17 (1985): 185-91.

————— "A Theistic Inductive Argument from Evil?" *International Journal for Philosophy of Religion* 22 (1987): 81-87.

————— "Reichenbach on Natural Evil." *Religious Studies* 24 (1988): 91-99.

————— *Atheism: A Philosophical Justification.* Philadelphia: Temple University Press, 1990.

Mavrodes, George. "Some Recent Philosophical Theology." *Review of Metaphysics* 24 (1970): 82-111.

————— "The Problem of Evil." *Belief in God: A Study in the Epistemology of Religion.* New York: Random House, 1970, chap. 4.

————— "Keith Yandell and the Problem of Evil." *International Journal for Philosophy of Religion* 20 (1986): 45-48.

Mesle, C. Robert. "Does God Hide from Us? John Hick and Process Theology on Faith, Freedom and Theodicy." *International Journal for Philosophy of Religion* 24 (1988): 93-111.

——— *John Hick's Theodicy: A Process Humanist Critique*. New York: St. Martin's Press, 1991.

Mijuskovic, Ben. "Camus and the Problem of Evil." *Sophia* (Australia) 15 (1976): 11-19.

Miller, Ed. "The Problem of Evil." *God and Reason*. New York: Macmillan, 1972.

Miller, Randolph Crump. "Process, Evil and God." *American Journal of Theology and Philosophy* 1 (1980): 60-70.

Milne, Peter. "Probability, God and Evil." *Heythrop Journal* 33 (1992): 434-36.

Monasterio, Xavier. "Plantinga and the Two Problems of Evil." *Lyceum* 4 (1992): 83-103.

Moore, Harold F. "Evidence, Evil and Religious Belief." *International Journal for Philosophy of Religion* 9 (1978): 241-45.

——— "Evidence—Once More: Reply to E. Wierenga's Reply to H. Moore's 'Evidence, Evil and Religious Belief.'" *International Journal for Philosophy of Religion* 9 (1978): 252-53.

Mora, Freya. "Thank God for Evil?" *Philosophy* 58 (1983): 399-401.

Morris, Thomas V. "A Response to the Problems of Evil." *Philosophia* (Israel) 14 (1984): 173-86.

——— "The Hidden God." *Philosophical Topics* 16 (1988).

Morriston, Wesley. "Gladness, Regret, God, and Evil." *Southern Journal of Philosophy* 20 (1982): 401-7.

——— "Is Plantinga's God Omnipotent?" *Sophia* (Australia) 23 (1984): 45-57.

——— "Is God 'Significantly Free'?" *Faith and Philosophy* 2 (1985): 257-64.

——— "Rowe's Bayesian Argument from Evil: A Response" (unpublished).

Moser, Paul K. "Natural Evil and the Free Will Defense." *International Journal for Philosophy of Religion* 15 (1984): 49-56.

Moulder, James. "Philosophy, Religion and Theodicy." *South African Journal of Philosophy* 3 (1984): 147-50.

Murphree, Wallace. "Can Theism Survive without the Devil?" *Religious Studies* 21 (1985): 231-44.

Murray, Michael J. "Coercion and the Hiddenness of God." *American Philosophical Quarterly* 30 (1993): 27-38.

Myers, C. Mason. "Free Will and the Problem of Evil." *Religious Studies* 23 (1987): 289-94.

Nash, Ronald. "The Problem of Evil." *Faith and Reason*. Grand Rapids: Zondervan, 1988, part 4.

Nelson, Mark T. "Naturalistic Ethics and the Argument from Evil." *Faith and Philosophy* 8 (1991): 368-79.

——— "Temporal Wholes and the Problem of Evil." *Religious Studies* 29 (1993): 313-24.

Nerny, Gayne. "Aristotle and Aquinas on Indignation: From Nemesis to Theodicy." *Faith and Philosophy* 8 (1991): 81-95.

Novak, Joseph A. "Comments on Calvert's 'Dualism and the Problem of Evil.'" *Sophia* (Australia) 26 (1987): 42-49.

Oakes, Robert A. "Actualities, Possibilities, and Free-Will Theodicy." *New Scholasticism* 46 (1972): 191-201.

——— "God, Evil, and Professor Ross." *Philosophy and Phenomenological Research* 35 (1974): 261-67.

——— "The Problem with the 'Problem of Evil.'" *Personalist* 55 (1974): 106-14.

——— "God, Suffering, and Conclusive Evidence." *Sophia* (Australia) 14 (1975): 16-20.

Oates, David. "Social Darwinism and Natural Theodicy." *Zygon* 23 (1988): 439-54.

O'Connor, David. "Swinburne on Natural Evil." *Religious Studies* 19 (1983): 65-74.

——— "Theism, Evil and the Onus of Proof—Reply to F. J. Fitzpatrick." *Religious Studies* 19 (1983): 241-47.

——— "A Skeptical Defense of Theism." *Proceedings of the Catholic Philosophical Association* 64 (1990): 211-20.

——— "On Natural Evil's Being Necessary for Free Will." *Sophia* (Australia) 24 (1985): 36-44.

——— "On the Problem of Evil's Not Being What It Seems." *Philosophical Quarterly* 37 (1987): 441-47.

——— "A Variation on the Free Will Defense." *Faith and Philosophy* 4 (1987): 160-67.

———— "In Defense of Theoretical Theodicy." *Modern Theology* 5 (1988): 61-74.

———— "On Failing to Resolve Theism-Versus-Atheism Empirically." *Religious Studies* 26 (1990): 91-103.

———— "On the Problem of Evil's Still Not Being What It Seems." *Philosophical Quarterly* 40 (1990): 72-78.

———— "Swinburne on Natural Evil from Natural Processes." *International Journal for Philosophy of Religion* (1991): 77-87.

———— "Ethical Naturalism and Evil." *Faith and Philosophy* 10 (1993): 389-93.

O'Hear, Anthony. *Experience, Explanation, and Faith.* London: Routledge and Kegan Paul, 1984.

O'Leary-Hawthorne, John. "Non-Organic Theories of Value and Pointless Evil." *Faith and Philosophy* 9 (1992): 387-91.

———— and Daniel Howard-Snyder. "God, Schmod and Gratuitous Evil." *Philosophy and Phenomenological Research* 53 (1993): 861-74.

———— and Daniel Howard-Snyder. "On the A Priori Rejection of Evidential Arguments from Evil." *Sophia* (Australia) 32 (1993).

Owens, Joseph. "Theodicy, Natural Theology, and Metaphysics." *Modern Schoolman* 28 (1951): 126-37.

Pargetter, Robert. "Evil as Evidence." *Sophia* (Australia) 21 (1982): 11-15.

———— "Evil as Evidence against the Existence of God." *Mind* 85 (1976): 242-45.

Parsons, Keith M. *God and the Burden of Proof: Plantinga, Swinburne, and the Analytic Defense of Theism.* Buffalo: Prometheus, 1989.

Paulsen, David L. "Divine Determinateness and the Free Will Defense." *Analysis* 41 (1981): 150-53.

Penelhum, Terence. "Divine Goodness and the Problem of Evil." *Religious Studies* 2 (1966): 95-107.

———— *God and Skepticism.* Dordrecht: Reidel, 1983.

Pentz, Rebecca D. "Rules and Values and the Problem of Evil." *Sophia* (Australia) 21 (1982): 23-29.

Perkins, R. K., Jr. "McHarry's Theodicy: A Reply." *Analysis* 40 (1980): 168-71.

Pestana, Mark. "Radical Freedom, Radical Evil and the Possibility of Eternal Damnation." *Faith and Philosophy* 9 (1994): 500-507.

Peterson, Michael. "Evil and Inconsistency." *Sophia* (Australia) 18 (1979): 20-27.

———— "God and Evil: Problems of Consistency and Gratuity." *Journal of Value Inquiry* 13 (1979): 305-13.

———— *Evil and the Christian God.* Grand Rapids: Baker, 1982.

———— "Recent Work on the Problem of Evil." *American Philosophical Quarterly* 20 (1983): 321-39.

———— "Evil as Evidence for the Existence of God." In *Kerygma and Praxis,* ed. W. Vanderhoof and D. Basinger. Rochester: Roberts Wesleyan College Press, 1984, 115-31.

———— "God and Evil in Process Theology." In *Process Theology,* ed. Ronald Nash. Grand Rapids: Baker, 1987, 117-39.

———— "The Problem of Evil: The Case Against God's Existence." In *Reason and Religious Belief: An Introduction to the Philosophy of Religion,* ed. Michael Peterson et al. New York: Oxford University Press, 1991, 92-116.

————, ed. *The Problem of Evil: Selected Readings.* Notre Dame: University of Notre Dame Press, 1992.

Petit, Francois. *The Problem of Evil.* New York: Hawthorne Books, 1959.

Petrie, Asenath. *Individuality in Pain and Suffering.* Chicago: University of Chicago Press, 1978.

Phifer, Kenneth. "Postscript." In *Reason and Religion,* ed. Stuart Brown. Ithaca: Cornell University Press, 1977, 134-39.

———— "Why Me; Why Now?" *Religious Humanism* 19 (1985): 40-45.

Phillips, D. Z. "The Problem of Evil." In *Reason and Religion,* ed. Stuart Brown Ithaca: Cornell University Press, 1977, 103-21.

Pike, Nelson. "God and Evil: A Reconsideration." *Ethics* 68 (1958): 116-24.

———— "Hume on Evil." *Philosophical Review* 72 (1963): 180-97.

————, ed. *God and Evil.* Englewood Cliffs: Prentice-Hall, 1964.

———— "Plantinga on the Free Will Defense: A Reply." *Journal of Philosophy* 63 (1966): 93-104.

———— "Of God and Freedom." *Philosophical Review* 75 (1966): 369-79.

———— "Plantinga on Free Will and Evil." *Religious Studies* 15 (1979): 449-73.

———— "Process Theodicy and the Concept of Power." *Process Studies* 12 (1982): 148-67.

———— "Over-Power and God's Responsibility for Sin." In *The Existence and Nature of God,* ed. Alfred Freddoso. Notre Dame: University of Notre Dame Press, 1983, 11-36.

Plantinga, Alvin. "The Free Will Defense." In *Philosophy in America,* ed. Max Black. London: George Allen and Unwin, 1965.

———— *God and Other Minds: A Study of the Rational Justification of Belief in God.* Ithaca: Cornell University Press, 1967.

———— "Which Worlds Could God Have Created?" *Journal of Philosophy* 70 (1973): 539-52.

———— *The Nature of Necessity.* Oxford: Clarendon Press, 1974.

———— *God, Freedom, and Evil.* Grand Rapids: Eerdmans, 1977.

———— "The Probabilistic Argument from Evil." *Philosophical Studies* 35 (1979): 1-53.

———— "Reply to the Basingers on Divine Omnipotence." *Process Studies* 11 (1981): 25-29.

———— "Tooley and Evil: A Reply." *Australian Journal of Philosophy* 60 (1982): 66-75.

———— "Self-Profile." In *Alvin Plantinga,* ed. James Tomberlin and Peter van Inwagen. Dordrecht: Reidel, 1985, esp. 36-55.

———— "Replies to Articles." In *Alvin Plantinga,* esp. 371-82.

———— "Is Theism Really a Miracle?" *Faith and Philosophy* 3 (1986): 122-23.

*———— "Epistemic Probability and Evil." *Archivio di filosofia* (Italy) 56 (1988): 557-84.

———— "Ad Walls." *Philosophy and Phenomenological Research* 54 (1991): 621-24.

———— *Warrant and Proper Function.* New York: Oxford University Press, 1993.

Plantinga, Theodore. *Learning to Live with Evil.* Grand Rapids: Eerdmans, 1982.

Platt, David. "God, Goodness and a Morally Perfect World." *Personalist* 46 (1965): 320-26.

Pontifex, Mark. "The Question of Evil." In *Prospect for Metaphysics,* ed. Ian Ramsey. London: George Allen and Unwin, 1961.

Puccetti, Roland. "The Concept of God." *Philosophical Quarterly* 14 (1964): 237-45.

———— "The Loving God: Some Observations on Hick's Theodicy." *Religious Studies* 2 (1967): 255-68.

Purtill, Richard. "Walton on Power and Evil." *International Journal for Philosophy of Religion* 6 (1975): 163-66.

Quinn, John M. "Triune Self-Giving: One Key to the Problem of Suffering." *Thomist* 44 (1980): 173-218.

Quinn, Michael. "Mustn't God Create the Best?" *Journal of Critical Analysis* 5 (1973): 2-8.

Quinn, Philip L. "A Pseudosolution to the Problem of Evil." *Zygon* 10 (1975): 444-46.

———— "God, Moral Perfection, and Possible Worlds." In *God: The Contemporary Discussion,* ed. Frederick Sontag and M. Darrol Bryant. New York: Rose of Sharon Press, 1982, 197-213. Also in *The Problem of Evil,* ed. Michael Peterson.

———— "Original Sin, Radical Evil and Moral Identity." *Faith and Philosophy* 1 (1984): 188-202.

———— "Social Evil: A Response to Adams." *Philosophical Studies* 69 (1993): 187-94.

Ramberan, Osmond G. "God, Evil and the Idea of a Perfect World." *Modern Schoolman* 53 (1976): 379-92.

———— "Evil and Theism." *Sophia* (Australia) 17 (1978): 28-36.

Reichenbach, Bruce. "Natural Evils and Natural Law: A Theodicy for Natural Evils." *International Philosophical Quarterly* 16 (1976): 179-96.

———— "The Inductive Argument from Evil." *American Philosophical Quarterly* 17 (1980): 221-27.

———— "The Deductive Argument from Evil." *Sophia* (Australia) 20 (April 1981): 25-42.

———— *Evil and a Good God.* New York: Fordham University Press, 1982.

———— "Evil and a Reformed View of God." *International Journal for Philosophy of Religion* 24 (1988): 67-85.

Resnick, Lawrence. "Evidence, Utility and God." *Analysis* 31 (1971): 87-90.

Richards, Norvin. "Gods and Viruses." *Analysis* 35 (1975): 102-4.

Richman, Robert J. "The Argument from Evil." *Religious Studies* 4 (1969): 203-11.

———— "Plantinga, God and (Yet) Other Minds." *Australasian Journal of Philosophy* 50 (1972): 40-54.

Rist, John. "Coherence and the Love of God." *Journal for Theological Studies* 22 (1972): 95-105.

Rosenberg, Alan, and Gerald Myers, eds. *Echoes from the Holocaust: Philosophical Reflections on a Dark Time.* Philadelphia: Temple University Press, 1988.

Rosenberg, Jay F. "The Problem of Evil Revisited." *Journal of Value Inquiry* 4 (1970): 212-18.

Rosenthal, Abigail L. *A Good Look at Evil.* Philadelphia: Temple University Press, 1987.

Ross, James. "Evil." *Introduction to the Philosophy of Religion.* New York: Macmillan, 1969, 113-48.

———— "'God is Good' and the Problem of Evil." *Philosophical Theology.* Indianapolis: Bobbs-Merrill, 1969, 222-78.

Roth, John K. "William James and Contemporary Religious Thought: The Problem of Evil." In *The Philosophy of William James,* ed. W. R. Corti. Hamburg: Felix Meiner, 1976.

———— *A Consuming Fire: Encounters with Elie Wiesel and the Holocaust.* Atlanta: Knox Press, 1979.

———— "A Theodicy of Protest." In *Encountering Evil: Live Options in Theodicy,* ed. Stephen T. Davis. Atlanta: Knox Press, 1981, 7-37.

———— "The Silence of God." *Faith and Philosophy* 1 (1984): 407-20.

Rowe, William L. "God and Other Minds." *Nous* 3 (1969): 259-84.

———— "Plantinga on Possible Worlds and Evil." *Journal of Philosophy* 70 (1973): 554-55.

*_____ "The Problem of Evil and Some Varieties of Atheism." *American Philosophical Quarterly* 16 (1979): 335-41.

———— "Evil and the Theistic Hypothesis: A Response to S. J. Wykstra." *International Journal for Philosophy of Religion* 16 (1984): 95-100.

———— "The Empirical Argument from Evil." In *Rationality, Religious Belief, and Moral Commitment,* ed. Robert Audi and William J. Wainwright. Ithaca: Cornell University Press, 1986.

———— "Evil and Theodicy." *Philosophical Topics* 16 (1988): 119-32.

———— "Ruminations about Evil." *Philosophical Perspectives* 5 (1991): 69-88.

———— "The Problem of Evil." *Philosophy of Religion: An Introduction,* 2d ed. Belmont: Wadsworth, 1993, 73-89.

———— "The Problem of Divine Perfection and Freedom." In *Reasoned Faith,* ed. Eleonore Stump. Ithaca: Cornell University Press, 1993.

———— "William Alston on the Problem of Evil." In *The Rationality of Belief and the Plurality of Faiths,* ed. Thomas D. Senor. Ithaca: Cornell University Press, 1994.

Runzo, Joseph. "Omniscience and Freedom for Evil." *International Journal for Philosophy of Religion* 12 (1981): 131-48.

Russell, Bruce. "The Persistent Problem of Evil." *Faith and Philosophy* 6 (1989): 121-39.

———— and Stephen Wykstra. "The 'Inductive' Argument from Evil: A Dialogue." *Philosophical Topics* 16 (1988): 133-60.

Russell, Robert John. "Entropy and Evil." *Zygon* 19 (1984): 449-68.

Sainsbury, R. M. "Benevolence and Evil." *Australasian Journal of Philosophy* 58 (1980): 128-34.

Salmon, Wesley. "Religion and Science: A New Look at Hume's *Dialogues.*" *Philosophical Studies* 33 (1978): 143-76.

Sanders, Paul. *Twentieth Century Interpretations of the Book of Job.* Englewood Cliffs: Prentice-Hall, 1968.

Schellenberg, J. L. "Alpha-Claims and the Problem of Evil." *Sophia* (Australia) 32 (1993): 56-61.

———— *Divine Hiddenness and Human Reason.* Ithaca: Cornell University Press, 1993.

Schilling, Paul. *God and Human Anguish.* Nashville: Abingdon, 1977.

Schlesinger, George. "The Problem of Evil and the Problem of Suffering." *American Philosophical Quarterly* 1 (1964): 244-47.

———— "On the Possibility of the Best of All Possible Worlds." *Journal of Value Inquiry* 4 (1970): 229-32.

———— *Religion and Scientific Method.* Dordrecht: D. Reidel, 1977.

———— "The Theological Implications of the Holocaust." *Philosophical Forum* (Boston) 16 (1984): 110-20.

———— "The Availability of Evidence in Support of Religious Belief." *Faith and Philosophy* 1 (1984): 422-27.

———— "The Moral Value of the Universe." *Journal of Value Inquiry* 22 (1988): 319-25.

———— *New Perspectives on Old-time Religion.* New York: Oxford University Press, 1988.

Schrader, David E. "Evil and the Best of Possible Worlds." *Sophia* (Australia) 27 (1988): 24-37.

Schuurman, Henry J. "The Concept of a Strong Theodicy." *International Journal for Philosophy of Religion* 27 (1990): 63-85.

———— "Two Concepts of Theodicy." *American Philosophical Quarterly* 30 (1993): 209-21.

Schwartz, Richard B. *Samuel Johnson and the Problem of Evil.* Madison: University of Wisconsin Press, 1975.

Seeskin, Kenneth. "Job and the Problem of Evil." *Philosophy and Literature* 11 (1987): 226-41.

Segal, Robert A. "A Jungian View of Evil." *Zygon* 20 (1985): 83-89.

Sennett, James F. "The Free Will Defense and Determinism." *Faith and Philosophy* (1991): 340-53.

———— "The Inscrutable Evil Defense." *Faith and Philosophy* 10 (1993): 220-29.

Settle, T. "A Prolegomenon to Intellectually Honest Theology." *Philosophical Forum* (Boston) 1 (1968): 136-70.

Shea, Winslow W. "God, Evil, and Professor Schlesinger." *Journal of Value Inquiry* 4 (1970): 219-28.

Silverstein, Harry S. "The Evil of Death." *Journal of Philosophy* 77 (1980): 401-23.

Smart, Ninian. "Omnipotence, Evil and Supermen." *Philosophy* 36 (1961): 188-95.

———— "Probably (Response to Flew)." *Philosophy* 37 (1962): 60.

Smith, Michael. "What's So Good about Feeling Bad?" *Faith and Philosophy* 2 (1985): 424-29.

Smith, Quentin. "An Atheological Argument from Evil Natural Laws." *International Journal for Philosophy of Religion* (1991): 159-74.

———— "The Anthropic Coincidence, Evil and the Disconfirmation of Theism." *Religious Studies* 28 (1992): 347-50.

Snyder, Daniel T. "Surplus Evil." *Philosophical Quarterly* 40 (1990): 78-86.

Soelle, Dorothee. *Suffering.* London: Darton, Longman, & Todd, 1975.

Solon, T. P. M and S. K. Wertz. "Hume's Argument from Evil." *Personalist* 50 (1969): 383-92.

Sontag, Frederick. "God and Evil." *Religion in Life* 34 (1965): 215-23.

———— *God, Why Did You Do That?* Philadelphia: Westminster Press, 1970.

———— *The God of Evil: An Argument from the Existence of the Devil.* New York: Harper & Row, 1970.

———— "Technology and Theodicy." *Nature and System* 1 (1979): 265-75.

Springsted, Eric O. "Is There a Problem with the Problem of Evil?" *International Philosophical Quarterly* 24 (1984): 303-32.

Stark, Judith C. "The Problem of Evil: Augustine and Ricoeur." *Augustinian Studies* (1982): 111-22.

Steuer, Axel D. "Once More on the Free Will Defense." *Religious Studies* 10 (1974): 301-11.

Stewart, Melville. *"O Felix Culpa,* Redemption, and the Greater Good Defense." *Sophia* (Australia) 25 (1986): 18-31.

———— *The Greater Good Defense.* London: Macmillan, 1993.

Stump, Eleonore. "Knowledge, Freedom, and the Problem of Evil." *International Journal for Philosophy of Religion* 14 (1983): 49-58.

———— "The Problem of Evil." *Faith and Philosophy* 2 (1985): 392-424.

———— "Suffering for Redemption: Reply to Smith's 'What's So Good About Feeling Bad?'" *Faith and Philosophy* 2 (1985): 430-35.

———— "Dante's Hell, Aquinas' Moral Theory, and the Love of God." *Candadian Journal of Philosophy* 16 (1986): 181-98.

———— "Faith and Goodness." In *The Philosophy in Christianity,* ed. Godfrey Vesey. Cambridge: Cambridge University Press, 1989, 167-91.

———— "Providence and the Problem of Evil." In *Christian Philosophy,* ed. Thomas P. Flint. Notre Dame: University of Notre Dame Press, 1990, 51-91.

*———— "Aquinas on the Sufferings of Job." In *Reasoned Faith,* ed. Eleonore Stump. Ithaca: Cornell University Press, 1993.

Surin, Kenneth. "The Impossibility of God and the Problem of Evil." *Scottish Journal of Theology* 35 (1982): 97-115.

———— "Theodicy?" *Harvard Theological Review* 76 (1983): 225-47.

———— *Theology and the Problem of Evil.* Oxford: Basil Blackwell, 1986.

Sutherland, Stewart. *Atheism and the Rejection of God: Contemporary Philosophy and "The Brothers Karamazov."* Oxford: Basil Blackwell, 1977.

———— "Horrendous Evils and the Goodness of God." *Aristotelian Society Supplementary Volume* 63 (1989): 311-23.

Suttle, Bruce B. "On God Tolerating Evil." *Sophia* (Australia) 26 (1987): 53-54.

Swinburne, Richard. "The Problem of Evil." In *Reason and Religion,* ed. Stuart Brown. Ithaca: Cornell University Press, 1977, 81-102.

———— "Postscript." In *Reason and Religion,* ed. Stuart Brown, 129-33.

———— "Natural Evil." *American Philosophical Quarterly* 15 (1978): 295-301.

———— "The Problem of Evil." *The Existence of God.* Oxford: Clarendon Press, 1979.

———— "A Theodicy of Heaven and Hell." In *The Existence and Nature of God,* ed. Alfred Freddoso. Notre Dame: University of Notre Dame Press, 1983, 37-54.

———— "Knowledge from Experience, and the Problem of Evil." In *The Rationality of Religious Belief,* ed. William Abraham and S. Holtzer. Oxford: Clarendon Press, 1987.

———— "Does Theism Need a Theodicy?" *Canadian Journal of Philosophy* 18 (1988): 287-311.

Talbott, Mark. "Is It Natural to Believe in God?" *Faith and Philosophy* 6 (1989).

Talbott, Thomas. "Providence, Freedom, and Human Destiny." *Religious Studies* 26 (1990): 227-45.

———— "The Doctrine of Everlasting Punishment." *Faith and Philosophy* 7 (1990): 19-42.

Taliaferro, Charles. "Imaginary Evil: A Sceptic's Wager." *Philosophia* 21 (1992): 221-33.

Tangwa, Godfrey. "God and the Problem of Evil." *Thought and Practice* 4 (1982): 79-85.

Thelakat, Paul. "Process and Privation: Aquinas and Whitehead on Evil." *International Philosophical Quarterly* 26 (1986): 287-96.

Tidman, Paul. "The Epistemology of Evil Possibilities." *Faith and Philosophy* 10 (1993): 181-97.

Tomberlin, James, and Frank McGuinness. "Good, Evil, and the Free Will Defense." *Religious Studies* 13 (1977): 455-75.

Tooley, Michael. "Alvin Plantinga and the Argument from Evil." *Australasian Journal of Philosophy* 58 (1980): 360-76.

———— "The Argument from Evil." *Philosophical Perspectives* 5 (1991): 89-134.

Tracy, Thomas F. "Victimization and the Problem of Evil: A Response to Ivan Karamazov." *Faith and Philosophy* 9 (1992): 301-29.

Trau, Jane Mary. "Fallacies in the Argument from Gratuitous Suffering." *New Scholasticism* 60 (1986): 585-89.

———— "The Positive Value of Evil." *International Journal for Philosophy of Religion* 24 (1988): 21-33.

Trethowan, Dom Illtyd. "Dr. Hick and the Problem of Evil." *Journal of Theological Studies* 18 (1967): 407-16.

Tweyman, Stanley. "Hume's Dialogues on Evil." *Hume Studies* 13 (1987): 74-85.

Van Der Hoeven, J. "The Problem of Evil—Crucible for the Authenticity and Modesty of Philosophizing: In Discussion with Paul Ricoeur." *South African Journal of Philosophy* 5 (1986): 44-52.

Van Inwagen, Peter. "The Place of Chance in a World Sustained by God." In *Divine and Human Action,* ed. Thomas V. Morris. Ithaca: Cornell University Press, 1988, 211-235.

———— "The Magnitude, Duration, and Distribution of Evil: A Theodicy." *Philosophical Topics* 16 (1988): 161-87.

*———— "The Problem of Evil, the Problem of Air, and the Problem of Silence." *Philosophical Perspectives* 5 (1991): 135-65.

Vicchio, Stephen J. *The Voice from the Whirlwind: The Problem of Evil and the Modern World.* Westminster: Christian Classics, 1989.

Vitali, Theodore R. "The Importance of the A Priori in Whiteheadian Theodicy." *Modern Schoolman* 62 (1985): 277-91.

Wachterhauser, Brice R. "The Problem of Evil and Moral Skepticism." *International Journal for Philosophy of Religion* 17 (1985): 167-74.

Wainwright, William. "The Presence of Evil and the Falsification of Theistic Assertions." *Religious Studies* 4 (1969): 213-16.

———— "God and the Necessity of Physical Evil." *Sophia* (Australia) 11 (1972): 16-19.

———— "Christian Theism and the Free Will Defense." *International Journal for Philosophy of Religion* 6 (1975): 243-50.

———— "The Problem of Evil." *Philosophy of Religion.* Belmont: Wadsworth, 1988, 66-98.

Wall, George. "Heaven and a Wholly Good God." *Personalist* 58 (1977): 352-57.

———— "A New Solution to an Old Problem." *Religious Studies* 15 (1979): 511-30.

———— "Other Worlds and the Comparison of Values." *Sophia* (Australia) 18 (1979): 10-19.

Wallace, Gerald. "The Problems of Moral and Physical Evil." *Philosophy* 46 (1971): 349-51.

Walls, Jerry. "The Free Will Defense, Calvinism, Wesley, and the Goodness of God." *Christian Scholar's Review* 13 (1983): 19-33.

———— "Hume on Divine Amorality." *Religious Studies* 26 (1990): 257-66.

———— "Why Plantinga Must Move from Defense to Theodicy." *Philosophy of Phenomenological Research* 51 (1991): 375-78.

———— *Hell: The Logic of Damnation.* Notre Dame: University of Notre Dame Press, 1992.

Walton, Douglas. "Modalities in the Free Will Defense." *Religious Studies* 10 (1974): 325-31.

———— "Language, God, and Evil." *International Journal for Philosophy of Religion* 6 (1975): 154-62.

———— "The Formalities of Evil." *Critica* 8 (1976): 3-9.

———— "Purtill on Power and Evil." *International Journal for Philosophy of Religion* 8 (1977): 263-67.

Ward, Keith. "Freedom and the Iranean Theodicy." *Journal of Theological Studies* 20 (1969): 249-54.

Weinstock, Jerome A. "What Theodicies Must But Do Not Do." *Philosophia* (Israel) 4 (1974): 449-67.

Wenham, John W. *The Goodness of God.* Downers Grove: InterVarsity Press, 1974.

Wennberg, Robert. "Animal Suffering and the Problem of Evil." *Christian Scholar's Review* 21 (1991): 120-40.

Wetzel, James. "Can Theodicy Be Avoided? The Claim of Unredeemed Evil." *Religious Studies* 25 (1989): 1-13.

Whale, J. S. *The Christian Answer to the Problem of Evil.* London: SCM Press, 1957.

Wharton, Robert V. "Evil in an Earthly Paradise: Dostoevsky's Theodicy." *Thomist* 41 (1977): 567-84.

Whitney, Barry L. "Process Theism: Does a Persuasive God Coerce?" *Southern Journal of Philosophy* 17 (1979): 133-43.

———— *Evil and the Process God.* New York: Mellen Press, 1985.

———— "Hartshorne and Theodicy." In *Hartshorne, Process Philosophy, and Theology,* ed. Robert Kane. Albany: SUNY Press, 1989, 53-69.

———— *Theodicy.* New York: Garland, 1993. (An annotated bibliography of 4,200 philosophical and theological works on the problem of evil written in English between 1960 and 1990.)

———— "An Aesthetic Solution to the Problem of Evil." *International Journal for Philosophy of Religion* 35 (1994): 21-37.

Wierenga, Edward. "Reply to Harold Moore's 'Evidence, Evil and Religious Belief.'" *International Journal for Philosophy of Religion* 9 (1978): 246-51.

Wilcox, John T. *The Bitterness of Job: A Philosophical Reading.* Ann Arbor: University of Michigan Press, 1989.

Windt, P. Y. "Plantinga's Unfortunate God." *Philosophical Studies* 24 (1973): 335-42.

Wisdom, John. "God and Evil." *Mind* 44 (1935): 1-20.

Wolterstorff, Nicholas. *Lament for a Son.* Grand Rapids: Eerdmans, 1987.

Wood, Forrest, Jr. "Some Whiteheadian Insights into the Problem of Evil." *Southwestern Journal of Philosophy* 10 (1979): 147-55.

Wykstra, Stephen J. "The Human Obstacle to Evidential Arguments from Suffering: On Avoiding the Evils of 'Appearance.'" *International Journal for Philosophy of Religion* 16 (1984): 73-94.

Yandell, Keith E. "A Premature Farewell to Theism (A Reply to Roland Puccetti)." *Religious Studies* 5 (1969): 251-55.

———— "Ethics, Evils and Theism." *Sophia* (Australia) 8 (1969): 18-28.

———— "The Problem of Evil." In *Basic Issues in the Philosophy of Religion.* Boston: Allyn and Bacon, 1971.

———— "Theism and Evil: A Reply." *Sophia* (Australia) 11 (1972): 1-7.

———— "The Greater Good Defense." *Sophia* (Australia) 13 (1974): 1-16.

———— "The Problem of Evil." *Philosophical Topics* 12 (1981): 7-38.

———— "The Problem of Evil and the Content of Morality." *International Journal for Philosophy of Religion* 17 (1985): 139-65.

———— "Gratuitous Evil and Divine Existence." *Religious Studies* 25 (1989): 15-30.

CONTRIBUTORS

William P. Alston is Professor Emeritus at Syracuse University. He has authored *Philosophy of Language, Perceiving God, The Reliability of Sense Perception,* and numerous articles, some of which are collected in *Epistemic Justification* and *Divine and Human Language.*

Paul Draper is Associate Professor of Philosophy at Florida University International. His papers have appeared in *Nous, Faith and Philosophy, International Journal for Philosophy of Religion,* and *Religious Studies.*

Richard M. Gale is Professor of Philosophy at the University of Pittsburgh. He has edited *The Philosophy of Time,* and he has authored *On the Nature and Existence of God* and many articles.

Daniel Howard-Snyder is Assistant Professor of Philosophy at Seattle Pacific University. He has co-edited *God, Freedom and Responsibility: Essays in the Philosophy of Religion.* His papers have appeared in *Philosophical Quarterly, Philosophy and Phenomenological Research, Faith and Philosophy, International Journal for Philosophy of Religion, Religious Studies,* and *Sophia.*

Alvin Plantinga is John A. O'Brien Professor of Philosophy at the University of Notre Dame. He has authored *God and Other Minds, The Nature of Necessity, God, Freedom and Evil, Does God Have a Nature?, Warrant: The Current Debate, Warrant and Proper Function,* and numerous articles.

William L. Rowe is Professor of Philosophy at Purdue University. He has authored *Religious Symbols and God: A Philosophical Study of Tillich's Theology, The Cosmological Argument, The Philosophy of Religion, Thomas Reid on Morality and Freedom,* and many articles.

Bruce Russell is Professor of Philosophy at Wayne State University. He authored many articles that have appeared in *American Philosophical Quarterly, Philosophical Studies, Philosophical Topics, Faith and Philosophy,* and various collections.

Eleonore Stump is Robert J. Henle Professor of Philosophy at Saint Louis University. She has translated and edited *Boethius's "De topicis differentiis," Boethius's "In Ciceronis Topica,"* and *Reasoned Faith,* and she has authored *Dialectic and Its Place in the Development of Medieval Logic* and many articles.

Richard G. Swinburne is the Nolloth Professor of the Philosophy of the Christian Religion at Oriel College, Oxford University. He has edited *The Justification of Induction,* and he has authored *Space and Time, The Concept of Miracle, An Introduction to Confirmation Theory, The Coherence of Theism, The Existence of God, Faith and Reason, Responsibility and Atonement, The Evolution of the Soul, Revelation,* and numerous articles.

Peter van Inwagen is Professor of Philosophy at Syracuse University. He has edited *Time and Cause: Essays Presented to Richard Taylor* and co-edited *Alvin Plantinga: A Profile,* and he has authored *An Essay on Free Will, Material Beings,* and numerous essays, some of which have been collected in *God, Knowledge and Mystery.*

Stephen John Wykstra is Professor of Philosophy at Calvin College. He has authored articles appearing in *Philosophical Topics, International Journal for Philosophy of Religion, Synthese, British Journal for the Philosophy of Science,* and various collections.

INDEX

Actualization: strong and weak, 77
Adams, Marilyn McCord: theodicy, 107-108, 114; mentioned, xvii
Adams, Robert: expanded theism, 20; middle knowledge, 27*n8*
Afterlife: relevance to theodicy, 51-64 *passim;* relevance to Rowe's "appears" version of evidential argument, 73-74, 141-45; effect of punishment, 104; mentioned, 207. *See also* Compensation to victims; Goods; Theodicy
Agnosticism: about God, 130-31, 138-39, 265, 271, 272-74, 304; about pointless evil, 98, 122; Rowe rejects, 10-11*n5*, 146-47
Ahern, M. B.: limited knowledge of goods, interconnections, 102
Alston, William: author, 97-125, 311-32; Rowe's "appears" version of evidential argument, 97-125 *passim,* 315, 316-22; Rowe's enumerative induction version of evidential argument, 109-10, 315-16, 322-27; Rowe's Bayesian versions of evidential argument, 312-15; cognitive limitations, 120, 316-22 *passim,* 323-27; Russell's crow, 319; progress argument, 109, 319-20; moral skepticism, 320; level confusion, 325-27, 332*n19;* Draper and HI, 327-30; *mentioned passim*
Aquinas: 49-68 *passim;* natural vs moral evil, 51-52 *passim;* sin as cancer of the soul, 54-56 *passim;* pain and suffering as spiritual chemotherapy, 54-64 *passim;* human happiness, 53-54; contrast with modern (Renaissance) view of undeserved suffering, 50, 57-64 *passim;* mentioned, 236
Aristotle, 164
Asceticism. *See* Simeon Stylites
Atheism: unfriendly, 8; indifferent, 8; friendly, 8-9, 11*n7;* atheistic stance, 145-47 *passim,* 309-10*n26*
Atlantis, 234
Atomism: 164-67, 217-18*n19;* atomicity, 165. *See also* Hypothesis of Independence; Hypothesis of Indifference
Augustine, 51
Austin, J. L., 74

Background knowledge: defined, 94, 265-66; problems with the concept, 94; importance in evaluating Draper's argument, 251; mentioned, 27*n2,* 195-96, 207, 216*n2,* 220-25, 304
Bayesian versions of the evidential argument. *See* Draper, Paul; Rowe, William
Bayes's Theorem, 76, 138, 146, 191*n19,* 195, 196, 203, 266, 293, 304
Biological utility of pain and pleasure: biologically useful, 15-18, 250, 252-54; biologically gratuitous, 16, 18-19, 254-57; biologically pathological, 19; biologically appropriate, 19. *See also* Draper, Paul; Plantinga, Alvin
Brown, Mark, 314

Calvin, John: on the *sensus divinitatis,* 91-92, 260
Camus, Albert, xvi
Chisholm, Roderick, 10*n5,* 72, 272
Christ: giving better than receiving, 42; resurrection, 60; atonement, 62; example, 62; consolation of, 62; to him who has, more given, 147; blessed is the one who hungers and thirsts, 147
Clifford, W., 89
Coherence. *See* Rationality
Compensation to victims, 45-46, 51, 111-12, 207
Complexity: argument from, 301-304 *passim*
Confirmation. *See* Evidence
Copernicus: on simplicity of theory, 294
CORNEA: 126-50 *passim;* adjunct principle (strong version), 129; Rowe's rendition of, 132-36; perspective on defeaters, 135-36, 271-72; revised adjunct principle (weak version), 136-39; revised adjunct principle and parent analogy, 145, 270-71; mentioned, 270
Cornman, James, 235
Crows: Bruce Russell's analogy, 194, 198; discussed by Howard-Snyder, 291-92; discussed by Alston, 319

Darwin, Charles, 25
Deception: incompatible with divine nature, 161
Defeaters: rebutters and undercutters distinguished, 133-34; propositional rebutters of evidential argument, xvi–xvii, 6-9 *passim,* 25-26, 87-88, 153-54, 203-204, 257-58; non-

Scriven, Michael: most memorable line, 91
Sensus divinitatis. See Calvin, John
Silence, divine: and parent analogy, 276, 285n35; argument from, 306; relation to argument from inscrutable evil, 305-307
Simeon Stylites: mistakes suffering for unconditional good, 59, 67n41
Simplicity: HI simpler than theism, 25; pointless evil hypothesis simpler than theism, 196-97, 293-94; determines a priori probability, 95n22; not truth-conducive, 293-94
Skepticism: as response to evidential argument, *mentioned passim;* defensive skepticism defined, 207; Gale's objections to defensive skepticism, 207-14; complete (wholesale, radical, generalized) skepticism, 120-21, 207-209, 235, 321-22; undermines belief in God, 188, 207; modal skepticism, 159-60, 163-64, 211-13, 235-39, 308; renders communion with God impossible, 209-11; cheapens religious life, 214; moral skepticism, 160-64, 197-98, 292-93, 320
Socrates: and Callicles in *Gorgias,* 56, 60, 63
Special creationism: Draper's analogy, 25; Russell's analogy, 196-98
Spinoza, 237
Stump, Eleonore: author, 49-68; on natural evil, 106-107; on sufferer-centered reasons requirement, 111; mentioned, xvii, 23. *See also* Aquinas
Suffering. *See* Evil
Swinburne, Richard: author, 30-48; theodicy, xvii; and Indifferent Deity Hypothesis, 28n12; mentioned, 164, 188, 215. *See also* Goods

Theism: generic (core), xi, 1-2, 12-13, 140-47 *passim;* expanded, 19-20. *See also* Explanation; Theodicy
Theistic story: defined, 180; aprobable, 180; good, 180; and counterdefense, 182-84; undefeated, 184; need for many independent stories, 184; unknown reasons, 185; free will, 185-86; natural law, 186-87, 191-92n23. *See also* Defense; Theodicy; van Inwagen, Peter; Weighted Average Principle (WAP)
Theodicy: defined, xvii, 19-20, 27n6, 30, 70, 121n3, 154; vs defense, 46n2; constraints on, 30-31, 51-52, 214-15; relation to evidential arguments, xvii, 206-207; relation to Draper's argument, 19-20, 179-80; as live possibility to rule out, 103-25, *passim;* free will, 20-24, 36-38, 112-14, 278-81; need for

knowledge, 22-24, 31-32; unknown goods, 24-25; punishment, 50, 103-104, 123n15, 278; sufferer-centered reasons, 103-109; martyrdom model, 107-108, 278; martyrdom model applied to perpetrators and onlookers, 114, 278; natural law, 114-18, 278; the Fall, 215-16; reincarnation, 216-17n4; soul-making, 20-21, 105-106, 216n1, 278. *See also* Defense; Goods; Theistic story
Thomas Aquinas. *See* Aquinas
Tilley, Terrence: on theodicies, 64
Tillich, Paul, 2
Tooley, Michael: overlooks explanatory arguments, 177; ignorance of intrinsic goods, 296-97

Undercutters. *See* Defeaters
Universe, deep and shallow: Wykstra defends relevance, 139-45 *passim;* Gale rejects, 210-11

van Fraassen, Bas: rationality as coherence, 79-80, 95n29
van Inwagen, Peter: author, 151-74, 219-43; on Draper-style evidential argument, 151-74 *passim,* 219-34; modal and moral skepticism, 159-64, 235-39; appeal to particular instances of evil, 173n11, 234-35. *See also* Draper, Paul; Gale, Richard; Russell, Bruce; Theistic story; Theodicy

Warrant: Plantinga on, 84-93 *passim;* internalist conception, 89-90, 259; externalist conception, 90-93, 259-60; as proper function, 92; and theistic belief, 92-93; its ontological roots, 92-93. *See also* Defeaters; Evidence
Weighted Average Principle (WAP): defined, 20; deployed by Draper, 20-25; and good, aprobable theistic stories, 181-82
Weikers, Norb: neighborly source of insight for Gale, 209
Whitney, Barry, ix
Wiesel, Elie, xvi
Wykstra, Stephen: author, 126-50; on Rowe's "appears" version of the evidential argument, 126-50 *passim;* on Rowe's enumerative induction version of the evidential argument, 128, 130, 133; assessment of explanatory argument, 145-47; mentioned, xviii, 19, 73, 102, 122-23, 202, 209, 210, 317. *See also* CORNEA; Parent Analogy; Rowe, William; Universe, deep and shallow

Zagaloops: Russell's analogy, 194, 198